THE ARCHITECTURAL INTERPRETATION
OF HISTORY

THE ARCHITECTURAL INTERPRETATION OF HISTORY

JOHN GLOAG

F.S.A., Hon. F.R.I.B.A., Hon. F.S.I.A.

ST. MARTIN'S PRESS
NEW YORK

First published in the USA 1977
St. Martin's Press, Inc.,
175 Fifth Avenue
New York, N.Y. 10010

Library of Congress Catalog Card Number
77–74665

Library of Congress Cataloging in Publication Data
Gloag, John, 1896–
    The architectural interpretation of history.

    Includes bibliographical references and index.
    1. Architecture and history. I. Title.
NA2543.H55G56   1977   720'.9   77–74665
ISBN 0–312–04812–2

Printed in Great Britain

Dedicated to

BRUCE ALLSOPP

CONTENTS

ILLUSTRATIONS IN THE TEXT,
INCLUDING DIAGRAMS AND MAPS

LIST OF PLATES

References to sources of quotations, to authorities and so forth are numbered consecutively throughout each chapter, and listed under their appropriate chapter numbers at the end of the text, beginning on page 319. Footnotes have been avoided.

ACKNOWLEDGEMENTS

The subject of this book was outlined in a paper on "The Significance of Historical Research in Architectural and Industrial Design" that I read before the Royal Society of Arts on March 20th, 1963, and later, at the suggestion of Mr. Bruce Allsopp, I wrote an essay that incorporated and amplified the architectural part of the paper, which was published in 1965 as a small book called *Enjoying Architecture*. That essay was in the nature of a sketch plan for the present book, which I was encouraged to write by the late J. D. Newth, whose constructive comments were invaluable to me, made as he read the typescript chapter by chapter, until his untimely death that occurred before the last four chapters were completed.

As my theme is the interpretative quality of architecture, and the revealing powers of that art and the purposes it has served at different times and in different places, to some extent this book has become a miniature history; but it is only incidentally an historical work. For authoritative studies the student and the general reader should turn to the works of Sir John Summerson, Sir Nikolaus Pevsner, Mr. James Lees-Milne, Miss Dorothy Stroud, Professor Henry-Russell Hitchcock, and the late Christopher Hussey, and in particular to those significant books by Bruce Allsopp, *A General History of Architecture*, and *The Study of Architectural History*.

I must acknowledge the help that I have received in collecting illustrations, in particular from Miss Ursula Clark, Mr. Bruce Allsopp, Mr. Alan Deller, Mr. Richard C. Grierson, and Mr. D. E. Dean, the Librarian of the Royal Institute of British Architects. For permission to reproduce some of their copyright drawings, I am indebted to Mr. Hulme Chadwick, Mr. Raymond McGrath, and Maureen Stafford. For reading and editing the typescript, my thanks are due to Mrs. Constance Bensley.

JOHN GLOAG.
May 1974.

THE INTERPRETATIVE QUALITY OF ARCHITECTURE

Buildings cannot lie; they tell the truth directly or by implication about those who made and used them and provide veracious records of the character and quality of past and present civilisations. Early in this century an original and perceptive architectural historian said: "The interpretative quality in architecture is its main fascination. There is no form of art which so faithfully portrays the character of its creators as this does." Those words, written by Lisle March Phillipps (1863–1917), appeared in a book of travel called *In the Desert*.[1]

The interpretative quality of architecture is the theme of the present work; its purpose is to suggest that architecture should be considered as a supplementary subject for the student of history, because the character of architecture may readjust some of the emotional and intellectual loyalties that we all hold, secretly or openly, and may also implant healthy doubts that modify the compulsive authority of the written or spoken word.

As buildings are candid statements they have a moral superiority as records over many of those made by historians, and subsequently revered and treasured by other historians. J. B. S. Haldane once observed that "history is written by people impressed with the importance of their own political and religious views, and inevitably takes on the character of propaganda for them."[2]

For instance, in many histories of mediaeval Europe, religious bias is exposed by the casual treatment or complete disregard of the achievements of the Arabs in Spain, where for centuries their civilisation illuminated the western world, intellectually and artistically; their achievements have been played down or ignored by Christian historians, who, until recently, appeared to be still subconsciously influenced by the shock of the great westward drive of

the Muslim conquerors who swept along North Africa, up into
Spain and over the Pyrenees into France. The flowering of that
oriental civilisation is illustrated by many examples of architecture
that still survive in Spain and fully reveal what the written word
has minimised; buildings such as the Giralda at Seville (Plate 29),
and the Alhambra at Granada (Plate 32).

An historian without opinions may become an intellectual
eunuch. Even old-fashioned, dry-as-dust historians had opinions;
the chief one being that history *should* be as dry as dust. Fortu-
nately the views of credulous doctrinaires or plodding pedants may
be corrected and humanised by evidence in brick and stone. "Historians have inevitably thought in terms of words," said J. B. S.
Haldane. "They have read many books and documents. They have
often been great stylists like Gibbon and Macaulay. They have
realised the power of words to move multitudes. They have not
been manual workers, and have seldom realized that man's hands
are as important as and more specifically human than his mouth."[3]

The history of a country comes alive through its buildings and
ruins; they are records with much to say, for architecture is a
living language that may be understood without acquiring a lot
of detailed technical knowledge. Hitherto, architectural history
has been thought of as a specialised subject, something apart, a
remote and segregated lake of knowledge instead of a tributary to
the main stream of history. This has happened because education
in western civilisation has a literary foundation. The late Stanley
Casson (1889–1945), in an article entitled "Written and Unwritten
Records",[4] described the growing dependence of literary scholars
on archaeologists who had helped them considerably by revealing
unsuspected records, such as the cuneiform of Babylonia and
Sumer and Egyptian hieroglyphics, thus adding another two
thousand years to written history.

Architecture is the most permanent and illuminating of unwritten records; but since the early nineteenth century the tendency to rely almost exclusively on what used to be called "book
learning" has made large sections of the English-speaking peoples
visually illiterate, so that they are unable to learn anything from
their architectural environment and are often unaware of its
existence. There are a few enclaves of enlightenment; but indiffer-
ence to the form, colour and composition of buildings has for over

a hundred years fostered visual insensitivity. This cultural infirmity is the subject of a later chapter; it accompanied, and was perhaps mainly caused by, economic and social changes and a revival of puritan ethics, so that moral earnestness was highly prized and art became suspect.

Until the second quarter of the nineteenth century, educated people had an alert awareness of their surroundings. Thereafter they lost their understanding of the interpretative quality of architecture. The last great historian who recognised that quality was Gibbon, but although he appreciated the rhythms of Greek and Roman architecture, he was blind to the merits of Byzantine. "Gibbon worked too much in the study and too little in collaboration with others," said Casson; "and the material remains of Byzantium meant nothing to him. Today the archaeologist and student of art can re-write his history in another vein. So that even the greatest historians can miscalculate if their work is not checked by the discoveries of archaeology."[5]

Gibbon's respect for classical architecture was natural enough in a Georgian man of letters; his occasional references to it are neither incidental nor casual; they are integral parts of his history of *The Decline and Fall of the Roman Empire*; and one passage in particular emphasises his consciousness of what buildings had to say. "Among innumerable monuments of architecture constructed by the Romans," he wrote, "how many have escaped the notice of history, how few have resisted the ravages of time and barbarism! And yet even the majestic ruins that are still scattered over Italy and the provinces, would be sufficient to prove, that those countries were once the seat of a polite and powerful empire. Their greatness alone, or their beauty, might deserve our attention: but they are rendered more interesting, by two important circumstances, which connect the agreeable history of the arts, with the more useful history of human manners. Many of those works were erected at private expense, and almost all were intended for public benefit."[6]

Gibbon could assert with serene confidence that "The practice of architecture is directed by a few general and even mechanical rules."[7] He was of course thinking only of the classic orders and the universal system of design that they represented. No special effort was then needed to place architecture in its historical context; nor have modern historians ignored its indicative powers. Dr. Northcote

Parkinson writing nearly two centuries after Gibbon, identified the sudden end of the Greek and Roman tradition in architectural design with the turn of the tide against the West, when, about 1845, "Europe began to lose confidence in its mission."[8] That mission, which began without conscious intention by the peaceful penetration of Asia Minor by Greek art and thought in the century before the conquests of Alexander, has for over two thousand years fostered an intermittent traffic in ideas between East and West, encouraged by commerce, unchecked and sometimes assisted by military adventures; though since the days of the Crusades, European architecture indicates that the East has given more inspiration to the West than the West to the East.

Several references to architecture are made by Arnold Toynbee in the twelve volumes of *A Study of History*, though he is concerned more with interpreting the meaning of architectural activities than with the revelations of architectural character. He recognises that the rebuilding of temples after a devastating war is symbolic of national recovery, and compares the vitality of Periclean Athens after the Persian war with that of France after the 1914–18 war. The French restored the ruins of Rheims Cathedral to their former condition, unlike the Athenians who, when they found the Hekatompedon burnt down to the foundations, let the foundations lie and, on a new site, built the Parthenon.[9]

Actually there was a preliminary structure, already begun when the Persian invasion disrupted the work; the stone platform on which the temple was to stand had been erected and the bottom drums for one colonnade laid out by 480 B.C. Dr. Rhys Carpenter presents the evidence for the subsequent changes that led to the building of another temple on the same site, which was stopped when half finished, and the final temple, designed and built on a more impressive scale, was completed structurally by 438 B.C. The ruins of that temple are those still standing on the Acropolis.[10] (Plate 9.)

Like the French at Rheims, the Belgians rebuilt the Cloth Hall at Ypres as an exact replica of the original destroyed by the Germans in 1914. When Coventry Cathedral was bombed in the Second World War the decision to build a new cathedral instead of carefully reconstructing the ruins asserted the national vitality of the British. (Plate 35.)

Disasters have often provided opportunities for rebuilding with fresh inspiration. When the central tower of Ely Cathedral fell in 1321, it was replaced by the magnificent octagon; when Canterbury Cathedral was burnt down in 1174 William of Sens was commissioned to superintend the rebuilding, and his work generated a structural revolution. At his home town of Sens the Cathedral of St. Etienne, one of the earliest Gothic buildings in France, was begun in 1140 and some of its character was impressed upon Canterbury. When old St. Paul's was largely destroyed in the Great Fire of 1666, the Commissioners took nine years to make up their minds to instruct Christopher Wren to build a new cathedral. Their caution was perhaps justified, for although the damage done to the mediaeval Gothic structure was enormous, a hopeful committee was formed to discuss ways and means of patching up the roofless fabric, and when the inevitable decision was reached to rebuild the cathedral to an entirely new design, courage was needed to make such a revolutionary break with the Gothic architectural tradition, which still showed sporadic signs of life. No such considerations held up the rebuilding of London after the Great Fire; the modern habit of delay for its own sake had not yet clogged the energies of the English, a habit that left London and many other cities dismal with ruins for nearly twenty years after the Second World War.

When such delays are prolonged, the civilisation that is resigned to living with ruins may be on its way out or in process of drastically changing its character, as British civilisation changed in the fifth and sixth centuries, when many of the Romano–British towns were abandoned. Some were never resettled and, haunted by half-starved squatters and bands of brigands, remained untenanted—quarries for later builders. The monumental temples and public buildings of Aquae Sulis, the luxurious spa, as famous in Roman Britain as it became under the name of Bath in Georgian England twelve centuries later, supplied stone for the mediaeval walls and abbey. Archaeologists have been able to recover by excavation the plans and, by careful reconstruction, the architectural character of some of those impressive structures, notably the great temple of Sulis Minerva and the Baths.[11] Kipling's description of the social life of the place in one of his Romano–British stories, written early in this century, was an inspired piece of imaginative writing, for

we then knew far less about Roman Bath than we do today.[12]
The once-important but long-deserted city of Verulamium was
broken up at the end of the tenth century to provide materials for
the Abbey Church of St. Albans, where Roman bricks and tiles
appear in the structure; and here, too, the street plan and the
nature of many of the buildings have been revealed by excavation.[13] In north Hampshire the walls of Silchester, rising to 15
feet, still enclose a hundred acres where the semi-rural Roman
town of Calleva once stood. Apart from some stretches of Hadrian's
Wall, that ran for seventy-three miles from Solway Firth to the
Tyne estuary, Roman ruins above ground are scattered and
scanty. Part of a Roman lighthouse survives in the precincts of
Dover Castle, and two views of it are shown on Plate 22. Dover
was the Roman Dubrae, and the port had two lighthouses, one on
each side of the harbour; the one on the western hill is now merely
a mass of fallen masonry. Another lighthouse across the Channel at
Boulogne, the Roman Gessoriacum, was built in A.D. 40 by order
of the Emperor Gaius (Caligula): that survived until the sixteenth
century when it was destroyed, but the site is known. Although
Roman walling was enormously strong, with layers of horizontal
tiles as binding courses and iron-hard cement, no structure, not
even walls as substantial as those of the Saxon Shore fort at Burgh
Castle shown on Plate 23, could defeat the stone robbers, who for
over fourteen hundred years have intently obliterated the remains
of Roman Britain.

As Stanley Casson pointed out, the work of archaeologists often
amplifies the facts historians draw from literary sources; the architectural historian in particular has a corresponding interest in
archaeology; there is, indeed, a close relationship between the two
branches of study though archaeology quickens public imagination in a way that few other learned subjects succeed in doing.
There is something dramatic, even glamorous, about recovering
long-kept secrets of history by digging them up. When the site of
the temple of Mithras by Walbrook was excavated in 1954, thousands of people queued up daily for weeks to view the remains.
Some may have realised that when Londoners were Roman
citizens sixteen hundred years ago they had worshipped in that
Mithraeum—men only, though, for women were excluded from
the cult. The dark curtain that separates us from the remote past

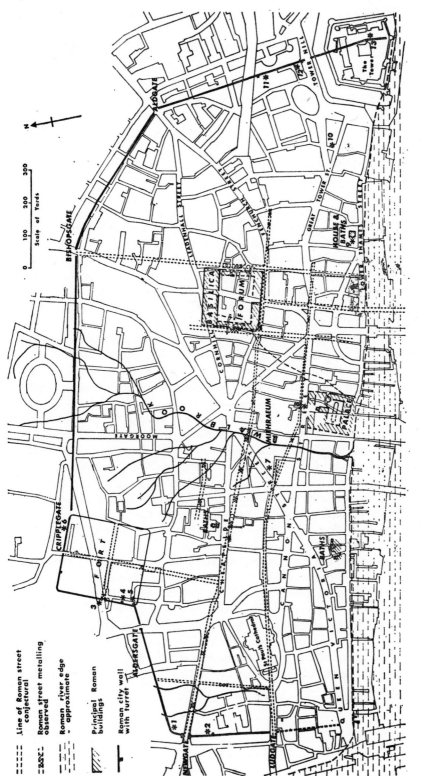

Map showing the principal features of Roman London, superimposed on the street-plan of the modern city. Reproduced from *Roman London*, by Ralph Merrifield, F.S.A., by permission of the author and the publishers, Cassell & Company Ltd.

was momentarily twitched aside; we caught a glimpse of the small, compact, cosmopolitan Roman city of Londinium, the city that W. R. Lethaby called "a little Rome in the west",[14] and saw too something of the power and significance of a religion that was a forerunner of Christianity and, until the fourth century, its strongest rival.[15]

Buildings nearly always say something; even their bones speak when disinterred after centuries, while standing ruins and ancient structures still in use retain the impress of the emotions, beliefs, fears and pleasures of their makers. The blithe hedonism of the Graeco–Roman world is recalled by the stupendous ruins of great baths; the passion for spectacles, impressive, trivial or ferocious, by the amphitheatres in or near so many Roman cities; even a remote garden city like Calleva had one with an arena about 150 by 120 feet;[16] small compared with the Flavian Amphitheatre at Rome, better known as the Colosseum, with its vast elliptical plan, 620 by 513 feet, and an arena measuring 287 by 180 feet. In ancient Egypt the power of the priestly order and the pre-occupation with life after death are proclaimed by immense temples and intimidating tombs. If nothing had survived of Egyptian, Greek and Roman civilisation except the remains of buildings and the sculptures that were so often intimately associated with their architectural design, we should still possess a key to the character of their makers. We know that the Athens of Pericles was the centre of the most aesthetically and intellectually alert civilisation that has ever existed in the West; the buildings that still stand on the Acropolis, though ruinous, have an intellectual quality that was absent from Roman and Gothic and Renaissance architecture, though the clarity of the Greek mind was reasserted in the design and construction of Justinian's great church, Santa Sophia at Constantinople, built in the sixth century.

Changes in the social, religious and military history of a country are marked by changes in the function of buildings. That monument to imperial grandeur, the Mausoleum of Hadrian at Rome, built A.D. 135, survived the destructive attentions of Goths and Vandals, and was transformed in the Middle Ages when it became a Papal fortress known as the Castle of St. Angelo; later it was used as a barracks and is now a museum. (See opposite). The great hall of the baths of Diocletian at Rome, built A.D. 302, was con-

The Mausoleum of Hadrian, Rome, A.D. 135. A monument that survived the destructive attentions of Goths and Vandals and its transformation in the Middle Ages when it became a Papal fortress and was christened the Castle of St. Angelo: it was used later as a barracks and finally as a museum. *Drawn by Maureen Stafford and reproduced by permission of the artist.*

9

verted over twelve and a half centuries later by Michelangelo and Vanvitelli into the church of Santa Maria degli Angeli (Plates 16 and 17). Santa Sophia at Constantinople was a Christian church until the Turkish conquest of the city in 1453, when it was converted to a mosque; now it is a forlorn museum, empty of sacred purpose, a cold reminder of the unemotional materialism of a modern state. (Plate 26.)

One of the three hills on which Ankara is built is crowned by three structures, two in ruins, one in active use, which mark the political and religious ups and downs of the last two thousand years. Ankara, now the capital of Turkey, was formerly the Roman city of Ancyra in the province of Galatia; imperial rule is commemorated by the temple of Augustus, a tall stone structure, roofless, empty, majestic, confirming by its size and flawless masonry Sir Mortimer Wheeler's view that "the crowning gift of the Roman Empire to architecture was magnitude."[17] (Plate 22.) Shadowed by those towering walls are the remains of a Byzantine church, which Christian builders erected without wholly demolishing its pagan predecessor, clearing only that part of the site which they wanted for their structure. Finally, the Ottoman Turks built a mosque, Haci Bayram, beside the temple, but made no use of its shell and ignored the Christian church.

In Spain the Muslims often exhibited a civilised spirit of tolerance towards other religions. At Cordova instead of demolishing the large Visigothic basilica of St. Vincent's, the Emir Abderrahaman bought half of it in 785 for use as a mosque and allowed the Christians to continue worshipping in the other part. "For some time this curious arrangement was successfully continued," observed Royall Tyler, "but one day Abderrahaman I had a vision which decided him to build a mosque worthy of his empire. For some reason or other it seemed essential that the new building should stand on the site of the old; Abderrahaman had little difficulty in persuading the Christians to sell him their share and to depart in peace."[18] After the Christians captured Cordova in 1236 they immediately reconsecrated the mosque to the Virgin but left it unaltered, for they appreciated the beauties of their new cathedral, and kept Moorish workmen constantly employed so that "the necessary repairs should have the true character, though the pig-headedness of a sixteenth century prelate brought about the erection of the coro and the capilla mayor, in spite of the protests of the Cordovese." (The coro is the choir; the capilla mayor a large or major chapel.) Royall Tyler added that it was only just to remember such facts, "when one reads the sweeping condemnations of Christian vandalism in destroying Moslem buildings. If the Moors had been half as respectful of what they found in Spain, we might still possess the wonderful Visigothic basilicas of Merida and Seville."[19] Religious zeal, like war, destroys and disfigures architecture. The intrusion of a large Christian church in the middle of the mosque at Cordova which now disrupts the perspectives between the columns, is one of many examples of damage wrought by the activities of the unintelligently devout; but the presence of that sixteenth century church built inside the mosque has probably been responsible for preserving it.[20] (Plate 28.)

The survival of any building is purely fortuitous; ancient monuments have more often inspired fear and awe than respect, and the idea of preservation is comparatively modern. Wren had no tenderness for the native English style so richly expressed in the Tudor palace at Hampton Court; much of the original building was demolished and replaced by stately classical compositions. Had Wren's plans been carried out, Hampton Court would have suffered the same fate as Richmond Palace, of which all but a fragment has disappeared. (See Plate 38 and page 221.) Demolition was halted, not for reasons that might be advanced today, but because Wren was spending far too much money. So the surviving Tudor work and Wren's additions visually contrast two phases of English civilisation. The mediaeval Gothic tradition, interrupted by the Italianate fashions of the mid-sixteenth century, was rejected by renaissance architects of the seventeenth as the classic tradition was to be rejected three hundred years later. The abrupt break between the two forms of architecture at Hampton Court is as disruptively violent as the break in the social and economic structure of English life in the latter part of Henry VIII's reign. The juxtaposition of such wholly different styles at Hampton Court, with no attempt to mollify their blatant disunity, asserts the finality of the social and aesthetic revolution that had changed the character of England over a century earlier. (See page 13.)

In periods when wealth is abundant and selectively distributed for the benefit of a cultivated, fastidious and selfish ruling class, the gifts of architects and the skill of craftsmen may be wantonly squandered; this occurred in eighteenth century France before the Revolution and, to a lesser extent, in the cluster of kingdoms and principalities of Central Europe. The results, if judged by the high level of accomplishment in architecture and the ancillary arts, suggest a correspondingly high level of civilisation; but the benefits were restricted and enjoyed only by the fortunate few who happened to have been born in the right bedrooms. When the French aristocracy was butchered or exiled, national respect for works of art preserved the monuments of the old régime, irrespective of the character of the government in power: skill survived and so did the classic architectural tradition.

In recessive periods of civilisation, when technical ability is either lost or so gravely diminished that it is ineffective, new adventures in building are halted. Old structures, preserved through sheer necessity, are patched up to prolong their life. In Western Europe during the disturbed fourth and fifth centuries the chief priorities for builders would have been walls, for, in H. A. L. Fisher's memorable phrase, "long before the Roman Empire went down, its cities had adopted the mediaeval livery of fear."[21] Within those cities many buildings were transformed and their function changed. Where solid construction recommended their use as strong points, they were fortified; the example of Hadrian's Mausoleum in Rome has already been cited; there were others, some of them lost for ever, because, as Gibbon said, "Whatever is fortified will be attacked; and whatever is attacked may be destroyed."[22] Many great works of architecture have been sacrificed to military necessity.

There were peaceful and gradual transformations in Roman provinces like Gaul, where imperial administrators and great landlords came to terms with the barbarian invaders, and settled down with them, side by side, forming a mixed society; great estates became the nuclei of rural communities and the Romano–Gallic villa the ancestor of the château. That mixed society, Christian in name though pagan in conduct, commanded enough trained skill for building to continue, and in fifth century Gaul churches of ambitious design were erected and luxurious additions made to existing houses.[23] French civilisation may justly

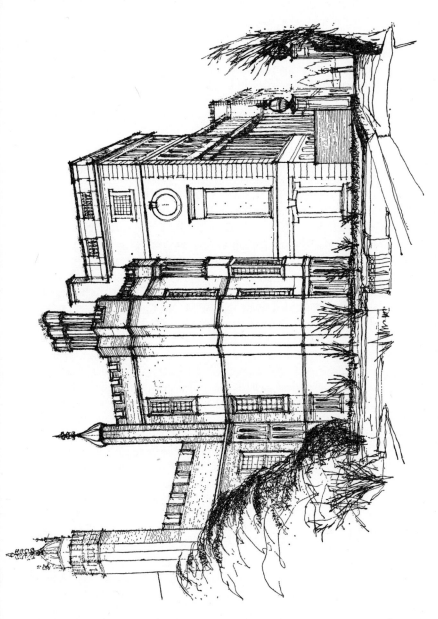

The meeting of two civilisations. The native English domestic style of the early sixteenth century at Hampton Court Palace, and the classic, late seventeenth century additions made by Sir Christopher Wren. *Drawn by Hulme Chadwick.*

claim continuity with the Roman province of Gaul, and thus with the art and culture of the Graeco–Roman world. In France as well as Italy, the remains of majestic buildings were a constant reminder of a former architectural competence, inviting emulation, and instructing the inheritors of an imperial legacy.

In Britain there was no collaboration between barbarian invaders and Romano–British citizens during the fifth and sixth centuries. The Saxons made no attempt to live in the well-built, clean cities, with their drains and unpolluted water supply, deserted by their former inhabitants but still standing, nor did they take over the abandoned villas, of which there were many, though there is evidence that some were lived in during the first half of the fifth century, perhaps later still. Collingwood and Myers have said that "Not a single villa in the country has been found underlying a Saxon dwelling or has yielded evidence of a permanent occupation in the Saxon period."[24] The invaders were pagans who honoured a grim company of gods and goddesses: Odin, Thor, Freya and the rest—very different from the deities of the Roman pantheon; different too from the native British gods. The temples of Roman Britain that had survived Christian iconoclasm were not adapted by the Saxons nor were they destroyed; like the cities and villas they stood empty, steadily assaulted by the weather, inhabited only by statues of the old gods, referred to by Gildas, the sixth century British historian, as "diabolical idols" which were "mouldering away within and without the deserted temples . . ."[25]

Some temples, like that of Claudius at Colchester, founded about A.D. 50, were very large; the massive podium which now lies beneath the Norman Castle was about 80 by 105 feet, and conjectural reconstructions, based on archaeological research, suggest an impressive pile, with colonnades of the Corinthian order.[26] At Lydney in Gloucestershire, a large-scale temple settlement was built, *circa* 364–367, for the worship of the native god, Nodens, and the accommodation of pilgrims; a considerable architectural enterprise to be undertaken in a province engaged at the time in a desperate war of defence against a concerted attack by Picts, Scots, Irish, Saxons and Attacotti. Again archaeological research has enabled the plan and purpose of a lost building to be recovered with some suggestion of its architectural character.[27] A

Reconstruction of the temple settlement at Lydney Park, Gloucestershire. The temple, dedicated to the god Nodens, is the isolated building on the left; the much larger building, surrounding a courtyard, is the guesthouse; beyond, at an angle, are the baths. The long building that runs behind the temple to the baths contains a range of small rooms, opening on to a verandah. This was the last large-scale group of buildings erected in Roman Britain, *circa* A.D. 364–367, at a time when the military forces of the province were fighting a defensive war against a coalition of barbarians. Reproduced by courtesy of the Society of Antiquaries of London from Fig. 7, of the *Report on the Excavation of the Prehistoric, Roman, and Post-Roman Site in Lydney Park, Gloucestershire*, by R. E. M. Wheeler and T. V. Wheeler. (Oxford University Press, 1932.)

reconstruction of the temple settlement is shown above: like uses beget like effects, and externally the group of late Romano-British buildings exhibits the characteristics of a mediaeval monastic establishment.

Today, throughout Europe, the towers and spires of Christian churches are familiar features of any stretch of countryside; a landscape without them would seem empty indeed, as it must have seemed before bell towers were built and the spire was invented, especially to those who remembered the world as it was before Christianity became the official state religion of the Roman Empire. In those tolerant pagan days, threads of smoke were stitched into the sky as they rose from temple altars, in every province from Wales to Syria.

Sacred sites have a long life; many churches have been built where Roman temples formerly stood; one of the oldest French Cathedrals, Notre Dame of Paris, covers the area once occupied by a temple of Jupiter when Paris was the small Roman city of Lutetia on an island in the Seine. A popular tradition that a temple of Diana was a forerunner of St. Paul's on Ludgate Hill in London is unsupported by any evidence, and when Christianity was reintroduced to Britain after St. Augustine's mission, the new bishop of London, Mellitus, created in 604, built the church of St. Paul in the southern portion of an early Roman cemetery, where a Romano–British Christian church may have existed, or at least some tradition that the site was sacred.[28] Bede quotes a letter sent by Pope Gregory to Mellitus when he was going to Britain instructing him to preserve the fabric of existing temples, to destroy the idols in them, and, after sprinkling the interior with holy water, to erect altars and place relics.[29] Some of those converted temples may have been well-built Romano–British structures, though the only known example in England of a Roman building having been subsequently incorporated in a Christian church is the ruined Church of Stone, near Faversham in Kent.[30] Bede records an early instance of the English genius for compromise, when Redwald, King of the East Saxons, attempted to make the best of both worlds by allowing Christian and pagan rites to be celebrated in the same building. While such a convenient arrangement was welcomed at a later date by the civilised Arabs and Christians of Cordova, the aggressive intolerance of Christianity in seventh century England would have none of it.[31]

When archaeologists recover the original plan of a building and the extent of subsequent additions and repairs, not only is material provided for imaginative reconstruction, as exemplified by the temple at Colchester and the temple settlement at Lydney; but long-dead architecture comes alive to support written records and, more rarely, oral traditions. One of the liveliest and most illuminating examinations of the scale and character of an ancient building is Dr. Gilbert Charles-Picard's study of the remains of Nero's fantastic Golden House in Rome, with its ancillary buildings and decoration and the extravagance of conception, which reveals the artistic ruthlessness of the imperial egomaniac who transformed the ancient temples of Castor and Vesta into vestibules to the palace, so that the citizens of Rome should be left in no doubt of his divine nature.[32] The mounting madness of the Emperor is proclaimed by the extent and complexity and continuous growth of one of the greatest architectural follies of the ancient world. The ruins still remain.

From the plan Dr. Charles-Picard deduces that the Golden House owed something to the royal palaces of Asian potentates who had come under Greek influence. That influence was first exerted after the Macedonian conquest of Hither Asia, and, as D. G. Hogarth wrote many years ago in *The Ancient East*, "the West did not assimilate the East except in very small measure then, and has not assimilated it in any very large measure to this day." His book was first published in 1914, and the statement that "the East is obstinately unreceptive of western influences" should perhaps be modified today, though the conclusion that the East has "more than once taken its captors captive" was valid until the mid-twentieth century.[33] The Romans borrowed more from the East than the Greeks, and the architectural disposition of Nero's Golden House and its relation to the spacious park that surrounded it, had Babylonian and Persian origins.[34] The scale of such Asiatic prototypes may be judged from the reconstruction, by Perrot and Chipiez, of the palaces of Persepolis, reproduced on page 61.

Architectural history seems to fit so conveniently into national compartments; but structural ideas and inventions are supernational; and throughout wide areas of civilisation the rise and decline of artistic and technical ability apparently mark cultural phases that transcend the gradations of national culture. Such phases related to Mediterranean civilisation were classified in eight periods by that great archaeologist, Sir William Flinders Petrie (1853–1942), in a remarkable little book, first published in

1911, and entitled *The Revolutions of Civilisation*.[35] He used sculpture to interpret the quality of civilisation, placed the first period in prehistoric times, and concluded the eighth in 1911—three years before the Great War that disrupted the political and social coherence of western civilisation. The eighth period began in A.D. 450, when the Roman Empire in the West was near its end, like the British Empire in 1911. The periods were shown by a diagram, which is reproduced opposite, with dotted lines indicating the growth of ability in painting, literature and mechanics, and the gradual expansion and accumulation of wealth. There are other notations on the diagram: for example the raid on Rome in 390 B.C. by Brennus, leader of the Senonian Gauls, is indicated by "Kelts" in Period VII; "Germans" in Period VIII marks a much later disaster, the sack of Rome by Germans under the Constable de Bourbon in A.D. 1527; while towards the end of that period "N" denotes the military adventures of Napoleon. The dates attributed to the early periods are invalid for, though he was a renowned Egyptologist, Flinders Petrie obstinately followed what Sir Mortimer Wheeler has called "an obsolete and untenable Egyptian chronology . . ."[36] But the fact that so great a man refused to discard a form of dating that he had used throughout his long career does not invalidate his general conclusion that cultural phases are superimposed on national history and are generated independently. Apart from his suspect dating, we should remember that in the past eminent archaeologists and art historians have inclined to mistake revolution in creative thought for decadence in executive skill. We must therefore be wary of the artistic taste of a Victorian archaeologist who, using sculpture as a yardstick, would approve the naturalism of, say, Bertel Thorwaldsen, Alfred Stevens or Lord Leighton, but faced with the abstract work of mid-twentieth century sculptors might regard their deliberate change of style as a device for concealing loss of ability. Such preoccupation with realism in sculpture has encouraged the misinterpretation of fourth and fifth century work, for at that time, as Dr. F. R. Cowell has said, "a curious thing happened. All the artistic skill of the preceding centuries seems to have vanished. Instead we have in sculpture very rough 'blocks' cut apparently without any skill, very primitively, without showing any ability to render the individual traits of the persons rendered or even the

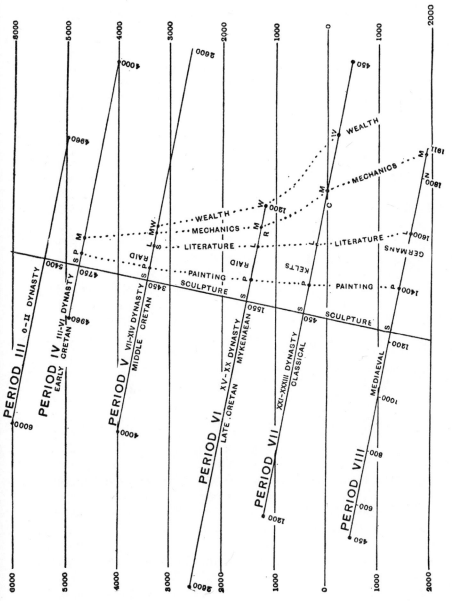

The periods and phases of Mediterranean Civilisation. Reproduced from *The Revolutions of Civilisation*, by W. M. Flinders Petrie (third edition, 1922). By courtesy of Harper and Row, Inc.

anatomy of the head and other parts of the human body." This is quoted from *History, Civilization and Culture*, Dr. Cowell's introduction to the historical and social philosophy of the Russian sociologist, Pitirim A. Sorokin (1889–1968), whose theories of social and cultural systems and historical relativity upset many accepted conclusions about the rise, maturity and decay of civilisations.[37] Dr. Cowell, after saying that the change of style in fourth and fifth century sculpture is usually explained as representing "the decay. degeneration, death and end of Roman art," quotes Sorokin's view that "this is to judge the matter by a very subjective evaluation, based on a mere assumption that there can be only one real style of artistic performance and that is the visual. The development of sculptural art in our own day," he continues, "illustrates Sorokin's views. Many of the works of modern sculptors, Eric Gill, Henry Moore, Epstein and others, may have a crude and unformed appearance . . . They are anything but visual. Yet nobody can doubt that such masters of their craft could produce excellent works in the traditional visual manner if they wished. The same may be true of the sculptors of the fourth and fifth centuries A.D."[38] Their work comes at the end of Period VII on Flinders Petrie's diagram, and he describes "the stumpy, clumsy figures of the age of Constantine, or the still coarser outlines from the catacomb tombs . . ."[39] He regards this departure from visual realism as evidence of decadence.

If some archaeologist with the same standards of artistic perception as Flinders Petrie should, three thousand years hence, recover examples of the work of Thorwaldsen and Henry Moore, separated in time by a mere century, he or she might draw the erroneous conclusion that Moore's work represented a decadent phase of civilisation. Change of style arising from a new creative awareness by a sculptor or an architect, so far from denoting degeneracy in skill or curtailed inventive powers, may indicate a fresh upsurge of cultural vitality. Naturally such revolutionary movements overset preconceived and established ideas of what is artistically permissible in sculpture or structurally possible in architecture; but modern ideas of form, like modern materials, are inherently revolutionary. Concrete, light alloys and plastics allow new freedoms, and tempt the creative designer to invent imaginative shapes, unlimited by the obduracy of stone or the faults and grain of timber; structures like Kennedy Airport in New York and the Sydney Opera House are the result.

The character of architecture asserts even more emphatically than contemporary sculpture that western civilisation has entered a new cultural period, the ninth if we accept the Flinders Petrie scale. Hitherto, to quote Professor David Pye, "the things we inherit from the past remind us that the men who made them were like us and give us a tangible link with them." (The technological revolution of the twentieth century has snapped such links.) "Hitherto it has been inconceivable," he continued, "that any one generation should discard all the equipment it has inherited and replace it completely. That may yet become possible. Even if it does, it will still be imperative for each generation deliberately to make some of its equipment so that it lasts and survives its makers."[40]

The character of modern architecture has been formed partly by the deliberate discarding of inherited equipment and the rejection of traditional building materials and methods; this flight from old and tested ideas followed the invention of new strucural methods and the use of industrially-produced materials in the nineteenth century; so that by 1910 Kipling's bricklayer, who tried to convince his hearers,

> "How very little since things were made,
> Things have altered in the building trade"[41]

was already archaic. The results of the building revolution, at first disguised, became apparent everywhere after the first quarter of the present century, and they are impersonal, orderly, and almost aggressively simple. Irregularities and fanciful human whims are excluded; the old, deep-rooted human love of ornament is ignored, or at most a piece of abstract sculpture is applied to a surface or erected in isolation, more as an intellectual stimulant than a concession to an ancient appetite. Mediaeval architecture differed as profoundly from the urbane classicism of the eighteenth century as Chaucer's earthy humour differed from the graceful wit of Horace Walpole; and contemporary architecture differs from all the previous works of man, and represents far more than a fashionable reaction against the aesthetic incertitudes and opulent vulgarity of the Victorian age. We are too close to its manifestations, too deeply, though perhaps unconsciously, influenced by the propaganda for what used to be called "the modern movement," to be able to interpret what the still immature architecture of our own century is saying about the society it serves, for it is certainly saying something. No building is dumb; a disused air-raid shelter cries *fear* as harshly as a city wall; a street of slums shouts *greed*; a modern office block asserts the economic facts of commercial life with the dry precision of an accountant. Irrespective of time or place, the interpretative quality in architecture persists, and in the chapters that follow architecture has been used as Flinders Petrie used sculpture to indicate phases of civilisation.

Stonehenge on Salisbury Plain, as it appeared in the mid-nineteenth century. This primitive example of post-and-lintel construction dates from the second millennium, B.C. Reproduced from *Wanderings of an Antiquary*, by Thomas Wright, F.S.A. (London: J. B. Nichols and Sons. 1854).

THE TYRANNY OF ETERNAL REPETITION

THE character of architecture has been developed by structural discoveries, of which the earliest was simply that two vertical members of equal height were able to support a horizontal member. This elementary form of post-and-lintel, post-and-beam, or trabeated architecture, as it is variously called, may be seen in primitive temples like Stonehenge, on Salisbury Plain, where the trilithons of the inner circle represent a crude version of the post-and-lintel construction of an Egyptian temple. The principle of vertical support for horizontal, weight-carrying beams, is still used, for walls act as posts and carry the beams that support floors and roofs. Even when walls have no structural function, they are often employed for visual satisfaction.

The Egyptians hit on the idea of using columns, upright members of uniform shape and circular section, that stood at equal distances apart, to support a continuous horizontal member. The use of columns in series originated the colonnade, about 2500 B.C. Post-and-lintel construction revealed the possibilities and the limitations of wood and stone; builders learned the maximum width of a gap that could be spanned by a lintel or a beam and what weight such a horizontal member could carry without breaking. To achieve stability and support weight were problems that faced builders directly they progressed beyond the stage of excavating shelters, by enlarging caves or burrowing into cliffs, and began to erect weather-proof structures on open ground. The art of architecture arose and developed in the valleys of the Nile and Tigris; the alluvial mud of those rivers not only gave abundant crops, but an inexhaustible supply of building material in the form of sun-baked bricks. The crops created a surplus of wealth for the endowment of architecture; in Egypt buildings ceased to be purely utilitarian shelters; tombs, temples and palaces began to reflect the complexities, mysteries and inhibitions of a sacerdotal civilisation, ruled by god-kings.

Although Egyptian builders made the next most important structural discovery, and as early as the thirtieth century B.C., first employed the arch in masonry,[1] they used it merely as a weight-distributing convenience, and remained faithful to the post-and-lintel principle. This reluctance to make the most of a new invention in building construction was not peculiar to the ancient Egyptians: later and more accomplished architects used the arch solely as a utilitarian device, and even concealed its structural significance by an external display of horizontal and vertical forms that had no function apart from comforting the eye of the beholder with something long-established and familiar.

Such inventions as the column and the colonnade had a profound effect upon the character of architecture that persisted until traditional reliance on the post-and-lintel principle was swept aside by the structural revolution of the industrial age as ruthlessly as the authority of religion was swept aside by nineteenth century science. Egyptian architecture seems to cry out: "Thus far, and no further. Stop! It is blasphemy to proceed." Such injunctions are invalid in a world that has lost its respect for priestly authority along with its ancient awe of magic. The Egyptians were specialists in awe, though Lisle March Phillipps regarded them as an intensely materialistic race because they were so impressed "by mere bulk and extent." (There was an excellent reason for massive bulk.) His view on the interpretative quality of architecture has already been quoted from one of his early and lesser-known books, *In the Desert*, published in 1905; by far his most important book, *The Works of Man*, followed in 1911 and it interprets the quality and character of successive civilisations through critical observation of their art and architecture.[2] The opening chapter presents the evidence for the arrested growth of Egyptian architectural design, petrified by the inert tyranny of eternal repetition.

"Thou art a rare noodle, master," says Shaw's St. Joan to Canon Courcelles; "do what was done last time is thy rule, eh?"[3] That common response to the uncomfortable challenge of change provides the cosiest of all excuses for doing what was done last time, especially when innovation is condemned by religious faith. In Ancient Egypt religion was an all-powerful and terrifying vested interest; priests and god-kings could and did insist that architects and sculptors, and to a lesser extent, painters, should do what was done last time: apart from religious subjects the artist was allowed to make full use of his imagination and to depict the animation and excitement of war and hunting as well as the diversions and routine of everyday life.

By comparison with the movement and vitality of Egyptian painting, architecture tells a sombre story; under the direction of the priestly caste, the architect was compelled to minimise the individual importance and even the stature of man by over-shadowing, overpowering structures. In the colonnaded halls of great temples humanity was dwarfed. The columns were visible from base to capital in the light that came through small openings high up in the solid walls and through horizontal slit windows immediately below the roof. Such internal colonnades were simple in form, like those in the temple of Amon at Luxor. (Plate 3.) Because those columns, with their plain bud capitals, now stand in a roofless ruin, exposed to the glare of Egyptian sunlight, their original architectural character has changed; intense shadow over-emphasises the break between shaft and capital, and the shafts plunge down darkly to almost invisible bases.

Of all royal tombs the pyramids are the most conspicuous and memorable, but other works of intimidating magnitude still exist, such as the avenue of ram-headed sphinxes between the temples of Amon at Karnak and Luxor, and gigantic statues that, like the tombs and temples, were intended to stand for ever. (Plate 4.) As impressive as the pyramids are the two seated statues of Amen-hotep III that rear their battered heads some fifty feet above the western plain of Thebes and once flanked the mortuary chapel of that pharaoh. They are known as the Memnon colossi, and the eastern statue has on a few occasions in the past emitted a melodious sound.[4] The figures, though badly damaged, have survived; the temple has disappeared. (Plate 1.)

The desire for permanence arose partly from the belief that earthly life was a transitory episode preceding a more impor-tant celestial hereafter;[5] the temples and tombs are architectural expressions of that hopeful desire: statues on the scale of the Memnon colossi assert the arrogant conviction that eternal fame was the royal due of pharoah. In Ozymandias of Egypt, Shelley exposed the glozing pride of those ancient god-kings, and the ineluctable destruction that awaited their monuments.

> "I met a traveller from an antique land
> Who said: Two vast and trunkless legs of stone
> Stand in the desert. Near them on the sand
> Half sunk, a shatter'd visage lies, whose frown
> And wrinkled lip and sneer of cold command
> Tell that its sculptor well those passions read
> Which yet survive, stamp'd on these lifeless things,
> The hand that mock'd them and the heart that fed;
> And on the pedestal these words appear:
> 'My name is Ozymandias, king of kings:
> Look on my works, ye Mighty, and despair!'
> Nothing beside remains. Round the decay
> Of that colossal wreck, boundless and bare,
> The lone and level sands stretch far away."

One hundred and fifty years after the reign of Amenhotep III ended (in 1375 B.C.), his mortuary chapel was destroyed by the pharaoh Merneptah (1225–1215 B.C.), and later still, in 525 B.C., Cambyses, the Persian conqueror of Egypt, defaced the twin colossi. The upper half of the eastern figure was thrown down by an earthquake in 27 B.C., which also damaged the western statue. Repairs were carried out late in the second or early in the third century A.D., when Egypt had long been a Roman province, and such public-spirited care for ancient monuments is ascribed to the emperor, Septimius Severus (A.D. 193–211). Only an emperor could have commanded the resources for such a considerable work of renovation. (Plate 1.)

Preoccupation with an after-life left a permanent mark on Egyptian art and architecture; and before the pyramids were built, spacious and magnificent tombs had become far more impressive in size and design than structures that served the living. The actual tomb chamber lay in the heart of a huge mass of brickwork, two or three hundred feet long and about a hundred and fifty feet wide; masterpieces of painting on the chamber walls were buried, along with the painted and gilt coffin containing the mummy—there they remained unseen in the spice-scented darkness until grave robbers centuries later looted the jewels and gold from the coffin,

Gateway to the Temple of Amon, Luxor, *circa* 1450 B.C. *Drawn by Maureen Stafford.*

and, later still, archaeologists sketched and photographed the murals. This *mastaba* type of tomb was enlarged by successive skins of sloping brickwork, built at a steep angle; the early step-pyramids were really enlarged *mastabas*, and it was from these that the smooth-sided pyramid form developed. The base of the Great Pyramid at Gizeh covers thirteen acres; the height to the apex is 482 feet; and the surface was cased with white polished stone. It was built by Khufu (or Cheops), the first pharaoh of the Fourth Dynasty, who began his reign in 2900 B.C. Herodotus, writing over two thousand four hundred years later mentions a tradition that the work employed 100,000 labourers for twenty years. The surplus wealth of the country was squandered on such structures, which, as Lisle March Phillipps has remarked, were devoid of intellectual significance.

"It would probably not be possible to find on the earth's surface buildings so vast yet so vacant of expression of any kind," he wrote. "They do not even express their own size, for the pyramidal or triangular outline carries the eye to its apex with such instant rapidity that the passage thereto seems no distance at all; and so, though we tell ourselves that the Great Pyramid covers thirteen acres and is taller than the dome of St. Peter's, though we walk round it and painfully climb up it, and impress by all means its bulk upon our minds, yet as an object of sight the building does not remain in the memory as of any considerable size."[6]

This view is far removed from the adulatory descriptions written with misplaced reverence by people who perhaps believe that the Great Pyramid confirms the vulgar notion that "bigger is better". Continuing his demolition of popular illusions, March Phillips said that "The idea of a pyramid suggests not greatness but a point, and is adequately represented by its image on a postcard. If it leaves a further impression on the mind, it must be one of wonder at the dullness, amounting, it would seem, to the atrophy of the intellectual faculties, which it indicates as characteristic of its builders. A uniform, solid triangle of masonry, mechanically accurate and utterly expressionless in its dead monotony, without any intelligible purpose, as is now admitted, save the stupid and ignoble one of hiding a wretched corpse in its bowels—that, I believe, is an architectural phenomenon absolutely without a parallel."[7]

The pyramids were not isolated monuments; each had a temple on the eastern side, dedicated to the buried pharaoh, and pyramids and temple were surrounded by paved, walled courts, like a cathedral precinct with its subsidiary buildings. The impressiveness of tombs and temples was accentuated by a majestic approach, which set a pattern that has been followed for fifty centuries. The avenue of sphinxes between the temples at Karnak and Luxor has its modern counterpart in the broad approach to the mausoleum of Kemal Ataturk at Ankara, which is flanked by sculptured lions.

Unlike the tomb and the temple with its adjacent buildings, the Egyptian town lacked impressive grandeur; it was merely a place for living in, and not, like a Greek city, calculated to generate civic pride. It was square or rectangular in plan with a regular pattern of streets and clearly defined quarters for different social classes: as death and the afterlife seemed so important, perhaps everyday existence was enjoyed without any desire for an indestructible environment. For slaves and the poorer classes life by modern standards was hardly worth living, for they inhabited mud-brick thatched houses, huddled in groups and masses, as devoid of amenities and privacy as the back-to-back houses of Victorian slums. Habit, religion and a benign climate kept them docile, though the patience of the unprivileged majority must have been severely strained when they contrasted their lives with the spacious leisure of their masters. Poverty may be less oppressive in a warm climate; rich and poor alike were devoted to outdoor life, and love of the open air tended to minimise the importance of the town. Well-planned houses were available for members of the ruling class, the royal entourage, high officials and wealthy noblemen; architecturally unpretentious, they were built of brick and timber, two or three storeys high. Their courts, colonnades, gardens, central water tanks, fish ponds and bathing pools provided the chief luxuries of life: shade and water. The garden was planted with fig, palm and sycamore trees; vines were laced over arbours, and seclusion ensured by thick walls that surrounded the whole estate.[8] The art of living gracefully and comfortably outside as well as inside a house had been perfected; the relationship of the garden to architecture was then established, and has been remembered and amplified ever since by other peoples in other places. Those lightly-built houses have not survived, but Egyptian paintings

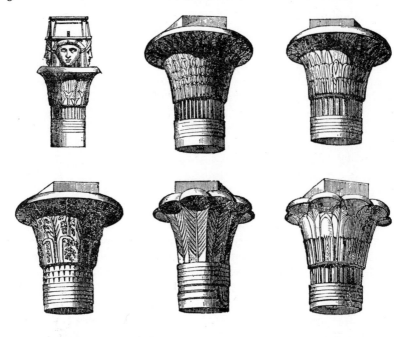

Each of these Egyptian capitals is separated from the column by a band, representing the cord that originally bound flowers, buds and leaves to a wooden post. Reproduced from *The British Museum: Egyptian Antiquities.* (London. M. A. Nattali, 1846.) Vol. 1, pages 107 and 110.

show us what they looked like. Windows lit the rooms; walls, ceilings and floors were painted with repetitive patterns of formalised flowers and plants, with vivid representations of birds, animals, hunting scenes, and the varied traffic on the Nile. Compared with the static quality of sculpture and architecture, Egyptian painting is animated by creative zest, struggling against and sometimes breaking free from the inflexible conventions of formal representation.

A timber-built Egyptian house, surrounded by a walled garden. *Restoration after Perrot and Chipiez.*

From early Egyptian paintings we may trace the evolution and development of many types of ornament and of the shape and decoration of the column. The prototype of the monolithic column, hewn from a single block of stone, was the wooden tent pole. Such columns were generally divided into three parts of unequal length, of which the longest was the shaft, rising from a base and crowned by a shaped, ornamented capital. The bulk and weight of a stone column bedded in the ground gave it the necessary stability; no

base was needed, but because the wooden prototypes had been
socketed into circular stone blocks, those blocks were perpetuated
as the bases of stone columns. The shape and ornamentation of the
capitals originated from the custom of tying flowers and leaves to
wooden posts; so formalised versions of the papyrus blossom, lotus
bud and palm leaf were carved in stone, precedent being honoured
even to the extent of separating the capital from the shaft by a band
representing the cord which had bound real flowers and buds and
leaves to a wooden post. Flinders Petrie has remarked on the slight
influence of the palm on early Egyptian architecture though it was
the most important tree in the land.[9] During the XIIth dynasty
(*circa* 2000–1788 B.C.), bundles of palm branches were imitated on
the capitals of columns, a decorative device that became common
in the XVIIIth dynasty (*circa* 1580–1350 B.C.). Before permanent
materials were used for pillars bundles of the flowering stem of the
papyrus reed were used. These reeds, lashed together in rolls,
probably originated the vertical convex ornament on columns
known as reeding.

Egyptian architects manipulated light and shade to give variety
to surfaces; mouldings drew bold dark lines across walls; coved
cornices, like those on the gateways on page 27 and Plate 2,
gained emphasis from deep bands of intense black; columns that
tapered towards the base appeared to rise from a pool of shadow
and their shape was not the result of aesthetic insensitivity, or
ignorance of structural necessity, as Lisle March Phillipps suggests, for although architecture tells the truth about those who
create its forms, modern minds may misinterpret the message.
March Phillipps, for instance, said that the shape of an Egyptian
column resembles "a gigantic sausage—that is to say, it is of great
bulk throughout, except at the base, where it suddenly and
violently contracts. Now, the base of a column is precisely the point
where its strength should be greatest; for, since it is evident that no
part of the column can exceed the strength of the base, any weakness
there cripples inevitably the whole body." A few sentences later,
he suggests that because of their bulging shape, Egyptian columns
"convey to the spectator an impression of softness. Resting on their
diminished bases," he continues, "their swollen masses have the
distended and, so to speak, dropsical aspect of matter divorced
from energy. Such forms as these strike the European mind as

abortions because they were not evolved by and do not express the function they perform. The giant shapes of the columns of Luxor and Karnak convey no idea of a definite power exercised or a definite duty fulfilled."[10]

The admission that such conclusions occur to "the European mind" significantly qualifies the statement: to an oriental mind the aesthetic intention of Egyptian architects might be sun-clear and the apparent sacrifice of structural stability condoned without any reservations. Those architects continued to use the same forms and ornamental conventions for thousands of years; the dynamic inspiration that originated the column and the colonnade and such shapes as the obelisk, deserted them, and though they knew about the arch, the vault and the dome, their knowledge was seldom applied; they were not free to make experiments, but their restricted liberty in matters of design was accompanied by a prodigious mastery over building materials.

"They certainly were the world's leaders in the craft of handling intractable stone," wrote Stanley Casson, in his book *Progress and Catastrophe*. "Their methods of craftsmanship in the Bronze Age were astonishing, for all their carving and finishing had to be done with instruments of stone except in the case of the carving of limestone, which was soft enough to be cut with copper and bronze. Their methods of masoning stone were equalled only in fifth century Greece, and were so precise and perfect that modern masons, even with the latest scientific appliances, cannot produce the effects of the Egyptian mason. To the Greeks also they transmitted some of the elements of temple-building, though the Greeks made an art of what the Egyptians had succeeded only in making a superb craft."

Magnificent craftsmanship has often been lavished on indifferent design. Casson, examining with the critical eye of an archaeologist the quality of the contribution made by various civilisations to progress and the sum of human knowledge, said that "In art, Egypt has bequeathed superb masterpieces, above all in the art of sculpture. But she also has to her credit enormous vulgarities. The tomb of Tutankhamen is proof enough of that. And in art Egypt has made what is almost her sole contribution to posterity. Otherwise she succeeded in putting civilisation into cold storage for an immense period of time."[11]

Egyptian architecture confirms that statement. If no other records existed, their monuments alone would reveal the nature of a society that was by choice unchanging, and in the course of countless generations, became incapable of change.

"From Egypt we seem, on reflection, to have inherited almost nothing," Casson said. "That some four thousand years of uninterrupted organised life in the Nile valley should have bequeathed us so little that we have to pause and rack our brains to think what is our 'legacy of Egypt', is a pathetic commentary on the Egyptian achievement. Not that civilisation ever broke down or was even destroyed at any time in Egyptian history. Nothing seriously interfered with the course of events. The Hyksos intrusion was, in a sense, a slight set-back, but the newcomers absorbed the system of Egyptian life almost as soon as they entered the valley. So, later, intrusive Greeks and Romans were absorbed by Egyptian ideas. Egypt imposed on Ptolemies and Emperors alike their ancient divine kingship, so that Greek princes rapidly learned to describe themselves as gods in a way which would have made Greeks elsewhere laugh with scorn, while Romans exalted the attenuated divinity that hedged a Roman Emperor into a real godhead. From start to finish in Egyptian history foreign ideas were quietly but firmly suffocated, while internal unorthodoxy was violently strangled."[12]

Apart from the spiritual desire for permanence and religious resistance to change, there was a compelling physical reason that committed Egyptian architects to massive structures. When they began to use brick and stone they had to contend with a seasonal instability of the ground they built on in the Nile Valley. In summer, when the river was at its lowest, the ground was dried up, but after the inundation as water penetrated the dry soil, the ground level rose, as much as twelve or twenty inches, settling down again to its original dry level when the water subsided, but never rising or falling evenly.[13] Temples erected beyond the range of seepage or surface flooding were immune, but those built near the river, like the temple at Karnak that stood on its bank, were designed to withstand the stresses and strains imposed by ground movement, and the success of the methods employed is proved by thirty centuries of survival.

Deliberate destruction has ruined far more buildings, great and small, than the attrition of time; destruction carried out for religious motives in the course of strangling unorthodoxy; or on the orders of some pharaoh who found the fame of his predecessors unbearable and defaced their temples and statues; or by the will of some conqueror, like Cambyses, determined to humble the national pride of the conquered. The last enemies of architecture, who appear only when civilisation has broken down, are the stone robbers.

The most outstanding example of suppressed innovation in Egyptian history, was the extirpation of the religious movement instigated by the pharaoh Amenhotep IV (1375–1358 B.C.), who changed his own name from Amenhotep to Ikhnaton, forsook Thebes, and built a new capital between Thebes and the sea which he called Akhetaton. The complexities of the theological struggle between the young pharaoh and the religious establishment, represented by the priests of Amon, are set forth in Professor Breasted's study, *The Dawn of Conscience*,[14] and in another work Breasted describes Ikhnaton as "the most remarkable of all the Pharaohs, and the first *individual* is human history."[15] During his reign and before his fall, the arts were released from the rigid formalism that sacred custom had ordained and perpetuated. Ikhnaton was a religious intellectual with a revolutionary mind; like lesser men before and after him he expunged from the great monuments of Thebes names that offended him, not through personal pride or self-aggrandisement, but because the name Amon was a constant reminder of the latent power of those who opposed him; not even the name of his father, Amenhotep III, escaped erasure.[16] He was unconcerned with worldly affairs or the welfare of the Egyptian Empire, and remained in his Sun-palace at Akhetaton, musing and dreaming about his great revolution, while the Hittites invaded and conquered his Asiatic provinces.[17] His portraits show the calm, kind, withdrawn countenance of a sensitive visionary.

A new chapter of Egyptian art opened and ended with the reign of Ikhnaton; during that time sculptors and painters rejoiced in their release from ancient controls; realism was vigorously triumphant; even royal figures were humanised; stiff, immobilised postures no longer conveyed an air of frozen dignity, and the modelling of the human form anticipated the easy plasticity of

Greek sculpture. Compositions of grouped figures were now conceived,[18] and the latent vivacity always apparent in Egyptian
painting at last found expression in three dimensions.

Little has survived. The intellectual dreamer not only lost the
Egyptian Empire, but the revolution in religion and art that he
had instigated. His city of Akhetaton lasted for a few years, but
was soon forsaken and deserted. It is known today as Tell el-
Amarna, and some ruins remain. The theological adventure, for
adventure rather than experiment is the right word for such a
defiant act of courage, and the brief period of liberation for the
arts, had no permanent effect; architecture and sculpture in
Egypt re-entered the shadows of tradition; the rule of eternal
repetition was re-established in the encircling gloom of the ancient
religion.

Sculpture has a special relationship with architecture, and there
is some truth in the plausible generalisation made by H. G. Wells
when he wrote: "Painting, sculpture, all furnishing and decoration, are the escaped subsidiaries of architecture, and may return
very largely to their old dependence."[19] Periodically, in different
ages and cultures, those arts and crafts have partly or wholly
resumed that dependence, a tendency already apparent in
western civilisation in the second half of the twentieth century, for
the belief that "The house is a machine for living in,"[20] has affected
the use and internal arrangement of space in dwellings, and externally sculpture has been reintroduced to punctuate the composition of groups of buildings or to variegate their surfaces.

In ancient Egypt the association of sculpture with buildings was
very close; an intimate connection that was repeated in many
later civilisations. Those stark, stiff figures that form the Osiris
pillars at Luxor (Plate 2), were the prototypes of the lighter and
far more graceful Greek caryatids; the Osiris figures are applied to
the vertical supports of the temple, unlike the Greek caryatids
which, either singly or in groups, were the actual supports, structurally incorporated with the building.

Large-scale sculptured figures in Egypt were usually detached
from a building, though they often formed an integral part of some
great architectural composition, like the Memnon colossi each side
of the mortuary chapel of Amenhotep III, or the four figures of
Rameses II, seated before the façade of the cliff temple of Abu

A restoration of the pavilion of Medinet-Abou, at Thebes. This shows the batter
on the outer walls and the pylons. *After Perrot and Chipiez.*

Simbel. (Egypt was so over-populated with statues of the god-
kings that the Israelites, with unhappy memories of their recent
bondage, probably welcomed the prohibition of the second commandment.) Far larger even than the Memnon colossi was the
monolithic granite statue of Rameses II (1292–1225 B.C.), ninety
feet high and weighing nine hundred tons, which overtopped the
huge pylons of his temple at Tanis, that flourishing city in the
Delta. His innumerable statues and splendid works of architecture
are everywhere in evidence: his placid face with full lips set in a
complacent half-smile stares down at the crowds of pygmy tourists
who from Roman times to our own visit the Nile valley. "Few of the
great temples of Egypt have not some chamber, hall, colonnade or
pylon which bears his name," wrote Breasted, "in perpetuating
which the king stopped at no desecration or destruction of the
ancient monuments of the country."[21]

The destruction of statues that celebrate the former fame of kings or great men still continues, in Egypt and elsewhere. After the short, abortive war over the control of the Suez Canal in October 1956 the statue of Ferdinand de Lesseps, the French engineer who made it, was violently removed by orders of President Gamal Abdel Nasser (1916–1970), who, after all, was only following the example of the pharaohs. The gesture, motivated by national emotion, was just as futile as the destruction of some former god-king's effigy, and nobody pretended to mourn the de Lesseps statue as the passing of a masterpiece of sculpture; it was never much more than a landmark.

Something about graven images seems to evoke boisterous passions, especially when they have a human likeness; they tempt sanctimonious hooligans to excesses of iconoclasm and release the uncreative forces of political fanaticism, and there was far deeper wisdom in the second commandment than the Children of Israel may have ever suspected, wisdom that was recognised by Mahomet many centuries later when he forbade the copying of human and natural forms, and thereby profoundly affected the character of Islamic art. In ancient Egypt there were, in addition to the multiplicity of statues of god-kings, priests and officials, innumerable copies of the sphinx, that fabulous hybrid in the form of a recumbent lion with a human head, sometimes carved with the features of the reigning pharaoh, or with the head of a ram, the sacred animal of Amon, or a falcon. When the head portrayed the god-king, the lion's body was retained to symbolise his power,[22] and the human face was surrounded by the lion's mane.[23] The Greeks gave this composite monster its name, and the most celebrated and largest example is at Gizeh, 189 feet long, carved from a single rock. (Plate 1.) The sphinx was often a unit in some large architectural complex of processional ways, courts and temples. It was adopted later by other civilisations; the Hittites, Assyrians, Greeks and Romans produced winged variations of the Egyptian original; when it reappeared during the Renaissance, it was regarded purely as an ornamental device, which would have horrified the Egyptians, if indeed they had been able to identify the classical version with the sacred and regal archetype. (See pages 50, 79, and 113).

Although the Egyptians were accomplished architects with a considerable knowledge of engineering, they never built any bridges; for crossing the Nile and other waterways they used ferry boats large enough to take animals and freight.[24] Despite their skill in handling building materials, they never altered their constructional methods. Their pylons and gateways were always built with a batter, sloped so the base of the wall was thicker than the top, which was essential to give stability to masses of sun-baked mud bricks, but unnecessary when stone was used; the form was retained though the material was changed, and battered walls and towers became and remained typical features of Egyptian architecture. (See pages 27, 37 and Plate 2.)

The strictures of Lisle March Phillipps on the rejection of visual stability, quoted earlier in connection with the shape of large columns, took no account of aesthetic intention; and it is conceivable that, apart altogether from the lure of the familiar, the batter on walls and pylons was never discarded because it was visually satisfying. But there is evidence for his contention that the simplicity of Egyptian art and architecture was primitive simplicity, not intellectual simplicity.[25] Egyptian craftsmanship was impressive, both in large-scale works like temples and tombs, or in small articles such as chairs and stools; but because precious and exotic materials are used, many modern admirers of that ancient furniture are oblivious of its inferior design. Beautifully carved legs, copied from animals, had no linear unity with the seat and back of a chair or throne; for example, the golden throne of Tutankhamen that glitters so alluringly is a conglomeration of well-executed but totally unrelated features. A painting of a chair with an X-shaped underframe, from the tomb of Nebamun, Thebes, *circa* 1400 B.C., illustrated on page 40, not only displays an incapacity for coherence in design, but structural weakness as well. Such defects appear chiefly in seat furniture: some stools, like tables and beds, have obvious stability, but the Egyptian cabinet-maker seldom achieved elegance and only with such receptacles as chests and caskets.

The panorama of Egyptian art and architecture, unrolled from the beginning of the third millennium B.C., to the early centuries of the Christian era, comes to an end in the last quarter of the seventh period of Mediterranean civilisation described by Flinders Petrie, when the cosmopolitan Graeco–Roman civilisation had established throughout the western world the standardised classic

Painting of a chair from the tomb of Nebamun, Thebes, *circa* 1400 B.C. The curved members of the X-shaped under-frame are unrelated, clumsy, and even unstable; the slight curve of the legs disrupts the line of the back and they cross at an angle that suggests structural instability, for the seat is not braced by members that could obviously support weight. This chair displays not only structural weakness, but an incapacity for coherence in design. Reproduced from *The British Museum: Egyptian Antiquities* (London: M. A. Nattali, 1846). Vol. II, page 64.

architecture and representational art originally developed and perfected in Greece. The repeating pattern of Egypt's intensely national art never changed, and the static character of Egyptian architecture throughout its long history apparently confirms Stanley Casson's conclusion, when he wrote: "If we look for anything to-day whose origin is Egyptian we shall look almost in vain."[26] But the Egyptian invention of the column and the colonnade liberated buildings from their complete dependence on walls, and later civilisations profited by this opening out of architectural composition: as we said earlier in this chapter, the results have endured wherever the post-and-lintel form of construction is still in use.

3

LOST EMPIRES

ARCHAEOLOGISTS have recovered the history of civilisations that were once as established and flourishing though not as widespread as western civilisation is to-day; by comparison with the Sumerians, the Hittites, and the Minoans, the the Roman Empire seems not only nearer to us in time but almost modern in its cosmopolitan character, and as the Roman past still survives in our present, so did the Sumerian past survive in the later civilisations of Mesopotamia and the Minoan past in the Mycenaean Empire and, later, in the Hellenic world. From the royal graves of Ur, the chief city of the Sumerians; from the excavated ruins of Hattusas, the capital of the Hittite empire; and from Cnossus in Crete, the island empire of the Minoans, we can assess the character of the architecture and art of those ancient peoples, as archaeologists may assess the architectural quality of London, Paris and New York, when, in Kipling's lines,

" . . . all our pomp of yesterday,
Is one with Nineveh and Tyre."

What they will make of our strenuous inconsistencies, our commercial aggrandisement and industrial squalor, is happily unknown to us; the jostling contrasts of wealth and poverty, the urge for movement, attested by sprawling airports and purposeful motorways, may lead savants of the thirtieth century to some odd and possibly unflattering conclusions about Western civilisation. Our buildings of steel and glass and concrete and other industrially-produced materials may have decayed beyond recognition or hope of restoration; and the archaeologists of futurity may be left with fragments as unrelated and puzzling as those in Salvador de Madariaga's romance, *The Sacred Giraffe*, which portrays a black African feminist civilisation of the seventieth century A.D., whose learned doctors attempt to reconstruct our life and times from the covers of the Oxford Book of English Verse, a tobacco tin, and an Eno's Fruit Salt bottle.[1]

Architecture to-day is seldom designed to endure; even if some buildings should escape demolition for economic reasons, modern methods of destruction are far more devastating than anything the military men and militant priests of the ancient world could command, so all that survives for the instruction of our remote descendants may be dust and ashes. We at least are better off when we seek evidence of the ways of our remote ancestors.

We may go back, perhaps, as early as 4000 B.C., to the Sumerians who founded a civilisation in Mesopotamia with Ur as their capital. That is further back in time than the first Egyptian dynasty, which began after Upper and Lower Egypt had been united. The date is uncertain; Breasted gives 3400 B.C. for the accession of that misty figure, Menes;[2] later authorities suggest 3100 B.C. as the beginning of the first dynasty, after the country had been united for over a century.[3] Long before Egyptian civilisation had established its characteristic architecture, the Sumerians were far advanced in that art, and had invented the ziggurat, a lofty temple tower of several storeys, each decreasing in area as the tower ascended. That forerunner of the zoned skyscraper had a celestial significance. Such towers stood in the centre of each town, an ever-visible link between heaven and earth, with the topmost platform inviting the gods to descend to earth, while earthly kings could humbly and arduously approach heaven. To build high is an ancient human ambition, and, as related in the eleventh chapter of Genesis, those who dwelt upon a plain in the land of Shinar made bricks and said, "let us build us a city and a tower, whose top may reach unto heaven . . ." Then "the Lord came down to see the city and the tower, which the children of men had builded."[4] Disliking what He saw, He confounded their language.

Centuries before the first Book of Moses was written, the Sumerians built their towers in order to invite such divine visits, and those lofty structures were the most conspicuous contribution to the architecture of Middle Eastern civilisations, and even the most famous tower of classical antiquity, the Pharos of Alexandria, seems to have been an elongated ziggurat, 500 feet high, and possibly the prototype of the Moslem minaret as described in a later chapter.

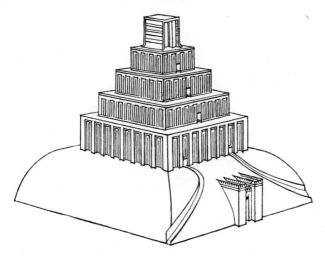

The central ziggurat of an Assyrian temple. *From a restoration after Perrot and Chipiez. Drawn by Maureen Stafford.*

The Babylonian Empire, derived from the Sumerian civilisation, was eventually transformed by Semitic invaders from the Arabian hinterland, and from a bustling, commercial state, became an aggressive military power, extending from Egypt and Syria eastwards to the Persian Gulf, and northwards to the territory of the Hittites, embracing the whole of Mesopotamia, and with Babylon, the chief city, straddling the Euphrates. That city was square in plan with a grid pattern of streets, and divided by the river into two approximately equal triangles. Herodotus, who went there about 450 B.C., wrote an exaggerated account of its size, though what he saw was probably very much what any modern traveller would see in a vast, strange city after exploring it without a street map. He recorded that the walls were of brick, 340 feet high and 90 feet thick. The houses rose to three or four storeys, and within the circuit of the walls were palaces, temples, open spaces planted with trees, an abundant water supply, a good drainage system, and an imposing processional way, broad and straight, running north and south and connecting the palaces with the temples. The famous hanging gardens, overlooking the walls,

Above: Restoration of north-eastern façade and grand entrance of Sennacherib's Palace. *After James Fergusson.* Reproduced from Layard's *Ninevah and Babylon.*

Right: Conjectural view of interior of an Assyrian Palace, showing the massive sculptured piers that support the galleries. From Jones's *Nineveh and its Story.* (See pages 48 and 49).

were laid out on different levels; and the walls, temples and palaces were unforgettably majestic. Not only great cities like Babylon, but the whole orderly countryside proclaimed the technical skill of a highly-organised civilisation: for centuries the land had been cultivated, irrigated by a system of canals, so old that their origin was attributed to the Gods, and between Armenia and the Persian Gulf a prosperous and settled world existed, irrespective of the ruling power, whether it was Babylonia or Assyria, divided or united or dominated by Semitic conquerors from the south, or Elamite conquerors from the north-east,[5] while the production of wealth, the progress of learning, and the practice of the arts continued unchecked by political changes and military adventures.

The different levels on which the large, lavish Babylonian palaces were built, were approached by flights of steps; for the peculiar impressiveness and dignity of steps had long been recognised, and they played a significant part in social, regal and religious ceremonies. Those long flights of steps may have generated the idea of rising tiers of seats about a circular or semi-circular space, so that an arena or stage was comfortably visible to a large crowd of spectators. This became the basic form of the open-air Greek theatre and the Roman amphitheatre, which still persists in Spanish and Mexican bull rings and in football and sports grounds.

The temples of Babylon, like the palaces, were built on different levels; the most imposing of all, the sanctuary of Bel, had eight towers or storeys, and followed the form of the Sumerian ziggurat, with the ascent to the temple, which stood on the topmost tower, winding about the other towers. In *The Golden Bough*, Sir James Frazer has described the furnishing and function of that temple, which contained a great bed, richly draped and cushioned, with a golden table beside it. There were no images, and the only person to spend a night there was a single woman, who, according to the priests, was chosen by the god from all the women of Babylon. The priests said that the god himself entered the temple at night and slept in the great bed, and the woman, as his consort, was thereafter forbidden to have intercourse with mortal men.[6]

The Assyrian civilisation that followed the Babylonian was a military autocracy, aggressive, ruthless, technically accomplished in architecture and the ancillary arts, and the way those arts were practised disclosed a coarse appetite for luxury and ostentation. Dean Inge once said, with some justice, that Assyria represented the Wolf State of antiquity,[7] an observation that gives sinister substance to Byron's lines:

"The Assyrian came down like the wolf on the fold,
    And his cohorts were gleaming in purple and gold . . ."

Their royal palaces were conceived on a gigantic scale and adorned with sculptured figures of gods, monarchs, animals, and, incorporated as structural elements, winged lions or bulls with bearded human heads. Those placidly smiling bearded faces looked wise and benevolent; but the Assyrians were anything but benevolent; the scenes depicted on their bas-reliefs often dwelt on the vilest aspects of war, the torture, flaying and impalement of captives, executed in spirited detail and exulting in the beastly cruelty that deformed the character of their rulers. The surfaces of their tall, brick-built structures shone with glazed tiles in varied colours and patterns, formalised leaves and flowers and geometrical motifs, and a voluptuous excess of ornament occasionally betrayed an innate vulgarity. The conjectural restorations of such palaces on page 44 show buildings totally different in character from the huge, passive immobility of Egyptian architecture. A predatory nation dedicated to war and persistently practising military aggression, whose Kings boasted of slaughter and the destruction of cities, would build boastfully, but with cautious regard for defence. The palace of King Sargon (722–705 B.C.) at Khorsabal, reconstructed externally by Perrot and Chipiez and shown opposite has the frowning strength of a castle, with guard towers flanking an arched gateway and battlements topping the towers and walls: a building designed to resist attack, a closed-in place. Heavy gates swinging on bronze pivots sunk in stone sockets protected the entrances to the inner courts of palaces and temples; but military precautions were not invariably dominant considerations in Assyrian architecture. The palace of Sennacherib, the son and successor of Sargon, is an open and airy building, according to Fergusson's version of the exterior reproduced at the top of page 44, a forerunner of the palaces built on platforms of masonry for the Persian monarchs who reigned over a later and far larger empire than the Wolf State of Assyria ever controlled.

Reconstruction of the palace of the Assyrian King Sargon (722–705 B.C.), with guard towers topped by battlements, an arched gateway, and winged bulls with human heads carved at the base of the towers. High walls guard and enclose the courts and buildings of the palace. *After Perrot and Chipiez.*

The arch was still regarded as essentially utilitarian; Assyrian builders used it for gateways, drains and sewers, but ignored its latent possibilities and capacity for transforming the whole conception of structure. Although they used domes, rounded and conical, they never departed from the post-and-lintel principle, and gave fresh life to it by developing the character of the colonnade. Columns sometimes rose from a base carved in the shape of a recumbent lion or a sphinx and were crowned by capitals on which rudimentary volutes occasionally appeared. Recessed galleries are formed by colonnades in Fergusson's drawing of the north-eastern

Human-headed winged lion. The Assyrian version of the sphinx form, though unlike the Egyptian sphinx it was often structurally incorporated with some large, royal building. (See page 44 also opposite.)

façade and grand entrance of Sennacherib's palace; the slender columns stand on a high, sculptured plinth, and the whole composition is orderly, with horizontal and vertical elements harmoniously related.

Architectural ostentation on this scale was enormously costly, and the continuous wars, undertaken for conquest or to crush revolts, depleted the wealth of the country; such wanton waste of economic resources and human life ultimately destroyed the Assyrian people. As a nation, they almost completely disappeared.[8]

Another civilisation that disappeared after flourishing for a few centuries in eastern Anatolia and north Syria, was the Hittite or Hatti Empire, a brief experiment in feudal urban life and imperial organisation. Stanley Casson has described it as "the shortest-lived empire in the history of the world."[9] The Hittites lasted as a military power from the sixteenth to the thirteenth century B.C.,

Human-headed winged bull. This example of Assyrian sculpture and that on the opposite page are reproduced from Jones's *Nineveh and its story*. (See also page 44.)

and during that time they created a massive and grandiose architecture, completely different from and uninfluenced by the architecture of neighbouring states, for it was asymmetrical, both in the lay-out of cities and the ground plan of buildings.[10] The column was unknown; square pillars were used for vertical supports, and Dr. Ekrem Akurgal, in his comprehensive study of Hittite art, suggests that they originated the corbel vault: a considerable structural discovery.[11] They were highly skilled in fortification, and the city walls of their capital, Hattusas, surpassed in strength and size all the defensive structures of antiquity.

The most imposing, as well as the largest buildings in Hattusas, were the temples, notably the temple of the Weather-God, of which the ground plan has been recovered, so that the extent and internal arrangement are now known. There were no vast, wastefully impressive tombs: the Hittites cremated their dead, and buried the

Pair of sphinxes with male and female heads, carved in basalt. They are slightly over 3 feet in height, and apparently formed part of the pedestal for a statue. These late examples of Hittite sculpture date from the eighth century B.C., when only the eastern fragment of the great Hittite Empire survived, and they are marked by Assyrian influence. In the Museum at Ankara. *Drawn by Maureen Stafford.*

ashes in urns of various kinds. Their sculpture was bold, vigorously executed; often carved in relief on palace walls or on a much larger scale on the faces of cliffs and isolated rocks.[12] The lion was a motif used with great frequency, on the plinths of statues and in pairs, ferociously represented, as the guardians of gateways. There is a lion gate at Hattusas.

The Hittites had their own versions of the sphinx. A pair, carved in basalt in the Museum at Ankara, are linked together; they are rather squat, feathered wings are folded along their bodies, and their male and female human faces have prominent chins, and elaborately curled hair. These are late examples from the eighth century B.C., and influenced by contemporary Assyrian work. By that time the Anatolian Empire of the Hittites had vanished: of their cities Carchemish survived, but Hattusas was a deserted ruin. Compare the Hittite sphinxes opposite with the Egyptian and Greek examples on Plate 1 and page 79. The linked pair at Ankara are in the round; another type carved in relief, from Carchemish, has a lion's body, with a human and a lion's head, and upraised wings.

The Hittite Empire was land-bound; although at its greatest extent it included the whole of what was later known as Cappadocia, reaching eastwards to the Euphrates, where the city of Carchemish stood, and most of north Syria, the Hittites made no use of the sea. There were no Hittite ports or maritime traffic; when north Syria was wrested from the Eygptians, the coastline remained undeveloped.[13] They had expanded southwards without much opposition from Egypt, for the pharoah Ikhnaton made no attempt to defend his Syrian possessions. Although the Hittite Empire disappeared, in the east such cities as Carchemish in northern Syria survived until the eighth century B.C., but the power that had dominated central and eastern Anatolia was forgotten, so completely that when the Greeks visited the country some centuries later and found the ruins of cities and the huge rock-sculptures, they could not identify their makers: no mention is made of Hittites in Greek legends or history.[14]

There are many references to the Hittites in the Old Testament; the first occurs in the fifteenth chapter of Genesis, when they are mentioned as one of several tribes inhabiting the area between Egypt and the Euphrates.[15] The power and possibly the very memory of their former empire had been forgotten; they had apparently reverted to tribal life like the Britons did when they were severed from the Roman Empire in the fifth century A.D. The Hittites, according to Stanley Casson, created nothing new, nothing "that had in it the germ of future development."[16] But if we accept Dr. Akurgal's view, that they invented the corbel vault, their contribution to the development of architecture was lasting.

The collapse of the Hittite Empire in Asia Minor was so complete, and the extinction of its power so devastatingly thorough that the successor states later established in Anatolia within the old imperial boundaries inherited nothing from their great forerunner. Nearly every Hittite site of the second millennium B.C. has so far disclosed a violent end. Dr. Akurgal records that "the Hittite cultural strata cease with a layer of conflagrations."[17] Phrygian culture, which developed after the Phrygian state emerged about 750 B.C., was uninfluenced by Hittite art and architecture; Phrygia and the neighbouring states of Lycaonia and Cappadocia, were separated from the former empire by some centuries of bleak barbarism, when most of Anatolia was probably occupied by nomadic savages, as averse to urban life as the Teutonic tribes that invaded the former Roman province of Britain in the fifth and sixth centuries. Mediaeval and modern England and Wales have tenuous links with Roman Britain, in the names of many cities; but no such links exist between the Hittite Empire and the city names of Central Anatolia, though some names in South Anatolia have a Hittite origin.[18]

Another empire that vanished catastrophically, flourished in the fertile island of Crete in the eastern Mediterranean from about 2600 to 1400 B.C. Unlike the Hittite Empire it was a non-military, peaceful state based on sea-power, and the lay-out of its cities and the character of the buildings in them suggested an untroubled, pacific type of social life. Some characteritics of the architecture created by that society were transmitted later to the less advanced Mycenaean civilisation that had been established in the third millennium B.C., by a pre-Hellenic people in Peloponnesus, that part of Greece which lies south of the Isthmus of Corinth. The Mycenaean civilisation was still in a semi-barbaric stage of development when Crete collapsed. The beginning of the great period of Cretan civilisation corresponds with the beginning of the sixth cultural phrase identified by Flinders Petrie, and it ended abruptly a couple of centuries before that phase also ended. (See diagram on page 19.)

The name Minoan has been adopted for the lost civilisation of Crete, because when the remains of the palace at Cnossus, the principal city of the island, were excavated, they were found to be an immense complex of halls, rooms, ante-rooms and corridors, so bewilderingly intricate that they were identified with the mythical Labyrinth, for Cnossus was the legendary home of the Minotaur, of King Minos, and of the Labyrinth.[19] This is one of many instances when the archaeologist has found the architectural substance of an ancient legend. Minos was apparently the royal title of the Hellenic kings who ruled in Crete early in the second

millennium B.C.[20] That royal palace was so extensive that it was
virtually a city itself and it lay in the heart of Cnossus, for Minos
was not an exclusive, holy autocrat; sacred, unapproachable and
segregated from his people, like the Egyptian pharoah; his royal
palace was accessible and closely identified with the social structure, which was totally dissimilar from that of the Hittite military
state or the mystical, priest-dominated and already ancient Egyptian civilisation.

The hills surrounding Cnossus were covered by innumerable
dwellings that housed a population estimated at about eighty
thousand, who appeared to be immune from the dark superstitions
that often passed for religious faith in the ancient world; indeed,
the Minoans seemed to be as happily insulated against religious
faith as they were against fear of external aggression or internal
revolution. The excavated remains of their architecture confirms
that. There were no majestic temples or swaggering tombs, only a
few modest shrines. Some religious symbols existed, but hardly any
representations of gods or priests, for Minoan art was free and
independent of any priestly control, and it was perhaps the first
free art in the world. Dr. Margaret Murray (1863–1964) has
asserted that not only Egyptian art but the art of all other countries
began in the service of religion,[21] but Minoan art had no sacred
origin: it was closely linked with life as it was lived every day, unconcerned with the insubstantial promises and rewards of some
imaginary hereafter, and it was an active and vigorous art that
depicted the occupations and reactions of people who seemed to
have lived gracefully and comfortably, if we may judge from the
subjects modelled in low relief or painted on the plastered walls of
their rooms.

In the palace at Cnossus there were halls with wooden columns
that tapered gently from capital to base, a form suitable for timber
construction, though inappropriate and structurally weak when
used in stone. Minoan architects designed porticoes with double
rows of columns, approached by broad flights of stairs; their houses
admitted daylight through windows that had frames with strong
upright members that carried the weight of the walls above; and
the plumbing would have satisfied Roman or even modern American standards, for running water was laid on to the palace and to
individual houses, which had bathrooms and water-closets.

Post-and-lintel construction was used, and there were abundant supplies of building materials: limestone, gypsum for slabs, brick earth, and timber from the wooded hills and valleys of the island. Heavy timbers were used for floors and roofs, and beams with a wide span were upheld by central columns. Partition walls were made from thin slabs of gypsum, laid in mortar. Minoan architecture was very largely domestic, and as materials and skill were never squandered on temples and tombs, and fortification was unknown, the cities of Crete were akin—albeit on a smaller scale— to European and American cities of the nineteenth and twentieth centuries, for they were open, unprotected and presumed to be safe from attack. The sea was the best wall in the world, and the Minoan navy the best defensive weapon. For at least twelve centuries that Minoan civilisation persisted in happy isolation, untroubled and unthreatened; a period far longer than the life span of the Roman Empire, longer than the history of England since the Norman conquest. The Minoan state was not completely isolated; some trade and traffic existed with Egypt, and a few artistic ideas were imported from that country; but for centuries no contacts with the outer world menaced the peace of the island, and as no town walls or forts were ever built, it has been conjectured that this peaceable people existed quite comfortably without an army or soldiers, apart perhaps from palace guards who were probably employed more for style than protection.

The end of the island state came suddenly at some time shortly after 1400 B.C., and destruction was as thorough as that which obliterated the Hittite civilisation; thereafter, for over thirty-three centuries, the power and glory of the Kingdom of Minos lived on in classical myths that, with the passage of time and the corrosive effect of Christian criticism, became increasingly implausible until in 1900 Sir Arthur Evans began to excavate the site of Cnossus. Various theories have been advanced to account for the overthrow of the Minoan culture, and one suggestion is that colonial expansion set up social stresses and strains, for early in the second millennium B.C. the Minoans established settlements in the adjacent islands of the Aegean, and followed these small-scale experiments in colonisation by settlements in Peloponnesus at Mycenae and Tiryns, and at Thebes in Boetia north of the Ishtmus of Corinth. These colonies inevitably brought about a closer association with the inhabitants of the mainland who were different in race and origin, and at a level of civilisation far below that of the cultivated and artistic inhabitants of Crete. Exposure to barbaric and possibly aggressive influences could have upset the social stability of the Minoans; perhaps the responsibility of running an overseas empire defeated their administrative capacity and over-taxed their maritime strength; internal revolution or foreign in-vasions may have combined to demolish national independence, or a convulsion of nature, such as an earthquake, may have dis-rupted social organisation beyond hope of recovery; but however the end came, troubles apparently began when the Minoans in-dulged imperial ambitions.[22]

The Minoan colonies in Peloponnesus formed the nucleus of the Mycenean Empire that grew in strength and power after the destruction of Cnossus. By comparison with the Minoans, the Myceneans were little better than savages, although they com-manded technical skills, and built houses and fortified cities of stone. They were certainly not house-trained; scraps of food littered the floors of their rooms; they were strangers to the refinements and security of Cnossus and the other cities of Crete; and they were afraid, as aggressive people are apt to be, of aggression from others. Huge fortifications enclosed their cities and restricted growth, and although the mainland was in the same climatic region as Crete, the Myceneans established the tradition of the hearth, so their houses differed fundamentally in plan from Minoan houses.[23] The fortress palaces of Mycenae, Tiryns and Argos all had rooms with hearths, and as civilisation spread to colder regions, the hearth moulded the character of domestic building in all those parts of Europe where winters were severe and prolonged, so the blazing log fire became a focal point for social life and the winter substitute for sunlight.

The Myceneans were accomplished builders, and used a type of masonry known as Cyclopean, that consisted of massive blocks of stone; the term is derived from the legend that the Cyclopes who build the wall at Tiryns for Proteus also built Mycenae;[24] but the method was known elsewhere by other peoples; the Hittites used it about the same period for the lower part of the outer and main walls of Hattusas.[25] A few Minoan architectural forms were adopted, such as the columns with downward-tapering shafts, that originally flanked the entrance to the Treasury of Atreus at

The Gate of the Lions, Mycenae, *circa* 1200 B.C. This has been described as the earliest example of European sculpture in association with an architectural feature. *Drawn by Maureen Stafford.* (See Plate 6.)

Mycenae (Plate 5), and a single column which separates the figures of lions carved on the slab of stone that fills the triangular space above the lintel of the Gate of the Lions. (See above.) That Mycenean architects had enlarged their knowledge of structure is attested by the use of triangular relieving spaces above the Gate of the Lions and the doorway to the Treasury of Atreus, and by the beehive roof of the Treasury, that was formed by encircling courses of masonry, progressively diminishing in diameter as they rose to the apex. The carved slab above the Gate of the Lions is an early European example of sculpture used in association with an architectural feature. (Plate 6.)

Mycenae stands on a hill at the edge of the Argive plain with Argos and the sea lying beyond, clearly visible. It has been in ruins for over two thousand five hundred years, and Pausanias in his *Description of Greece* gives the reason for its destruction by the

Argives. "For though they took no part against the Medes, the people of Mycenae sent to Thermopylae 80 men, who shared in the glory of the famous 300. This public spirit brought about their destruction, by provoking the Argives to jealousy. But there are still some remains of the precincts and the gate, and there are some lions on it . . ."[26] Pausanias visited Mycenae in the second century A.D., and the ruins were already ancient when he described them.

The city consisted of the Acropolis and a lower town, both surrounded by strong walls, with the Acropolis occupying the summit of a steep hill that was really a spur of a mountain that rose behind it; and this citadel was surmounted by the royal palace. The architecture of the mainland was strongly influenced by Minoan practice, and Bruce Allsopp considers that the most interesting examples are the citadels of Tiryns and Mycenae, which display considerable skill in the planning of the living quarters and the fortifications.[27] From the ruins that remain it is possible to trace the plan of the palace at Mycenae, though the details of the architectural treatment are tantalisingly fragmentary. Worn stone discs rising above floor level mark the bases of columns; the walls, mainly of dry construction, have some crudely-laid courses bound with cement; and from traces of plaster that still adhere to the stonework it may be assumed that the walls of the rooms were smooth and painted. There is some evidence that painted floors were used. But despite such refinements of interior decoration, the inhabitants of Mycenae and other mainland cities were very different from the "gay, intelligent and sophisticated people" of Cnossus, and after that assessment of the character of the Minoans, deduced from their architecture, Bruce Allsopp concludes that "the sack of Cnossus was one of the greatest tragedies in the history of mankind."[28]

In the Mycenean empire the acropolis of a city was invariably fortified and the rest of the city subordinated as a mere appendage to this lofty, dominant strong point. The cities of Crete were conceived differently, with a central palace or an agora, that was an open-air assembly place. Both the acropolis and the agora reappeared centuries after in Greek cities, long after the death of Minoan and Mycenean civilisation.

THE CLASSICAL PHASE: PERSIA AND GREECE

DURING the eighth and seventh centuries B.C., changes in the character of architecture in Mesopotamia, Anatolia and the Balkan peninsula indicated a fresh and sensitive awareness of the shape and relationship of masses, that led to greater discernment in composition. These changes marked the beginning of the classical phase that occupied three quarters of period seven in the Flinders Petrie diagram (page 19), and lasted until Graeco-Roman civilisation had lost momentum and was in decline. The architectural forms perfected during that period have influenced visual standards in Western civilisation ever since.

After inventing the arch (which they ignored) and the colonnade (which they continued to use with ponderous impressiveness), no new creative or adventurous experiments were made by the Egyptians; the next contributors to the growth and flexibility of architecture were the Babylonians, Assyrians and Persians. When the Persians overthrew the Assyrian Empire in the sixth century B.C., they adopted architectural ideas from the vanquished as, centuries earlier, the Assyrians had adopted those of Babylon.

The brutal ostentation and military strength of Assyrian palaces were modified by Persian architects. The shapes of columns were refined, their shafts reduced in section so that they became less bulky and obvious supports, while slight surface variations and enriched mouldings gave an agreeable liveliness to the entablatures that united rows of columns horizontally above their carved capitals. A new and sensitive awareness which adjusted the relationship of vertical and horizontal elements, indicated that architects were seeking, perhaps unconsciously, a master key or scale to establish a general rhythm that would give greater visual satisfaction than a plain statement of structural soundness. Those oriental architects were moving towards the system of architectural design that the Greeks ultimately perfected.

As the Persians built in lands where strong sunlight prevailed, they became as adept as the Egyptians in manipulating shadows, but the sections of their horizontal mouldings, their coves and cornices, were less pronounced than such Egyptian features and the shadows they cast never frowned. Persian palaces had an airy lightness of form, marred only by ornate and excessive decoration, for their designers had a barbaric reluctance to leave blank space alone; the temptation to overload surfaces with ornamental intricacies, with repetitive and often very boring patterns, was seldom resisted, so elegant lines and good proportions were occasionally blurred and sometimes obscured; but the boredom of excessive repetition was mitigated by the skilful use of glazed and coloured brickwork.

The Persian debt to Assyrian architecture is apparent in the tombs and palaces at Persepolis and Susa; the same winged hybrid monsters, the inevitable lions, the stiff, bearded warriors, all appear on bas-reliefs or on glazed tiles, and at Persepolis the palaces are built on an immense platform that rises forty feet above the level of the plain, partly cut from the solid rock, partly built up from big blocks of stone, held in place by metal cramps; a large-scale example of dry construction. This raised platform is approached on the north-west side by a flight of steps, shallow enough to allow horses to ascend them. The raised platform is an Assyrian device, which exalted the dignity and importance of the buildings it carried. At Persepolis the Propylaea, built by Xerxes (485–465 B.C.), forms an entrance of monumental grandeur, to the platform, but by far the most impressive structure is the Hall of the Hundred Columns, built for Darius (511–484 B.C.), which appears to have been used as a throne room. The columns were 37 feet high, with fluted shafts and intricate capitals consisting of vertical volutes, four each side, and twin bulls above, with the roof beams resting on their backs. Double bull and double unicorn capitals were used on the columns of the Propylaea, boldly carved; the formalised creatures crouching, linked like Siamese twins, and rather top-heavy as the capitals seemed to be unrelated to the shafts of the columns. (See page 64.)

Although Persian architecture anticipated some of the Greek

classical forms, it was recognisably the product of an exotic and uncontrollably luxurious civilisation; materially triumphant but intellectually sterile. The basic difference between the civilised standards of a Greek city state like Athens and the large, well-ordered Persian Empire was described by Clive Bell when he wrote: "The Athenians wished to live richly rather than to be rich; which is why we reckon them to be the most highly civilised people in history."[1] The Persians rejoiced in the material evidence of wealth as flamboyantly as the Elizabethans of the sixteenth century or the Victorians of the nineteenth; they had riches, but unlike the Greeks never mastered the art of living richly. The efficiency of their state planning and the exclusive luxury of their palaces proclaim a rigid authoritarian approach to government; for although they established a system of posts for transmitting news and made splendid roads, of which the Royal Road that ran from Ephesus and Sardes in Lydia to Susa was one of the great trade routes of the ancient world, there was a flaw in the pattern of Persian life; they were accomplished administrators, but notwithstanding the competence of their bureaucracy and the relative justice of their laws, their empire was essentially an oriental despotism.

In 500 B.C., that empire had, in the words of Sir Mark Sykes, "dominated the world by reason of its toleration, moderation, honesty and efficiency."[2] But as an empire it sprawled over an enormous area, from Thrace in the west to India in the east; at its greatest extent it included Syria and Egypt and the whole of Asia Minor; this lack of geographical cohesion might have been compensated for had the system of government been as effective as that of the Roman Empire; but a despotism is unstable. The people did not continue to benefit from "toleration, moderation, honesty and efficiency"; and after a couple of hundred years, as Sykes records, "its kings had become the playthings of women and eunuchs; its satraps disloyal, incompetent, and rapacious officials; its marvellous system of posts and communications, mere channels of spies' reports and intrigues; its armies, hordes of untrained, undisciplined polyglot slaves and blackguards. . . ."[3]

After their conquest of Assyria the Persians dominated the whole of the Middle East and brought unity to the various kingdoms and petty principalities that had grown up after the demise of the

The royal palaces of Persian monarchs were sited on large, raised platforms, amid gardens and trees, aggressively proclaiming the wealth and luxury of rulers who, in time, adopted the title of King of Kings. *After Perrot and Chipiez.*

Hittite Empire in Anatolia, ending the wars and border raids that had occupied those turbulent little states on and off for centuries; by absorbing them and controlling their administration, Persia performed a civilising mission, and because Persian control extended to the Greek colonies established on the coasts and islands of the Aegean and eastern Mediterranean and the southern shore of the Black Sea, Greek fashions and art were observed and imitated, though Greek ideas of the state and the obligations of citizens were unable to take root in the barren soil of an empire whose ruler never considered the interests of his subjects or gave them anything in return for the taxes they paid.[4] The people as such were there to do what they were told and to accept without question the control of those set in authority over them: a condition of social life that was alien to the restless, innovating, challenging Greek mind.

The Persians were ultimately corrupted by riches; the belief that gold could buy anything, including military prowess, ensured their defeat in later wars with the Greeks and their final overthrow by Alexander the Great. Their architecture achieved magnificence, and over-ornamentation could not wholly conceal a mastery of composition; their architects were certainly capable of something nobler than satisfying the demands of royal and wealthy patrons whose prodigal taste easily degenerated into voluptuous vulgarity. By comparison, the serene simplicity of the temples and public buildings in the Greek states on the western borders of the empire, made Persian design seem tawdry.

There was nothing ornate or lavish about the Greeks. Their way of life was frugal; their clothes just adequate; their manners free and easy; and though Persians might regard them as poverty-stricken, lacking in personal dignity, and far too talkative, they were ready enough to imitate Greek art and some Greek ways, though they never abandoned their rich, voluminous clothes or restricted their appetite for luxury. The Greeks lived temperately; moderation in all things informed and guided their conception of the good life; with them the word temperance was invested with a civilised significance that has been forgotten since puritan teetotallers in the nineteenth century perverted its meaning by confusing it with abstinence; but *proportion* is the right word for describing the basis of the Greek character.[5] The tranquil beauty of a Doric

Conjectural restoration of the palace of Darius, the walls clad with coloured tiles, and the columns surmounted by double-bull capitals. See view of raised platform, with palaces and gardens, on page 61. *Drawn by Maureen Stafford.*

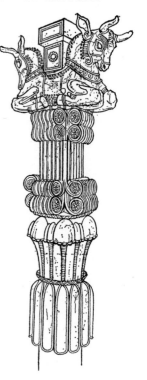

Double bull capital, resting on a scrolled and fluted support. The scrolls are forerunners of the Ionic volute (pages 70 and 71), but are much simpler, with a central rosette. Such capitals appear on the columns of the Propylaea of Xerxes at Persepolis, 485–465 B.C., one of the buildings on the great platform of palaces. (See restoration after Perrot and Chipiez, page 61.)
Drawn by Maureen Stafford.

temple shows the Greek sense of proportion in action; no architecture before or since has attained such faultless harmony, such perfect balance between horizontal and vertical elements, where each part of the building contributes to the general rhythm. The character of civic and sacred buildings in the Greek city states and colonies was shaped and controlled by the orders of architecture, of which the first two were Doric and Ionic, with an ornate variation of the Ionic that was invented in the fifth century B.C., known as Corinthian, and used less than the other two. These "orders" represented a flexible system of design that determined the proportions and spacing of columns, the form of the capitals that crowned them, the depth, vertical divisions and moulded detail of the entablature supported by the columns, the profiles of mouldings and the formalised ornament that enriched them. The Doric entablature was divided into three: the architrave, frieze, and cornice, and of these the frieze was the deepest, with blocks called triglyphs, grooved by vertical channels, separating panels called metopes that were either left as plain surfaces or filled with sculptured subjects. The drawing on page 66 shows the proportions and characteristics of the order. The columns have no bases and stand directly upon a substructure, the stylobate, which formed a continuous platform. The shaft of each column, circular in section, gradually diminished from bottom to top on a line that was, by intention, slightly convex, which corrected the slightly hollow appearance tapering columns with perfectly straight sides would otherwise have. This graduated swelling or outward curvature of the column from bottom to top is called the entasis, and is one of many devices used by the Greeks to minimise the imperfections of human eyesight, for their visual perception was so sensitive and demanding that they took infinite trouble to ensure that the human eye would be converted from a fallible organ into a perfect optical instrument.

Of the three orders, the Doric was the earliest and has been traced back in its archaic form to the ninth century B.C., before the Hellenic period had become a cultural verity. On Plate 7 three examples are shown: the remains of the temple of Apollo at Corinth, dating from the sixth century B.C., with archaic capitals and monolithic fluted columns; the temple of Demeter at Segesta in Sicily, 430–420 B.C., with plain columns built up in sections; and the Parthenon at Athens, 454–438 B.C. Two views of the Parthenon are given on Plates 8 and 9. A drawing on page 67, shows the Treasury of the Athenians at Delphi, a small building of the Doric order, extensively but skilfully restored.

The Parthenon has been described as the most intelligent extrovert building that the world has ever seen.[6] This was not an exclusive characteristic of the Doric order, for all Hellenic architecture was essentially extrovert. Externally the Parthenon exhibits an orderly array of columns, supporting an entablature with heroic themes carved on the metopes of the frieze. Erected in the time of Pericles, it was dedicated to Athena Parthenos, the virgin Athena, and it housed a vast statue of her in gold and ivory; so despite its extrovert character as a building it was, in Sir Mortimer Wheeler's descriptive phrase, "a religious safe-deposit."[7] The architects were Ictinus and Callicrates: Pheidias was the master sculptor. The

The Greek Doric order. The column has no base, and the shaft gradually diminishes from bottom to top, and is generally divided into twenty shallow flutes, though the number varies. *After Nicholson.* (See Plates 7, 8, and 9.)

The Treasury of the Athenians at Delphi. This example of the Greek Doric order has been extensively restored. The shaft of the right-hand column has been replaced; but the middle section of the left-hand column is original, so are the capitals of both, also the entablature and the pediment. *Drawn by Maureen Stafford.*

Parthenon, which they created, was the supreme expression of the Greek exaltation of the sense of sight, for the builders corrected by an infinitude of inflections the defects of ordinary vision; the use of the entasis on the shafts of columns has been mentioned, but in the Parthenon, and in other Doric temples, subtle adjustments were made that modified the vertical and horizontal lines of colonnades; masons exercised their skill to bring before the eyes of men the real, rather than the apparent, shape of horizontal and vertical elements. That long platform, the stylobate, which carried the colonnades, would normally appear slightly concave in the middle, although it was actually straight; but Greek masons deflected that straight line so it became slightly convex in fact, and consequently straight in appearance. Some vertical lines were deliberately slanted in order to appear vertical; and in some small and imperceptible degree every stone of the Parthenon has some slight irregularity; level surfaces are made unlevel in order to appear level, and all ascending and lateral lines adjusted to achieve the placid perfection of form that alone satisfied Greek eyes.

This intentional rejection of mechanical regularity was not suspected until an English architect named Francis Cranmer Penrose (1817–1903) made detailed measurements of the Parthenon in the second half of the nineteenth century. Before that time, students of Greek architecture had detected a profound but inexplicable difference between Greek and Roman buildings, some property of design which remained unidentified until Penrose's measurements revealed what appeared to be an astonishing partnership between creative and mathematical minds. For some years it was believed that all those subtle corrections of man's visual disabilities had been worked out by master-mathematicians, who imposed their minute and elaborate calculations on the executant craftsmen who built the Parthenon; a drawing-board view that was held by many architectural historians in the latter part of the nineteenth century and the early years of the twentieth, though a penetrating writer like Lisle March Phillipps, who dwells on the "infinity of labour and skill and expense" needed for "carrying out these inflections," left the matter of their execution unresolved.[8]

The drawing-board outlook, so comfortably acceptable to the late Victorians and Edwardians, implied the domination of the draughtsman over the mason working on the site; only a few dissentient voices asserted that adjustments and modifications to lines and surfaces were made by the men who actually handled and carved the Pentelic marble of the Parthenon. That was the view, emphatically expressed, of John T. Emmet, an abrasive contemporary critic of Victorian architects and architecture, who realised that master masons and carvers who think with their hands were far more likely to be responsible for the grace and refinement of a great temple than master-mathematicians making their calculations in isolation at two removes from reality. This assumption of remote control for artistic inspiration and responsible skill was, he said, absurd; a suggestion that "may commend itself to specially dull people; others will discern its fallacy and folly." While admitting that drawings for the general design of the Parthenon were probably made and used, he qualified that admission by saying, "All the curves of mouldings, entasis, and stylobate, are purely building work; and were set out, full size, by the chief master workmen, with the grace and delicate refinement that men of plastic art invent, and add to their mere graphic studies. They are at the building, and they see where form, beyond the draughtsman's lines, and various expressive modulation should be given."[9] Authorities like Dr. Rhys Carpenter endorse the view that such mathematical precision "was achieved empirically at the time of execution rather than by previous arithmetical or geometrical calculation."[10]

The Parthenon is an enduring monument to the lucidity of the Greek mind; even the ruins proclaim that intellectual quality, and for centuries after the end of Hellenic civilisation the building survived changes of culture and religion, its beauty unimpaired until in the late seventeenth century A.D., the structure was shattered in war. Pericles spent the war chest contributed by the allies of Athens upon the beautification of the city and the adornment of the Acropolis with noble buildings. "This was an unrighteous thing to do by our modern standards," as H. G. Wells has observed, "but it was not a base or greedy thing to do. Athens had accomplished the work of the Delian League, and is not the labourer worthy of his hire?"[11]

The English might have done the same for London after the Great Fire of 1666, but were content to give their capital a great cathedral and some noble churches; the opportunity came again after the bombs of the Second World War, but London had no Pericles to authorise a glorious transformation.

When the temples on the Acropolis at Athens were completed perhaps the Greeks said all they had to say about architecture.[12] They were erected between 454 and 393 B.C., and it is strange that such superb buildings were omitted from that select group of works of art, known as the Seven Wonders of the World. Tourism is an

Greek Ionic capital with the necking below the volutes decorated by the anthe-mion ornament, a formalised version of the honeysuckle flower and leaves: above and below the band of honeysuckle are two borders of the bead-and-reel ornament, enriching an astragal moulding, and above that is an ovolo moulding enriched with the egg-and-dart or egg-and-tongue ornament, based on arrow-heads and eggs arranged alternately. The edge of the abacus, the upper mem-ber of the capital on which the architrave of the entablature rests, is also carved with the egg-and-tongue device. *After Nicholson*. A simpler form of the Greek Ionic capital is shown opposite.

ancient industry and has flourished always when peace, security and good communications exist over large areas. Guide-books for tourists were current in the Graeco-Roman world; and from those circulating in the second century B.C., the epigrammatist, Anti-pater of Sidon, probably compiled his list of Wonders, which in-cluded the following: (1) the pyramids of Egypt, (2) the gardens of Semiramis at Babylon, (3) the statue of Zeus in gold and ivory, by Pheidias at Olympia, (4) the Ionic temple of Artemis (Diana) at Ephesus, (5) the Mausoleum at Halicarnassus, (6) the Colossus at

The Greek Ionic and Corinthian orders. The Ionic capitals have spiral volutes; the Corinthian capitals have smaller volutes above the band of formalised acanthus leaves. *After Nicholson.*

Rhodes, and (7) the Pharos at Alexandria. Later lists have included the Walls of Babylon as well as the hanging gardens of Semiramis.[13]

The Parthenon was the supreme example of the mature Doric order; the elegance and delicacy of the Ionic are exemplified by the Erechtheion and the temple of Nike Apteros. (Plates 10 and 11) The Propylaea combined the Doric and Ionic. The Plan on page 75 shows the siting of those buildings on the Acropolis, also the position at a lower level on the south side of the Odeion of Herodes Atticus, the Stoa of Eumenes, and the Theatre of Dionysos: the seating of that theatre is shown on Plate 12.

The Ionic order like the Doric had columns that supported an entablature with the lateral divisions of architrave, frieze and cornice, but the columns rose from circular moulded bases and their capitals had scrolls or volutes, a spiral form that was anticipated by the Persians who used, as mentioned earlier in this chapter, pairs of vertical volutes on their double-bull capitals. The spiral is a natural shape, found in the nautilus shell, and the Greek formalised version was carved on the rectangular block of the Ionic capital. An example used as the base of the Greek sphinx appears on page 79; the general character of the order, column, capital and entablature, is shown on page 71. The capital was sometimes varied by a band of honeysuckle ornament carved below the volutes. (Page 70.) The columns were fluted and the entasis less marked than the Doric. Everything that Persian architects strove for was realised by the Ionic order, which had a lightness and gaiety of form that made Persian composition seem by comparison a fussy and tumescent exercise.

The Erechtheion, which stands to the north of the Parthenon, was built 420–393 B.C., on the site of an older temple that the Persians had destroyed sixty years earlier. The architect, Mnesicles, also designed the Propylaea. Human figures rarely appear as supports in Greek architecture; the best known example of their use is on the southern portico of the Erechtheion, where six draped female Caryatids, spaced like columns and each 7' 9" high, support a deep entablature and stand on a high plinth of solid marble. (Plate 11.) The incorporation of human figures as vertical elements originated in Egypt; the Osiris pillars at Luxor (Plate 2) are prototypes of the Greek caryatid, but with the difference already

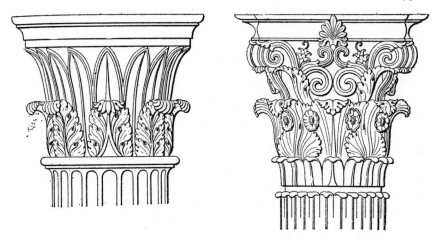

Left: Capital from the Tower of the Winds, Athens, with formalised palm leaves above a band of acanthus leaves.
Right: Detail of Greek Corinthian capital from the Choragic Monument of Lysicrates, Athens. (See Plate 13.) *After Nicholson.*

mentioned in chapter two: the Osiris pillars have formalised figures applied to the supporting uprights: the caryatids of the Erechtheion are structurally valid and bear the weight of the entablature. Although the term caryatid was not in use before the Roman conquest of Greece, the word suggests that the burdened female figures preserve the memory of an ancient political error and its punishment, for Caryatid is derived from Caryatis, a woman of Caryae, a city in Laconia that sided with the Persians at Thermopylae, and was afterwards destroyed by the Greeks who killed the men and enslaved the women. At Delphi, two caryatids support the entablature of the Treasury of the people of Cnidus, a city in Caria. A variation of the caryatid was the canephora, a sculptured female figure bearing a basket in the form of a bell-shaped capital, structurally incorporated like the caryatid; the canephorae from Delphi illustrated on page 77 differ greatly from the rigid, formal figures on the Erechtheion; they are strenuous rather than placid, their swirling draperies suggest movement, their faces and limbs assert a lively vitality, unlike the air of resigned endurance that characterises the static caryatid; even the

Ruins of the Erechtheion, the Ionic temple on the Acropolis at Athens, to the north of the Parthenon. The relative position of the buildings on the Acropolis is shown on the map opposite; the Caryatid porch that appears in the drawing is shown in greater detail on Plate 11 together with the fluted Ionic columns. The Erechtheion, designed by Mnesicles, was built 420–393 B.C., on the site of an older temple that was destroyed by the Persians in 480 B.C. *Drawn by Raymond McGrath, and reproduced by permission of the artist.*

baskets balanced on their carefully-dressed hair seem light burdens. Unfortunately the group is detached from its architectural context.

The small Ionic temple of Nike Apteros on the south-western spur of the Acropolis was dedicated to "Wingless Victory". Designed by Callicrates and built 438 B.C., it survived until A.D. 1687, when the Turks, then engaged in their war with the Venetians, took it down and used the materials in a battery. In A.D. 1836 the battery was demolished, and the temple was reconstructed from its original materials on its former site, with nearly all the

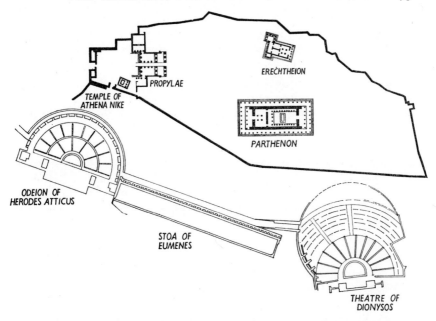

ERECHTHEION

PROPYLAE

TEMPLE OF
ATHENA NIKE

PARTHENON

ODEION OF
HERODES ATTICUS

STOA OF
EUMENES

THEATRE OF
DIONYSOS

The Acropolis at Athens, showing the relative positions of the Parthenon, the Erechtheion, the Propylae, and the Temple of Athena Nike. The Odeion of Herodes Atticus and the Theatre of Dionysos are on the south side of the Acropolis and on a much lower level. *Drawn by Marcelle Barton.* See Plates 9, 10, and 11 for views of the Parthenon, the temple of Athena Nike and the Erechtheion: a general view of the Erechtheion is shown in the drawing opposite.

slabs of its famous frieze, carved in high relief, replaced on the entablature. (Plate 10.)

The largest and most celebrated of all Greek temples of the Ionic order was that of Artemis at Ephesus in Lydia, built in 356 B.C. to the design of Deinocrates, a Macedonian architect, with Scopas as the master sculptor. The huge, impressive building, known as the Hellenistic temple, was 391 feet long and 211 wide. It occupied the site of two earlier temples. Few traces of it remain, for although it survived after the Goths sacked it in A.D. 262, the Edict of the Emperor Theodosius one hundred and thirty years later, ended the life of all pagan temples, and thereafter it was progressively demolished and robbed of its rich marbles to provide materials for Christian churches. (Eight columns of dark green marble were ultimately used in Santa Sophia at Constantinople.) After Christianity became the state religion of the Roman Empire, classic temples were everywhere despoiled; fragments of columns and mutilated sculptures were embedded in the walls of the churches that replaced them; and this quarrying of materials from the architectural triumphs of the classic phase continued for centuries. (Part of a white marble Ionic column with the capital and delicately carved volutes is built into the north wall of the Byzantine church at Daphni on the Sacred Way from Athens to Eleusis, all that survives of the temple of Apollo which stood there before the ninth century Christian church was built.) Another lost Ionic monument sufficiently famous in its day to be counted as one of the Seven Wonders of the World was the gigantic tomb of Mausolus, the ruler of Caria in Asia Minor (377–353 B.C.), erected at Halicarnassus by his widow Aremisia who succeeded him. The architects were Satyros and Pythios, and Scopas who had worked on the Ephesian temple of Artemis was the master sculptor. The tomb has not survived, though various fragments of the sculptures that adorned it have been recovered and some are preserved in the British Museum; the ruins which were excavated in A.D. 1857 have inspired several conjectural restorations of the original appearance. The building consisted of a square podium, on which stood the tomb chamber, surrounded by Ionic columns, with a stepped pyramidal roof above the entablature, the apex crowned by a marble quadriga and a group of figures. The podium, constructed of greenstone blocks, was faced with marble. Such posthumous ostentation was alien to Greek ideas; but Mausolus was a Persian satrap who had assumed authority as an independent ruler; his widow's taste for large-scale magnificence thus ensured immortality for his name, as Mausoleum has been used ever since to describe a monumental tomb.

The Corinthian order was an elaboration of the Ionic, with smaller volutes on the capital and a band of acanthus leaves carved below them. Another form of capital, used more rarely, had a similar band of formalised acanthus leaves, with a band of outward-curving blade-shaped palm leaves above, but no volutes: an example of this type from the Tower of the Winds (100–135 B.C.) appears on page 73 side by side with a Corinthian capital from the Choragic monument of Lysicrates (335 B.C.), both at Athens.

Group of Greek canephorae, draped female figures bearing baskets on their heads. See caryatid porch of the Erechtheion, Athens, on Plate 11, and compare with the Osiris pillars at Luxor, Plate 2. These Greek examples are from Delphi. *Drawn by Maureen Stafford.*

(Plate 13.) Some evidence suggests that the Corinthian capital had originated at Bassae at the temple of Apollo Epicurius (430 B.C.), which was designed by Ictinus, one of the architects of the Parthenon.[14] The invention of the capital is also attributed to Callimachus, a worker in bronze. Vitruvius, a Roman architect who lived in the first century B.C., relates in the fourth book of his work on architecture how Callimachus passing the tomb of a young Corinthian girl had noticed a basket put there by the girl's old nurse, who had filled it with small articles that the child had been fond of in her lifetime, with a tile on top to preserve them. The basket had been placed by accident on the root of an acanthus plant, which "pressed by the weight, shot forth, towards spring, its stems and large foliage, and in the course of growth reached the angles of the tile, and thus formed volutes at the extremities."[15] Whether the decorative possibilities of the acanthus were accidentally discovered or not, the formalised leaves of that plant have appeared, in an infinity of variations, for twenty-four centuries on buildings in Europe and lands influenced by European architecture. Two species of acanthus grow in southern Europe: *acanthus spinosus*, with spiny leaves, that the Greeks used with elegant effect, and *acanthus mollis*, with large, deeply-cut hairy leaves, which the Romans used with voluptuous gusto. No other natural form has commanded such universal popularity or retained its popularity so long; even after the end of the classic phase, when Graeco-Roman civilisation was no more than a dim memory of an almost legendary golden age, versions of the Corinthian capital and proliferating acanthus foliations appeared in many parts of Italy during the Middle Ages, until the resurrection of classic architecture in the early fifteenth century A.D. Thereafter acanthus leaves and scrolls and tendrils made an irresistible appeal to creative artists and designers in every field, and were used with lively imagination by Renaissance architects, by painters, sculptors, woodcarvers, gold and silversmiths, armourers, embroiderers, French and Italian ornamentalists and artist-craftsmen of the seventeenth and eighteenth centuries and great English cabinet-makers of the Georgian period. Every craftsman in Europe, from those who worked for fastidious aristocrats to the humblest village or estate carpenter, knew how, when and where the ubiquitous acanthus leaves should be placed. They were essential components in the decorative character of Baroque and

The Greek version of the Sphinx. This example, standing on an Ionic capital, is from the museum at Delphi. *Drawn by Maureen Stafford.*

Rococo, nor did they lose their vitality until the mid-nineteenth century, when they became withered patterns, mechanically and thoughtlessly applied, often unrelated to the design of whatever it was they were supposed to embellish.

All the florid and intricate developments of Baroque and Rococo are traceable to the Corinthian order, which the Greeks seldom used, and the Romans amplified. Moderation in all things was not a precept that attracted Roman respect, though when they were not being insanely extravagant, like Nero with his Golden House, Romans could achieve and appreciate dignity in architectural design: size, as we have already seen, impressed them.

One large-scale example of the use of the Corinthian order in Greece is the Olympieion at Athens, that stands on the site of an earlier Doric temple, though as it was designed by the Roman architect Cossutius it is really a Roman building on a Greek site. (Plate 12.) It was begun in 174 B.C., by Antiochus Epiphanes of Syria, but left incomplete; in 80 B.C., some of the columns were removed to Rome and reused in the temple of Jupiter Capitolinus; it was ultimately completed in A.D. 117 by the authority of Hadrian.

The character and design of Greek temples suggest that the Greek gods were never taken particularly seriously; although they were terrible in their rages and likes and dislikes and their capricious vengeances, they did not inspire awe; the myths and legends about them reveal a jovial, lascivious, utterly irresponsible crew of deities with understandable human failings and no nonsense about moral earnestness; indeed no morals of any kind, merely appetites which ordinary men and women could understand and condone. All Greek temples looked outwards; they were designed for external effect; Sir Mortimer Wheeler's description of the Parthenon as the most intelligent extrovert building the world has ever seen was quoted earlier; there it stood, "a plain and sturdy exterior set squarely and possessively on its rock and owing its sturdiness to infinite judgement and finesse." But although it housed the massive statue of Athena in gold and ivory, "neither the building nor its decoration had any inner life . . ."[16] There was nothing secret about a Greek temple, or for that matter about Greek architecture, though mystery was certainly not rejected or despised in the Hellenic world. At Eleusis in Attica the most famous of ancient Mysteries

were celebrated until the sacred buildings there were destroyed in
A.D. 396 by Alaric, the Gothic leader who had invaded Greece in
his attack on the Eastern Roman Empire. It is unlikely that the
great Doric temple of the Mysteries was ever restored, for after
the Edict of Theodosius (A.D. 392), all pagan rites were forbidden.

Although militant Christians wrecked and pillaged pagan
temples with all the ardour they brought to the persecution of
those still faithful to the old gods or to members of heretical sects,
some of the great Greek buildings escaped. On the Acropolis at
Athens, the Erechtheion stood unharmed for hundreds of years,
serving different purposes but more or less kept in repair. In the
sixth century Justinian transformed it into a Christian church; in
the fifteenth, after the Turkish conquest, it was used as a harem; it
became a casualty in 1829 during the Greek Revolution, when
much of it was destroyed. Some restorations were carried out in
1838, and in 1845 the southern portico with the Caryatids was
rebuilt, but seven years later a storm did further damage. What
we see today is a skilfully-preserved shell.

The Parthenon remained unchanged until early in the fifth
century A.D. when the colossal statue of Athena was removed, and
the temple consecrated as a church, dedicated to St. Sophia. In the
following century, it was rededicated to the Virgin Mother of God,
and the inner columns were removed from the interior, also the
roof, and at the eastern end an apse was formed. Six hundred
years later, at the close of the twelfth century, it was still almost
entire, uninjured by time, with the sculptures on the metopes and
pediments intact.[17] On the walls were frescoes, executed by order
of Basil II (*circa* 958–1025), known as Bulgaroktonos (slayer of
Bulgarians), Roman Emperor of the East, who presented rich gifts
to the church, which attracted many pilgrims from the islands and
provinces of the Eastern Empire, to attend the feast of the Virgin.
In A.D. 1456 Athens was captured by the Turks, and the Parthenon
became a mosque, without any alteration to the structure. Christian symbols were of course removed, and a minaret was added.
Apart from superficial alterations and additions, the Parthenon
was unchanged, until in A.D. 1687 the Turks used it as a powder
magazine, when the Venetians were besieging Athens. The building was blown up and the columns overthrown as a result of a new
technique of plunging fire invented by a German artillery officer,

for a descending shell pierced the roof and exploded in the magazine. A little later a small mosque was built amid the ruins, and rather squalid houses gradually invaded the site, with fragments of sculpture embedded in their walls. (Plate 8.) In 1801 Lord Elgin obtained authority from the Turkish government to pull down these houses, and to rescue and remove many of the sculptures that would otherwise have been irreparably damaged or lost. When in 1831 Greece became an independent kingdom, the significance of the Parthenon as an historic monument of incomparable beauty was recognised and although it was never included among the Seven Wonders of the World, it has taken its place as one of the greatest works of man.

When they built cities the Greeks asserted their sense of civic and social responsibility; from the remote and forgotten towns of the Mycenaean Empire they had inherited such features as the agora and the acropolis; roads entering a city from the surrounding countryside converged upon the agora, that Greek equivalent of the Roman forum, while public buildings such as the council house and the town hall, and those detached colonnades called *stoas*, which provided shade and shelter for the pleasures of scandalous conversation, philosophical discussion or political intrigue, were dotted about without any planned relationship, though occasionally they were grouped upon the acropolis. In common with the cities of western civilisation in the eighteenth, nineteenth and twentieth centuries, A.D., ancient Greek cities were built on the assumption that they would never be attacked; they were not surrounded and restricted by walls; town-planners and architects were not intimidated by the need for defence. Professor Wycherley in his work on the design of Greek cities states that the wall "was loosely flung around the city; it was not the frame into which the rest was fitted, and it was not normally a dominant factor in the plan." Even when walls were recognised as necessities, as they were in the later towns, "a circuit might be marked out and built up at an early phase, for the sake of immediate security; but still the outline was irregular and did not conform to a type."[18] The function of walls was often confined to the protection of the citadel.

Many Greek cities were built on hills; no rivers like the Nile, Tigris or Euphrates, the Danube or the Seine bisected or encircled them or influenced their plan and character, though inland cities that had grown up round an acropolis were often linked with some coastal town, as Athens was linked with the Piraeus by a straight road, just over four miles long, protected by the famous Long Walls. Theoretically that guarded route made Athens impregnable; no siege could be successful so long as the Athenian fleet had command of the sea, so that cargoes could be unloaded at the Piraeus, and the city provisioned; but when the city was captured by the Spartans in 404 B.C., the victors destroyed the Long Walls and the fortifications of the Piraeus. They were restored in 393 B.C. by Conon, the Athenian general, but did not endure. Even before the Roman conquest of Greece they had fallen into decay, and were finally demolished by the Roman general, Lucius Cornelius Sulla (138–78 B.C.).

The Greek city has the same open, extrovert character as the Greek temple; the climate encouraged outdoor life, and in the early cities the absence of walls secured a healthy partnership with the fields beyond the city limits, a partnership that was never lost, for the life of the city-state was based on agriculture, and even when cities grew and their populations became too large for dependence on locally-grown corn, olives and vines, and food had to be imported, Greek civilisation never became unhealthily urban. Many recreations and social activities took place in the open air: the gymnasium, the stadium and the theatre had no roof but the sky. No Greek town would have been complete without its gymnasium; it was as essential to civilised life as the agora, more important perhaps than any temple.

In plan the early cities seemed to contradict the orderly quality of the Greek mind; eventually the variety and interest created by irregularity were sacrificed, and Hippodamus of Miletus introduced the grid plan, with straight, broad streets. Haverfield suggested in 1913 that this form of town-planning was copied from eastern cities,[19] and excavation has since revealed that cities in the Indus valley, like Harappa, were town-planned[20] as early as the third millennium B.C., long before such planning was practised at Babylon about 2000 B.C. Hippodamus worked for Pericles, and made the street plan for the Piraeus; later in the fifth century B.C. he planned the new city of Rhodes, which was adorned with a very short-lived Wonder of the World in the form of a huge bronze statue 105 feet high of the sun-god Helios, by Chares of Lindus, that stood overlooking one of the city's two harbours, though the exact site is unknown. It was once believed that it bestrode the entrance to one of them, and that ships passed between its legs. It took twelve years to make, and stood for fifty-six, until overthrown by an earthquake in 224 B.C. It was never re-erected, and its fragments remained until the island was conquered by the Saracens in A.D. 656, when they were removed and sold as scrap metal.

At the Piraeus, Hippodamus had demonstrated on a small scale how convenient a geometric plan could be, with the streets crossing at right angles, though a grid plan in a large city could become an imprisoning net that strangled originality; but Greek architects avoided the threat of oppressive uniformity by driving broad processional ways through the grid, leaving spacious island sites for temples and public buildings. An adventurous spirit encouraged Greek town-planners to try out new ideas; sometimes these were fantastic, but an indulgent patron like Alexander the Great seriously considered a scheme for carving Mount Athos at the end of the peninsula of Acte into a colossal statue of a man, with a spacious city built on the palm of his left hand, and a vast cup held in his right, into which all the mountain streams would flow, pouring from thence into the sea. This would not have seemed a particularly fantastic plan in the ancient world, and it was only turned down after Alexander had investigated the site and found that it was too bleak and infertile for enough food to be grown in the vicinity, so that the city would have to depend on sea-borne supplies. The idea was suggested by Deinocrates, who had designed the temple of Artemis at Ephesus, and his originality and reputation commended him to Alexander, who appointed him to supervise the building of a new city in Egypt at the western end of the Nile Delta, that was to be named Alexandria.[21]

The city was destined to become second only to Rome in fame, luxury and wealth. Egypt had been seized by Alexander in 332 B.C., and the new city became the Hellenic capital of that ancient land; utterly un-Egyptian in character, a cosmopolitan meeting place for every race, every creed and every vice, with three main regions, Jewish, Greek and native Egyptian, and as a great port and market and trading centre, it had a floating population of merchants, mariners, soldiers and travellers, who were expertly plundered by the permanent residents. The ground plan of the city was conceived by Alexander, but when he died, his architect Deinocrates was superseded by Cleomenes of Naucratis, who carried on the work, that continued until the city was completed during the reign of Ptolemy II Philadelphus (285–247 B.C.), though new buildings were added century after century under the Ptolemies until in 30 B.C. Egypt became a Roman province. Even before that, Alexandria stood in relation to the Graeco–Roman world much as twentieth-century New York stood to the Western world: it was the most uncharacteristic of Greek cities, as New York is the most uncharacteristic of American, and the site and street plan had certain superficial affinities with Manhattan, for the city was confined between the waters of the harbour and Lake Mareotis. While American architects have adorned New York with arrogant and exciting towers, Greek architects overcame the limitations of the grid plan and the compressed area by the variety, size and brilliance of the buildings that stood on rectangular sites between the streets, for they were constructed of dazzling white marble, shaded by colonnades, and below them lay a labyrinth of water cisterns, four or five storeys deep, upheld by thousands of columns. There was also a tower that became as famous as the city itself, one of the Seven Wonders of the World, the Pharos, the lighthouse that rose to a height estimated at 500 feet, progenitor of all high isolated towers, designed by Sostratus of Cnidos, and built in the third century B.C. It stood on the north-east corner of the Island of Pharos and was connected with the city by the Heptastadium, a long causeway raised on arches. Although the Pharos remained intact until the Arab Conquest of Egypt in A.D. 641, the lantern collapsed shortly after that date; the lower storeys survived until the fourteenth century, when they were destroyed by an earthquake; but the graceful form of the great tower lives on in the Egyptian minaret. As long ago as 1880. Dr. Alfred Butler suggested that the Pharos was the original model of the minaret,[22] and expanded the theory in his later work, *The Arab Conquest of Egypt*, when he said: "Though the mediaeval minarets of Cairo vary in combination of design, in many of them one may see an exact reproduction of the design of Sostratus, which was a tower springing four-square from the ground, then changing to a smaller octagonal and from the octagonal to a still smaller circular shaft, and crowned at the top with a lantern."[23]

Ancient Alexandria was celebrated as a seat of learning, of science and art, and infamous for its racial disturbances, and (particularly in the Christian era) for its religious disputes, its sectarian intolerance and savage persecutions. As a great trading city it was culturally superior to that other North African market place and business centre, Carthage, for unlike Carthage it was not dedicated almost exclusively to commerce and money-making, and though the Carthaginian way of life appeared to be one of peaceful commerce[24] it was shadowed by dark religious beliefs which condoned and even compelled human sacrifices.[25] The architectural remains of Carthage are scanty, and, like the surviving artifacts, unimpressive; Carthaginian civilisation made little impact on the cultural phases of Mediterranean life; it turned out uninspired low-grade consumer goods for export and not much else; it took a profit and gave nothing to the art of living.

Although Alexandria was the most uncharacteristic of all Greek cities, it owed to Greek inspiration the nobility of its architecture and the establishment of such institutions as the library, the museum, the medical school, and the theatre for lectures and assemblies. The site is different, but perhaps the mid-twentieth century city with its varied, vicious and pulsating life described in Lawrence Durrell's *Alexandria Quartet*[26] is not dissimilar in character from the city that Julius Ceasar and Mark Antony knew.

Alexandria was not the only African outpost of Hellenism; five hundred miles to the west Cyrene had been founded in the seventh century B.C., and became one of the greatest of all Greek colonies and the capital of ancient Cyrenaica. Greek art and influence had gradually spread along the north African littoral, checked only at the frontier of Carthaginian territory. Eastwards Greek cultural influence extended as far as India, though its impact on Indian art has been greatly exaggerated. The effective rule of the Macedonian Greek generals in India did not survive the death of Alexander.[27] There was no fusion between the humanistic classic art of Greece and the mystical, emotional art of India; the chief and most constructive result of Alexander's expedition was the establishment of contact between India and the civilisations of Greece and Persia.[28]

Long before Alexander conquered the Persian empire, Greek ideas were exerting their power on the Persians, who were probably unaware that they were being subjected to very subtle intellectual and artistic infiltration; invasion without visible military means of support was unknown to oriental states. Marching and riding armies their rulers could see and resist, but the Persians never recognised the unarmed advance guard of a coming Greek raid; so they welcomed the first wave of invaders, the artists and architects, philosophers and commercial travellers, and allowed them to penetrate and change the tone of the social and cultural life of their cities. Thus was the way prepared for Alexander's conquests and the transplanting of classic architecture and Greek art and civilisation. After his death the imperial system he created fell apart. The fleeting promise of a great universal state, dominated by the west, was unfulfilled, though the idea of such a state has never died. The bits and pieces of Alexander's still-born empire were scrambled for and inherited by the Ptolemys, the kings of Pergamum and the Selucids, who made no attempt to achieve political unity. They preserved the external forms of Greek civilisation, founded new cities, like Antioch, and rebuilt existing cities, and gave them temples, theatres, gymnasia, palaces and public buildings. Meanwhile the Romans—disciplined, efficient and often insensitive—were expanding and consolidating the area they ruled, ultimately moving in on the empire Alexander might have ruled had he lived, and absorbing Greece, Macedonia, Anatolia, Syria, Egypt and then turning westwards, leaving their monuments and ruins all round the shores of the Mediterranean, and throughout the provinces of Spain, Gaul and Belgica, and, ultimately, in the island of Britain south of Caledonia. What their architecture tells us about their character, sharply differentiated from the Greek character, is the subject of the next chapter.

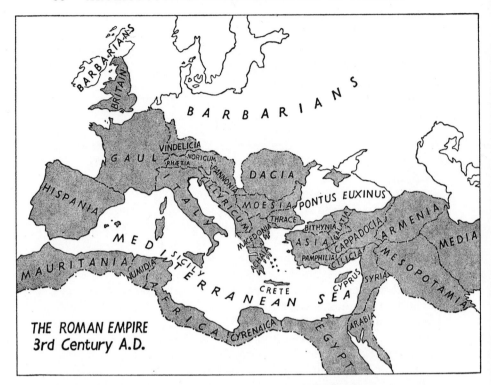

THE ROMAN EMPIRE
3rd Century A.D.

The Roman Empire at its greatest extent, third century A.D. Everywhere throughout this vast administrative area the standardised classic orders of architecture were permanent reminders of the all-pervading Roman power. They appeared on triumphal arches, temples, government buildings, monuments to emperors, public baths and the colonnades of every city forum. Sometimes the price of protecting a distant province was too high, and in the third quarter of the third century the emperor Aurelian (270–275) cut his losses and abandoned Dacia. Compare with the map on page 135. *Drawn by Marcelle Barton.*

THE CLASSICAL PHASE: ROMAN POWER

THE Romans were practical, orderly and ambitious, with a taste for grand effects that were often majestic, and occasionally vulgar. They adopted the architectural ideas of other nations, and the view that their crowning gift to architecture was magnitude is confirmed by tall structures that rear their columns and entablatures and pediments throughout the former provinces of the Empire. The Roman desire to build high was by no means ignoble, it was a visible assertion of imperial pride, though it occasionally denoted plutocratic vanity. Ruskin discerningly observed that whenever men became skilful architects they tended to build high, "not in any religious feeling, but in mere exuberance of spirit and power—as they dance or sing—with a certain mingling of vanity—like the feeling in which a child builds a tower of cards; and, in nobler instances, with also a strong sense of, and delight in, the majesty, height, and strength of the building itself, such as we have in that of a lofty tree or a peaked mountain."[1]

The Romans built high not from lighthearted joy of life, but to impress; height was often the architectural expression of that sober quality, the Roman *gravitas*. They never used towers or domes to give additional height to their buildings. Towers had a defensive function or were otherwise strictly utilitarian; domes had no external significance; they were convex lids, conveniently roofing some space, as exemplified by the Pantheon at Rome (Plates 18 and 19); lofty effects were gained by the use of gigantic columns, like those in the great temple complex at Baalbek in Syria: the Olympieion at Athens (Plate 12) or at Rome on the Temple of Mars Ultor in the Forum of Augustus (page 90), and within the Baths of Diocletian (Plate 16).

Roman architecture gained its coherence and authoritative dignity from the system of design the Greeks had invented; to the

The three remaining columns and pilaster of the Temple of Mars Ultor in the Forum of Augustus, Rome, 42 B.C. The columns are 58 feet high, and, like the ruins of Baalbek, support Sir Mortimer Wheeler's view that "the crowning gift of the Roman Empire to architecture was magnitude." *Drawn by Maureen Stafford, and reproduced by permission of the artist.*

three classic orders, Doric, Ionic and Corinthian, they added two others, the Tuscan and Composite. In the middle years of the last century, Ralph Wornum pointed out in his *Analysis of Ornament*, that Roman art was simply an enlargement or enrichment of the Greek, which did not add a single important element, but elaborated the established elements with ever possible variety of effect; from which he concluded that Roman art was still Greek art, and that it was more than probable that nearly all the great artists employed by the Romans were Greeks.[2] The Roman versions of the Doric, Ionic and Corinthian orders were not developed in the intellectual and artistic climate of a Greek city state: they lacked the subtle inflexions of Greek Doric, the formal elegance of Ionic, and the controlled gaiety of Corinthian. The two orders invented by the Romans were adapted, without much imagination, from the Greek originals: Tuscan was a variation of Doric; Composite a showy version of Corinthian. In Roman hands Greek ornament was over-elaborated in the pursuit of magnificence.[3] The most florid example of the Greek Corinthian order appears on the choragic monument of Lysicrates at Athens (Plate 13): compare the capital from that monument on page 73 with the six Corinthian capitals from Roman temples on pages 95 and 97; the Roman choice of the *acanthus mollis* with its bold rather coarsely-shaped leaves committed them to a profuse effect, and when they renounced restraint and invented the Composite order, the result was as ornate as the capital from the Arch of Titus at Rome on page 97.

The Etruscans, who had established a flourishing civilisation in central Italy about the eighth century B.C., were inventive and innovating builders. They lost their national identity after six or seven hundred years, and were incorporated in the Roman state; and to Rome they gave the arch, the vault, and the dome. The Romans used the arch almost exclusively as a structural device. Vitruvius advised that the weight of walls should be discharged "by arches consisting of wedges concentrically arranged; for if these are turned over beams or lintels, the beam, being relieved from the weight, will not sag . . ."[4] Ostensibly Roman architects were faithful to post-and-lintel construction; the arch was only used openly and without any attempt to mask its shape or function in bridges and aqueducts, of which many examples still exist, such as the Pont du Gard at Nîmes, France—part of the twenty-five mile

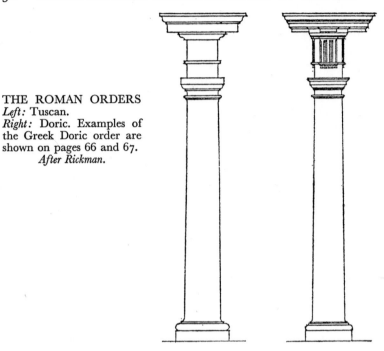

THE ROMAN ORDERS
Left: Tuscan.
Right: Doric. Examples of
the Greek Doric order are
shown on pages 66 and 67.
After Rickman.

long aqueduct built in 19 B.C., by Agrippa—and those that brought water to Rome, notably the Aqua Marcia (144 B.C.) and the Aqua Claudia (A.D. 38). These engineering works certainly suggested the dormant possibilities of the arch form; but the suggestion was ignored and arches were excluded from any significant part in the design of temples, palaces and public buildings. Arches might be supporting a vast structure but must not be visibly acknowledged. Vitruvius thought only in terms of relieving arches.

An outstanding example of this obscurantism on the part of Roman architects is the Colosseum, the Flavian amphitheatre, begun in A.D. 70 and completed twelve years later. Tiers of arches are raised on massive piers, and the structural ingenuity of the whole building, and the adventurous use of concrete internally for corridors and walls and vaults, are hidden as, very often, the triumphs of Victorian engineering were hidden by the application of spurious architectural details culled from some dead or dying style. The architects of the Colosseum used the classic orders for disguising their structural triumphs. The tiers of arches appear to be incidental elements in the composition, and the attached columns on the face of the piers, and the entablatures that they pretend to support, introduce the hackneyed vertical and horizontal features of the Tuscan, Ionic and Corinthian orders on the three lower storeys. The top storey, with Corinthian pilasters on a solid masonry face, was added in the third century. (Page 98.) The same rejection of structural reality may be seen in other great amphitheatres, at Arles, for instance, the ancient Roman town of Arelate, where attached Corinthian columns on the piers that carry the arches have no function apart from decoration. (Plate 23.)

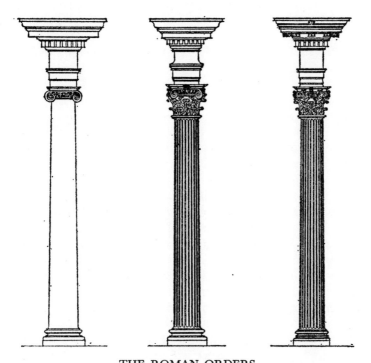

THE ROMAN ORDERS

Left: Ionic. *Centre:* Composite. *Right:* Corinthian. See opposite page, also pages 90, 95, 97, and Plates 14, 18 and 19. *After Rickman.*

From this reluctance to acknowledge structural facts we may deduce a weakness of the Roman character, a weakness that was not incompatible with Roman *gravitas*; for serious, conventional people are apt to distrust experiments and to prefer an unenterprising reliance on settled and proved methods. This aspect of Roman architecture accords with a suspicion of ideas and a hardened reluctance to change anything. Military organisation, for example, was inflexible for centuries; the legions marched in the same formations, were deployed by the same tactics, equipped with the same weapons and pattern of armour, from the Punic wars to the civil struggles of the third and fourth centuries A.D., when the legions fought each other as often as they fought the barbarians who were constantly probing the frontiers of the declining Empire. In architectural design and ornament, the familiar was respected; the classic orders were as visually reassuring as the forms and practices of Roman law were morally and socially reassuring; and early in the fourth century the social and economic order was petrified by the decrees of Diocletian. Thereafter, the iron collar of bureaucracy throttled initiative, so that social and economic collapse became inevitable. Long before those repressive decrees were enforced, inertia had slowed up the whole life of the Empire. The arch, which "never sleeps," was the visible negation of inertia. Perhaps Roman architects were too tactful or too nervous to challenge the complacency of the establishment by exhibiting such an example of disruptive energy.

As a mere outline the arch was, of course, quite innocuous, and the imperious triumphal arches that were dotted about all over the Empire were acceptably respectable decorative shapes: nothing more. Those arches slumbered. They were not arches in action; nor were they conceived as such; in fact their only entitlement to the name of arch was based on the fact that they had apertures with semi-circular heads, pierced through a mass of masonry, supporting nothing, not even distributing weight like a relieving arch.

The Arch of Constantine at Rome, erected in A.D. 312, shows how blandly oblivious Roman architects were to the virtues of structural frankness. The main and flanking arches which give passage through the stonework are pleasantly formal shapes; the eight detached monolithic Corinthian columns, rising from carved plinths to an entablature that breaks forward above the capitals,

VARIATIONS OF THE ROMAN CORINTHIAN CAPITAL

Left: From the temple of Mars Ultor. (See page 90.) *Right:* Temple of Jupiter Tonans, built by Augustus on the Capitoline Hill. *After Nicholson.*

Left: Temple of Antonius and Faustina, Rome. *Right:* The Pantheon, Rome. Both examples surmount plain shafts. *After Nicholson.*

are purely ornamental; neither arches nor columns have any structural function, they do not distribute or support the weight of the attic storey above the entablature or the quadriga that formerly surmounted it; but their noble proportions serve the purpose of the monument, which was to glorify the Emperor and to record his victories and achievements. By the beginning of the fourth century few skilled sculptors were available for adorning such examples of imperial self-advertisement, and reliefs were removed from the Arch of Trajan (A.D. 114), and re-used on Constantine's arch. (Plates 14 and 15.) Triumphal arches were proclamations in three dimensions of the Empire's military power. At Rome the Arch of Titus (A.D. 81) commemorated the capture of Jerusalem in A.D. 70; the arch of Septimius Severus (A.D. 204) honours the Parthian victories of the Emperor and his two sons, Caracalla and Geta; and the idea of the triumphal arch has endured and asserted the military pride of later nations. (A distinguished example is the Arc de Triomphe in Paris, built between A.D. 1806 and 1836.) In the provinces triumphal arches were declarations of imperial grandeur, rather less useful than the monuments erected throughout Britain in the late nineteenth century to celebrate Queen Victoria's Jubilee; for while a Jubilee memorial often provided a clock-tower or a drinking fountain, a triumphal arch had no practical function, only a political purpose as a reminder of the respect due not only to the Emperor but to Roman law and order; a covert threat to newly-conquered peoples or restless provincials of their duty to be docile and pay their taxes.

Those isolated triumphal arches were not gateways. The gateway of a city often resembled that of a fort, with guard-towers, which might be as simple as the gate of the reconstructed fort at Saalburg on the old, dangerous German frontier of the Empire (page 104), or as impressive as the Porta Nigra at Trier (Plate 21), which was part of the wall of the Roman city of Augusta Treverorum, in Belgic Gaul, some eighty miles west of that frontier. The military gateway was standardised, with twin portals, surmounted or flanked by guard-houses, as at the west gate of the fort at Housesteads on Hadrian's Wall in Northumberland (page 105). Such structures, devoid of any decorative features, were bleakly functional.[5] But whether they were simple or as elaborate as the Black Gate at Trier, the standard form was perpetuated all over

VARIATIONS OF THE ROMAN CORINTHIAN CAPITAL

Left: Temple of Vesta at Tivoli. *Right:* Temple of Vesta at Rome. *After Nicholson.*

CAPITAL OF THE COMPOSITE ORDER

This florid example is from the Arch of Titus, Rome, which was erected to commemorate the capture of Jerusalem, and represents one of the earliest known uses of the Composite order. *After Nicholson.*

The Flavian Amphitheatre at Rome, generally called the Colosseum, begun A.D. 70 and completed A.D. 82. The three lower storeys are pierced by arches, and on the façade the Tuscan, Ionic and Corinthian orders are used; their attached columns and their entablatures have no function apart from decoration. The top storey, with its Corinthian pilasters, was added in the third century. The tiers of arcades are supported by massive piers and the arcuated construction and the extensive use of concrete for corridors, cells and vaults are deliberately hidden. *Drawn by Maureen Stafford.*

the Empire: two main arches for traffic, and in some cities, two smaller arches for pedestrians. With their adjacent guard-chambers, they were the prototypes of the gate-house. The gate towers as well as the walls of many mediaeval European cities and castles rose from Roman foundations. Pevensey Castle in Sussex incorporates the Roman material of Anderida, the last Saxon Shore fort built for the defence of Roman Britain. The masonry of innumerable siege-resisting walls and bastions, gripped by Roman cement, put their mediaeval defenders in the debt of long-forgotten legionaries whose building skills had originally reared such stalwart defences. The titanic scale of Roman city walls may be gauged by the remains of those at Constantinople and Antioch (Plate 20); the staunchness imparted to stonework by layers of horizontal tiles used as binding courses is shown by the walls of the Saxon Shore fort at Burgh Castle, Norfolk (Plate 23.)

Roman taste for monuments of commanding height was expressed by memorial columns, pillars of victory that recorded military successes, and of these Trajan's column in Rome (A.D. 114) is the most famous, and for the student of history the most illuminating, for the bas-reliefs carved on the shaft illustrate incidents of the Emperor's Dacian campaign. Some two thousand five hundred human figures appear on a spiral band that winds upwards about the column. Details of costume, armour, weapons and equipment and the varied activities of an army in the field, the preparation of fortifications, building operations and religious ceremonies as well as battle scenes are vividly depicted. The column, which is of the Doric order, is 115 ft. 7 ins. high, and stands on a pedestal that contained the tomb chamber of the Emperor. The shaft has a diameter of 12 ft. 2 ins., and within a spiral staircase ascends, lit by small apertures. Originally the column bore a statue of Trajan, which was later replaced by one of St. Peter. Two pillars of victory of comparable design, both in Rome, are those of Antoninus Pius (A.D. 161) and Marcus Aurelius (A.D. 174); many others were erected in cities of the Empire. Sometimes they were sycophantic expressions of gratitude like the pillar at Alexandria, subscribed for by the citizens in acknowledgement of Diocletian's gift to them of part of the corn tribute. That emperor had beseiged Alexandria in A.D. 297, and the gift was made after the troubles were over and the province of Egypt had been reorganised. The pillar was erected near the Serapeion, and some centuries later became known as Pompey's Pillar, a name erroneously bestowed by crusaders.

Victories at sea were celebrated by Rostral columns, a name derived from the rostra, or prows, of ships captured in battle, which were affixed to the shaft of the column. The solitary column has never lost favour as a monument of victory or occasionally as a reminder of disaster, like Wren's Monument to the Great Fire of London. (Page 251.) Victorious generals and admirals as well as innumerable royal and noble celebrities (and nonentities) look down from such columns in cities all over Europe. Sometimes those figures standing high above the roof tops were tricked out in a Roman toga, unless they wore becoming and distinguished uniform (like Nelson in Trafalgar Square); for latter-day clothes, even those of the seventeenth and eighteenth centuries, seldom look well when petrified in bronze or marble.

The Roman attitude to religion differed profoundly from the Greek, and this showed in the design of temples. For more than a thousand years the Roman religion, with all its complicated ceremonies and rituals, gave spiritual satisfaction to a diversity of peoples, largely because it offered an acceptable and easily comprehended interpretation of life and the world, and the Roman gods were involved with human activities, unlike the remote and detached and irresponsibly mischievous Greek gods. As Mr. R. M. Ogilvie has pointed out in *The Romans and their Gods in the Age of Augustus*: "The ultimate test of a religion is that it works; and the Romans truly believed that their religion worked. Otherwise Roman civilisation would have collapsed with Augustus. For the social and constitutional recovery that he engineered could not have succeeded unless it had been based on a widely diffused religious confidence to make it succeed."[6]

The Roman gods and goddesses performed specific functions, and specially-built houses were provided for their accommodation. Thus the Roman temple was essentially a shelter for the god, and architects were concerned primarily with the adornment of the interior: the exterior was of secondary importance, though the entrance demanded dignity, which was often conveyed by a formal portico, like that of the Pantheon at Rome (Plate 19). As a sanctuary, and with certain deities a secret sanctuary, the Roman

Remains of the Roman Theatre at Taormina, Sicily. This is mainly hewn from the rock of the hillside, and is of Greek origin, but entirely reconstructed in the Roman period. Most of the seats have gone; mediaeval stone robbers have removed the marble sheathing that formerly concealed the brickwork and the arcuated construction. *Drawn by Raymond McGrath, and reproduced by permission of the artist.*

temple was the antithesis of the "extrovert" Greek type. When in the later years of the Empire various oriental religions began to compete with the old gods of Rome, secrecy and mystery and exotic rites were introduced, for the Romans were hospitable to gods, and in provinces like Gaul and Britain were prepared to assimilate native gods with the familiar and traditional deities. An example of this is the assimilation of Sulis, a British water-goddess, with Minerva, for whom an imposing classical temple was built at Bath, the Roman Aquae Sulis, perhaps as early as the first century A.D., though some authorities suggest a later date.[7]

Some religions deliberately concealed their god or gods from worshippers; the touchy and jealous Jehovah of the Hebrews was one of those hidden gods, and one moreover who would have

seemed intolerable to reasonable Greeks and incomprehensible
to practical Romans. Some religions began as secret cults, and,
through fear of persecution, long remained so; Christianity began
like that, for its adherents were forced to meet in caves and cata-
combs; other cults, like that of Mithras, sought seclusion in order
to protect their sacred rituals from the uninitiated. The buildings
that served both religions were designed to reproduce the dim
atmosphere of a cave.

The Pantheon in Rome was probably the first major monument
to be composed entirely as an interior;[8] the external part ends with
the octastyle portico of unfluted monolithic Corinthian columns in
marble and granite with the capitals carved in white Pentelic
marble. Within, the Rotunda is roofed by a hemi-spherical dome,
formed by horizontal brick courses set in cement, and not cast in
concrete as was once supposed. The inner surface is coffered in five
diminishing ranges, that provide ornament and reduce weight. A
circular unglazed aperture at the crown admits a shaft of light that
illuminates the whole interior. (Plates 18 and 19.) The building,
erected A.D. 120–124, is in a perfect state of preservation, though
many bronze and marble sculptures and ornaments have been
removed, notably the bronze relief that once filled the pediment
of the portico, and the colossal statues of Augustus and Agrippa
that stood in niches behind the columns. Walls, vaulting and the
colonnaded portico remain in their original condition, having
happily survived extensive restoration.

Roman rectangular temples bear a superficial resemblance to
Greek. Vitruvius classified five species, based on the disposition of
the columns and not related to the plan.[9] He referred to the Greek
respect for proportion. The design of temples, he said, depended on
symmetry and symmetry arose from proportion, and proportion
was "a due adjustment of the size of the different parts to each
other and to the whole; on this proper adjustment symmetry
depends. Hence no building can be said to be well designed which
wants symmetry and proportion."

Best-preserved of all the rectangular Roman temples that still
stand is the Maison Carrée at Nîmes, the ancient city of Nemausus.
It has symmetry, proportion and cold dignity, with Corinthian
columns standing on a 12 foot podium, and a flight of steps leading
to the entrance. Like the Pantheon it is designed as an interior; like

nearly all Roman temples it provided not only a residence for the god or gods, but a secluded and private place where the individual could have direct and secret communion with the god he was praying to or petitioning; no priest was interpolated between worshipper and deity, though priests conducted sacrifices and ceremonies at the altar or altars outside the temple. Religion in the Graeco–Roman world was easy-going, non-sectarian, and free from the bitter righteousness that made Judaism intractably exclusive and Christianity savagely intolerant. The variety of cults for which temples were built in Rome and lesser cities attests the open-mindedness of Roman religiosity; all the different peoples in the Empire were allowed to worship their own gods in their accustomed way; only such native cults as Druidism were proscribed, and not because the Romans disapproved of human sacrifice— which had occasionally disfigured their own history—but because Druidism exercised an authority which competed with that of the state. Temples built in honour of a deified emperor had an indirect political significance; sometimes they recorded imperial interest in a locality, but such dedicated temples represented a very small proportion of the huge number of sacred buildings, and everywhere their design illustrated the basic difference between the Greek and Roman view of religion and life.

The difference is emphasised by the character of secular buildings, in particular those devoted to entertainment. The Greek theatre, with its semi-circle of seats rising in tiers, was designed for dramatic performances; the Roman amphitheatre for spectacles, not always edifying. Perhaps too much has been made of their alleged horrific nature; the games were largely exhibitions of skill, particularly the chariot races, which took place on seventeen days of the year in the time of Augustus and on sixty-six in the fourth century.[10] True, there was plenty of bloodshed, but the victims were often wild animals, brought to Rome and other cities at considerable expense, and they were pitted against highly-trained professional gladiators who gave the audience the thrill and excitement of watching a wild beast hunt. Gladiatorial shows with men fighting each other did not represent a large element in the regular public games;[11] perhaps such turns, put on without regard for human rights or dignity were too wasteful; professional gladiators were costly, and the appetite for bloodshed could be satisfied more

Reconstruction of a Roman frontier fort, at Saalburg, on the German limes. *Above:* The principal gate, with double arches and guard towers. *Below:* The north gate, seen from the inside, showing the embankment on either side of the guard towers that gave rapid access to the battlemented wall. *Drawn by Maureen Stafford.*

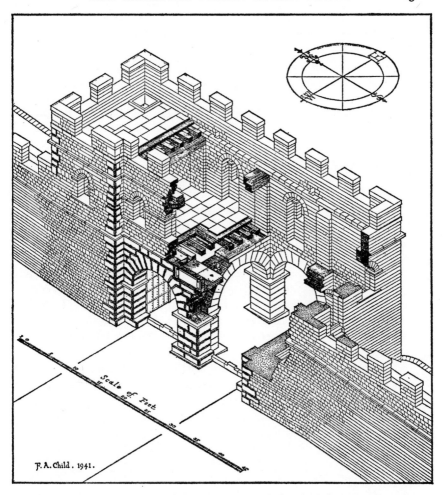

F. A. Child. 1941.

Restoration of the West Gate at Housesteads on Hadrian's Wall, showing the double arches, and the guard chambers above and at one side. Compare with the two gateways on the opposite page, from the reconstructed fort at Saalburg on the German frontier of the Empire. From *The Roman Imperial Army*, by Graham Webster, Fig. 32, page 181. (A. & C. Black Ltd. 1969.) Reproduced by permission of the Society of Antiquaries of Newcastle-upon-Tyne and the late F. Austin Child, F.R.I.B.A.

cheaply by making military prisoners fight each other or by providing lions and tigers with a meal of condemned criminals.The number of circuses, amphitheatres, and hippodromes increased in Rome during the imperial era, and in every important municipality in the provinces. The ruins of these places of entertainment have inflamed the imagination of so many painters and writers that what went on in the arena has long become familiar through scenes realistically depicted on canvasses, particularly in the nineteenth century, in historical novels, and their film versions, and in the writings of social historians, like Mr. Lewis Mumford, who tells us that "Terrorism, violence, lust were organized and systematized on a scale that passes belief: people lived from day to day in the vicarious enjoyment of the most ingenious brutalities that have ever depraved the human soul. The Romans became esthetes of torture."[12] What the architecture of the amphitheatres and circuses reveals is that thousands of spectators saw these shows in reasonable comfort; quite as comfortably as modern spectators at a bull-fight, a ball game or a cup-final though they were not as cosy and secluded as those who watch the streamlined pornography and violence of some modern television features. Behind all the appurtenances of a highly-organised civilisation, behind law and order, safe communications, well-planned cities with drains and aqueducts and fountains, magnificent public baths and splendid buildings, was the evidence of a casual and condoned brutality, inseparable, perhaps, from a bureaucratic slave state.

The contrast between Roman and Greek ideas of civilised life is illustrated by the way Roman cities were planned. Many of them began as camps, for the Roman provinces were nearly all acquired by military conquest, so the needs of a fortified camp determined the plan, which was four-square with a gate in the centre of each wall and a geometric grid of streets within, the main streets leading from the gates forming a carfax in the city centre. This was not invariable, for some cities even in remote provinces such as Britain were residential from their foundation, like Silchester, the ancient Calleva, planned on Roman lines with a grid of streets but irregular in shape. In Italy there were residential and pleasure cities, planned as such, and only fortified in the later, dangerous years of the Empire. But even with these there were exceptions. Pompeii, as we know it today, is about 160 acres in extent, an irregular oval in shape, built on a small hill, and encircled by a stone wall nearly two miles in circumference, with eight gates. The place had been fortified long before it became a colony for time-expired Roman veterans about 80 B.C., and a summer resort for wealthy aristocrats, until it was destroyed by an eruption of Vesuvius (long believed to be extinct) in A.D. 79. The streets of Pompeii, although approaching symmetrical arrangement, are not really symmetrical, as there is hardly a right angle or any approach to a right angle at any street corner.

In the centre of the Roman city was the forum which corresponded to the Greek agora; about it were grouped the public buildings, and it was the focal point of social, political and commercial life and a market as well, with shops. One side or the middle might be occupied by a basilica, a large building, rectangular in plan, twice as long as it was wide, with two or four rows of columns forming three or five aisles, running the entire length, with galleries above which had upper columns that supported the roof. The entrance was either at the side or at one end; at the other end was a tribunal on a raised platform, usually in a semi-circular space called an apse. The basilica was a hall of justice, where legal business was transacted, also the town hall and a public meeting place and commercial exchange. On the platform in the apse were seats for law officers, and an altar where sacrifices were made by a priest before legal business began.

In Rome the basilica of Trajan, designed by Apollodorus of Damascus and built in A.D. 98, was entered through a portico from the adjoining forum of Trajan; in provincial cities the basilica often occupied one side of the forum. The great basilica of Roman London was on the north side of the forum; part of the southern side of the building seems to have been an open portico.[13] (See map on page 7.) At Silchester the forum and basilica covered nearly two acres of ground. The forum consisted of a large open court, surrounded on three sides by shops and offices, with the basilica on the fourth.[14] However remote the locality, the forum and basilica dignified the city centre. Those excavated in British towns are much simpler in plan compared with those in Italian, south European or North African cities.[15]

Public buildings had prestige value; their scale was monumental; and the major structures in any city, temples, baths and the forum and basilica, were ennobled by the proportions of one or other of the orders of architecture, of which the Corinthian was the most favoured. From Wales to Syria, from the Sahara to the Alps, the system of architectural design represented by the classic orders gave an impassive, standardised solemnity to everything the Romans built. Temples, tombs, altars, triumphal arches, colonnades and porticoes, all repeated over and over again the unalterable profiles of mouldings and the formalised ornament appropriate for each order; and this standardisation educated the eyes of Roman citizens everywhere and accustomed them to accept the classic orders as the only conceivable type of civilised architecture: to reject them was to surrender to barbarism. Wherever stone was used, masons reproduced the forms originally perfected by Greek architects and sculptors; and throughout the Graeco–Roman world those forms denoted the vitality of the cultural system that flourished during period seven on the Flinders Petrie diagram (page 19). The maturity and decline of this classic phase of western civilisation coincided with the rise and decline of the Roman Empire in the west.

The Romans excelled in architecture because they were a practical people, and architecture is a practical art. Beyond the northern and western frontiers of the Empire the untutored natives built straw-thatched wattle-and-daub huts: the Irish in their island, the Picts of Caledonia north of the Antonine Wall, and the innumerable Germanic tribes across the Rhine, all living tax-free disorderly lives, congenially occupied with internecine tribal wars, and—except possibly the Irish—intimidated by the reputation and apparently unassailable might of Rome, a little bewildered, perhaps, by the spectacle of an orderly civilisation, and more than a little envious of its wealth. When tribesmen served in the Roman army as legionaries—as many did in increasing numbers during the third and fourth centuries—or were settled in some frontier province as *foederati*, every structure they saw reminded them of Roman supremacy, the technical perfection of Roman arts and engineering, and the ubiquity of Roman law and order.

The scale and splendour of imperial palaces in Rome and elsewhere may be judged from existing ruins; the extravagance of Nero's Golden House in Rome has been mentioned in chapter one, but for size and magnificence it was surpassed by Diocletian's palace in Dalmatia, which resembled a miniature city, occupying eight acres and extending along the sea-front of the Adriatic, with halls, temples, a basilica for entertainments and innumerable apartments for officials as well as the imperial suite and servants' quarters. The palace, erected between A.D. 290 and 310, was incorporated in the mediaeval town of Spalatro. (A detailed record of the surviving building was made by Robert Adam, who published in 1764 a volume with engravings by Bartolozzi, entitled *Ruins of the Palace of the Emperor Diocletian at Spalatro.*) The official palaces of provincial governors were extensive and luxurious. Even in remote Londinium the governor's palace was a large building with considerable architectural pretensions.[16]

The plan and character of Roman houses, whether in a town or in the country, suggest that their owners placed a high value on privacy. Town houses presented blank, windowless walls to the street; or else, on either side of the portico, the frontage would be rented to shopkeepers; but this combination of private dwelling with commercial activity was usually confined to a few principal streets. The central feature of a small house was a hall, the *atrium*, with smaller rooms grouped round it, and a large central opening in the roof that admitted light and air. The house was essentially inward-looking, and more spacious types had one or more internal courts, with rooms opening out on them; they were usually of one storey, and the living rooms were heated by hot air passing below the floors and up hollow tiles in the walls, supplemented by braziers in which charcoal was burned.

In Rome and some other cities there were tenement dwellings, known as *insula*, rising to several storeys, with a height limit of 75 feet, which had been imposed by Augustus. They sometimes collapsed, because faulty construction and dishonest building contractors were not unknown in the ancient world.

The villa or country house was spaciously planned; the term villa included not only the residence, but the farm-buildings, offices, granaries, and the living quarters of the staff, slaves and freedmen, and also the estate of the landed proprietor. To some extent the Roman villa resembled the mediaeval manor, though there was no connection between them.[17] The large country houses in Italy and many of the provinces with their gardens and orchards and groves of trees were as extensive as a small town; as mentioned in chapter one, the great estates of Roman Gaul were gradually transformed into rural communities in the Middle Ages and the Romano–Gallic villa was the ancestor of the château.

In Britain the remains of many large houses have been excavated, but nothing comparable with the scale and luxury of the late first century palace at Fishbourne in Sussex.[18] It is conjectured that it was built for a Roman client-king, Cogidubnus, who ruled at that time in the Chichester area, and it lay a few miles from the city that was then called Noviomagus. Although some of the country houses of Roman Britain were extensive and even sumptuous, with mosaic floors and painted walls, the general standard of domestic architecture cannot be judged from a few palatial examples. But even more modest homes in the countryside and small country towns were commodious and comfortable, with central heating, running water, latrines, baths and competent drainage.

Windows were glazed, with glass cast in small panes, cemented into place.[19] Glass was made in Britain, and some evidence of the manufacture has been found at Wilderspool near Warrington in Lancashire.[20] It is uncertain whether Roman window glass was transparent: fragments found on many sites suggest that the panes were translucent. In the large houses of Italy, planned for ease and pleasure, the window became the frame for a view. Pliny describing his Laurentine villa in a letter to Gallus mentions "a roomy bedroom, then a smaller one, with one window to let in the dawn, another to hold the sunset; with a view too of the sea below—farther off, certainly, but safer." This translation, by W. G. Newton, is quoted by Robert Atkinson and Hope Bagenal in *Theory and Elements of Architecture*, and they observe that those last two words, *but safer*, recall an "early apprehension—a last breath of primeval terror of the elements which we have forgotten today but from which we were first emancipated by the great Greeks and Romans."[21] Translucent glass would have obscured the view from such carefully placed windows; either they were unglazed or the glass must have been far superior in quality to that used in provincial villa houses. Window glass in the first and second centuries A.D. was 3 to 6 mm. thick, pale blue or sea-green in tint, and sometimes brownish. In the third and fourth centuries the manufacture had obviously improved, and although the prevailing colour was still pale green, the glass was clearer and approached more closely to modern window glass.[22]

Roman domestic architecture gives us a picture of a settled, secure, and materially accomplished civilisation, with nearly every modern convenience. Perhaps the crowning and most lasting achievement of Roman organisation and technical ability was the road. Roads paved with stone were originated by the Carthaginians; the Romans adopted their constructional method, and on a large scale also adopted the Persian system of linking the provinces of their Empire by well-made, well-guarded highways. Nothing is known about Carthaginian roads, though it seems likely that the Roman roads of North Africa and Spain followed the same routes.[23] A great deal is known about Roman roads, those purposeful ways that were driven across plains and deserts, through mountain passes, and in hilly or undulating country surveyed from skyline to skyline, and cleared of undergrowth for the length of a bow-shot on either side when they passed through woodlands or forests. In the provinces that had been acquired originally by conquest, many roads were laid out to suit military needs in the initial campaigns against the native tribes; after the conquered country was pacified and occupied, later roads were made to meet the requirements of trade and to carry local traffic. One of the most distinctive characteristics of Roman roads was their straight alignments. As Mr. Ivan D. Margary explains in his study of *Roman Roads in Britain.* "The real purpose of the straight alignments was merely for convenience in setting out the course of the road, for sighting marks could be quickly aligned from one high point to another, with intermediate marks adjusted between, probably by the use of moving beacons, shifted alternately to the right and left until all were brought into line . . ."[24] Those alignments on main roads were laid out with great accuracy for considerable distances. The alignment angles were very distinctive features, for the road followed each right up to the angle, unlike the curving courses of later roads.[25]

Long after Rome had sunk to a name, those superb highways survived to remind the struggling, semi-barbaric European states of a lost world of order and technical efficiency that was rapidly passing from memory to myth. In the old provinces of the Western

Empire, the survival and condition of the Roman roads recorded the fluctuations of civilisation, nowhere more clearly than in Britain, for many of the main roads today follow the same lines and in some places are built upon the same foundations as their Roman predecessors. A comparison of the ordnance map of England and Wales with a map of Roman Britain shows the debt we owe to Roman engineers.[26] Where there are divergencies from the original straight alignments, some forgotten piece of local history such as the greed of some Tudor landlord who diverted a highway to enlarge his parkland, or the demands of the Industrial Revolution, which devoured acres of land, or, very far back indeed in the dim post-Roman age, lack of technical skill, may account for the change of direction. One of those drastic changes mentioned by the late M. P. Charlesworth in *The Lost Province* occurs near Lichfield in Staffordshire, where Watling Street, heading north-west in an unbroken line on the map of Roman Britain, now swings through two right-angled turns to avoid crossing marshy ground. The Roman road crossed the marsh on piles of alder wood; a simple piece of engineering that was not even attempted in later times.[27] On the ordnance map the diversion is shown, and the original line of the Roman road is also marked, cutting through Lawton Grange as a footpath, passing below a railway, then running straight for Wall, the Roman Letocetum, where the road turned west to Wroxeter where the city of Viroconium once stood. In many English localities the old line of Roman roads remain, sometimes as a footpath, a grass-grown lane, or a parish boundary.

Although road-making ceased in the fifth century, when the Western Empire was slowly collapsing, building did not, though in the frontier provinces and in Britain building craftsmen were engaged chiefly on fortification and repairing walls. The only new buildings were churches. The last large-scale non-military building in Britain, was the temple settlement at Lydney, described in chapter one, and dedicated to the native god Nodens. (Page 15.) Late in the fourth century St. Ninian is supposed to have built a church at Whithorn, north of Hadrian's Wall, in what is now Galloway. This is mentioned by Bede, and the church was alleged to have been dedicated to St. Martin. The actual site was on the western side of Wigtown Bay; Ninian called the place Leukopia, and the church became known as the White House (Candida

Roman winged figures, both from Pompeii. *Left:* One of the ends of a white marble table, with two winged leopards on a pedestal and a cornucopia cut in relief between them. From the house of Meleager. *Right:* White marble table with a sphinx forming the supporting pedestal. From the house of the Faun. Both reproduced from *Illustrations of Ancient Art*, by Edward Trollope, F.S.A. (London: George Bell. 1854.) Plate XX. (Compare with the Greek sphinx on page 79.)

Casa). He is said to have visited St. Martin at Tours, when he was returning from his period of training at Rome, "and obtained from him masons for the purpose of building a church after the Roman manner . . ."[28] That legend, long accepted, has often been re-peated in various historical works. But the conclusions of the modern archaeologist, based on excavated evidence and the archi-tectural character that it reveals, often modifies conclusions derived from folklore or piety.

Now there is a small, rectangular building on a site in Galloway, just to the east of Whithorn Priory Church, though it is doubtful whether that chapel had any direct connection with Ninian. The foundations have been excavated, originally by the Marquess of Bute, and later by Dr. C. V. Ralegh Radford. Professor Antony Charles Thomas discounts the slender evidence that the outer face of the building was daubed with coarse, cream-coloured mortar, or indeed with white plaster, and doubts whether this was the church built by Ninian, or even in the late fourth or early fifth century. He believes that it was merely a subsidiary chapel of seventh century date or even later, built when the site of Whithorn had become a monastery under Irish influence.[29] The connection with St. Ninian is slender; no convincing archaeological evidence supports the claim that the excavated ruins are those of the White House; but the legend of the Candida Casa has lived on for generations, until the cold, hard light of archaeological research has dispelled its claim to authenticity.

Church building gave new direction and inspiration to architectural design, and this activity commanded nearly all of the available skill in the still surviving parts of the Empire, though some was left over for the adornment of large country houses, like that of Apollinaris Sidonius, at Avitacum.[30] Sidonius, who was born about 430, probably at Lyons, wrote descriptions of the building, appointments and abundant luxury of his house. But these were isolated instances; the architects who worked in that twilit period served the now dominant and unworldly religion of Christianity; and the rejection of the material world that such a faith encouraged may have been one of the causes for the rejection of representational art in the fourth and fifth centuries. The classical phase of Mediterranean civilisation was ending, overcome by the pressures of change, and reflecting the power of those pressures by a new style in sculpture and architecture. That style, as noted in chapter one, was not a result of loss of artistic skill and as such to be regarded as evidence of decadence, but was a change deliberately made, and generated by a fresh creative awareness that enlightened sculptors and architects. The art and architecture of the fourth and fifth centuries, that troubled period of transition, represents triumphant change: not decay.

6

THE DEATH OF THE GODS AND THE
AGE OF FAITH

EARLY in the fourth century the Christian religion ceased to be condemned officially as a subversive social influence; after the Edict of Toleration of A.D. 313 members of the sect were free to design and build their own churches, and these they modelled on the Roman basilica, with a semi-circular apse at one end, which often faced to the west; a broad central aisle or nave, flanked by one or two lesser aisles; and a wide, deep, arcaded entrance porch called a narthex. An open square or rectangular forecourt lay in front, and like the entrance court of a Roman house this was called the atrium. Very often columns from ruined temples were used inside, and whether borrowed or new, were closely set in rows and supported an entablature that separated the nave from the flanking aisles. When the columns carried arches they stood further apart, and the arches rested on the abacus—the square, flat uppermost member of the capital. A simple type of flat or pitched timber roof was used. The vault and the dome were neglected.

Those early Christian churches derived their architectural character largely from Roman basilicas: there was nothing revolutionary or distinctive about their design: they continued the classic tradition, though the long nave, with its procession of Corinthian or Ionic columns, had an impressive solemnity that transcended the dignity of secular prototypes. The tower, which became a characteristic feature of Christian churches, was probably added late in the fourth century or early in the fifth; but towers were not apparently used for bells until early in the seventh century, when Pope Sabinianus (A.D. 604–606) is said to have introduced bell-ringing at the canonical hours. A church with two high round towers and a rounded apse is carved as a symbol of Jerusalem on some ivory tablets from the Werden casket that dates from about A.D. 400, looking, as Lethaby remarks, like a twelfth century Romanesque church.[1] Those carved tablets are now in the Victoria and Albert Museum. (Plate 24). The towers resemble those depicted on the reverse of a large gold medallion, found near Arras, that was struck to commemorate the relief of Londinium when Britain was restored to the Empire by Constantius Chlorus after the defeat of the usurper Allectus in A.D. 296. The goddess of Londinium kneels to welcome Constantius who appears on horseback, approaching the city gates; the twin towers with their conical tops are in the background, and the abbreviation LON is placed below the kneeling goddess.[2] They are probably look-out towers, forming an integral part of the gateway and guard house, contiguous with the city wall. That compressed, symbolic view is the only authentic picture we have of Roman London. (Plate 24.)

When the first emancipated Christian communities began to build churches, they did so almost furtively. The habit of secret worship was not easily shaken off; and as they were still poor and unendowed, they were content with the simplest of shelters, often constructed from materials taken from old and abandoned buildings. But the Church became materially prosperous during the fourth century, and as its power and influence expanded, so did the arrogance and intolerance of its prelates. The first of the ruthless wars of religion began, waged with all the bitterness that self-righteousness engenders, between the Church militant and the old gods of the happy-go-lucky pagan world. The Edict of Theodosius in A.D. 380 stigmatised all religions other than Catholic Christianity as heretical; in the sixty-seven years between 313 and 380 organised Christianity acquired secular powers comparable with those of the state; it was the spiritual department of the administration, and during the period of growing ascendency churches were built in every province of the Empire, even in far-away Britain. At Silchester (Calleva) the remains of a building that has all the features of an early Christian church were uncovered in the southeast corner of the Forum Insula in May 1892, when the site of the city was originally excavated. Another building, excavated at Caerwent (Venta), could be a church, but no proof in the form of altars or objects marked with Christian symbols were found.[3] Mr.

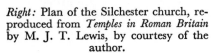

Imaginative reconstruction of the building at Silchester that may have been a
church. Reproduced from *Roman Silchester* by George C. Boon (1957 edition),
by courtesy of the author.

Right: Plan of the Silchester church, reproduced from *Temples in Roman Britain*
by M. J. T. Lewis, by courtesy of the
author.

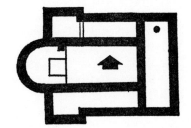

George Boon has described the Silchester church as "one of the
most discussed buildings of Roman Britain."[4] An imaginative
reconstruction of the exterior, from his book, *Roman Silchester*, is
given above; a small, modest structure that has the features of
an early Christian church; the plan of the building, reproduced
from Dr. M. J. T. Lewis's *Temples in Roman Britain*, shows a central
nave, with an apsidal west end, 29 ft. 3 in. long and about 10 ft.
wide, flanked by small aisles 5 ft. wide, and a narthex, 24 ft. 3 in.
by 6 ft. 9 in., at the east end.[5] That type of plan was not confined
to churches; and the Silchester building could have served as a
mithraeum, for the various esoteric mystery cults demanded closed
places of worship.[6]

In many provinces of the Empire, especially in the Middle East,
Christian churches were erected at the expense of the magnificent
temples that had been officially condemned. Fanatical iconoclasts
tore down the columns and carved capitals and marble wall facings
from those older sacred edifices, which were then re-used, often

with scant regard for their proportions. Ruins in Syria and Asia Minor, dating from those early centuries of Christian looting, indicate the scale of religious building enterprise; but gradually the new state religion developed confident architectural character, and one of the earliest examples indicative of new inspiration in design was the Church of the Nativity at Bethlehem, founded in A.D. 330 by Constantine, and built over the traditional birthplace of Christ. That church was simple and spacious, with a nave, double aisles, and a sanctuary with triple apses.

In Italy, where Christianity as a religion has had a continuous history since the days of its persecution in the early Empire, many churches still remain that incorporate some part of an original structure, or have been carefully reconstructed like the basilican church of St. Paul's-outside-the-Walls at Rome, which was founded about A.D. 380, destroyed in 1823, and rebuilt exactly to its original design. (Opposite.) Many others, like St. John Lateran at Rome, first built A.D. 330, have been so extensively remodelled that the early Christian character has been lost.

The basilican form persisted from the fourth to the seventh centuries, and in countries where sunlight was not so powerful as in Italy and Greece and Syria, windows acquired a new significance, which forecast the ultimate conquest of voids over solids that was the final architectural triumph of the Gothic builders of the late mediaeval period. A contemporary fifth century description has survived in the letters and poems of Apollinaris Sidonius of a church built by Patiens, the Bishop of Lugdunum, the Roman Lyons, which shows how dark walls gave way to brilliant areas of light. Dimness withdrew from the interior of the church, for, as the writer said, "the light flashes and the sunshine is so tempted to the gilded ceiling that it travels over tawny metal, matching its hue." Coloured marbles covered the vaulting, the floor, and the window frames, forming on the latter "designs of diverse colour, a verdant grass-green encrustation" that brought "winding lines of sapphire-hued stones over the leek-green glass".[7] The building was destroyed by the Huguenots in 1562.

Early Christian basilican churches showed no advance in the use or understanding of the arch principle. Their builders continued to depend on post-and-lintel construction; nothing new emerged from their combination and adaptation of old forms,

The early Christian basilican church of St. Paul's-outside-the-Walls, Rome. Founded in A.D. 380, destroyed in 1823, and rebuilt to the original design. There are eighty granite columns in the nave, with arches springing from the capitals. This early example of Christian church building is indistinguishable from the official public buildings of Imperial Rome: it could serve equally well as a law court or a pagan temple. *Drawn by Maureen Stafford.*

though richness and depth of colour came from painted surfaces and mosaics. Walls became warmly pictorial, and the holy figures depicted displayed their complete severance from representational art.

Christian architecture remained static in the West, for the power of Rome, though challenged and assailed in the second half of the fourth century with greater boldness and frequency by the barbarian tribes beyond the frontiers of the Empire, still imposed immobility on design, and the first indications of new thought in structure and composition came from the Eastern Empire. The Empire had been divided by Constantine who moved the capital from Rome to Byzantium in Thrace on the Bosphorus; enlarging and rebuilding an ancient town that had originally been a Greek colony, and laying out a spacious city, that for political reasons was named New Rome, though—more flattering to its founder—it was also known as Constantinople. Rather confusingly the original name of Byzantium was used as well. At first it was pre-eminently a Roman city, lavishly magnificent in appearance, with the slopes of what is now Seraglio Point adorned with palaces, the Acropolis and its Forum Augusteum rising beyond, and the imperial residence facing the sea.

The city was dedicated to the Virgin in A.D. 330, and though nominally Christian, it long remained a tolerantly half-pagan cosmopolitan place; as permissively vicious and easygoing as pre-Christian Alexandria had been. Zosimus, the Greek historical writer, who lived in Constantinople in the latter part of the fifth century, said that Constantine's palace was little inferior to that of Rome, that he embellished the Hippodrome, and took into it the temple of Castor and Pollux, whose statues remained in the porticoes. On one side of the Hippodrome the Emperor placed "the tripod that belonged to the Delphian Apollo, on which stood an image of the deity." There was a very large market place at Byzantium, said Zosimus, consisting of four porticoes, and at the end of one the Emperor erected two temples; one housing the statue of Rhea, the mother of the gods; the other the statue of the Fortune of Rome.[8] An odd gesture of respect for the old gods coming from a Christian Emperor; though Constantine the Great was as yet unbaptised when he made it.

This transformation of a distant provincial town into the capital of a vast empire had a stimulating effect on trade, art and eventually on architectural design, comparable with the founding of Alexandria, six hundred years before. Constantinople, like that earlier city, became a melting pot for the ideas and cultures of different races. Asia lay across the Bosphorus. Oriental ideas of colour and form and ornament flowed into the new, expanding city, and were interpreted by the native architects and artists of Byzantium, for whom the patronage of an opulent society provided opportunities to build ambitiously and extravagantly. Roman dignity suffered a little, and during the fifth century the latent genius of Greek artists inaugurated a phase of culture that was eventually to succeed the classic phase. Apart from the patronage of affluent aristocrats, the Church that had grown in strength and wealth was able to employ architects on buildings that eclipsed the splendour of those erected for personal aggrandisement or public entertainment. Roman imperial architecture in the hands of talented Byzantine Greeks acquired intellectual animation. Presently they liberated the arch from its subordination to the exigent lines of post-and-lintel construction, and created a new arcuated style; a triumph of reason, as brilliantly celebrated by Christian Byzantine Greeks as nine centuries earlier it had been celebrated by the Doric temple builders. Their intellectual achievement was not diminished by the darkness of the Age of Faith.

Although the old gods had been officially banished by Theodosius, it was impossible to change traditional loyalties and beliefs by decree overnight, so the familiar deities lingered on in the affections of men for centuries, though their temples were destroyed or fell into ruin and they were no longer honoured by new buildings. The only attempt to reinstate them officially had failed, when during his short reign, the Emperor Julian (A.D. 331–363), restored freedom of worship throughout the Empire, to the dismay and fury of the Christians, although, in the words of Gibbon, the only hardship he inflicted on them "was to deprive them of the power of tormenting their fellow-subjects, whom they stigmatised with the odious titles of idolators and heretics."[9] Many ancient temples had then enjoyed a brief respite from the destructive forces of Christianity; a few were rebuilt, though Julian's attempts to enforce restoration at the expense of the Church were usually defeated, because on the ruins of the ancient temples, "the Christians had frequently erected their own religious edifices: and as it was necessary to re-move the church before the temple could be rebuilt, the justice and piety of the emperor were applauded by one party, while the other deplored and execrated his sacrilegious violence. After the ground was cleared," Gibbon continued, "the restitution of those stately structures, which had been levelled with the dust; and of the precious ornaments, which had been converted to Christian uses; swelled into a very large account for damages and debt."[10] As the power of the Christians had increased, and with it their appetite for persecution, the priests of many temples had buried their treasured works of art, their sacred sculptures and jewels, and they remained safely hidden far below the feet of the holy wreckers, and there they stayed while the ruins above them decayed, or were plundered for building materials; some, like the Walbrook Mithraeum, kept their secrets until the twentieth century. A few famous buildings changed their function though not their form; in earlier chapters we have described how the Parthenon and the Pantheon prolonged their lives as Christian churches, but such adaptations contributed nothing to the development of architec-tural design; they indicated the operation of a ulitilitarian spirit, a desire to make use of an existing structure, nothing more. The buildings of this darkening world, when reason was inarticulate, have little to say until the fifth century when the Greek genius was gloriously reasserted, not in works of philosophic or scientific speculation, but through a decisive change in the whole concep-tion of architectural composition, which brought structural facts into the open by the agile use of the arch, the vault, the dome and the semi-dome.

This new arcuated style became the most enduring monument of the Eastern Roman Empire, and preserved the name of Byzan-tium for nearly a thousand years. At the beginning of the fifth century the Eastern Empire included the Balkans, Anatolia, Syria and Egypt, with Constantinople as the focal point of the old civilization. Behind the enormously strong walls of that city, the cultural heritage of the ancient world was defended, and this out-post of a progressively shrinking Empire survived until the Turkish conquest in 1453. After the second flowering of the Greek genius which generated the Byzantine style, architects were content to continue that style with local variations of decoration, but no fundamental changes. After the intellectual rejuvenations of architecture had ended allegiance to post-and-lintel construction, no new adventures were encouraged in the corrupt atmosphere of the later Byzantine Empire. Before the decline of that Empire there was a short period of political expansion, military achievement, and activity in the arts. The Emperor Justinian I, who reigned from 527 until his death in 565, reconquered Italy, the south-east part of Spain, and the whole of North Africa from Egypt to the Atlantic, leaving the Empire economically exhausted by those temporary triumphs. Far more important for what remained of Western civilisation was the Emperor's patronage of architecture.

In A.D. 532 work began on the great church of Santa Sophia at Constantinople, which was completed in five years. The architects, Anthemius of Tralles and Isodorus of Miletus, tactfully admitted that their design had been guided by the celestial inspiration of the Emperor, an acceptable tribute to their patron who was a humourless fanatic, a great maker of laws, and a typical product of the Age of Faith. He ended classical studies and killed intellectual adventure by closing the schools of Athens, but never suspected that Santa Sophia was as great an intellectual adventure in terms of architecture as the Parthenon, or that his architects were using the arch and the dome to reinterpret Western conceptions of form, and using the soft, plastic and infinitely flexible material, mosaic, to introduce Oriental conceptions of colour.

Byzantine builders used brickwork and concrete in construction, which provided an internal surface admirably adapted for applying marble and mosaic. Clarity of form was blurred by a coloured mist, as mosaics flowed over walls and gave to the surfaces of arches and domes and semi-domes rich, darkly gleaming compositions in ruby and gold, deep blue and soft olive green. The emotional impact of Byzantine interiors was more intense than anything Oriental architects had hitherto achieved, for they had relied on colour alone: the assault on the emotions was irresistible when the Byzantine Greeks united mastery of colour with their traditional mastery of form.

Byzantine churches were square or polygonal in plan, and by an adroit use of arches, semi-domes and pendentives, their architects could float a large shallow dome over a central space.

Santa Sophia is the supreme example of this technique of arcuated construction. The church has an oval nave, 225 feet long by 107 feet wide, and the great dome, that rises to a height of 180 feet, seems to hover above the central area, which is a square, uninterrupted open space, with massive stone piers at each corner that support the four semi-circular arches and the pendentives on which the dome rests. The pendentives are the curved triangular spaces, formed between the arches, which give a continuous supporting surface for the dome. (Plate 26 and opposite). East and west of the central area are semi-circular spaces, roofed by half-domes and flanked by tall alcoves also rising to half-domes, and at the far eastern end there is a great apse.

Arches, pendentives and domes melt into each other, and create an illusion of movement, as though the semi-domes and the great dome are gently oscillating, an effect produced possibly by the play of daylight on the dull gold of the mosaics, helped too by the figures of six-winged cherubim that fill the pendentives and seem to carry aloft the great dome on their pale green and brown pinions. That dome is lit by forty small arched windows, pierced in the lower part, which, according to some authorities were not originally part of the design, but were openings left for scaffolding when building was in progress. North and south of the square below the dome are two arcades, one above the other, with the piers at the corners of the square pierced to allow the aisles and galleries to pass through. (See page 126.)

Lethaby and Swainson in their detailed study of the building and materials of Santa Sophia, observed that "After more than a thousand years of working marble through one complete development, Greek builders, by considering afresh the prime necessities of the material, and a rational system of craftsmanship, opened the great quarry of ideas in constructive art which is exhaustless. In a hundred years architecture became truly *organic*, features that had become mere 'vestiges' dropped away, and a new style was complete; one, not perhaps so completely winning as some forms of Gothic, but the supremely logical building art that has been."[11]

With the example of the Ionic and Corinthian orders before them, the architects of Santa Sophia invented what was virtually a new order, with capitals shaped to achieve a graceful transition from the column to the cube of marble that it supported, and those

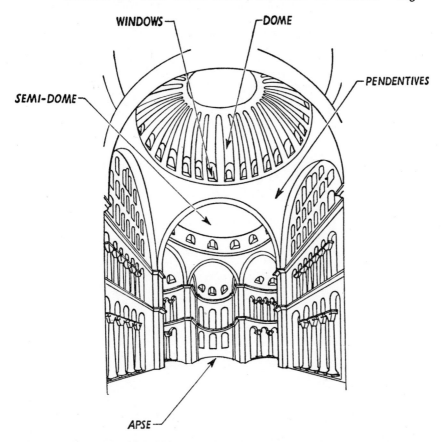

Diagram of the interior of Santa Sophia, looking towards the apse. This shows the pendentives, the triangular curved overhanging surfaces, that support the dome. (See West to East section page 126.) "All these parts surprisingly joined one to another, and resting only on that which is next to them, form the work into one admirably harmonious whole, which spectators do not dwell upon for long in the mass, as each individual part attracts the eye to itself. The sight causes men constantly to change their point of view, and the spectator can nowhere point to any part which he admires more than the rest." Procopius, translated by Aubrey Stewart and quoted by W. R. Lethaby and Harold Swainson in *The Church of Sancta Sophia Constantinople* (Macmillan & Co. London: 1894.) Chap. II, Page 26. *Drawn by Marcel Barton.* (See also Plate 26.)

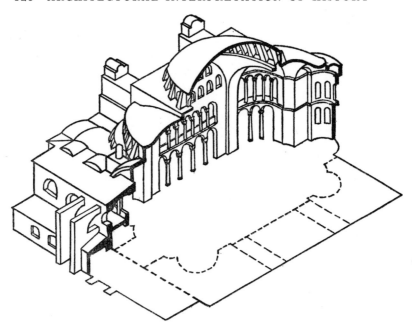

Section through Santa Sophia, Constantinople, showing the structural use of arches, domes and semi-domes, and the pendentives on which the domes are supported. See previous page for diagram of the interior, also Plate 26. *Drawn by Marcelle Barton.*

capitals, intricately carved with lace-like ornament, earned the severe disapproval of Gibbon because they failed to follow the familiar forms and proportions. Gibbon asserted that many of the columns in Santa Sophia represented "the last spoils of Paganism" though many came "from the quarries of Asia Minor, the isles and continent of Greece, Egypt, Africa and Gaul." He added that "Eight columns of porphyry, which Aurelian had placed in the temple of the sun, were offered by the piety of a Roman matron; eight others of green marble were presented by the ambitious zeal of the magistrates of Ephesus: both are admirable by their size and beauty, but every order of architecture disclaims their fantastic capitals."[12]

Gibbon apparently based his statement about columns from the temple of the sun on an account by a writer generally known as the Anonymous of Combesis, whose work is probably not earlier than the twelfth century; but a contemporary writer, Paulus, one of the Royal Silentiaries, states that those columns came direct from the porphyry quarries at Mons Porphyrites in Egypt, and were brought from the quarry to the Red Sea, and thence by the Nile canal to the Lower Nile and into the Mediterranean. (The Nile canal remained open to shipping until the Moslem conquest.) Lethaby and Swainson conclude from this evidence that the porphyry used at Constantinople in the time of Justinian was quarried for the purpose, and not looted from Roman buildings.[13]

Wherever the materials came from, they contributed to a grave richness of effect; the conception of an obscured, mysterious sanctuary has been abandoned; light descending from above, light pouring through innumerable arched windows, gives new exotic values to form and colour. The shadows of the Mithraeum and the catacomb have withdrawn, and light animates the mosaic compositions and paintings that clothe the walls.

Nothing like Santa Sophia was ever built again. Byzantine churches with a principal dome and various minor domes and semi-domes were erected, but nowhere was the arch principle employed with the mathematical precision and intellectual felicity which gave to the interior of Justinian's church that vivacious interplay of ascending and expanding curves. The masterpiece was never repeated; not even on a smaller scale. St. Mark's at Venice, built five centuries later, was inspired less by Santa Sophia than by the Church of the Apostles at Constantinople, which was demolished in 1463 and replaced by the mosque of Sultan Mahomet II. The Byzantine Greeks had rescued and glorified the arch, opening up a new world of architectural possibilities; but they did not explore it fully. Like the Egyptians before them, they established a set style and remained blindly faithful to it, building in the same way and repeating the same ideas for over nine hundred years, losing the challenging clarity of their earlier work, and forgetting the transfiguring effect of light. Structural lines, masked by the deep hues of mosaics, are drowned in gloom, deliberately contrived. The voice of reason, so clearly heard in Santa Sophia, is muted: we are back in the whispering dusk.

That return to obscurity with an increasing dependence on rich colour at the expense of form reflected the character of the later

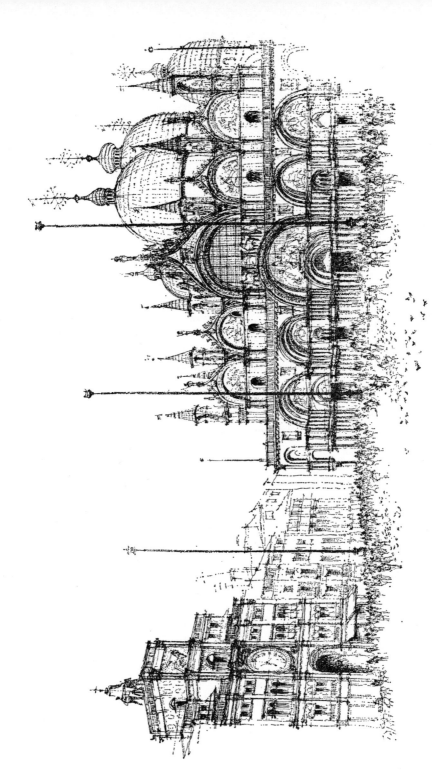

The west façade of St. Mark, Venice. *From a drawing by Hulme Chadwick. Reproduced by permission of the artist.*

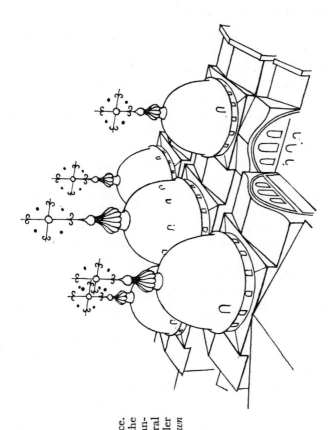

The five domes of St. Mark, Venice. These were probably copied from the Church of the Apostles at Constantinople. The diameter of the central dome is 42 feet; and there is a smaller dome over the arm of each cross. *Drawn by Maureen Stafford.*

Byzantine Empire, stifling in an atmosphere of superstition and corruption, when innovations were repressed and intellectual activity equated with heresy. Working in such conditions, architects inevitably sacrificed form, which expressed logic and reason and mental lucidity, and relied more and more on colour, the vehicle of emotion and faith. In Santa Sophia alone was the mystical character of a sacred building enhanced by daylight, and the emotional appeal of the interior was so powerful that the Crusaders who sacked Constantinople at the beginning of the thirteenth century believed that the great dome had been raised by magic, suspiciously like the work of devils.

Byzantine architecture speaks continuously and consistently of the Age of Faith; in Santa Sophia only is the brief resurgence of intellectual life asserted; and it is not altogether fanciful to deduce from later Byzantine work that the Greek mind, lively and independent as ever, deliberately disguised the ancient attachment to reason by subduing form and exalting colour. The influence of Byzantine art and architecture permeated the east Roman Empire, spread into Asia Minor, westward to Sicily and Italy, and north and westward to Russia, where in the tenth century Greek artists were invited to advise on the construction and decoration of new churches at Kiev.[14]

After Santa Sophia the greatest example of Byzantine architecture is St. Mark's at Venice, built between A.D. 1042 and 1071 on the site of an earlier church of basilican type founded about 864. The façade, with its five arched portals, faces the great Piazza, and exhibits a perplexing assembly of decorative features: panels of mosaic, trophies, alabaster and porphyry columns from Constantinople and Alexandria, united by the framework of arches. (See pages 128 and 129.) The plan is that of a Greek cross, with a dome above each arm of the cross and a large central dome, 42 feet in diameter. The five domes do not correspond externally with the shapes that swell up above the façade of the narthex; those are of timber, added in the thirteenth century to increase the height of the dome cluster. Within, some of the structural frankness of Santa Sophia is recalled, though dimly. The domes float above the arches and pendentives; all curved surfaces are covered by a glowing, unbroken skin of mosaic that spreads over vaults, apses, arches, pendentives and domes; the entire upper

St. Fosca, on the island of Torcello, in the lagoons north-west of Venice. The church is close by the cathedral of St. Maria. It has a central dome on a drum, and externally an arcade shades five sides of the building. *Drawn by Raymond McGrath, and reproduced by the artist's permission.*

part is composed of curves; no flat expanse, sharp edge or right angle appears, for angles are filled in and rounded; vaults and deep recesses flow into each other. (Plate 27.) Comparing St. Mark's with Santa Sophia, Lisle March Phillipps concluded that while Santa Sophia elaborated the dome theory as an architectural motive, St. Mark's was wholly different in conception. The domes of Santa Sophia owed nothing of their real power to the mosaics, which were purely decorative in character, but St. Mark's owed everything to them. It was, he said, "the elaboration of the mosaic theory as an architectural motive."[15] That view was expressed in *Form and Colour*, a book which expounds the theory that form is the art idiom of the West and colour the art idiom of the East; a theory that the late Sir Herbert Read dismissed, perhaps a little abruptly, as "a doubtful proposition."[16]

What St. Mark's has to say as a building makes that theory at least plausible. Inside, the ascendancy of the East is asserted through the dominance of colour; form is minimised, lost in a multi-hued haze; the whole church speaks of the rising influence of oriental ideas and art. Venice was the great mercantile meeting place of East and West. Perhaps the penetration of such non-Christian influence was unsuspected; perhaps it was recognised and surreptitiously welcomed in that prosperous community of educated and artistic business men. The architecture of Venice, the gorgeous palaces and public buildings, openly advertised the power of an independent commercial state, and proved that its rulers and citizens were as artistically sensitive and perceptive as those of the ancient Greek city states. (Plate 30.)

What the smaller Byzantine churches have to say is often boring; a tale told over and over again of static faith and artistic paralysis. The break with representational art made in the fourth and fifth centuries that had promised new creative adventures and helped to form the eighth cultural period of Mediterranean civilisation

The Byzantine churches of the monastery of St. Luke of Stiris, near Delphi, Greece. Eleventh century. *Drawn by Maureen Stafford.*

The Church of St. Saviour in the Chora, Constantinople (Istanbul), showing the central dome and the smaller domes. The domes are on drums, pierced by arched windows. The minaret is a Turkish addition. Eleventh century. *Drawn by Maureen Stafford.*

classified by Flinders Petrie, seems to have been made in vain. The patronage of the Church and the dark superstitions of the Eastern emperors were too repressive; few of those emperors had the genius or greatness of Justinian, though they shared his fanaticism. The renewal of intellectual vigour in architectural design had produced the arcuated style; but that moment of freedom for Greek minds passed, and thereafter Byzantine architects and artists built and carved and devised vast mosaics in much the same way from the sixth century to the fifteenth. The external characteristics of the smaller buildings had a family likeness; small shallow alcoves, blind arcading and slender attached columns provided surface variation; domes were mounted on circular or octagonal drums. (See pages 132 and 133.) But the enduring glory of Byzantine art was mosaic. The late Cecil Stewart in his masterly study, *Byzantine Legacy*, stated that mosaic alone as a surface decoration is enhanced by the minimum amount of light. "Those vitreous cubes," he said, "which in some peculiar way sparkle and glitter with inherent brilliancy behind a candle flame, would in the light of day be severely toned and modified by the surrounding brightness." This subdued effect was intentional, for when the early Christian churches were designed, their architects mindful of the secret, underground worship formerly imposed on congregations by official persecution, preserved the atmosphere of the catacomb and the cave, and "took particular care to ensure just that minimum of light necessary to illuminate glistening walls. And there can be no doubt," Stewart continues, "that it is that strange, almost unbegotten light which pervades the mosaiced churches of the Byzantine Empire that lends them their particular mystery and charm."[17]

In Constantinople he describes the mosaics of the mosque of Karich Djami as the final and supreme achievement of this Byzantine art. This became known as the mosaic mosque, but it was originally the Church of St. Saviour in the Chora, founded in the fourth century, repaired by Justinian, and restored and largely rebuilt in the latter part of the eleventh century, about the time of the Norman Conquest of England. (Page 133.) Most of the mosaics within are of fourteenth century workmanship: some of the designs are crisply defined by the introduction of black and white, and the whole interior seems to be clad in cloth of gold, with figures that are, in Stewart's words, "flat symbols elongated to unhuman proportion and are there primarily to illustrate the Gospel story." Those rugged figures are as remote from representational art as the work of Picasso, Graham Sutherland or Henry Moore, and as fervidly vital. The transformation of holy figures into symbols was partly a protective device, intended to save them from the attentions of ardent iconoclasts and image-breakers, who were outraged when saints and apostles were given a human likeness. This rejection of realism and the injunction that forbade the construction of idols, are responsible for the eastern sculptor's consistent avoidance of any representation of the human figure in the round. The artist who composed mosaics worked in two dimensions only when he drew the etiolated figures that symbolized the ascetic character of saints and martyrs. "The Byzantine artist," as Stewart says, "was never limited by the more or less outward appearance of things." His pictures often portrayed "not a single incident, but a series, all dependent upon each other."[18] Occasionally the subjects included

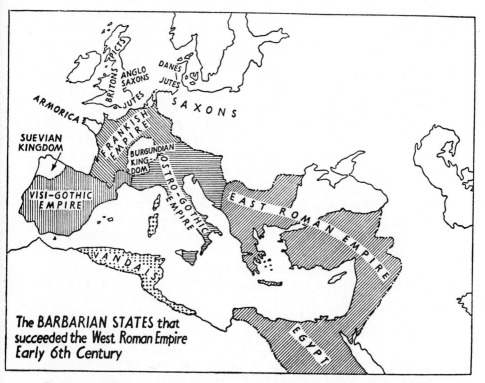

The BARBARIAN STATES that succeeded the West Roman Empire Early 6th Century

Roman architecture still stood in all the former provinces of the Western Empire, where the new rulers took over the great estates and cities; the East Roman Empire was still intact and Byzantine builders had developed arcuated construction and adorned many cities with fine churches. Of all the invading barbarians, the Visigoths were the most accomplished in the arts, and after settling in Spain they created a distinctive architecture for their churches and palaces. (See map on page 88). *Drawn by Marcelle Barton.*

regal as well as saintly figures; for example, the mosaics that enrich the interior of St. Vitale at Ravenna show the Emperor Justinian and his Empress, Theodora, surrounded by ministers of the imperial court, as rigid and formal as the kings and queens of a pack of cards. Both figures are adorned with spangled haloes, and their carefully drawn faces almost recapture the long-abandoned realism of earlier centuries: clearly they are intended to be portraits.

Throughout the area of the old East Roman Empire, Byzantine architecture displayed commanding technical competence; but it also told a tale of lost endeavour, of immense artistic powers withering in the torpid climate of the Age of Faith. In the West, the emergent barbarian states of Europe were inspired by that age, and the architecture that presently arose in the Frankish, Visigothic and Ostrogothic kingdoms that were established in the former provinces of Gaul, Spain, Italy and Illyricum, exhibited an arrogant, adventurous sense of power. Those provinces were still served by buildings and roads and bridges and aqueducts, inherited from the Western Empire intact and in good repair. The new rulers had settled down to enjoy their shared property and they preserved the administrative forms and civic titles of Rome, for like all barbarians they were still overawed by the ancient prestige of the Empire, although the power and the glory had gone and there was no longer an Emperor in the West. Britain alone was fighting a long rearguard action against the barbarians; and the civilisation of that far western Roman province was being precariously preserved by local chieftains and confederations of kings, as Dr. John Morris has described in comprehensive detail in *The Age of Arthur*.[19]

The remains of Roman Britain disclose standards of material welfare that were not equalled until the late eighteenth century. There was no abrupt destruction apparently; but a progressive decline of technical ability in the building arts and crafts. Anything built in the fifth and sixth centuries was largely made of impermanent materials; chiefly wood, but the example of Roman construction was not forgotten. In the excavations of the fifth century buildings at Cadbury–Camelot (1966–1970), dressed stone was found that had been quarried from derelict Roman buildings, but as Mr. Leslie Alcock observes, in an account of the

View of walled town, with watch towers and angle guard towers, depicted by a ninth century artist. The walls were certainly Roman, for courses of dressed stone are shown, and Roman masonry lasted for centuries. (See Plates 20 and 24.) The drawing was copied by F. W. Fairholt from an Anglo-Saxon manuscript of the Psalms (MS. Harl., No. 603), and included in *A History of Domestic Manners and Sentiments in England*, by Thomas Wright. (London: 1862.)

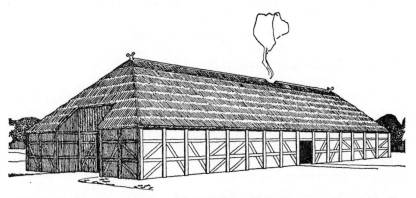

The Saxon forerunner of the mediaeval Great Hall. By comparison with the commodius, well-appointed Romano–British houses, this was little more than a large and squalid hut. The Saxon barbarians were competent wood-workers, and as they were skilled shipwrights some of that expert knowledge was transferred to house building. Their spacious halls were timber-framed and thatched, heated by open fires, from which the smoke escaped eventually through holes in the roof. *Drawn by A. S. Cook.*

excavations, "it was used in an un-Roman manner, without mortar." The timber gate-tower had, he said, "a clearly Roman ancestry, for it was derived from the simplest type of auxiliary fort gate. It is interesting to see how much of military technology had been preserved, and how much had been lost, by A.D. 500."[20]

Legend and folklore have glorified those squalid halls and huts and fortified hilltops, and transformed them into palaces and castles. There seems to be some evidence for accepting Artorius, the legendary King Arthur, as an historical personage; he is a shadowy figure but may well have been a harassed Romano–British general, trying to persuade temperamental British leaders to work together against the Teutonic barbarians instead of fighting among themselves. He lived in a land of decaying cities, though few of them seem to have been destroyed; a land that was nominally Christian, which probably had very few churches; a land where everything was breaking down.

The barbarian invaders of Britain unlike those on the continent, were not sufficiently enlightened to enjoy the amenities of a Roman province in going order; as we said in chapter one, they made no attempt to live in the well-planned cities. They occupied the southern and eastern parts of the province, content with a grubby, communal life in timber-built halls with no architectural pretensions and few comforts. Inside, sleeping benches or shut beds stood against the walls; windows were mere holes, protected from weather by shutters or wooden slats; the very word window is derived from the old Norwegian *vindauga*, which meant "wind eye"; and for heating a log fire burnt night and day on a raised stone hearth or in a long fire-trench, dug in the stamped earthen floor, smoke eventually eddying its way through a hole in the thatched roof. Those wooden halls of the sixth, seventh and eighth centuries were the crude forerunners of the great halls of mediaeval castles and manor houses, and their structural form long persisted in barns and country cottages.

Within a generation the destructive warriors and looters had settled down as farmers, clearing dense woodland, ploughing and sowing and reaping their crops, and changing the face of the land. Only one vestige of the Roman past was preserved: the roads.

THE SUCCESSOR STATES AND THE
MUSLIM WORLD

In Europe after the political extinction of the Western Empire, architecture in the successor states still followed the guide lines of classical Roman tradition, though no longer adhering strictly to the proportions and standardised moulded details and ornament of the classic orders. This post-Roman architecture formed a recognisable style, since called Romanesque, which lasted from the eighth to the twelfth century. In Italy and what had been Gaul, Byzantine influence fostered a variation of that style, described rather clumsily by Lethaby as "Byzanto–Romanesque or even Byzantesque."[1] An example of this amalgam of Byzantine and Romanesque is the Cathedral built by the Emperor Charlemagne at Aix-la-Chapelle (Aachen) between 796 and 804. This had a classical ancestry, for it was modelled on the Byzantine church of St. Vitale, Ravenna (526–547), which had derived its architectural character from the Minerva Medica at Rome, an arcuated, domical building that was probably a nymphaeum of the Baths of Gallienus (A.D. 266). As Romanesque evolved when the new European states were slowly shedding their barbaric heritage and their rulers were salvaging the remains of Roman civilisation, the style reflected the energy, passionate religious zeal, and ambitions of those kings and princes, who, a few generations earlier would have aspired to no higher title than chieftain. Those new masters of Europe were served by a strong, simple, dynamic architecture, unencumbered by inessential accretions, for the architects who created it had seen through the external deceits of contrived magnificence to the bones and sinews of the building art.

The round arch, barrel-vault, cross-vault and dome were used, their powers and purpose frankly acknowledged and displayed,

Romano–British group of a lion devouring a stag, found in the cistern of a house excavated at Corbridge, the Roman station of Corstopitum, south of Hadrian's Wall, Northumberland. Second or third century A.D. Probably a tomb monument originally and adapted later as a fountain ornament. The group could easily be mistaken for a vigorous example of mediaeval carving, and, like the Medusa mask on page 143, suggests the latent artistic powers and incipient nationalism smouldering in the remote, far western province of Britain. *Drawn by Maureen Stafford.* (In the Corbridge Museum.)

and the inventive genius of native craftsmen, long restrained by officially imposed standardisation, was released. Masons and carvers, hitherto regarded as little more than disciplined hands, skilled in repetitive work, were able to indulge their talents with greater freedom. Even in the Roman world the wanton and insubordinate faculty of native imagination had occasionally burst out. For instance in Britain there were some unforgettable examples of rebellious inspiration having its way, such as the Medusa mask on the central shield of the pediment on the Temple of Sulis-Minerva at Bath, and the Corbridge group showing a lion devouring a stag; the latter was probably a tomb monument originally, adapted at some later time as a fountain ornament.[2] The Corbridge group could easily be mistaken for a piece of vigorous mediaeval carving. Such evidence of repressed artistic powers finding expression in a remote province of the Empire, indicates that an incipient nationalism was awaiting the day of opportunity. (Pages 140 and 143.)

The barbarians who had founded the new successor states were by no means untutored savages; they practised a number of crafts with sufficient skill, though their taste in ornament would have repelled an educated Greek or Roman citizen. Among the hordes that had flooded into the territory of the moribund Empire, the Visigoths were far the most advanced in the arts of war and peace. They were natives of Dacia, the province that corresponds roughly with modern Rumania, which the Emperor Aurelian had abandoned in the third quarter of the third century; they were Christians, and the kingdom they founded in Spain attained higher standards of civilisation than any other of the new western states. Few of their buildings now exist, and the churches that remain are basilican in type, exhibiting debased Roman forms and some Byzantine characteristics. Their decoration is lost but accounts have survived that describe the mosaics, marbles and rare stones that once adorned them. There is evidence that the horseshoe arch was known in Spain before the Arab conquest, for Arab chronicles record that some of the eighth century windows of the mosque at Cordova were removed from Visigothic buildings, and a double horseshoe window from the Visigothic ducal palace is in the museum at Merida, which was formerly the Roman city of Emerita Augusta, the capital of Lusitania.[3] The Arabs were pre-eminently horsemen, and are supposed to have used the shape of their horses' shoes as a pattern for their arches, though the decorative attributes of that shape may have been discovered in the Middle East long before the seventh century warrior missionaries of a new religion attacked the Graeco–Roman world and the barbarian states that were trying to become civilised. There is substance in Royall Tyler's suggestion that the horseshoe shape was introduced to pre-Muslim Spain from the East as a decorative motive which may possibly have possessed some symbolic import. The Visigothic builders used it at the heads of doors and windows, and the Arabs appropriated it after their conquest.[4] This challenges the long-held belief that the horseshoe arch is an infallible indication of Muslim influence, but evidence of its use in Visigothic Spain seems to be incontestable. Religious intolerance, war, and the depredations of stone-robbers have obliterated nearly every trace of the Visigothic churches and palaces, splendid barbaric structures that rivalled in size and magnificence the massive Roman monuments that had survived from the age of Trajan. The Arabs did their best to destroy all the sacred buildings of Merida; Roman temples and Christian churches alike, a task, as Royall Tyler observes, "in which the Spaniards and the Napoleonic invaders also lent a hand."[5]

Many of the Muslim conquerors of Spain were imperfectly civilised; but even so they were not always out for plunder and destruction. Sometimes the primitive, nomadic contingents of the invading armies demolished buildings casually to meet a momentary need, light-heartedly ignoring the permanent effect of such destruction. The Arab historian, Ibn Khaldun (A.D. 1332–1406) explained, though he did not excuse, this almost childish carelessness. The Arabs, he said, were a fierce people who enjoyed a rough life because it gave them freedom from authority and political domination; an attitude that modern hippies would readily understand. Their favourite occupation, he continued, "is trekking and roaming in the desert, and this is opposed to the establishment of a quiet and sedentary life, on which the growth of civilisation depends. Thus, for instance, they will meet the need for stones to prop up their cooking vessels by demolishing a building. In the same way they will get their tent poles and pegs from the roof of a house. As a result of their mode of living, their very presence is inimical to the existence of buildings, which are the very foundation of civilisation."[6]

The Arab historian was describing the wandering Bedouin who were incapable of living a settled, orderly life; very different in character from the accomplished military and civil administrators who consolidated conquered territories. That such men were inclined to be mild and indulgent towards the vanquished, and tolerant of other religions, was shown by their transactions with the Christians over the Visigothic basilica at Cordova, described in chapter one.

Medusa mask on the central shield of the pediment on the front elevation of the temple of Sulis-Minerva, Bath, the Roman Aquae Sulis. Detailed restorations of the temple façade show the entablature and pediment supported by four fluted Corinthian columns, so this ferocious mask glares from a correct classical setting, an intimidating example of Romano–British sculpture. *Drawn by Maureen Stafford*. (In the Roman Baths Museum, Bath.)

The Arab Conquest arrested the development of Romanesque architecture in Spain, though the subsequent implanting of oriental ideas of decoration and colour was a rich compensation of incalculable significance not only for Spain, but for the adjacent Frankish kingdoms. The new cultural phase that followed the Graeco–Roman period was generated in those kingdoms. Technical ability in the arts and industries that serve architecture had survived, though on a reduced scale. Opportunities for using the skill of masons and carpenters and metal workers were limited; priorities were determined by military needs and essential repairs. Luxury building in the West had disappeared by the middle of the sixth century; only the Church had the wealth and the will to sponsor ambitious architecture, and what the Church wanted largely controlled the supply of building materials. For example, in the Seine–Rhine glass industry, the production of domestic and ornamental glass in the sixth, seventh and eighth centuries shifted to broad glass, that is to glass plates for windows. The Church wanted windows, also the influence of the Church indirectly interfered with the management of that particular industry, for glass-making was largely in the hands of Syrians and Jews, and during the late sixth and early seventh centuries anti-Semitism had appeared in Merovingian Gaul, partly a religious and partly a racial movement.[7]

The successor states of the Empire, struggling to establish law and order, were hampered by military adventures that were sparked off by recurrent memories of imperial greatness. It is a commonplace that the ghost of the Roman Empire has never been laid; in an attenuated, commercial form it has even reappeared in the second half of the twentieth century, for the trading area of the European Common Market roughly corresponds with the Italian and north-western provinces of the Empire; and from the sixth to the tenth century that ghost actively haunted the minds of European monarchs and inflamed their ambitions. Justinian I, as related in the last chapter, had reconquered some of the lost provinces of the Western Empire and temporarily reimposed imperial rule; his example was followed over two centuries later by Charlemagne (*circa* 742–814), King of the Franks, who engaged in almost continuous warfare and succeeded before his death in ruling over France, northern Italy, and a great part of Germany

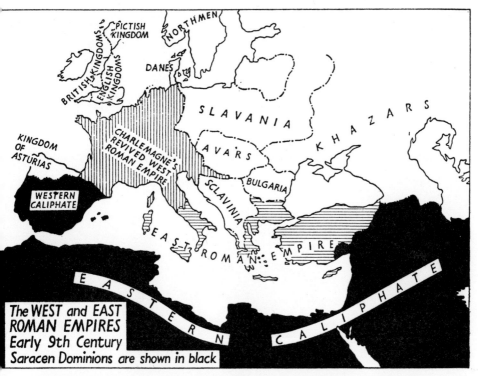

The WEST and EAST
ROMAN EMPIRES
Early 9th Century
Saracen Dominions are shown in black

The impact of Islam on Europe, the Middle East, and North Africa may be
gauged from the extent of Muslim territory, won at the expense of the East
Roman Empire and the successor states in North Africa and Spain. The
Frankish Empire that occupied what is now France, the Low Countries and
Western Germany early in the sixth century was expanded by Charlemagne
(*circa* 742–814), in his attempt to revive the Western Roman Empire. (See map
on page 135, showing the successor states of Rome, early in the sixth century.)
The Muslim conquests changed the character of Mediterranean civilisation, and
invigorated the arts and architecture of the adjacent Christian states and
islands. *Drawn by Marcelle Barton.*

and Austria; territory large enough to support the title of Roman
Emperor, which he assumed; but after his death that Frankish
version of the Empire fell apart. (See maps on pages 88 and 135.)

As the Romanesque style came to maturity during those centuries of strife, the regional variations seemed dimly to forecast
European nationalism in architectural terms, long before it became

a political reality. As mentioned earlier, the men who created that style had discarded the external trappings of Roman architecture, and by returning to structural realities impressed upon the character of their buildings an austere beauty. This simplicity of form and a sparing use of ornament marked not only the advent of a new cultural phase, but the transition from antiquity to mediaeval civilisation, from classical architecture to Gothic.

The dynamic character of Gothic owed much to the adventurous spirit of mediaeval architects, but something also to the impact of Islam on Europe, and especially to the stimulation of Oriental

Early Muslim tomb at Akhlat, above Lake Van, in Kurdistan. A conical roof, varying in pitch, was characteristic of these small buildings. Reproduced from Layard's *Discoveries in the Ruins of Nineveh and Babylon* (London: 1853). See opposite page.

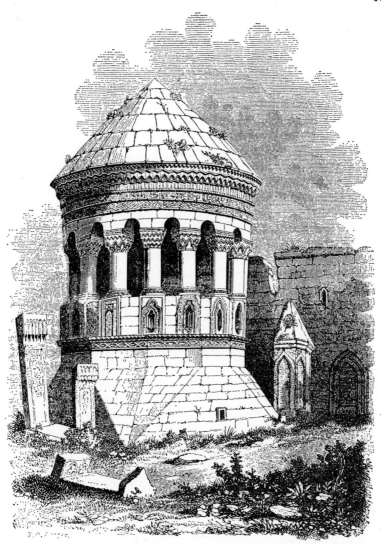

Tomb of the Sultan Baiandour, one of the few structures left standing, when the city of Akhlat was destroyed in the thirteenth century by the Mongols. Like the example shown opposite this is an early Muslim tomb, richly decorated with geometric patterns and arabesques. Reproduced from Layard's *Discoveries in the Ruins of Nineveh and Babylon* (London: 1853).

ideas that radiated from the bridgehead of Muslim art and learning established in Spain, and later refreshed and reinforced by those brought home by the impressionable nobles and knights who survived the Crusades. Early in the seventh century, Mahomet, "the Prophet of God," had founded a new religion that Europeans called Mohammedanism, though the founder named it Islam or Hanifism. This newly-minted faith made a potent appeal to the nations of the Middle East, for it inspired them with a sense of collective purpose, and brought to the Arab peoples unity in place of inter-tribal jealousies and strife. A sacred book, the Koran, perpetuated the revelations and injunctions of the Prophet, whose avowed intention was the conversion of the whole world to Islam, if necessary by force. When Mahomet died in 632, Muslim power extended over Arabia, Persia, Armenia and Syria. The Holy War continued; fresh converts reinforced the Muslim armies, until eventually the Caliph, the Commander of the Faithful, could claim spiritual dominion over a vast area from Turkestan on the north, India on the east, the whole of North Africa from Egypt to the Atlantic, and, after the defeat of the Visigoths in A.D. 711, all Spain save for a small strip in the north where the Basques and the Kingdom of Asturias remained independent. The Visigothic kingdom had included the south-east corner of France, which also came under Muslim control and was used as a jumping-off place for invading the Frankish kingdom. That enterprise was attempted, but it failed, and the Muslim army was defeated in A. D. 732 by Charles Martel at Moussais-la-Bataille, between Tours and Poitiers. (See map on page 145.)

In Spain the Muslim colonists were known as Moors, for the first and subsequent waves of invaders came from Morocco, though their leaders were Arabs. Professor Trend has likened the Moors to the Spanish conquistadores of the sixteenth century, for they were inspired, as the Spaniards were in South America and Mexico, by "a triumphant, proselytizing faith," and sustained by the conviction that they were God's elect.[8]

Europeans generally used the name Saracen for the various races unified by Islam, and Saracenic is the familiar descriptive term for their vivacious and varied styles of architecture, so different from anything created in Europe, so full of convulsive energy and passionate colour and perplexing intricacies. In Spain it was, and is still, called Moorish. One basic difference between Muslim architecture and that familiar to the west, arose from Mahomet's injunction that, like the second of Jehovah's Ten Commandments, forbade the making of any graven image. Although this did not entirely exclude the sculptor from participation in architectural design and composition, it debarred him from the whole realm of representational art. His skill and that of the painter was deflected to devising geometrical patterns and the interlacing and elaborate scrolls that came to be known as arabesques. (Characteristic examples of such ornamental forms are shown on the tombs at Akhlat illustrated on pages 146 and 147, and on the sides and cornice of the Giralda at Seville, on Plate 29.)

Geometrical patterns such as the fret and key, had been used by the Greeks, and Roman mosaics often had borders and centrepieces composed of orderly and rather dull variations of linked circles and running scrolls; but nothing in classical art approached the restless animation of arabesques. Such sinuous forms curled and wound their way across surfaces of wood and stone and plaster in all the countries subjected to Muslim rule. As their civilisation mellowed and patrons of architecture acquired a sophisticated taste, the prohibitions of the Prophet were occasionally ignored, and in Spain the Moors began to imitate their Christian neighbours, "in their dress and ornaments and indeed in many of their customs and institutions, even to the extent of having statues and pictures on the walls of their houses and shops," as Ibn Khaldun recorded, adding that the careful observer would mark such lapses as "a sign of inferiority."[9]

In early Muslim architecture, the arch was used as a dominant form, often with impulsive disregard for structural probity and common sense, so that arches, variously shaped, became openwork arabesques on a large scale, as in the great mosque at Cordova. (Plate 28.) Arches were curved, twisted, inverted and interlaced; there were horseshoe, semi-circular, pointed, stilted, ogee or keel arches, the latter formed like the keel of a ship; and arches with three, five or more cusps and foils. In Spain and North Africa, Egypt and Syria, Muslim architects rejected the plain arch and the vault and the calm stability of post-and-lintel construction: such forms, in which Greek thought still lingered, were anathema to romantic minds governed by the whims of emotion. Habitual disrespect for stable forms marked many of the first tentative experiments of Muslim architecture; the desert was still close; the brigand codes of nomadic life and blind devotion to the Muslim faith prompted the conquerors to rip precious materials from sacred and secular buildings and rearrange them, like trophies, piling them into the new mosques that they ran up everywhere. It was an architecture of loot.

Totally different interpretations of Arab architecture are given by Lisle March Phillipps and W. R. Lethaby. In *The Works of Man*, March Phillipps said: "That memorable onslaught of the Arabs which swept before it the old social landmarks in a common ruin is so closely echoed by the general smash-up under his hands of established structural forms that it is impossible not to see in both processes a manifestation of one and the same force. The whimsical civilisation which accompanied the Arab dominion and broke into so wild a frenzy of necromantic and astrological speculations is paralleled with curious felicity in the odd and freakish shapes, the flamelike mounting spirals and fantastically curved and twisted arches, into which the new architecture instantly developed."[10] Those words originally appeared in 1911, in the first edition of the book; in the same year Lethaby had set down some contrary views. "Early and late the Arabian is a style of great splendour and clearness of expression," he wrote. "Save for its refusal of human interest in sculpture and painting, which were ruled out by the Mohammedan employers, it is one of the most intellectual styles. All is direct structure or frank ornamentation, and there is no survival of misunderstood forms."[11]

Actually the conclusions of both writers are supported by architectural evidence. The clarity of expression that Lethaby describes appears in some of the earliest examples of Muslim architecture, like the Dome of the Rock in Jerusalem and the Great Mosque at Damascus. Both were, he said, "almost perfectly Byzantine buildings except for some touch of added energy."[12]

That energy, and the impetuousness it begot, are the characteristics that offended March Phillipps, and prompted his strictures on the Mosque at Cordova. (Plate 28.) Such quotations from the writings of eminent architectural historians, far from invalidating the interpretative quality of architecture merely show that personal bias may distort the message. Herbert Read in his introduction to the 1950 edition of *The Works of Man* remarked on the author's tendency to impatience with fantasy, which coloured his views on Arab architecture, and showed, said Read, "that he had not finally exorcised one of the fatal limitations of English art criticism—the puritanical bias. . . ."[13]

William Richard Lethaby (1857–1931) who was an antiquary, a gifted writer and teacher, a practising architect, and an impartial critic with practical experience of structural problems, does justice to the creative contribution Arab art and architecture made to the western world. But the buildings in the Muslim domains speak clearly for themselves; unlike some of those in times closer to our own, they have nothing to conceal.

Unfortunately, the creative contribution made by the Arabs to the Mediterranean civilisation was offset by the destruction they wrought. Many towns and cities in the vast territories they conquered sank to the level of squalid villages; those that survived lost their architectural identity as their street plans were blurred and finally obliterated by houses packed closely into small spaces, so that the relationship of one building to another was ignored, the unity of the street disrupted, and what had been a fine Graeco–Roman city became a congested and insanitary slum. For example, Roman Ancyra in Anatolia gradually shrank in size and importtance after it was taken first by the Persians, then by the Arabs, and later by the Seljuk Turks. Crusaders occupied and held it for eighteen years, and in 1360 it finally passed into the hands of the Ottoman Turks. (We referred in chapter one to the Roman temple there and the adjacent church and mosque.) It was known through the Middle Ages as Angola and is now Ankara, the capital of modern Turkey; once more a fine, well-planned and well-watered city, inspired by the vision and created by the authority of Kemal Ataturk.

With the exception of Spain, the Emirate of Cordova, which became the most highly-civilised country of mediaeval Europe, Arab domination was disastrous. Ibn Khaldun describes the devastation of Iraq and Syria, and how, in North Africa, the two Arabian tribes, Banu Hilal and Banu Sulaim, early in the eleventh century invaded the prosperous lands that had survived the Vandal settlement, Justinian's war of reconquest, and the original assault by the Arabs that, led by Uqba ibn Nafi had reached the Atlantic in the last quarter of the eighth century. North Africa never re-covered from the eleventh century invasion. The Banu Sulaim stayed in Cyrenaica, but the Banu Hilal pushed on westwards, far into the interior, and the ravages of both tribes of marauding nomads continued for some three hundred and fifty years. Ibn Khaldun likened the Hilalian invasion to a swarm of locusts, devouring the whole country over which it passed.[14] Up to that time it had been possible, according to some Arab writers, to walk from one end of North Africa to the other in the shade, which meant that the legendary African forests were untouched in the first centuries of the occupation; but thereafter the aspect and the climate of what had been a well-wooded, fertile countryside were transformed by those inveterate enemies of cultivation, the nomadic Bedouin and their herds of goats.[15] Towns, villages, farmsteads, dams, cisterns, aqueducts, and all the evidence of Roman archi-tectural skill, engineering and husbandry were obliterated. Popu-lous centres like Leptis Magna, the birthplace of Septimius Severus, resplendent with imperial largesse in the shape of noble buildings and monuments, lay empty and desolate. Ports were idle, their harbours silted up, and inland the desert took over, drawing a golden shroud of wind-blown sand over dead cities and a dying countryside.

Of all the former Roman provinces in Africa, Egypt alone was indestructible. Alexandria lived on; its splendours awed the con-querors, and we owe to Arab writers many detailed descriptions of them.[16] Muslim architects laid out a new city some hundred and thirty miles south-east of Alexandria, which became famous as Cairo, and its magnificence was such that Ibn Khaldun, quoting a statement by one of his former teachers, said that "What one sees in dreams surpasses reality, but all that one could dream of Cairo falls short of the truth."[17]

Six national styles of Muslim architecture developed during the centuries after the conquests: Syrian, Egyptian, Spanish, Persian, Turkish and Indian; and of these the first three influenced Euro-pean ideas. The principal buildings were mosques, tombs, palaces and markets. The early mosques had big open courtyards sur-rounded by arcades with a hall on the eastward or Mecca side. These were the caravanserai mosques, resting places for travellers and pilgrims, built wherever the Arabs had penetrated. In towns they became more complicated; the area of the central courtyard was reduced in size and the surrounding buildings raised to several storeys with separate apartments, not unlike the large European inns of much later date. The interior of the mosque became the most important part, and in some of the earliest examples the halls were very large, with slim columns supporting the roof. In Arabia no tradition of temple building existed, and until the Muslims became warrior missionaries with subject peoples to convert they felt no urge to build. Apart from the Great Mosque at Mecca, there is no distinctive Arabian variation of Muslim architecture.

In Syria many of the first mosques were adapted Christian churches; rebuilt and enlarged in the course of centuries. The Dome of the Rock in Jerusalem, often wrongly called the Mosque of Omar, stands on the Temple platform and dates from A.D. 688. It is an octagonal building with a ribbed central dome rising from a drum, with Roman columns and Byzantine capitals used in the interior. In Egypt the oldest mosque is that of Amr in Cairo, originally built in A.D. 641-642; a simple, unpretentious structure, since rebuilt and enlarged, with arcades added that are supported by classic columns removed from older buildings.

Sacred buildings in the Middle East, whether mosques or adapted churches, impressed the Crusaders by their splendour as much as the towns impressed them by their almost impregnable fortifications. But the initial impact of Islam on the semi-barbaric Christian states of Europe came through Spain, for there, once the invaders had consolidated their gains, a vigorous oriental state came into being. Muslim Spain was a magnet that drew artists and craftsmen and scholars from all Europe, until the Spanish Christians gradually reconquered province after province during the Middle Ages, and finally crushed the prosperous and sophisticated Oriental civilisation that was so far in advance of their own, and permanently affected their architecture, art and language. The accomplishments of that most westerly of eastern civilisations may be read very clearly indeed from the buildings that still stand at Cordova, Seville and Granada.

The amicable agreement between Muslims and Christians over the sharing of the Visigothic church of St. Vincent's at Cordova has been described, and when the Emir Abderrahaman, inspired by a vision, built a new mosque, he chose the same site, perhaps because it had for many centuries been a sacred site, for before the Visigothic church a Roman temple of Janus had stood there. The Great Mosque eventually occupied an area far larger than the Christian church. Externally the rectangular ground plan is 570 feet long by 425 feet wide. There are nineteen aisles, running North and South, each aisle with thirty-three bays; and the whole structure, which is only thirty feet high, is supported by 1200 columns, mostly of porphyry and coloured marbles, removed from older buildings, often cut down to a suitable length with complete disregard for their proportions, with the intertwined arches springing from their capitals. (Plate 28.) The arches with their alternate quoins of red and white, while opulently decorative in effect, suggest that the builders were fumbling in their endeavour to find structural solutions, uninformed by any building traditions, but nevertheless building with enormous gusto, though hardly deserving the strictures of March Phillipps who described those interlacing cusped arches as a "ribald exhibition . . . of forms which have parted with their last shred of intellectual self-respect."[18]

Far greater ability was shown by Jebir, the architect who designed the tower of the mosque at Seville for Yusuf I in A.D. 1196. That tower, the Giralda, 45 feet square and 230 feet high, was formerly surmounted by a platform that supported four large brazen balls. It stands at the north-east angle of the Christian cathedral that replaced the mosque, and was not apparently a minaret, but an architectural outburst of high spirits, like the exuberant tower-building described by Ruskin. Only the lower part, to the height of 185 feet, now retains the original Moorish decoration, and the refinement and delicacy of those frets and arches tell us much about the quality of the civilisation that was condemned by Christendom as infidel. In 1568 the top was demolished and an open bell chamber added, with diminishing stages above, and the belfry crowned with a bronze figure representing Faith. The bell chamber and belfry were designed by Fernando Ruiz, the statue was the work of Bartholome Morel; those Renaissance additions disrupt the graceful ascending lines of the Moorish tower, that has a warmer relationship with the adjacent Gothic cathedral, for Spanish Gothic exhibits the same jewelled intricacy and sparkle of Moorish work. (Plate 29.)

The contrast between the civilised standards of life in Muslim

Spain and those of the neighbouring Christian states is shown by the architecture of the Alhambra at Granada, the pleasure palace built between A.D. 1248 and 1354. In the Alhambra the Moorish style had attained maturity and become established as a style in its own right, perfected by architects of commanding ability and sensitive imagination. The slender, delicately-proportioned columns of the arcades that surround the courts, alternately single and coupled, are crowned with stalactite capitals. The courts are cool and spacious; the oblong Court of the Lions, 116 by 66 feet, has a fountain with an alabaster basin supported by twelve carved lions; in the Court of Alberca, 140 by 74 feet, a large fish-pond is set in a marble pavement. With its fountains, baths, bedrooms and summer rooms, its cleanliness, santitation and abundant water supply, the palace possessed standards of comfort and luxury that were not even remote memories in the lands north of the Pyrenees. (Plate 32.) Those arcades and courts had something of the fantastic, half-magical quality of palaces described in the *Arabian Nights*. But united Christendom condemned it all: Moorish or Saracenic, such work was infidel and therefore accursed. Nevertheless, those nominally Christian states borrowed freely from infidel architects, and most significant of all such borrowings was the pointed arch.

The sparkling gaiety of Muslim ornament was transmitted to many Christian buildings, and that transmission of eastern forms to the West began before the twelfth century, when the traffic in ideas between the Muslim and Christian worlds was intensified by the Crusades. Over much of Europe the influence of Muslim art is discernible; in southern Italy and Sicily, in the cloisters of Monreale Cathedral, for example, and even as far west as Norfolk in England, where the blind arcading at Castle Rising has eastern affinities. (Plates 32 and 34.) But the chief and most enduring effect of eastern art and architecture was in Spain, and Spanish Gothic buildings reveal through their intricately carved decoration how much Christian Spanish craftsmen owed to their Moorish brethren. Such debts might be officially repudiated, but the strength and extent of Muslim influence on Spain, and to a lesser extent on mediaeval Europe, cannot be denied: the message in stone defies contradiction.

PRELUDE TO GOTHIC

ROMANESQUE architecture gradually developed characteristic forms in Italy and France from the eighth to the twelfth century; in Germany the period of development was longer, for it lasted from the eighth to the thirteenth century; and in England it was delayed until the ninth and tenth, for the country had been devastated by the Great Army of the invading Danes and was not free from such troubles until after A.D. 886, when King Alfred recovered London, and by 897 an effective English fleet had checked further sea-borne Danish raids.[1] English Romanesque came to maturity at the hands of Norman builders in the eleventh and twelfth centuries. Although the regional variations of the style seemed to predict European nationalism, any such fragmentation would have been unthinkable in what was then United Christendom, for the European states were spiritually united, and the strength and moral sustenance derived from that spiritual unity presently created an architecture which affirmed with rapturous urgency that this was indeed the Age of living and active Faith; the cathedrals and churches that raised their towers and spires in every Christian land were the earthly gateways to the Heavenly Kingdom; and to such uplifting visual reminders of the life to come there were aural reminders, bells that called the faithful to prayer and, day and night, gave to the cities of Europe a melodious pattern of sound.

Italian, French, German and English Romanesque buildings shared a common relationship to such functionally frank Roman structures as aqueducts, bridges, town gateways and gate-houses, watch towers and fortified posts; there were some traces of Byzantine influence; but most emphatic and outstanding of all variations of the style was Norman, which was pre-eminently an architecture of power, asserting the efficiency of a formidable race of warriors and administrators. Every line of Norman architecture suggests the unabating virility of the Northmen who had established themselves in France early in the tenth century. Those northmen—soon to be known, respected and dreaded as Normans—adopted the language and social customs of France; and in their own land of Normandy, and in Apulia which they conquered in 1042, and in Sicily, where they took Messina in 1060 and the whole island in 1090, they built splendidly.

At Caen one of the finest examples of Norman architecture is the Abbaye-aux-Dames, "La Trinite", built 1062–1066, and founded by Matilda, wife of William the Conqueror. (Plate 34.) But the greatest triumphs of the style were the Anglo-Norman cathedrals and abbey churches. In England the Normans built arrogantly. The castles with their high, square keeps and towering walls say as clearly as words shouted in anger: "*We* are the masters now." For a century after the Conquest of 1066 Norman architecture in England records an unholy alliance between Church and State, formed and maintained to overawe a subject people, for that was what the English had become, and for several generations they remained a servile and inferior though never docile people. The fortress-like cathedrals and abbey churches, especially those in the North, show the extensive support the Church could and did give to the secular power. "We are at one with the state," is the message of the church militant.

The suggestion that large-scale sacred buildings had a secondary and military function has been made convincingly by Mr. Frank Morley in his book, *The Great North Road*,[2] and a great deal of architectural evidence confirms it. For example, the fortress element is certainly present in the tower of St. Albans Abbey, in the hill-top cathedral at Lincoln, also in the Cathedral Monastery of Durham, sited on a rocky peninsula above the River Wear with the Castle of the Bishops perched on an eminence to the north. That particular castle was a military structure, built to protect the monastery from raiding Scots and sea rovers, but also useful for intimidating the townsmen. In the territory of the Danelaw, that extended from the Thames to the Cheviots and in the North Midlands from the Lancashire coast to the North Sea, temporal interests determined the siting and architectural character of monastic institutions. The territory was turbulent and unruly; in the towns especially sporadic outbreaks of independent spirit were brutally repressed by the Norman rulers, and permanent re-minders of their authority were established, not only by such structures as watch towers and fortified posts, but by a strongly-built cathedral church in the town centre; proclaiming yet again the unity of Church and state. This occupation of the town centre by Norman monks who were hand-in-glove with the hated Norman ruling class originated the conflict between "town and gown" which has lasted for centuries; in some university cities an annual bout of fisticuffs between undergraduates and townees took place as late as Victorian times, as we may read very cheerfully in Edward Bradley's *Verdant Green*, published in the mid-nineteenth century.[3] The antipathy of town and gown still persists in a mildly snobbish form.

Norman ideas had penetrated England before the Conquest, when Norman masons began to influence the English version of Romanesque, for there was an international traffic in skill: despite the disturbed state of many European countries, the unsafe roads, the brigands and predatory landlords, craftsmen apparently moved about as freely as churchmen. Stone churches had been built in the Anglo-Saxon kingdoms since the late seventh century. As a matter of policy, the Normans minimised Saxon achievements in the arts, so Saxon churches were rebuilt, and tombs and inscrip-tions in them defaced. A few small churches survived, like Escombe in Durham and St. Lawrence's, Bradford-on-Avon, Wiltshire (Plate 25), which both date from the early eighth century. We referred in chapter one to the use of materials taken from the deserted Roman city of Verulamium for building the Abbey Church of St. Albans, a task begun by the Saxon abbots, Ealdred and Ealmer at the close of the tenth century. Work continued slowly until the building was completed in 1077, by the first Norman abbot, Paul of Caen, who in the interests of political propaganda, destroyed the tombs of his predecessors.

Ely, Durham and Winchester cathedrals, Tewkesbury Abbey and the ruins of Buildwas and Fountains show the command of Norman builders over their materials and the satisfaction they found in leaving undisturbed the purity of structural lines. Arches were piled on arches, arcades were interlaced, and the massive cylindrical piers and the round-headed arches were serene state-

East end of the Presbytery, Ely Cathedral, built 1235–1252, by Bishop Hugh de Northwold. The tabernacles are empty; the windows of the side aisles have been inserted; and the large square piers from which the gable ascends were probably never completed. Reproduced from Plate 12 of Stewart's *Architectural History of Ely Cathedral* (London: John Van Voorst, 1868).

ments of power and stability. Those piers and arches were never ponderous, whether striding down some vast cathedral nave or swinging their shadows inside some small country church. In early Norman work carved ornament was used sparingly, usually to give slight accentuation to a curve or the moulding of a capital, never for its own sake. But during the twelfth and thirteenth centuries Saracenic influence infiltrated the West, and ornament was used to enrich as well as to emphasise mouldings, as on the façade of Castle Rising, Norfolk (Plate 34), the eastern end of the Presbytery of Ely Cathedral and the north porch of Southwell Minster (pages 159 and opposite).

The castles and fortresses were statements of naked power, and of these the Tower of London was intended to remind the tiresomely independent Londoners of the realities of military force, as well as every mariner who used the port. A fort had stood five centuries earlier at the north-west part of Roman London, between Cripplegate and Aldersgate, but although Normans and mediaeval builders were always prepared to use Roman foundations and to incorporate ancient, well-built walls, as at Pevensey Castle in Sussex which was originally the Saxon Shore fort of Anderida, the Tower of London was raised on a new site, where the eastern line of the city wall ran down to the river. (See map on page 7.) There it provided a threatening symbol of royal authority; but London was rich enough to tame kings, who were always short of money and would sell charters and concessions and respect the rights of the often disrespectful citizens, and under financial strain would even extend those rights. (Page 163.)

In the countryside, manor houses like castles were fortified, and although the great hall of a castle or a manor house was often built of stone, and occasionally had a stone-hooded fireplace with a chimney instead of an open central hearth, the hall, the houseplace, was cold, draughty and by Roman and modern standards, impossibly uncomfortable. Glass was for church windows, not for houses. In towns, some houses were built of stone, and a few have survived in England and Normandy; but as wood was chiefly used for domestic building, whole streets were periodically destroyed by fire.

France, which had preserved a tenuous tradition of civilised amenity from Roman times, could, as we suggested in chapter one,

The north porch of Southwell Minster, Nottinghamshire, showing the interlaced arcading within, and the enriched mouldings on the inner arch and the
triple windows in the pediment above the porch. Reproduced from Thomas
Rickman's *Styles of Architecture in England* (Oxford: seventh edition, 1881.)

claim unbroken continuity with fifth century Gaul; although few Romano–Gallic secular buildings remained undamaged, churches were comparatively immune, unless they happened to be in regions ravaged by the Great Army of the Danes in the latter part of the ninth century. The description of the fifth century church at Lyons, dedicated to St. Justus and built by Bishop Patiens, has been quoted in chapter six. When Romanesque architecture was evolving in France that church was barely four hundred years old, and probably as well preserved as many of Wren's London churches are today. There were doubtless many other examples of early Christian basilical churches in France; but they were not imitated by the Romanesque builders, who perfected a new and strenuously vital style, for French Romanesque was structurally experimental: what Lethaby called "The Architecture of Adventure" was arising.[4]

The Roman barrel vault was used and much enlarged, so wooden roofs over the naves of churches could be dispensed with: the congregation looked upwards at a prolonged stone arch, heavy, secure and demanding the sturdy support of stout piers instead of columns. The side aisles of those early Romanesque churches were also vaulted, so throughout its length the weight of the main vault above the nave was partly distributed by those above the aisles. At the eastern end of the church, the thrust of the nave and aisle vaults was taken by a main apse with smaller apses on either side, so three semi-circular structures corresponding with the width of the nave and aisles held up one end of the building; at the other, the entrance porch was enlarged, strengthened and flanked by two towers; so a great mass of masonry stabilised the thrust of the vaults, and those twin western towers became a characteristic feature of French Romanesque and Gothic churches.

The discovery that masses of masonry were thrust-absorbers led to the use of buttresses against walls to counter the pressure from within of an arch or a vault. The half-barrel vaults over the aisles of a church were thrust-absorbers of a lighter kind, carrying down the pressure of the nave vault by a semi-circular path to the side walls. The design of these French Romanesque churches announces the advent of a new age of structural innovations; openly made, triumphantly acknowledged; the days of Roman concealment were already remote. The next advance in securing structural

The Tower of London, as it was recorded by Wenceslaus Hollar in 1647. The square keep with its four angle towers was originally white, though it was no longer so when Hollar made his drawings for the engraving. This intimidating Norman fortress was built by William the Conqueror to command the river approach to London and to remind the eleventh century cockneys that might was right, at least until kings and those in authority ran short of money: then Londoners could relish their own special kind of power. *Reproduced by courtesy of the Trustees of the British Museum.*

equilibrium was the building of independent piers, from which half-arches curved up to abut against the outside walls, redistributing the pressure from within and relieving the side walls from the full force of cumulative thrusts. This device became architecturally famous as the flying buttress. Another architectural invention was ribbed vaulting, which may have been originated by Romanesque builders or imported from some eastern source.[5] Dynamic invention was far more characteristic of French Romanesque than unconscious imitation and adaptation; and the use of the barrel-vault led to the creation of other types. Where two barrel vaults intersected, a groined vault was formed, and as the groins tended to be weak, Romanesque masons—good engineers in stone—rein-forced them by an arch or groin rib, a device that initiated rib vaulting.

Freedom to invent and to make structural experiments was possible under the patronage of a wealthy Church; freedom in other fields of human endeavour was strictly and often savagely circumscribed; but Romanesque architecture in France and other parts of Europe showed that below the surface of the still half-barbaric civilisation of the Christian states an unwonted creative restlessness was astir. Italy was, and for long remained, the brilliant exception, for the Italians, the heirs of Imperial Rome, never surrendered to barbarism. Italian Romanesque architecture con-firms that triumphant resistance by every nuance of design, by every subtle choice of ornament, by the immutability of the Greek-given sense of proportion.

In Italy the classic orders were never out of sight or out of mind. The monuments of the Imperial age remained, and Italian archi-tects were in closer visual and artistic accord with their Roman predecessors than other Europeans. But they were not intimidated by ancient examples; the innate gaiety of the Italian character escaped from the bonds of Roman discipline; in the south their interpretation of Romanesque was refreshed and stimulated by Saracenic influences; in the north Lombardic art developed, en-riched and amplified by the use of various marbles; and in all parts of Italy characteristic forms evolved; lighter and more graceful than the French, German and Anglo-Norman varieties of the style. The arch was used structurally, but its weight-lifting and distributing powers were never unduly emphasised, and the decorative proper-ties of arcading were elegantly employed to cool with round-headed shadows the walls of buildings bathed in strong sunlight. Arcading accentuated the delicate proportions of the famous group at Pisa, the Cathedral, Baptistry and Campanile. (Plates 30 and 31.) The cathedral was built in 1063–92, the Baptistry in 1153–1278, and the campanile, the Leaning Tower, in 1174. One of the distinctive features of Italian Romanesque churches is the detached bell

Arched Norman windows, with small attached columns flanking the opening. *Circa* 1130. *Left:* Castle Hedingham, Essex. *Right:* Rochester Castle, Kent. The original form of the windows is shown. *Drawn by A. S. Cook.*

tower, the campanile, always standing alone, though sometimes linked with the church by cloisters.

Early in the eleventh century, the church of St. Miniato at Florence showed that Italian architects, while acknowledging their debt to the Roman past, were no longer obsessed by weight and mere size. That church has a light and graceful façade, with five semi-circular arches springing from the capitals of slender versions of Corinthian columns; the exterior and interior are banded and panelled in black and white marble which gives a sprightly air to what is after all a sacred edifice; the whole gleaming composition recalling the unrepressed joyousness of paganism, as if the old gods had stirred in their sleep, and the amoral gaiety of pre-Christian Rome was about to be restored. Italian Romanesque architecture is untouched by Roman *gravitas*: solemnity had been expelled, never to return to the nimble-minded Italians. (Plate 31.) In Milan, Florence, Pisa, Genoa and Verona, splendid public buildings showed how such an artistic and gifted people pursued beauty for its own sake and with a zest and discrimination that gave to everything they built a fabulous vitality.

In Germany the Romanesque style had some likeness to Lombardic architecture, especially in the use and treatment of the arch; and this similarity was an indication of the cultural and political relationship that existed between northern Italy and Germany. The structural frankness of French and Norman building is absent, but there is greater variety of composition and an unconsciously picturesque grouping of features. Circular and octagonal turrets, polygonal domes, and blind arcading on walls and below eaves begot a multiplicity of angles, which occasionally produced an appearance of conflict and confusion. But not always: for example horizontal and vertical elements are smoothly united in the Church of the Apostles at Cologne, shown opposite. In this church the choir ends in three apses, and the curved bases of the twin towers form five semi-circular external features which flow into each other, and are linked by tiers of blind arcading and arcaded galleries running under the eaves. Instead of the gaiety that distinguishes Italian Romanesque, German Romanesque churches are sober statements of strength.

Over a period of four hundred years, from the eighth to the twelfth century, the growth and regional development of western European architecture show great advances in technical accomplishment and command over materials. Romanesque was essentially an architecture of stone, which architects learnt to use with increasing ingenuity and confidence. They had found that by balancing the play of forces in their buildings, by controlling thrust and counter-thrust, they could achieve both equilibrium and elasticity; their structures were no longer inert, settled heavily on their foundations, achieving stability through bulk and weight; they stood erect, tall, splendid, secure, and with the diminished surface area of walls, the expansion of church windows increased the dominance of voids over solids. By the twelfth century the prelude to Gothic was over: a structural revolution began, and, as usual, technical discoveries and creative ability were far ahead of political conventions and the limited comprehension of mediaeval kings and ruling classes.

The Church of the Apostles, Cologne, an example of German Romanesque,
A.D. 1220–1250. The small building with pointed windows in the foreground is
later in date. The three apses at the eastern end have blind arcading externally, rising to two storeys, with arcading on a smaller scale below the eaves.
(From Thomas Hope's *Essay on Architecture*.)

THE MEDIAEVAL CIVILISATION

EDIAEVAL civilisation was generated during the so-called
Dark Ages, which were not so consistently dark as historians of the last century believed; there were a few
highlights, and records of architectural achievement and
technical experiments in building refute the assumption that the
interlude between the decline of the Graeco–Roman world and the
end of the first millennium A.D. was a time of unrelieved anarchy,
chaos and artistic sterility. In Britain a short-lived but brilliant
civilisation had thrived in the kingdom of Northumbria during the
seventh and eighth centuries. At that time Northumbria extended
from the Humber to the Forth, westwards to the Lancashire coast,
with the British kingdom of Strathclyde on the north-west border.
While it lasted it seemed to be a little Golden Age. Such ages, as
Sir Charles Oman has remarked, are often "the result of the good
work of a previous generation, rather than the start of a continuous
period of activity destined to endure."[1]

Bede the scholar and historian writing in the comparative
security of the monastery at Jarrow allows a faint hint of apprehension about the future to diminish the optimism of his review of
contemporary life in the year A.D. 731. His world was tranquil;
that he admitted, but he also doubted, and with good reason.
"Such being the peaceable and calm disposition of the times," he
wrote, "many of the Northumbrians, as well of the nobility as
private persons, laying aside their weapons, rather incline to dedi-
cate both themselves and their children to the tonsure and monastic
vows, than to study martial discipline. What will be the end
hereof, the next age will show."[2] On a far smaller scale, the history
of the religious intellectual pharaoh, Ikhnaton, was repeated by
the Northumbrians, who believed the service of religion to be
more important than the safety of the realm. Ikhnaton lost the

Asiatic provinces of his Empire which were conquered by the Hittites: the Northumbrians lost their civilisation, which was shattered by the Danish invasions during the second half of the ninth century.

Little survives of that Northumbrian golden age: the Danes had no respect for churches and monasteries. They destroyed the buildings and butchered the monks. Bede describes a church built "in the Roman manner," in A.D. 675, by the Abbot of Wearmouth, Benedict called Biscop, who brought masons over from Gaul—then incorporated in the Frankish kingdom—which suggests a shortage of skilled craftsmen in Northumbria. That church and monastery at the mouth of the Wear had glass windows, and both glass and glaziers were also brought from Gaul. The glass-making industry in the Seine–Rhine area had continued from Roman times, as described in chapter seven; but in Britain glass-making, like brick and tile-making, was a lost art. Those Frankish artisans instructed local English craftsmen in glass manufacture; but the art was soon forgotten, for eighty-three years later, Cuthbert, another Abbot of Wearmouth, asked Lullus, the Archbishop of Mainz, to send him some artisans who could make glass for vessels and windows. Bede, who was the first English architectural historian, mentions a less permanent structure, built in A.D. 652 on the Isle of Lindisfarne, with an oak framework, walled and thatched with reeds, that were later removed by Bishop Eadbert who then covered walls and roof with lead plates.[3] Such descriptions, brief though they are, indicate a volume of building activity in that lost civilisation.

Although architectural remains are scattered and scanty, innumerable carved crosses and some major works of sculpture have survived, and many examples of manuscripts and drawings. This Anglo-Saxon Renaissance in the arts occurred in the sixty-six years between the arrival of Theodore of Tarsus, who was appointed Archbishop of Canterbury in A.D. 665, and the death of Bede in A.D. 735, and during that time, in the words of Sir Thomas Kendrick, "the remote province of England, happily aloof from a continent made miserable by barbarian wars and the Arab invasion, achieved a position that without exaggeration may be described as supreme in western civilisation."[4]

The time interval between the collapse of the Roman Empire in the West and the emergence of the independent Christian states of Europe was about five hundred years; thus mediaeval civilisation became established midway in the eighth cultural period classified by Flinders Petrie, the period in which we are still living. (See diagram on page 19.) The architecture that arose in the three centuries between A.D. 1200 and 1500 was as different from that of the Graeco–Roman world as the new Western architecture of the late nineteenth and twentieth centuries is different from the resurrected and revitalised classic of the Renaissance.

The name Gothic which has been given to the architecture of the Middle Ages, is both inappropriate and misleading, for the Goths, who sacked Rome in A.D. 410 and helped to destroy the Western Empire, had no remote connection with, or influence on, the character or design of the cathedrals, abbeys, civic buildings, palaces and great mansions of mediaeval Europe. The term was first used and in a most unflattering sense of Giorgio Vasari (1511–1574), an Italian art historian, for in the sixteenth century Renaissance noblemen and their architects dismissed the Middle Ages as barbaric. That term the Middle Ages, was also used in a derogatory sense to describe the interlude between the ancient world and the Renaissance, which was formerly believed to be crude and unenlightened; a belief utterly refuted by the architectural evidence. A German scholar named Keller or Celarius invented the term some three hundred years ago.

The achievements of mediaeval architects have been dramatically described as "solutions of problems of how to throw stones high into the air, and balance them there."[5] Gothic architecture was boldly experimental, imbued with confident vitality, and though it in no way resembled the architecture of the Age of Reason, it had no kinship either with the architecture of the Age of Faith that Justinian had consolidated, which led to the repetitious conventions of Byzantine art. The first manifestations of this new spirit in architectural design appeared in France in the middle of the twelfth century, with revolutionary uses of the arch and vault, and it soon spread to Germany, to the Low Countries, to England, Scotland and Ireland, Scandinavia, and in a tentative rather unsure manner to Italy (for there architects were always looking over their shoulder at the classic orders and all that they implied), and also to northern Spain, gradually advancing south-

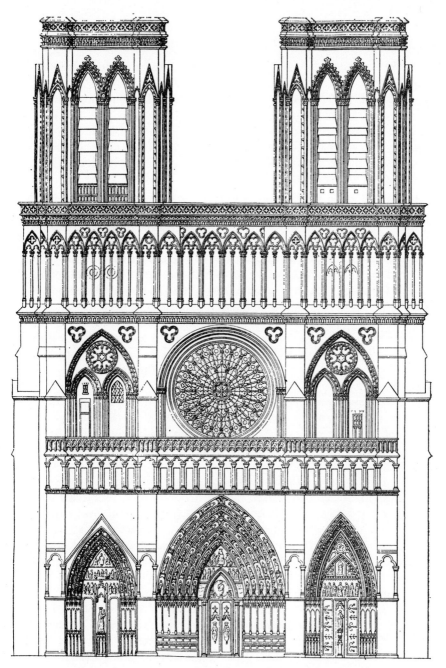

The west front of Notre Dame, Paris, A.D. 1163–1235. From a drawing by
W. B. Clarke, engraved by E. Turrell, included in *A Theoretical and Practical
Treatise on the Five Orders of Architecture*, Plate XCVIII. (London: Thomas Kelly
1840.)

wards, as the Muslim states declined in power under Christian pressure.

The arts and crafts related to building had become increasingly cosmopolitan; interchanges of technical skill had helped to extend Romanesque architecture throughout Europe, and Gothic had partly evolved from Romanesque. By the twelfth century a mason, carver, painter or metal worker was at home with his fellow-craftsmen wherever his skill was needed, in places as far apart as York or Seville, Rouen or Venice. They may well have shared a common vocabulary of technical terms; and their work, in all parts of Western Europe, shows a common attitude of mind towards the use of materials, an innate respect for quality, not only in the choice of materials but in the application of their own skills. This conferred on their work a lively and varied character, wholly different from the standardised and formalised patterns executed by highly-trained slaves that adorned Roman buildings. Gothic ornament, largely naturalistic in character, and occasionally whimsical, was never disorderly. In the fourteenth, fifteenth and early sixteenth centuries, heraldic motifs were used, and later in this chapter the influence of heraldry on architecture and the industrial arts is examined.

Mediaeval builders with the means at their disposal gave new meaning to the arch; they solved by empirical methods the problem of throwing stones high into the air and balancing them there; they rejected Roman rules, though they knew about them, and they made rules of their own. Unlike the early Arab builders, they were not amateurs improvising structural solutions in a state of emotional frenzy; they were highly accomplished architects who had learned to control a material that invited structural experiments. The Romans imprisoned the arch: the Greeks of the Eastern Empire released it, and Byzantine churches, great and small, showed how the secrets of its strength and flexibility could be mastered. Gothic builders revealed an intellectual awareness that was not incompatible with the Faith that united Christendom. The architecture they created was highly charged with emotion, conveyed by form as well as colour, and churches, assured of immunity from physical danger in the twelfth and thirteenth centuries, lost the fortress-like solidity of their Romanesque predecessors. The challenging spirit of Christendom is proclaimed by the vast

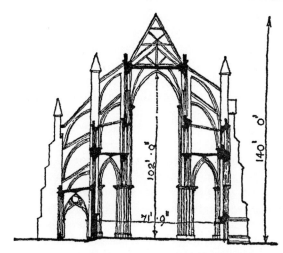

Section through the nave of Westminster Abbey, the highest Gothic vault in England. Flying buttresses over the aisles and north cloister absorb and distribute the thrust of the vault. *From a drawing by A. S. Cook.*

cathedrals constructed in Western Europe and England. The form conveyed heavenly aspirations but the plan was sometimes distorted, conceivably for some symbolic reason, for it was an age of symbols, with shapes and ornament conveying secret and not always Christian meanings; petrified folklore. Some very odd carvings found their way into churches, and Dr. Margaret Murray suggested that a faith far older than Christianity survived throughout the Middle Ages, actively competitive with the teaching of the Church, and ultimately degenerating into witchcraft; a view that might explain the presence of imps and animals that appear occasionally in sedate and sacred surroundings.[6]

Gothic architecture drew the eye upwards, away from earthly concerns; towers and spires were signposts to the Heavens above, visible from afar, and within the great cathedrals every line fortified the illusion of ascent. From tall slender columns arches spurt up in frozen jets to meet and form a web of radiating ribs high above nave and sanctuary; so strong is the illusion of vertical striving, that what is really a reversal of structural fact is automatically accepted, for those columns and climbing arches are really bringing weight down to earth by innumerable paths while apparently flinging weight skywards. That soaring, strenuous architecture was the visible manifestation of the immense pressures of spiritual power in Christendom; power that became the driving force of the Crusades, and gave the Christian states of Europe a sense of valiant purpose, so that kings and princes and great nobles sank their habitual animosities and united to reconquer the lost provinces of the Middle East. That they failed eventually to hold what little they did reconquer, does not diminish the splendour of their attempt. The architecture of the thirteenth and fourteenth centuries suggests the restoration of confidence in the western world; the achievements are the result of trial and error; new knowledge of what could and could not be done with stone and timber was won occasionally by some accident—a collapsed roof, a fallen tower, an arch breaking beneath too great a strain. But the urgent spirit of experiment gave sustained encouragement to builders, who must have known that their trial of some new technique was not always to blame when things went wrong, for in some of the French and English cathedrals carelessness and cheap construction obviously caused disaster.

Some of the Gothic cathedrals had a vast internal spaciousness; from the carved capitals of tall, delicate columns a mesh of curving ribs and arches rose high above nave and transepts and choir. Compared with the stout piers and rounded arches of Romanesque buildings, the single or clustered shafts of Gothic columns seem strikingly light and slender, the moulded ribs of vaults almost fragile; excessively visible bulk and strength have been replaced by a lithe stone structure, bearing and distributing weight and drawing assertive pressures downwards along innumerable curved paths within the church while diverting those pressures externally through flying buttresses. The scale was astounding. The vault at Beauvais, the highest in Europe, is over 157 feet, some three and a half times its span, and the cathedral is perhaps the greatest and most courageous example of French Gothic. The building was begun in A.D. 1225; the roof collapsed in 1284, and the choir was reconstructed and strengthened between 1337 and 1347. The transepts were not built until the sixteenth century and west of them the cathedral remained unfinished.

The mediaeval habit of building by fits and starts, with architectural second thoughts disrupting or obliterating the original conception, often signified the capricious whims of some prelate; the steadily accumulating wealth of the Church allowed ambitious churchmen to underwrite enterprises that even a Roman Emperor might have hesitated to sanction, not because of the cost but because of the structural risk; churchmen of the thirteenth and fourteenth centuries took risks and spent money with the lavish abandon of modern politicians backing some technological gamble. Intent on glorifying God and His saints by great works, they enriched the European heritage. Patrons in later ages might be satisfied by essential repairs to existing buildings, by a few minor extensions or adornments, but not those pioneers of Gothic. In France and England cathedrals and abbeys and occasionally the smaller churches of the countryside were enlarged or rebuilt without any sentimental regard for existing work which was pulled down without scruple to make room for new ideas; nobody cherished ruins; nothing was preserved unless it still had some useful purpose. Nostaglia for the past usually occurs when the fire of creative inspiration has sunk low. A disused castle evoked no admiration; to the predominantly practical men of the Middle Ages it was neither romantic nor picturesque, merely a quarry, like the Roman cities of Britain had been some centuries earlier. William the Conqueror's castle at Cambridge, for example, provided materials for the college builders of the fourteenth century. Nobody thought of copying an ancient building while a living tradition of architecture flourished. The past was without influence, unless some dim memory of the vanished might of the Roman Empire was recalled; but in England there were few traces left of Roman rule, apart from the roads; architecturally the past was dead; as for the future, that was not an earthly matter at all, for it concerned Heaven and Hell, so everything about the design and decoration of churches was deliberately intended to remind illiterate Christians of the life to come.

No large church in France or England was altogether free from scaffolding during the centuries when Gothic architecture was passing through its three main periods of development, for additions and alterations were constantly made. Growth and change attested the unflagging vitality of an architecture that was universal in general character, though by the thirteenth century it had become nationally distinctive in France, Italy, Germany, England, the Netherlands and the Christian states of northern Spain. Architecture, the vehicle of creative vision, had through those national interpretations of Gothic drawn an approximation to the map of

Part of the north side of the nave of Salisbury Cathedral. The main body of the cathedral was built between 1220 and 1260: after an interval work was resumed in the late thirteenth century, and the spire completed in the middle of the fourteenth. The cathedral is almost entirely in the Early English Gothic style. Reproduced from part of Plate XX, Britton's *History and Antiquities of the Cathedral Church of Salisbury* (See opposite page.)

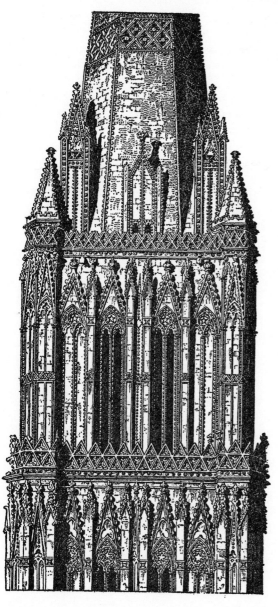

Part of the two upper storeys of the tower and the base of the spire of Salisbury Cathedral. Compared with the frugal use of ornament in the interior, the tower is opulently decorated, and is indeed an early example of the period classified as Decorated Gothic. The steeple was the work of the mason, Richard of Farleigh, and was completed in the mid-fourteenth century. Reproduced on a slightly smaller scale from Britton's *History and Antiquities of the Cathedral Church of Salisbury*, Plate VII. (See opposite page.)

Western Europe, which remained valid until the present century, irrespective of the fluctuations of political frontiers.

French Gothic, known generally as *Style Ogivale*, originated late in the twelfth century and has three main periods, identified by name conveniently through perhaps rather superficially with the form and tracery of church windows. The first is *Gothique à Lancettes*, when pointed arches and lancet windows were first used, the window heads being filled by stone plates pierced by geometric patterns. This form of filling was called plate tracery, and from it bar tracery developed, with carved stone members spraying out from the mullions to form interlacing patterns. The next period began in the thirteenth century and was named *Rayonnant*, when circular windows with wheel tracery were introduced, justifying the name *Rayonnant* by the radiant and sparkling effect they created. The brilliancy of this form of tracery may be seen in Notre Dame, Paris, at Amiens and Rouen. (See page 171.) The final period was *Flamboyant*, descriptive of the wavering, flame-like tracery that filled church windows in the fourteenth and fifteenth centuries. Those periods melted into each other; there were no sharp divisions; and this fluidity of growth and transition characterised the corresponding periods of English Gothic.

The form of society in Western Europe was perfected in the thirteenth century; in France the new social coherence was accompanied by a great expansion in the establishment of monastic institutions. Altogether it was an expansive age: artistically and intellectually. Theological philosophy engaged some of the best minds in Europe; the arts prospered, and Paris soon became recognised as the capital of European culture: a position that city has retained for centuries. The new ebullient style of architecture, expressive of adventurous originality in building theory, arose in a period of intellectual, religious and artistic ferment. To Gothic art French genius contributed clarity, gaiety, and the same tense energy that characterised the best work of Arab artists and architects; there was passion and mystery in the early phase of French Gothic, and a partly submerged symbolism that has led to much perplexed speculation and fostered some conflicting theories about the intentions and abilities of mediaeval builders.

In England the development of Gothic was comparable with the French, though exhibiting the nascent nationalism that was for so

The octagonal Chapter House, Salisbury Cathedral. Windows were already beginning their conquest of walls, foreshadowing the final phase of English Gothic, when voids dominated solids. Reproduced from Britton's *History and Antiquities of the Cathedral Church of Salisbury*.

long unsuspected by the spiritual and temporal rulers of Europe. To the Church any conception of civilisation other than United Christendom was tantamount to blasphemy; to Kings and Princes nationalism was a subversive and treasonable idea, for the loyalty of all classes had to be given to their rightful Lords; not to some locality. But the marked differences between English and French and German Gothic broadened the hint already given earlier by the variations of Romanesque architecture, that at some future time nationalism would become established, and the unity of Christendom be overthrown as ruthlessly as the Roman Empire had been overthrown.

The now familiar terms describing the periods of English Gothic are Early English, Decorated and Perpendicular. They were first used by Thomas Rickman (1776–1841), an architect who had made a systematic study of Gothic architecture, and in 1817 published a work entitled *An Attempt to Discriminate the Styles of*

Architecture in England From the Conquest to the Reformation.[7] Rickman described four periods beginning with Norman, though as that was the eleventh century form of Romanesque it cannot be classified as Gothic. The Early English period began in the late twelfth century, and the first break with Anglo-Norman forms came when the French master-mason, William of Sens, was appointed to rebuild the choir of Canterbury Cathedral which had been burnt down in 1174. Some fifteen years later, Lincoln Cathedral was rebuilt by St. Hugh of Avalon, who employed Geoffrey de Noiers as master-mason. The western part of the choir, known as St. Hugh's, was constructed between 1168 and 1204. An Early English screen was erected later across the original Norman front, and in the last quarter of the fourteenth century the upper parts of the west towers were rebuilt. (Plate 37.) Evidence of contemporary awareness of the audacity and beauty of the new work at Lincoln is provided by an account in *The Metrical Life of St. Hugh.* An abbreviated version of it quoted by Dr. G. G. Coulton in his *Social Life in Britain from the Conquest to the Reformation,* reads as follows:

"With wondrous art he built the fabric of the Cathedral; whereunto he supplied not only his own wealth, and the labours of his servants, but even the sweat of his own brow; for he oftentimes bore the hod-load of hewn stone or of binding lime. In this structure, the art equals the precious materials; for the vault may be compared to a bird stretching out her broad wings to fly; planted on its firm columns, it soars to the clouds. On the other hand, the work is supported by precious columns of swarthy stone, not confined to one sole colour, nor loose of pore, but flecked with glittering stars and close-set in all its grain. This stone disdains to be tamed with steel until it have first been subdued by art; for its surface must first be softened by long grinding with sand, and its hardness is relaxed with strong vinegar. Moreover, it may suspend the mind in doubt whether it be jasper or marble; it is dull indeed for jasper, yet, for marble, of a most noble nature. Of this are formed those slender columns which stand round the great piers, even as a bevy of maidens stand marshalled for a dance."[8]

The "swarthy stone" was Purbeck marble. The urgent curves of the choir vault seem indeed to be poised for flight. The vaulting at Lincoln influenced cathedral-builders elsewhere; at York, Beverley and in Scotland at Holyrood. The account of St. Hugh

of Lincoln implies that he was an architect and an executant craftsman, though bearing a "hod-load of hewn stone or of binding
lime" is the job of a builders' labourer not a skilled workman. This,
as the late Dr. Salzman has suggested, was rather a gesture, "like
that of Edward I when he wheeled a barrow on the fortifications of
Berwick. . . ."[9] Such anecdotes are suspect and give little support to the belief that churchmen of exalted rank combined the
creative vision of an architect with the exacting skills of a mason, a
carver or a painter. Some of the brethren in a monastery may well
have possessed special aptitudes and were trained to use them,
though many probably assisted hired workmen, acting as unskilled
labourers. Salzman cites the Chronicles of Evesham Abbey where
about A.D. 1300 the infirmary buildings were "constructed by the
devotion and industry of the monks."[10] The picture drawn by
nineteenth century romanticists of mediaeval craftsmen as a band
of pious brothers joyously chipping at stone, carving wood, and
painting and gilding this and that while they sang the praises of
God is emotionally overcharged, altogether too highly coloured.
Teams of specialists in various crafts obviously did work together
on the great Gothic buildings, and may sometimes have worked in
amity, though they probably quarrelled bitterly now and then,
and were mutually abusive, jealous and crotchety and egoistical
as creative people so often are, but the results of their combined
work glorified the civilisation of Europe.

The overall responsibility for a great church was that of the
architect, the man who had the imaginative power to envisage the
building as a complete entity, the master designer who could convey his vision to the men who worked the stone and fashioned the
timber. Historians and critics have written thousands of explanatory words about this division of creative activities, occasionally
confusing the skill that directs with the skill that executes. Professor David Pye condensed into one sentence the simple truth
when he said: "Design is what, for practical purposes, can be conveyed in words and by drawing: workmanship is what, for practical purposes, can not."[11]

The borrowing and adaptation of structural methods and ornamental devices showed how receptive and open-minded the members of the building fraternity were; though individuals probably
cherished well-guarded secrets and passed them on perhaps to their

favourite apprentices or to relatives who were also practising crafts-men. Eventually the craft guilds became "closed shops", guarding their mysteries, and preserving standards of workmanship, restrict-ing the numbers of those entitled to share their privileges as strictly as any modern trade union. The work at Lincoln was far from being a solitary inspirational source. At Westminster Abbey, which had the highest vault in England, rising to 102 feet, the flying buttresses with their double tiers of arches were copied at St. Albans, and the Chapter House and cloisters copied at Salis-bury, just as the windows at Westminster had been copied from those at the cathedrals of Rheims and Amiens. (See page 173.)

The cathedral-builders constantly challenged gravity, and as they increased their mastery over materials they reared their lofty naves with an ample margin of safety, depending less and less on thick supporting masonry, until at last the dominance of voids over solids, of windows over walls, was established in the architecture of northern, central and western Europe and England. This did not happen in Spain, southern Italy or Sicily, where light was too intense to allow a great expansion of window space. In France and England particularly that expansion continued, until the church became, in Lethaby's phrase, "a cage of stone", a colossal lantern of coloured glass. The artists and glaziers who designed those high, glowing windows were relating over and over again the story of Christianity for the benefit of congregations who, with very few exceptions, were unable to read. Christian Barman has likened the mediaeval church with its fiery pictorial windows to a celestial cinema.[12] The illiterate worshippers were surrounded by reiterated affirmations of the Christian faith, for competitive cults still existed; some secret, others openly practised, surviving with an obstinate vitality that troubled churchmen greatly. Architects could never forget that when they designed a church the building had a dual function: it was an instrument for the praise and wor-ship of God, also a weapon for fighting the ancient magic of pre-Christian Europe. (The beastliness of that magic, as it flourished in the Graeco–Roman world, is described in dark and bloody detail in *The Golden Ass*, the novel by Lucius Apuleius written in the second century A.D.)

Churches had to give their message, over and over again un-ceasingly to all who entered. The glories of heaven and the flames of hell blazed through the windows during the daylight hours. But not always. Some windows were restful, calm, serene, emotionally passive. Such were grisaille windows, that consisted almost entirely of white glass with the surface ornamented with patterns, delicately painted in line. The warmth and variegation of the surface were due partly to the imperfections of mediaeval glass manufacture; the patterns were the work of accomplished artists. The finest examples in England, that date from about 1260 A.D., are the "Five Sisters" at York Minster, five lancets over 50 feet high that fill the end of the north transept. There is evidence that the lower windows of Westminster Abbey were glazed with grisaille patterns in the mid-thirteenth century, and there are early thirteenth century French examples at Angers and Soissons and some, a little later in date, at Chartres.[13] The grisaille window may have developed partly as a result of the Cistercian ban on the use of colour, a rule enforced in the twelfth century, and partly to allow more light to penetrate to the nave and aisles of churches, for little could pass through the dark, intense coloured glass that filled so many windows; perhaps an even more mundane reason was the comparative cheapness of white glass.

Wherever the eye roved within a church, some solace for troubled souls or promise of salvation for the faithful was visible. Carved and gilded saints and angels looked down benignly from roof beams; mural paintings recorded the triumphs and sufferings of the noble army of marytrs; and, as mentioned earlier, even the occasional distortion of the cruciform plan of a church, whether large or small, may have been a symbolical reminder of Christ's sacrifice. The distortion of the plan occurs when the chancel is out of line with the nave, inclining either to the right or the left, and this "weeping" or "skew" chancel appears in some English and French cathedrals, and elsewhere in Western Europe and in many small churches. In large structures the deflection is very obvious, for example at Lichfield Cathedral, where the inclination of the chancel to the north exaggerates the length of the interior when it is viewed from the west end of the nave, so much so that the apse with the Lady Chapel becomes indistinct, almost lost in the distance. The view down the nave and chancel is unobstructed at Lichfield for the rood screen is light, with open tracery, and comparatively low: looking over it the south side of the chancel is

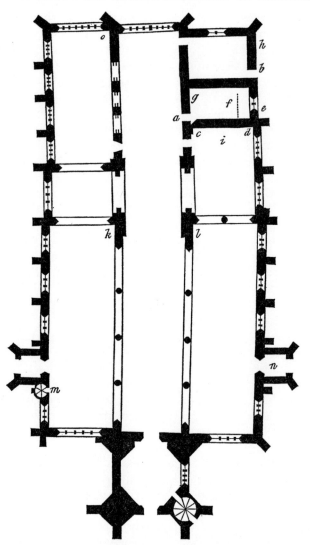

Plan of St. Editha, the Collegiate Church of Tamworth, Staffordshire, showing the marked deflection of the chancel from the line of the nave. Reproduced from *The History and Antiquities of the Collegiate Church of Tamworth*, by Charles Ferrers R. Palmer. (Tamworth: J. Thompson. London: Simpkin, Marshall & Co. 1871). Facing page 59.

clearly visible, but not the north: the bend hides it. The inclination varies: at Ely, Canterbury and York Minster it is to the south: in the small mid-fourteenth century Collegiate parish church of St. Editha at Tamworth, Staffordshire, it is to the north. In western and northern Europe the inclination is usually to the north, though the south bend does occur, as in the cathedral choirs of Geneva and Stuttgart. (See plan on page opposite.)

Although the weeping chancel is not confined to any particular period of Gothic architecture, there are no marked examples before A.D. 1200 and the feature is most observable during the fourteenth century.[14] Three theories are advanced to explain this break in alignment: the accidental, the aesthetic and the symbolical. The first assumes that mediaeval architects were unable to set out a church accurately; an implausible assumption, for the technical competence of Gothic designers and church builders is overwhelmingly evident all over Europe, Britain and Ireland. Accident is far less likely than deliberate design, but if intentional what then was the purpose and significance of the design?

The aesthetic theory suggests an exercise in optical deceit, as the bent plan with the chancel inclined to the north or south tends to make the choir fade out of sight, so together nave and choir appear to be far longer than they really are; an illusion impressively achieved at Lichfield. Was this manipulated perspective intentional like the minutely deflected vertical and horizontal lines of a Greek Doric temple? The aim was different: the skew chancel was not devised like those Greek modulations to correct the imperfections of human vision but to exaggerate them in order to create an illusion of overpowering immensity in a large church, though in a small one the change of axis would be hardly perceptible, and if perceived, merely puzzling.

The symbolical theory is attuned to the ideas of an age when men relied on symbolism to an extent scarcely credible to those living in a literate civilisation, for it suggests that the plan of the church represented the death of Christ on the cross, with His head inclined to the left or right. To accept this solution demands no blind or strenuous act of faith: the church with a cruciform plan was a symbol on a large scale: the deflection of the chancel reinforced the original symbolical significance.

The position of a mediaeval cathedral in relation to a city also

Front elevation of Westminster Hall, completed in 1402, but, to quote Sir Nikolaus Pevsner, "severely restored in 1810–12." From *A Theoretical and Practical Treatise on the Five Orders of Architecture*, Plate XCI. (London: Thomas Kelly, 1840.) See opposite page for the appearance and surroundings of the Hall according to Hollar, 1647.

Westminster Hall as it appeared from the Thames in the mid-seventeenth century. From part of an engraving by Wenceslaus Hollar made in 1647. (See front elevation of the Hall opposite.) *Reproduced by courtesy of the Trustees of the British Museum.*

had a symbolic significance. In Norman England, as we have said, the cathedral could be a sinister reminder of the united authority of Church and State, but only in regions where social unrest was a recurrent threat to Norman rule. French cathedrals, unlike English, did not originate as part of some monastic establishment, though there were exceptions, such as Soissons Cathedral, built between 1160 and 1212, which was the church of a Royal Abbey. In France and elsewhere in Europe the cathedral became a focal point, the hub of city life, occupying a central position, approached by processional ways that wound between tall houses which leaned towards each other across the narrow street. (Plate 36.) The great church usually stood in a large open space, and rose high above the roof tops, dominating all other buildings until that dominance was challenged when secular power, financed by commerce, boldly advertised its strength by ambitious architecture. The Belfry at Bruges, built in 1280, soared up to 352 feet; that at Ghent to 400, the latter built between 1300 and 1339; both rose from public buildings that displayed the formidable quality of civic pride. In the Low Countries secular architecture became increasingly magnificent: not only the Halles and Belfry at Bruges, and the town hall of Ghent, but those at Brussels and Louvain and the great Cloth Hall at Ypres. Churches like St. Gudule at Brussels (1226–1280) and the cathedral at Tournai (1066–1338) were eclipsed by civic stateliness. In every part of Europe fine buildings were rising, changing the character of cities and the face of the land. Churches, monasteries, universities and public buildings, were everywhere enlarged and beautified. Cities acquired greater dignity, with a large market square surrounding or adjoining the cathedral, which became the mediaeval equivalent of the Greek agora and the Roman forum, like the Binnenhof at the Hague or St. Mark's Square at Venice.

Architecture, the infallible witness of social change and archaic survivals, shows the beginnings of the struggle between inherited power and privilege and the orderly, enterprising civilisation of the trading ports and cities. One sign of that long-drawn-out conflict is the anti-social character of princes and great noblemen when they built their town houses without any consideration for the convenience of their neighbours or the amenities and traffic of the city. Those houses were extravagant assertions of aristocratic authority, half-palace and half-fortress; but those princes, dukes and lords were compelled eventually to recognise the power of civic authority, which became stronger than their own hereditary rights and privileges, for it was nourished by trade and commerce, activities that aristocrats despised, for at heart they were brigands, believing that wealth could come only from loot, ransoms and tolls. That it could be created by honest trade was beyond their comprehension. They were still barbarians, and their fortified dwellings, whether in town or countryside, showed it all too plainly. Castles and strongholds

St. John's Gate, Clerkenwell; a fragment of the Priory of St. John of Jerusalem.
The church was destroyed by Wat Tyler's rabble, but was rebuilt, and destroyed in the mid-twentieth century by German bombs. The gateway that
survives, was built at the beginning of the sixteenth century by Prior Docwra;
and this shows its appearance in the late eighteenth century, an isolated
mediaeval relic amid the domestic buildings of the Georgian age. Reproduced
from *Some Account of London*, by Thomas Pennant. Fifth edition, 1813.

betray the poverty of their standards, for amenities were sacrificed
to safety. Blood and treasure were squandered in constructing these
monstrous hide-outs, ill-lit, ill-ventilated, ill-heated, with walls
20 feet thick, girdled by a moat that might be noisome with sewage
or clean and stocked with fish. The moat was crossed by a drawbridge let down over it, with a massive gateway behind, protected
by an iron portcullis that was lowered when the drawbridge was
raised and the gates closed. The gate-house had a barbican, a
strong tower with projecting bartizans, or hanging turrets, and
was a self-contained fort. Behind the moat was the first line of

defence, a curtain wall, guarded by towers, and behind that was the high, thick main wall of the castle, with towers and semi-circular projections called bastions rising at intervals. The space between the curtain and main wall was the outer ward; behind the main wall was the inner ward, with the living quarters and store houses, the great hall, the chapel, and a high central tower, the keep or donjon, strong enough to hold out when every other defence had fallen.

Windows that faced outwards were high up and small, too small for anybody to climb in, or for much light to pass through; so the civilised delight of a room with a view was denied to those who lived in castles or fortified manor houses. The countryside could be seen only by climbing a tower, or walking behind the battlements of the main wall. Only windows that opened on the inner ward were big enough to admit daylight, but as they admitted wind and rain and snow also, they were usually shuttered except in fine weather.

The castles of the early Middle Ages, those of the eleventh, twelfth and thirteenth centuries, point to a life of repressions and emergencies, a life *driven* inwards, *looking* inwards, never outwards, of a self-contained community cut off from the chance of change or the hope of expansion; an isolation that was intermittently relieved by the Crusades, which uprooted many great landlords and their followers. When the survivors returned, they had learnt a thing or two about castle design from Byzantine engineers, for the Crusaders' castles in Palestine were built with the help of technical specialists from the Eastern Empire. After the twelfth century the defensive efficiency of castles in Europe and England greatly increased but their standards of comfort and hygiene were those of a nineteenth century industrial slum. Mediaeval European cities, though greatly inferior to the well-planned, well-drained, sanitary cities of the ancient world, were infinitely superior to the cramped little communities confined by castle walls.

Castles represented the architecture of brute strength, though military needs occasionally gave them some advantages in siting, when they were built on the summit of a hill, as at Halton near Runcorn in Cheshire and Beeston in the same county. Beeston is perched on an isolated rock, 700 feet high. Such airy and healthy positions could be peacefully enjoyed when castles were trans-

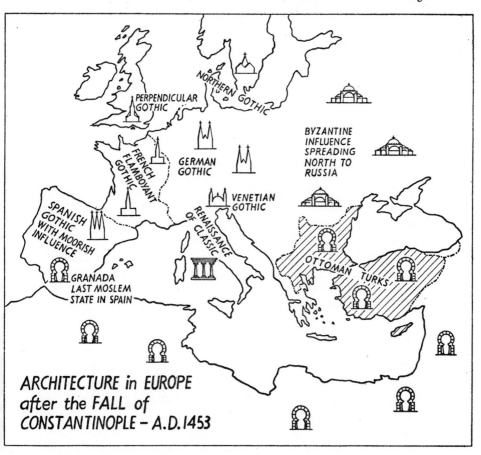

ARCHITECTURE in EUROPE
after the FALL of
CONSTANTINOPLE – A.D. 1453

During the fifteenth century Gothic architecture attained a vigorous maturity; in Western Europe master-masons and craftsmen were working in a living and still creative tradition, as yet undisturbed by the new concept of architectural design that reflected the new concept of culture that had arisen in the first half of the century in Italy, at Florence, Rome and Venice. In Spain, Muslim power was in retreat: in the remains of the old Eastern Roman Empire it had advanced, and Constantinople, the hitherto impregnable city, fell to the Ottoman Turks in A.D. 1453. Compare with the map on page 145. *Drawn by Marcelle Barton.*

formed into country houses, as many were when the need for fortification had passed, though many in England were destroyed
during the Commonwealth when, in the unhappy Civil War of the
mid-seventeenth century they had resumed their former military
character. (Halton and Beeston are ruins, though at Halton an
hotel now occupies part of the castle area.) Other sites chosen for
their natural defensive character were islands in lakes and rivers.
The most famous in Europe are those on the Rhine, that were in-
conveniently cramped by the limited area they occupied, and incapable of expansion, unlike French strongholds when the *château
fort* was converted to the commodious *château de plaisance*, particularly those built along the river Loire. The *château fort* was often a
huge building that resembled a walled town in miniature, with
residential towers and dwelling houses inside the defences, and their
conversion to spacious, well-lit country mansions was delayed until
the fifteenth and sixteenth centuries. In England such changes
came earlier, for by the fourteenth century castles and fortified
manors were out of date in the Midlands and the south; only in the
northern counties adjacent to the Kingdom of Scotland and in the
Welsh marches were walls kept strong and weapons sharp.

The pattern of English mediaeval country life changed, and the
remains of castles such as Stokesay in Shropshire record the social
readjustments that took place, the segregation of classes that ultimately divided the household, an insistent desire for privacy by the
privileged and the withdrawal of the lord and lady, their relatives
and more important dependants, from the rough-and-tumble of
communal living. At Stokesay the great hall was an example of
what is now called open-planning; all the activities of the numerous
household took place there, paternally regarded and even regulated
by the lord: eating, drinking, recreation and, for the lower orders,
sleeping too, so the place was as noisy and smelly and chaotic as
the original Saxon halls of wood and thatch that had replaced the
well-built Roman villa houses centuries earlier. Smaller apartments budded off the great hall; bedrooms, a privy parlour or
solar, on a higher level, with a window opening on to the hall so
the lord could see what went on below. The threat that "Big
Brother is watching you" is as old as serfdom, which, under other
names, still exists in many unhappy states. William Langland
(*circa* 1332–1400) regretted this desertion of the great hall when he

Exterior view of the great hall of Stokesay Castle, Shropshire, *circa* 1240–90. The gate-house, of much later date, is shown below. *Drawn by Maureen Stafford.*

The detached half-timbered gate-house at Stokesay Castle, Shropshire. *Circa* 1600. The need for a fortified entrance had long passed: wood and plaster was used, and the place was a residence for the gate-keepers, not a strong point. *Drawn by Maureen Stafford.*

The Great Hall was the social core of the mediaeval house. This mid-fourteenth century example is at Penshurst Place, Kent. The screens are late sixteenth century and include some modern work. The central hearth had a double-ended fire-dog. Drawn by Maureen Stafford and reproduced from *Guide to Furniture Styles: English and French, 1450–1850.*

wrote: "There the lorde ne the lady liketh noute to sytte."[15] Stokesay Castle was built between A.D. 1240 and 1290, and a far more spacious example of a great hall is at Penshurst Place in Kent, built in the mid-fourteenth century, with a lofty roof and generous windows, though the archaic central hearth was retained. (See opposite page.)

The transformation of the castle and fortified manor from a military machine to a dwelling with some elementary amenities was accompanied by an increase in rural domestic building in England as rich merchants moved out of the cramped towns, bought country estates, and had large, comfortable houses designed for them, unhampered by any need for fortification. By the beginning of the fifteenth century the character of such houses, where window space reduced the area of solid wall, showed that the land was enjoying a settled, orderly peace, that almost recalled the days of the Roman province; almost but not completely. Drains, aqueducts and well-made and well-kept roads were missing. (See page 202.) Disaster overtook Europe and England when the plague, the Black Death of the fourteenth century, killed millions of people, amounting to perhaps a quarter of the total population of the continent. Some parts of England never recovered from it, and the huge, cathedral-like churches of East Anglia that were built originally in populous and prosperous areas have for over five hundred years served only a few villages and hamlets. But European civilisation was resilient; the great plague was far less disastrous than the barbarian incursions that destroyed the Roman Empire in the West, and the Church gave spiritual strength, though not political unity, to the European states. The expanding power of commerce was asserted not only by the splendour of civil buildings, but in the Low Countries, Germany and Italy by the great houses built for the new merchant princes. In England the wealthy merchant was content with a comfortable, spacious and well-appointed home: in many parts of Europe, particularly in Italy, leaders of the business community satisfied their appetite for display by building ornate palaces untouched by vulgarity, for an appreciation of art and architectural design was widely diffused in mediaeval civilisation. Occasionally the new patrons of the arts were tempted to make boastful gestures, but never to the detriment of the community; they built no threatening castles, but now and then they built towers, and in one Italian town, San Gimignano near Florence, as many as seventy residential towers competed for attention, status symbols that gave the place an exuberant vertical diversity. Even to-day, when many of the original towers have gone, the skyline of San Gimignano suggests that of down-town New York when seen from a distance. (Plate 33.)

The Italians had built many bell towers, with an airy grace of form and a delicacy of detail and ornament that may, occasionally, have owed something to oriental influence. The elegance of the Romanesque leaning tower at Pisa with its eight storeys of en-circling arcades is apt to be ignored because in the eyes of most beholders it is an amusing freak; few observe its intrinsic merit or recognise the subtle control of vertical and horizontal elements by architects who had never forgotten the proportions and concinnity of the Roman orders. (Plate 31.) In all their buildings, apart from those with a purely military function, or like the towers of San Gimignano built for pure swank, vertical character was modified by horizontal features, string courses that drew thin dark lines across sunlit façades and arcades and galleries that gave cool depths of shadow, like those on the Doge's Palace at Venice. (Plate 30.) Italian Gothic was not strikingly different from Italian Roman-esque; the spires and lofty vaults of French and English churches are seldom found in Italy, though there are exceptions, such as Milan Cathedral, built between 1385 and 1485, that amalgamated the traditions of Northern Gothic with the invincible orderliness and symmetry inseparable from the work of Italian architects. Sculpture, so intimately linked with the design of French and English cathedrals, seems to have been an afterthought in Italy, unrelated to the general composition, perched on pinnacles (as at Milan) or on the capital of some column. No niches were provided for sculptured figures which then became essential elements of a façade, like those on the west front and towers of Wells Cathedral in Somerset, or, much later, at Rouen.

Italian interpretations of Gothic have the same sprightly vitality that enlivens Italian Romanesque, and indicate the eager response to new ideas, and the acceptance of the challenge of change by the aristocratic or commercial oligarchies that governed the prosperous city states, and by the well-endowed Church. Citizens and church-men shared an alert appreciation of the visual arts, and the citizens and their rulers possessed an equally alert sense of civic responsibility. In Venice the interpretation of Gothic differed from that of every other Italian or European city, just as Venice differed from every other city in the Western world; in that affluent and highly civilised place Oriental, Byzantine, classical and Gothic influences mingled; patronage was generous and enterprising; architects, painters, sculptors and skilled craftsmen knew that in Venice rewards were lavish, encouragement discerning and generous, and the opportunities limitless. In chapter six we said that the rulers and citizens of Venice were as sensitive and perceptive as those of the ancient Greek city states; but Venice was infinitely richer than Athens or Rhodes; while Greek architecture conveys the calm, level tones of reason, the fantastic, gay and luxurious palaces that line the canals prove by the elegance of their design that while the Venetians enjoyed their wealth, they were not corrupted or vulgarised by it; in that cosmopolitan city business seemed more like a festive adventure than an earnest preoccupation. Largest and most commanding of all those splendid buildings is the Doge's Palace, with its arcades, slender columns and lace-like tracery. The Palace was begun in the ninth century, rebuilt several times, and the façades were completed between 1309 and 1424; it towers above St. Mark's, screening the church from the lagoon so that only the crosses on the five domes are visible over the roof. (Plate 30 and pages 128 and 129.)

In France, England, Italy and Spain, Gothic architecture was largely the result of building with stone; but in some countries, like Holland, Belgium and North Germany, the use of brick altered the character of Gothic so far as church design was concerned, though the material stimulated progress in civic and domestic building. In Germany, Gothic began to replace Romanesque architecture after the mid-thirteenth century; but because of the structural limitations of the material, mediaeval German churches never acquired the tense, lithe vitality of French and English churches. Although distinguished by fine towers and spires, they had a static quality; no arches took flight, no soaring vaults or sweeping lines of ascent drew the eye upwards. In some German cathedrals the eye had plenty of occupation, for they were ornamented with an almost barbaric profusion; blank space was not allowed; the technical ability of sculptors and wood carvers betrayed their discretion, and tempted them to over-burden every surface with extravagant decoration. Only the smaller churches escaped such excesses and retained a pleasing and restful simplicity. In Holland a national taste for simplicity and comfort was satisfied by domestic architecture of a warm and inviting character. The extensive use of brickwork, agreeable in texture and of rich red colour, diminished the desire for ornament; the decorative quality of the material was sufficient.

In the Low Countries and Germany and northern Europe, the scale of secular architecture showed the strength of commercial power, one of the most potent of formative influences in the Western world. During the centuries after the fall of the Roman Empire many of the ancient centres of culture and civilisation declined; Rome itself was a name, sacred and revered, not a power. The vitality and enterprise inherent in the European peoples flourished in the north and north-west, far removed from the Mediterranean. Northern trade routes through Russia linked the Baltic with the Black Sea; trading cities in Central Europe grew up along the route that led to Venice where the seaways through the Adriatic and the Aegean began. The retreat from the Mediterranean followed the conquest and occupation of the North African littoral and the invasion of Spain by the Arabs. Thereafter the coastlines of the Eastern Empire, Italy and southern France became the frontier of Christian Europe. The importance of the inland trade routes was enhanced when command of the sea was local and limited, exercised only by such maritime powers as Venice and Genoa; but sea-borne trade flourished in north-west Europe and England, where good ports were numerous, busy, and well defended. By the thirteenth century trading agreements between north German towns led to federation, and ultimately to the formation of the Henseatic League, an international trading organisation with business affiliations extending from Norway and England in the north and west, to Russia and Constantinople in the east, and southwards to Genoa and Venice. (Map on opposite page.)

The number of cities actually in the League varied from time to time, and though many centres in France, Spain, Portugal and England had dealings with the League they were not Hanseatic cities.[16] The League attained its maximum power and prosperity during the fourteenth century; but its power was financial, not

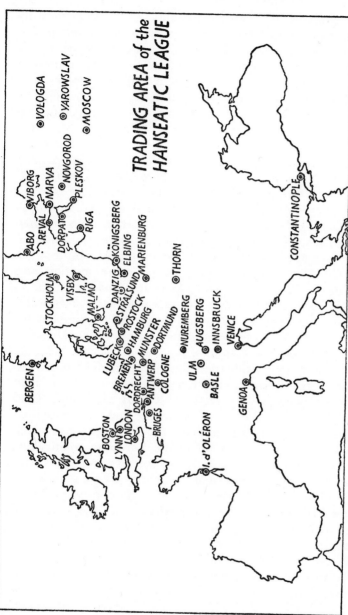

The growing power of commerce in Europe was marked by the extent and influence of the Hanseatic League. Many of the important towns of Germany and the Low Countries belonged to the League at some time during the thirteenth, fourteenth and fifteenth centuries; protected by strong walls those towns created and accumulated wealth, and patronage for architecture became one of the prerogatives of merchants and traders. The business affiliations of the League extended from England to Turkey, from Genoa and Venice to Russia. *Drawn by Marcelle Barton.*

political or military; the Hansa merchants were only incidentally politicians, and avoided any type of permanent federation that could have given them political control of Northern Europe and the Baltic.[17] They were particularly careful not to become embroiled with rulers who could command destructive military power, for in Europe cities that paraded their wealth too ostentatiously or boasted too openly of their civic rights and independence, attracted the malice of their royal or noble overlords, who enjoyed teaching the civilised bourgeois an occasional lesson. Those chivalrous noblemen were ruthless savages, as Charles the Bold, Duke of Burgundy abundantly proved in 1468 when his soldiers sacked the rich industrial city of Liége, and razed it to the ground.

European cities could not take the risk of being undefended, so centuries passed before they dismantled the fortifications that had often restricted their growth and imposed an unhealthy compression on streets and houses; but after the mid-fifteenth century thick walls and faithful garrisons no longer guaranteed exemption from conquest, for the Turks had used artillery to attack cities, and in 1453 had breached the walls of Constantinople: strong walls, like plate armour, could never again be regarded as impregnable. Thereafter no city could feel completely secure, no nobleman or knight armed *cap-à-pie* be certain of superior protection. With the use of gunpowder as a missile propellant, attack gained the ascendency over defence: even the great castles that crouched like sullen and menacing monsters all over Europe were vulnerable. Civil wars, foreign invasions, lean years of famine and the devastation of some great pestilence like the Black Death, maintained a high standard of misery in large areas of the European countryside. Villages and hamlets were expendable: cottages and small farm houses, built of impermanent materials, were looted and burnt, though their inhabitants, if they were warned in time, were able to seek shelter in the castles of their overlords who recognised the obligation to protect their dependants. Churches and monastic establishments while not wholly immune were moderately safe, though to mercenary troops nothing was sacred.

England was far more fortunate: the development of domestic architecture, and the growth of unwalled towns, like Chipping Campden in Gloucestershire, and the casual habit of city fathers who allowed their walls to disintegrate and even pulled down sections

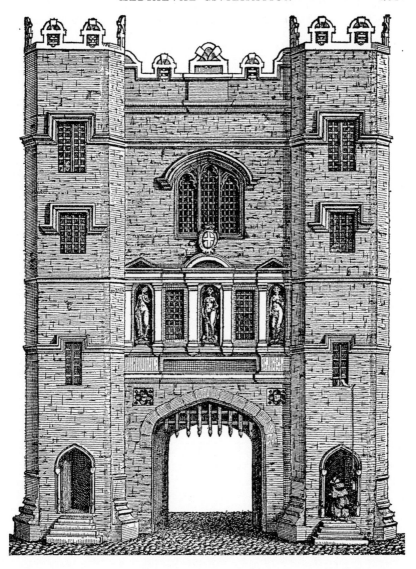

The mediaeval gates of many cities survived long after the walls had decayed, and some became partly residential. Newgate as it appeared in the late eighteenth century was included in J. T. Smith's *Antiquities of London*, and is reproduced from that work on a smaller scale. (See also page 189.)

The house of Sir William Grevel in the main street of Chipping Campden, Gloucestershire, built in the late fifteenth century of Cotswold stone, with a bay window ascending through two storeys. *Drawn by Maureen Stafford.*

of them in the interests of commercial and residential development, showed how rich and varied were the freedoms enjoyed by the English people. By the fifteenth century the country was comparatively immune from the destructive consequences of civil war. Philippe de Commines (*circa* 1445–1511), the French historian, observed that "there are no buildings destroyed or demolished by war, and there the mischief of it falls on those who make the war." He added: "This England is among the world's lordships of which I have knowledge, that where public weal is best ordered, and where least violence reigns over the people. . . ."[18] The bland, comfortable native English style of domestic architecture confirms the words of that contemporary historian. Whether of stone, like Sir William Grevel's house in Chipping Campden (above), or warm red brick, like Compton Wynyates, in Warwickshire (page

205), built for the London merchant Sir William Compton, such houses were first and foremost, homes. So were early Tudor palaces like Hampton Court, the Bishop's Palace at Croydon in Surrey, and Fulham Palace, London. In church architecture, the ruling temper of mature English Gothic was, according to Lethaby, "a spirit of sweetness which contrasts with the soaring grandeur of the French cathedrals."[19] Architecture emphasised the basic differences between French and English taste: the down-to-earth common sense that informs late mediaeval domestic buildings in England reflects the unpretentiousness and stolidity of the national character; in France the love of magnificence and sumptuous decoration was expressed by the scale and splendour of royal palaces and those of the French nobility.

The last phase of Gothic architecture coincided with the decay and loss of what Flinders Petrie described as the true style of the eighth period of civilisation.[20] The mediaeval world was changing; even the great cathedrals and churches built during that final period showed how churchmen and architects had surrendered to a growing appetite for ornament. This was especially marked in Spain, where the impact of Saracenic art had been greater than anywhere else in Europe. The dazzling richness of Spanish Gothic ornament, with its multiplicity of saintly figures, delicate tracery, sprouting pinnacles burred with crockets, outshines in decorative brilliancy the Moorish examples from which so much was learnt. Seville Cathedral, the largest mediaeval cathedral in Europe, was built between A.D. 1401 and 1520, and there the juxtaposition of the Moorish Giralda with its vertical panels of restrained geometrical decoration, still surviving on the lower part of the tower, and the intricacy and dynamic, sparkling ornamental fabric of the Gothic west front show how two greatly differing cultures could become mutually stimulating. (Plate 29.) Spanish churches built between the eleventh and sixteenth centuries could never be mistaken for oriental buildings; Moorish influence might occasionally bring a warm, exotic quality to some of the ornament, possibly because Moorish craftsmen were employed now and then on Christian structures; they may have been responsible for introducing pierced stone tracery, geometrical patterns, and far more gaiety than, left to themselves, the rather sombre Spaniards would have permitted in a sacred building.

In France the tracery that adorned the upper part of church windows in the last period of Gothic had a sinuous intricacy that justified the name *Flamboyant*: civic buildings and town houses were enriched with crisply carved ornament, like the tower of the Hôtel de Ville at Bourges; and the men who carved stone and wood and decorated walls and ceilings with paintings were fluent in a symbolic language that began, early in the Middle Ages, as a military recognition device, and developed into a gloriously fanciful visual code that has been called "The Shorthand of History."[21] This code in time became a comprehensive system of communication known as the Science of Heraldry: it was invented when the use of armour made some type of identification essential in order to distinguish friend from foe in the mixed-up free-for-all battles of the twelfth and thirteenth centuries, and it originally took the form of easily recognised marks, bold, simple and unmistakable, painted on shields, and later elaborated as crests surmounting helmets.

By the fourteenth and fifteenth centuries, the signs, symbols and colours of heraldry were understood throughout Christian Europe, and were related not only to the members and branches of royal and noble families but to civic authorities, companies of merchants, craft guilds and trade associations. Men to whom the alphabet was a meaningless mystery were familiar with the graphic vocabulary that was built up by the various hues known as tinctures and the shapes of the lines which separated them when more than one appeared on a shield, and with the various symbols that included a zoo of fabulous creatures, far exceeding in anatomical diversity anything in the mythology of the ancient world, and when used in conjunction with inanimate objects, such as buildings or parts of buildings, they occasionally resembled the visions (or hallucinations) that had troubled the early Christian anchorites in their desert solitudes. Birds, beasts, reptiles and fishes, complete or detached bits of them—heads, limbs or wings—jostled such chimerical monsters as the dragon, cockatrice and wivern. Flowers, trees, wreaths, crowns, turbans, turrets, castles, battlements, bridges, gates, chains, ropes—looped and knotted—ships and keys; or armour: helmets, breastplates, gauntlets, and shields. In their various combinations, such symbols could disclose reliable (and frank) information about families entitled to bear arms, and about merchants, guilds, companies or cities that had been granted them.

Domestic architecture in England matured during the second half of the fifteenth century; half-timbered buildings with brick infilling between the oak beams and comfortable associations of brick and stone suggested one of the virtues of the national character: moderation in all things. Ostentation was rejected, whether in a royal or episcopal palace or the country house of a rich London merchant, like Compton Wynyates, completed in 1520 for Sir William Compton. There is a family likeness between that spacious Warwickshire country seat and the remains of Richmond Palace and the Tudor parts of Hampton Court. (See page 221.) All three were built during the first quarter of the sixteenth century. Reproduced from Parker's *Domestic Architecture in England* (Oxford: 1859).

Heraldic devices emblazoned tradesmen's signs in city streets, glowed in the coloured glass windows of churches and private chapels, civic buildings and private dwellings, and on carved and painted woodwork. The names of inns, particularly in England, owe as much to heraldry as they do to hunting and victorious soldiers and sailors.

The last period of English Gothic, the Perpendicular, also known as Rectilinear, was by far the most decorative, though ornament was never unduly extravagant. The mathematical precision of fan vaulting, like that in the nave of Bath Abbey, King's College Chapel, Cambridge, or Henry VII's Chapel at Westminster Abbey (opposite), and the use of blind tracery on walls and woodwork gave richness of texture that was never indigestibly rich: the English, churchmen and laymen alike, were satisfied by the appearance of moderate opulence. Perpendicular Gothic, like the native English style in domestic architecture, continued throughout the sixteenth century, and beyond, into the reign of Charles I and the Commonwealth; in some country districts it survived much later. England was the last country in Europe to acknowledge the architectural inspiration of a new age; perhaps because the vitality of national forms of workmanship was unimpaired. Perhaps reluctance to change to a new style was yet another assertion of the stubborn conservative quality in the English character, a declaration of isolated self-sufficiency, for though England and Europe were bound together by ties of trade, after the wasteful and inconclusive wars with France, England had cut her losses and deliberately detached herself from the Continent. English architecture of the late fifteenth and early sixteenth centuries and English resistance to the "Italianate" fashions that accompanied the new phase of European civilisation show the strength of national independence.

Henry VII's Chapel, Westminster (1502–1515). perhaps the finest example of
the last phase of English Gothic, the Perpendicular. *Drawn by A. S. Cook.*

RENAISSANCE AND REVOLUTION

ARLY in the fifteenth century the art and literature of the
Graeco–Roman world were revived in Italy, and at Florence,
Rome and Venice, some men of exceptional genius were able
by the example of their work to change the whole character
of European architecture for over four hundred years. This revival
was more potent and far-reaching than any intellectual fashion or
antiquarian exercise; it began as a natural and a national expression of the Italian sense of continuity with the Roman past; as a
national movement it meant infinitely more than a sifting and
picking over of antique patterns and ideas; it was a reawakening
of ways of thought and approaches to life and art, long dormant
but never extinct. The very foundations of the Age of Faith
trembled; the Church became alarmed, and with good reason, for
the old gods began to whisper the most heretical suggestions to
intellectual members of the Italian nobility. Pagan mysteries were
disinterred by scholars; painters glorified the exploits and lubri-
cious eccentricities of ancient divinities.[1] The age of Humanism
ennobled by the resurrection of Vitruvian rules for architectural
composition, had dawned.

This restoration of the visual felicities of the ancient world was
at first confined to Italy; elsewhere in Europe it was regarded not
as a fundamental change in the approach to architectural composition, but as an "Italianate" fashion, flavoured with long-
forgotten learning and beset by arbitrary rules for the proportions
of horizontal and vertical elements. The initial attempts to amal-
gamate the precepts of Vitruvius with the living Gothic tradition
of building were obstructed. Even in France, where the ruling
class welcomed and encouraged new fashions, mediaeval forms in
the building arts were cherished and stubbornly followed by men
with tenacious loyalties to old ways. What was good enough for

my father is good enough for me, they said, or, if they practised a craft: what my master taught is the right and only way. Such sentiments did not necessarily exclude or condemn all interest in novelty. Chaucer had written: "Men loven of propre kinde new-fangelnesse."[2] But the novelty of a transitory mode was very different from the comprehensive change in visual values demanded when the Roman Empire, in terms of architectural design, marched back into Europe.

The Renaissance which came in the eighth period of Mediterranean culture, coincided with the decline of mediaeval civilisation, the loss of spiritual unity in Europe and the ideal of united Christendom. Flinders Petrie asserted that the Renaissance was merely a resort to copying the earlier seventh period, because the mediaeval age of art had decayed and the true style had been lost.[3] But the Renaissance cannot be dismissed as mere copyism because the system of design represented by the classic orders of architecture had been reintroduced. That system was revitalised. In the interval between the collapse of the western Roman Empire and the rise, maturity and decline of mediaeval civilisation, advances in technology had expanded the powers of builders; all the structural knowledge gained by the daring experiments that had created Gothic architecture was now available and gave Renaissance architects a super-Roman ability for using the classic orders. They saw far beyond the convenient regulation of proportions and began to explore spatial possibilities that had eluded their Roman predecessors. They glorified the dome, and the result was such structures as Bramante's Tempietto of San Pietro in Montorio in Rome (1502–10), and Santa Maria della Consolazione (1508–1604), at Todi, designed by Cola da Caprarola. (Page 211.) The dome of the Roman Pantheon had no external significance, nor did the shallow domes of many Byzantine churches, even when they were mounted on drums. (Pages 132 and 133.) The greatest of all Byzantine achievements, Santa Sophia in Constantinople, is from the outside an undistinguished mass; squat, dull and featureless, conspicuously improved by the vertical punctuation of four minarets added by the Turks after they transformed the church into a mosque.

Not only in Italy, but presently in France and Spain and Germany, Renaissance architects rescued the dome from its old dull function as a mere lid, and allowed it to swell up as a curved continuation of a cylindrical or octagonal tower, establishing a new curvilinear triumph of design. High domes were topped by lanterns with a gleaming gilded cross above, and those nobly swelling forms gave fresh emphasis to the forest of mediaeval church spires. The skyline of every European city began to change. In Russia the Byzantine dome was reshaped to resemble an oriental cupola; and, mounted on tall drums, like the Cathedral of the Assumption in the Kremlin at Moscow, or carried aloft to crown bell towers, those slightly bulbous shapes were a constant reminder that Russia was the most westerly of eastern nations. (Pages 212 and 213.)

Although architects and patrons now looked back to ancient Rome, there was no loss of vitality or inspiration because of that backward glance; far from it, for in every European country architectural design was regenerated, and the only loss sustained was the diminishing of oriental influence. England was the last country to use the classic system with creative originality. In Italy alone, during the fifteenth century, was that system thoroughly understood; in France it was accepted in a tentative way, and everywhere the acceptance of ancient Roman rules established dual standards of taste, and began to separate popular art from fashionable or exclusive art. This brought into the open the undying conflict between office and workshop. The classically correct compositions architects worked out on their drawing boards had to be interpreted, and more often misinterpreted, by building craftsmen who cherished their own individual ideas and were stubbornly devoted to traditional methods and forms of ornament. The men who worked on the scaffolding were as conservative as the ancient Egyptian priests who had once controlled and petrified architectural design.

Gothic had been a dynamic growth, adventurous and experimental and by no means exhausted or bereft of animation in the fifteenth century, but the reintroduction of the classic orders gave fresh direction to all imaginative effort, and sometimes extinguished it, leaving in its place obstructive resentment. This showed in many buildings of the late fifteenth and early sixteenth centuries, not only by their proportions, but by the admixture of classic detail and Gothic features. One of the most famous of the Loire châteaux, that of Chambord, illustrates the incompatability of the

Santa Maria della Consolazione, Todi, 1508–1604, designed by Cola da Caprarola; an early Renaissance building on a Byzantine plan with an impressive central dome on a high drum, pierced by windows, and rising to a height of 180 feet. Corinthian pilasters are superimposed on the exterior. *Drawn by Maureen Stafford.*

The Cathedral of the Assumption, in the Kremlin, Moscow, built in 1479. Unlike the cluster of domes on St. Mark, Venice, these Russian domes derive their bulbous shapes from Tartar sources: they are far more oriental in character than the Byzantine buildings of Venice or Constantinople (See pages 128 and 133.) *Drawn by Hulme Chadwick, and reproduced by permission of the artist.*

two cultures. It was built in A.D. 1520, a large, semi-fortified symmetrical structure with thick round towers, a clear architectural statement of the transition from the Middle Ages to the Renaissance. The Château displays a strenuous skyline; Gothic features and Renaissance detail are in virile competition, yet the whole building has an air of placid stability. (Plate 39.)

The texture and finish of wall surfaces and the enlargement and increased significance of windows changed the character of

The bell tower in the Kremlin, Moscow, built in 1600 by Boris Godunov, which rises to a height of 271 feet (318 feet to the top of the cross). Byzantine and Lombardic influences are apparent, also the far-distant influence of the classic pharos. *Drawn by Hulme Chadwick, and reproduced by permission of the artist.*

When fortification was no longer an imperative need, windows began to dissolve solid walls in isolated country houses, and the whole character of such domestic architecture in the countryside reflected immunity from external attacks, an immunity unknown in central and southern Britain since the days of the Roman province. This shows part of the interior of the Hall at Ockwells Manor, Bray, Berkshire, a half-timbered house built about 1465. Drawn by Maureen Stafford and reproduced from *Guide to Furniture Styles: English and French, 1450–1850.*

domestic architecture drastically. In palaces and houses windows were no longer mean apertures for admitting daylight; they resumed a partnership with the outer world, something well known in the Graeco–Roman civilisation but forgotten during the dark centuries of fear and fortification. Windows now threw rooms open to gardens, parks and distant views, and in towns to the flowing colour and life of streets. The rediscovery that windows had a two-way function, to admit light to a room and to give visual pleasure, indicated that Europeans were acquiring a healthier and more reasonable idea of the art of living. Windows had grown in size during the fourteenth and fifteenth centuries, not only in great churches and civic buildings but in town and country houses, and the making of glass had improved so that by the end of the sixteenth century, what were virtually transparent walls ascended in great bays from ground level to roof, rising through three or four storeys. An early example of a window ascending through two storeys, is in the house of Sir William Grevel at Chipping Campden in Gloucestershire. (Page 202.) There were also horizontal extensions of glazed areas and in some of the large half-timbered English country houses of the late fifteenth century windows formed a transparent frieze above the interior panelling of halls and large living rooms, as at Ockwells Manor in Berkshire, built about 1465 and restored during the nineteenth century. (Page opposite.)

Such devices as a frieze window disturbed the external symmetry of an elevation; but the men who developed and perfected the native English domestic style could and did achieve balance and harmony without depending on symmetrical arrangement, as exemplified by such buildings as the George Inn at Glastonbury (page 216), erected by Abbot John Selwood about 1480 as a hostelry for pilgrims to the Abbey. Those pre-eminently practical builders were guided by a typically English principle long before it was put into words by Francis Bacon, who said: "Houses are built to live in and not to look on; therefore let use be preferred before uniformity, except where both may be had."[4] Every building craftsman would have agreed with that, especially those who worked and continued to work in the Gothic tradition, quietly resisting the intrusive fashions of the Renaissance and the increasing professionalism of the architects who imposed them in order to gratify the "Italianate" taste of their well-travelled patrons. The resentment of the traditionalists showed in their misinterpretation of classic ornament and maltreatment of the Roman orders.

The contrast between the extant tradition of native Gothic and the imported classic style is vividly illustrated by two examples, less than a century apart: the entrance to the court at Compton Wynyates, page 218, and the doorway at York Manor, page 219. The latter shows not only the English carver's capacity for misinterpretation, but the malign influence of the drawing board

The George Inn at Glastonbury, Somerset, built about 1480 by Abbot John Selwood as a hostelry for pilgrims to the Abbey. Reproduced from a drawing by William Twopeny in Parker's *Domestic Architecture in England* (Oxford: 1859.)

extended by the printing press, for Flemish and German engravers invented fantastic versions of the classic orders and classic ornament, mixing the latter with scrolls, diamond-shaped protruberances and strapwork; a witches' brew of grotesque and sometimes sinister motifs ladled out in hundreds of workshops. That such mixtures were acceptable at all showed how civilisation in England had changed drastically: it had changed elsewhere, for in every European country fashion was climbing into the saddle. In that distraught period of transition, architectural design recorded the incertitudes and divided loyalties that troubled patrons, architects and executant craftsmen. The work of some English architects showed that use and uniformity could both be had, as in mansions like Montacute in Somerset (1580–1599) and Hardwick Hall in Derbyshire (1590–1597); designs that stood midway between full comprehension and use of the classic idiom and the late Gothic of Henry VII's Palace at Richmond, Wolsey's great house at Hampton, and Compton Wynyates. (Plates 38 and 40: pages 221, 218, and 205.)

Where windows were arranged in a formal pattern, the daylight reflected from the glass panes gave glittering animation to a façade. Fenestration became an integral part of architectural design and a benign influence, unknown in the ancient world, though anticipated by mediaeval builders who had progressively enlarged window space in churches and civic structures. Windows in such houses as the Château de Chambord regulated the composition by unifying horizontal lines, so conflict between Gothic survivals and Renaissance innovations while still apparent was partially resolved; in English houses like Hardwick windows dominated to such an extent that they justified the popular jingle: "Hardwick Hall, more glass than wall." (Below.)

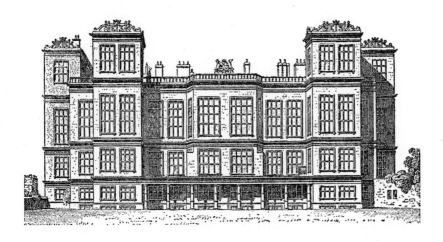

The east wing of Hardwick Hall, Derbyshire, built 1590–1597. Like Montacute House (Plate 40) this is an example of the new native style of domestic architecture that developed during the latter part of the sixteenth century, with generous windows that brought rooms and galleries into visual partnership with the surrounding gardens and parkland. From Lyson's *Magna Britannia*, Volume V, Derbyshire. (London: 1817.)

Entrance to the court at Compton Wynyates, Warwickshire, the country house built in the reign of Henry VIII for Sir William Compton. This example of an established and flourishing native style of domestic architecture was unaffected by the Renaissance; "Italianate" influence had not yet invaded England; how disastrously it was to confuse English craftsmen and designers is suggested by the doorway shown opposite, though to be sure the German and Flemish engravers who illustrated copy books were responsible for much of the mischief. (See also illustration on page 205.) *Drawn by Maureen Stafford.*

Entrance to the Manor, York. A Jacobean nightmare of misrepresentation, with
the grossest liberties taken in the use of classic ornament. Compare this muddle,
with the controlled opulence of the baroque composition at the Villa d'Este,
Tivoli, on Plate 43. Compare it also with the bold, confident simplicity of the
early Tudor doorway shown opposite. *Drawn by Maureen Stafford.*

European architecture in the fifteenth and sixteenth centuries illustrates the profound changes that were taking place in the spiritual climate of civilisation. The artistic and intellectual achievements of Italy were emulated in other countries; gradually the scientific attitude became established. Experiment was more exciting than the authority of precedent. The day of the mediaeval schoolmen had passed. All this social and spiritual ferment was reflected in the design and ornamentation of buildings and the changing shape of cities. The urgent restlessness of scientific enquiry encouraged advances in applied science of which the most rapid was in the field of engineering. Hitherto architect and engineer had been one and the same person: early in the seventeenth century they separated: an age of specialisation was foreshadowed.

The architect, fundamentally an artist and secondarily an organiser, was recognised as the master designer; the controller and collator of all work connected with building, from the initial planning down to the smallest ornamental details within and without; he was himself controlled by the rules set forth by Vitruvius, and unless he enjoyed a powerful and rebellious imagination could be as constrained as imperial Roman architects before him. After the first creative raptures of the Renaissance, the architect became very much a professional man with all the attendant limitations, sometimes supporting a superstructure of professional dignity that diminished the man and injured the artist. Architects all over Europe began to accept new and extensive responsibilities, and one conspicuous result of their attentions was the restoration of an ancient orderliness to many cities.

The streets of mediaeval cities exhibited an aggressive individualism: the Gothic façades of the houses were splendidly ornamental, each site treated as a separate unit, the ascending storeys projecting slightly, elbowing each other companionably, varied in colour and decoration, or comparatively plain like the street in York on Plate 36; but individually and collectively asserting the irrepressible vitality of a society that rejoiced in diversity. Renaissance architects rediscovered the architectural significance of the street. The processional ways of ancient cities had been adorned with temples and public buildings standing on isolated sites; those of mediaeval cities had wound towards a central space where a cathedral or a large abbey church dominated by height and

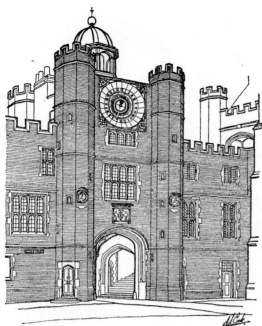

The native English style of the early sixteenth century before the intrusion of Italianate fashions. It was a homely, domestic style, with a straightforward use of red brick and stone. *Left:* The Clock Tower in the Clock Court (1515–1530), sometimes called the Stone Court: the chief inner part of Cardinal Wolsey's palace at Hampton.

The gate-house of Richmond Palace, facing Richmond Green; all that remains of a building that once covered nearly ten acres of ground. Built for Henry VII, and completed in 1501. (See Plate 38.) *Both drawings by A. S. Cook.*

Timber-framed house in Butcher Row, Shrewsbury. Late fifteenth century.
Such houses were stout cages of wood, with infilling of plaster or brick between
the vertical and horizontal members: sometimes the entire front was plastered,
like the houses in the street in York on Plate 36. Even so, they were highly inflammable, and uncontrollable fires often swept away whole streets of mediaeval
cities. From Parker's *Domestic Architecure in England*.

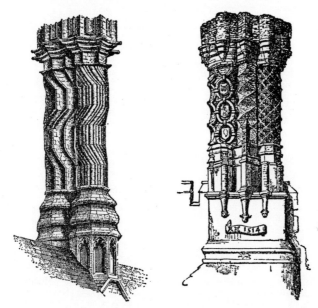

Moulded brick chimney-shafts were characteristic of the native English style of the earlier part of the sixteenth century; flamboyantly ornamental and patterned with geometric devices invented by craftsmen who were as yet independent of Renaissance models, they rose as proudly as towers, and roused the admiration and astonishment of men who had grown old during the Tudor reigns, and, in William Harrison's words, regarded them as chief of "things to be marvellouslie altered in England within their sound remembrance. . . ." (*Description of England*, see page 235.) *Right:* Droitwich. Worcestershire. *Left:* Thornbury Castle, Gloucestershire. From Parker's *Glossary* and *Domestic Architecture in England*.

magnificence every other structure; but now long straight streets composed of related units replaced the old, haphazard pattern. This changed the look of some cities, but by depriving them of their intimate neighbourliness left a social gap of which we are still conscious, and which town-planners in the second half of the twentieth century have attempted to remedy by creating artificial "neighbourhood units", as though the rich human growth of centuries could be brought to life on paper. In many cities mediaeval individualism was never abandoned. London lost most of its Roman street plan after it ceased to be Londinium Augusta in the fifth century and became just another squalid barbarian town; but

The Villa Capra, Vincenza, also known as the Rotonda, designed by Andrea Palladio (1518–1580), with a portico in the Ionic order on each of the four faces. The design and the classic features were adapted by Lord Burlington for his ornamental villa at Chiswick, Middlesex, built in 1725. (See page 260.) *Drawn by Maureen Stafford.*

the mediaeval city was established in general lay-out before the Norman Conquest, and it is still there; not buried twenty to twenty-five feet below ground like its Roman forerunner, but alive and confusing with its twisted maze of streets which survived the fire of 1666 and the air raids of 1940.

Opportunities for replanning were often created by disasters; and one of the greatest in the long history of Rome occurred in 1525 during the Italian wars of the Emperor Charles V, when the city was sacked by twelve thousand Lutheran *Landsknechts* who, united with the imperial forces commanded by the Constable of Bourbon, indulged their lust and religious zeal during eight days of hideous violence that left two-thirds of Rome in ruins.[5] Thereafter the city was a patchwork of splendid reconstruction interspersed with areas of dismal wreckage. (Plate 42.) The ruins remained and during the eighteenth century became familiar to men of taste through the work of Giovanni Battista Piranesi, an Italian engraver who not only depicted ancient architectural fragments, but supplied missing parts and with the informed imagination of an antiquary reconstructed the original design.

In Italy the revival of classic architecture was unhampered by any conflict with a robust mediaeval tradition; Italian architects of the fifteenth century worked with a sense of continuity; after a long interlude of semi-darkness, ancient lights were rekindled, brightening creative imagination which advanced to new triumphs. The charge that the Renaissance was no more than a rehash of Roman architecture is refuted by such works as St. Peter's at Rome, where the Cathedral, Piazza and Vatican form a noble and imposing group, and the classic orders are used with a pliant grace hitherto unknown. St. Peter's, built between 1506 and 1626, was the work of many architects, and the entrance piazza, designed by Bernini was built between 1655 and 1667. Throughout the fifteenth and sixteenth centuries, Italian architects satisfied the taste of a radiant and cultivated society. Of these, Andrea Palladio had the most potent and prolonged influence. Born in 1518 he lived until 1580, and his principal work was done at his own home town of Vincenza, where he designed many buildings, among them the Villa Capra, known also as the Rotonda; a square structure with an Ionic portico on each face, and a shallow dome above a circular central hall. (See opposite.) His design for the Teatro Olimpico at Vincenza, that was completed by Vincenzo Scamozzi (1552–1616), inspired the English architect Inigo Jones to transform the character of the theatre. The stage ceased to be a central feature, an arena or an elevated platform surrounded by the audience; it became a moving picture with a curtained frame, a proscenium that separated the audience from the players and concealed the mechanics of scene-shifting.

Italian architects continued to refresh the classic system with bold and exciting innovations. The Italian spirit, as Professor Huizinga has remarked, "could expand freely and naturally in the restored forms of classic expression."[6] "Italianate" implied far more than a label for modish design, for controlled splendour in building and decoration, for polished manners and fastidious attention to the luxurious trifles that contributed to the art of graceful living; it stood for heightened sensibility, an alert regard for visual excellence in every necessary and unnecessary thing; and as a term it aroused both admiration and contempt. In the bleak moral and

Native English Gothic, late fifteenth century, and "Italianate" fashion. *Left*: Doorway at Place House, Cornwall. *Right*: North entrance, Wollaton Hall, Northamptonshire, the house designed by Robert Smythson, 1580–88. Reproduced on a slightly smaller scale from Ralph N. Wornum's *Analysis of Ornament*.

physical climate of north-western Europe, and, to a lesser extent in England, "Italianate" ideas were suspect, especially in the first half of the sixteenth century. Meanwhile Italian architects and their noble patrons revelled happily in the bright garden of their fancies; taking liberties with the classic system of design, bringing sculpture and ornament into fresh relationships with architectural composition, liberating imagination while elsewhere in Europe the classic orders were restricting it, or, when architects and builders were seduced by the work of German and Flemish draftsmen, distorting it: from Italy alone came the dynamic power that established the next phase of the Renaissance: the baroque.

Italian leadership in the arts during the fifteenth, sixteenth and seventeenth centuries was comparable with that of Greece in the

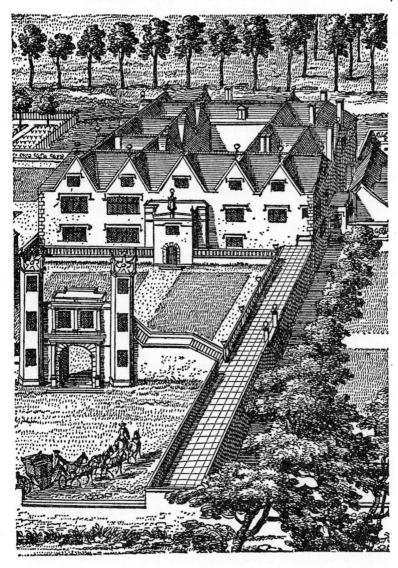

A sixteenth century house that follows the traditional English style perfected in
the previous century. The Renaissance is cursorily acknowledged by the classic
features on the façade of the gate-house. This view of Shipton Moyne was engraved by Kip in the late seventeenth century. Only part of the engraving is
reproduced.

ancient world: in architecture the Romans never cast off Greek leading strings, and until the genius of French taste was splendidly asserted in the second half of the seventeenth century, all Europe had looked to Italy for artistic inspiration and guidance. In the baroque phase of Renaissance architecture ornamental riches were lavished upon buildings; new possibilities of decoration in depth were explored; highlights and shadows were adventurously manipulated; the treasury of classical themes expertly raided and ancient motifs reinterpreted and invigorated. Such compositions as the fountains of the Villa d'Este at Tivoli illustrate the masterly control exercised by Italian architects as well as displaying the fantastic scope of their imagination; sculpture was restored to joyous association with design; and classic proportions maintained a serene unity. The façade of the Fountain of the Hydraulic Organ, by Pirro Ligorio with a central feature by Bernini, shown on Plate 43, is the product of a civilisation that has achieved far more than the revival and revision of Roman architecture. Liberties have been taken with classic ornament and motifs, but they are not gross liberties, like those that disfigure the doorway at York Manor on page 219. The Villa d'Este, begun in 1550, was sited on a steep slope with many terraces and innumerable fountains; originally designed for Cardinal Ippolito d'Este, it represents the work of a team of architects, working over a long period, and is perhaps the finest example of a Renaissance garden in Italy; an example, too, of the establishment and recognition of the relationship of architectural and garden design, a relationship presently extended to an entire landscape.

The buildings and civic projects of sixteenth century Europe show that the Italian states were far in advance of the rest of western civilisation; but in England the vicissitudes of architectural design at that time and the neglect (not the decay) of native Gothic, relate a story of economic and social revolution, when a new rich class rose like scum to the surface of life, old arts and skills were driven underground, and the plundered ruins of great mediaeval religious buildings stood open to the sky in every county. New ideas had to fight for their right to exist at all in England; they could be introduced and favoured by royal autocrats and wealthy noblemen, but were not generally acceptable and were often resisted, for the English were quite satisfied with their national

The Talbot Inn, in the Borough, as it appeared in the early nineteenth century.
Reproduced from an engraving of the drawing by Thomas H. Shepherd.

arts, customs and ideas, looked down rather pityingly on all
foreigners, and as Andrea Trevisano the Venetian ambassador to
the court of Henry VII in 1497 noted, "were great lovers of themselves and everything belonging to them; they think that there are
no other men than themselves, and no other world but England. . . ."[7] Early Tudor England was a thicket of prejudices;
classicism made little progress, and would have been effectually
barred had it not been for that glowing young enthusiast for the
new learning and the revived antique arts and architecture who
succeeded to the throne in 1509 as Henry VIII. A few brilliant
Italian craftsmen had been commissioned for special work like the
monument to Henry VII and Elizabeth of York in Westminster
Abbey, and for isolated additions and embellishments to existing
buildings; royal and noble patronage had coaxed artists like
Torrigiano from Florence; others followed. But what they did
failed to establish the new classicism, and this false dawn of the

The Guild Houses in the Grande Place at Brussels are shown above and opposite. These buildings proclaim not only the prosperity of the fraternities of craftsmen that erected them, but their civic pride and appreciation of archi- tectural design.

The Guild Houses were built in the last decade of the seventeenth century; but
the Butchers is later, 1720, and the Brewers, 1752. They represent a luxuriant
amalgam of mediaeval Gothic, contained by the formal framework of classic
design. *Drawn by Maureen Stafford.* (See opposite.)

English Renaissance faded after Italian Catholic artists became unwelcome and a religious revolution changed the character of the country.

That revolution which culminated in the Dissolution of the Monasteries (1536–39) not only ended church building but destroyed the livelihood of master-masons and other skilled craftsmen. In a few rare cases work in progress on some church was slowly completed, like Bath Abbey Church, a fine example of late Perpendicular Gothic, begun in 1499 and finished in 1616. The suppression of the Chantries, Guilds and Collegiate foundations in 1546 and 1547 not only led to the demolition of many buildings, but a widespread redistribution of property so that the religious revolution was accompanied by an economic upheaval which provided the new mercantile aristocracy with abundant opportunities for profitable speculation. A royal grant or sale of church lands was often followed by speculative resale. Miss Jane Wight, in her summary of the architectural consequences, has noted that this process was so complete and "so identified with it was the governing class that Mary Tudor and Cardinal Reginald Pole, who reversed all the doctrinal changes, could not touch this property revolution. They had to let all the new owners—including the members of the Privy Council itself—enjoy their gains 'without scruple of conscience' even."[8]

The new aristocrats, enriched by the acquisition of church lands and their speculations in real estate, began to build large houses, and to some extent this relieved unemployment among master-masons and other craftsmen. Such patrons, desiring to be modish and therefore "Italianate", were satisfied with almost any version of classical character. The men who built for them lacked informed guidance; they often relied on the crudities depicted in the plates of those disastrous Flemish and German copy books. Meanwhile craftsmen from Flanders and Germany, good reliable Protestants with impeccable religious beliefs but doubtful taste, were welcomed in England after the Catholic Italians had been expelled or had left of their own accord. The consequent changes in architectural character and decoration correspond with what Mr. James Lees-Milne has called the metamorphosis of Henry VIII, for the insularity of the English in the early part of his reign had obstructed the establishment of Italian classicism "before the

Dr. Jekyll of the king turned to Mr. Hyde."[9] The study of domestic architecture in the first half of the sixteenth century has tempted some writers to take sides and become partisans for the native early Tudor style or champions of the nascent classicism that was deferred by national obstinacy and religious intolerance. Fidelity to the late Gothic native style indicated the deep satisfaction it gave to the home-loving English people. Loyalty to that style became embedded in the national consciousness and, like a dim folk-memory, periodically re-emerged. In some regions, notably the West Country and East Anglia, it never died out, for as late as the first quarter of the present century local builders were still using early Tudor arches and mouldings for fireplaces and doorways, unconsciously working in the manner of their forefathers, for at that time many long-established family businesses flourished. Such authentic survivals of the native style were different in quality and kind from the sorry profusion of Tudor parodies erected during the last hundred years by speculative builders and popularised by estate agents. Miles of suburban streets in southern England are lined with houses that are superficially linked with the substantial timber-framed houses built in the reigns of Henry VII and Henry VIII. Their false half-timbering, leaded casement windows and gables with flimsy barge-boards are as remote from the sturdy reality of the early Tudor house as an electric heater with imitation logs of moulded and coloured glass that flicker mechanically is remote from the crackle and scented warmth of a blazing wood fire.

In the mid-sixteenth century the inappropriate use of classic details may occasionally have indicated tactful avoidance of a religious quandary. Such adaptable clerics as the legendary Vicar of Bray in Berkshire, who between 1520 and 1560 was twice a Papist and twice a Protestant, certainly demonstrated the easy-going English gift for compromise. Some architectural evidence of conflict appears at the small parish church of St. Leonard at Sunningwell, also in Berkshire. Cultural and perhaps theological pliability is suggested by a sexagonal porch, reputedly added to the church in 1552, by John Jewel who was made vicar of Sunningwell in that year, and ultimately became Bishop of Salisbury and trusted advisor to Queen Elizabeth I. (This porch with its association of traditional Gothic and imperfectly understood classic is shown on

Plate 40.) Jewel had a distinguished career at Oxford, and in the year of his appointment to Sunningwell had graduated B.D., and been made public orator to the University. He had a sketchy knowledge of classic architecture, but no eye for the proportions and details of the Ionic order used on his porch, and he was probably unaware of the conflict of the clumsy columns and deep entablature with the nondescript Gothic windows. A different stone is used for the walls of the porch and the columns, so it is possible that the former already existed and Jewel merely added the columns and entablature. Those classic additions may have reflected a desire to display architectural erudition, hoping thereby to catch the eye of some well-travelled potential patron, and his retention of the Gothic windows a prudent gesture of respect to the old religion. This is, of course, conjectural, but those conflicting features on the porch provoke speculation. The potential bishop certainly believed in placating the establishment, and as public orator of Oxford had composed a congratulatory epistle to Queen Mary on her accession. All the same, he became a suspect and in 1555 fled to Germany, remaining abroad until 1558.

The religious and economic revolution that changed England in Henry VIII's reign destroyed a way of life, and the shells of monastic buildings, great and small, still inform us of the thoroughness of that revolution. The system they represented may have been tyrannical and corrupt, but the large, pretentious and restlessly ornamental mansions that were built on the forfeited church lands and often partly constructed from materials looted from the ruins of abbeys and priories, represented a new and totally different pattern of English life; indicative of a carefully-guarded exclusiveness, and extending to England the class-consciousness in art and architecture that was one of the social infirmities of the Renaissance. Perhaps it was then, in the unsettled years of the mid-sixteenth century, that people began to speak of the "good old times", and the legend of "Merry England" was invented, which was expanded and glorified nearly three hundred years later by William Cobbett in his most misleading work.[10]

Perhaps countrymen with their long memories identified "the good old times" with the matey social life enjoyed by the lower orders in the Great Hall of mediaeval houses and castles, which was to some extent shared, at least in matters of noise and smells, by the lord and lady until the days lamented by Langland when the desire for privacy separated them from the rest of the household. Already, in the fifteenth century, traces of mediaeval layout in the arrangement of a country house were rare, and by the middle of the sixteenth very few buildings were grouped about a courtyard; the shape of the house as a complete entity was now immediately visible, and for the first time since the days of the castle keep and the pele-tower of the fortified manor, buildings in the countryside were over two storeys in height, with wings occasionally rising to four. Improved glazing and heating had a marked external effect: the orderly array of windows smiled, the forest of chimneys, with cut and moulded brickwork on their shafts, sent up columns of smoke like those ascending from the temples of Roman Britain, twelve hundred years earlier. Those chimneys for long astonished men of an older generation, as William Harrison, the rector of Radwinter in Essex, records in his *Description of England*. . "There are old men yet dwelling in the village where I remaine", he wrote, "which have noted three things to be marvellouslie altred in England within their sound remembrance. . . . One is, the multitude of chimnies latelie erected, whereas in their yoong daies there were not above two or three, if so manie, in most uplandith townes of the realme (the religious houses, and manour places of their lords alwaies excepted, and peradventure some great personages) but ech one made his fire against a reredosse in the hall, where he dined and dressed his meat."[11]

Loyalty to mediaeval methods of timber-framed construction was unshaken by the revival of brick building in the late fifteenth century. Bricks had been used at the end of the twelfth century; brick-making as an art had been dormant in England for eight hundred years, since the land ceased to be a Roman province, and when bricks were reintroduced they were used chiefly for churches and monastic establishments.[12] By the early sixteenth century, brickwork had become fashionable: but even so, as Harrison says, "The ancient manours and houses of our gentlemen are yet, and for the most part of strong timber (in framing whereof our carpenters have been and are worthilie preferred before those of like science among all other nations)." He noted the change to more permanent materials. "Hobeit such as be latelie builded," he said, "are commonlie either of brick or hard stone (or both); their rooms large and comlie, and houses of office further distant from their lodgings. Those of the nobilitie are likewise wrought with brick and hard stone, as provision may best be made: but so magnificent and statelie, as the basest house of a baron doth often match (in our daies) with some honours of princes in old time. So that if ever curious building did flourish in England, it is in these our years, wherein our workmen excell, and are in manner comparable with skill with old *Vitruvius*, (*Leo Baptisa*), and *Serlo*."[13]

For the building of town houses, the joiner and the carpenter long remained the leading craftsmen; their work was completed by the bricklayer or the plasterer, who supplied the infilling for the strong wooden framework that locked floors and walls together. Small, neat bricks, set in mortar, occupied the space between the timber uprights, a form of walling common in the eastern counties of England, but elsewhere rubble was used and plastered over. The plastering of walls, inside and out, was a precaution against fire, especially applicable to buildings where fire risk was high. As early as 1212 the city council of London had made an order that all cookshops on the Thames were to be plastered, and at the same time forbade the use of thatch for new buildings anywhere in the city. Fires often began in cookshops. Trades with a high fire risk were confined to certain areas; for example, an Order of Common Council, dated October 12, 1463, restricted basketmakers with their inflammable materials to the Manor of Blanche Appleton (now the site of Fenchurch Street railway station). Fire was the terror of mediaeval cities, especially in those where wood-and-plaster houses predominated. Such houses were often three or four storeys high, for as William Langland had recorded, they were regarded as a good investment.[14]

From the late fourteenth to the early eighteenth century, there was little difference in the external appearance of timber-framed town houses, apart from an increase of glazed windows; well-built houses lasted for three or four hundred years; when the framework was skimped and plaster of poor quality was slapped on carelessly, the whole street decayed, becoming known as Rotten Row or "ruinous street".[15] The anti-social property developer, the jerry-builder, and the slums spawned by their greed are not modern afflictions. Many of the streets in mediaeval European cities would seem like slums to contemporary western eyes. The architectural individualism of those streets fomented congestion and disorder in the trading areas. The price paid for the pleasure and excitement of diversity was high: a continuous performance of salesmanship could and did lead to chaos. Shopkeepers and stall-holders were centuries away from the trading maxim that "the customer is always right"; their main concern was that the customer should be caught and held and bullied into buying; regarding the street as a trap for their prey, they did all they could to obstruct through traffic so that crowds would collect round their displays of merchandise. The colour and movement, noise and smell probably resembled an oriental bazaar, but there the resemblance ended: no European city, however haphazard its growth, could ever be mistaken for an oriental city. Wherever situated, the cities of Europe had a family likeness, which was strengthened by the Renaissance, for thereafter Europe recovered its ancient classical order. That family likeness was preserved, even in Spain where oriental influence was still powerful, for the proportions and symmetrical disposition of door and window openings and their mouldings and detail were now controlled by classic prototypes; and in Central and Southern Europe balconies and external window shutters, and flat or barely visible roofs masked by parapets above the top storey, were characteristic features of town houses. Squares, crescents, circuses, long avenues, gardens and parks, began to diversify cities, sometimes as the result of royal imagination, sometimes because an aristocratic landlord with vision and financial acumen, recognised that fine buildings and spacious town-planning would pay handsome dividends. Buildings that occupied one or more sides of a square, were designed as a grand composition and the ground storey was often arcaded, like the early seventeenth century houses in the Place des Vosges in Paris (formerly the Place Royale); but apart from the studied magnificence of such compositions, evidence of expanding wealth and a rising regard for comfort was to be found in large cities and small towns alike, for an influential middle class was making a civilisation in its own image; settled, stable, quietly accomplished, with its own characteristic arts and crafts. The stability and cultural standards of the bourgeoisie were everywhere asserted by the quality of their domestic architecture; and even in countries crippled by aristocratic privilege and clerical obscurantism, merchants and traders could employ and, what was even more important, *pay* architects and builders, perhaps more promptly than noblemen and churchmen. The wealthy middle class in Northern and Central Europe impressed their innately conservative outlook on their houses; by loyalty to mediaeval traditions they encouraged hybrid designs, half-Gothic, half-classical.

Renaissance architecture came to Germany from France, as Gothic had come three centuries earlier; and the initial period was marked by classic additions to existing mediaeval buildings, like the portico applied to the façade of the Rath-haus at Cologne in 1571. In Holland and Belgium the full and lucid comprehension of classic design was delayed. Buildings like the Town Hall at Leyden (A.D. 1579) and the Guild Houses in the Grand Place at Brussels represent a luxuriant amalgam of mediaeval Gothic and Renaissance detail contained by a formal classic framework. In Belgium this rather overloaded form of architectural design continued until the mid-eighteenth century. The guild house of the Butchers at Brussels was built in 1720; that of the Brewers in 1752. (See pages 230 and 231.)

In Spain the introduction of Renaissance architecture followed the conquest in 1492 of Granada, the last independent Muslim state, and this opening phase of reinstated classic design was richly decorative. Buildings had a scintillating quality, derived from the association of Gothic, Oriental and classic forms and ornament; and during the sixteenth and seventeenth centuries Spanish and Portuguese architects transplanted the classic orders to Central and South America, as the Dutch, English and French did later to their colonies in North America. This architectural invasion marked the steady advance of European control in the New World and recorded the cultural dominance of a more sophisticated civilisation as today the steel and glass and concrete buildings that rise in nearly every city in the world record the technical dominance of the scientific-commercial west.

In the sixteenth and seventeenth centuries, as in the twentieth, the imposition of a new system of design tended to replace and arrest the development of indigenous architecture, although in the Inca cities of Peru builders had surpassed the technical accomplishments of the Hittites and Mycenaeans, using mortarless

The monument to Sir Thomas Gorges who died in 1610. This stands at the east
end of the north aisle of Salisbury Cathedral and presents a congested assort-
ment of architectural oddments, almost certainly culled from German and
Flemish copy books. The twisted columns at the angles hint at Baroque influence, badly interpreted. (See frontispiece.) The design is typical of the uncontrolled lavishness of Jacobean architecture and decoration. Reproduced
from Britton's *History and Antiquities of the Cathedral Church of Salisbury*.

ashlars for their temples and palaces, cut and laid with a precision far in advance of Cyclopean masonry.[16] In South and Central America the potency of native art, though weakened was not wholly lost, for the Spanish conquerors who settled down to build their own towns employed and trained native craftsmen. The classic orders when used in the cathedrals and palaces of Peru, Ecuador, Colombia, Venezuela and further north in Mexico, assumed an exotic character; Indian art, partly submerged and directed into unfamiliar channels, gave florid emphasis to the acanthus scrolls and foliations and other formalised Renaissance ornament. In North America no such fusion of cultures occurred, for the Indians there had not advanced beyond a primitive stage of nomadic life, though they were not without arts and crafts, so the Dutch, French and English settlers had no contact with organised societies comparable with those discovered by the Spaniards. Consequently the architectural character of European settlements on the eastern seaboard was contemporary English with contemporary French in Canada, French Florida and Louisiana.

In the East, the Portuguese and Dutch, and later on the English, carried the classic orders far beyond the range of Alexander's conquests. By the beginning of the seventeenth century the prosperity of the Portuguese settlements in India had reached its highest point, and Goa was the mercantile and the ecclesiastical capital of their Asiatic empire. It justified the name of "Goa the Golden", for the innumerable churches, public buildings, great squares and markets, the harbour crowded with shipping, and the sumptuous architecture, all proclaimed the wealth and lavish luxury of the place.[17] By the early eighteenth century it was far gone in decay, and survived for another couple of hundred years as an impoverished European enclave, with ruinous and neglected churches, until it was ultimately incorporated in the Indian state.

As Rome had left imposing reminders of the law and order and power and wealth of its Empire all over Europe, North Africa and the Middle East, so the European states of the sixteenth and seventeenth centuries left architectural monuments of their commercial enterprise, military prowess and tireless energy in India and the East Indies. Until the nineteenth century that architecture still honoured the classic orders in the regulation of proportions and the character of ornament. That projection of Renaissance design far beyond the confines of Europe, announced to the world the dominance of western civilisation. Architecture thus recorded a social and an imperial illusion, apparent to us now, but unsuspected by the architects or their patrons.

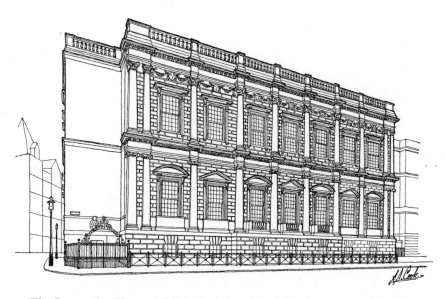

The Banqueting House, Whitehall, designed by Inigo Jones, A.D. 1619–1622. The first example of English mastery of the classic system of architectural design. *Drawn by A. S. Cook.*

The classic orders and the system of design they represented, controlled the proportions of architectural styles, even when they were as florid and exuberant as Baroque. The chimneypiece of the North Drawing Room at Ham House, Petersham, Surrey. The plaster frieze and ceiling date from 1637; the columns flanking the fireplace may have been influenced by the work of the German artist, Francis Cleyn (1582–1658). Drawn by Maureen Stafford and reproduced from *Guide to Furniture Styles: English and French, 1450–1850.* (*By courtesy of the Victoria and Albert Museum.*)

THE GOLDEN AGE OF TASTE AND REASON

THE transition of European civilisation from the Age of Faith to an age of humanism is partly recorded by the three main periods of Renaissance architecture. The mediaeval world lived on, not only in the memories and affections of old-fashioned people, but in building methods; and such traditional constancy survived the challenging revelations of the art and architecture of classical antiquity which had charged the opening period of Renaissance design with emotional excitement. The fervour of a great adventure was subdued by a growing respect for authority that accumulated strength during the second period which became one of artistic consolidation. As Geoffrey Scott wrote in *The Architecture of Humanism*: "We are confronted with a period of architecture at once daring and pedantic, and with a succession of masters the orthodoxy of whose professions is often equalled only by the licence of their practice." Men, it seems, especially when they are practising a profession, cannot reject authority. Scott added: "In spite of its liberty of thought, in spite of its keen individualism, the Renaissance is yet an age of authority; and Rome, but pagan Rome this time, is once more the arbiter. Every architect confesses allegiance to the antique; none would dispute the inspiration of Vitruvius."[1]

The works of that Roman architect, which were known in the Middle Ages, reappeared in book form late in the fifteenth century, and during the sixteenth nine editions were printed; French, Italian and German versions were also published in that century but nothing in Spanish until 1602, or in English until, in 1624, Sir Henry Wotton issued his paraphrase of Vitruvius under the title of *The Elements of Architecture*. Apart from translations of the original ten books of Vitruvius, the ever-expanding interest in classical architecture and the demand for reliable information about the

243

Roman orders were satisfied by a variety of works, illustrated by engraved plates with dimensions and commentaries and learned notes and directions, of which by far the most influential were those of Sebastiano Serlio (1475–1552), a north Italian architect who was accepted throughout Europe as *the* supreme authority on the classic orders. (He is the *Serlo* mentioned by William Harrison in the passage from his *Description of England* quoted in the previous chapter.) From France came two reliable guides: du Cerceau's *Architectura* (1559) and Philip de l'Orme's *Nouvelles Inventions* (1561), and from England, John Shute's book, *The First and Chief Groundes of Architecture* (1563), with copperplate engravings of the five orders. The Italian treatises of Giacomo Barozzi da Vignola (1563) and Andrea Palladio (1570), were reissued in successive translations and editions and accepted as authoritative guides for the next two centuries. Such works were free from the nightmare quality of those printed in Holland, Belgium and Germany. Perhaps the most harmful were the draughtsman's follies of Jan Vredeman de Vries of Antwerp, who published his *Architectura* in 1563 and, three years later, his *Compartimenta*; while between 1594 and 1598, Wendel Ditterlin's *Architectura* came out in Nuremberg. (The results of those copy books endured until far into the present century, in the form of applied ornament on machine-made versions of Jacobean furniture and chimneypieces.)

When Sir Thomas More (1478–1535) described an ideal city in the second book of his *Utopia*, he was unconcerned with classic proportions and details, though the spacious ideas of the Renaissance clearly influenced his conception of Amaurote, as he called his city. "The streets be appointed and set forth very commodious and handsome," he wrote, "both for carriage, and also against the winds. The houses be of fair and gorgeous building, and on the street side they stand joined together in a long row through the whole street without any partition or separation. The streets be twenty feet broad. On the back side of the houses through the whole length of the street, lie large gardens inclosed round about with the back part of the streets. Every house hath two doors, one into the street, and a postern door on the back side into the garden. These doors be made with two leaves, never locked nor bolted, so easy to be opened, that they will follow the least drawing of a finger, and shut again alone." The houses had three storeys and were "curiously builded after a gorgeous and gallant sort", with external walls of "hard flint, or of plaster, or else of brick", the inner sides being strengthened with timber. "The roofs," he continued, "be plain and flat, covered with a certain kind of plaster that is of no cost, and yet so tempered that no fire can hurt or perish it, and withstandeth the violence of the weather better than any lead. They keep the wind out of the windows with glass, for it is there much used, and sometimes also with fine linen cloth dipped in oil of amber, and that for two commodities. For by this means more light cometh in, and the wind is better kept out."

The book, originally written in Latin, was first published in 1516 at Louvain, and went into many editions and was translated into various European languages, but no English translation appeared until 1551, sixteen years after the author had been executed for refusing to change his view that no king could be the supreme head of the Church. (Henry VIII had then reached the point of no return in the character of Mr. Hyde.) More's *Utopia* with its revolutionary vision of a well-adjusted society had a great and continuing influence on social theorists, and some of the practical common sense about terrace housing and access to streets and gardens was applied a couple of hundred years later in the towns of Georgian England. When Bath was replanned and rebuilt in the eighteenth century, with its "commodious and handsome" streets and houses "of fair and gorgeous building", More's Amaurote came to life in stone in the last of the three main periods of Renaissance architecture. (Plate 46.)

Those three periods overlapped and developed their characteristic forms far later in England than in Europe. The early, opening period was followed by the classical, with its strict adherence to Vitruvian rules, until Italian architects created baroque and released a new surge of inventiveness. Thereafter fresh interpretations of the classic orders were introduced, and in the second half of the eighteenth century Greek art was rediscovered and Greece hailed as the great progenitor of classic design.

In England, early in the seventeenth century, a visual revolution occurred that changed the character of building, and established a discerning and beneficent understanding of the classic orders as a universal system of design, that ultimately affected the shape and ornamentation of every article of use. This revolution began when Inigo Jones (1573–1652) designed the Banqueting House for the Palace of Whitehall, the only part of that palace that was ever completed. (See page 241.) This architect's buildings were not merely Italian transcripts or scissors-and-paste compositions, made up from snippets from Flemish and German copy books; they were as English as their designer, who, despite his Welsh name was a Londoner, the son of a Smithfield clothworker. The Banqueting House in Whitehall marks the real beginning of the English classic style. Presently Sir Henry Wotton's *Elements of Architecture* improved the knowledge of the nobility and gentry and gave the classic orders a genial familiarity, for the author fully appreciated the interpretative quality of architecture, and described the characteristics of each order "according to their dignity and perfection."[2]

The English Renaissance was established by the revealing genius of Inigo Jones, while the educational potency of Wotton's essay cleared away many of the misconceptions that had hitherto encouraged the confusion of ornament with design, for in that respect the wealthy subjects of Elizabeth I and James I resembled those of Queen Victoria. The Jacobean English ultimately accepted and employed the classic idiom; two centuries later the Victorians rejected it, for everything that Henry Wotton found admirable about the orders, John Ruskin detested.

Wotton's descriptions of their characteristics made the five Roman orders very much alive. He began with the Tuscan, which, he said, "is a plain, massie rural Pillar, resembling some sturdy well limb'd Labourer, homely clad . . ." It was "of all the Rudest Pillar, and his Principal Character *Simplicity*". The Doric was "the gravest that hath been received into civil use, preserving, in comparison of those that follow, a more *Masculine Aspect* and a little trimmer than the Tuscan that went before, save a sober garnishment now and then of *Lions heads* in the *Cornice*, and of *Tryglyphs* and *Metopes* always in the *Frize* . . . The *Ionique Order* doth represent a kind of Feminine slenderness, yet saith *Vitruvius*, not like a light Housewife, but in decent dressing, hath much of the *Matron* . . . The *Corinthian*, is a *Columne* lasciviously decked like a Curtesan, and therein much participating (as all Inventions do) of the place where they were first born: *Corinth* having been (without controversie) one of the wantonest Towns in the World . . .

The last is the Compounded *Order*: His *name* being a brief of his *nature*. For this Pillar is nothing in effect, but a *medly*, or an *amasse* of all the precedent *Ornaments*, making a new kind, by stealth; and though the most richly tricked yet the poorest in this, that he is a borrower of all his Beauty . . ."

Wotton began his essay with words which have been quoted ever since by architects and writers on architecture. "In *Architecture*, as in all other *Operative* Arts, the *End* must direct the *Operation*," he wrote. "The *End* is to build well. *Well-building* hath three Conditions, *Commodity*, *Firmness* and *Delight*."

Wherever the conflict between loyalty to mediaeval tradition and acceptance of the classic orders had been resolved, delight in building was restored: in Italy it had never been lost, and during the baroque phase of the Renaissance, delight was uninhibited. In seventeenth century Italy, France, Spain, and Central Europe, buildings were lavishly, almost voluptuously embellished; in England baroque was delayed until the second half of the century. A few isolated forerunners of English baroque had appeared earlier, notably the south porch of the University Church of St. Mary the Virgin, Oxford, built in 1637, under the influence of Archbishop Laud, (1573–1645), and executed and probably designed by John Jackson, a master-mason. (See frontispiece.) The antagonistic elements of this design, with Corinthian capitals perched on ungainly twisted columns, a broken pediment, overloaded with scrolls, and a shell niche framing a statue of the Virgin and Child, on a plinth with a Gothic boss below, were more Flemish than English in character. The statue, added by Laud, was used later as evidence against him by his Puritan accusers; but the whole muddled composition suggests unreconcilable differences of taste between prelate and designer. *Commodity* is honoured, for the porch afforded shelter, thus fulfilling its function; but *Firmness* is doubtful, and *Delight* is absent. Those twisted columns deny structural function, exalt ornamental effect, and make us doubt firmness. The great twisted columns that support the bronze canopy of Bernini's baldacchino in St. Peter's, Rome, arouse no such doubts; apart from the difference in scale, the twist is relatively slight and there is no suggestion that strength has been sacrificed. Is delight absent from that porch at Oxford because the struggle between patron and mason was too bitter, or because Laud was using architecture to assert his unpopular religious views in an increasingly hostile Puritan England? The assumption that he was influencing architectural design in the interests of a movement that he and like-minded clerics had initiated is doubtful. This movement for rehabilitating the transcendental character of the liturgy and the significance of its setting has been called the "Laudian Revival," and began to be effective after Laud became Bishop of London in 1628. Sir John Summerson has described the architectural results of this revival as "highly curious". Although there were some instances of a faint stylistic revivalism, in most cases there were none, and "Laud himself does not seem to have had any stylistic prejudices." Laud had been made Chancellor of Oxford University in 1629, and the work he sponsored at St. John's College (Plate 41), like the porch of St. Mary the Virgin, was Anglo-Flemish, and the traces of mediaeval character were, as Summerson observes, "accidental rather than deliberate."[3]

It is surprising that Laud's porch at St. Mary's escaped destruction or mutilation, as England was distracted by civil war, inflamed partly by religious intolerance; and the iconoclastic zeal of those dedicated art-haters, the English Puritans, did almost as much damage to mediaeval art as the official despoilers employed by Henry VIII when they demolished the monasteries. The battered sculptures and missing glass in so many English cathedrals and churches expose the dark face of religion, distorted by fanaticism. Possibly Laud's porch at St. Mary had immunity as an important exhibit needed for his prosecution.

When new churches were built in England in the second quarter of the seventeenth century and during the Commonwealth they were in Perpendicular style and represented unbroken continuity with tradition rather than conscious revival of Gothic. As Summerson points out, "the fact that they are Gothic is neither more nor less significant than the fact that they are churches. To build a church was an act of conservative colour; and the conception of a church was by the overwhelming force of tradition a Gothic conception."[4] Such new churches were usually small, unpretentious and situated in country parishes, like the church of St. Paul's at Hammersmith, Middlesex, opened in 1631, that was described by William Morris as "a harmless silly old thing" when it was demolished in 1882 and replaced by a mock-Gothic design which

The parish church of St. Paul's, Hammersmith, built to serve what was then a small Middlesex village and opened in 1631. Few new churches were built at that time, but when they were the Gothic tradition determined their design. The church was demolished in 1882 and replaced by a Gothic revival structure in pallid brick with stone dressings. (See illustrations on page 305.) Reproduced from a print, *circa* 1809. *In the author's possession.*

he condemned as an "excrescence".[5] The original church is shown above; the late Victorian replacement on page 305.

The emotive association of the Gothic style with the design of almost any sacred edifice persisted. To many sincere and devout Englishmen, a change to the classic idiom for church-building seemed like a change of religion, or worse—a reversion to paganism. The strength of this feeling partly accounts for the protracted delay before a decision was reached to replace the Gothic ruin of old St. Paul's, hopelessly damaged in the Great Fire of 1666, with a new cathedral. Wren's design may have shocked sensitive people who recalled Wotton's description of the Corinthian order and its origin in "one of the wantonest Towns in the world"; but his classic composition was a masterpiece. The great dome still dominates the skyline of London, a splendid shape that shames the modern rabble of see-through glass and steel office blocks. (See early nineteenth century views of west front and south façade on pages 252 and 253.)

Inigo Jones, the pioneer of English classic architecture, belonged spiritually to mediaeval civilisation, for he remained loyal to the old faith and was stigmatised as a "malignant" and fined by the intolerant Puritans, but he fully understood and used the artistic bounty of the Renaissance; so did Sir Christopher Wren who followed him and became the great national architect of England. Wren was born in 1632 and lived to be ninety-one; he was essentially a man of the new age of scientific enquiry and intellectual illumination; a many-sided genius, a mathematician, an inventor, an architect who used what he called "a good Roman manner" and never completely discarded his amateur status, a prominent member of the Royal Society who read papers and conducted experiments for the edification of that assembly of lively minds; and withal a cultivated English gentleman with quiet taste who rejected the copious, florid decoration that so often clothed European examples of baroque. The comparative sobriety of English baroque reflects not only Wren's personal taste but a long-established national suspicion of anything excessive, whether it was an intemperate display of wealth or the austerity and spiritual invigilation enforced by the Puritans.

Despite the political and religious disturbances and the bitterness engendered by the Civil War, a great deal of building was done in mid-seventeenth century England and one effect of the Puritan dictatorship was to drive abroad people who were too civilised to be partisans and wealthy enough to travel. Later on a new generation of well-travelled gentlemen returned to England with their ideas enriched by what they had seen in the cities of

The Monument on Fish Street Hill, erected to commemorate the Great Fire of London in 1666, the greatest disaster that had overtaken the city since it was sacked by Boudicca in A.D. 60. It was built to the design of Sir Christopher Wren, 1671–1676, with some possible assistance from Robert Hooke, for John Aubrey attributes "the Piller", as he called it, to Hooke. Reproduced from *London and its Environs* (1766), Vol. V.

The west front of St. Paul's Cathedral, London. Sir Christopher Wren's classic design replaced the Gothic church that was largely destroyed in the fire of 1666. The view is continued on the opposite page.

Drawn and engraved in the early nineteenth century. The houses in the background were destroyed in the air raids of 1940–1941.

The south façade of St. Paul's. Above is the drum with the Corinthian peristyle, gallery and attic supporting the dome. The weight of the lantern, ball and cross is carried by an inner conical brick dome.

Both views by John Coney and reproduced from *Booth's Architectural Series of London Churches*. (Published, 1818.)

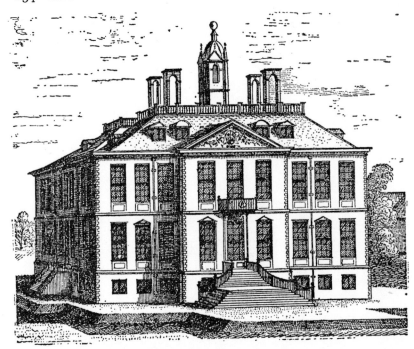

Melton Constable Hall, Norfolk, built in 1687. The robust, comfortable characteristics of the native English style are apparent, though the proportions and
moulded details accord with the classic system of design. The fenestration is
orderly, but not mannered. The grandeur of the design has not descended to
mere ostentation, though it approaches the continental conception of what was
fitting and proper for a country house to be occupied by a nobleman or a gentleman. Reproduced from a view published by Samuel and Nathaniel Buck in
1741. Only a part of the engraving has been reproduced.

France, Central Europe and Italy. Many made their peace with
the Puritan régime and lived quietly in the country where they
attracted little attention to themselves and became patrons of
architecture and learning and extended their own knowledge by
scientific studies.

When the Puritans came to power the extravagant, over-
decorative Jacobean architecture was discontinued and the serious
study of the disciplines of pure classic began. Meanwhile the native

English domestic style perfected in the late fifteenth century and throughout the sixteenth, still flourished. In the countryside great estates were laid out and planned. Gardens and groves, plantations, parkland, villages, were all related to some large house that was approached by avenues and the whole estate encircled by walls.

One of the greatest opportunities for the advance and improvement of civic architecture came after 1666 when London was largely destroyed by the great fire. The opportunity for replanning the city was missed then, as it was nearly three hundred years later after the air raids of the Second World War. Some excellent plans were made, and won the approval of that witty and much-maligned monarch, Charles II; but property-owners, wary and jealous of their legal rights, were too conservative to allow any of the imaginative proposals made by Wren, John Evelyn and Robert Hooke to be adopted, so the whole problem was relegated to the Royal Commissioners and City surveyors and eventually sank into a bureaucratic morass. At first the prospect seemed hopeful, for as Mr. T. F. Reddaway records, "No more sympathetic body could have been found".[6] Wren was one of the commissioners. His great contribution to London, apart from St. Paul's Cathedral, was the array of steeples that still raise their slender, graceful shapes and show how he discovered in the Roman orders an infinitude of variations, often by grouping their columns in diminishing tiers, like those of St. Mary-le-Bow, Cheapside and St. Bride's, Fleet Street. The suspicion of anything logical that is an English characteristic may have helped to defeat the post-fire plans; but although the city was not replanned it was rebuilt, and the new houses, of brick chiefly with stone trimmings, must have seemed as strange to Londoners as the classic cathedral which surpassed the splendour of ancient Roman temples.

A technical improvement in the mechanism of windows made as great a change in the appearance of houses as the adoption of classic mouldings. The hinged casement with its small lead-framed panes, diamond-shaped, square, or rectangular, was replaced by the double-hung sash that slid up and down, controlled by concealed weights. This sliding sash had originated in Holland, and wherever it was introduced, the proportions of rooms were improved and their comfort increased; moreover the sash frames were usually made in the form of a double square which fitted in with the classic character of the new houses of London, and imposed an urbane but by no means monotonous lateral unity on streets. Politicians presently recognised a source of revenue in the abundance of windows, which could be tapped by the sacrifice of a few unimportant amenities, such as daylight, so in 1697 a window tax was imposed that was not repealed until 1851. This was levied on all houses with more than six windows and worth over £5 a year, which led to an architectural form of tax-avoidance, for windows were blocked up in old houses, and in new houses blank spaces were left, complete with architraves, keystones and cills and either a brick or painted plastered surface instead of glass. This preserved the proportions of the façade, and such blind depressions remain in many eighteenth and early nineteenth century houses as reminders of the unending greed of governments. The tax netted £1,200,000 in the first year it was imposed, and thereafter brought in an annual revenue of over a million pounds. Successive governments renewed it, six increases were made between 1747 and 1803, but in 1823 it was reduced, and finally abolished in the year of the Great Exhibition. This unhealthy fiscal policy penalised the middle classes and left the wealthy gentry and the poor cottager unaffected; but did not halt technical advances in glass manufacture. The painted wood glazing bars that had enclosed the panes of the original sashes were flat and thick, becoming progressively thinner and more delicate in section during the eighteenth century; by the close of the Georgian period they were reduced to a knife-edge fineness and during the Victorian age disappeared altogether, as makers could then produce plate and sheet glass in bigger sizes so that the double-hung sash could have two large square expanses of glass instead of twelve small rectangular panes. This stupid and sordid story of political interference with comfort and the progress of window design has an equally stupid sentimental sequel. When the tax was finally abolished and householders could have as many windows as they liked, in the generous sizes made possible by improved methods of flat glass manufacture, the admission of daylight to rooms was deliberately restricted by filling window openings with tracery, so that the disciples of Ruskin, among whom were thousands of speculative jerry-builders, could pay their cheap tribute to the Gothic revival.

In the century and a half that preceded the Victorian rejection

Two totally different conceptions of the use, proportion and placing of windows. *Above*: Early seventeenth century houses behind the Charterhouse, London, as they appeared in the late eighteenth century. Disorderly fenestration. *Below*: Goose-Pie House, Whitehall, designed for his own residence by Sir John Vanbrugh, 1699–1700. Orderly, well-balanced fenestration. The wings were added later, and when this engraving was published it was the town house of Lord Cathcart. Both illustrations reproduced from *The European Magazine*, February, 1797.

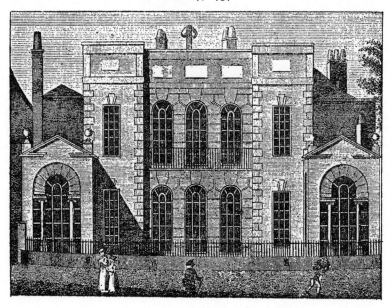

of the classic idiom, English architects had created a national style, urbane and graceful and reflecting the love of comfort and moderation that informed the taste of the nobility and gentry. The author of *The History of the Royal Society*, Dr. Thomas Sprat who became Bishop of Rochester, had remarked that "the usual course of Life of the *English Gentleman* is so well plac'd between the troublesome Noise of pompous Magnificence, and the Baseness of avaricious Sordidness; that the true Happiness of living according to the Rules and Pleasures of uncorrupt *Nature*, is more in their power than any others. To them, in this way of Life, there can nothing offer itself which may not be turn'd to a *Philosophical Use*. Their Country Seats being remov'd from the Tumults of *Cities*, give them the best Opportunity, and Freedom of *Observations*." After enumerating the varied pleasures and pursuits and neighbourliness of country life, he said that "the *English Gentry* has the Advantage of those of *France, Spain, Italy*, or *Germany*; who are generally either shut up in *Towns*, and dream away their Lives in the Diversions of *Cities*; or else are engag'd to follow their *Princes* Wills to foreign Wars."[7] Praise of rural pastimes and the countryside is a recurrent theme in English literature, pastoral scenes are the favourite subject of painters, family groups are often portrayed with a wooded glade or rolling parkland as a background, with perhaps a distant view of a commodious and elegant country house. Bishop Sprat's inventory of the English way of country life may sound like an example of insular complacency, but the architectural evidence from the second half of the seventeenth century to the early nineteenth supports his claims.

The national style in domestic architecture was graciously and comfortably expressed in houses of moderate size rather than in town or country mansions built in the grand manner. In many European countries houses were designed to be impressive, a comparatively light structure rising from a ponderous base, indicative of a social formalism that was the antithesis of the air of welcome that English houses conveyed. For men of taste Italy remained the great examplar. "Northampton, having been lately burnt and re-edified, is now become a town that for the beauty of the buildings, especially the church and town-house, may compare with the neatest in Italy itself," John Evelyn wrote in his *Diary* (July 23rd, 1688). The greater part of that town had been destroyed by fire in

Early Georgian houses at Richmond, Surrey. *Left*: The south-west corner of The Green. *Right*: Ormond Road, formerly known as Ormond Row. *Drawings by A. S. Cook.*

1675.[8] Although classic details followed Italian prototypes and the works of Serlio and Vignola were sedulously studied, architects and builders Anglicised their borrowings, often content with a simple unpretentious porch or a projecting canopy over an entrance door flanked by pilasters like the Georgian houses at Richmond, Surrey, shown above and on page 261.

Whether large or small, in town or countryside, English houses looked friendly and comfortable; in the country they diffused an

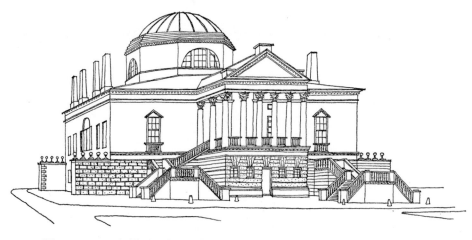

The ornamental villa, probably designed entirely by the third Earl of Burlington (1694–1753), and modelled on Palladio's Villa Capra or Villa Rotonda. This villa at Chiswick, Middlesex, was one of the results of Burlington's studies at Vincenza. Built in 1725. (See page 224.)

Sudbrooke Lodge, Petersham, Surrey, built for the second Duke of Argyll, 1726–1728, to the design of James Gibbs. Brick with stone dressings and an imposing portico with Corinthian columns with a raised balustrade above the entablature. *Both drawings by David Owen.*

An early Georgian example of the elegance of English domestic architecture.
Maids of Honour Row, Richmond Green, Surrey, built in 1724 for the Maids of
Honour attending the Princess of Wales. *Drawn by A. S. Cook.*

air of easygoing leisure; their owners, as Bishop Sprat had pointed
out, were part of a rural society, not aloof from it, and as their
lives were less circumscribed by precedent and etiquette than those
of the Continental aristocracy, their homes were unmarked by the
formidable and oppressive dignity of so many German castles,
Austrian palaces and French châteaux. This is apparent even in
large-scale works like Wren's additions to Hampton Court Palace
(page 13), while such accomplished exponents of grandeur in
architectural design as Sir John Vanbrugh could confer an air of
robust gaiety on baroque compositions like Blenheim and Castle
Howard. (Plate 44.) The conscientious imitation of some Italian
model occasionally eliminated English characteristics, as the third
Earl of Burlington succeeded in doing with his ornamental villa
at Chiswick, Middlesex, which was based on Palladio's Villa Capra
at Vicenza. (Page 224.) Palladio had used the Roman Ionic order
for the porticos; Lord Burlington chose the Corinthian. (Opposite.)
When noble amateurs practised architecture, their creative
work was exposed to a well-informed and sharply critical society.
Horace Walpole condescended to some diluted approval of Burlington's Chiswick villa, which, he said, was "a model of taste,
though not without faults, some of which are occasioned by too

strict adherence to rules and symmetry. Such are too many correspondent doors in spaces so contracted; chimneys between
windows, and which is worse, windows between chimneys; and
vestibules, however beautiful, yet too little secured from the damps
of this climate. The trusses that support the ceiling of the corner
drawing-room are beyond measure massive, and the ground
apartment is rather a diminutive-catacomb, than a library in a
northern latitude. Yet these blemishes, and Lord Hervey's wit, who
said *the house was too small to inhabit, and too large to hang to one's watch,*
cannot depreciate the taste that reigns in the whole."[9]

The critical foundation of English taste in the eighteenth century
was described in four lines by Pope in the verses addressed to Lord
Burlington:—

> "Something there is more needful than expense,
> And something previous even to taste—'tis sense:
> Good sense, which only is the gift of Heaven,
> And, though no science, fairly worth the seven. . . ."

Architects and their patrons knew where to stop, and such
restraint and moderation earned the slightly astonished approval
of visitors from Europe. But it was a century of moderation; even
the European wars have been described as wars of limited liability,
and were fought with good manners.

"Gentlemen of the French Guard, fire first!" was Lord Charles
Hay's invitation to the French commander at the Battle of Fonte-
noy (1745). The invitation was not accepted. The French suspected that there might be a catch in it, as there so often was in
English propositions.

No French visitor to England could ignore the fundamental
differences between the two peoples: everything in the countryside
and the towns illustrated a social pattern unknown in France, or
indeed in the rest of Europe. The compact neatness of the houses
was either taken for granted or ignored. One acute observer,
François de la Rochefoucauld, who visited England in 1784, remarked on the general lack of stone in the country so that it was a
sign of magnificence to use stone for public buildings. "Houses are
generally built of brick or plaster and timber," he wrote, "and
consequently are low in height and lacking in architectural distinction. At the same time their form is pleasing. The houses in a

From the late seventeenth century to the early nineteenth, towers on English churches and secular buildings were gay and graceful. They brought to the skylines of towns and cities in England and the North American Colonies a cheerful and exciting diversity, and, like the two examples illustrated, showed that a church need not exhibit an oppressively solemn exterior, nor a military establishment an air of grim purpose. *Left*: The upper part of the tower of St. Anne's, Soho, designed by William Talman in 1714, and added to the church that was built by Wren, 1680–1686. Wren's original tower, which this replaced, is shown in Kip's view of London (1710). Talman's tower was rebuilt by S. P. Cockerell in 1802–1806, and it still remains, having survived the bombs of 1940–1941 which destroyed the rest of the church. Reproduced from a print by B. Cole, 1754. *Right*: The east front of the Horse Guards, Whitehall, built to the designs of William Kent after his death, by John Vardy and William Robinson, 1750–1758. Although the tower is not a light, airy structure like that of St. Anne's, it shares the same gay elegance.

town or village are small, since they never accommodate more than one household; the general custom, when the children marry, is for them to take a house and to set up their own establishment, which leads to their marrying at a later age than in France."[10]

In that same year the Comte de Mirabeau also travelled in England, and set down in some detail his impressions after arrival. "From Lewes," he wrote, "we traversed the finest country in Europe, for variety and verdure, for beauty and richness, for rural neatness and elegance. It was a feast for the sight, a charm for the mind, which it is impossible to exaggerate. The approaches to London are through a country for which Holland affords no parallel (I should compare to it some of the vallies of Switzerland), for, and this remarkable observation seizes immediately an experienced mind, this sovereign people are, above all, farmers in the bosom of their island; and that is what has so long saved it from its own convulsions. I felt my mind deeply and strongly interested as I travelled through this well cultivated and prosperous country, and I said to myself, whence this new emotion. Their castles, compared to ours, are but pigeon houses. Several cantons in France, even in the poorest provinces, and all Normandy, which I have just visited, are finer by nature than these fields. Here we find in this place, and that place, but every where in our country, fine edifices, proud buildings, great public works, the traces of the most wonderful works of man; and yet this contents me more than those things astonish me. It is that nature is here ameliorated and not forced . . . that the high state of cultivation here announces the respect for property; that this care and universal neatness is a living system of well being; that all this rural wealth is in nature, by nature, according to nature, and does not disclose that extreme inequality of fortune, source of so many evils, like the sumptuous edifice surrounded by cottages; it is that here every thing informs me that the people are something; that every man has the development and free exercise of his faculties, and that thus I am in a new order of things."[11]

England was singularly free from provocative social contrasts that were so common in many European countries; "the sumptuous edifice surrounded by cottages" was a comparative rarity, for the English nobility and gentry possessed a sense of fitness and social obligation; villages, hamlets and rows of cottages were separated from the great estates, screened from the windows of the landlord's mansion by plantations, but the countrymen often had glimpses of life as it was lived at "the big house", for gardens and parks, originally hidden by high brick walls, were sometimes partly opened to public view, the brickwork rising only two or three feet for a hundred yards or so, with fine wrought iron railings above. These railed openings had a two-way function, for the rustics could look in and, as they were carefully sited, a pleasant vista over fields and woodland, with perhaps a church tower, could be enjoyed by those privileged to look from the windows of the house or the surrounding terraces. Frequently their eyes were diverted by some mediaeval remains, for on many estates, especially those acquired in the middle years of the sixteenth century that had included former church lands, ruined chapels and chantries and fragments of monastic buildings still survived: a broken arch, the skeleton of a tall window, a stretch of roofless cloisters. When William Stukeley, the antiquary, visited Glastonbury about 1723 the Abbot's House was still standing, and in his *Itinerary* he described its appearance. At that time the Abbey buildings were owned by a presbyterian named Thomas Prew, who was systematically destroying the remains, blowing up the vaults with gunpowder, and ultimately demolishing the Abbot's house. He used the materials for building a new house for himself, selling the surplus stone for repairing roads.

Ruins were everywhere exciting the interest of cultivated people, though few attempts were made to preserve or protect them from stone-robbers or religious fanatics who took a morbid pleasure in breaking up buildings that had served the old faith; men like Thomas Prew the landlord of Glastonbury and his successor, John Down, another presbyterian, who continued demolition throughout the latter part of the eighteenth century and the opening decades of the nineteenth. Although such destructive activities were regretted, the loss of authentic remains continued unchecked. Their survival very often depended on whether parts of them could be used by farmers, and small chapels and the naves of disused churches made admirable barns.[12]

After the first quarter of the eighteenth century romantic interest in mediaeval remains degenerated into fashionable absurdity, especially when false ruins were lovingly contrived, with dead trees planted as mournful adjuncts to a faked archway or an embattled tower. Perhaps the local rustics, with realistic common sense, were the first to call them "follies"; in England and some parts of Europe such architectural eccentricities indicated the anti-quarian preoccupations of modish society. Although fashion gained partial control of taste and tended to debilitate the sense of fitness, patrons everywhere retained their appreciation of graceful shapes and good proportions. From the seventeenth century to the early nineteenth, visual propriety and a sense of proportion were main-tained, for architecture and the industrial arts and crafts were con-trolled by the universal system of classic design that everybody understood, from the nobleman who employed a fashionable archi-tect to the country squire who instructed his estate carpenter; and this respect and acceptance of the system which related every shape and every form of ornament to one or other of the Greek or Roman classic orders, was common to western civilisation, as manifested throughout Europe and in young nations, like the United States of America. The new federal capital of that republic was a classic composition: Washington had the spaciousness and dignity of an ancient Greek or Roman city. Almost any style or whimsical fancy could be accommodated within the classic framework, for those golden proportions could be imposed alike on the vibrant shapes and shadow-play of baroque or the bubbling effervescence of rococo. Everything ornamental, from the acanthus arabesques on a jewelled snuff-box or watch-case to the carving on the cabriole legs of a card table, the cornice of a bookcase, or the spokes of a coach wheel, derived decorative character from some Roman prototype; and everywhere the influence of the architect, the master-designer, was apparent; his standards of judgement dominated the studio, drawing-office and workshop.

The assumption of such wide responsibilities had begun as we have seen in the sixteenth century in France, Germany and Spain; much earlier in Italy, and much later in England. During the seventeenth century the architect shed one significant responsibility when architecture and engineering became separate professions. The first record of this distinction was in 1620, when the French architect Jacques Lemercier (*circa* 1583–1654) was sent to report on a bridge near Rouen, accompanied by an engineer. This formal separation of art from science was ultimately as injurious to archi-

Interiors in the palaces and great mansions of France possessed an almost
Roman magnitude, and the likeness to the architecture of the Roman world was
heightened by classic mouldings and ornament, used with far more imagination
and freedom than the Romans could ever command. This lofty late seventeenth
century salon is reproduced on a smaller scale from Jean Le Pautre's book of
designs. *By courtesy of the Victoria and Albert Museum.*

The palaces and great mansions of France in the reign of Louis XIV had an almost Roman magnitude. The late seventeenth century salon, reproduced on page 269 from Jean Le Pautre's book of designs, recalls in relation to human scale the soaring loftiness of the Baths of Diocletian. (Plate 16.) The likeness to buildings of the ancient world was heightened by classic mouldings and ornament, which the Renaissance designers used with far greater flexibility of imagination than Roman architects were permitted. A Roman patrician would have been visually at home in a Versailles salon; but aghast at the dirt and the smells. The beautifully-dressed people who adorned the French court seldom used soap and water: they drenched themselves with perfume. Washing facilities were limited: hygiene, in the modern sense, was non-existent. Although there were baths and bathrooms in a few palaces and large houses, they were rarities; in the seventeenth and early eighteenth centuries people irrespective of class or wealth were denied the comfort of thorough cleanliness; and the only parts of Europe where facilities for bathing were as common as they had been in the Roman world were the western provinces of the Turkish Empire. Lady Mary Wortley Montagu, whose husband was appointed ambassador at Constantinople in 1716, described in detail her visit to the baths at Sophia, while on her way to the Turkish capital. Sophia she thought was "one of the most beautiful towns in the Turkish empire, and famous for its hot baths, that are resorted to both for diversion and health."[13] The Turks preserved the design and character of the Roman bath, and gave their name to it; for the so-called Turkish bath is indistinguishable from its Roman forerunner.

While noses in the seventeenth and eighteenth centuries were less easily outraged than those of Roman patricians or modern Americans and Europeans, eyes were continuously delighted and intrigued by the work of architects and artists and those fertile and ingenious ornamentalists who invented rococo; the frivolous sequel to baroque. That gaily decorative and intricate style, conceived on the drawing board and developed by the skill of engravers, had originated with the work of Pierre Le Pautre, the eldest child of Jean Le Pautre (1618–1682); both were designers and engravers, and Jean Le Pautre's book of designs was an indispensable source for ornamentalists, so too were the lively and original compositions of another French designer and engraver, Jean Bérain (1638–1711).

Jean Le Pautre reanimated classical ornament, and endowed the fabulous fauna of antiquity with energetic vitality; mythical monsters disported themselves amid formalised foliage of oak and laurel and sinuous acanthus leaves, and of all those hybrids—centaurs, satyrs, griffins, winged leopards and sea horses with webbed feet—the sphinx alone was static, crouching or sitting, invariably passive. Fluttering in and out of the carved or painted decoration were plump cupids, for such carnal figures had ousted the angels and suffering saints of Gothic art who, banished from the salon, were relegated to the oratory. Imaginative flourishes by a gifted engraver and designer could easily be transposed from two dimensions to three without losing that essential characteristic of the classic idiom: symmetry. Externally mass balanced mass: the wings of a palace or a large house were exactly alike and united by a dominant central feature, a symmetrical arrangement that was usually followed in the principal interiors by the relative positions of doors, windows and chimneypieces. Classic proportions and well-balanced features charmed the eye, so did the diversity of beautifully-executed ornament on walls, ceilings and furniture.

Rococo, far less robust than baroque, delicate, involved, but never confused, though inclined to be finical, forsook strictly symmetrical composition. The name, derived from *rocaille*, meaning rock-work, was first used to describe the fountains and artificial grottoes in the gardens Le Nôtre designed and executed at Versailles, between 1662 and 1688. As a style it lacked the depth and bold surface variation of baroque; reminders of its origin in the engravers' skill and flamboyant fancifulness were never absent. Rococo ornament covered surfaces like a web, softening and sometimes smudging and obliterating structural lines.

The strength and dignity of baroque remained during the reign of Louis XIV; but thereafter rococo developed in France and spread through Europe. The architect had less to do with changing rococo from a linear art to decoration in three dimensions than the ornamentalists, the carvers and *ébénistes*, and although asymmetrical shapes began to invade interiors and to weaken the structural anatomy of furniture, externally the architecture of the Louis XV period was unrelated to the delirious instabilities of the rococo

The Petit Trianon, Versailles, designed by Ange Jacques Gabriel for Madame du Barry and built, 1762–1768. The placid dignity of the façade, with its elegant classic detail and fluted Corinthian columns, suggests an orderly and well-balanced society, with no hint of the social wrath to come; externally most of the buildings of this extravagant and frivolous period of French history gave an impression of eternal stability. Only within was the truth revealed by decorative turmoil and fantastic ornament. *Drawn by Maureen Stafford.*

salons and boudoirs that rioted behind tranquil classic façades. Rococo was basically a style of decoration rather than of architecture, and as such divulged the social ill health of eighteenth century France. The style has been wrongly linked with the name of La Pompadour (1721–1764), but was already on the wane when she was established as "maîtresse en titre" at Versailles in 1745, and although she encouraged the far more restrained Neo-classical taste that followed rococo, the complexity and extravagance of her surroundings, and the reckless squandering of wealth that characterised the French court and aristocracy, justified her prophetic remark "Après nous le déluge".

The classic calm of such buildings as the Petit Trianon at Versailles, might suggest a placid and secure state of society: within, far different conclusions would inevitably be formed. (Opposite.) No illusions of social stability could survive the impact of rococo. No society that rejoiced in ornamental turbulence and lived at such a distance from reality could long survive. The French Revolution was predicted by the most prodigal style ever invented.

A characteristic motif in rococo decoration was the C-shaped scroll, interlaced with acanthus foliations and delicately carved and gilded flowers, wreaths, shells, also trophies of Roman arms—helmets, breastplates and weapons—and beribboned musical instruments; exotic birds stalked about or spread their wings, and monkeys, actively acrobatic or pensively nibbling at fruit, enlivened the scene. Early in the development of rococo, Chinese architectural features were introduced: the umbrella roof and the pagoda, and railings formed from geometric frets: attempts were also made to portray celestial landscapes on painted and lacquered panels, with strangely-shaped trees and unfamiliar blossoms and stiff, stylised figures in oriental costumes. Such borrowings were mere ingredients for decorative fantasies: they had no significant influence on architectural design, for Chinese architecture was basically asymmetrical, and visually unacceptable to those accustomed to the stability and balanced proportions of baroque.

In his references to the Emperor's palace in China, Père Le Comte said, "in the decorations there is little regularity; one sees nothing of the harmonious arrangement which gives to our own palaces their pleasing and commodious character. Moreover, there is everywhere evidently—what shall I say?—something unshape (if I may use the expression), which is displeasing to Europeans, and which must be distressing to all who have a feeling for good architecture."[14] The ultimate acceptance of "something unshape" which happened late in the eighteenth century indicated the decay of the golden age of taste and reason and the onset of romantic disorder. Significantly, the romantic and picturesque movement received greater encouragement in England than in Europe; for the English were all unknowingly in the early phase of a revolution, not a dramatic and bloodthirsty revolution like the French, but one that created wealth, degraded whole classes of workpeople, injured the natural environment, and with the recrudescence of puritanism led to loss of visual sensitivity and the triumph of moral earnestness. This, as architecture accurately recorded, was the price paid for becoming the workshop of the world.

Long before such afflictions lowered civilised standards in the British Isles, oriental influences had returned to Europe by devious routes. The far-eastern commercial interests of Holland, Portugal and France and, later, England, fostered a taste for oriental art and architecture. The static quality of that architecture— particularly Chinese—was unsuspected by enthusiastic European admirers, the men and women of fashion who had never seen a real Chinese building, and were unaware that the Chinese, while producing superb porcelain and lacquer, had, like the ancient Egyptians, reached the dead end of constant and boring repetition in architectural design. French taste for *Chinoiserie*—a term that embraced every branch of Chinese art—had in the late seventeenth and early eighteenth century contributed to the character of rococo; and when that style became acceptably modish, many so-called Chinese and Japanese palaces were built in France and Germany, though they were little more than open garden houses, lightly constructed for use in summertime. There was an air of gay impermanence about them; they were only architectural fireworks that gave a transitory sparkle to the scene; unlike the far more solid pagodas that adorned some gardens. Sir William Chambers (1723–1796), one of the few architects who had visited China, published a book in 1757, entitled *Designs of Chinese Buildings, Furniture, Dresses, Machines and Utensils*, and in that year built a pagoda when he planned Kew Gardens in Surrey for the Dowager Princess of Wales, a sober and admirably-proportioned example of the Chinese taste. (Plate 46).

One of the oriental influences that gradually encouraged English tolerance for irregular composition was a form of taste known as *sharawadgi*, a word first used by Sir William Temple in his *Essay on Gardening*, written about 1685, in which he described the advantages of regularity and irregularity in the design and planting of gardens, approving—with some reservations—the asymmetrical effects contrived by Chinese gardeners. The *sharawadgi* taste prepared the fashionable world of Georgian England for the flight from symmetry that began with the growth of the picturesque movement, and led finally to the desertion of the classic idiom.

No. 7 Adam Street, Adelphi, London: an elegant interpretation of the classic idiom characteristic of the work of the Brothers Adam, who used Greek and Roman ornament with a delicacy that gave light and fresh graces to Georgian architecture. Designed by Robert Adam, *circa* 1770. *Drawn by David Owen.*

Periodically the architectural virtues of the classic system of design were reassessed; fashions like the Chinese, Indian and Gothic taste might attract the passing interest of the modish, but the increase of travel among educated and observant Europeans, and the study of remains in the old Roman provinces that were under Muslim rule and either part of the Turkish Empire or in alliance with it, encouraged attempts to return to the initial purity of ancient forms. The discovery and excavation of the Roman cities of Pompeii and Herculaneum, buried in lava and ashes when Vesuvius erupted in A.D. 79, supplemented existing knowledge of classical art. The very sites of those cities had been forgotten during the Middle Ages. The buried ruins were discovered in 1748; systematic excavation began in 1763 and was continued during the

Pelham Crescent, Hastings, Sussex, designed by Joseph Kay (1775–1847) and built between 1824–1828, with a private chapel in the centre. The façades of the Crescent have been restored by the Old Hastings Preservation Society. (See Plate 48.) *Reproduced from a drawing by Richard A. Haskell, A.R.I.B.A., A.M.T.P.I., by courtesy of the artist.*

rest of the eighteenth century and, far more methodically, during the early nineteenth by the French government under Napoleon and rather less methodically under the Bourbon kings, until after 1861 the work was carried on by the Italians. Other and more accessible Roman sites had been explored, and two Scottish architects, Robert and James Adam, made detailed and extensive records of the Palace of Diocletian at Spalatro, in the old Roman province of Illyricum, east of the Adriatic. (See map on page 88.) Robert Adam had lived in Italy from 1754 to 1757, and those records, illustrated by Bartolozzi and other engravers, were published in 1764 under the title of *Ruins of the Palace of the Emperor Diocletian at Spalatro*. The brothers Adam created a delicate version of classic architecture, based on authentic Roman models, light, gay and elegant, which became the national English style during the last third of the eighteenth century.

In 1734 a group of wealthy English noblemen and gentlemen who had travelled extensively in Italy, Greece and Asia Minor, founded the Society of Dilettanti, so they could share the fruits of their archaeological and architectural studies, and encourage and maintain interest and knowledge of classical art in England. The society began informally as a dining club, but soon acquired the authority of a learned body.[15] The most important of their activities was the financing of expeditions to make records of remains in Greece and the more inaccessible of the ancient Roman provinces, and when in 1748 James Stuart and Nicholas Revett issued their "Proposals for publishing an Accurate Description of the Antiquities of Athens" the Society sponsored them, and the two "painters and architects" as they described themselves, arrived in Athens in 1751 and began work.[16] The first of the four volumes of *The Antiquities of Athens* was published in 1762, and thereafter interest in the original source of classic architecture was increased, until in the last decade of the eighteenth century, a Greek revival found expression in architecture, interior decoration and the design of furniture.

The debt to Greece had been acknowledged in 1728 by the English architect Robert Morris who deplored the lack of original subjects for study. "As no Footsteps of the *Grecian* Buildings now remain", he wrote, "we must of necessity have recourse to the *Antiquities* of the *Romans*, who received the Rules and Methods

Gardens ran down to the Thames, and elegant villas and small, ornamental buildings diversified both banks of the river, which until the early nineteenth century was unpolluted in the upper reaches. Although here and there the pinnacles of some Georgian Gothic edifice rose in spiky profusion, the classic orders usually determined the form and character of dwellings and smaller structures like the Duke of Northumberland's boathouse, near Syon House on the Middlesex bank. This graceful design is often wrongly attributed to Robert Adam, but it was the work of James Wyatt. From a drawing by J. D. Harding, engraved by W. B. Cooke, and reproduced from *Richmond and its Surrounding Scenery*, by Barbara Hofland. (London, 1832.)

immediately from the *Grecians*."[17] That lament was no longer valid by the end of the eighteenth century, for the activities of scholars, antiquaries and artists had multiplied the records of Greek architecture, and art collectors, like the seventh Earl of Elgin (1766–1841), had saved many treasures of sculpture from neglect or destruction. Lord Elgin during his appointment as envoy extraordinary at the Porte had, as mentioned in chapter four, been allowed by the Turkish authorities to clear the area round the ruins of the Parthenon at Athens and to remove the sculptures that became known as the Elgin marbles and are now housed in the British Museum. (Plate 8.)

No extraneous influences or fashions diminished the authority of the architectural establishment in eighteenth century Europe; the classic orders and all that they implied survived the impact of oriental taste; even that "symphony of hilarity",[18] as Mr. James Lees-Milne has so aptly called the rococo style, made no fundamental change, but merely contributed to the ultimate tolerance of asymmetrical composition. Respect for the Graeco–Roman past was unshaken by the French Revolution, and ornamentalists and architects still relied on antique ornament and obeyed the discipline of the orders. Classic ornament was occasionally supplemented by forms drawn from sources far older than those provided by Greece and Rome; the sphinxes and hawk-headed and jackal-headed Gods of Ancient Egypt, palm-leaves and lotus and papyrus buds, began to appear over a decade before Napoleon's Egyptian campaign, and such features of the French Empire style were introduced as a part of a minor fashion in the reign of Louis XVI.

In the early years of the French Revolution some abortive attempts were made to give ideological substance to ornaments of various kinds. Revolutionary symbols in the form of workmen's tools appeared amid the conventional acanthus foliations and scrolls: *liberty, equality* and *fraternity* were represented respectively by the Phrygian cap, the spirit-level and clasped hands, while pikes, somewhat abstrusely, stood for *freedom of man*. Such incongruities might gratify demagogues, but the innate common sense and good taste of the French people limited their use. The Revolution inspired no distinctive architectural style; loyalty to the classic system of design was undiminished; and in the earlier American revolution, the founding fathers of the United States were as impressed by the art and institutions of ancient Rome as the rulers of the country they had repudiated. The thirteen English colonies in North America made no break with Georgian architectural tradition when they became independent. Like every European state they were, below the threshold of national consciousness, still under the spell of Rome. The eagle with outspread wings became the

American emblem; ever since that martial bird was borne on the standards of the Roman legions it had secured the enduring respect of European rulers, and in heraldry was accounted one of the most noble bearings, often appearing as double-headed on the arms of emperors. It reappeared during Napoleon's French Empire, surmounting the staves of infantry colours, and in that form was occasionally used as a decorative motif in architectural compositions.

In the last phase of Renaissance architecture, the classic system was still intact, though erosive influences were already threatening the authority of the Roman and Greek orders. Until the opening decades of the nineteenth century the ruling classes in Europe habitually sought classical precedents for their arts and often for their political actions; educated men could read Greek and Latin and make orations in those tongues, and the surviving literature of the ancient world was as familiar as the urbane architectural forms that had changed the appearance of every European city since the end of the Middle Ages. Although the inspiration that had revolutionised European life and art and thought since the fifteenth century was dying down at the beginning of the nineteenth, the architectural evidence shows no loss of faith in the supremacy of the classic idiom. Splendid buildings were designed, such as the Madeleine in Paris; the arcaded Rue de Rivoli; the Paris Bourse; and the Arc de Triomphe de L'Etoile, built to celebrate the victories of the Grande Armée.

In England the final graces of the Georgian period appeared in the elegant terraces, crescents and circuses of the West End of London, with façades of delicately moulded stucco, painted white or cream; classic proportions were preserved though moulded cornices were replaced by plain slightly projecting bands and ornament was used sparingly. Buildings of comparable design and finish rose in towns dedicated to the enjoyment of leisure, fashionable spas like Cheltenham and Leamington, and watering places like Ramsgate, Herne Bay, Hastings, Tenby, Brighton and Hove. This last phase of creative classic design was as consistently well-mannered as anything built in the eighteenth century, and John Nash (1752–1835), who helped to perfect the style that is associated with the Regency period, gave London Regent Street, at that time one of the finest shopping streets in Europe. That street

View of Mount Arrarat, the seat of Edward Clarke Esq. Published by I.
Stockdale, Piccadilly, London, December 2nd, 1797. Indian architecture has
contributed to the design: the verandah, the flat roof and the cornice projecting on brackets, which casts a deep band of shadow on the upper part of the
walls. The pointed heads of the windows and the arches of the verandah acknowledge the Gothic taste. *Reproduced from an engraving in the author's possession.*

Seizincote House, near Moreton-in-the-Marsh, Gloucestershire, designed in the so-called "Moorish" style by Samuel Pepys Cockrell (*circa* 1754–1827) for his brother, Sir Charles Cockrell, and built in 1805. The style was more Indian than Moorish, which was appropriate as it was designed for a nabob who had acquired his fortune in the service of the East India Company. The plan of the house was as English as any other large late-Georgian country mansion; the arrangement and proportions of the windows were controlled by the classic system of design, and the multi-foil arches, deep projecting bracketed cornice and swelling onion dome gave the house its pseudo-oriental character. Reproduced from a drawing by J. P. Neale included in John Britton's historical and descriptive views of *Bath and Bristol with the Counties of Somerset and Gloucester.* (London. W. Evans & Co. 1829.)

with its quadrant and colonnades survived for nearly a hundred years, though the colonnades were removed in 1848. Carlton House Terrace and the terraces of Regent's Park escaped the destruction that in the twentieth century turned a sunny shopping street into a shadowed thoroughfare, pulsating with traffic and lined with non-descript, unrelated buildings.

Some engaging fantasies were built, of which the most famous is the Royal Pavilion at Brighton, a semi-oriental conglomeration of features, held together by classic proportions, designed by Nash who was the personal architect of the Prince Regent. (Plate 46.) The Pavilion was a very expensive royal joke, but it owed something to the interest in Indian art and architecture that was generated by the increasing number of men who had served in India, either as soldiers or in the administration of the British possessions. Many had made large fortunes, and when such wealthy "Nabobs" retired they often built large white houses on some eminence, over-looking the countryside, in imitation of the stucco-covered mansions of Calcutta or Madras.[19] The roofed gallery or balcony was introduced from India in the late eighteenth century, and the name verandah, that was common to several Indian languages, was adopted as well as a most convenient and agreeable form of shelter. Other eastern influences—not often acknowledged—improved domestic architecture in the West. For example nineteenth century houses were normally equipped with bathrooms, apart of course from the slums of industrial centres, because Europeans changed their attitude to personal cleanliness; having learned from India the value of cold water. Kim, in Kipling's novel, when he went to school at St. Xavier's, "learned to wash himself with the Levitical scrupulosity of the native-born, who in his heart considers the Englishman rather dirty."[20] India and other eastern countries had a long-established tradition of cleanliness, for they had never been subjected to the grubby beliefs of mediaeval churchmen who like the early Christians equated bathing with immorality.

Some future historian, five hundred or a thousand years hence, may conclude by a study of European architecture from the early seventeenth to the late eighteenth century, that western civilisation had then reached its climax. The reinterpretation of the classic idiom by Renaissance architects and artists had provided an environment of unsurpassed beauty and order for a well-balanced and stable society.

LOOKING BACKWARDS

ARLY in the nineteenth century the decline of the eighth cultural period of Mediterranean and western civilisation began; not, as Flinders Petrie suggests, at the Renaissance. His dismissal of the intellectual and artistic invigoration of Europe as an unoriginal sequel to mediaeval art is based on the assumption that sculpture and engraving had reached their highest point in the latter part of the thirteenth century, and thereafter decayed.[1] The last two chapters have shown that European architecture refutes the theory of cultural collapse in the sixteenth, seventeenth and eighteenth centuries. At the end of *The Revolutions of Civilisation*, Flinders Petrie suggested that the production of a new European art lay far ahead in the future. Referring to his diagram of periods (page 19), he remarked "that the widening apart of the stages means that wealth of improvements can be accumulated later in each stage, and the maximum of wealth in Europe promises in our own stage to reach to near the end of our period, when an entire mixture with another race will be requisite."[2] He qualified his conclusions by asking: "But are not the conditions of the world so radically altered that no past phenomena will be repeated again?"

The ancient cycle of national or imperial rise, decline and collapse, followed by barbarian conquest, changes in the system of breeding and consequent hybridisation, might be ended by some new form of revolution in civilisation, unforeseen by old-fashioned social theorists. We are inclined to be intimidated by a belief in the immutability of historical patterns, but architecture while illustrating historical relationships and revealing origins, denies that history repeats itself. The growth of wealth and the expanding knowledge of mechanics shown on the Flinders Petrie diagram indicated an accumulation of power that could become uncontrollable, and did indeed lead to destructive wars very soon after that diagram was first published, wars that changed the map of Europe and the character of European civilisation.

An unforseen and long unrecognised revolution originated in England in the late seventeenth century, and a few of the creative and destructive results were apparent during the next hundred years, though not extensive enough to arouse alarm. At first this industrial revolution, as we now call it, affected only a few manufacturing districts, like Coalbrookdale in Shropshire, threatening the "universal neatness" of the rural scene that Mirabeau had observed and commended, and it remained an unacknowledged revolution until the mid-nineteenth century, when its implications became so disturbing that sensitive English people, who could no longer pretend that it hadn't happened, sought refuge in nostalgic dreams. Nostalgia is a powerful drug to which intelligent and sensitive people resort when they are bored or frightened by the times they are living in; and comforting doses are increased as their dislike of the present is reinforced by dread of the future. Their apprehensions and need for artistic and intellectual solace encourage architectural revivals; not revivals intended to enlarge and purify existing knowledge of original sources, like the Greek Revival, but revivals with a moral and spiritual potential, that begin as innocent, well-mannered fashions. Of all these the Gothic Revival produced the most lasting and in some respects the most disastrous architectural results, and the most unflattering disclosures about social life. In England fidelity to Gothic had never completely faded; examples of seventeenth century Gothic were mentioned in chapter eleven, and in that century the style, as Dr. Mordaunt Crook states in his introduction to the 1970 reprint of Eastlake's *A History of the Gothic Revival* "had again been given artificial respiration", notably in London, Oxford and Cambridge.[3]

Some of Wren's City churches were Gothic, and in 1713 he had recommended the style for the western towers of Westminster Abbey, which were designed in their present form by Nicholas Hawksmoor (1661–1736), completed by John James (1672–1746), and built 1735–1746. Such designs by architects of the calibre of Wren and Hawksmoor had valid continuity with Perpendicular English Gothic; in such hands the style was under orderly control, and preserved a sedate and restrained character until it was taken up by amateur antiquaries and changed into a gay and volatile fashion. By the middle years of the eighteenth century a few superficial Gothic features invaded domestic architecture; the heads of windows and doorways were pointed; battlements ran above cornices; turrets and tourelles were silhouetted against the sky; but such occasional tributes to Gothic remained superficial, they had no effect upon structure or proportions. This was the gentlemanly, elegant stage of the revival that was still guided by classic discipline. The irregularities of Horace Walpole's villa at Strawberry Hill were external: the rooms had mediaeval decoration and classic proportions. (Below.)

Walpole's "little plaything house" as he called it, became the most influential and best-remembered harbinger of the Gothic

Strawberry Hill, Horace Walpole's Gothic fantasy, as it appeared in the early nineteenth century. The house, which he acquired in 1747, became the most conspicuous and best-remembered example of the "Gothic Taste", and was nothing more than the charming whim of a cultivated nobleman with considerable architectural knowledge. It was as innocent of spiritual purpose as the later works of the morally earnest Gothic Revivalists were devoid of charm or whimsicality. Reproduced from an engraving dated June 4th, 1810, included in the eleventh edition of *The Ambulator* (London: 1811).

South-west view of Fonthill Abbey, Wiltshire, designed by James Wyatt for
William Beckford, and built between 1796 and 1807. This was a large-scale
example of the revived Gothic taste, pretentious and structurally unsound. The
tower, an elegant piece of stage scenery and about as stable, collapsed in 1807.
Although Beckford had originally envisaged a large artificial ruin, with a few
rooms sound enough for temporary residence, the place developed into a huge
house, as owner and architect allowed imagination and enthusiasm to take
control. The final result was a dramatic conglomeration; not even a gay joke
like Strawberry Hill, really a gargantuan "folly". Reproduced from the
frontispiece of John Rutter's *Description of Fonthill Abbey*. Third edition, 1822.

taste; agreeably devoid of serious purpose it was the charming
whim of a cultivated nobleman possessed of considerable architectural knowledge and the selective eye of a discriminating collector. There were other examples of Georgian Gothic, such as the
designs of Walpole's contemporary, Sanderson Miller, an amateur
architect, whose work enriched the character without increasing

the momentum of the revival, for until the last quarter of the eighteenth century no crusading revivalist spirit disturbed the placid enjoyment of a diverting fashion.

Not all the manifestations of that fashion were as modest in scale as Strawberry Hill. Fonthill Abbey, in Wiltshire, designed by James Wyatt for William Beckford and built between 1796 and 1807, was enormous: a central octagonal tower rose to a height of 278 feet, an elegant piece of stage scenery and about as stable, for in 1807 it collapsed. (See page 287.) Beckford had originally envisaged a large mock ruin, with some parts sound enough to act as an occasional residence; but the enthusiasm and imagination of owner and architect expanded as the work progressed, and Beckford's great fortune could bear the strain. While Strawberry Hill still exists, and now houses St. Mary's Roman Catholic Training

Old Battersea Church as it appeared in the mid-eighteenth century; a simple, unpretentious mediaeval building, which was demolished in the 1770s and replaced by the classic design shown opposite. Although the interest in Gothic ruins had swollen into a considerable fashion, few, if any, attempts were made to preserve churches like this that were still in use. *From a contemporary engraving, circa 1750, in the author's possession.*

From the late seventeenth century to the early nineteenth church architecture
ceased to be exclusively Gothic, and throughout England graceful and modest
churches of classic design replaced mediaeval structures, nor was the style discarded until the Gothic revival gathered strength. St. Mary's Church, Battersea,
attributed to the architect Joseph Dixon, and built in 1777 in place of an older
Gothic church. *Drawn by A. S. Cook.* (See opposite page.)

College, Fonthill Abbey has disappeared, apart from some fragments at the end of the north wing. Another vast Gothic house, Eaton Hall, Cheshire, was designed by William Porden for Lord Grosvenor, and built 1804–1812. In 1870 it was completely remodelled by Alfred Waterhouse. Eastlake thought it "one of the most important attempts at Pointed architecture" and described the design as "a mixture of Early and Late Gothic." He rather unkindly referred to Porden as "an architect whose name has been long forgotten, but who, no doubt, had considerable practice in his day."[4] The unwieldy Victorian Gothic building that replaced Porden's original, gracious design, has like Fonthill been demolished.

While Gothic was engaging the favourable regard of the nobility and gentry, there were religious rumblings about the suitability of classical architecture as a background for Christian worship. Even St. Paul's came in for some muted disapproval, and was compared unfavourably with Westminster Abbey by William Woty, who wrote in 1780 the following lines on Church-Langton.

> "On yon proud eminence where LANGTON stands,
> That yields a prospect of the richest lands,
> There shall the grand collegiate CHURCH arise,
> A welcome, free-will off'ring to the skies.
> *Gothic* the Stile, and tending to excite
> Free-thinkers to a sense of what is right,
> With length'ning ayles, and windows that impart
> A gloomy steady light to chear the heart,
> Such as affects the soul, and which I see
> With joy, celestial *Westminster*! in thee.
> Not like Saint PAUL's, beneath whose ample dome,
> No thought arises of the life to come.
> For, tho' superb, not solemn is the place,
> That mind but wanders o'er the distant space,
> Where 'stead of thinking on the GOD, most men
> Forget his presence to remember *Wren*."[5]

Such pious sentiments inspired no movement for safeguarding existing mediaeval churches; many were pulled down, sometimes quite needlessly, and replaced by new buildings in the classic style. Occasionally there were protests, as at Banbury in Oxfordshire, where a survey conducted in 1773 pronounced the tower of the old church to be structurally sound though the nave was not; so, despite considerable local opposition, the church was rebuilt, 1792–1797, to the design of Samuel Pepys Cockerell, the tower being completed in 1822 by his second son, Charles Robert Cockerell.[6] At Battersea, Surrey, the original parish church of St. Mary was rebuilt by Act of Parliament and a new church with a classic portico opened in 1777.[7] The painted glass from the old church was preserved and reused in the east window. (See pages 288 and 289.)

Spiritual sanctions for using the Gothic style in church building accumulated about the same time as the taste for ruins increased in popularity, for they were regarded as essential in the creation of picturesque effects, and were by reason of the erosions of time, pleasingly irregular. The case *for* irregularity, which was also the case *against* symmetrical design, had been put with charming persuasiveness by Sir Uvedale Price (1747–1829) in his famous *Essays on the Picturesque* (1794), which, like Sir William Temple's *Essay on Gardening*, written over a hundred years earlier, condoned, but without any of Temple's reservations, the use of asymmetrical composition. As we said in the previous chapter, the *sharawadgi* taste had prepared the Georgian nobility and gentry for a flight from symmetry: until the picturesque movement became influential, it was no more than a flight of fancy, but Price and those who thought like him had justified the movement, and were, perhaps unknowingly, helping to change—as the rococo style had already tended to change—the belief that beauty and symmetry were identical in architectural design. Price recognised the contribution that Gothic architecture could make to the movement, for it was, he wrote, "generally considered as more picturesque, though less beautiful, than Grecian; and upon the same principle that a ruin is more so than a new edifice. The first thing that strikes the eye in approaching any building, is the general outline, and effect of the opening. In Grecian buildings, the general lines of the roof are straight; and even when varied and adorned by a dome or a pediment, the whole has a character of symmetry and regularity. But symmetry, which in works of art particularly accords with the beautiful, is in the same degree adverse to the picturesque; and among the various causes of the superior picturesqueness of ruins,

The domestic architecture of the first half of the nineteenth century maintained the good proportions and classical character of the Georgian period, and this terrace of small houses, built about 1835, is an example of the appropriate use of materials. The houses were of red brick, with moulded plaster door and window architraves, and slate roofs. They stood formerly on the Lower Richmond Road facing the north side of Mortlake Green. They were demolished in 1960. *Drawn by David Owen.*

compared with entire buildings, the destruction of symmetry is by no means the least powerful."[8]

His advocacy of Gothic anticipated some of the arguments John Ruskin used half a century later, though without Ruskin's irate passion; Price never departed from a standpoint of sweet reasonableness, although the form of taste he was justifying was the visual negation of everything that the golden age of taste and reason had honoured. "In Gothic buildings," he said, "the outline of the summit presents such a variety of forms, of turrets and pinnacles, some open, some fretted and variously enriched, that even where there is an exact correspondence of parts, it is often disguised by an appearance of splended confusion and irregularity." He recognised the incompatability of Gothic with the classic system of design. "In the doors and windows of Gothic churches," he continued, "the pointed arch has as much variety as any regular figure can well have; the eye, too, is less strongly conducted than by the parallel lines in the Grecian style, from the top of one aperture to that of another; and every person must be struck by the extreme richness of some of the principal windows of our cathedrals and ruined abbeys. In these last is displayed the triumph of the picturesque; and their charms to a painter's eye are often so great, as to rival those which arise from the chaste ornaments, and the noble and elegant simplicity of Grecian architecture."

The contriving of picturesque effects and attempts to copy the methods and recapture the outlook of mediaeval builders led to architectural chaos; inspired by literary fashions in the eighteenth century, the revival of Gothic by the early nineteenth was identified with spiritual obligation, for as William Woty had insisted it was the style that promoted and sustained reverence and piety. By implication classic architecture seemed to suggest if not actual immorality at least an easy-going pagan tolerance that condoned levity. Moral earnestness was gathering power, and in the second quarter of the nineteenth century the revival of Gothic expressed the views of an influential section of society that was suspicious of pleasure, nervous of art, and inclined to confuse comfort, hygienic convenience and respectability with civilisation.

The industrial revolution had created a new rich class, confident, enterprising, innocently ignorant and never suspecting that within a hundred years huge areas of the English countryside would be sentenced to death by the spread of industry and the architectural character of many towns irreparably injured. The portly mansions and public buildings of the Victorians are memorials of their inability to distinguish between ornament and design. Like the new rich of every country and every period, they spent lavishly on showing-off; but they were also religious and public-spirited, and subsidised the building of Gothic churches, town halls, and memorial halls. Many such records of their generosity demonstrated the energetic decadence of a period in which architecture had become separated from life, for Victorian Gothic was born dead on the drawing-board. Gothic had never represented a system of design in any way comparable with classic, and new life could not be given to mediaeval forms as new life had been given to the classic orders at the Renaissance. The architect became little more than a diligent copyist, studying historic buildings and reproducing with the accuracy of a skilled draughtsman the work of masons and builders, far removed in time, and remote in spiritual and artistic sensibility.

In Britain a writer of genius whose influence on contemporary taste was profound, had dismissed the Renaissance as "a foul tor-rent". His name was John Ruskin (1819–1900), and in burning words he condemned the classic idiom. "Whatever has any con-nection with the five orders, or with any one of the orders," he said, "whatever is Doric or Ionic or Corinthian or Composite, or in any way Grecised or Romanised; whatever betrays the smallest respect for Vitruvian laws or conformity with Palladian work . . . that we are to endure no more."

His persistent advocacy of Gothic forms for every type of build-ing encouraged the destruction of urbane uniformity in streets. The late Sir Charles Reilly, an architect, critic and gifted teacher, saw Ruskin as pre-eminently a destroyer. "Ruskin simply turned us, or rather our houses, upside down," he wrote. "The quiet dignified old England of Rowlandson's drawings—I refer to the houses not to the people—were changed to the speckled red and white, the pink and blue irregularly strewn crumbs of any awkward pointed shape of which Bournemouth, wholly built in Ruskinian and post-Ruskinian times, provided the supreme example."[9]

The attempt to restore mediaeval individualism only achieved clumsy disorder or drab monotony, with a mechanical repetition of pointed arches on doorways and unrelated Gothic ornament spotted here and there on façades; nothing resembling the spark-ling, coloured variety of a mediaeval street. The popularity of Ruskin's views prevented even perceptive people from recognising the emergence of a new form of architecture, largely the work of engineers, which more than any conscious attempt to create a fresh style or to reinterpret the principles of an old one, suggested the birth of another cultural period, destined to follow the eighth on Petrie's diagram, though still in its raw infancy, as strident and in-continent as infants are apt to be.

After the first quarter of the nineteenth century changes in architectural fashions suggested a concerted reluctance on the part of the British upper and middle classes to acknowledge that any such birth had occurred; like other socially embarrassing happen-ings it was hushed-up; the fruit of a union between engineering and organised industry incurred the odium of artistic impropriety. Since the early seventeenth century, when architects and engineers went their separate ways, creative art and applied science were insulated in what J. B. S. Haldane once called "idea-tight" compartments. Many of the versatile and promising materials, such as cast-iron and glass, were either ignored, used in the interests of disguise—like fluted Doric columns of cast-iron painted to look like stone—or pontifically condemned, as Ruskin condemned them in the first of his lectures on architecture and painting delivered in 1854 at Edinburgh. Invoking Biblical authority he quoted the words spoken by the Lord to Jeremiah. "For, behold, I have made thee this day a defenced city, and an iron pillar, and brasen walls, against the whole land."[10]

A mid-nineteenth century Scottish audience would respect the quotation and respond to Ruskin's general conclusions, when he went on to say: "But I do not find that iron is ever alluded to as likely to become *familiar* to the minds of men; but, on the contrary, that an architecture of carved stone is continually employed as a source of the most important illustrations. A simple instance must occur to you all at once. The force of the image of the Corner Stone, as used throughout Scripture, would be completely lost, if the Christian and civilised world were ever extensively to employ any other material than earth and rock in their domestic buildings: I firmly believe that they never will; but that as the laws of beauty are more perfectly established, we shall be content still to build as our forefathers built . . ."[11]

He had admitted earlier that everything he said in his lecture "rested on the assumption that all architecture was to be of brick and stone; and may meet with some hesitation in its acceptance, on account of the probable use of iron, glass, and such other materials in our future edifices." As the Great Exhibition of 1851 had been housed in a vast structure, formed by pre-fabricated units of glass and iron, he could hardly ignore those materials, though Ruskin and his disciples failed to recognise the Crystal Palace as an architectural portent. They did not classify such buildings as architecture at all. In their eyes, Sir Joseph Paxton had erected no more than an ingenious exaggeration of a conservatory. Even Pugin who, as a practising architect might have taken a more perceptive view of such a structural achievement, was repelled by the materials. "Cast-iron pillars were odious things in his sight, and notwithstanding the astonishing mechanical skill shown in the conception of the building," he "viewed the whole scheme with feelings of aversion".[12] On one of his visits to the building when it was nearly completed, he met Paxton, who asked him what he thought of the design. Pugin was blunt, and replied "you had better keep to building greenhouses, and I will keep to my churches and cathedrals."

Ruskin and Pugin, two totally different types of genius, both had their eyes on the past; unfortunately their eyes were out of focus; they saw only what they wanted to see. Augustus Northmore Welby Pugin (1811–1852) was one of those prickly, eccentric characters, whose gifts and opinions upset comfortable people. He refused to restrict his activities to his creative work as an artist and an architect, and did not regard the Gothic revival as a romantic escape from the brutal disorder that had invaded and destroyed ancient towns, with factories sprouting sooty chimneys, gas-works with clusters of corpulent gas-holders, and, darkest part of the squalid scene, unhappy streets of back-to-back, cheaply-built brick houses for the factory hands and their families. He assessed the dubious gains and mounting losses of contemporary civilisation in an extraordinary book, written and illustrated with savage originality, published in 1836 at his own expense and at a considerable loss, which he called *Contrasts: or a Parallel between the noble edifices of the Middle Ages and corresponding buildings of the present day, showing the present decay of taste*. Five years later it was reissued, and from that second edition two illustrations are reproduced on pages 298 and 299, which show an English town in 1440 and the same town in 1840.[13]

Pugin believed that European civilisation had taken a wrong and disastrous turning at the Reformation. Almost inevitably he became a Catholic convert, so his writings thereafter were suspect and apt to be discounted as mere Catholic propaganda. He made no secret of his championship of the old religion and felt passionately that only by returning to mediaeval beliefs and standards could European culture be salvaged. He elaborated a method of graphic criticism, applied particularly to civic life and architecture, that has never been forgotten. His book of *Contrasts* has inspired many of the illustrated commentaries published since the end of the 1914–18 war, when people began to be worried about pollution not only in Britain but throughout the western world. Of these later commentaries the most outstanding are Osbert Lancaster's *Progress at Pelvis Bay* and *Drayneflete Revealed*,[14] written and illustrated with a sophisticated humour, quite unlike Pugin's bitter moralising, but equally effective in castigating civic and bureaucratic stupidity.

Lord Clark has described Pugin as "the Janus of the Gothic Revival; his buildings look back to the picturesque past, and his writings look forward to the ethical future."[15] Alone of all the Gothic Revival architects Pugin was able to give the breath of life to his versions of mediaeval art; his interpretations were illuminated by something more profound than love of his subject; he was happily at home in the spiritual atmosphere of the Middle Ages; sympathetically identified with the beliefs and skills of the painters and carvers and masons of the thirteenth and fourteenth centuries; whereas scholarly copyists could only make sketches and measured drawings and erudite notes; thin nourishment for creative inspiration. Pugin was a great artist like Ruskin, but Ruskin was an artist in words; visually he was finical and obsessed by unimportant ornamental details, and he disapproved of Pugin's work, against which some of his more obnoxious architectural criticisms were directed. Like a great many Victorians, Ruskin had an almost pathological suspicion of Roman Catholics, and his unjust strictures on Pugin were inflamed by bigotry.

Those two great men made their characteristic contributions to the Gothic Revival: the architect with noble buildings and interior decoration that reanimated mediaeval art: the writer with splendid-sounding phrases that glorified it: both rejected the materials, techniques, and potential promise of the scientific industrial age in which they lived. Like Ruskin, Pugin denigrated classic architecture and everything associated with its lucidity and discipline. Like Ruskin he also rejected the Georgian Gothic of the eighteenth and early nineteenth centuries.

Ruskin had been particularly pained that Sir Walter Scott, whom he greatly admired, was unable to detect the difference between true Gothic, as at Glasgow cathedral, and "false Gothic at Abbotsford."[16] Abbotsford House near Melrose in Roxburghshire was designed for Scott by Edward Blore, begun in 1816 and completed by William Atkinson in 1822–23. This richly congested assembly of mediaeval features was a forerunner of the Scottish baronial style; an appropriate residence for the author of the Waverley novels. Scott's romances, especially those like *Ivanhoe*,

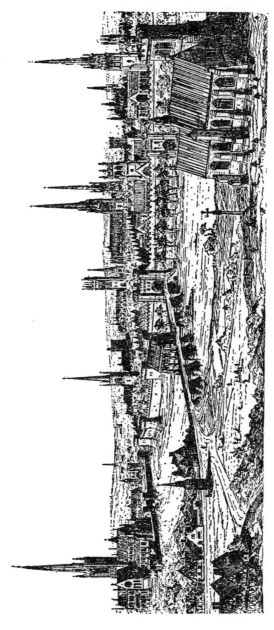

Two views of an English town, reproduced on a slightly smaller scale from Pugin's book of *Contrasts*. (London. Charles Dolman. Second edition, 1841.) *Above*: "A Catholic town in 1440." (Pugin's description.) On the left a great abbey stands, separated from the town by a broad river; within the town itself, behind the encircling walls, the towers and spires of churches and monastic buildings endow the scene with celestial splendour. This idealised view was drawn by a passionate advocate of the Gothic Revival. What the view looked like four centuries later is shown opposite.

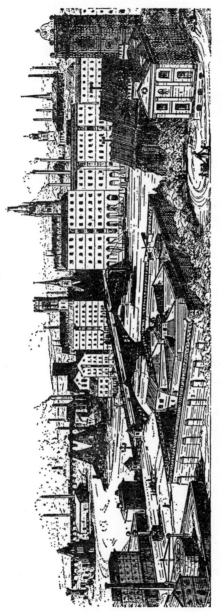

The same town in 1840. Industry has moved in; cliff-like warehouses have replaced the walls; the stone arches of the mediaeval bridge have been replaced by two elliptical arches of cast-iron; the abbey is in ruins; the spires of other churches are truncated, the pinnacles on church towers chopped off, and some of the churches rebuilt in the classic style that Pugin abominated; gas works face the abbey ruins across the stream; factory chimneys raise sooty shafts all over the town; and in the foreground is a grim new Jail. Up and down the country, such transformations were taking place, unremarked and apparently condoned by all save a few gifted, and sometimes eccentric, observers like Pugin. See view on opposite page. Reproduced on a slightly smaller scale from Pugin's book of *Contrasts*.

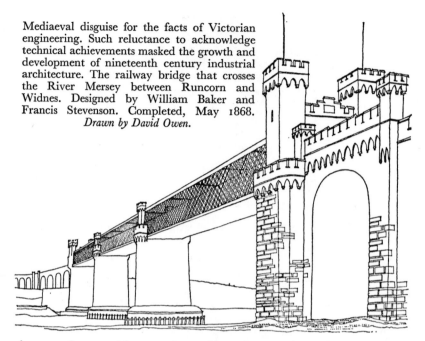

Mediaeval disguise for the facts of Victorian engineering. Such reluctance to acknowledge technical achievements masked the growth and development of nineteenth century industrial architecture. The railway bridge that crosses the River Mersey between Runcorn and Widnes. Designed by William Baker and Francis Stevenson. Completed, May 1868.
Drawn by David Owen.

increased general interest in mediaeval art and architecture, as in France the popularity of Victor Hugo's *Notre-Dame de Paris*, published in 1831, encouraged the so-called "Cathedral" and "Troubadour" styles; but those were ephemeral fashions in decoration, sustained only by superficial interest, unlike the taste for Gothic which in the second quarter of the century became identified with spiritual rectitude. Any perplexity about what particular period of architecture should be favoured by the Gothic revivalists was resolved by Ruskin. "I have no doubt," he declared, "that the only style proper for modern northern work, is the Northern Gothic of the thirteenth century, as exemplified, in England, pre-eminently by the cathedrals of Lincoln and Wells, and, in France, by those of Paris, Amiens, Chartres, Rheims, and Bourges, and by the transepts of that of Rouen."[17]

The proselytising zeal and exhortations of Ruskin made the escape route from contemporary life seem easy and rewarding, though he offered no hedonistic satisfactions; the fulfilment of moral duty was its own reward, and it became almost a matter of moral duty to reject the pagan architecture of Rome and to replace it with what passed for Gothic. "Do not be afraid of incongruities," he urged; "do not think of unities of effect. Introduce your Gothic line by line and stone by stone; never mind mixing it with your present architecture; your existing houses will be none the worse for having little bits of better work fitted to them; build a porch, or point a window, if you can do nothing else; and remember that it is the glory of Gothic architecture that it can do *anything*. Whatever you really and seriously want, Gothic will do it for you; but it must be an *earnest* want."[18] Such words gave unlimited licence to the scissors-and-paste school of design; moreover they were sanctified by moral earnestness.

Travels with a sketch-book had long been rendered unnecessary in order to collect and record scraps and oddments of Gothic ornament, for innumerable copy books were published, including one best-seller that became the stand-by of architects and speculative builders for over half a century. This was *The Encyclopaedia of Cottage, Farm, and Villa Architecture, and Furniture*, compiled and largely written by an industrious Scot named John Claudius Loudon (1783–1843), first published in 1833 and running to 1138 pages, which were increased to 1317 in later editions. The illustrations included the "Castellated style", "Monastic Gothic", "Old English", and even "Indian Gothic".[19] The whole conception of the service architecture could and should offer to a community was distorted; the style-fanciers offered visual diversions and disguises for all kinds of structures; frowning mock fortifications guarded railway bridges like that crossing the Mersey at Runcorn (opposite); in London the Tower Bridge, a fine piece of engineering, was dolled-up in Scottish baronial trappings; factories masqueraded externally as Venetian palaces; and everywhere in Britain the Gothic monsters of the Victorian wonderland of wealth and scientific and industrial progress helped to suppress the authentic architecture of a new cultural period, struggling into existence.

Lewis Mumford has suggested that the Gothic Revival slightly checked what he called "the centralizing, exploitative, and deregionalizing processes of the machine civilization."[20] The revival certainly checked acceptance of the facts of industrial life, providing a refuge from their upsetting intrusion and supplying a proper and agreeably romantic covering for their shocking nakedness. The Victorians have been accused of hypocrisy, which has been defined as "feigning to be what one is not; concealment of true character."[21] By that definition very many Victorian buildings represented something altogether new in the history of art: an architecture of hypocrisy. Many of the public buildings were impossibly inconvenient, like the Law Courts in the Strand, London, built to the designs of George Edmund Street (1824–1881), begun in 1868 and completed in 1882. The façade has been described by Sir Nikolaus Pevsner as "an object lesson in free composition, with none of the symmetry of the classics, yet not undisciplined where symmetry is abandoned."[22] It satisfies Ruskin's choice for "modern northern work" as the style imitates thirteenth century English Gothic. (Below.) The windows of the Great Hall admit the minimum of daylight, as they are narrow lancets, with geometrical tracery; gloom pervades the interior, for, as Pevsner observes, "the conception of a light and efficient secular building to please those who work in it, did not yet exist."

The expensive and wasteful game of make-believe that the Gothic revivalists were playing had a large and responsive audi-

The Law Courts in the Strand. The last large public building in London to be designed in the revived Gothic style. The architect was George Edmund Street, and work was begun in 1868 and completed in 1882, two years after Street's death. This Victorian version of thirteenth century English Gothic reveals much about the character of the Victorians and their passion for inconvenient make-believe.
Drawn by A. S. Cook.

The Victoria Tower of the Houses of Parliament, London. The building, designed by Sir Charles Barry, was erected between 1840 and 1858: the Tower was completed in 1860. After Barry's death in that year the work was finished by his son, Edward Middleton Barry. *Drawn by A. S. Cook.*

ence, for the fairy-tale visions of the Middle Ages, of an illusory "Merry England", had grown and multiplied, and an attempt to restore lost or failing arts and crafts was one of the later accompaniments of the revival, inspired and initiated by William Morris (1834–1896). Like Ruskin and Pugin, Morris viewed the Renaissance as a disaster; the separation of art from everyday life which had then occurred outraged him emotionally; the revival of classic architecture had fostered a hateful professionalism; neither St. Paul's Cathedral in London nor St. Peter's in Rome were "built to be beautiful, or to be beautiful and convenient," he declared. "They were built to be the homes of a decent unenthusiastic ecclesiasticism, of those whom we sometimes call Dons now-a-days. Beauty and Romance were outside the aspirations of their builders."[23] So away with it all: back to dreams of an idealised past, and a London that had never existed.

> "Forget the spreading of the hideous town;
> Think rather of the pack-horse on the down,
> And dream of London, small and white and clean,
> The clear Thames bordered by its gardens green . . ."[24]

Until the early nineteenth century the Thames had been clear and reasonably clean; on both banks the gardens of elegant country villas ran down to the river's lip; but London had not been "small and white and clean" since the far-off days when it was Londinium Augusta, and, when Morris wrote those lines the city was only just beginning to have efficient sanitation like its Roman predecessor. Mediaeval London, which Morris had in mind, was a noisome slum, rank with filth and a plague-breeder; but nostalgia is as blind as love and it is unfair to dissect a poet's imagery.

Though the champions of the Gothic Revival were sincerely convinced that they were restoring old English traditions submerged since the sixteenth century, they were really depriving architects and builders of a known and reliable system of design; and the guiding influence of that system was often reasserted. The new Houses of Parliament, designed by Sir Charles Barry (1795–1860), built between 1840 and 1868, and completed by his third son, Edward Middleton Barry, was a classic composition, veneered with late Gothic ornament. Pugin, who had designed most of the decoration, had no illusions about the real architectural character of the building. "All Grecian, Sir!" he said to a friend, when they saw the riverside frontage from the deck of a Thames steam-boat; "Tudor details on a classic body."[25]

The Victorians were not always faithful to Gothic; hundreds of architects whose diligence surpassed their creative abilities, copied other styles: Romanesque, Byzantine, and compounded a restless amalgam of oriental features, horseshoe and cusped arches and geometrical patternings, stirred together and labelled Moorish, and from the sixteenth and seventeenth centuries they culled raw mixtures described as Elizabethan and Jacobean. Architects and their patrons both liked towers, so the status symbols of San Gimignano were repeated on a smaller scale and with some very peculiar variations in country houses, suburban villas, civic

St. Paul's, Hammersmith, built 1882, to the designs of
Hugh Roumien Gough and John Pollard Seddon. From
a photograph, about 1910, with adjoining eighteenth
century houses. *Below*: The same church today, with the
Hammersmith fly-over alongside. *Drawn by Maureen
Stafford*. (See page 249.)

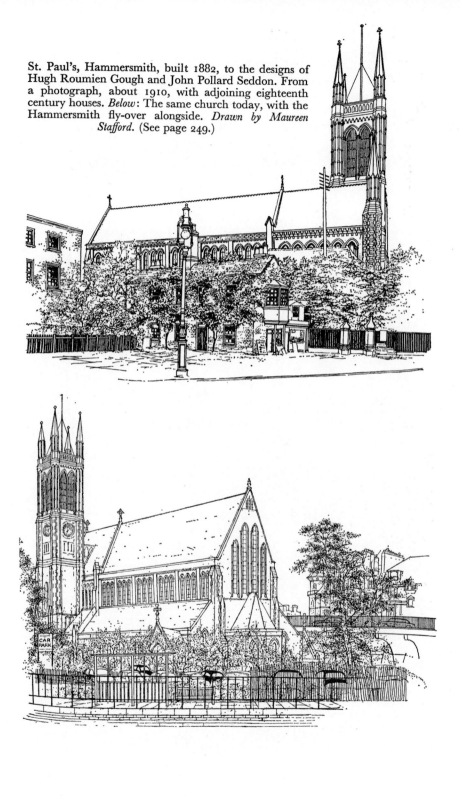

Fashions in architecture have always affected the form and ornament of rooms and furniture, and the Gothic Revival left its mark on Victorian furniture. This massive bookcase at least showed that cabinet-makers and carvers had preserved their skill, though all sense of proportion was lost. This was one of the exhibits sent by the firm of C. Hindley and Sons, of 134 Oxford Street, London to the International Exhibition of 1862. Reproduced from *The Art Journal Illustrated Catalogue*, 1862, page 177.

buildings and large, pretentious hotels. The Natural History Museum, fronting Cromwell Road in South Kensington, was designed in the Romanesque style by Alfred Waterhouse (1830–1905), and built 1873–1881. The composition is symmetrical; the building is faced with hard-wearing terracotta slabs of repellent colour, and the façade is diversified with zoological motifs.

Although the warm tide of humanism was receding, classic architecture continued in use, occasionally recapturing the urbanity of the Golden Age and enriching cities with monumental and magnificent works. Some were outstanding, like St. George's Hall, Liverpool, 1842–1854; the Greek Doric portico at Euston Station, the terminus of the London and North Western Railway, 1833–1857, wantonly and, as later established, quite needlessly demolished in 1960; the British Museum in Bloomsbury, built between 1823 and 1847; the Fitzwilliam Museum, Cambridge, 1837–1847, and the National Gallery of Scotland, Edinburgh, 1850–1854. In the new residential suburbs of London and other cities, broad streets, squares and crescents were lined with terraces of spacious houses, with façades of painted stucco, well-proportioned doors and windows, the profile of every moulding in accord with classical precedent, and often with sheltering porches, approached by a short flight of stone steps and usually flanked by Tuscan or Doric columns. The standardised type of Georgian town-house was still built in the third quarter of the nineteenth century; a little coarsened in detail perhaps, but with good windows and lofty rooms.

Dr. Northcote Parkinson's conclusion, quoted in chapter one, that the abandonment of the classic idiom about 1845 coincided with the turn of the tide against the West, when "Europe began to lose confidence in its mission" has a disturbing plausibility. "After that date," he said, "the known methods ceased to work. The classic proportions were lost as rooms gained a new height— Anglo-Indian influence providing space for an imaginary punkah. The magic had gone out of the formula and buildings varied from the mediocre to the drab."[26]

The "splendid confusion" of Gothic that Sir Uvedale Price had praised, all too often degenerated into architectural anarchy, afflicting alike the buildings of Britain and the British Dominions overseas, and those of the United States. In Europe the classic tradition continued, with a certain lush emphasis on ornament in France. In England, city streets and country houses told a story of wealth misused; of reliance on thick, solid evidence of prosperity; and because the solidity of Victorian houses and their contents recall the cosy stability of the period, nostalgic affection has cast a tender-coloured haze over its visual shortcomings, though no passing fashion in taste can alter the fact that the period was remarkable for more ugliness than any other in the history of civilisation.

SHADOWS OF THE FUTURE

FROM the closing decades of the nineteenth century to the third quarter of the twentieth, the character and design of buildings gave the brutally clear message that Western civilisation had crossed a vital threshold. We are, apparently, in the early growth stages of another period of culture that, according to the Flinders Petrie diagram, is due to begin when the eighth period ends about A.D. 2000. We may have to pass through another Dark Age before any new cultural period is consolidated, but as we are now living in a time of transition it is a capital mistake to assume either triumphant progress or inevitable disaster. Sorokin, whose theories were referred to in chapter one, takes the catastrophic view, and Dr. Cowell in his introduction to the Russian sociologist's work mentions his prophecy that crisis and disaster are about to overtake Western society and culture in its present form. Already he sees evidence of "a sensate super-system in disintegration and decay. Its values are dissolving, and there is no way of halting the process which has already begun to remove the distinction between right and wrong, beautiful and ugly, true and false."[1] The final result will be anarchy, when "our world will become a kind of bazaar, a cultural dumping-place into which are thrust all manner of miscellaneous cultural elements devoid of any unity or individuality."

Sir John Betjeman, with the incisive economy of genius, has described such a world in "The Planster's Vision."

> "I have a Vision of the Future, chum,
>   The workers' flats in fields of soya beans
>   Tower up like silver pencils, score on score:
>   And Surging Millions hear the Challenge come
>   From microphones in communal canteens
>   "No Right! No Wrong! All's perfect, everymore."[2]

The evidence of contemporary architecture could be manipulated to suggest either triumph or disaster; for the changes in character and intention, not only in architecture but in sculpture and the graphic arts, have been encouraged and partly controlled by the technological revolution that has stealthily and almost secretly assumed partial control of social, commercial and industrial life in the Western World. The power of this revolution could be hailed as a triumph of progress, or an ominous warning. The by-products of a triumphant and expanding technology include pollution, over-population, overcrowding, the continuous and remorseless destruction of human scale and the steady erosion of individual independence and liberty. The involvement of architects with sociology has encouraged social engineering; a sinister phrase that really means, pushing people around without their consent and filing them away in approved accommodation units, as inanimate documents are tidily disposed of in a filing cabinet.

The tall residential towers of modern cities constitute an architecture of inhumanism unknown in previous civilisations, and made possible by the industrially-produced materials and new structural techniques developed since the last quarter of the nineteenth century. Until then buildings depended on one or other (or both) of the two structural inventions, post-and-lintel and the arch. To these a third was added: the cantilever, which is a horizontal support or elongated bracket, fixed at one end and free at the other, projecting from an upright member or a vertical surface. The length and supporting power of a cantilever is controlled by anchoring the fixed end either by a great weight or by securing it with anchor plates and ties. The cantilever principle was known and used in the Far East before it was employed by Europeans and Americans. The projecting roofs that jutted out from pagodas, temples and palaces were supported by a system of timber brackets and lever arms; and though the superficial characteristics of Chinese pagodas had been imitated in the eighteenth century by French and English architects, the structural principle apparently escaped their notice. The cantilever was eventually employed when steel construction and reinforced concrete were introduced. The internal steel supporting skeleton took over the ancient duties of the wall, which became a skin instead of a support, and though this structural transformation changed the whole character of architecture, its implications were not acknowledged. Like so many works designed by nineteenth century engineers, such as railway stations and bridges, disguise was sought; structural and functional frankness were still frightening. The first American skyscrapers in Chicago and New York looked like immense exaggerations of traditional buildings and they announced (though few got the message) that after two hundred and fifty years of separation the activities of the architect and the engineer were tending to merge, a merger that became dramatically apparent when architects discovered the promise of reinforced concrete and took advantage of its infinite plasticity to create buildings that were in effect great sculptured masses. The spirit of adventure returned to architectural design when those ambitious towers rose in American cities. The first men who were openly aware that a new architecture was struggling to break through the stylistic confusions of the late nineteenth century, were the Americans: Louis Sullivan (1850–1924) and Frank Lloyd Wright (1869–1959); the Austrians: Otto Wagner (1841–1918) and Adolph Loos (1870–1933); and the Belgian: Henry van de Velde (1863–1957). They were exceptionally perceptive pioneers.

During the last decade of the nineteenth century revivals still flourished, though the Gothic had lost spiritual momentum, and the Romanesque and Byzantine had never had any. In London one large pseudo-Byzantine building was erected between 1895 and 1903, the Roman Catholic cathedral at Westminster, designed by John Francis Bentley (1839–1902). Something called free classic was also introduced, the use of the word free presumably excusing almost as many garbled versions of the classic orders as those on the plates of sixteenth century Flemish and German copy books. An attempt to make an effective break with traditional styles, and to cut loose from all historical ties, resulted in a restless ornamental fashion known as *Art Nouveau*, based on the intertwining undulations of naturalistic forms, snakey arabesques and bursting blossoms, asymmetrically disposed on flat or curved surfaces and punctuated with heart-shaped bosses and apertures. It was not an architectural style, and, like rococo, had more influence on interior decoration and furniture than on buildings. This was a long way from being the opening phase of a new period of European art and architecture: it was, and deserved to be, short-lived.

In Britain a few architects possessed the vision and ability to exercise civilised control over the febrile exuberance of *Art Nouveau*, and of these the most outstanding were Charles Rennie Mackintosh (1868–1928), whose principal building, the Glasgow School of Art (1898–1899), was far ahead of its time; and Charles Francis Annesley Voysey (1857–1941), who built houses that seemed revolutionary in the 1890s, but left an enduring mark on the character of domestic architecture in England.[3] Like many of their contemporaries they used traditional materials, thus reflecting a cautious reluctance to experiment frankly with the new structural techniques and materials, a reluctance that deferred the emergence of a new Western architecture, that was destined to spread over Europe and America, and to the former Asiatic empires of Britain, France and Holland, as classic architecture had spread in the sixteenth, seventeenth and eighteenth centuries. The persistent power of nationalism is asserted by the distinctive architecture that has arisen in Europe, North and South America, Australia, South Africa and the Middle East.

A suggestion of impermanence is conveyed by the glittering glass cubes that have in so many cities replaced old, overcrowded offices which had become business slums; the new office blocks have an economic life, calculated by actuaries; so much floor space, so much rent, so many years of earning power as premises, and then demolition; just as the former transatlantic liners had an economic life, from the proud day of their launch to their last journey to the shipbreakers. Controlled by such utilitarian considerations, the imagination of an architect, hitherto an essential ingredient in design, may be diminished or even dispensed with as something unwanted and uneconomic. A purely commercial state, some modern, mechanised Carthage, could unconsciously suppress inspired architecture because inspiration, beyond the ken of accountants, is excluded from balance sheets. Architectural evidence of creative bankruptcy occurs in modern totalitarian states: like Sparta, the ancient Greek forerunner of a fascist military state, they lack dynamic artistic powers, and like Sparta contribute nothing to the history of art or architecture. Hitlerite Germany produced a harsh, abruptly brutal type of building, of which the Brown House at Munich was typical, and the big programmes of domestic housing were intentionally traditional in character. The unfamiliar forms of the Modern Movement in the 1930s were rejected outright; they were identified with revolutionary sentiments, for Nazi propaganda extended to architectural design, and had officially condemned the flat roof and the monotonous concrete boxes that were functionally perfect and as dull as ditchwater. So for rural housing, farms and farm buildings, it was back to the thatch and traditional building methods.[4]

During a visit to Nazi Germany, made in October 1938, soon after the Munich Agreement, the writer was told by officials of the Reichsheimstat-tenamt that the Modern Movement in architecture had been abandoned because the State wanted a nation of home-lovers. They explained in detail just how potent an instrument of propaganda domestic architecture had become under National Socialism. What they encouraged (indeed, insisted on) was homely-looking stuff that would never disturb the inhabitants by any of the revolutionary notions that clamoured for attention in modern buildings. So all apartment blocks and houses had to have pitched roofs, red tiles, cosy rooms, and little touches here and there of romantic ornament to furnish a picturesque note of subdued individualism.[5] Those officials were emphatically frank. "We don't want experiments in structure or materials," they said. The needs of a family were known, and accommodation was designed to create a comfortable setting for traditional family life. "We *must* make a difference between the factory and the home," said one of them, and unexpectedly quoted Le Corbusier's dictum, by adding: "We won't have house machines."

Early in the second quarter of the twentieth century, European architects, particularly in Germany and France, were beginning to shape their ideas of architectural design to accord with social theories that were based on spurious logic and were apt to ignore human relationships. The domestic architecture of that time, in the 1930s especially, reflects a growing contempt for privacy, a desire to change traditional patterns of life, and a new, confident arrogance on the part of a young generation of architects, often muddled with ill-digested Marxism, who saw themselves as pioneers of social reconstruction. They forgot about people as human beings with little peculiar ways and tastes, and were bedevilled by that chilled abstraction, *The People*. Open planning enforced proximity, and denied the blessings of seclusion in homes. This architectural reversion to the great hall, with its communal life, in one large all-purpose room, was part of the reaction against the bourgeois comforts and standards of the nine-teenth century; quite unlike sentimental attempts on Pugin-Ruskin-William Morris lines to revive mediaeval ways and beliefs; open planning was advocated in the interests of mechanised effi-ciency in dwellings. The infernal plausibility of Le Corbusier's phrase, "the house is a machine for living in",[6] captivated a whole generation of European architects, and ensnared them into believ-ing that life could be ordered and regulated and tidied-up on drawing boards; they became impersonal arbiters of lives they never saw, as far removed from the social results of their work as gunners firing at targets twenty miles away are removed from the men their shells have disembowelled.

An English architect taking part in a series of talks broadcast in 1933 on "Design in Modern Life", said: "We have redivided the house into a compact working space; a space given over to the act of sleeping, planned to be no bigger than it need be; and the rest, spacious, subdivisible at will, is there to live in spaciously, served by controlled heat, made of beautiful but easily cleaned materials, thrown open to the air in fine weather—a flexible, airy dwelling."[7]

This was the specification for Le Corbusier's "house machine": a model of petrified convenience, from which the warmth and welcome of a home were efficiently expelled. The whole con-ception implied impermanence; and during the second and third quarters of the twentieth century the character of architecture in the Western World denied the belief once expressed by Sir Christopher Wren that "Building certainly ought to have the Attribute of Eternal, and therefore the only Thing uncapable of new Fashions."

In every previous cultural period, the permanence of secular and sacred buildings had been taken for granted: temples and churches and monumental tombs, palaces and great mansions, were built not only for present use and display but for posterity. After the mid-twentieth century, apart from churches and civic buildings, few works possessed the quality of permanence; the tall office blocks and residential towers had, as we said earlier, an economic expectation of life: nothing beyond. Structures transcending that meagre expectation are often built of traditional materials, like Ragnar Östberg's Town Hall at Stockholm (1909–1923), the last romantic building in Europe; the new cathedral at Coventry, by Sir Basil Spence; or that serene and impressive monument, the Mausoleum of Kemal Ataturk, at Ankara.

The commercial preoccupations of states in the free world sometimes discourage the erection of noble and enduring buildings; in democracies, edging towards collectivism and bureaucracy, business interests often feel obliged to be reticent, to play down their successes, so their buildings become architectural apologies for prosperity, except in the United States of America, where a vivacious partnership exists between art and commerce, comparable with that of mediaeval Venice. Splendid towers adorn American cities, as varied and exciting and magnificent as the towers and spires of mediaeval and Renaissance Europe. "The business of America is business," said Calvin Coolidge. American architecture repeats that message in every state of the Union. The tall buildings are expressions of pride and confidence; but although zoning regulations exist, civic character has often been debased, and nearly every big North American city has suffered from uncontrolled and over-rapid growth. The processional ways that used to dignify and unite the quarters of ancient cities have been replaced by speedways that slice a roaring path through everything, wholly in the interests of locomotion. Cities like Los Angeles seem to have adopted the motto Kipling invented in the opening decade of this century, when he looked ahead a hundred years and imagined a world state governed by a technocratic body called the Aerial Board of Control, that believed *Transportation is Civilisation.* The citizens of that united world were, theoretically, allowed to do as they pleased, so long as they did not interfere with traffic, "and all it implies."[8]

The much-criticised traffic system of Los Angeles may eventually be imposed everywhere in the Western World, so that cities are no longer planned and built for man; a prospect that some specialists accept with bland approval. At a conference on "Transport and Environment" held in 1966 under the auspices of the Town and Country Planning Association, Dr. Peter Hall contended that the Los Angeles system worked aesthetically and emotionally, "provided you accept the principle that this is a city to be seen from the view-point of the car, not from the traditionally urban vantage point of the pedestrian."[9] The acceptance of such a principle could change the whole conception of city planning and transmogrify the visual function of architecture. The interests of vehicles would become paramount and pedestrian traffic segregated, driven underground or carried overhead, with special precincts for leisurely strolling: eventually the residential and business quarters might be raised over, or buried below, ground level. The French architect, Yona Friedman has visualised cities hanging in space above ground, freeing land for agriculture, and relieving the congestion of existing cities by suspending mobile, airy buildings from huge metal frames above the streets, parks, and waterways.

Meanwhile the throughways and their speeding serpents of bumper-to-bumper vehicles continue to disintegrate existing cities, unlike the nineteenth century railways that, in the United States, created towns and helped to populate the vast territory of the Republic. In America the railroad was not only the new road, but often the only road. As the tracks were laid, radiating North, South and West from the eastern seaboard, they became life-lines for small, scattered settlements. Those settlements expanded; the railroad soon ran down the main street of a village; stores, saloons, a few shacks, a church or a meeting house, and a pinewood hotel, grew up on either side of the tracks; and this collection of timber-framed structures followed the siting of the depot, often a mere shanty beside a water tank and coal dump for locomotives. Many of those haphazard groups of temporary buildings became the focal point of agricultural and industrial interests, and eventually the core of a humming modern city. The pace of growth was accelerated by the indigenous architecture of wood that exists in America. Pre-fabricated frame houses could be run up in a few days. From Main Street, with its subsequent traffic complicated by the railroad that had originally determined its direction, the city was laid out on a grid plan, so future development was predictable, as speculators and far-sighted citizens soon realised. Those young, flourishing timber-built cities were as vulnerable as their mediaeval forerunners: fires were frequent and sometimes devastating, as in 1871 when Chicago was largely destroyed.

The growth and character of American cities were stimulated by two inventions: the steam locomotive and the elevator. The generative powers of technology were replacing the social and spiritual forces that had in the past made and unmade civilisations. The buildings of the second and third quarters of the twentieth century exhibit a purposeful and naked efficiency that differentiates them from all previous architectural works. They are as incompatible and disruptive when sited amid traditional buildings as a Neanderthal man armed with a club would be in the ranks of a Guards regiment. Theorists are already beginning to suggest that architecture as hitherto understood is no longer necessary, and that the term itself has lost or is rapidly losing its meaning.[10] But even the bitterly efficient buildings of a new age in the making can speak. Perhaps they are beginning to say that technology is taking over; that the ninth period of Western civilisation that has developed from the ancient Mediterranean culture may be characterised by a progressive separation of man from his natural environment. Already a creative American engineer, Buckminster Fuller, has suggested the covering of lower Manhattan by a colossal transparent dome. This is not a new idea. In 1899, H. G. Wells envisaged London in the twenty-third century as a city roofed entirely by glass, weather-proof, artificially lit, heated and ventilated, so that day and night and the seasons no longer had any significance.[11]

Extremes of climate have been conquered by modern technology. Architecture in the process of becoming super-shelter may cease to be autogenous, and the diverse creative gifts of the architect may wither away. Hitherto new structural inventions, new materials, and the challenge of new social problems have encouraged adventurous imagination; but the technological revolution may remove human society to new regions of achievement, especially if computers become more and more sophisticated, so that men are largely superseded by their own artifacts.[12] Computerised architecture might conceivably produce higher and larger buildings, condensing whole towns into one colossal structure five miles high; *commodity* and *firmness* would still be achieved, but *delight* might well be missing.

Technical advances have already helped to change the character of painting and sculpture; Dr. Desmond Morris suggests that abstract art has been stimulated by the perfection of photographic techniques and colour processes.[13] Those techniques have taken over the communication element inherent in representational art but omitted from abstract art. Alike with architecture, which has hitherto always had something to say; but we may be too close to the architecture of our own day to hear its message. Many buildings seem to be stuttering out something; some are forbidding, and seem to support Sorokin's catastrophic predictions mentioned at the beginning of this chapter. They should not perhaps be taken too seriously. Pitrim Sorokin was a renowned sociologist but also a dedicated pessimist, and some years ago at Harvard after giving a particularly depressing lecture a young student asked him if he could possibly say anything optimistic. "Yes," Sorokin replied; "we have not yet hit the bottom."[14]

As we said in the opening chapter, past changes of style in art and architecture have often been mistaken for decadence, especially those that occurred in the fourth and fifth centuries A.D., when the classical period, the seventh, was ending; now that the succeeding period, the eighth, is ending too, we are everywhere confronted with the evidence of change though not necessarily of decay. Although contemporary architecture because of its impermanent character may leave little for future archaeologists to read, there is an undeniable and aspiring vitality about much of it, which refutes the gloom of Sorokin. The faith in material progress, that sustained nineteenth century enterprise, has been shaken by two devastating world wars. That faith appears to be recovering strength and influence; encouraged perhaps by such recent achievements as the first landings on the moon and the prospect of exploring outer space. Temporarily our technology may have outstripped our culture, and our bewildered arts and congested cities and pollution problems are ever-present reminders of this imbalance of civilisation; but occasionally contemporary architecture suggests the abounding optimism that G. K. Chesterton condensed into one line when he wrote:

"For there is good news yet to hear and fine things to be seen . . ."

LIST OF REFERENCES IN THE TEXT

Chapter 1

(1) *In the Desert*, by Lisle March Phillipps. (London: Edward Arnold, 1905.) Chap. XVII, page 240.

(2) *The Inequality of Man*, by J. B. S. Haldane. (London: Chatto & Windus, 1932.) "Is History a Fraud?" page 62.

(3) Haldane, *opus cit*, page 62.

(4) "Written and Unwritten Records," by Stanley Casson. Originally published in the *Fortnightly Review*, February 1937, and reprinted in *Antiquity*, March 1951, Vol. XXV, No. 97. Pages 22–27.

(5) *Opus cit*, page 27.

(6) *The Decline and Fall of the Roman Empire*, by Edward Gibbon. (Quoted from the edition published in twelve volumes, London 1807.) Chap. II.

(7) *Opus cit*, Chap. XIII.

(8) *East and West*, by C. Northcote Parkinson. (London: John Murray 1963.) Chap. 18, page 227.

(9) *A Study of History*, by Arnold J. Toynbee. (Oxford University Press, 1934.) Vol. II, pages 110–111.

(10) *The Architects of the Parthenon*, by Rhys Carpenter. (Penguin Books Ltd., 1970.) Section 1, page 67.

(11) *Roman Bath*, by Barry Cunliffe, M.A., Ph.D. F.S.A. No. XXIV of Reports of the Research Committee of the Society of Antiquaries of London (Oxford University Press, 1969).

(12) *Puck of Pook's Hill*, by Rudyard Kipling. (London: Macmillan and Co. 1906.) Story entitled: "A Centurion of the Thirtieth".

(13) Reports of the Research Committee of the Society of Antiquaries of London. Nos: XI and XXVIII (Oxford University Press, 1936 and 1972).

(14) *Londinium: Architecture and the Crafts*, by W. R. Lethaby. (London: Duckworth & Co. 1923.) Chap. III, page 83.

(15) *Mithras, The Secret God*, by M. J. Vermaseren. (Translated by

Therese and Vincent Megaw from Mithras de geheimzinnige God. Elsevier, Amsterdam, 1959. London: Chatto & Windus, 1963.) Chap. 21, pages 186–192.

(16) *Roman Silchester*, by George C. Boon, B.A., F.S.A. (London: Max Parrish, 1957.) Chap. 4, page 114.

(17) "Size and Baalbek," by Sir Mortimer Wheeler. *Antiquity*, 1962, Vol XXXVI, page 6.

(18) *Spain: A Study of Her Life and Arts*, by Royall Tyler. (London: Sidgwick & Jackson, 1913. Originally published, 1909.) Chap. XX, page 500.

(19) *Opus cit*, page 501.

(20) *The Civilisation of Spain*, by J. B. Trend. (Oxford University Press, 1944.) Chap. II, page 31.

(21) *A History of Europe*, by H. A. L. Fisher. (London: Edward Arnold & Co. Complete edition in one volume, 1936.) Book I, Chap. VIII, page 95.

(22) Gibbon, *opus cit.* Chap. LXXI.

(23) *Sidonius, Poems and Letters*, translated by W. B. Anderson. (The Loeb Classical Library. London: William Heinemann Ltd., 1936.) Vol. I, Letters, Book II.

(24) *Roman Britain and the English Settlements*, by R. G. Collingwood and J. N. L. Myres. (Oxford: Clarendon Press, 1936.) Book IV, Chap. XIX, pages 317–318.

(25) *The Works of Gildas and Nennius*, translated by J. A. Giles, LL.D. (London: James Bohn, 1841.) Section II, "The History," page 8.

(26) *Temples in Roman Britain*, by M. J. T. Lewis, F.S.A. (Cambridge University Press, 1966.) II, pages 61–66 and plate IIa.

(27) *Excavation of the Prehistoric, Roman, and Post-Roman Site in Lydney, Gloucestershire*. By R. E. M. Wheeler, D.Lit., F.S.A., and T. V. Wheeler, F.S.A. (Reports of the Research Committee of the Society of Antiquaries of London, No. IX. Oxford University Press, 1932).

(28) *Roman London*, by Ralph Merrifield, F.S.A. (London: Cassell & Company Ltd. 1969.) Chap. X, page 202.

(29) *The Ecclesiastical History of the English Nation*, by the Venerable Bede. (London: J. M. Dent & Sons. Everyman Library edition, 1910.) Book I, Chap. XXX.

(30) "The Ruined Church of Stone-by-Faversham," by Sir Eric

Fletcher, F.S.A., and Lt.-Col. G. W. Meates, F.S.A. *The Antiquaries Journal*, Vol. XLIX, pages 273–294. (1969).

(31) Bede, *opus cit*. Book II, Chap. XV.

(32) *Augustus and Nero*, by Gilbert Charles-Picard. (Thomas Y. Crowell Company, New York, 1965. Translated by Len Ortzen from *Auguste et Néron*. Hatchette, 1962.) Part Two, Chaps. IV and V, pages 95–108.

(33) *The Ancient East*, by D. G. Hogarth, M.A., F.B.A., F.S.A. (Quoted from the sixth impression. London: Thornton. Butterworth Ltd., 1939.) Introduction, page 13.

(34) Charles-Picard, *opus cit*. Chap. V, page 102.

(35) *The Revolutions of Civilisation*, by W. M. Flinders Petrie. (Harper & Brothers, London & New York, 1911. The third edition, 1922, has been used for quotation).

(36) "Adventure and Flinders Petrie," the Presidential address to the Royal Archaeological Institute, by Sir Mortimer Wheeler, May 13th 1953. Reprinted in *Antiquity*, Vol. XXVII, No: 106, pages 87–93.

(37) *History, Civilization and Culture, An Introduction to the Historical and Social Philosophy of Pitirim A. Sorokin*, by F. R. Cowell (London: Adam and Charles Black, 1952).

(38) Cowell, *opus cit*. Chap. III, page 31.

(39) Flinders Petrie, *opus cit*., Chap. III, page 59.

(40) *The Nature and Art of Workmanship*, by David Pye. (Cambridge University Press, 1968.) Chap. 8, page 43.

(41) "A Truthful Song," by Rudyard Kipling. *Rewards and Fairies* (London: Macmillan and Co. Ltd., 1910).

Chapter 2

(1) *A History of Egypt*, by James Henry Breasted. (Originally published in 1905, by Charles Scribner's Sons, New York, and many times reprinted. The reprint of January, 1939, issued by Hodder and Stoughton, London, in 1946, has been used for reference.) Chap. V, page 101, fig. 47.

(2) *The Works of Man*, by Lisle March Phillipps. (London: Duckworth and Co. 1911. The second edition issued in 1914 has been used for quotation: the book has been reprinted several

times, later editions having an introduction by the late Sir Herbert Read.) Chap I, p. 8.

(3) *Saint Joan*, by Bernard Shaw. Scene VI.

(4) The Memnon Colossi, of which the eastern statue is celebrated for producing a melodious sound. In the course of centuries this was only heard on rare occasions, and the most detailed account of the vocal statue is in Lieut.-Commander Rupert T. Gould's book, *Enigmas*. (London, Geoffrey Bles, 1929).

(5) *The Dawn of Conscience*, by James Henry Breasted. (Charles Scribner's Sons. New York, London, 1935.) Chap. VI, pages 82–93.

(6) *The Works of Man*, Chap. I, page 8.

(7) *Ibid*, pages 8 and 9.

(8) *A History of Egypt*, by J. H. Breasted. Book II, Chap. V.

(9) *Egyptian Decorative Art*, by W. M. Flinders Petrie. (Originally a course of lectures delivered at the Royal Institution. Published in book form by Methuen & Co. Ltd. London, 1895. Second edition, which has been used for reference, 1920.) Chap. III, pages 78–79.

(10) *The Works of Man*, Chap. I, pages 14–15.

(11) *Progress and Catastrophe; An Anatomy of Human Adventure*, by Stanley Casson. (Hamish Hamilton. London, 1937.) Chap. IX, pages 145–147.

(12) *Ibid*. pages 143–144.

(13) *The Splendour that was Egypt*, by Margaret A. Murray, D.Litt. (Sidgwick and Jackson, Ltd. London, 1949.) Chap. V, page 229.

(14) *The Dawn of Conscience*, by J. H. Breasted. (Charles Scribner's Sons. New York, 1935.) Chapters XV and XVI.

(15) *A History of Egypt*. Chap. XVIII, page 356.

(16) *The Dawn of Conscience*, Chap. XV, page 280.

(17) *Ibid*, Chap. XVI, page 309.

(18) *A History of Egypt*, Chap. XVIII, page 378.

(19) *The Work, Wealth and Happiness of Mankind*, by H. G. Wells. (William Heinemann Limited, London, 1932.) Chap. XIV, page 711.

(20) *Towards a New Architecture*, by Le Corbusier. Translated from the thirteenth French edition by Frederick Etchells. (John Rodker. London, 1927.) Page 4.

(21) *A History of Egypt*, by J. H. Breasted. Chap. XXII, page 443.

(22) *Ibid*, Chap. VI, page 120.

(23) *The Splendour That Was Egypt*, by Margaret Murray. Chap. V, page 259.

(24) *Ibid*. Chap. V, page 285.

(25) *The Works of Man*, Chap. I, pages 9–10.

(26) *Progress and Catastrophe*, Chap. IX, page 147.

Chapter 3

(1) *The Sacred Giraffe*, Salvador de Madariaga, (London: Martin Hopkinson & Co. Ltd. 1925).

(2) *A History of Egypt*, by J. H. Breasted. Chronological Table of Kings, page 597.

(3) "The Egyptian 1st Dynasty Royal Cemetery," by Barry J. Kemp. *Antiquity*, Vol. XLI, No. 161, March, 1967, pages 22–32.

(4) Genesis, Chap. XI, 4, 5.

(5) *The Caliphs' Last Heritage*, by Sir Mark Sykes. (London: Macmillan and Co., Ltd., 1915.) Chap. II, page 10.

(6) *The Golden Bough*, by Sir James George Frazer, F.R.S. F.B.A. (London: Macmillan and Co. Ltd. Abridged edition, 1922.) Chap. XII, page 142.

(7) *The End of an Age*, by William Ralph Inge. (London: Putnam, 1948.) Chap. III, page 110.

(8) *The Ancient World*, by T. R. Glover. (Cambridge University Press, 1935. The Pelican Books edition, 1944, has been used.) Chap. IV, page 66.

(9) *Progress and Catastrophe*, by Stanley Casson. Chap. X, page 152.

(10) *The Art of the Hittites*, by Ekrem Akurgal. (London: Thames and Hudson, 1962.) Section IV, page 107.

(11) *Opus cit*, page 108.

(12) *Progress and Catastrophe*, by Stanley Casson. Chap. X, page 171. *Art of the Hittites*, by Ekrem Akurgal, Section IV, pages 108–114.

(13) *Progress and Catastrophe*, by Stanley Casson. Chap. X, page 172.

(14) *Opus cit*, page 174.

(15) Genesis, Chap. XV, 18–21.

(16) *Progress and Catastrophe*, Chap. X, page 173.

(17) *The Art of the Hittites*, by Ekrem Akurgal. Section V, page 124.
(18) *Opus cit.*, page 124.
(19) *The Discovery of Man*, by Stanley Casson. (London: Hamish Hamilton, 1940.) Chap. V., page 252.
(20) *Greek Myths*, by Robert Graves. (London: Cassell & Company Ltd., 1958.) Section 88, 1, page 295.
(21) *The Splendour that was Egypt*, by Margaret Murray. Chap. V, Page 224.
(22) *Progress and Catastrophe*, by Stanley Casson. Chap. X, page 165.
(23) *Theory and Elements of Architecture*, by Robert Atkinson and Hope Bagenal. (London: Ernest Benn Ltd. 1926.) Vol. 1, Part 1, Chap. II, page 20.
(24) *Pausanias' Description of Greece*. Translated by Arthur Richard Shilleto. (London: George Bell and Sons, 1886.) Vol. 1, Chap. XVI, page 121.
(25) *The Art of the Hittites*, by Ekrem Akurgal. Section IV, page 96.
(26) *Pausanias. Opus cit.* Vol. I, Chap. XVI, p. 121.
(27) *A General History of Architecture*, by Bruce Allsopp, F. R. I. B. A., F.S.A. (London: Sir Isaac Pitman & Sons. 1955. The 1962 edition has been used.) Chap. III, page 32.
(28) *Opus cit*, Chap. III, page 32.

Chapter 4

(1) *Civilization*, by Clive Bell. (London: Chatto and Windus, 1928. Chap. IV, page 95. Quoted from the Phoenix Library edition, 1932).
(2) *The Caliphs' Last Heritage*, by Sir Mark Sykes. Chap. III, page 15.
(3) *Ibid.*
(4) *The Ancient East*, by D. G. Hogarth. (London: Thornton Butterworth Ltd. Sixth edition 1939.) Chap. IV, page 171.
(5) *East and West*, by C. Northcote Parkinson. Chap. V, pages 53–54.
(6) "Size and Baalbek", by Sir Mortimer Wheeler. *Antiquity*, 1962, Vol. XXXVI, pages 6–7.
(7) *Ibid.*
(8) *The Works of Man*, by Lisle March Phillipps. Chap. IV, page 10.

(9) "The Bane of English Architecture." Reprinted from *The British Quarterly Review*, April 1881, and included as the fourth section of *Six Essays*, by John T. Emmett. (London: Unwin Brothers. 1891.) Page 39.

(10) *The Architects of the Parthenon*, by Rhys Carpenter. (Penguin Books Ltd. 1970.) Section 4, page 118.

(11) *The Outline of History*, by H. G. Wells. (London: Cassell & Company Ltd. Revised edition, January 1972.) Chap. XXI, page 275.

(12) "Size and Baalbek," by Sir Mortimer Wheeler. *Antiquity*, 1962. Vol. XXXVI, page 6.

(13) *Encyclopaedia Britannica*. (Eleventh edition, 1910–11).

(14) *The Architects of the Parthenon*, by Rhys Carpenter. Section 4, pages 152–156.

(15) *The Architecture of Marcus Vitruvius Pollio*, In Ten Books. Translated from the Latin by Joseph Gwilt. (London: Priestley and Weale, 1826.) Book IV, Chap. I, pages 101–102.

(16) "Size and Baalbek," by Sir Mortimer Wheeler. *Antiquity*, 1962. Vol. XXXVI, page 7.

(17) *The Latins in the Levant*. A History of Frankish Greece (1204–1566), by William Miller, M.A. (London: John Murray, 1908) pages 15–19.

(18) *How the Greeks Built Cities*, by R. B. Wycherley. (London: Macmillan & Co., Ltd. 1949.) Chap. III, page 39.

(19) *Ancient Town-Planning*, by F. Haverfield. (Oxford University Press 1913.) Chaps. II and III, pages 29–30.

(20) *The Discovery of Man*, by Stanley Casson. (London: Hamish Hamilton, 1940.) Chap. VI, page 308.

(21) *Vitruvius*. Book II, Introduction, pages 34–35.

(22) *The Athenaeum*, November 20th, 1880.

(23) *The Arab Conquest of Egypt, and the Last Thirty Years of Roman Dominion*, by Alfred J. Butler, D.Litt., F.S.A. (Oxford: the Clarendon Press, 1902.) Chap. XXIV, page 398.

(24) *Carthage*, by B. H. Warmington. (London: Robert Hale, 1960. Quotations and references to the Pelican Book edition, 1964.) Chap. 6, page 145.

(25) *Ibid*. Pages 159–160.

(26) The Alexandria Quartet, by Lawrence Durrell, consisting of the four novels: *Justine. Balthazar. Mountolive. Clea.* (London:

Faber and Faber. Published during the 1950s).

(27) *The Art and Architecture of India*, by Benjamin Rowland. The Pelican History of Art. (London: Penguin Books Limited. 1953. The revised second edition of 1959 has been used.) Part III, chap. 9. Pages 69 and 72.

(28) Rowland, *opus cit.* Part II, chap. 5. Page 35.

Chapter 5

(1) *Lectures on Architecture and Painting*, by John Ruskin. (London: 1854.) Lecture 1.

(2) *Analysis of Ornament*, by Ralph N. Wornum. (London: Chapman and Hall. The sixth edition, 1879, has been used. The first was published in 1855.) Chap. VIII, pages 66–73.

(3) *Ibid*, page 73.

(4) *Vitruvius*. Book VI, Chap. XI, page 187.

(5) *The Roman Imperial Army*, by Graham Webster, M.A., Ph.D., F.S.A. (London: Adam & Charles Black Ltd., 1969.) Chap. IV, pages 180–181.

(6) *The Romans and their Gods in the Age of Augustus*, by R. M. Ogilvie. (London: Chatto & Windus, 1969.) Conclusion. Page 124.

(7) *Britannia, a History of Roman Britain*, by Sheppard Frere, M.A., F.S.A. (London: Routledge and Kegan Paul. 1967.) Chap. XV, page 328. Also *Roman Bath*, by Barry Cunliffe, M.A., Ph.D., F.S.A. (Reports of the Research Committee of the Society of Antiquaries of London, XXIV. Oxford University Press, 1969.) Part II, Section, Sec. 9, pages 36–38.

(8) J. B. Ward-Perkins in *Proceedings of the British Academy*, XXXIII, 1947, page 169. Quoted by Sir Mortimer Wheeler, *Antiquity*, Vol. XXXVI 1962, page 7.

(9) *Vitruvius*. Book III, Chap. II, pages 83–87.

(10) *Life and Leisure in Ancient Rome*, by J. P. V. D. Balsdon. (London: The Bodley Head, 1969.) Chap. VIII. Page 268.

(11) Balsdon, *opus cit.* Chap. VIII. Page 251.

(12) *The Condition of Man*, by Lewis Mumford. (London: Martin Secker and Warburg Ltd. 1944.) Chap. I, Sec. 8, Page 45.

(13) *Roman London*, by Ralph Merrifield, F.S.A. (London: Cassell & Company Ltd. 1969.) Chap. V. Page 82.

(14) *Roman Silchester,* by George C. Boon, B.A., F.S.A. (London: Max Parrish, 1957.) Chap. IV. Pages 90–97.

(15) *Britain in the Roman Empire,* by Joan Liversidge, M.Litt., F.S.A. (London: Routledge & Kegan Paul, 1968.) Chap. III, page 41.

(16) *Roman London* by Ralph Merrifield, F.S.A. Chap. V, pages 78–81.

(17) *Romano-British Buildings and Earthworks,* by John Ward, F.S.A. (London: Methuen & Co. 1911.) Chap. VI. Page 156.

(18) *Fishbourne: The Roman Palace and its History.* Written and edited by Professor Barry Cunliffe, Patricia Connor, and Kenneth Pearson. (Published by the *Sunday Times.*) *Excavations at Fishbourne: 1967: Seventh and Final Interim Report,* by Barry Cunliffe, F.S.A. *The Antiquaries Journal,* Vol. XLVIII, Oxford University Press, 1968. Pages 32–40.

(19) *Londinium: Architecture and the Crafts,* by W. R. Lethaby. (London: Duckworth & Co. 1923.) Chap. II. Pages 31–32.

(20) *Warrington's Roman Remains,* by Thomas May, F.E.I., F.S.A. Scot. (Warrington: Mackie & Co. Ltd., Guardian Office, 1904.) Section IX. Pages 37–39.

(21) *Theory and Elements of Architecture,* by Robert Atkinson, F.R.I.B.A. and Hope Bagenal, A.R.I.B.A., D.C.M. (London: Ernest Benn Ltd. 1926.) Vol. I. Part I. Chap. IX. Page 319. The sentence from Pliny's letter appeared in "Imperial Building: What we may learn from Rome," by W. G. Newton. *Journal of the R.I.B.A.* March 5th 1921.

(22) *Glass in Architecture and Decoration.* New edition revised by Raymond McGrath, B.Arch. (Sydney), A.R.H.A., F.R.I.B.A. (London: The Architectural Press, 1961.) Section I. Pages 29–30.

(23) *Communication has been Established,* by Astley J. H. Goodwin. (London: Methuen & Co. 1937.) Chap. XII. Page 202.

(24) *Roman Roads in Britain,* by Ivan D. Margary, M.A., F.S.A. (London: Phoenix House. 1955.) Vol. I. Chap. I. Pages 12–13

(25) *Ibid,* page 13.

(26) *Map of Roman Britain.* (The Ordnance Survey. Third edition, 1956).

(27) *The Lost Province,* by M. P. Charlesworth, F.B.A., F.S.A. (Cardiff: University of Wales Press. 1949.) Chap. IV. Page 68.

(28) *Celtic Scotland*: a History of Ancient Alban, by William Skene, D.C.L., LL.D. (Edinburgh: David Douglas. Second edition, 1887.) Vol. II. Chap. I, page 2; and Chap. II, page 46.

(29) *The Early Christian Archaeology of Northern Britain*, by Charles Thomas, M.A., F.S.A. (Published for the University of Glasgow by the Oxford University Press. 1971.) Chap. II. Pages 14–15.

(30) *Sidonius: Poems and Letters*, translated by W. B. Anderson. (London: William Heinemann Ltd. Cambridge, Massachusetts: Harvard University Press. 1961.) Vol. I. Book II. Letter II to Domitus. Page 417.

Chapter 6

(1) *Architecture: An Introduction to the History and Theory of the Art of Building*, by W. R. Lethaby. (London: Williams and Norgate Home University Library, original edition.) Chap. VIII. Page 136.

(2) *Britain in the Roman Empire*, by Joan Liversidge, M.Litt., F.S.A. (London: Routledge & Kegan Paul Ltd. 1968.) Chap. VII. Pages 172–173. *Britannia*, by Sheppard Frere, M.A., F.B.A., F.S.A. London: Routledge and Kegan Paul Ltd. 1967.) Chap. XVI, page 340.

(3) *Britain in the Roman Empire*, by Joan Liversidge, M.Litt., F.S.A. Chap. XV. Pages 458–459.

(4) *Roman Silchester*, by George C. Boon, B.A., F.S.A. (London: Max Parrish. 1957.) Chap. V. Pages 128–130.

(5) *Temples in Roman Britain*, by M. J. T. Lewis, M.A., Ph.D., F.S.A. (Cambridge University Press. 1966.) Chap. III. Pages 108–109.

(6) Boon, *opus cit*. Page 130.

(7) *Sidonius: Poems and Letters*, translated by W. B. Anderson. Vol. I Book II. Letter to Hesperius. Pages 465–467.

(8) *The History of Count Zosimus*. (London: printed for J. Davis. 1814.) Book II. Pages 52–53.

(9) *The Decline and Fall of the Roman Empire*, by Edward Gibbon. Chap. XXIII.

(10) Gibbon. *Opus cit*. Chap. XXIII.

(11) *The Church of Sancta Sophia Constantinople: A Study of Byzantine*

Building, by W. R. Lethaby and Harold Swainson. (London: Macmillan & Co. 1894.) Chap. XI. Sec. 4, Page 247.
(12) Gibbon. *Opus cit*. Chap. XL.
(13) *The Church of Sancta Sophia Constantinople*. Lethaby and Swainson. Chap. XI. Sec. 2. Page 236.
(14) *Byzantine Legacy*, by Cecil Stewart, D.A. (Edin.), A.R.I.B.A. (London: George Allen & Unwin Ltd. 1947.) Chap. VI. Page 118.
(15) *Form and Colour*, by Lisle March Phillipps. (London: Duckworth and Co. 1915.) Chap. IV. Pages 83–84.
(16) Introduction by Herbert Read to the 1950 edition of *The Works of Man*. (Gerald Duckworth and Co. Ltd.) Page vi.
(17) *Byzantine Legacy*, by Cecil Stewart, D.A. (Edin.), A.R.I.B.A. Chap. V. Pages 102–105.
(18) Stewart, *opus cit*. Chap. VII. Page 146.
(19) *The Age of Arthur: A History of the British Isles from 350 to 650*, by John Morris (London: Weidenfeld and Nicolson. 1973).
(20) "Excavations at Cadbury-Camelot, 1966–70," by Leslie Alcock, F.S.A. *Antiquity*, Vol. XLVI. 1972. Page 35. See also Summary Report, 1970, of the Excavations. *The Antiquaries Journal*, Vol. LI. 1971. Pages 1–7.

Chapter 7
(1) *Architecture: An Introduction to the History and Theory of the Art of Building*, by W. R. Lethaby. (London: Williams and Norgate. Home University Library: Original Edition.) Chap. X. Page 171.
(2) *Art in Roman Britain*, by J. M. C. Toynbee, M.A., D.Phil., F.B.A., F.S.A. (London: The Phaidon Press: published for The Society for the Promotion of Roman Studies. 1962.) Plates 96 and 51. Pages 148 and 162.
(3) *Spain: A Study of her Life and Arts*, by Royall Tyler. (London: Sidgwick and Jackson. Second edition, 1913.) Chap. II. Pages 35–36.
(4) *Opus cit*. Pages 36–37.
(5) *Opus cit*. Chap. XII. Page 270.
(6) *An Arab Philosophy of History*. Selections from the Prolegomena Of Ibn Khaldun of Tunis (1332–1406). Translated and

arranged by Charles Issawi, M.A. (London: John Murray. 1950.) Chap. II. Pages 55–56.

(7) *English Glass*, by W. A. Thorpe. (London: Adam & Charles Black Ltd. Second edition, 1949.) Chap. II. Pages 77–78.

(8) *The Civilization of Spain*, by J. B. Trend. (Oxford University Press. 1944.) Chap. II. Page 23.

(9) *An Arab Philosophy of History*. Chap. II. Page 54.

(10) *The Works of Man*, by Lisle March Phillipps. (Second edition. 1914.) Chap. VI. Page 166.

(11) *Architecture: An Introduction to the History and Theory of the Art of Building*, by W. R. Lethaby. Chap. IX. Page 163.

(12) Lethaby. *Opus cit.* Chap. IX. Page 159.

(13) *The Works of Man*. (New edition. 1950.) Introduction. Page viii.

(14) *An Arab Philosophy of History*. Chap. II. Pages 57–58. Also *The Golden Trade of the Moors*, by E. W. Bovill. (Oxford University Press. 1958. The paperback edition of 1970 has been used for reference.) Chap. VI. Pages 58–59.

(15) *The Golden Trade of the Moors. Opus cit.* Also *Fountains in the Sand*, by Norman Douglas. (London: Martin Secker, 1912. New Adelphi Library edition, 1926, used for reference.) Chap. XVII. "Roman Olive-Culture." Page 145.

(16) *The Arab Conquest of Egypt*, by Alfred J. Butler, D.Litt., F.S.A. (Oxford. 1902.) Chap. XXIV.

(17) *An Arab Philosophy of History*. Introduction. Page 4.

(18) *The Works of Man*, by Lisle March Phillipps. (Illustrated edition, 1914.) This quotation is from the caption of the plate showing the interior of the Mosque at Cordova, facing page 166. This plate is omitted from the 1950 edition.

Chapter 8

(1) *England Before the Norman Conquest*, by Sir Charles Oman. (London: Methuen & Co. Ltd. Sixth edition, 1924.) Chap. XXIII. Pages 464–467.

(2) *The Great North Road*, by Frank Morley. (London: Hutchinson and Co. 1961.) "The Questing Beast." Page 121.

(3) *The Adventures of Mr. Verdant Green*, by Cuthbert Bede, which was the pen name of Edward Bradley. (London: James Black-

wood & Co. 1853–56.) Part II. Chap. IV.

(4) "The Architecture of Adventure": title of paper given by W. R. Lethaby before the Royal Institute of British Architects, April 18th, 1910. Included in his collected papers on Art and Labour, under the title of *Form in Civilization*. (Oxford University Press. 1922.) VII. Pages 66–95.

(5) *Architecture: An Introduction to the History and Theory of the Art of Building*, by W. R. Lethaby. (London: Williams & Norgate. Home University Library. Original Edition.) Chap. X. Page 180.

Chapter 9

(1) *England Before the Norman Conquest*, by Sir Charles Oman. (London: Methuen & Co. Ltd. Sixth edition, 1924.) Chap. XVI. Page 319.

(2) *The Ecclestical History of the English Nation*, by the Venerable Bede. (London: J. M. Dent & Sons Ltd. Everyman Library Edition.) Book V. Chap. XXIII.

(3) Bede, *Opus cit.* Lives of the Holy Abbots of Weremouth and Jarrow.

(4) *Anglo-Saxon Art*, by T. D. Kendrick, M.A., F.S.A. (London: Methuen & Co. 1938.) Chap. VI. Page 119.

(5) *Form in Civilization*, by W. R. Lethaby. (Oxford University Press, 1922.) VII. "The Architecture of Adventure." Page 73.

(6) *The God of the Witches*, by Margaret Alice Murray, D.Litt. (London: Samson Low, Marston & Co. Ltd. No date.) Also *The Divine King in England*, a later work. (London: Faber & Faber Ltd. 1954.) Both books expound theories of religious survivals that have occasioned considerable controversy.

(7) *A Biographical Dictionary of English Architects, 1660–1840*, by H. M. Colvin, C.B.E., M.A., F.B.A. (London: John Murray, 1954).

(8) *The Metrical Life of St. Hugh*, edited by J. F. Dimock, from two MSS. in the British Museum and Bodleian Library. (London: 1860.) Quoted by G. G. Coulton in *Social Life in Britain, from the Conquest to the Reformation*. (Cambridge University Press 1919.) Sec. XIII, page 472.

(9) *Building in England, down to 1540*, by L. F. Salzman, F.S.A. (Oxford, 1952.) Chap. I. Page 3.

(10) Salzman. *Ibid.*

(11) *The Nature and Art of Workmanship*, by David Pye. (Cambridge University Press, 1968.) Sec. 1. Page 1.

(12) *Architecture*, by Christian Barman, O.B.E., F.R.I.B.A., R.D.I. (London: Ernest Benn Ltd. 1928.) Chap. IV. Pages 47–48.

(13) *Westminster Abbey and the Kings' Craftsmen*, by W. R. Lethaby. (London: Duckworth & Co. 1906.) Chap. I. Pages 29–30. *Stained Glass of the Middle Ages in England and France*, by Lawrence B. Saint and Hugh Arnold. (London: Adam & Charles Black, Ltd. 1913.) Chap. VIII. Pages 115–120.

(14) *Byways in British Archaeology*, by Walter Johnson, F.G.S. (Cambridge University Press, 1912.) Chap. V. Pages 229–237.

(15) *Social Life in the days of Piers Plowman*, by D. Chadwick. (Cambridge University Press, 1922.) Page 55.

(16) *The Hansa*, by E. Gee Nash. (London: John Lane, 1929.) Chap. II, pages 15–16.

(17) *A History of Europe*, by H. A. L. Fisher. (London: Edward Arnold. Complete edition, 1936.) Chap. XXI. Pages 256–257.

(18) Quoted by G. G. Coulton in *Mediaeval Panorama*. (Cambridge University Press, 1938.) Chap. XXXIX. Page 515.

(19) *Architecture: An Introduction to the History and Theory of the Art of Building*, by W. R. Lethaby. (London: Williams and Norgate, 1911.) Chap. XIII. Page 228.

(20) *The Revolutions of Civilisation*, by W. M. Flinders Petrie. Chap. III. Page 74.

(21) *The Manual of Heraldry*, edited by Francis J. Grant, Rothesay Herald. (New and revised edition. Edinburgh: John Grant, 1924.) Preface. Page vi.

Chapter 10

(1) *Pagan Mysteries in the Renaissance*, by Edgar Wind. (London: Faber and Faber, 1958.)

(2) *The Canterbury Tales.* "The Squieres Tale." Line 610.

(3) *The Revolutions of Civilisation*, by W. M. Flinders Petrie. Chap. III. Page 74.

(4) Francis Bacon (1561–1626). *Essays.* "On Building."

(5) *A History of Europe*, by H. A. L. Fisher. (Complete edition. London: Edward Arnold & Co. 1936.) Chap. X. Page 536.

(6) *The Waning of the Middle Ages*, by J. Huizings. (London: Edward Arnold & Co. 1924.) Chap. XXIII. Page 297.

(7) *England as Seen by Foreigners*, by William Brenchley Rye. (London: John Russell Smith. 1865.) Introduction. Pages xliii and xliv.

(8) *Brick Building in England* by Jane A. Wight. (London: John Baker, 1972.) Chap. V. "Ecclesiastical buildings and the reformation conversions." Page 169.

(9) *Tudor Renaissance*, by James Lees-Milne, F.S.A. (London: B. T. Batsford Ltd. 1951.) Chap. II. Page 19.

(10) *A History of the Protestant "Reformation", in England and Ireland*, by William Cobbett. (London: Charles Clement. 1824).

(11) *Harrison's Description of England in Shakespere's Youth*, edited by Frederick J. Furnival. (Published for the New Shakespere Society by N. Trubner & Co., London, 1877.) Book II. Chap. XII. Pages 239–40.

(12) *Brick Building in England* by Jane A. Wight. (London: John Baker. 1972.) Introduction and Chap. I.

(13) Harrison. *Opus cit.* Book II. Chap. XII.

(14) *Social Life in the Days of Piers Plowman*, by D. Chadwick. (Cambridge University Press, 1922.) Sec. V. Page 81.

(15) *The Evolution of the English House*, by S. O. Addy. (London: George Allen & Unwin Limited. Revised and enlarged by John Summerson from the author's notes. 1933.) Chap. VI. Page 120.

(16) *The Conquest of the Incas*, by John Hemming. (London: Macmillan London Limited, 1970.) Chap. VI.

(17) *The Land of the Great Image*, by Maurice Collis. (London: Faber and Faber. 1946.) Chap. III. Pages 24–34.

Chapter 11

(1) *The Architecture of Humanism*, by Geoffrey Scott. (London: Constable and Company Ltd. Second revised edition, 1924.) Chap. I. Pages 16–17.

(2) *The Elements of Architecture*, collected by Henry Wotton Kt., from the Best Authors and Examples. The two books of this work were included in *Reliquiae Wottonianae*. The third edition,

printed in London in 1672, has been used. The date of Wotton's original essay was 1624.

(3) *Architecture in Britain, 1530 to 1830*, by Sir John Summerson, C.B.E., F.B.A., F.S.A., A.R.I.B.A. (The Pelican History of Art. London: Penguin Books, 1953 edition.) Chap. 11. Page 107.

(4) Summerson. *Ibid.*

(5) *Life of William Morris*, by J. W. Mackill. (London: Longmans, Green and Co. 1899.) Vol. II, page 97.

(6) *The Rebuilding of London after the Great Fire*, by T. F. Reddaway. (London: Jonathan Cape, 1940.) Pages 311–312.

(7) *The History of the Royal Society of London for the Improving of Natural Knowledge*, by Thomas Sprat, D.D. (London: Third edition, corrected. 1722.) Sec. XXXIV. Pages 405–406.

(8) *Diary and Correspondence of John Evelyn*, edited by William Bray. (London: Henry Colburn. 1854.) Vol. II. Page 279.

(9) *Anecdotes of Painting in England*, collected by George Vertue and digested and published by Horace Walpole from the original MSS. (London: J. Dodsley. Third edition, 1786.) Vol. IV. Pages 232–233.

(10) *A Frenchman in England, 1784*. Being the *Melanges sur l'Angleterre* of François de la Rochefoucauld. Edited from the MS by Jean Marchand and translated with Notes by S. C. Roberts. (Cambridge University Press, 1933.) Page 40.

(11) The extract from the Comte de Mirabeau's letter was included in *La Decade Philosophique Literaire et Politique*, and the translation quoted was published in *The European Magazine*, November 1798.

(12) *Ruined and Deserted Churches*, by Lucy Elizabeth Beedham. (London: Elliot Stock. 1908.) Chap. III. Pages 25–32.

(13) *The Letters and Works of Lady Mary Wortley Montagu*, edited by her great-grandson, Lord Wharncliffe. (London: Richard Bentley. 1837. Second edition, revised.) Vol. I. Letter to Lady Rich. Adrianople, April 1, O.S. 1717. Pages 353–357.

(14) *Nouveaux memoires sur l'etat present de la Chine*, by Père Le Comte. (1699.) Quoted by Adolf Reichwein, in *China and Europe*. (London: Kegan Paul. Trench Trubner & Co. 1925.) Page 56.

(15) *Georgian Grace*, by John Gloag. (London: Spring Books.

Second edition 1967.) Appendix IV. The Society of Dilettanti. Pages 385–387.

(16) *A Biographical Dictionary of English Architects, 1660–1840*, by H. M. Colvin, C.B.E., F.B.A. (London: John Murray. 1954.) Pages 493–495 and 581–584.

(17) *An Essay in Defence of Ancient Architecture; or, a Parallel of the Ancient Buildings with the Modern, Shewing the Beauty and Harmony of the Former, and the Irregularity of the Latter*, by Robert Morris, of Twickenham. (London: 1728.) Chap. III. Page 20.

(18) *Roman Mornings*, by James Lees-Milne, F.S.A. (London: Alan Wingate, 1956.) "Rococo." Page 147.

(19) *East and West* by C. Northcote Parkinson. (London: John Murray. 1963.) Chap. XV. Page 199.

(20) *Kim*, by Rudyard Kipling. (London: Macmillan and Co. 1901.) Chap. VII. Page 175.

Chapter 12

(1) *The Revolutions of Civilisation*, by W. M. Flinders Petrie. Chap. III. Page 74.

(2) *Opus cit.* Chap. VII. Page 130.

(3) *A History of the Gothic Revival*, by Charles L. Eastlake. Edited with an Introduction by J. Mordaunt Crook. (First published in 1872. Reissued, with Dr. Crook's introduction by Leicester University Press, 1970.) Introduction, page 29.

(4) *A History of the Gothic Revival*, by Charles L. Eastlake. Chap. V. Page 77.

(5) *Poems on Several Occasions*, by William Woty. (Derby. Printed for the Author, by J. Drewry. M,DCC,LXXX).

(6) *A Biographical Dictionary of English Architects, 1660–1830*, by H. M. Colvin, C.B.E., F.B.A. (London. John Murray, 1954.) Pages 107, 146, and 148.

(7) Colvin, *opus cit.* Pages 175–176.

(8) *Essays on the Picturesque*, by Uvedale Price. (London: Printed for J. Mawman. 1810. Vol. I. Chap. III. Pages 51–53. The first edition was published by J. Robson in 1794.)

(9) *Some Architectural Problems of To-day*, by C. H. Reilly. (The University Press of Liverpool. 1924.) Chap. X. Page 60.

(10) Jeremiah. I. 18.

(11) *Lectures on Architecture and Painting*, by John Ruskin. (Published in book form, 1854.) Lecture I.

(12) *Recollections of A. N. Welby Pugin, and his father, Augustus Pugin*, by Benjamin Ferry, F.R.I.B.A. (London: Edward Stanford. 1861.) Chap XX. Pages 257–258.

(13) *Contrasts*, by A. Welby Pugin. (London: Charles Dolman. Second edition. 1841).

(14) *Progress at Pelvis Bay*, by Osbert Lancaster. (Originally published 1936, and many times reprinted. London: John Murray.) *Drayneflete Revealed* (John Murray. 1949).

(15) *The Gothic Revival*, by Kenneth Clark. (Originally published in 1928 by Constable and Co. The quotation is from the Pelican paper-back reprint of the revised 1962 edition, published by John Murray.) Chap. 7. Page 122.

(16) *The Seven Lamps of Architecture*, by John Ruskin. (First published, 1849.) Preface to the second edition.

(17) Ruskin. *Opus cit.* Preface to the second edition.

(18) *Lectures on Architecture and Painting*, by John Ruskin. (1854.) Lecture II.

(19) *Mr. Loudon's England*, by John Gloag. (Newcastle-upon-Tyne. The Oriel Press Limited. 1970.) Chap. VIII. Pages 82–85, 91, 93–95.

(20) *Technics and Civilization*, by Lewis Mumford. (London. George Routledge & Sons Ltd. 1934.) Chap. VI. Sec. 7. Page 290.

(21) *Chambers Twentieth Century Dictionary*.

(22) *The Buildings of England, London. I The Cities of London and Westminster*. By Nikolaus Pevsner. (Penguin Books. 1957.) Page 275.

(23) *Gothic Architecture*, an address by William Morris to the Arts and Crafts Exhibition Society, 1889. Printed at the Kelmscott Press, 1893.

(24) *The Wanderers*. Opening lines.

(25) *Recollections of A. N. Welby Pugin, and his father Augustus Pugin*, by Benjamin Ferry, F.R.I.B.A. Chap. XVIII. Pages 247–248.

(26) *East and West*, by C. Northcote Parkinson. (London: John Murray. 1963.) Chap. 18. Page 227.

Chapter 13

(1) *History, Civilization and Culture: An Introduction to the Historical and Social Philosophy of Pitirim A. Sorokin*, by F. R. Cowell. (London: Adam & Charles Black, 1952.) Chap. XI. Page 242.

(2) *New Bats in Old Belfries*, by John Betjeman. (London: John Murray, 1945).

(3) The works of Charles Rennie Mackintosh and C. F. A. Voysey are listed in Dora Ware's *A Short Dictionary of British Architects*. (London: George Allen & Unwin Ltd. 1967).

(4) *Word Warfare. Some Aspects of German Propaganda and English Liberty*, by John Gloag. (London: Nicholson and Watson 1939.) Chap. VII. Pages 52–61.

(5) *Ibid.* Page 55.

(6) *Towards a New Architecture*, by Le Corbusier. Translated by Frederick Etchells. (London. John Rodker, 1937.) Page 4.

(7) *Design in Modern Life*, edited by John Gloag. (London: George Allen & Unwin Ltd, 1934. Second impression, 1946.) Chapter II, by E. Maxwell Fry. Page 36.

(8) Described in two stories, "With the Night Mail," and "As Easy as A.B.C." The first included in *Actions and Reactions*, by Rudyard Kipling. (London: Macmillan and Co. Limited. 1909.) The second, written in 1912, and included in *A Diversity of Creatures* (Macmillan. 1917).

(9) "The Remaining Third," by John Gloag. *The Architectural Review*, September 1967. Pages 179–180.

(10) *The Architectural Review.* November 1973. Pages 289–297.

(11) *When the Sleeper Wakes*, by H. G. Wells. (Reissued by Nelson in 1909 under the revised title of *The Sleeper Awakes*.)

(12) "Revolution by Computer," by Professor N. S. Sutherland. *The Observer*, April 9th 1967. Page 21.

(13) *The Biology of Art*, by Desmond Morris. (London: Methuen & Co Ltd. 1962.) Chap. V. Pages 149–151.

(14) *The New Yorker*, April 8th, 1974. Page 144. In a review of Konrad Lorenz's book, *Civilized Man's Eight Deadly Sins*.

THE PLATES

The forty-eight plates that follow correspond with the historical
sequence of chapters one to twelve, though some are intentionally
placed out of sequence to illustrate some contrast or to facilitate
some comparison, as on plates 33 and 35.

338

PLATE I.   *Above:* The two seated statues of Amenhotep III (1411–1375 B.C.),
known as the Memnon colossi. *Below:* The Great Sphinx of Gizeh, with the
pyramid of Khafre in the background. (Fourth Dynasty, 2900–2750 B.C.).
Both subjects reproduced by courtesy of the Egyptian Tourist Information Centre.

PLATE 2. *Right:* Entrance to temple precincts at Luxor. This shows the batter on the external wall. (See also drawing on page 27.) *Below:* Osiris pillars at Luxor, prototypes of the Greek caryatid, which emphasise the impressive power of repetition. (See Plate 11.) *Photographs by Alan Deller.*

PLATE 3. Columns in the temple of Amon, Luxor. These colonnades within the temple stood in perpetual gloom; the glare of sunlight in the roofless ruin gives them a totally different architectural character from their original symbolic quality which conveyed a sense of power and mystery. *Photograph by Alan Deller.*

PLATE 4. The avenue of ram-headed sphinxes connecting the temples at Karnak and Luxor, carved in stone, each bearing a statue of the Pharaoh between its forepaws. Erected during the reign of Amenhotep III. (See Plate 1.) *Both illustrations reproduced by courtesy of the Egyptian Tourist Information Centre.*

PLATE 5.   Entrance to the Treasury of Atreus, Mycenae, showing the massive masonry of the dromos, the passage that approaches the entrance. Above the solid lintel of the entrance is a corbelled triangular aperture. Built in the fourteenth century B.C. *Reproduced by courtesy of the National Tourist Organisation of Greece.* (See also Plate 6.)

PLATE 6. *Above:* View of the Royal Tombs on the Acropolis at Mycenae, taken over the top of the Lion Gate. The thin slab of lime-stone on which the lions are carved is a rudimentary pediment. *Reproduced by courtesy of the National Tourist Organisation of Greece. Right:* Inner side of the Lion Gate, showing masonry above the lintel and behind the limestone slab. *Photograph by the author.* (See drawing on page 56.)

PLATE 7. Monolithic Doric columns of the temple of Apollo, Corinth. *Circa* 540 B.C. *Reproduced by courtesy of the National Tourist Organisation of Greece.*

Above: Doric columns of the Parthenon, Athens, 454–438 B.C. *Photograph by the author. Left:* Temple of Demeter, Segesta, Sicily. *Circa* 430–420 B.C. *Photograph by Julian Gloag.*

PLATE 8. The eastern portico of the Parthenon as it appeared in the late eighteenth century, with a Turkish mosque in the centre of the temple and houses crowded untidily on the Acropolis. From a drawing by William Pars, reproduced from Volume II of *The Antiquities of Athens*, by James "Athenian" Stuart and Nicholas Revett, which was dated 1787 though not actually published until 1789. (See plate 9 opposite.)

PLATE 9.   The eastern portico of the Parthenon as it is today. The Turkish houses shown on plate 8 cluttering up the site and surrounding the ruins were removed early in the nineteenth century, Thomas Bruce, the 7th Earl of Elgin (1766–1841) having secured an order from the Sultan for clearing the area. (See page 279.) *Photograph : Richard C. Grierson.*

Plate 10. The small Ionic temple of Nike
Apteros (Athena Nike), dedicated to "Wingless
Victory", designed by the architect Callicrates,
and built, 438 B.C., on the south-western spur of
the Acropolis at Athens. *Photograph above: by Alan
Deller. To the right: by the author.*

PLATE 11. The Caryatid porch of the Erechtheion, the temple that stands on the Acropolis
at Athens, north of the Parthenon. The drawing
on page 74 shows the position of the porch in
relation to the rest of the temple: the fluted
Ionic columns are shown to the left. *Photograph
above: by Alan Deller: left: by the author.*

PLATE 12. *Left:* The Olympieion, Athens, begun in 174 B.C., by Antiochus Epiphanes of Syria and built from the designs of Cossutius, a Roman architect. It was not completed, and some of the columns were taken to Rome in 80 B.C., and used for the temple of Jupiter Capitolinus. It was finished in A.D. 117, by Hadrian.

Rising tiers of seats in the theatre of Dionysos, Athens, that could accommodate an audience of thirty thousand. It was completed in 340 B.C., and is sited in an excavated space on the slope of the Acropolis. *Photographs by the author.*

PLATE 13. *Above:* The Choragic Monument of Lysicrates, Athens, as it is today. *Photograph: Oriel. Right:* Restoration of the Monument. *After Stuart and Revett.*

Left: Tomb of the Julii at St. Remy, Provence. *Photograph: Julian Gloag.*

PLATE 14. *Above:* The Arch of Constantine, Rome, A.D. 312. The triple arches have little structural significance: they are tunnelled through a mass of masonry, over 67 ft. high and 82 ft. wide. The eight monolithic detached Corinthian columns, four on each face, have no structural significance at all: they are there in order to supply vertical elements in the composition. (See Plate 13 opposite for detail of sculptures.) *Photograph: Oriel. Below:* The siting of the arch in relationship to the Colosseum. A.D. 70–82. *Photograph: G. M. Gloag.*

PLATE 15.   Detail of the reliefs and ornament above one of the flanking arches.
(See Plate opposite.) Some authorities suggest that by the early fourth century,
few sculptors had enough skill to adorn imperial monuments, and reliefs were
taken from the arch of Trajan and re-used on the arch of Constantine. *Reproduced
by courtesy of the Italian State Tourist Office.*

PLATE 16. The Baths of Diocletian, completed during the opening years of the fourth century A.D. Reconstruction by Edmond Paulin, reproduced from *Thermes de Diocletian* (Paris, 1877). The great central hall was converted by Michelangelo in 1563 into the Church of St. Maria degli Angeli. (See Plate 17, opposite.)

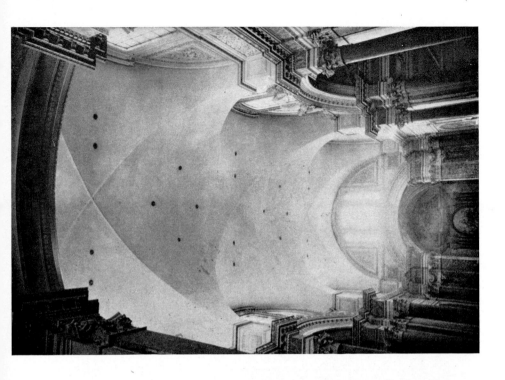

PLATE 17. The great central hall of the Baths of Diocletian was converted in 1563 by Michelangelo and became the Church of St. Maria degli Angeli. (See Plate 16 opposite, also chapter one, page 10.) This hall, the tepidarium of the Roman baths, was 200 ft. by 80 ft. and 90 ft. high. *Right:* Interior view showing the Corinthian capitals and details of entablature. *Photograph: Oriel. Below:* Mid-nineteenth century interior view that includes decoration which no longer exists. Reproduced from *Kunsthistorischen Bilderatlas,* by Theodor Schreiber. Vol. I. (Leipzig, 1884–85.) English Translation, 1895.

PLATE 18.   Interior of the Pantheon, Rome, showing the coffered hemispherical dome, with light entering through the circular hole at the top. The exterior is shown on the Plate opposite. *Photograph: Oriel.*

PLATE 19.   The Pantheon, Rome, the best preserved of all the ancient buildings in the city. This large circular structure was composed entirely as an interior; the external part ends with the Corinthian octostyle portico; the dome is a hemisphere, coffered and rising to an unglazed circular aperture that admits a shaft of daylight. The rotunda was built by the Emperor Hadrian, A.D. 120–124, and the structure has survived unchanged for over eighteen-and-a-half centuries. It became a Christian church, and early in the seventh century was dedicated to St. Maria by Pope Boniface IV, and is now known as St. Maria Rotunda. The interior is shown on the Plate opposite. *Photograph: Oriel.*

PLATE 20.   Remains of the walls of Antioch, at the southern end of the city. Reproduced from plate 7 of *Voyage Pittoresque de la Syrie, de la Palestine, et de la Basse-Egypte*, engraved by Louis François Cassas (1756–1827), who visited Antioch between 1784 and 1787. (Published in Paris, 1799.) *Reproduced by courtesy of the Royal Institute of British Architects.*

Right: The Golden Gate and walls of Constantinople. Roman masonry was intended to defeat the ravages of time and the onslaught of enemies. *Photograph: Oriel.*

PLATE 21.   The Porta Nigra, Trier, early fourth century A.D., which was part
of the city wall. This large fortified gateway is built of sandstone blocks, so
darkened by age that they are almost black: hence the name. The whole
structure, with the bow-fronted gate-houses, is 115 ft. long and 29 ft. deep:
the height varies from 75 to 93 ft. Trier in Roman times was Augusta Treverorum, within eighty miles of the dangerous eastern frontier of the Empire.
Photograph: Oriel. (See other examples of Roman fortification on Plates 20, 23
and pages 104 and 105.)

PLATE 22. *Right:* Example of fine Roman masonry on one of the surviving walls of the Temple of Augustus at Ankara. *Photograph by the author.*

The surviving part of the Roman lighthouse in the precincts of Dover Castle. The landward side is shown at the left, the seaward side at the right. There were two lighthouses at Dover, the Roman Dubrae, one on each side of the harbour; the one on the western hill is now merely a mass of fallen masonry. Across the Channel at Boulogne, Gessoriacum, there was another lighthouse, built to the order of the Emperor Gaius in A.D. 40. This was destroyed in the sixteenth-century, though its site is known. *Photographs by Patrick Deller.*

PLATE 23. *Right:* Roman masonry on the upper tier of the amphitheatre at Arles, showing the capital of one of the attached Corinthian columns. *Photograph by Richard Grierson*

Left: Roman walling with binding courses of three layers of horizontal tiles, south-east bastion of Burgh Castle, in Norfolk, the most easterly of the Saxon Shore forts of Roman Britain in the third century. *Photograph by W. L. D. Bayley.*

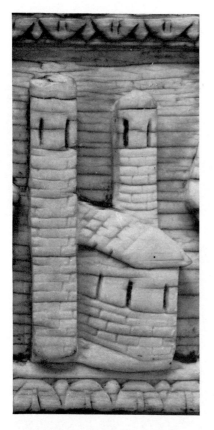

PLATE 24. *Left:* An early Christian church with two lofty round towers, carved on an ivory tablet from the Werden Casket, *circa* A.D. 400. Such towers with rounded or conical tops resembled those that often flanked the gateways of Roman cities. Compare them with the twin towers depicted on the reverse of the medallion struck to commemorate the relief of Londinium (London) when Britain was reunited to the Empire after the defeat of the usurper Allectus in A.D. 296. *Reproduced by courtesy of the Victoria and Albert Museum. Crown copyright.*

Actual size of medallion.

Slight enlargement of the reverse side of the medallion struck to commemorate the relief of Londinium by Constantius Chlorus in A.D. 296. The gate towers and part of the city wall are shown. (See page 116.) *Reproduced by courtesy of the Trustees of the British Museum.*

PLATE 25. *Right:* The Saxon church of St. Lawrence at Bradford-on-Avon, Wiltshire. *Circa* A.D. 700. Compare this with the reconstruction of the Silchester church on page 117. Reproduced by courtesy of *The National Monuments Record.*

Left: Interior of Escombe Church, Durham. Early eighth century. Both churches on this Plate are extremely simple structures and may well have derived their form from the early Christian churches of Roman Britain. *Photograph: Ursula Clark.*

PLATE 26.   Interior of Santa Sophia, Constantinople, A.D. 532–37. This view, looking towards the apse, shows how the genius of Greek architects interpreted and employed the arch principle. Reproduced from the drawing made by Gaspard Fossati, published in 1852, after the building had been restored by order of the sultan, Abdul Medjid. (See drawings on pages 125 and 126.)

PLATE 27.   Interior view, St. Mark, Venice. (1042–1071.) An unbroken skin of mosaic spreads over all surfaces, curved or flat. (See drawings of exterior on pages 128 and 129.) *Photograph: Oriel.*

PLATE 28.   Interior of the Mosque at Cordova, 786–990, with arches springing from columns and Corinthian capitals, taken from Roman buildings. *Photograph: Oriel.*

PLATE 29.   Part of the west front of Seville cathedral, with the Giralda at the left. This tower originally adjoined the mosque that formerly stood on the site of the cathedral; it was not a minaret, but a magnificently decorative expression of architectural high spirits. Built in 1196 by Jebir, architect to Yusuf I. The lower part, to the height of 185 ft. still retains its Moorish character. *Photograph: Oriel.*

PLATE 30. The façades of the Doge's Palace at Venice, the finest example of mediaeval civic architecture in the city. The palace dates from 1309–1424: Oriental, Byzantine, classic and Gothic influences have contributed to the design. *Photograph by the author.*

The east end of the cathedral at Pisa. 1063–1092. *Photograph: Oriel.*

PLATE 31. *Right:* Façade of St. Miniato, Florence, 1013, with five semi-circular arches springing from the capitals of slender versions of Corinthian columns. Bands and panels of black and white marble enliven the composition, and the proportions of classic architecture have been happily preserved. *Photograph by Richard C. Grierson.*

Left: The Campanile, Pisa. 1174. The last of the Pisan group to be built, though it was completed before the Baptistry. The eight storeys of encircling arcades give an elegant slenderness to the famous leaning tower, which is 52 ft. in diameter. The east end of the cathedral is shown on the plate opposite. *Photograph by the author.*

PLATE 32. Coupled capitals and columns in the cloisters of Monreale Cathedral, south-west of Palermo, Sicily. The columns on the left are encrusted with glass mosaics; all the capitals are elaborate variations of the Corinthian order. The cathedral, built in 1174, records Norman rule in the island. The cloisters are the only remaining part of the Benedictine monastery. *Photographs by Danielle Haase-Dubosc.*

Court of the Lions at the Alhambra, Granada, a royal pleasure palace built between 1248 and 1354. *Photograph by the author.*

PLATE 33. The towers of San Gimignano, a small Italian town near Florence, where as many as seventy were built by wealthy merchants, all in the great cause of self-advertisement. Thirteen of those monuments to exuberant pride still exist, and give to this remote town the likeness of an American city, albeit on a reduced scale. *Photograph: Oriel.*

The skyline of New York, seen from the Harbour and showing the down-town skyscrapers. The Ferry Building is in the foreground. *Photograph by the author.*

PLATE 34. *Above:* Abbaye-aux-Dames, at Caen, 1062–1066. Founded by Matilda, wife of William the Conqueror. The typical round-headed Norman arch appears on the doors of the west front, and on the arcaded stages of the towers. *Photograph: Oriel. Right:* The west façade, Castle Rising, Norfolk. The arcading and the enrichment of the mouldings indicate Saracenic influence. *Circa* 1160. By that date ideas from the architecture of the Middle East were beginning to invade the West. *Photograph by the author.*

PLATE 35. *Above:* The ruins of Coventry Cathedral. *Photograph by the author. Right:* The new Cathedral, completed in 1962 to the design of Sir Basil Spence. *Photograph: Oriel.*

PLATE 36. Despite restorations and additions, the mediaeval character of this street in York survives. One of the towers of the Minster in the background shows how the great churches of the Middle Ages dominated the streets of cities. (See air view of the Minster on the Plate opposite.) *Photograph: The Times.*

PLATE 37. Lincoln Minster: the Cathedral Church of the Virgin Mary. This air view shows the Early English screen built across the Norman front, and the west towers rising behind. *Photograph: Aerofilms.*

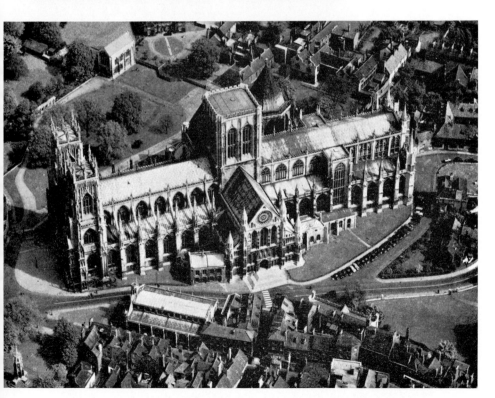

Air view of York Minster, the Cathedral Church of St. Peter, showing the cruciform plan. *Photograph: Aerofilms.* (See Plate 36.)

PLATE 38. View of Richmond Palace, looking across the Thames from the Middlesex bank. The Palace, built at Sheen for Henry VII, was completed in 1501, and occupied an area of about ten acres between Richmond Green and the River. The Palace replaced a much older building that had been burnt down in 1497, and was one of Henry VII's few extravagances. It was built of brick, round a courtyard; a large irregular structure of three storeys, with twelve rounded and octagonal towers, with decorative lead crowns flaring up to their summits and surmounted by vanes. (See drawing of the gate-house on page 221.) This view is from a painting in oils on an oak panel, $12\frac{3}{4}''$ by $30\frac{3}{4}''$, *circa* 1650, by an unknown artist. *Reproduced by courtesy of the Society of Antiquaries of London.*

PLATE 39. Château de Chambord, from the north, built 1520, and one of the most famous of the Loire châteaux. This large, semi-fortified building, with its thick round towers and impeccably symmetrical composition, strenuous skyline, Gothic features and Renaissance detail, shows the conflict, as yet unresolved, between mediaeval tradition and the revival of the architectural harmonies of the ancient world. The design marks the transition from the Middle Ages to the new classical civilisation that was becoming established in Europe. *Reproduced by courtesy of the French Government Tourist Office.*

PLATE 40. *Above:* General view and detail of columns and entablature of the sexagonal porch added about 1552 to the parish church of St. Leonard, Sunningwell, Berkshire. This represents a clumsy association of traditional Gothic and imperfectly understood classic. The addition is attributed to John Jewel, of Corpus Christi College, Oxford, who had graduated B.D. in 1552, and in that year was appointed vicar of Sunningwell and public orator of the University. *Photographs by the author.*

Above: Montacute House, Somerset, completed *circa* 1599. Built for Edward Phelips, a lawyer, it has three storeys, with attic rooms in the two wings lit by small windows in the curved Flemish gables. This is an example of the new native style that developed during the second half of the sixteenth-century. *Photograph: Ursula Clark.*

PLATE 41. *Above:* The gateway, Canterbury Quadrangle, St. John's College, Oxford. 1632–36. Flemish influence is apparent, comparable to that in the south porch of St. Mary's. (See frontispiece.) *Left:* The Customs House, King's Lynn, Norfolk. Designed by Henry Bell, alderman and architect of that town, and built in 1683: originally the Exchange. *Photographs: Ursula Clark.*

PLATE 42. Part of the entrance piazza, St. Peter, Rome, showing the southern sweep of Bernini's Tuscan colonnades. Erected 1655–1667. *Photograph by S. M. Sternfeldt, L.R.I.B.A.*

The Capitol, Rome, 1540–1644, Michelangelo's imposing civic design. This view, reduced from an engraving by Piranesi, shows the remains of older buildings and the general appearance of the site in the mid-eighteenth-century.

PLATE 43. The fountain of the Hydraulic Organ at the Villa d'Este, Tivoli, by Pirro Ligorio. The central feature by Bernini. Work on the water gardens of the Villa began in 1550, directed by Pirro Ligorio as master designer: G. A. Galvani was architect and Muziano, Zuccari and Agresti were associated with the work. The villa and gardens were originally designed for Cardinal Ippolito d'Este. *Photograph: Ursula Clark.*

PLATE 44. Architecture in the grand manner. *Above:* Part of the Orangery at the Palace of Versailles, built for Louis XIV. *Reproduced by courtesy of the French Government Tourist Office. Below:* Castle Howard, Yorkshire, 1699–1712. Designed by Sir John Vanbrugh for the Earl of Carlisle. Reduced from plates 5 and 6 of *Vitruvius Britannicus*, Vol. III.

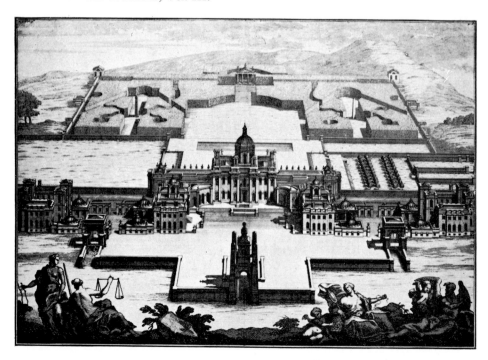

PLATE 45. Independence Hall, Philadelphia, Pennsylvania, designed by the Speaker of the Assembly, Andrew Hamilton (1676–1741). The foundations were laid in 1731 and the building completed twenty years later. The characteristics of contemporary Georgian architecture were reproduced with marked and agreeable regional variations in the towns and countryside of the English colonies, and an American school of design revitalised and maintained the classic tradition throughout the eighteenth and nineteenth centuries. *U.S.A. National Park Service Photograph.*

PLATE 46. Roman splendour and eastern eccentricity. *Above:* The Royal Crescent, Bath. *Left:* The Pagoda, Kew Gardens. 1757–62. By Sir William Chambers. *Below:* Royal Pavilion, Brighton. 1815–1818. Chiefly by John Nash. *Photographs: Ursula Clark.*

PLATE 47. *Above:* York Station: an example of the new architecture of iron and glass, conceived and carried out by engineers, who were unable to resist dumping a pseudo-Corinthian capital on a cast iron column. *Below:* Exterior of the station at Buxton, Derbyshire, *circa* 1863. A combination of sandstone, glass and iron. Both illustrations reproduced by courtesy of *British Railways.*

PLATE 48. Knightsbridge, London. North side looking east towards Hyde Park Corner. The tall, plain mass of the contemporary building asserts the impersonal character of the scientific industrial age: the late Victorian houses and shops in the foreground are different in scale, structure and materials, and belong to a dying age.

Right: Part of Pelham Crescent, Hastings. (See page 276.) The pseudo-Gothic intrusion is the result of John Ruskin's advocacy for Gothic forms. *Photograph: Oriel.*

INDEX

Names and places are included, also the titles of works quoted or referred to in the text.

341

An Episode
in Anti-Catholicism:

The American Protective Association

by Donald L. Kinzer

University of Washington Press: Seattle

Copyright © 1964
by the University of Washington Press
Library of Congress Catalog Card Number 64-10948
Manufactured by Vail-Ballou Press, Inc., Binghamton, N.Y.
Printed in the United States of America

Preface

The American Protective Association was not the creator of the anti-Catholicism of its time, nor was it exclusively the manipulator of prejudice. The organization was the beneficiary of its era, and an instrument which both its supporters and its opponents used to gain political support and to mold public opinion. The story of its career is a part of the story of the 1890's. Like previous anti-Catholic political organizations in the history of this country, the A.P.A. was nationalistic and patriotic; unlike them, it did not limit membership to the native-born. Like them, the A.P.A. engaged in politics; unlike them, it utilized existing political parties rather than seeking to create a new party. There is ample room, consequently, for a detailed study of the career of the American Protective Association, since it varied from other anti-Catholic political groups.

There is one previous book-length study of the A.P.A.; that of Humphrey J. Desmond, *The A.P.A. Movement: A Sketch,* which appeared in 1912. As the notes in this study will show, Mr. Desmond was a trained historian, a lawyer, a newspaperman, and was as well a participant in the crusade against the A.P.A. His account does not lack objectivity because of his beliefs or activities; it is, in fact, a *source* for this study because of its nature. Mr. Desmond recognized his book's limitations when he designated it a "sketch." In seeking to provide a study which will fill out the story of the A.P.A. and provide the detail which most students of the era recognize to be lacking, I have received nothing but encouragement from my fellow scholars.

There are, apparently, no organizational records of the A.P.A. in existence—no minute books, membership lists, not even a constitution—to provide the student with basic materials. This study,

thus, has had to depend on a search through the existing files of the remnants of the self-styled "patriotic press" that carried the news of the A.P.A. during its lifetime. Of somewhere near one hundred of these periodicals for which titles and places of publication were found, the files of seventeen were used, most of them partial rather than complete. Several of these periodicals are used here for the first time by anyone pursuing this subject, or a theme related to it. Supplementing these periodicals and the rather favorable impression they provide were files of Catholic diocesan newspapers as well as daily and weekly newspapers and weekly and monthly magazines of general circulation.

Since the A.P.A. took part in the political struggles of its time, personal records of local and national figures on deposit in several libraries were surveyed with good results. The story that grew out of these sources was augmented by use of memoirs, biographies, and published collections of personal documents. The legislative career of the organization was followed in the records of several state legislatures and the national Congress.

The narrative was enriched by additional information and insights gained from reading the propagandistic literature, books and pamphlets alike, that appeared during the lifetime of the organization, in its favor and in opposition. These materials are now somewhat fugitive so that the obtaining of them was partly a matter of good fortune and partly a matter of search.

The obligation to archivists and librarians consequently is very great. My appreciation to the custodians, the archivists, and the librarians (as well as their assistants) in the several depositories where these materials were found is more than can be expressed. I am confident that their attention to my requests was not unusual; this patron is humbly grateful.

At various stages this study received substantial criticism from Professors W. Stull Holt, Thomas J. Pressly, the late Charles M. Gates, Max Savelle, and Scott Lytle of the University of Washington. In revising the manuscript, I received assistance in 1956 from the University of Delaware Faculty Research fellowship funds; I also appreciate the encouragement and stimulus given by Professors John A. Munroe and H. Clay Reed of Delaware.

Anyone working in the field of patriotic or nativistic organizations must be grateful to John Higham for his *Strangers in the Land*. Mr. Higham extended a hand to me, however, before his book was in print and I am indebted to him. I also wish to thank William Duffy, Jr., of Wilmington, Delaware, for his generous assistance.

Some parts of the study have already appeared in print as an article, "The Political Uses of Anti-Catholicism: Michigan and Wisconsin, 1890–1894," in *Michigan History,* XXXIX, 312–26.

The time spent on completing this study was subtracted from that on which my family had some claim. I want to extend belated thanks to my parents, and particular gratitude to my wife.

Donald L. Kinzer

February, 1963
Trenton, N.J.

Contents

An Episode in Anti-Catholicism:
The American Protective Association

1 Setting

Anti-Catholicism in the post-Civil War United States was the child of two related, but separable, heritages. First, within the Christian community there was a long history of divisions that extended back so far into the past that one could sense, intuitively if not by direct evidence, that there never had been unity in Christendom except in the person of its Founder. Within the same frame, there was the historical knowledge of dissent from a unity that at one time did exist. Second, within the United States rationalism and secularism had a history, not so long perhaps or so well known as the other heritage, extending at least back to the inauguration of the new government under the Constitution, so that the man of the last half of the nineteenth century could find precedent for his acceptance of them. The rationalism was antireligious because it held that religion was a superstitious fetter on the freedom of man's mind. Consequently it was anti-Catholic, but no more than it was anti-Lutheran or anti-Mormon.

The religious tradition in America was colored by the first of these heritages, so that folk memories of the Protestant Reformation and its religious wars with their horrors and rancors were just below the level of consciousness. Not only was it a matter of religion; national loyalties were involved as well. In his intellectual baggage, the "American" had brought with him from Europe the recollection of national churches with their respective relationships to the Roman Catholic Church. Thus, antagonism toward Catholicism was always in reserve, ready to spring into life when it was appealed to as an aspect of nativism. The American tradition was Protestant, bulwarked by the preponderantly non-Catholic composition of the people of the United States.[1]

The rationalistic tradition had won a victory in the writing of the first amendment to the Constitution, inaugurating thereby a problem in the relationship of church and state. Practically, the rationalists' victory was the result of compromising the argument as to established churches on the least common denominator—no establishment and no prohibition of the free exercise of religion—thus placing all faiths on an equal footing before the law. Actually, the first amendment represented a positive attitude. This positive conception, that the law provided for religious freedom for individuals and not simple toleration for corporate bodies, was to gain surprising strength in the latter half of the nineteenth century.[2]

Another string to the rationalists' bow was added in 1859 when the challenging announcement of Charles Darwin appeared. Darwin's statement seemed, to its enthusiastic adherents at least, to cut the ground from under revealed religion. One of its results was to secularize American thought further, adding weight to the rationalists' positive attitude.[3]

Simple toleration permitted Catholicism to exist as an act of good will. Religious freedom, meaning equality of individuals and freedom of choice under law, was something else. Under the American concept of it, the Catholic Church was one of the sects of Christendom, entitled to all the privileges and freedoms enjoyed by other religious groups, entitled also to all the criticisms and injustices the others were subjected to on occasion.[4] The Catholic interpretation of religious freedom, with its tendency to emphasize the corporate body, was not identical with the view held by other segments of American society, which looked to the first amendment as the source of the individual's religious liberties. In the post-Civil War period a series of events demonstrated these differences between Catholic and non-Catholic views of religious liberty and the relationship between church and state.

Anti-Catholicism requires a Catholic position to oppose, and certain "aggressive" tendencies on the part of Catholics can be discerned. Quite spontaneously and without direction from the church hierarchy, Catholics throughout the country began to

seek "religious liberty" by accomplishing certain objectives. Their moves were a reflection of an increase in Catholic population that produced a self-confidence not hitherto enjoyed by the Catholic minority. A search for some solution to the school question that would not violate Catholic consciences was one of these moves. This, in so far as it insisted on a separate Catholic school system, could be expected to conflict with the growing public school system, which many of its supporters regarded as the best means of achieving national unity. Another move on the part of Catholics was toward securing tax support for Catholic institutions of all kinds on the same basis as state aid to non-Catholic institutions. This move would tend to conflict with the growing acceptance of state support on a nonsectarian basis for charities, correctional activities, hospitals, and so forth, as a proper function of the state rather than of private action. Furthermore, Catholics began more actively to seek election to public office and thus to end the widely accepted exclusion of Catholics from political preferment because of their religion. In addition to these three major moves, an additional one, of minor importance but still troublesome, was the obtaining for inmates of public institutions a free choice of religious counselors. This last move raised the entire question of chaplains and also led to a discussion of whether administrative officials could operate their institutional charges as though they were completely nonsectarian.[5]

Catholic action and anti-Catholic reaction on these issues are evident in the presidential election of 1876 and became increasingly strong in the decade of the eighties. The first well-publicized incident occurred in Cincinnati, Ohio, as early as 1869. Its roots could be traced back to 1842, when Bishop Purcell of Cincinnati had objected to the use of the King James Version of the Bible in the public schools and to the continued use of McGuffey readers because they contained statements "obnoxious" to Catholics.[6] The local school board sought to compromise; in return for banning the Bible from the public schools, local parochial schools would be incorporated within the public system by purchase. Over Purcell's objection that his church regarded moral instruction as a churchly function, the school board went ahead with

its plans. The courts enjoined the school board, and a court hearing followed. In the course of the arguments, Attorney Rufus King stated that of the twenty-two members of the board, ten were Catholics who had been elected by some "strange coalition." He wondered how it was that suddenly ten Catholics should have been elected to the board when the usual number was about three.[7] By a decision of two to one, the court judges voted to continue the injunction, but on appeal to the higher state court the lower court was overruled and the Bible was eliminated from the schools.[8] Thus, in the name of religious freedom the King James Version was barred from public school use so that Catholic children attending the public schools would not hear an unauthorized version. The result, moreover, was satisfactory to secularists as well as to Catholics.[9]

The centennial year of 1876 provided the next series of incidents. Patriotism and nationalistic fervor were injected into the story by centennial enthusiasm. A concerted, organized, and ramified attack on the great principles of religious freedom would, in the judgment of a writer in the *Catholic World,* signalize a revival of "irreligious fanaticism" during the centennial year. "Wild exhibitions of anti-Catholicism and anti-American fanaticism" were predicted, which the author hoped would be met with "forbearance, charity, and conciliation."[10] The writer was hardly describing a situation which was in the future; it was, in fact, painfully evident when his article appeared that exhibitions of anti-Catholicism had already occurred. The accuracy of his picture of the centennial year hinged on his interpretation of the content of anti-Catholicism, its identification in his mind with "anti-American fanaticism," and the particular meaning he gave to religious freedom. The centennial year was also a presidential election year, so that the context was political. The events involved the presidential race and a proposed amendment to the Constitution.

The re-election of President Grant in 1872 had been opposed by the *Irish World* of New York City, which published twenty-five reasons for its support of Horace Greeley. Among these reasons were the facts that Grant was on the same ticket as Henry

Wilson, the "unrepentant Know-Nothing," that he was supported by all the "proscriptive sectarians" in the country, and that the "interests of England" demanded his re-election.[11] This New York paper appealed directly to the "Irish vote," and its statements should be interpreted against the background of the Tammany-Tweed Ring scandals and the alleged influence of the Irish as part of the Ring domination of New York's Democratic party.[12]

As his second term drew to its close, President Grant, whose church affiliation was always somewhat obscure, made a speech to his former comrades of the Army of The Tennessee in a convention at Des Moines, Iowa. His political purpose was to appeal to the nation's schoolteachers, who had been hit financially by the Panic of 1873, and to demonstrate that his party favored free public education.[13] Grant advised his comrades to work for the preservation of "free thought, free speech, a free press, pure morals, unfettered religious sentiment, and equal rights for all before the law"; to resolve that neither state nor nation should support institutions of learning which mixed education with sectarian, pagan, or atheistic dogmas. He concluded, "Leave the matter of religion to the family altar, the church, and the private school, supported entirely by private contributions. Keep the church and the state forever separate. With these safeguards, I believe that the battles which created the Army of The Tennessee will not have been fought in vain."

When the President's remarks were reported in the *Catholic World,* they were agreed with in the following context: no tax money should be expended to support sectarian schools, but the existing system of public schools was in fact sectarian because they used the Protestant Bible, or because they did *not* teach religion; schools where "God was ignored" were pagan; if religious teaching was not permitted, the school was "godless"; if God were to be denied by instruction in a "science falsely so-called," the atheistic school so teaching should not under the President's strictures receive support from tax money.[14] Admittedly, this argument did not represent *the* Catholic position; it was the view of one Catholic. But it served to present points of

view that many Catholics did accept in later discussions, and it illustrated the difficulties surrounding any public airing of the public school question as it involved Catholics.

To the Congress convening in December of 1875, Grant submitted a recommendation for an amendment to the Constitution making it mandatory on the states to establish and maintain free public schools adequate to instruct all pupils in the elementary branches of learning. This far, the proposal may be regarded as a continuation of Reconstruction in that it would extend educational privileges to freed Negroes. But Grant suggested further that a clause be added forbidding the use of public funds for institutions supported by "any religious sect or denomination," and he recommended a policy of taxing all church property except, possibly, burial grounds and church edifices.[15]

One week later, Congressman James G. Blaine introduced a resolution containing less than the President had asked for but providing for a sixteenth amendment to the Constitution:

No State shall make any law respecting an establishment of religion or prohibiting the free exercise thereof; and no money raised by taxation in any State for the support of public schools, or derived from any public fund therefor, nor any public lands devoted thereto, shall ever be under the control of any religious sect, nor shall any money so raised or lands so devoted be divided between religious sects or denominations.

Congress took no action on the proposed resolution for nearly a year, so that its debate and decision actually took place in the months just preceding the presidential election of 1876.[16]

Meanwhile, the spotlight swung back to the state of Ohio, from which the Republican presidential candidate would come. Rutherford B. Hayes, who had been governor from 1868 to 1872, was elected again in the fall of 1875 after a Democratic interlude. The "Catholic question" was one of the leading topics of his second gubernatorial campaign, the current issue being the "Geghan Law" passed by the Democratic legislature, which permitted Catholic priests to minister to inmates of state penal and benevolent institutions if the inmates so desired. Hayes's position was that the law was unnecessary, since the practice was not

forbidden in the existing law, and that therefore the only reason for enactment of a new law was to demonstrate the extent to which Catholics controlled the Democratic party.[17] Hayes was elected and the law was repealed on his recommendation.[18]

Nominated for the presidency, Hayes endorsed the proposed sixteenth amendment as placing the public school beyond "all danger of sectarian control or interference" and failed to become worried at the statement that he was an anti-Catholic. He viewed the charge as an attempt to put him and his party on the defensive, and he refused to be pushed into such a position.[19]

In August of 1876, Congress debated the proposed Blaine amendment. The obvious purpose of the resolution was to expand and extend the idea of separate church and state, which the first amendment had applied to the actions of the federal government, so as to include the actions of state governments. Amid some assumption that the fourteenth amendment had already made such an extension of the first,[20] the debates probably indicated more of a desire to gain partisan advantage in the campaign than an attempt to resolve a constitutional problem. The Archbishop of Baltimore, Cardinal Gibbons, added to the confusion by pointing out that Grant's proposal for universal compulsory elementary education was more extensive than the Blaine amendment, since it led in the direction of federal control of schooling so that the individual would tend to be "absorbed by the state." [21]

Combined in the circumstances, then, were several issues aside from the religious one: extension of federal power over the states, limitation of state powers, and federal insistence on equal education for all children regardless of color. In debate on the floor of Congress the proposed amendment was described as unobjectionable to anyone because it was so "broad you can drive an omnibus through it." Senator Frelinghuysen of New Jersey deplored the charge that the proposal was against religion, holding that there was a "pure and undefiled religion which appertains to the relationship and responsibility of man to God; and it is readily distinguishable from the creeds of sects." Infringement of state rights was acknowledged in the debates, but some who were conscious of the threat of federal power were willing

to risk it in order to "quiet those groundless fears" as to the use of tax money for support of nonpublic schools. The papal Syllabus of Errors, the Geghan Law, and the "godless" charge against the public schools were all mentioned. One Democrat suggested that Republicans were attempting to wave a "bloody shirt" against the Pope now that the Negro issue was dead. When the Senate voted, supporters of the resolution drew twenty-eight votes, the opponents sixteen, while twenty-seven failed to cast a vote. Without the necessary two-thirds majority, the resolution failed to pass, but the division in voting was along party lines, with Republicans generally for passage and Democrats against.[22]

As if to bulwark Republican opposition to Catholicism, President Hayes appointed as his Secretary of the Navy a man from Indiana named Richard Wigginton Thompson, whose book on *The Papacy and the Civil Power* appeared in 1876. In it, Thompson expounded his belief that there was an irreconcilable conflict between papal theory and popular government.[23] The total effect, then, of the election of 1876 was to saddle a willing Republican party with the reputation of champion of the public schools and anti-Catholicism, a position to which it continued to give lip service, at least, in succeeding party platforms for years.[24] Yet the issues could not be separated from the question that the Democrats had mentioned during the debates; in the minds of many, the school question was closely connected with compulsory education for Negroes. Robert Ingersoll, the Republican orator and agnostic, expressed his summary of the matter by saying that he wished the South to have prosperity and a "schoolhouse in every town [and] books in the hands of every child" so that "all the civilization of the nineteenth century [may] enter every home in the South." He believed that this could be accomplished and that the result would be to fill "that section full of good Republicans." [25]

After the election of 1876, there was a temporary decline in the importance of anti-Catholicism as an issue. But attempts continued to define more clearly the proper relationship of church to state. Two organizations spearheaded the movement, one of them rationalist and secularist and seeking to remove all legal

privileges granted by government to religious groups, the other seeking a formal and legal recognition of God as the source of law. The National Liberal League drew together in 1876 a number of existing local groups to support the "Nine Demands of Liberalism." These demands included equal taxation of all property, including church-owned property; abolition of chaplains paid from public funds in the armed services or in public institutions; abolition of sectarian appropriations of any kind from public funds; prohibition of the use of the Bible in public schools for any purpose; abolition of all religious feasts as legal holidays; abolition of oaths in court, to be replaced with affirmations; repeal of Sabbath laws; an understanding of all references to morality in the law as relating to a "natural morality"; and no privileges or advantages for any faith, Christian or otherwise, in governmental administration.[26] Robert Ingersoll was one of the leaders of the movement, and he was willing to forgo his usual Republicanism to inaugurate a new political party in 1879 to obtain the goals of the Liberals.[27]

Quite the opposite in its goals, the National Reform Association, dating from 1864, held that "Almighty God is the source of all power and authority in civil government and Jesus is the ruler of all nations." Its legislative objective, the so-called "God-in-the-Constitution" movement, was the enactment of an amendment to the Constitution that would acknowledge God as the source of law. This organization was actually Protestant in inspiration and leadership,[28] but its objective eventually came to be regarded as a Catholic move by anti-Catholics. Of it and its objectives, the Liberal Robert Ingersoll said, "If we should put God in the Constitution, there would be no room left for man." Any attempt to enforce a particular religious belief or dogma would be contrary to the scientific knowledge gained during recent years; in the schools, "Baptist botany" would be as foolish as "Catholic chemistry." [29]

Of the two groups, the Liberals were apparently more in sympathy with their times, for lawmaking bodies accepted some of the planks in their platform. Constitutional prohibitions on appropriations of public funds for sectarian purposes, specifically

mentioning public school funds in many instances, were passed by at least twenty-four of the states between 1870 and 1900.[30] However, the force of these prohibitions was not so clear in specific instances. For example, the Bible was often eliminated from the schools on the grounds that it was a "sectarian" book. No state enacted a law which forbade use of the Bible, but there were many court cases in which its use was an issue.[31] In summary, the secularization of the American public school which characterized the period after 1850 eliminated religious and church influences from publicly supported education. Two propositions guided this development: the first was that maintenance of the republic demanded an educated citizenry, and to obtain this compulsory education laws were necessary; the second held that to protect private religious beliefs any source of controversy should be eliminated from the schools.[32]

To anti-Catholics, compulsory education in public schools and retention of the Bible were necessary because, between them, "the Bible and the Common Schools were the two stones of the mill that would grind Catholicity out of Catholics." [33] Struggling to retain the Bible, these extremists blamed Catholics for taking cases to court, which eliminated it; with the Bible gone, however, they continued to fight for compulsory school legislation.[34] To a Catholic writer, the results of the drive were dangerous in that compulsory attendance at public schools would deny Catholics the opportunity to teach their own youth, while elimination of Bible-reading would destroy Protestantism, an outcome which he hardly disapproved,[35] but which was admittedly a little hard on religion.

That Protestantism had already failed was the opinion expressed by the English historian, James Anthony Froude, in a magazine article that pointed to the remarkable growth of Catholic population in the United States. He referred to a figure of six and a half million as the current Catholic population, noting that the rate of increase was likely to continue. He gave as the cause of the increase the prolific and ignorant Irish peasantry which had furnished the bulk of Irish immigration to America. Protestantism had once been the opponent of Catholicism, he believed, but now

a new foe, rationalism, had appeared in "an intellectual revolution" that was sweeping over the world. But rationalism was weak
in that when the rationalist's "rationality tells him to abandon
Christianity, he replies by falling back into the Roman Communion." [36] His message was obviously intended to encourage
liberals and rationalists and to make vivid the strength and
growth of their "enemy."

In 1884, the "enemy" dramatized its achievements in America
at the Third Plenary Council of the hierarchy at Baltimore in
November. Since the last meeting of the bishops in 1866, the
Catholic population of the country had almost doubled; an
American archbishop had been elevated to the first cardinalate
within the United States; and each year after 1880 saw some
change in diocesan boundaries to accommodate growth. Expansion was particularly noticeable in the West.[37] After some deliberations, the consulting bishops announced that the wearing
of the Roman collar would thereafter be obligatory for priests,
who were advised to "leave to worldlings the cares and anxieties
of political partizanship, the struggles for ascendancy, and the
manifestations of disappointed ambition." As a means of publicity, the bishops hoped that "Catholic" books and newspapers
would soon appear, specifically mentioning a desire for a diocesan newspaper in each diocese and a newspaper, not necessarily
bearing the designation "Catholic" in its title, which would one
day equal the largest and best metropolitan dailies.[38] On education, the decision was to encourage parochial schools so that
Catholic children would not obtain schooling where their faith
was put in jeopardy. Parochial curricula should be on a par with
those in the public schools, while pastors were warned not to use
excessive zeal in enforcing attendance at them. A specific reference to the zeal to be avoided was the recommendation that
priests should not deny the sacraments to parents in order to
coerce their children's attendance. Training in United States
history was specifically mentioned as a part of the curriculum.[39]

In a pastoral letter, the bishops took note of the current antagonism toward their church and expressed a desire for moderation on the part of Catholics in return. They were sure that the

"right-minded American nowhere finds himself more at home than in the Catholic Church," and they repudiated the idea that Catholics were hostile to the American republic.[40] Moderate and wise as the bishops were in their public announcements, they indicated no retreat from principles. In fact, on the matter of clerical garb, newspapers, and the public schools, they had indicated an attitude toward which anti-Catholics would point as illustrating "aggression."

Though seemingly united against attacks from without, the church was torn by internal dissensions and faced as well problems created by an influx of immigrants. One group within the church—some of them followers of the Reverend Isaac Hecker, editor of the *Catholic World* from 1865 to 1888—was generally of American birth and upbringing and had little knowledge of the peasant faith of the immigrant. Their interest lay in proselytizing Americans like themselves and they felt that this could be best done if the church demonstrated its adaptability to American conditions. The parochial school and the public school system were reconcilable in their thinking, while Catholicism and republicanism were likewise compatible. Another group of clerics, however, wished to emphasize the nonnational tradition of the church and felt that maintenance of the faith among immigrants was the first job of the hierarchy. These two groups were usually designated as the "Irish" and the "German," the "Irish" representing the older and "American" group while "German" summarized the views of the others.[41] This terminology was misleading. For example, one of the leaders of the so-called "German" group was the obviously Irish-American Archbishop Corrigan of New York City. Moreover, the term "American" as applied to the "Irish" group frequently led to a misconception of their position, particularly after "Americanism" was denounced by the papacy. From the differences of the two factions, however, derived the expressions of nativism by Catholics, expressions which demonstrated the appeal and force of nativistic sentiment, but which also discouraged understanding.

One specific example of the differences between the "Ameri-

cans" and their colleagues within the hierarchy was to be noted in the attempts to get Catholic immigrants out of the crowded cities of the East and into rural areas in the West.[42] The bishops of the "German" camp felt that the immigrants' religion would be jeopardized if they were removed from the close spiritual guidance that could be more easily, and practically, administered in an urban setting at a time when the number of available parish priests was limited. The differences were thus really only differences in method, but they did reflect light on the expansion of the church in the United States and on the occurrences from which anti-Catholics drew some evidence. Undeniably, the Catholic Church in the United States was no longer an immigrants' church; it had become as "American" as any other. At the same time, however, it faced the problem of retaining the recent immigrant who was now in unfamiliar surroundings that might very likely put his faith to the test. Anything like official figures showing Catholic growth awaited the federal census of 1890, but the fact of Catholic expansion was evident and being publicized. Much of the growth came from recent immigration,[43] but much of its strength lay with the second- and third-generation American who disliked being regarded as deficient in national loyalty merely because of church affiliation.

Just as secularization proved to be the apparent wish of the majority in educational matters, some restriction on immigration and some limitation on the immigrants' quick naturalization was another of the dominant moods of the era. Anti-Catholicism accompanied this mood too as a minor theme. Western states had been extremely lenient in permitting aliens the right to vote immediately after declaration of intent to become citizens.[44] This leniency reached its greatest extent in 1875, but even before then it had begun to recede in some places. The last state constitutions to grant aliens of declared intent full rights of suffrage were those of the Dakotas in 1889; the movement to withdraw suffrage before citizenship was attained began in 1848 in Illinois. By 1900, only half the states that had granted the privilege at one time still retained it.[45] Literacy tests before suffrage was granted were also

a feature of attempts to control the suffrage. They were intended in part as a restriction on Negro voting but were also an expression of nativism.[46]

Not until 1906 was the basic law regarding naturalization altered; the campaign that led to change was based on the belief that because of an "alliance with political grafters" naturalization processes had become a source of political scandal.[47] Closely allied to the problem of naturalization was the widespread belief that in some way immigration should be restricted. In fact, the temper of the times may be described as concerned not with whether, but with how, the goal of restriction could be achieved.[48]

These two factors, immigration and suffrage restriction, composed the nativistic sentiment of the period, and were related to anti-Catholicism in that large numbers of the immigrants coming to the country at the time were adherents of the Catholic Church. But it should also be remembered that probably the most sensitive group among Catholics, those most likely to resent antagonisms, were the second- and third-generation Catholic Americans. With literacy regarded as a prerequisite to the proper exercise of the suffrage, education and school questions were emphasized. With nationalism as an objective, the unity achieved through common experience in the public school was considered preferable to the religious division that the parochial school depended on (and magnified, according to those who opposed it). With widespread fear that the ignorant immigrant was the cat's-paw of unscrupulous politicians, a fear that was certainly not restricted to anti-Catholics, plus the belief that Catholic leadership operated to control the vote of the church's adherents, Catholic immigration was regarded as a particular threat. Extremist groups on both the Catholic side and the anti-Catholic side tended to unite many elements into a composite picture; thus the anti-Catholic would accept the idea of a "Catholic conspiracy" against those things he held dear and would find the evidence supporting his fears to be overwhelming. A Catholic, on the other hand, could easily compose opposition to immigration, limitation of naturalization, opposition to parochial schools, and many other attitudes into a generalized picture of anti-Catholicism. Both of these

groups would exaggerate their fears and magnify the opposition.

In the developing anti-Catholicism that characterized the eighties, certain distant events provided background. Both the publication of the Syllabus of Errors in 1864, which, in effect, tended to place Catholicism in opposition to the secularistic and liberalist tendencies of the century, and the Vatican Council of 1870, which agreed to accept papal infallibility, were significant.[49] No less important were the *Kulturkampf* in Germany, Gladstone's attitude toward Catholicism in England, and anti-clericalism in France. In Italy, 1870 brought an end to the temporal domain of the Pope. The effect within the United States of these occurrences abroad was to stimulate awareness of Catholicism, to cause debate on whether any person or institution could be really infallible, and to bring an influx of refugees from Europe's quarrels to America.

One of the immediate results of the *Kulturkampf* was to bring to the United States priests and members of religious orders fleeing from Germany. Their coming was fortunate for the church in that they provided pastors for immigrants speaking German and teachers for parochial schools;[50] but their advent was unfortunate, too, in that the refugees tended to retain their native languages and to support the most conservative elements within the church, to look with alarm on the freer attitude of Americans toward religion in general, and to draw excessive criticism from nativists and anti-Catholics.[51]

Americans were not unaware, nor were anti-Catholics ignorant, of the dogma of infallibility and the importance of the ending of papal dominion in Italy. Actually, these events were merely proof to the anti-Catholic of what he had maintained in his arsenal of arguments at all times. To him, the Pope was the guiding light of a conspiracy, directing all the actions of his subordinates without consulting the bishops who, in turn, carried out the Pope's directions without question. The distinction between temporal and spiritual had always been made in anti-Catholic literature and did not alter the interpretation of the "conspiracy" to be found there. In fact, the anti-Catholic did not believe that the Pope's temporal power *had* come to an end in

1870; for him, the Pope's power transcended both time and political boundaries.[52]

But anti-Catholicism was much more concerned with immediate events in the United States and what it saw there as direct threats than it was with an abstract and generalized picture. Obvious and widely discussed facts and incidents in the decade of the eighties formed the foundation upon which anti-Catholics constructed interpretations creating for themselves a pattern of domestic Catholic aggression. Three fears—the so-called Catholic vote, the public school question, and Catholic influence on organized labor—were the sources of specific anti-Catholicism. The most significant explanation of the apparent success of anti-Catholicism, however, derives from the fact that many men who were not essentially anti-Catholic were concerned with these same problems, finding solutions to them not in religious antagonisms but in social reform. One of these men was the Reverend Josiah Strong, who became secretary of the Evangelical Alliance in 1886, thus placing himself among the leaders of the "social gospel" movement among Protestant clergymen.[53]

Strong's important and stimulating book, *Our Country: Its Possible Future and Its Present Crisis,* appeared in 1885 and sold 167,000 copies by 1891.[54] Strong was urgent, graphic, and vigorous; undoubtedly the style accounted for some of the book's success. Actually, however, the author struck nearly every current chord that could be sounded. Chapter headings show that the following topics were among those discussed: natural resources, the West, immigration, "Romanism," religion and the public schools, Mormonism, intemperance, socialism, wealth and poverty, the city, exhaustion of the public lands, Anglo-Saxonism, and the money question.

Immigration brought unquestioned benefits, said Strong, but it complicated every problem and furnished the soil from which came the noxious growths threatening American civilization. Low morality and pauperism followed the immigrant into the cities where he congregated, for when he left his home country the migrant did not take his standards of morality or his religious training with him. Mormonism, Catholicism, and socialism all

derived their political potential from the immigrants, he said. He argued further, "Rome has never favored popular education," and that Catholics owed their highest allegiance to their church, not the nation. With its characteristic foresight, Rome was said to be "concentrating her strength in the western territories. As the West is to dominate the nation, she intends to dominate the West. In the United States a little more than one-eighth of the population is Catholic; in the territories taken together, more than one-third." On the public school question, "the principal digestive organ of the body politic," Strong believed that for a continuation of democracy compulsory education was essential in order to Americanize the children of the immigrants. Extreme secularism was dangerous, too; separation of church and state should not mean abolition of religion or the failure to teach morality, but, he maintained, "Sectarian dogmas are not essential to popular morality."

Strong's book appeared in the year following the presidential election of 1884, in which the phrase "Rum, Romanism, and Rebellion" played its debatable part in electing a Democrat. The book was at least six years ahead of the point at which anti-Catholics were able to effect a degree of organizational unity among themselves in order to carry their program into effect. It struck the popular fancy but its effect was diffused. The book can hardly be charged with having given any particular direction to anti-Catholicism. Its importance derived from the fact that it so neatly tied together the themes that were stimulating social and political thinking among religious people of the Protestant persuasion.

Contemporary interpretation of the results of the presidential election of 1884 placed emphasis on the Reverend Mr. Burchard's alliterative "Rum, Romanism, and Rebellion" as a factor in causing New York City's Irish-Catholics to vote for Cleveland instead of for Blaine. In this shift of votes, anti-Catholics saw evidence of the conspiratorial guidance of the hierarchy, illustrating a "peril to the Republic" in that, without opportunity for argument, a bloc of votes could be switched in the last moments of a campaign from one candidate to another.[55] Commenting on

the election results at the time, the noted Catholic historian John Gilmary Shea referred to the revival of "know nothingism" during the campaign, and believed that the Burchard incident had the effect of giving victory to the "unworthy Cleveland." [56]

The incident provides an illustration of the cross-purposes and false positions that the injection of Catholicism and anti-Catholicism into politics forced upon candidates. Traditionally, the New York Irish had been affiliated with the Democrats. The alliance had flourished under the notorious Tweed Ring and had been criticized in 1880 by Dexter Hawkins, a New York attorney, as a natural consequence of the Ring's subsidizing Catholic charities in New York City. This subsidy allegedly paid for the Irish-Catholic support of the Democratic Ring and was supported from public funds distributed through Catholic charitable institutions.[57] As governor of New York, Cleveland had vetoed an appropriation bill extending funds to the Catholic Protectory, a church institution for children, and was consequently regarded as anti-Catholic.[58] Yet this was the man who benefited from the last-minute switch of Irish-Catholic votes during the campaign of 1884, as the anti-Catholics viewed the story.

On the other hand, the defeated Republican James G. Blaine was throughout his career suspected for "Catholic connections" because members of his family were practicing Catholics.[59] Moreover, Blaine was the Republican party leader to whom the "Blaine Irish" were so enthusiastically loyal that he appeared to be the man whose nomination for the presidency would break the traditional Irish-Democratic alliance. Yet, Blaine's record as a congressman and the fact that he had introduced the proposed sixteenth amendment meant that he was acceptable to anti-Catholics, too, who continued to insist thereafter that Cleveland was the darling of the Romanists.

Despite this demonstration of hazards involved in manipulating prejudices where anything so temperamental as the "Irish vote" was involved, the pursuit of the Irish continued among New York politicians. For example, David B. Hill, Cleveland's successor as governor, in contrast to his predecessor's position on the Protectory, supported a "freedom of worship" bill that

would permit priests to minister to Catholic inmates in public institutions. The legislators failed to agree with him, but the gesture was an attempt to retain Irish votes for the Democrats.[60]

New York's mayor, Abram Hewitt, felt the revenge of the Irish in 1888 over the issue of flags flying from the city hall. He had permitted the national flag to fly at half-mast out of respect for the death of the German Kaiser in 1888 but would not permit the display of a green flag over the city hall on St. Patrick's day. The city council tried to take the decision from his hands, but Hewitt vetoed their ordinance. In his veto message, Hewitt pointed out that the Irish accounted for only 16.4 per cent of the city's population, yet, of twenty-six aldermen, seven (27 per cent) were of Irish birth; very nearly the same ratio existed among city employees, but he singled out the police department, in which 28.1 per cent were "Irishmen born." Such figures might have reflected Irish superiority, but Hewitt could not permit the figures to imply this compliment. He referred to the "institutions under the care of the Commissioners of Charities and Correction," where the Irish furnished nearly double their population ratio in inmates. Making a comparison to the Germans, Mayor Hewitt said that if any complaints of discrimination were to be lodged, the Germans should lodge them. He suggested that his facts should "impose a modest restraint" on those asking for special privileges from the city. His chances for re-election, consequently, went glimmering.[61]

Hewitt's stand and his publicity made him the choice as nominee for a new political party, the American party, which made a brief national appearance in 1888. Hewitt was not willing to accept the nomination, but the group succeeded in participating in the election without him. A "flag" resolution, a statement on religious freedom, and an affirmation of belief in the complete separation of church and state were subordinated in its platform to the main emphasis on immigration restriction. If anything, the American party of 1888 demonstrated that nativism had no appeal at the time as the offering of a third party;[62] nativism was in fact quite at home in the two major parties.

In the national campaign of 1888, Irish hatred of England

was played upon by Republicans in the notorious "Murchison letter" to take votes from Cleveland.[63] More specifically related to anti-Catholicism, however, was the reappearance of the Reverend Justin D. Fulton, a Baptist minister of Boston, in the role of publicist. Fulton had written the *Outlook of Freedom, Or, The Roman Catholic Element in American History* in 1856 and had been an active participant in Know-Nothing affairs. His *Rome in America,* dedicated to the "lovers and defenders of Education, of Liberty, and of Truth . . . ," appeared in 1887, while his *Washington in the Lap of Rome* [64] appeared in 1888, to assert that Romanism was attempting in America what it had already "achieved in Europe, to awe the state, control the people, and banish liberty." [65] The book was obviously intended to have a bearing on the presidential election, for it stated in its preface: "If it be not true, as is charged, that a private wire runs from the White House, in Washington, to the Cardinal's Palace, in Baltimore, and that every important question touching the interests of Romanism in America is placed before his eye, before it becomes a public act, it is true that the Cardinal is a factor in politics." [66]

Fulton's main objective was to charge that the national capital had come under the domination of Catholics, but his evidence was of less importance to his book than his positive charges. Without citing a source for his figures, he stated that fifteen thousand government employees were Catholics and consequently under the surveillance of priests, to whom they paid contributions in support of Catholic institutions as the price for retaining their places in government service. One may conclude that Fulton intended his readers to believe that whatever government business was not communicated to Catholic headquarters over the private wire from the White House was surreptitiously forwarded from clerical help strategically situated in government offices.[67] While "headquarters" were in Baltimore in 1888, the decision to build the Catholic University of America at Washington meant that soon the center of the conspiracy would have a seat in the capital city. Fulton's picture was obviously untrue and unnecessarily suspicious and relied for effect on a preconceived belief in his

reader that all Catholics were engaged in a priest-directed conspiracy. Thus, to him, the great trust inherent in popular government had been betrayed.

If, as Fulton feared, Irish political victories meant Catholic domination, he had cause for alarm. Besides New York City, which had elected its first Irish-Catholic mayor in 1880, the New England cities of Lawrence (in 1881), Lowell (in 1882), and Boston (in 1884) each chose an Irish-Catholic as mayor for the first time. By 1887, Boston's municipal government was said to be dominated by Irish-Catholics.[68] To New England, then, the anti-Catholic could also look with fear at the menace of Irish-Catholic political power; there, however, the fight soon concentrated on the school question.

In addition to its Irish-Catholic population, Boston was well supplied with vigorous Protestants. Minor anti-Irish organizations had waxed and waned in Boston for many years. One of these groups was called the "British-American Association." This group had rented Faneuil Hall for a celebration of Queen Victoria's Golden Jubilee in the spring of 1887. An Irish outcry was voiced immediately, terming the meeting a desecration of that "sanctuary of liberty," and a public protest meeting was called. By fall, the British-American Association had increased its membership phenomenally and had started publication of its own newspaper, the *British-American Citizen*. Meanwhile, the Reverend Mr. Fulton had stepped in. Resigning his pulpit to give full time to the crusade, he directed his efforts toward organizing and heading the "Pauline Propaganda," a society of dues-paying members which, among other activities, published his books. By the fall of 1887, Fulton was conducting regular weekly evening meetings with large paid attendances. One drawing card was his offer, to each purchaser of admission, of a copy of his book *Why Priests Should Wed.*[69]

Still one more crusader appeared in the person of Mrs. Margaret Lisle Shepherd. In August of 1887, Mrs. Shepherd was baptized and joined the Trinity Baptist Church of East Boston. Her autobiography, published first in 1887, relates how this woman had been reared in all the comforts; after an idyllic

childhood she had entered a convent and become a contented nun. One day, quite accidentally, a copy of the Bible fell into her hands. Her life was changed; she left the nunnery and the church. Welcoming Protestantism, impelled by the Faneuil Hall incident, she offered herself to the crusade against Rome. Mrs. Shepherd began a series of weekly lectures at Boston's Tremont Temple in December of 1887. Advertised as an "escaped nun," she continued her lectures until the early summer of 1888 to audiences avid for the inside story. She then conceived the idea of organizing and leading a woman's crusade; the "Loyal Women of American Liberty" resulted, with Mrs. Shepherd as its leader. Her career as a lecturer continued through the nineties with tours to many states.

Her effectiveness as a lecturer, however, depended on her success in remaining one jump ahead of the truth concerning her life before the Boston conversion. Margaret Shepherd was born Isabella Marron, the daughter of an Irish-Catholic soldier in the British Army, and had been brought up in India. Her earlier life had been marked by the birth of an illegitimate child, participation in a swindling racket, and a term in jail for theft. Punctuating these activities were an interval as a Salvation Army worker and two years as the repentant inmate of a refuge for fallen women operated by the Sisters of the Good Shepherd at Bristol in England. Dismissed from the refuge as beyond reform in 1885, she left for Canada to conduct a "Gospel Army" in Ontario and Prince Edward Island, and from there she came to Maine. She had acquired a husband but had deserted him, and she arrived in Boston in 1887, equipped in a limited fashion to describe the inner life of a "nunnery" and possessing the vocabulary of emotional religion as well as a convenient set of morals. Not until 1891 was her sordid story revealed in Boston. By that time her field of operations had been enlarged, both as lecturer and as leader of the Loyal Women, so that the revelations did not curtail —perhaps they even enhanced—her drawing power as a lecturer. After the exposure, she wrote another autobiography, *My Life in the Convent,* which differed in many details from her first attempt. In this account she described herself as a naive and trust-

ing girl subjected to a life of tragedy; she admitted the illegitimacy of her child but implied that a priest had promised to give up the church for her love. Her misplaced confidence in this heartless fiend, his lust, and her innocence resulted in the child.[70]

Beginning as it did in Boston as an incident growing out of anti-Irish rather than anti-Catholic sentiment, the 1888 campaign was able to turn directly on Catholic school policy shortly after January and to pick up much more respectable leadership. The state board of education recommended to the Massachusetts legislature the passage of a bill for the inspection of private schools by public boards. Its stated purpose was to seek conformity of private with public schools, but the final result was a law permitting public boards to require certain reports from private schools to prevent truancy. Considerable opposition to the original bill had arisen from non-Catholic private schools. In Haverhill, an overzealous public school superintendent sought to enforce the law to the letter and met the opposition of French-Canadian Catholic parents. A court decision resulted, favoring the private school position, so that the legislature of 1889 then enacted a compulsory school attendance law.[71]

Viewed as anti-Catholic action, these incidents were somewhat of a tempest in a teapot, inasmuch as Archbishop Cummings had been reluctant to enforce the parish school requirement of the Third Plenary Council in his diocese. Consequently, few parochial schools were in existence. Some of his priests enthusiastically prodded the Archbishop, seeking to enforce attendance at the existing parochial schools by denying the sacraments to nonconforming parents. Others of his priests went to the opposite extreme and opposed outright the announced school policy of the hierarchy.[72] In this instance, the single-mindedness attributed to Catholics by their critics was nonexistent. Yet the following incident was one on which most Catholics could agree.

In April, a public school history teacher at the English High School in Boston was asked in class to define "indulgences." When a Catholic pupil objected to the answer given, the teacher retired behind the authority of the text then in use, Swinton's *Out-*

lines of the World's History. After a Catholic protest, the Boston
School Committee took three steps: the teacher was reprimanded;
he was transferred from history to English, "a safer subject"; and
Swinton's text was dropped from use.[73]

The British-American Association, the British-American
Women's Association, and the Loyal Women of American
Liberty were led into the resulting fray by a new group acting
under the title of the "Boston Committee of One Hundred,"
organized in 1888 with the Reverend James B. Dunn as its secretary. Women could vote in school elections in Massachusetts,
a fact which accounted for the part taken by women. A "League
of Independent Women Voters" began publication of the
Women's Voice and Public School Champion, while the Boston
Committee of One Hundred published a series of pamphlets.
These pamphlets stressed the divided loyalty of Catholics and
requested that the ballot should be denied to Catholics until
they took an oath of allegiance to the United States and another
renouncing the supremacy of the Pope. Referring to Utah, the
pamphlets held that a church oath, such as the one the Mormons
were supposed to take, was inimical to the public welfare. On the
specific issue of schools, the statement was made that education
was a function of the state—not of the church; while the Civil
War idea of an irrepressible conflict, this time between Romanism
and the public welfare, was applied.[74]

The objective of all this furor was to gain a majority of members on the elected Boston School Committee. The campaign
continued for many years, during which the Boston schools degenerated while political capital was made of religious prejudices.[75] Irish-Catholic control of Boston's municipal affairs was
terminated for a time in that no Irishman was elected mayor for
another twelve years. The long-term victim of the campaign was
the Boston school system. The two contending groups of narrow-
minded zealots were concerned not so much with the fate of
public education as with winning victory over each other. But
cooler heads viewed the results with alarm, seeing in the origins
of the conflict implications which raised considerably broader

questions of educational policy. The ban on Swinton's text was seen as an action involving a question of teaching historical fact even though the truth were unpalatable to Catholics. Unlike the Bible cases, this one involved freedom of inquiry and teaching. Since compulsory education laws were also at issue, the quality of schooling offered in alternative systems was discussed. Moreover, since the Catholic attack was on the "godless" nature of the public schools, the problem included not only whether, but also how, ethics and morality could be taught in the public schools without offending religious minorities. The Boston incident illustrated how simple prejudice could easily enjoy the prestige that accompanies discussions on the broadest of public policies.

The debate eventually involved Boston intellectuals, prominent historians, politicians, prelates, and professional educators. Its origins were to be found in the long-continuing discussion of policies, rather than in the particular situation at Boston. In fact, the two should be considered as aspects, differing in intensity and significance, of the same problem. The Reverend Daniel Dorchester, soon to be an appointee of President Harrison as Commissioner of Indian Education, was not able to surmount a basic anti-Catholic prejudice in his approach to the problem. His appeal to the nation was not to permit Boston's experience elsewhere.[76] Francis Parkman, historian, was impelled by a growing personal bias against Catholicism and its clergy to write a pamphlet in defense of the public schools for publication by the "Citizen's Public School Union" of Boston.[77] Another Bostonian, Edwin D. Mead, editor of the *New England Magazine,* annotator and editor of many of the *Old South Leaflets,* and Universalist in religious belief,[78] found the virulence of the ministers more to be blamed for the intolerable situation in his home city than the counterattack of their chosen enemies. He warned, however, "Bigotry is bigotry, whether Catholic or Protestant, and we want none of it." His statement was made at a public meeting in October of 1888 protesting the extremism already apparent. To him, no other national problem was so important as that of pub-

lic education, but he did not wish to see it decided as a politically partisan issue; rather he desired that it be referred to the calm and reasonable decision of the American people.[79]

In an attempt to see the problem historically, Philip Schaff, historian, presented his findings to the American Historical Association.[80] He could see no solution to the problem without compromises, and he expected no compromise from the Catholic side. Senator Henry W. Blair, of New Hampshire, on May 25, 1885, introduced another proposed constitutional amendment, similar in most respects to that introduced by Congressman Blaine in 1875. Blair considered his amendment, in its prohibitions on established churches, to have a specific bearing on Mormonism in Utah, and he also sought to require compulsory education for all children in the South. Moreover, his amendment would have required the public schools to teach virtue, morality, and the Christian religion. Loaded with so much, the resolution stood no chance of passing the Congress and it never came to a vote.[81]

Professional educators of the National Education Association endorsed the Blair resolution as an aid to the South in overcoming illiteracy. During its sessions for the years 1887 and 1888, the association heard discussions on "Current Criticisms of the Public Schools." The problem was so intense that the N.E.A. decided to come to grips with it in the annual session for 1889, when the major addresses at its convention were on the subject of "Denominational Schools." Cardinal Gibbons and Bishop John J. Keane, newly appointed rector of the recently established Catholic University of America, represented the Catholic position. Edwin Mead of Boston and John Jay of New York, historian and president of the American Historical Association for 1890, represented the non-Catholic position. Neither of the Catholics agreed that the essential moral teachings could be given in public schools and consequently advised that a system of denominational schools be recognized as a necessity. Mead argued for breadth and liberality in education, saying that "parochialism fosters the narrowness and disproportion which

are falsehood," while John Jay contended that the goals of the
public school and those of the Catholic parochial school were
antagonistic. In rebuttal, Keane denounced Mead's statement
as an attack on Catholicism.[82] No agreement was reached at the
time and the debate continued for years afterward with almost
undiminished intensity and, probably more than any other issue,
provided ammunition for anti-Catholicism.

Those priests in the archdiocese of Boston who by their disagreement with their superior on the school issue had illustrated
a cleavage among Catholic clergy were of minor importance to
anti-Catholicism as compared to the Reverend Dr. Edward
McGlynn of New York. Father McGlynn had been an active
participant in the Irish Land League and had solicited funds to
carry on its agitation for Irish Home Rule.[83] He had also supported Henry George in his attempt to become mayor of New
York in 1886 and had urged for several years the teachings of
Progress and Poverty. His ecclesiastical superior was disturbed
by McGlynn's nonclerical public activity and had ordered him
not to participate further. Archbishop Corrigan was thus applying the advisory statement of the Plenary Council that politics
be left to "worldlings." But McGlynn continued to take part, and
was found disobedient and insubordinate; he was then removed
from his pastorate and excommunicated in 1887.[84] Out of his
pulpit, McGlynn was neither apologetic nor forgiving. He would
not appeal his case to Rome because he believed that Corrigan
had exceeded his authority.[85] There was evidence that McGlynn,
who had not accepted the Bishop's school policies, was being
chastised in part for his statements in favor of the public
schools.[86]

McGlynn's case was hardly a good illustration for anti-Catholic
propaganda. His Irish sympathies were well known, and his refusal to accept his superior's judgment on matters not involving
faith and morals only disproved the anti-Catholic's favorite
charge of hierarchical unanimity. The removal of his excommunication at a later date confirmed his, rather than Corrigan's,
position. In the meantime, however, anti-Catholics found evi-

dence in the incident to prove that Archbishop Corrigan was manipulating the Irish-Catholic vote in order to support Tammany Hall and municipal corruption.[87]

In the spring of 1887, Cardinal Gibbons went to Rome. One of his purposes was to prevent condemnation of Henry George's works by the papacy. Gibbons did not approve of George's thought, but he did believe that the books did not violate Catholic teaching on the sanctity of private property. He believed further that a condemnation would seem to reveal little sympathy on the part of the church for the problems of contemporary society. But Gibbons' position on Henry George was misunderstood in America, just as was his plea, made at the same time, that there be no papal condemnation of the Knights of Labor. His views on the labor organization were the same as his position on George: there was nothing on which a condemnation could be based, and, practically, the church would be damaged more by condemnation, in the long run, than it would be helped in its relations with laborers. In the short view of the anti-Catholics, however, Gibbons' actions were ascribed to favoritism among Catholics for the "socialism" of George and the "anarchism" of the Knights of Labor.[88]

Back of the eagerness to connect Catholic leadership with social disturbance was a history of reputed domination of the Knights of Labor by Irish laborers. Stemming from Molly Maguire incidents in Pennsylvania and the belief that the Ancient Order of Hibernians had furnished the leadership for the Mollies in the coal strike violence of the seventies, and despite the fact that many leading Catholic clergy were outspokenly opposed to the Knights, the idea persisted. Terence Powderly, the Knights of Labor leader, was a known Catholic and was further proof, to those willing to believe it, that Catholic authority extended through him into the union he headed; this in spite of the fact that Powderly was himself in difficulties with his bishop.[89] In 1886, the year of the Haymarket Affair, the Catholic press had been generous in its praise of Powderly and the Knights, in spite of the discussions that same year among the bishops as to the possibility of condemning the union. *Puck* published a cartoon

with a caption asking, "Does the Catholic Church sanction mob law?" [90] Opportunely for the anti-Catholics, a certain Dr. Cronin was found murdered at Chicago, in May of 1889, with the evidence pointing toward the Clan-Na-Gael, an Irish terrorist organization likewise denounced by many of the clergy, as the perpetrators.[91]

As it turned out, this belief in an affinity between Catholics and violence was the weakest of the three fears which stimulated anti-Catholicism in the eighties, although it was as persistent as the others. Of the three, however, it demonstrated most clearly that the anti-Catholic could find evidence of Catholic "aggression" anywhere he chose to look, and in spite of the facts. The essential element in the anti-Catholic attitude was the idea of a "conspiracy," operating by devious and illogical means to attain the end of Catholic world supremacy.

The decade also produced the forerunners of a flood of anti-Catholic literature. From St. Louis came a plea to "let the light shine" by the publication of a series of debates conducted by the *American Baptist* in opposition to the *Church Progress*. The meat of the argument was whether the Catholic Church's claim to be the emissary of God on earth was a valid one.[92] A series of lectures given during 1888 at Worcester, Massachusetts, by the Reverend Isaac J. Lansing, appeared in print. Lansing proposed to "diminish prejudice by increasing intelligence," and referred to the McGlynn case as an example of churchly thought control. Lansing named the Jesuits as the agents of the papacy in its conspiratorial activities, and asserted that Abraham Lincoln had been assassinated as a result of a particular conspiracy of Catholics.[93]

The growing anti-Catholicism of the decade fed on a book that was probably the first-ranking, certainly no less than second, of all anti-Catholic best sellers. Charles P. T. Chiniquy's *Fifty Years in the Church of Rome* appeared first in 1885 and had reached a fortieth edition by 1891. Chiniquy was a former priest who had left the church in 1858 to become a Presbyterian minister. He was the source for the legend that Abraham Lincoln was aware of the "Catholic menace," asserting that Lincoln had told

him during a visit to the White House in the midst of the Civil War, "I do not pretend to be a prophet. But though not a prophet, I see a dark cloud on our horizon. And that dark cloud is coming from Rome. . . ." [94] This quotation was used constantly throughout the ensuing crusade, and Lincoln became a brooding spirit whose premonition was a warning to his fellow countrymen less well equipped with prophetic vision.

The year 1889 provided another centennial celebration in that it was the end of one century under the Constitution. This event, like the centennial of 1876, undoubtedly stimulated the patriotic sentiments and nationalistic fervor of self-appointed protectors of the nation. Moreover, it was the hundredth anniversary of the appointment of the first Catholic bishop in the United States and thus the occasion for Catholic rejoicing. Archbishop John Ireland of St. Paul, speaking on this occasion, laid out a program for the members of his church. During the coming century, he asked Catholics to endeavor "to make America Catholic," saying that "America is at heart a Christian country. As a religious system, Protestantism is in process of dissolution; it is without value as a doctrinal or moral power, and it is no longer a foe with which we need to reckon." [95] Ireland advocated as a method a program to seek out and eradicate social evils that was similar to that of the social gospel movement supported by some Protestants. Anti-Catholics, however, who probably neither heard nor read his speech, were already convinced that the objective of Catholics was to "make America Catholic" and were prepared to resist any such design, seeking aid wherever it was to be found.

2 The American Protective Association Appears

During the last quarter of the nineteenth century, Americans showed they valued membership in secret and fraternal societies by joining them in increasing numbers. Profiting, perhaps, from the individual's desire to belong to a defined group at a time when urbanization and industrialization tended to submerge personality, these lodges offered their members a feeling of exclusiveness, something to set the individual apart from the mass and yet to provide him with a feeling of fellowship. Ritualistic lodges, with secret oaths and colorful ceremonies, answered part of the demand; the Freemasons, Odd Fellows, Knights of Pythias, and the Ancient Order of United Workmen were the most successful in obtaining members. Except for the Masonic societies, which had a European origin, the emphasis in the period was on lodges that were native in origin.[1]

Among the lodges, not secret but attaining exclusiveness by another means, were those whose members were Catholics. The Catholic Knights of America was organized in 1877, and the Catholic Order of Foresters began in 1883.[2] In 1882, the Knights of Columbus began the career that eventually made it the outstanding Catholic men's organization.[3] Secrecy in Catholic societies was not permitted, inasmuch as the church disapproved of it. However, secrecy was difficult to maintain even among the so-called "secret" lodges, and the term had little real meaning except that it indicated the presence of rituals, oaths, and ceremonials. Life insurance plans frequently appeared as features of these societies.

33

The centennials of national independence and of the Constitution stimulated development of patriotic and hereditary societies, too, which depended on ancestry for exclusiveness. Usually excessive in their emphasis on patriotism, a concept so vague as to be extremely useful, these groups were nationalistic and conscious of the need for inculcating patriotism in the schools. The teaching of national history, for example, was almost a fetish with them. The Daughters of the American Revolution, the Colonial Dames of America, and the Society of New England Women were only a few of these on the distaff side. The power of the Grand Army of the Republic, which owed its origin to the war for preserving national unity, was at its height.[4]

Nativistic and anti-Catholic, secret, ritualistic organizations, such as the United American Mechanics, founded in 1843, survived from Know-Nothing days. The Junior Order of United American Mechanics separated from it because the parent order did not prosecute its program with sufficient zeal. A women's auxiliary, the Daughters of Liberty, appeared in 1875. The Patriotic Order of the Sons of America, dating from 1847, limited its membership as had the Junior Order to American-born white males over sixteen years of age.[5] Organized in 1843, the American Protestant Association was composed of Protestant ministers in its early days,[6] and it remained alive as a militantly Protestant group with a wider membership. These groups were generally native products.

Imports from abroad appeared in the post-Civil War period. The Loyal Orange Institution made its debut formally in 1870, although the term "Orange" as an adjective had been used to describe the anti-Irish element for many years previously. Its appearance in the United States was marked by riots in New York City in 1870 and 1871, during which numbers of people were killed in the street fighting between Orangemen and Irishmen.[7] With Masonic antecedents, the founding date for the Orange society may be placed as 1795 in Ireland, where it was organized to oppose the Catholic Church and to support the occupant of the British throne. It may have been the inspiration for —certainly it was involved with—most of the postwar political,

patriotic, and secret societies that maintained an enmity toward Catholicism.[8] Many groups developed from this source in America, lived for a short time, and then expired.[9] The Templars of Liberty (1881), the Patriotic League of the Revolution (1882), the Order of American Freedom (1884), the American Patriotic League (1885), and the National Order of the Videttes (1886), were only a few of the many attempts to capitalize on anti-Catholic sentiment. These groups were usually self-styled "patriotic societies," and they included in their principles a stand for the public schools, separation of church and state, and opposition to Catholicism.[10]

The organization of anti-Catholics that was to gain the largest membership in the latter part of the nineteenth century and was to give the name the "American Protective Association"—or its initials, the "A.P.A."—to the entire anti-Catholic movement for the decade of the nineties, was founded on a Sunday afternoon, March 13, 1887, in the city of Clinton, Iowa. Clinton claimed to be the largest manufacturing town in Iowa in 1887, with a population of approximately 15,000. Four railroad lines served it and provided it with a large payroll; of first importance, however, were the lumber mills and sash-and-door factories. Two-fifths of the population were foreign-born; the largest single group was Irish and the second, German. Undoubtedly a sizable number of the Irish were Catholic in religion. Clinton's Catholic parish was expanding its facilities and adding a pastor to accommodate the growth.[11] Iowa's Catholic population had increased sufficiently to warrant division of the state into two dioceses as recently as 1881;[12] Clinton's expansion was thus quite natural. The center of Catholic strength within the state was Dubuque, where there were rumors that Catholic pressures had been applied so that the catechism was being taught in the public schools of some Iowa towns and villages.[13]

March of 1887 was election time in Clinton, with its citizens casting votes both in the annual mayoralty election and in a separate school election. In both, Catholicism came to be regarded as an issue by some residents. In the election for mayor, the incumbent, Arnold Walliker, was defeated. One year before,

Walliker had been elected in a three-way race that he won handily. At that time, he had had the open support of the local Knights of Labor and also had enjoyed the confidence of the businessmen. As mayor, however, he antagonized the largest employer in Clinton, a local lumber firm, which had for some time made a practice of using city streets to stack lumber awaiting shipment. The business community apparently regarded the mayor's insistence on keeping the streets clear as an attack on business enterprise. When the election came around, then, the obstructionist Walliker was opposed by a candidate campaigning on the issue of Clinton's unhampered future as a metropolis. Most telling in the election results, however, was the refusal of the Knights of Labor to support Walliker, although they had endorsed him the year before. When the votes were counted, the fourth ward appeared to be the source of the defeat. In that ward lived the majority of the lumber company's employees, the members of the Knights. Walliker believed that it was Catholic influence within the union which had caused its failure to endorse him and consequently his defeat. In the school election, Clinton voters approved a proposition to purchase land from the local Catholic parish as the site for a new public high school. The local press did not mention any public dispute over the contemplated purchase.[14] The city election occurred in one week; the school election took place during the following week. Sunday, March 13, the date of the organizational meeting for the American Protective Association, intervened between these two elections.

Henry Francis Bowers called a meeting of seven men at his law office in downtown Clinton on Sunday to discuss a new organization designed to protect the country from Catholics. Arnold Walliker and his brother, Jacob H. Walliker, were in attendance. These three men were lawyers; Bowers had been one of Mayor Walliker's advisers during the campaign.[15] None of the others in attendance had taken an active part in Clinton public affairs, nor did they play any part in the life of the organization they helped to establish after it had gotten under way.[16]

Local political affairs were undoubtedly the incidents which caused the men to gather at the time they did. But when they met, the founders were probably already convinced that a "Catholic menace" existed and found only confirmation and illustration in Clinton's politics. The explanation, then, for their action was to be found in circumstances which they could see all about them. Henry Bowers was the key figure in the meeting; several years later when the association was at its height, he was asked to describe the original meeting. His version was as follows:

The condition of affairs in this country in 1887, and up to that time, was such that the institutions of our Government were controlled and the patronage was doled out by an ecclesiastical element under the direction and heavy hand of a foreign ecclesiastical potentate. This power became so influential that it stood as a unit in many places against the institutions of the country. Through the legislature of Maryland at one time it destroyed the public school system of that State. Seeing these things, I felt that it was necessary that something be done. Gathering around me six men who had the courage of their convictions, we met in my office in Clinton on March 13, 1887, and laid the foundations of the order. That same day we formulated the ritualistic work and adopted a constitution. The chief idea we had in view in the constitution was this, that we had not the right under the Constitution of this country to oppose any religious body on account of its dogmatic views, faith, etc., but we did believe we had a right to oppose it when it became a great political factor. We believed then, and we believe now, that every man in this country has a right to worship God according to the dictates of his conscience, but we did not believe that the Constitution intended to convey the right to any set of men to control and manipulate the political affairs of this country to the aggrandizement of any ecclesiastical power.[17]

While it gives a few facts and indicates in general terms the motives for organizing, this recollection does not reveal very much. So obvious, though, to Bowers was the need for such a group that his oversight of the other founders indicates that in his mind each of them had already taken on the coloration of "Everyman" resisting an encroaching and easily apparent menace. By being anonymous, then, the founders became representative. The effect was an impression that, because the impulses generat-

ing it were so universally felt, an organization such as the American Protective Association could very well have been established in any town in the country by any group of citizens. In view of the fact that many other organizations with the same or similar objectives had already been established, the impression was not altogether a false one.

In spite of all the information about him that can be unearthed, Henry Francis Bowers remains somewhat of an enigma. The pattern of his life suggests adversity in youth with a fair amount of success after struggle; a close attachment to his mother, punctuated by a brief marriage, with the attachment to his children not so close; and an interest in things and organizations rather than in people or in learning. The evidence of his speeches and the very few examples of his writing that exist suggest that he did not submit to the discipline of facts. He approached truth by intuition, accepting or rejecting evidence according to his intuitive conception, so that the results amounted often to self-deception and acceptance of that which he chose to believe. His face was bearded, placid, and ordinary, above a figure with suggestions of rotundity. The enigma was that of an ordinary man who found himself in an extraordinary situation as the founder of an order that attained a spectacular reputation. There was force in the man, determination and strength, but the power was that of a convinced zealot who did not regard his convictions as unusual or his purposes as anything but worthy.[18]

Bowers was born in Maryland on August 12, 1837, and left there for Iowa in 1857, so that he had been a resident of Maryland as an adolescent throughout the Know-Nothing era. The maintenance of the public schools against Catholic threats was always uppermost in his mind as the explanation for the A.P.A. He placed the source of his fears on this score in an incident that he believed had occurred in Maryland when Catholic pressure on the state legislature had forced the closing of public schools. No such incident actually had occurred in the manner of his recollection, but his belief that it had permitted Bowers to rationalize his own failure to secure a basic schooling. He was thus led to vow that no other child should undergo a similar ex-

perience at the hands of Catholics if he could prevent it. What Bowers was actually recalling was the controversy in Maryland when pre-Civil War anti-Catholicism was strong. Undoubtedly the roots of his own anti-Catholicism may be traced to real incidents in those years; certainly his own belief was that his fears had a basis in fact.[19]

The Bowers family name had been altered in spelling from Bauer. His father was a German Lutheran immigrant who had married the daughter of a New England Methodist family. The mother was a dominant force in Bowers' life, as his father had died at sea while making a return trip to Europe. An only child, the son was reared by his mother, who was in her early thirties at his birth, and he accepted her church affiliation. In 1857, mother and son arrived in eastern Iowa to settle on a farm. For three years, crop failures discouraged them, and they then moved into Clinton. Bowers became a cabinetmaker. His Civil War enlistment was brief; he contracted typhoid fever and used crutches for two years. Always a Republican in politics, he became a deputy county clerk in 1863; in 1869, a deputy county recorder; in 1870, he ran for the office of county recorder with success and was re-elected in 1872. He capped his political career by being appointed a special aide-de-camp to Governor John Gear in 1878, with the honorary rank of lieutenant colonel. Thereafter he was frequently referred to as "Colonel" Bowers, sweet compensation for one whose military career had been so brief and inglorious.

The year 1870 was a banner year. In addition to his election to office, he was admitted to the bar after long self-education under his mother's tutelage. His law career was a successful one, with admission to practice before the Iowa Supreme Court coming in a few years. Also in 1870 he was married to Miss Emma B. Crawford of Ohio. Two sons and a daughter were born to the couple, before Mrs. Bowers died in 1878 at the birth of her daughter. The senior Mrs. Bowers then returned to her role as the manager of her son's household until her death at eighty-eight in 1893.[20]

An amateur geologist, Bowers was the author of the article on

geology in Wolfe's *History of Clinton County*. He maintained a private museum at his home, which was always open to visitors; in it he kept a collection of geological specimens and a shell collection, as well as miscellaneous Indian relics. He also liked to crochet, and was an amateur painter.[21]

Some evidence of Bowers' nature was revealed in his family relationships. In a published interview, a friendly reporter described Bowers as visibly moved to tears when describing his happy but short married life. Likewise, the closeness between mother and son was featured in the same story. There was a strong note of sentimentality recorded in the interview and the impression of an upright, self-made man bereft of his loved one and bearing up nobly under the blows of fate, which suggested close family attachments.[22] But a measure of coldness also appeared as a part of his nature. After their mother's death, the three children were separated and reared by different relatives on her side of the family. The children never became well acquainted with one another or, with the exception of one son, with their father.[23]

His antagonism toward "political Romanism" had not extended into his personal or professional relationships with individual Catholics or with church activities. Bowers was friendly with Catholics in Clinton; two of his Irish-Catholic friends made a call on him as he lay on his deathbed. He donated his own needlework to money-raising raffles in the local Catholic parish, and he was reputed to have provided legal assistance, without fee, to numerous Catholic families whose homes were threatened with foreclosure during the hard times of the nineties. In his bedroom there was a picture of a Catholic nun who had befriended him as a child.[24]

Bowers did not come to the A.P.A. unprepared in the paraphernalia of lodge work. From the 1870's he had been an enthusiastic Mason, a member of the Blue Lodge and of the thirty-second degree of the Scottish Rite. He also served for seven years as grand orator for the DeMolay Consistory of Iowa. So thoroughly did Bowers believe Americanism and Catholicism to be incompatible that he argued that the American Republic

was founded by Masons against the wishes of Rome; furthermore, he considered the A.P.A. an offspring of Masonry, protecting the republican institutions the Masons had established.[25]

According to Bowers' recollection, the group meeting in his office drew up a ritual and wrote a constitution on that Sunday afternoon. There is no reason for doubting that so much was accomplished, but the probability is that Bowers brought with him a model that he had worked on beforehand; perhaps he had consulted with his friends even before the meeting on the content of the two documents. The society organized there was a secret and fraternal order, similar to other ritualistic lodges. Its name, "American Protective Association," was adopted because it expressed what the order was intended to do—to protect America. Some question arose later over the failure to utilize "Protestant" somewhere in the title. All of the men present at the founding were Protestants, with the possible exception of one, who had no church affiliation. The explanation was a simple one; the order was intended to have the broadest appeal to all who were in opposition to the designs of Romanism. While it was to be committed definitely to political action, the order was to be nonpartisan. Secrecy was to bind the members because of the nature of the battle; going to war, one does not divulge one's plans to the enemy.[26]

Details of the constitution and ritual that were drawn up at Clinton were probably altered and amended in later meetings of the association. With only two exceptions, as far as can be learned, these changes were minor and were unimportant in explaining either the success or the failure of the order. During the time the A.P.A. was a national organization, its constitutional structure was almost static. The two exceptions that caused concern both came to a head at the national meetings that just preceded the decline of the order and were closely connected with the internal reasons for decline.[27]

The membership of the order was theoretically supreme in the government of the A.P.A., but practical authority resided with the officers, the various boards, and committees defined by the constitution. An annual convention of the supreme legislative

body within the organization was held each spring, usually in May, at which the will of the membership operated through delegates. This annual convention was both a business and a ceremonial meeting. Committee work dominated the convention day, with routine meetings of committees functioning on matters of ritual, agitation and education, political goals and action, and the various other areas in which the order operated. Several daytime sessions of all delegates took place, at which convention business was decided. An annual address by the president and an annual report by the secretary were highlights. Secrecy concealed the daytime meetings from the public, except for the publicity handouts to the press, but the evening meetings were frequently open to all comers.[28]

The most important order of business at conventions was the election of officers for the ensuing year. By title, national officers were designated "supreme," as an addition to the title of the office they held; thus there was a supreme president, a supreme vice-president, and so on through a double secretaryship, a treasurer, chaplain, sergeant-at-arms, guard, sentinel, and three trustees. One secretary, called the supreme secretary of state, was an honorary and ceremonial officeholder, while the other, designated the supreme secretary, was the record keeper. These officials, who served one-year terms with possibility of re-election, constituted a supreme executive board, which wielded sole power in the intervals between annual conventions. The presidents of the various state councils and past national officers were also members of the supreme board. Until the convention of 1896 decreed otherwise, the supreme president could remove state officers at will, so the control he had over a majority of the members on the supreme board was nearly absolute until that time. Outright opposition to the president, then, could come to a head only in an annual convention and would, of necessity, represent the result of considerable organizational dissent.

Of these officers, the supreme president and secretary (working) were paid an annual salary plus their traveling expenses incurred in the order's work. Until 1896, national headquarters were located in Chicago, for 1896 and 1897 they were in Wash-

ington, D.C., and after that time they were apparently located wherever the national secretary resided.[29]

Except for the office of honorary secretary, the titles of offices were repeated on the two lower levels of organization. On an organizational chart, a state council and officers would appear as an intermediate step between the local councils and the national officers. However, the state council was the product of cooperation among the local councils, so that chronologically it was the last of the three levels of organization to develop. Properly designated as the "Superior Council," the state body represented the local units within the boundaries of states or territories. Some of the states in which only a small number of local units were formed never succeeded in accomplishing this intermediate level. Thus, the superior council, consisting of all state officers, did not become an automatic link in the chain of command from the top, but actually represented an increase in local autonomy for those states in which the order achieved a degree of success. Annual state conventions were the legislative sessions that determined the course of action for state councils; meetings were held in the early spring so that delegates to the state convention could elect delegates to the coming national convention. Authority for developing a state council derived from the national headquarters, although the council represented the local units within the region it supervised. With state presidents removable at the will of the national president, however, possibility for controversy existed concerning "dictatorship" from above.

For those states and territories in which no superior council was organized, the chain of authority was direct from the national headquarters to the local unit. In this instance, the local council itself sent delegates to the national convention.[30] Since local units of this sort were under the jurisdiction of the national officers, a further opportunity for "dictatorship" appeared, particularly as the delegates from local units had a convention vote equal to that of state delegates.

Local units had a set of officers with the same titles as officers on state and national levels. There was no limit to the number of

councils that could be organized in any given locality, the only criterion being the number of people who could be induced to join. After a state council had been organized, it issued charters for new councils; before the state council developed, the authority for new councils came from the national office. State organizers were frequently used to spread the order into new localities, or interested persons were asked to communicate their desire to join by mail to the state secretary. The smallest number of persons who could inaugurate a new unit was twenty-five; for that number, or more, a charter could be issued. An initiation fee of one dollar was charged each member, in addition to which he paid annual dues of a dollar a year, quarterly if he desired.[31]

Thus, while the founders may have desired to work out an organization in which the members were supreme (in effect criticizing the hierarchical government of the institution they opposed), and an outline of democratic control was certainly to be found in the structure of the order, the A.P.A. was in its workings a centralized body with great power in the hands of the supreme president. One additional feature of this control was the provision that in disputes between officers, or between national and state officers, the supreme council could act as the court of settlement. On the other hand, the existence of the state councils gave to the regions with the greatest membership considerable freedom and control of their own operations. And the existence of the annual convention meant that internal dissensions could always be aired, but not necessarily solved.

Further decentralization was possible as the result of the power that in the nature of things accrued to the advisory boards. On each level of organization, a group of members or officers served the council as a body to investigate political issues and candidates. On the basis of its investigation, the advisory board would recommend political action to the council, and the assumption was that the membership would heed the advice of the experts. Here, more than any other place, was the greatest potential source of discord. Since the American Protective Association was politically minded in its purposes, the advisory boards were probably the most powerful bodies within the order. And since politics

in the United States has always been a local game, the American Protective Association was, in practice, as decentralized as the political circumstances in which it dabbled.

In 1894, a statement of principles representing what may be termed the platform of the order was approved by the annual convention and given to the public. To be sure, some such statement had been drawn up by the founders, but, according to the arguments of 1894, the original statement had only "feebly indicated" the aims of the order.[32] The thirteen-point statement of principles as clarified and adopted in 1894 illustrated the political emphasis of the order:

First: Loyalty to true Americanism, which knows neither birthplace, race, creed, or party, is the first requisite for membership in the American Protective Association.

Second: The American Protective Association is not a political party and does not control the political affiliations of its members.

Third: While tolerant of all creeds, it holds that subjection to and support of any ecclesiastical power, not created and controlled by American citizens, and which claims equal, if not greater, sovereignty than the government of the United States of America, is irreconcilable with American citizenship. It is therefore opposed to the holding of offices in National, State, or Municipal government by any subject or supporter of such ecclesiastical power.

Fourth: We uphold the Constitution of the United States of America, and no portion of it more than its guaranty of religious liberty, but we hold this religious liberty to be guaranteed to the individual and not to mean that under its protection any un-American ecclesiastical power can claim absolute control over the education of children growing up under the Stars and Stripes.

Fifth: We consider the non-sectarian free public schools, the bulwark of American institutions, the best place for the education of American children. To keep them as such we protest against the employment of subjects of any un-American ecclesiastical power as officers or teachers of our public schools.

Sixth: We condemn the support out of the public treasury by direct appropriations or by contract with any sectarian school, reformatory, or other institution now owned or controlled by the public authority.

Seventh: Believing that an exemption from taxation is equivalent to a grant of public funds, we demand that no real or personal property

be exempt from taxation, the title to which is not vested in the National or State governments, or in any of their subdivisions.

Eighth: We protest against the enlistment in the United States army, navy, or the militia of any State, of any persons not an actual citizen of the United States.

Ninth: We demand for the protection of our citizen laborers, the prohibition of the importation of pauper labor, and the restriction of immigration to persons who can show their ability and honest intention to become self-supporting American citizens.

Tenth: We demand the change of the national naturalization laws by the repeal of the act authorizing the naturalization of minors without a previous declaration of intention, and by providing that no alien shall be naturalized or permitted to vote in any State in the Union, who cannot speak the language of the land, and who cannot prove seven years continuous residence in this country from the date of his declaration of intention.

Eleventh: We protest against the gross negligence and laxity with which the Judiciary of our land administer the present naturalization laws, and against the practice of naturalizing aliens at the expense of committees of candidates, as the most prolific source of the present prostitution of American citizenship to the basest uses.

Twelfth: We demand that all hospitals, asylums, reformatories, or other institutions in which people are under restraint, be at all times subject to public inspection, whether they are maintained by the public or private corporations or individuals.

Thirteenth: We demand that all National or State legislation affecting financial, commercial, or industrial interests be general in character and in no instance in favor of any one section of the country, or of any class of people.[33]

As was indicated by the first plank in the platform, membership in the order was not limited by place of birth or by race. While the A.P.A. had definitely nativistic planks in its set of principles, it did not limit its membership to the native-born citizen. In fact, it often faced the charge that it was an importation from abroad. Actually, two of the founders were admittedly not native-born, and one of its supreme presidents was born in Canada. The following song, sung to the tune of "Marching Through Georgia," illustrated this cosmopolitan aspect, which

was peculiar to the A.P.A. and distinguished it from other extreme nationalistic societies in United States history:

> From the workshop and the factories
>   Comes the loyal Swedish man,
> Who left King Oscar long ago
>   To become American,
> While the loyal Scotch and Orangeman
>   Are leading in the van,
> Marching to the tune of Yankee Doodle.[34]

Negroes were members of the order and served as delegates representing their state councils at national conventions. Their presence may have been "window-dressing" in the same way that Negro delegates appeared at national Republican party conventions during the same period. That racial mixing was not a universally accepted practice within the order, however, was shown when segregated "colored" councils were reported from the St. Louis area.[35] While there was no evidence that Jews accepted membership within the order, and the oaths that members were required to take would prohibit the conscientious Jew from membership, there was also no evidence of anti-Semitism as a feature of the propaganda of the order.[36]

Strictly speaking, membership was limited to males. Very shortly after the order had begun to function, however, a "Women's American Protective Association" was organized as an auxiliary. A Mrs. Blanche E. Reynolds, of Lombard, Illinois, was the first president, and the group was organized sometime prior to September of 1891. Mrs. Reynolds was an active worker in the Loyal Orange Institution at the time of her entry into the W.A.P.A.[37] At the national meeting of the A.P.A. in 1892, a resolution was passed recognizing the official character of the work already done by the issuance of a charter naming this group an auxiliary; thereafter it operated directly under the control of the supreme council. Mrs. Reynolds was confirmed as president and a Mrs. M. S. Coffin, of Detroit, was listed as supreme secretary.

Immediately a charge of highhanded action was launched

against the supreme president, Mr. Bowers. A Mrs. Addie Scamman protested that she had organized an auxiliary group of women and argued that the parent organization should have recognized her group. Bowers' offense, in her mind, was that he had ignored the prior claim of Mrs. Scamman and her ladies. The tiff was resolved by the orderly retirement of Mrs. Scamman in the interests of the larger fight against Rome. The two groups of ladies cooperated thereafter as one auxiliary, holding an annual convention at the same time and in the same city as the A.P.A.[38]

On two other levels, the order attempted to encompass larger groups in its support. In 1895, at the annual convention, a "Junior A.P.A." was projected for the age group of from fourteen to twenty-one. Obviously an attempt to train recruits, this action revealed that the minimum age requirement for the senior groups was twenty-one years, voting age. The following year, the Juniors were placed under the motherly jurisdiction of the W.A.P.A., but no other news was forthcoming about their career. At the same 1895 convention, an international order was envisioned. Under the title of the "International Protective Association," it was to oppose international Romanism on the international level. Occasional instances of cooperation across boundaries followed, with the Protestant Protective Association and the Canadian Protective Association representing Canada, the Constitutional Reform Club under the leadership of one Filomena Mita taking care of Mexico, while a reported, but unnamed, order existed in Manchester, England, to save the British Isles.[39]

In order to enter the A.P.A., the prospective member made an application to join, which was endorsed by two members. The application was then presented to a regular lodge meeting, and a period of time elapsed while the applicant was being investigated. Actual election to membership was by vote of the council when the results of the investigation were made known to it by the committee. The applicant paid an initiation fee of one dollar, of which twenty-five cents were forwarded to the national office. The applicant was thereupon notified to appear for the initiation ceremony.

The initiate was permitted to proceed with the ceremony only after he had first obligated himself to keep secret the ritual to follow.[40] Within the council's chambers, where the installing officers were arranged in positions so as to form a cross, the blindfolded initiate took four oaths of increasing intensity and varying content. The first was a general avowal of justice among men; the second, an oath to preserve the purity of the ballot, to encourage political honesty, to defend the government against foreign invasion by either national or ecclesiastical foes, and to support the complete separation of church and state. After the second oath, the initiate could withdraw if he was unwilling to complete the initiation.

Then followed the third and fourth oaths, which contained the substance of the obligation taken by a member. Before the council chaplain, with his hand on his heart, the initiate swore not to permit a Roman Catholic to become a member of the order, not to employ a Catholic when a Protestant was available, not to aid the Catholic Church or any of its institutions, not to enter a controversy with a Catholic on the subject of the A.P.A., not to vote for or countenance the nomination of a Catholic for public office, and not to go on strike in a labor dispute with a Catholic.[41] This completed, the blindfold was removed, symbolically relieving the initiate of "mental darkness" so that he could take the final vows in full possession of his faculties. With his right hand on the "assumed emblem of the Catholic church" (the Cross?), and his left hand on the "book of your faith" (the Bible? King James Version, no doubt!), he repeated:

I hereby denounce Roman Catholicism. I hereby denounce the Pope, sitting at Rome or elsewhere. I denounce his priests and emissaries, and the diabolical work of the Roman Catholic church, and hereby pledge myself to the cause of Protestantism to the end that there may be no interference with the discharge of the duties of citizenship, and I solemnly bind myself to protect at all times, and with all the means in my power, the good name of the order and its members, so help me God. Amen.

In view of the wording of these oaths, the statement that the A.P.A. was intended to appeal to all non-Catholics indicated an

obtuseness on the part of its founders as to the meaning of the ritual. As they stood, the oaths could appeal only to Protestants. One who did not accept the Bible, the Cross as a symbol, or a sworn oath could become a member only after thorough rationalization. Moreover, the oaths were distinctly negative in the character of their anti-Catholic obligations. Not until 1896, when the importance of the order was waning, did this negative quality disappear. In that year, the national convention removed all references to Roman Catholicism from the ritual, retaining only those provisions against sectarianism in government. The fact is worth only passing comment, since it came too late in the history of the A.P.A. to be of any moment.[42]

Comparison of the initiation oaths with the statement of principles leads to the conclusion that the order had a public face differing from its private one. To the public, it was intended to appear as a society with a positive and fairly respectable set of goals to be attained by political action. To its members, the order was anti-Catholic not only in politics but in personal relationships. Recognition of this distinction between the public and positive aims of the order, and the secret and negative obligations required of its members, is essential to an understanding of the order.

Officers wore black robes trimmed with yellow, more elaborate for the higher offices than for the lower. Each officer also had a prescribed pin, decorated with jewels, to be worn on the left breast during meetings. A triangle formed the basic design of the pin for all offices, but the eagle, a flag, a schoolhouse, the open Bible, balance scales, swords, and daggers embellished with red, white, and blue colors appeared as recurrent symbols in various combinations. Of these, the "little red schoolhouse" and the balance scales were used most frequently to symbolize free public education and justice as the cherished goals of the order. When addressing one another, the members were expected to use "Friend" followed by the surname of the person addressed, this formality being used in official correspondence to people not members of the order as well as to those within the pale. A motto was suggested by the recurrent use of the letters, "F.P. and P.,"

which meant "Friendship, Purity, and Protection." Correspondence was brought to a close with the phrase, "Yours in F.P. and P.," which was too bland for the exuberant Montana members, who added the letters "T.H.W.T.P.," meaning "Yours in Friendship, Purity, and Protection and To Hell With The Pope." [43]

Local council meetings were either public or private, depending on the kind of business transacted. Business meetings, for members only, were concerned with new members, discipline of those already in, election of officers, and the general "good of the order" in political matters, as well as the ceremonial of initiation. Rapid growth indicated a heavy burden of membership problems and frequent initiations. The inner life of the order could very well have become burdensome on the more active members, a fact which was recognized in 1895 with the proposal that several advanced "degrees" be instituted so that especially active members could receive additional honors for their services.[44] Such an alteration would have enhanced the "lodge" appeal of the order, but no decision on it was reached.

Educational and social meetings were open to the public; usually weekly, these meetings gave to the order the appearance of activity. Attendants were members and their guests, usually prospective candidates for initiation, and the curious. A seasonal variation in attendance and in the quality of interest displayed was illustrated when the national office sent out prepared programs to occupy the faithful during the winter and spring, when political interest was usually at a low ebb. These prepared lessons were worked up by "authorities." Some of the subjects and their authors were: "The Jesuit Lobby in Washington," and "The Hand of the Pope in the American Press," by Joseph Bradfield, member of the Washington, D.C., council; "Investments in American Commerce by the Pope," by Henry Bowers, founder and first national president; "The Vatican and the Labor Unions," by W. J. H. Traynor, national president after Bowers; "Vaticanism and Crime," by the Reverend Adam Fawcett, supreme vicepresident in 1894; "The Vatican and the Secret Societies," by C. P. Johnson, superior president for Illinois; "The Grand Army of the Papacy in the United States," by Charles T. Beatty,

supreme secretary from 1893 to 1896; and "The Papacy and the American Indian," by Thomas J. Morgan, Indian Commissioner under President Benjamin Harrison.[45]

The "Friendship" of the motto was emphasized as the keynote for the personal relations of one member with another. A sense of unity sustained the membership, derived in part from common purposes and in part from the need to aid each other in a world dominated by unfriendly Catholic conspirators. The subjects listed above indicate what the A.P.A. member believed the Papacy had accomplished within the United States. Songs were sung in meetings to verbalize and strengthen the bonds of unity; thus, "Tramp! Tramp! Tramp!" was sung with the following words:

> Come ye sons of Uncle Sam,
> Come join the gallant band,
> Come unite with us to fight our country's foe.
> For our God is with the right,
> We will conquer by His might,
> And the slick and wily Jesuit must go.
>
> Noble men are in our ranks—
> We are not a band of cranks—
> We are not a lot of bigots or of fools.
> But, ye Roman Catholic hordes,
> We will buckle on our swords,
> If you dare to meddle with our public schools.[46]

A collection of such songs was compiled, and distribution was arranged at a cost of twenty-five cents a copy. The booklet had a replica of a little red schoolhouse on its cover and was advertised in the patriotic press. It challenged its readers to

> Dare to be an A.P.A.,
> Dare to stand alone.
> Dare to work for Freedom's cause,
> Dare to make it known.[47]

A businessman expressed his desire for his "friends'" patronage by advertising in a friendly paper with an acrostic:

> Artistic
> Printing
> A Specialty.[48]

Scattered evidence that members were somewhat closely supervised in their private lives appeared from time to time. For example, the order interceded at one time to demand recognition at the funeral of one of its deceased members. Because the man's wife was a Catholic, he had not achieved full status within the order, even though he allegedly agreed with its objectives. During his last illness, his wife had called a priest to attend the husband; after his death she made plans for his funeral despite protests from the local council of the A.P.A.,[49] which was apparently operating on the assumption that affiliation with the order continued at least to and perhaps beyond the grave. In Washington, D.C., in another case, a young lady's decision was applauded in the following resolution, published by Council No. 8.

Whereas, it has come to the notice of this Council that the accomplished young lady, Miss Cora Lane, of this city, a Protestant and the daughter of Rev. William Lane of Baltimore, did reject a man by the name of Hunter Ware, in suit of marriage because he would not give up his oaths and vows of the Roman hierarchy, and become an American citizen, it is

Resolved: That this Council congratulate Miss Lane on her escape from the fetters of ignorance and superstition; and it is further

Resolved: That this Council esteem and cherish Miss Lane's admiration for our American flag, American homes, and American institutions, in granting these constitutional lessons (as monuments to the liberty of our country) the first place in her heart; and it is still further

Resolved: That this Council notify Miss Lane of our action in this matter by sending her a copy of these resolutions and that they be printed in the *United American*.[50]

An attempt to give the A.P.A. an additional feature of the fraternal lodge finally succeeded after long consideration. Beginning in 1892, there had been talk of including an insurance plan. After the convention of 1895, the plans were carried forward. Judge John H. D. Stevens, of Ironwood, Michigan, was the organizer. His plans called for a mutual benefit policy similar to that offered by the Knights of Pythias or the Masonic lodges.

Insurance was to be furnished through eleven of the old-line companies, of which the Equitable, Northwestern Mutual, Mutual Life, and the American Union companies were mentioned. Early in 1896, an announcement appeared that a new organization, called the "American Minute Men," had been created to coordinate the patriotic and beneficial objectives of the "patriots." Incorporated under the laws of Missouri on November 22, 1895, with headquarters at St. Louis, the Minute Men were supposed to have made arrangements to carry the insurance needs of the A.P.A. Policies were to be guaranteed by the Knights Templars and the Masons' Life Indemnity Company of Chicago. Judge Stevens was designated Judge Advocate General of the Minute Men to manage the plan.[51] The A.P.A. thus did not succeed in developing its own insurance plan, but worked with other patriotic societies in a cooperative plan.

The organization created by the men who met in Bowers' office had its roots in the Know-Nothing period, was a secret, ritualistic, fraternal, and beneficial society, which announced a platform broad enough to attract many adherents. The oaths required of initiated members, however, were narrow to the point of excluding many who might otherwise consider affiliating with it.

For the first few years, Iowa and its neighboring states were the scene of the slow growth of the new organization. Very little is known of these years. It was obscurity rather than secrecy which hid it, however. Henry Bowers was the first organizer, and he spread the society by his own efforts, paying expenses from his own pocket when fees did not cover costs. His activities took him across the Mississippi River into Illinois and westward into Nebraska during 1887–88. By 1890, councils had been organized in several towns and cities across Iowa; at Omaha and perhaps a few other places in Nebraska; at Rock Island, Rockford, Freeport, Peoria, and Bloomington in Illinois; at Janesville in Wisconsin; and at Detroit in Michigan.[52] Bowers was responsible for the growth in the areas east and west of Clinton; the Detroit council, however, was the responsibility of W. J. H. Traynor, who would have much to do with the order in later years. Assuming that the place of the first convention (Belle Plaine) was near the hub of existing councils, that choice would suggest that the early efforts at expansion were more successful west of Clinton than they were east of it.

Belle Plaine, Iowa, was a small town approximately one third of the distance from Clinton to the western border of Iowa, and it became the choice for the first "national" convention, which met on December 18, 1889. Sometime between the date of the founding at Clinton and the time of the convention, a decision had been reached to make the A.P.A. a national society. Early in its career, then, the objective of nationwide activity was decided upon; what was already a regional organization had signified its intent to strike for the larger scene.

Already within the Clinton council dissension had appeared. Bowers, now the national president rather than simply the leader of the Clinton group, had appointed a personal friend to represent the Clinton council at the Belle Plaine meeting. The council members were disturbed by Bowers' oversight in failing to notify them in sufficient time for them to choose their delegate. Outraged at what it believed to be Bowers' highhanded method, the group condemned Bowers. Loss of members in the home town followed this incident.[53] That this was in its origins a "vest pocket" organization was strongly suggested by Bowers' control of it.

For six years Bowers was to dominate the A.P.A. so thoroughly that the name of no other national officer became known then or later. After 1890, an increasing measure of publicity accompanied the growing reputation of the order. Friendly weeklies and occasional references in the public press mentioned the national A.P.A., but the only figure identified with it was Bowers. Officials of the ladies' auxiliary, as well as state and local officers, were mentioned, but the national organization was unquestionably Bowers' through six years of growth.[54]

But Bowers was not the only "patriot" active during those years. In May of 1889, a man named Henry Baldwin, of New Haven, Connecticut, had called a meeting of the heads of all prominent "patriotic orders" at New York City for a conference from which he hoped to secure cooperation among them on a national scale. A similar conference was held in Philadelphia in 1890, but no formal unity was achieved until 1891. Organizations were represented at the first two conferences from Chicago, California, and Wisconsin, but the American Protective Association was not among them.[55] Thus, the various organizations that had responded to calls of patriotism, nativism, and anti-Catholicism of the previous decade were seeking unity. In doing so, they invited the stronger groups to send delegates to the conferences. Obviously, the spreading A.P.A. was as yet of insufficient importance to attract attention among its potential colleagues. As late as 1890, its name did not appear in another list of organizations fighting Catholicism and dedicated to the protection of the public school system.[56] Yet the public mind was being prepared to accept the necessity of some sort of united opposition to the alleged designs of the Catholic hierarchy, particularly on the issues of public schools and the use of tax funds, and to the existing Irish political leadership.

A certain respectability was given to this swelling antagonism by the National League for the Protection of American Institutions, which was organized in 1889. Its platform was directed solely "to secure constitutional and legislative safeguards for the protection of the common school system and other American institutions, to promote public instruction in harmony with such institutions, and to prevent all sectarian or denominational appropriations of public funds." Its law committee proposed a sixteenth amendment to the federal Constitution, similar to the Blaine amendment, to carry these objectives into law. Where other flourishing groups depended for their strength on number of members, the N.L.P.A.I. was almost a paper organization, with a large number of respectable leaders lending their names to it while its general secretary carried on the business of the league. The Reverend James M. King, pastor of the Union Methodist Church in New York City, was the general secretary throughout the career of the group; the historian John Jay was its first president.[57] The league's work was carried on by corresponding secretaries in reputedly "over 200 cities," but its in-

fluence derived from the battery of prominent persons whose names were listed on its letterheads. The officers included William H. Parsons and Dorman B. Eaton; Francis P. Bellamy, William Fellowes Morgan, Churchill H. Cutting, and seventeen others were its incorporators. Among the membership were General Francis Amasa Walker, President of the Massachusetts Institute of Technology; David Starr Jordan, President of Stanford University; presidents Andrews of Brown and Rogers of Northwestern; Rufus W. Peckham, later a member of the United States Supreme Court; Judge William Strong, formerly a member of the Court; Henry Hitchcock, former president of the American Bar Association; Levi P. Morton, Cornelius Bliss, J. Pierpont Morgan, Cornelius Vanderbilt, Cyrus W. Field, Rutherford B. Hayes, and others.[58]

As the decade closed, then, the A.P.A. was struggling to make its way at a time when several other organizations with similar objectives were more active and more successful. That the A.P.A. was aware of these other organizations and that it too saw the possibility of cooperation was revealed in one of the sections of its ritual. At one place, the initiate swore not to make known to anyone what he saw, heard, or discovered "in this order, unless directed by the proper authority to confer this degree or communicate this work to a regularly organized and recognized body of Amoreans, and neither to any of them unless duly advised of the genuineness of the body to be so instructed." The word "Amorean" was usually assumed by the critics of the A.P.A. during the nineties to represent a secret name for the order so that its members could deny membership in the A.P.A., if asked.[59] However, all the various self-styled "patriotic orders" also called themselves the "*Am*erican *or*ders," with their own special meaning of "American." If the first two letters of each of these two words were combined, the word "Amoreans" would result, and its appearance in the oath as quoted above showed that the A.P.A. had made its plans for unity among the many anti-Catholic societies.

3 The Years of "Guerrilla Warfare"

To describe the struggle against tremendous odds opposing the American Protective Association in the years between 1890 and its annual convention of 1893, a leader of the order used the descriptive term "guerrilla warfare." He meant that the forces of patriotism fought as best they could, where they could, in scattered or close-knit bands forced by necessity to practice secrecy because their enemy was unscrupulous, powerful, far-reaching, and successful. Boycotts, newspaper opposition and exposures, nonrecognition by politicians, all kinds of difficulties were the lot of this David as he faced his Goliath; so, at least, it appeared to David.[1] Actually, the A.P.A. faced in these years only the problem of making itself the most prominent of the various anti-Catholic societies; the struggle that took place was competitive among like-minded groups, rather than a contest against Catholicism. The psychology of the David-Goliath interpretation, however, illustrates the defensive attitude characteristic of the A.P.A. The secret of the eventual prominence of the A.P.A. as *the* anti-Catholic organization of its era lay in its willingness to take part in political contests. From the viewpoint of the order, its defensive attitude led it to interpret the political developments of the years from 1890 to 1893 as demonstrations of Catholic success.

In these years of "guerrilla warfare," the locale was the Middle West. A definite pattern may be noted in the defensive interpretation. First, the congressional elections of 1890 and the presidential election of 1892 produced a general impression of

58

Catholic strength; second, issues involving the public schools provided the A.P.A. with contests in which it could advertise itself; third, confederation and cooperation among the various "patriotic orders" were accomplished; and fourth, the group learned certain successful political techniques, including the tactics of attack rather than defense, concentration on local rather than national campaign issues, the use of existing parties rather than a third party, and the practice of using current events to illustrate the truth of its own propaganda. Opposition was met, to be sure, but divisions among Catholics lessened organized opposition from that source. By 1893, with an established "patriotic press" in operation, the A.P.A. had gone a long way toward establishing itself.

In several localities, the A.P.A. did not create the anti-Catholic feeling but was the beneficiary of campaigns launched by others. In Michigan, for example, was the *Patriotic American,* a weekly edited by W. J. H. Traynor, a man prominent in the Loyal Orange lodges. During the election of 1890, this weekly conducted a campaign against two Republicans: the candidate for state treasurer, on the grounds that he was a Catholic, and Congressman Julius C. Burrows, on the grounds that he had advocated the erection of a commemorative statue of Queen Isabella of "Catholic" Spain for the coming Columbus centennial. Burrows survived the opposition, but the Republican candidate for state treasurer was defeated in a series of Democratic victories. Newspaper reporters, seeking the source of anti-Catholicism, were unable to detect the participation of the A.P.A. and gave credit to the "Sons of America." By the spring of 1891, however, there was an A.P.A. council flourishing in Detroit, with Traynor as its president and reportedly initiating a hundred new members a week. The council was, in this instance, apparently acting as a clearinghouse for members of the Patriotic Order of the Sons of America, the Orange lodges, and the Junior Order of United American Mechanics who were dissatisfied with the pallid political behavior of their own organizations.[2]

For many years prior to the nineties Detroit had been regarded as "normally" a Democratic city. It was the second most

important port of entry for immigrants arriving in the United States, and it suffered from the same conditions that burdened New York City.[3] A reform campaign in 1889 had resulted in the election of Hazen S. Pingree as mayor and in a general defeat for the Democrats. In his successful re-election campaign in 1891, Pingree had advocated the abolition of parochial schools, while Catholic priests had opposed the use of Freeman's *General Sketch of History* in the public schools for reasons similar to those advanced in Boston.[4] Mayor Pingree received the support of anti-Catholic groups in his city campaigns, yet in state politics he was constantly at odds with the Republican machine dominated by United States Senator James McMillan. Since anti-Catholicism in Michigan, like anti-Catholicism elsewhere, tended to find itself committed to Republicans because Catholics were generally thought to be Democrats, the operations of the A.P.A. were to be within Michigan's Republican ranks and were a factor in determining party control between the Pingree and McMillan forces.

In the spring of 1892, William S. Linton, who had been defeated for lieutenant governor in 1890, was elected mayor of Saginaw, a victory that made him a prospect for nomination to a higher office in the fall. Linton, a former lumberman, former president of the state league of building and loan associations, a member of the Saginaw Water Board, and a state legislator in 1887–88, was a member of the Maccabees, Independent Order of Foresters, and the Masons. His election as mayor signaled an anti-Catholic victory, and politicians thereafter had to face clearly drawn Catholic and anti-Catholic lines in their political plans for Saginaw and its vicinity.[5]

As Republicans prepared for their nominating convention in the fall of 1892, Linton made his position stronger with both factions by staying clear of the Pingree-McMillan struggle. The goal of the anti-Catholics was to get the governorship nomination for one of their own, and to defeat the nomination of Joseph Moore for state treasurer because of his Catholicism. Pingree was said to be acceptable to the anti-Catholics because he was a member of the Patriotic Order of the Sons of America.[6] The

reason for Linton's neutrality in the struggle for party control was that he wished to become the party nominee for Congress. There appeared to be little doubt that the Pingree group could muster organized labor as well as anti-Catholic support.[7]

In the convention, however, the nomination for governor went to John Rich, McMillan's candidate, while the Catholic was not nominated for state treasurer. This in outline would seem to demonstrate that the McMillan forces outwitted the Pingree group on the governorship by conceding the treasury nomination in return for anti-Catholic support for Rich. Linton was not a part of the compromise, for he took the nomination in the Eighth Congressional District. In the general election that followed, Republicans won and captured control of the state.[8]

The closeness of the cooperation between the Republicans and the A.P.A. was shown in election post-mortems in Linton's district. On official stationery of the Eighth Congressional District Republican committee, its chairman conducted the business of the A.P.A. advisory board, of which he was also chairman, in writing to another party leader. According to his analysis, the A.P.A. group in Saginaw County numbered five thousand voters, of whom approximately 30 per cent were formerly Democrats. Of these, about 22 per cent had been persuaded to switch to the Republican candidates for governor, congressman, and presidential elector, thereby providing the winning margin. In recognition, the chairman asked that one of these former Democrats be appointed to a minor post in the state house so that the others would stay with the Republicans. Moreover, the correspondent continued, the election had been a pertinent demonstration of A.P.A. strength in Saginaw, so that its membership was now increasing rapidly with "our best citizens coming into line with us." Whether the former Democrat received his political plum was not clear, but the writer of the letter, George W. Hill, was recognized for his contribution with an appointment as state salt inspector by the new governor.[9]

In Nebraska, too, the stage was set by non-A.P.A. anti-Catholic groups, whose activity was also political. The Omaha *American* had begun publication in 1891 under the editorship

of John C. Thompson, who was Superior Councillor of the Nebraska state Junior Order of United American Mechanics. Both the Junior Order and the Patriotic Order of the Sons of America were already active in Nebraska.[10] The A.P.A. claimed to have obtained four thousand members in Omaha by the autumn of 1891, although it had come into prominence only the preceding summer. According to Edward Rosewater, a Republican leader and editor, as well as owner, of the daily Omaha *Bee,* the town was "boiling over with sectarian contention" rising from a "deep-seated feeling . . . that a radical change was demanded in local government. The preponderance of Irish office-holders had created a revulsion," so that people, including many Catholics, "massed their votes in favor of the Republican county and city tickets, although a majority of the nominees were avowed and reputed A.P.A.'s." Rosewater and his newspaper had supported this combination for the following reasons:

First, because it was my honest conviction that a general cleaning out of the courthouse and city hall were essential to the public welfare. Second, because I am a Republican and, as five-sixths of the A.P.A.'s were Republicans, it is impossible to break up the old courthouse ring, and antagonize the A.P.A.'s at the same time.[11]

Rosewater's reasoning was that of a practical politician, used to putting first things first, and it proved to be an accurate summary, which many another political leader might use to explain an alliance with the A.P.A.

George P. Bemis, the Republican candidate for mayor, and every other man endorsed by the A.P.A. were victorious over "Roman intrigue" with the saloon element and corruption; the results were an "A.P.A. victory" for political morality as viewed by its local mouthpiece, the Omaha *American.*[12] The paper's interpretation was more lurid than Rosewater's, but it was essentially the same. Even so, it must be remembered that it was a Republican victory that Rosewater celebrated.

In the following spring the separate municipality of South Omaha elected C. P. Miller as its mayor against "priestly interference." That fall, Mayor Miller became a martyr, according to anti-Catholics for their propaganda purposes. He was murdered

in a vacant lot by an unknown assailant. Since the murderer was never identified, he was easily described as a Catholic conspirator by Miller's friends. The *Patriotic American* charged in addition that a local meat-packing plant discharged all of its employees who attended Miller's funeral,[13] using the incident to show its readers how tightly Rome controlled Omaha and its vicinity.

Editor Rosewater and the *Bee* began to find certain aspects of the Republican–A.P.A. alliance distasteful by the time the gubernatorial election of 1892 arrived. At that time, Lorenzo Crounse was the Republican nominee for governor. But a Thomas Majors had been the A.P.A. choice prior to the nominations. Since Majors represented to Rosewater all that was bad in Nebraska politics because of his being the "railroad candidate" as well, the *Bee* supported Crounse. The newspaper and its editor could not view with equanimity the continued growth of the "railroad" element within the party by the addition of A.P.A. strength. Rosewater's switch to the antirailroad Populists in 1894 was forecast when the election of 1892 resulted in Crounse's victory as governor with a Populist-controlled legislature.[14]

That the A.P.A. had also gained some strength in the legislature was demonstrated by the necessity of considering its men in electing a United States Senator in January of 1893. The supporters of William Jennings Bryan found it advisable to look into the religious affiliation of legislators in the hope of discovering Catholics who would vote for him. Political independents were expected to swing to the Republican side, Bryan's supporters feared, because the "A.P.A. business" was complicating matters. The independents, however, swung to William V. Allen, a Populist, who was elected without A.P.A. support.[15]

Patronage matters, particularly the membership of the Omaha Board of Police and Fire Commissioners, became the concern of the A.P.A. for the time being. This board, which was at one and the same time a limitation on city home rule and a further source of patronage, provided the backbone for the A.P.A. struggle in Omaha for the next few years. The A.P.A. advisory board for Omaha asked Governor Crounse to accept its recommendations for appointment to the police board. A list was

submitted, with men from both political parties mentioned, and at least one of the men on the A.P.A. list was appointed. From these patronage requests, it is known that there were forty-five councils of the A.P.A. within Nebraska by the early spring of 1893. A state council, with C. B. Campbell as president, had been organized in 1892, and J. S. Hatfield succeeded Campbell in 1893. Undoubtedly, the major strength of the order was concentrated in Omaha and Douglas County.[16]

Thus, the political lines for the A.P.A. were established in Nebraska. The growth of the order was probably stimulated by the publicity received in the columns of the Omaha *Bee,* whose editor found the A.P.A. working with the hated "railroad" interests. Moreover, since the *Bee* was the source for wire service news emanating from Omaha, Rosewater's interpretation gave an illusion of A.P.A. success to a national audience, which learned therefrom that the A.P.A. was being given more credit for achievement than it was entitled to have.

In Wisconsin, Illinois, Ohio, and Minnesota, school questions provided the stimulus for anti-Catholicism and the growth of the A.P.A. In both Wisconsin and Illinois, compulsory school attendance laws became issues in the elections of 1890. Neither the Bennett Law in Wisconsin nor the Edwards Law in Illinois had been regarded as anti-Catholic legislation when enacted by the respective legislatures. Both laws were in line with compulsory attendance laws being inaugurated in many of the states, requiring attendance at some school for children between seven and fourteen years of age for either twelve weeks (in the case of the Bennett Law) or sixteen weeks (in the Edwards Law) out of each year.[17] Instruction was to be required in "reading, writing, arithmetic, and United States history, in the English language." No inspection of parochial schools was provided for or intended, and attendance at a private school that met the laws' requirements was not discouraged. Both laws were in the form of amendments to previous legislation. It is obvious that the laws were not causes of anti-Catholicism, but were made into issues with partisan value in political contests, which then precipitated partisan use of religious divisions.

Hostile reaction to the laws first appeared in the spring of 1890 among German Lutherans, incensed at the English language requirement. George W. Peck, author of *Peck's Bad Boy,* was elected Democratic mayor of Milwaukee apparently on the strength of his opposition to the Bennett Law. In the gubernatorial election that fall, Republican incumbent William D. Hoard was opposed by this same George Peck as the Democratic candidate. The Democrats offered repeal of the Bennett Law at the next legislative session if they were elected; the Republicans, caught unawares by the apparently sudden shift in public opinion, defended the law. A Democratic victory resulted, with the governorship, the state legislature, and the full congressional delegation except one falling to Democrats. This astonishing turnover in a staunch Republican state was generally blamed on German Lutheran and Catholic antagonism toward the Bennett Law, but anti-Catholics saw in it proof of the strength of "foreign influences" within the state.[18]

The plain fact was that the Lutherans had been the first to oppose the law. Soon they were joined by Catholic priests and bishops. Democratic party leadership saw the opportunity to develop an issue with which to gather German votes from the Republicans, while Republicans complacently regarded the law as unopposed. Much was said in the campaign concerning the "language of Luther," while Catholics were appealed to on the basis of state invasion of parental rights. Joining the Bennett Law in their minds with current agitation on liquor prohibition, some Germans regarded the trend as an invasion of their "personal liberties." Neither Catholic nor German opposition to the law was universal, however. Archbishop Ireland, of St. Paul, was in favor of the Bennett Law, and the Turner organizations of Milwaukee also favored it. On the other hand, Archbishop Katzer of Milwaukee, a leader of German Catholics, was quite sensitive on the retention of German in his parish work.[19] Republicans defending the law utilized the "little red schoolhouse" as a symbol and were defeated. For the next four years, they faced the necessity of recovering their losses among the Germans, while the Democrats were constantly on the lookout for evidence

that would demonstrate undue friendship among Republicans for either anti-Germanism or anti-Catholicism.[20] The A.P.A. flourished in this fertile seed bed.

The Democratic legislature repealed the Bennett Law and elected William F. Vilas, a member of President Cleveland's cabinet during the first administration, as United States senator from Wisconsin. Senator Vilas was well aware of the importance of the Bennett Law to his party.[21] Edward C. Wall, chairman of the Democratic State Central Committee, had recognized the importance of the school issue in lining up German Lutherans and Catholics behind the Democrats to bring party victory in 1890. He now wished to preserve the alliance, although he nervously anticipated breaches in it in his reports to Senator Vilas. His difficulty lay, as he saw it, in attempting to reconcile within the same alliance the divergent forces of a traditional German liberalism, which opposed coercion by the state, such as that represented by the Bennett Law, with an extremely conservative German Catholic group, which regarded the law as an interference with strict church control over educational matters.[22]

A Milwaukee city election in the spring of 1892 tested the precarious Democratic alliance. With many misgivings, Chairman Wall found himself in the difficult position of supporting a ticket "loaded down with Catholics, Irish, and Saloon keepers," which he knew did not appeal to the Lutherans and the independent voters. His "boys" felt confident that victory could be "managed," but Wall did not. Nevertheless, the coalition did hold, and Wall rejoiced by telegram to Vilas: "Over three thousand for Somers; great victory; our Lutheran friends stood solid." [23]

Even with a municipal victory under his belt, Wall could not rest easily, for he feared that the liberal Germans were "going back on us," while the German Catholics were said to be complaining because they were not getting enough patronage.[24] As the fall elections approached, the Democrats renominated Governor Peck and again repudiated the Bennett Law, as though their repeal of it two years before had not been enough.[25]

In the campaign, Republicans avoided outright support of the Bennett Law and blamed the Democrats for injecting religion into politics. Former Senator John C. Spooner, replaced by Vilas in 1891, was the Republican choice for governor. At Baraboo, Spooner denounced the Bennett Law and stated that he disliked any man who would drag religion into politics, saying "I despise a Know-Nothing." Hearing him thus cut the heart from the Republican position, a member of one of the patriotic societies wrote to protest, asking, "If it was right in '90 why is it wrong in '92?" Spooner was also reminded that fifty thousand people in Wisconsin were organized to "protect American institutions" and that such a large number could accomplish in Wisconsin what had already been done in Chicago, Omaha, and Detroit. With that happy faculty of enthusiasts to see greater success in distant fields, this man reported that fifty thousand Illinois citizens were supporting "Americanism" and that this kind of person was essential for Republican victories. Since Spooner by his statement was apparently rejecting this support, the correspondent thought their votes would go Prohibition.[26] Whether or not the votes of the "patriots" were siphoned off into the Prohibition totals, it is certain that Chairman Wall's fears were not yet justified. The Democrats again were victorious. The overwhelming fact, to the anti-Catholic at least, was that the Catholics had won another victory.

In Illinois, the outline of the struggle was similar, but there was no gubernatorial office at stake in 1890. As in Wisconsin, the newly elected Democratic legislature repealed the Edwards Law. In 1892, the Democrats nominated John Peter Altgeld for governor. In a shrewd move, Altgeld fastened responsibility for the Edwards Law on his Republican opponent, although Altgeld had approved the law in principle before he was nominated and perhaps even had something to do with writing the original bill at the time of its submission to the legislature in 1889.[27] Altgeld's election was assured, but the loss of the state's presidential vote to the Democrats was a surprise; for it, German Lutherans and Catholics were regarded as responsible.[28]

A Catholic priest's antagonism to the Ohio compulsory school

attendance law was responsible for producing an issue there on which the A.P.A. could flourish. Father Patrick F. Quigley, of Toledo, sought to test the constitutionality of the existing law. His method was to refuse compliance by failing to make the required attendance report. He was arrested in April of 1890 and indicted in June. A jury found him guilty a year later. The case was appealed to the Ohio Supreme Court, where the law was upheld. Father Quigley was then arrested again, this time for failure to comply with the court ruling, and it was necessary for his bishop to advise submission and compliance before the priest would submit. Yielding, though unconvinced that justice had been done, Quigley took his case to the court of public opinion by publishing a book in 1894 in which he expressed his views.[29]

Toledo, Cleveland, and Columbus were the sites of the first A.P.A. penetration of Ohio. In Toledo, the two chief leaders were B. F. Reno, attorney, and Captain Egbert Doville, chief of police. The intransigent Father Quigley and his court case were the evidence used to demonstrate need for an anti-Catholic organization. By November of 1892, one member of the Toledo school board was assertedly acting for the A.P.A. in seeking to discharge all Catholic teachers from the schools.[30] Toledo was also the site of the organization of the Ohio superior council of the A.P.A., with Captain Doville as the first state president, elected in 1892.[31]

Fully established with six councils in Cleveland by March of 1892, the order was already participating in a school board election through the Republican party organization. The Cleveland *Plain Dealer* put a reporter on the trail of the facts, and learned that the A.P.A. had come to Cleveland from Chicago sometime during 1891. Ship captains had been responsible for bringing word of the new organization and had used the quarters of the Shipmaster's Marine Benevolent Association as a center where captains discussed the issue as they sat out the winter lull in lake shipping. The A.P.A. was accurately described by the *Plain Dealer* as a distinct group acting in concert with the Junior Order of United American Mechanics through a joint

committee. This committee had prepared a recommended list of school board candidates, on which a large "C" indicated a Catholic, a small "c" designated a "Catholic sympathizer," while a "P" marked the candidate endorsed by the two orders. Despite the publicity, which was intended to harm the anti-Catholics, plus the outright editorial opposition of the *Plain Dealer,* Republicans won the election, and the men designated with "P" received the largest vote.[32]

Not until July of 1892 was there mention of the A.P.A. operating in Columbus, but its entry there must also be dated sometime in 1891. Perhaps the most active organizer was the Reverend Adam Fawcett of the Hildreth Baptist Church, but Fawcett was only one of an "original thirteen" founders in Columbus. The incident that assertedly stirred these men to action was one in which Bishop Watterson supposedly refused a Catholic girl permission to sing at a Protestant entertainment. In April of 1892, the *Catholic Columbian* stated that a member of the Patriotic Order of the Sons of America was on the school board, where he was supported by the local Junior Order of United American Mechanics. On July 1, the daily *Ohio State Journal* reported an anonymous flourishing secret society with fourteen branches, one having a thousand members, already operating within the city. The *Journal* believed that these groups were affiliated in turn with an anti-Catholic order active in the "Northwestern states." The next day the *Catholic Columbian* discovered the same thing. Then the Columbus *Record,* shortly to be acknowledged as the spokesman of the Ohio A.P.A., joined the guessing game but still did not identify the organization. The *Record,* in the same issue, however, did publish a document that was to be used constantly by the A.P.A. as propaganda, the "Instructions to True Catholics," said to be a letter from the hierarchy advising Catholics to remember their papal allegiance and to oppose the public schools. This weekly also printed the inflammatory information that Columbus' city population was only one-tenth Catholic while the majority of its municipal employees were of that faith. Near the end of July, the Catholic weekly broke the news that the organization was the A.P.A., at

about the same time that the Reverend Justin D. Fulton of Boston spoke under the auspices of the Reverend Mr. Fawcett.[33] By September, Fawcett claimed ten thousand voters as supporters of the A.P.A. program,[34] but since he was indulging in the speculative venture of tabulating voters without a casting of the ballot, his estimate was probably excessive.

As a protest, the Reverend Washington Gladden, a Congregational minister of Columbus and a leader in the "social gospel" movement, preached a Sunday evening sermon (which eventually appeared in the pages of a national magazine) on the subject of the "Revival of Know-Nothingism" in Columbus.[35] Gladden's disapproving words were met with a barrage laid down by Fawcett, who said that Gladden was seeing ghosts if he saw Know-Nothingism revived. Evangelism and patriotism were joined in Fawcett's oratorical plea for a "starry flag over every school," an open Bible on each teacher's desk, a love for the common schools in every breast, and a government by all the people, not just the Catholic minority.[36] The main contribution of Fawcett's reply, however, was its clear indication that to him there was no middle ground; one was either opposed to Catholicism or was its supporter.

As the election approached, two county officers, both Democrats, were singled out for defeat "because of their religious association." When election day passed, these two men were the only incumbents defeated. The newspapers reported that Catholic Republicans had voted for them, but that enough Democrats had scratched them to account for their defeat.[37]

Just before the election, on November 7, the *Ohio State Journal* had published a front-page exposure of the A.P.A.[38] Based on information secured by a local private detective agency that placed its men within A.P.A. councils, the exposure merely repeated statements in a campaign pamphlet; who had hired the detectives was not disclosed. The revelation said that eight thousand members belonged to the order in Franklin County and Columbus, and there was a total of forty councils in the state. The news story used the initials "A.P.A." and the word "Amoreans" interchangeably, however, so that the total of membership

probably included the Junior Order and the Patriotic Order of the Sons of America along with the A.P.A.

The success of the order in Minnesota was more moderate. Some localized anti-Catholicism had existed at Rochester for some time, incidental to arrangements made by the Mayo Clinic with a Catholic hospital. More significantly and to the point, a compulsory school law had been in force since 1885. In August of 1891, the parish priest at Faribault informed the local school board that his parochial school would not open that fall. By law, the board was required to provide accommodations for the 150 or so pupils involved. Almost immediately, the priest presented a plan that became the board's solution.[39] It called for the parochial school to be leased to the school board at one dollar per year, to be operated under the supervision of the city superintendent. Its teaching staff was to continue to be members of the Dominican Order, who would be certified under state law and paid regular salaries. The same texts as were used in the public school were to be used, no religious symbols were to appear in classrooms, but the teaching sisters could wear their habits. Any religious instruction would take place after regular school hours. This agreement was acceptable to the community, apparently, since there was no outright dissent. A similar plan was offered by the parish priest at Stillwater and was accepted by the school board there.

The Faribault-Stillwater plans were ones that eventually engendered as bitter opposition from within Catholic ranks as from without. The results, thus, had a broader effect than merely to explain the incidence of the A.P.A. in Minnesota. The center of the controversy, according to both sources of dissent, was Archbishop John Ireland of St. Paul, an outspoken and controversial church leader whose opinions were freely expressed on many current issues, including education. Those of his parish priests who were responsible for the school plans at Faribault and Stillwater were apparently without specific instructions from him, but they knew without being told that he was in sympathy.[40] Neither plan was original, inasmuch as a similar scheme had been operating at Poughkeepsie, New York, for some eight-

een years, while in some fifteen to twenty districts of Stearns County, Minnesota, the Benedictine Sisters had operated a similar arrangement. The Faribault plan, however, was the one widely publicized. Immediate opposition to it came from within the state; Catholic opposition came a year or more later.

The Reverend Gulian L. ("Go-Lightly") Morrill, a Protestant of Minneapolis, immediately attacked the plans as a "Jesuit wooden-horse" and made an inspection visit to the schools at Faribault and Stillwater. He found a picture of the Pope in a classroom at Faribault, and certain unspecified "Catholic paraphernalia" displayed in rooms at Stillwater. On Thanksgiving Day, some of the Protestant ministers of St. Paul preached their alarm. In early December, a conference of ministers in Minneapolis was told that the plans were an instance of the "Catholic camel getting its nose under the canvas of American free institutions," and the ministers thereupon adopted a resolution denouncing the plans as unconstitutional. No court suit was instituted, however, to test the legality of the plan, and the debate continued as a political issue.

The Stillwater experiment ended after only one year's operation. The Faribault plan extended into the second year. After the first year, the community expressed its judgment in an election at which the issue was clearly placed before the electorate. An unprecedented number of ballots was cast, with 60 per cent of the voters opposing the plan's continuation. But the contract had already been made for the succeeding year, so termination was postponed. In the meantime, the school board made no plans to include the parochial school children within the public system when termination should occur. In the fall of 1893, the contract was renewed again. Its termination came, however, when the superintendent transferred one of the Catholic sisters to a public school and sent two Protestant teachers into the former parochial school. The parish priest protested, but the board refused to alter the assignments, and the contract was broken. With as little fanfare as it had begun, then, the Faribault plan came to a close. But it did stimulate the growth of the A.P.A. in

Minnesota, and it was cited elsewhere to illustrate "Catholic duplicity." [41]

Actually, the first appearance of an A.P.A. unit within the state took place at Duluth, and the origin was apparently unrelated to the Faribault incidents. Rather, a somewhat nativistic opposition to "Austrian" Catholic workers in the ore fields seems to provide the explanation for appearance of an A.P.A. council sometime in late 1891 or early 1892. The purchase of a flag to fly over the Duluth High School created the first public controversy. A Minnesota superior council was organized at Duluth in May of 1893 with Thomas Clark, Superintendent of the St. Louis County (Duluth) Poor Farm, as the first state secretary. [42]

Secretary Clark was responsible for organizing the first council in the Twin Cities, but this did not occur until May of 1893. Nevertheless, anti-Catholicism, stirred by the Faribault incident for over a year, preceded the organizational effort. Orange lodges were already in existence, and a weekly newspaper had been established as early as December of 1892. It was named the *Loyal American* and was edited by Edwards J. Doyle, a member of the local Orange lodge. Moreover, sufficient native antagonism toward Scandinavians and, on the other hand, anti-Catholicism on the part of Protestant Scandinavians existed so that Minnesota's experience with the A.P.A. illustrated the peculiar uses to which political nativism and anti-Catholicism could be put. The Scandinavian-born Knute Nelson, Republican, in his race for the governorship in 1892, faced opposition because he was foreign-born and also because he was supported by anti-Catholics. Despite this somewhat unusual combination among his opponents, Nelson won a three-way contest against a Democrat and a Populist. [43]

Thus, many state and local incidents provided issues and personalities that gave political contests in 1892 the aspect of a Catholic and anti-Catholic struggle for power. The national race for the presidency in that year had its own developments along the same lines. At the Republican convention, James G. Blaine's bid for the nomination was hampered by the fact that

his son-in-law, Colonel Coppinger, was a Catholic and by the fact that Blaine's son had only recently been divorced after a runaway marriage performed by a Catholic priest. The priest involved had written to Mrs. Blaine protesting the divorce, and Blaine had replied, taking the priest to task for having performed the ceremony for a minor and for having criticized Mrs. Blaine. In the judgment of one editorial writer at least, this incident had put Blaine in a bad position to appeal to Catholic support.[44] The renomination of President Harrison was assured even before the convention was held, however, so that the Blaine affair was of no great importance. After the convention, Harrison replaced the national chairman, James S. Clarkson, with Thomas Carter, a former commissioner of the General Land Office and a well-known Roman Catholic from Montana.[45] In the opinion of Thomas J. Morgan, who was to be the real target of Catholic attack in the campaign to follow, Catholics had opposed Harrison at the convention and continued to do so through the campaign.[46] President Cleveland's nomination for a delayed second term on the Democratic ticket was the signal for a renewal of the charges that his friendship for Cardinal Gibbons was too close.

The "issue" that stimulated Catholics and anti-Catholics during the election of 1892 was Indian school policy. Since the inauguration of President Grant's "peace policy," the federal government had sought the cooperation of the various Christian sects in providing education on Indian reservations. One method was the contract system, whereby church missionaries operated Indian schools under annual contracts with the federal government. A Catholic Bureau of Indian Missions had been established in 1874 to oversee the Catholic missions and schools, while the Protestant churches handled theirs individually.[47] During Cleveland's first administration, his Secretary of the Interior expressed a determination to begin limiting government funds for contract schools and to begin the building of a government school system for the Indians. The Dawes Act of 1887 established a policy that sought to merge the Indian into the general population by ending his status as a ward of the government. The two policies were, thus, not contradictory; in fact they complemented each

other. Shortly, each of the Protestant sects adopted resolutions in annual meetings asking the government to end the contract system, and notifying it that each of them intended to enter into no more contracts. Back of this development stood the National League for the Protection of American Institutions, which, through its secretary, James M. King, claimed credit for persuading the Protestant sects to take this step and for asking Catholics to do likewise. Soon, only the Catholics had not done so.[48] This situation had been accepted by the Harrison administration in 1889, and a new Indian Commissioner, Thomas J. Morgan, was then appointed to carry out the policy.

Morgan was not a newcomer to educational circles, and his position on current school questions was well known. At the time of the appointment as commissioner, he was principal of the state normal school at Providence, Rhode Island.[49] His standing among educators was shown by his election to the vice-presidency of the National Education Association in 1887–88 and again in 1888–89. He was prominent at N.E.A. meetings, where his firmly held convictions probably provided some basis for his reputation as an anti-Catholic. Any anti-Catholicism he expressed until after his career as Indian Commissioner, however, was incidental and secondary to his overwhelming enthusiasm for free and compulsory education in the English language for all children. He believed firmly that the public school was the unifying experience for the diversities in Americans.[50] He also thought the schools should provide a "high moral, and if possible, religious tone." [51] Morgan was a man of varied experience and accomplishments. An ordained Baptist minister, he had risen during the Civil War through the commissioned ranks, part of the time in command of colored troops, until brevetted a brigadier-general shortly before the end of the war.[52] As a consequence of his career, his titles presented an impressive array; he was addressed as "Reverend," "Doctor," or "General," a combination of any two, or all three at once.

President Harrison appointed Morgan as Commissioner of Indian Affairs, and chose the Reverend Daniel Dorchester, whose book *Romanism and the Public Schools* had appeared in 1888

as a part of the Boston school difficulties, as Commissioner of Indian Education. Dorchester was probably the more offensive to Catholics at the time of appointment, but it was his superior, Morgan, who eventually received the greater criticism. Confirmation of these appointments was delayed by bitter opposition led by Democratic Senators James K. Jones of Arkansas and George Vest of Missouri. One of the charges that Morgan faced had to do with the court-martial he had undergone during the Civil War. Form petitions against the confirmation were printed in the *Kansas Catholic* of Leavenworth and the *Catholic Columbian* of Ohio to be signed and sent to the Senate. Despite opposition, however, the two men were confirmed, Morgan by a vote of twenty-eight to sixteen, and took office.[53]

Morgan began to put into effect his policies so that Indians would receive a training equal to that received in the public schools. He knew that his reforms could not be accomplished overnight; in fact, statistics showed that the contract schools were still being operated at the end of his term of office.[54] There was no evidence that President Harrison disapproved of his plans or his work. Criticism of Morgan continued throughout his entire term of office, including references to his personal life, his military career, and his work as commissioner. The court-martial incident was constantly publicized, although the failure to convict was overlooked, while his wife's presence on the public payroll was called nepotism. Morgan replied to the last charge that his wife understood his objectives and could be trusted to aid in carrying them out.[55]

The center from which criticism of Morgan originated was the Catholic Bureau of Indian Missions in Washington, and its director, Father Joseph Stephan. In his efforts, Father Stephan did not have the unqualified support of either Cardinal Gibbons or Archbishop Ireland.[56] So virulent did the attacks become that Morgan felt compelled to sever all relationships between his office and that of the Bureau in the summer of 1891.[57] After this the disputes became more bitter, and the Bureau was charged by its enemies with misappropriating government funds intended for Indian use and using them for church purposes.[58]

Almost a year later, in time for it to become a part of the presidential campaign of 1892, Father Stephan presented his version of the story and his condemnation of Morgan's policies. Stephan placed the responsibility on the President, and his report was intended solely for his superiors and not for publication. But the report, or the salient parts of it, did become public property. One of Stephan's striking phrases referred to Morgan and Harrison as the "bigoted commissioner and not much less bigoted president," and Stephan was aware that these words, if publicized, would be used to arouse prejudice. He asked for secrecy, and when the report was publicized with these words he blamed the printer for releasing it. In any case, the Catholic press utilized excerpts to chastise Harrison and Morgan and predicted the coming defeat of the President.[59] The nondenominational Protestant weekly *Independent* of New York editorially described the attack as a "still hunt" on Morgan and lamented the fact that it introduced Catholicism into the campaign.[60]

Father Stephan was an active participant in the campaign of 1892, according to one observer:

There was a wonderful old man about Washington in those days, Father Stephan, a priest with a long white beard who spent much time among the Indians and was zealous in the propagation of his religion among them. When Harrison refused to remove Morgan and it was known that the Commissioner would continue in his course, Father Stephan procured letters from the prelates. These letters said nothing about politics or the approaching election; they simply commended Father Stephan to the consideration of the churchmen. That was enough. Father Stephan did the rest, and as he was no novice as a politician, the result of his work was shown in the returns from every place he visited during the campaign. He told leading Catholics what the Harrison administration had done in regard to the Indian schools, and created a spirit of hostility against the Republican party which was far-reaching in its effects upon the election.[61]

The Catholic press rather generally ascribed Harrison's defeat to Morgan's Indian policies. Other commentators concluded that the tariff was the most decisive factor in the outcome, while lethargy on the part of Republicans also was said to have contributed a share to his defeat. But the author of the above

statement thought these explanations were insufficient and concluded that the Indian policies had cost Harrison "thousands
upon thousands of Catholic votes." [62] Certainly the press reports,
both before and after election day, from the Catholic as well as
from the daily press, would indicate that the controversy over
Indian school policy might have had some such effect.

To summarize its effect on the election outcome, anti-Catholicism had become a factor in a number of states. Of these
states, the A.P.A. had become established in strength in Wisconsin and Illinois, which swung to the Democratic columns for the
first time since the Civil War. It was generally assumed that this
was the result of the compulsory education laws in both states,
driving German voters into Democratic ranks. In other states
where A.P.A. councils existed, five of Michigan's fourteen electoral votes went Democratic, while Ohio's vote was so close that
an official tabulation was necessary to determine finally that the
Republicans had carried it; Minnesota, Nebraska, and Iowa remained in the Republican van.[63] It is quite likely that where
A.P.A. members could overlook Chairman Carter's religious
affiliation they voted for Harrison and Republicans. Despite,
then, the results in local and state elections that seemed to favor
their cause, the victory of Cleveland and the Democrats in 1892
was regarded by anti-Catholics as a defeat for their cause and a
significant victory for "political Romanism."

The presidential election of 1892 did favor the A.P.A. by
bringing it forward as a political agent and by forcing it to assess
its own behavior. In October of 1892 a Catholic newspaper in
New York announced that a "secret anti-Catholic society called
the American Protective Association" had been established
within the country, and described its membership as "active,
aggressive, persistent, and unscrupulous." Catholics were warned
to prepare for a religious conflict and for falsehoods, forgeries,
and boycotts.[64] This news was somewhat belated. The most important effect of the election was that the A.P.A. had found a
political home within the Republican party, while Democrats in
opposing it had discovered a means of retaining the "Catholic
vote."

In the Morgan case, the A.P.A. had found a martyr and a legislative goal. Morgan became the darling of the A.P.A. press, and the demand for the cessation of government appropriations for contract schools became a rallying cry.[65] By accepting the bonanza of the Morgan case, the A.P.A. attached itself to a considerably larger and quite respectable point of view, which held that government appropriations to any religious group under contract terms should be abolished.[66] Those Catholics who chose to make an issue of this opposition to sectarian appropriations were acting unwisely, especially as they contributed to the misjudgment that the A.P.A. had been responsible for creating sentiment in favor of termination. It had not. Because of their allegations, Catholics can be charged with helping to create a legend of A.P.A. strength. The movement for termination was well under way—in fact, it had practically achieved its goal— while the A.P.A. was only gaining momentum, and the order was not responsible for its eventual success. The opportunity to capitalize on it, and to accept credit for its success, given to it so gratuitously by its enemies, was more than the A.P.A. could be expected to overlook.[67]

At the same time that its name was entering the national political currency, the A.P.A. was taking leadership among the self-styled "patriotic orders." The growth of unity among them had a brief history. Centering in Chicago, with the Edwards school law as its object, a "Committee of One Hundred" had been established in September of 1890 with the cooperation of the usual patriotic societies, including the A.P.A. The committee claimed a total of eighteen thousand adherents from among its member societies.[68] But it had been defeated in its goals during the elections of 1890.

Beginning in January of 1891, the Reverend Oliver E. Murray of the Wabash Avenue Methodist Church in Chicago presented a series of lectures. Murray was the lecturer, but each Sunday afternoon a different patriotic leader served as presiding officer for the meeting. Harry C. Gano, who was currently president of the A.P.A. state council, presided over the first meeting, and Henry F. Bowers was a chairman later. The talks were in opposi-

tion to alcohol, Catholicism, and municipal corruption. It was alleged that ten thousand incorrigible children of school age were wandering the streets of Chicago because of the inoperative school attendance law. The Catholic "menace" was illustrated by chilling references to the "Catholic Cadets," a volunteer marching group, and by references to the arsenal in every Catholic church basement. Since the state election was already past, the only hope for saving the schools was to elect a mayor and city council for Chicago. In the spring of 1891, the coalition supported a third-party candidate on a "Citizen's Party" ticket and suffered a defeat.[69]

Two immediate results grew out of the Murray meetings. A magazine, entitled *Patriot,* began publication to carry the lectures and news to a wider audience, and the "National American Patriotic Union" was projected in March of 1891 as a joint effort of those interested in various issues of the day, including votes for women, naturalization, immigration, school matters, and Indian affairs. No distinction of "sect, sex, or party" was permitted within this union, which chose Mr. Murray as its president, while electing as vice-presidents the national leaders of the various patriotic societies. Thus, Henry F. Bowers became a vice-president.[70] For those who wished to learn them, two lessons had been presented: third-party tactics were unlikely to be successful, and the more generalized a platform was the more useful it was in attracting support.

Within a month, the third national Conference of Patriotic Organizations met in Chicago. For the first time, this group, which had been meeting each year for two years in order to achieve unity among the patriotic groups, included the A.P.A. Fifty-nine societies from twenty-five states were represented. A platform in favor of immigration restriction, free public schools, free press, free speech, and the sale of public lands only to American citizens was adopted. National officers were elected and permanent plans were made, including one for an annual conference.[71] By March of 1891, then, the A.P.A. had succeeded in winning its way into the circle of patriotic societies and demonstrated its willingness to cooperate with them. The next prob-

lem was the identification of the entire anti-Catholic and "patriotic" movement with the American Protective Association, whose initials provided so convenient a label. Its own publicity, but more probably its recognition by others, provided the A.P.A. with this boon; elements of luck, and of coincidence, again operated to enhance the reputation of the order.

A.P.A. publicists were quick to capitalize on any event or issue that could be utilized as propaganda to attach individuals or groups to the order. Perhaps one of the reasons why the W.A.P.A. was organized may be found in the fact that women could vote in school elections in many localities. The *Patriotic American* found this "noble and humane," and argued that women should have the full franchise before it was given to the "ignorant naturalized foreigner or a dominated Romanist." Prohibition was another issue in many areas, and the A.P.A. press frequently noted a close relationship between Catholics and saloonkeepers and asserted that the Catholic press was subsidized by "whiskey dominated" advertising.[72] The story that the public press was controlled by Catholics was told frequently. When the Chicago *Advance* made this charge, specifically naming the new Associated Press as being unfair to the A.P.A. and excessively friendly to Catholicism, the criticism was answered privately by the newly chosen head of the press association:

What an industrious and crafty army of Jesuitical agents these men who serve the daily press of the world! And what very stupid people the proprietors of all these hundreds of papers served, never to have discovered the imposition daily practiced by the Catholic management! No greater tribute was ever paid to the overmastering ability of the Roman Catholic Church, or, if intellectual superiority is to control, stronger reason given for the universal domination of that Church.

More soberly, he then listed the religious affiliations of the chief officers of the news service and ended with a general plea for toleration.[73]

To the anti-Catholic enthusiast, the borderline between fact and fiction was elastic. Since Catholicism was to him so obviously a menace, he was disposed to manufacture proof of evil Catholic

intentions where the facts were not available. One product of this kind was the forged "Pastoral Letter," assertedly a statement of American Catholic bishops, which advocated the formation of a papal political party, viewed the spread of intelligence with alarm, and suggested that education and the true faith were incompatible.[74] Still another forgery was a set of "Instructions to Catholics," which began to appear in 1892 and continued to be the most successful of A.P.A. propaganda devices. It purported to be a papal encyclical dated December 25, 1891. Its concluding paragraph announced:

Moreover, we proclaim the people of the United States to have forfeited all right to rule said Republic and also all dominion, dignity, and privilege appertaining to it. We likewise declare that all subjects of every rank and condition in the United States and every individual who has taken any oath of loyalty to the United States in any way whatsoever, may be absolved from said oath, as also from all duty, fidelity, or obedience on or about the 5th of September, 1893, when the Catholic Congress shall convene at Chicago, Illinois, as we shall exonerate them from all engagements, and on or about the feast of Ignatius Loyola in the year of our Lord, 1893, it will be the duty of the faithful to exterminate all heretics found within the jurisdiction of the United States of America.[75]

This "encyclical," with its threat of an uprising of Catholics to murder all non-Catholics, gave point to the references repeated with consistent emphasis in the anti-Catholic press to the different marching groups that drilled in anticipation of a coming bloodbath.[76] The forgery at least had the virtue of designating a date for the uprising, although the dates were somewhat confused. The Feast of Ignatius Loyola, July 31, was to occur before, instead of after, the Chicago meeting that apparently was to be the signal for the uprising.

Anti-Catholic propaganda was dispensed with a personal touch by itinerant lecturers and organizers who went from town to town. Claiming to be "ex-priests" in some cases, these men drew their audiences by promising to reveal the secrets of the confessional or to describe the inside story of convents and monasteries in lurid terms. They were sometimes referred to as "Reverend," and the title occasionally meant that they were or-

dained in one of the Protestant denominations. The Reverend Joseph Slattery was one, and George Rudolph was another. Slattery was working his way through the Midwest in the spring of 1893, and Rudolph appeared in Iowa in December of 1892, challenging his hearers to brave the "Romish boycott" and join the A.P.A. He announced that almost every town in Iowa had an A.P.A. council, considering this incentive enough for joining. One anti-Catholic lecturer, appearing in Muscatine, Iowa, in 1892, was stoned in the streets by an outraged crowd.[77] William Lloyd Clark became a speaker for the order and worked out of Jacksonville, Illinois, as an organizer. He also took subscriptions to his newspaper, *Our True Friend,* the name of which had a significant "relation to the ritualistic work of the order." Mr. Clark's partner in the publishing business was more interested in the financial return from the paper than in the gospel of anti-Catholicism, so that the partnership eventually dissolved and Clark lost his investment. His experience did not dampen his animosity toward the "Scarlet Beast, Rome," however, and he spent the remainder of his life pursuing the struggle.[78]

Immediate results of the propaganda campaign were felt in election returns from numerous municipal and school board elections in the spring of 1893. Just how these returns were to be interpreted, however, was not clear. Some indicated A.P.A. success; others merely constituted favorable publicity for it. In Chicago, for example, the Democrat Carter Harrison successfully recaptured the mayoralty, with one side picturing him as acceptable to Catholics and the other side seeing him as a representative of the A.P.A.[79] Harrison was realist enough to accept votes from any source, but there was little reason why he should seriously have been considered an A.P.A. choice. An avowed A.P.A. man, the Reverend Adam Fawcett, did manage to secure election to the board of education in Columbus, Ohio; at the same time victories were reported for the order from Keokuk and Fort Madison, Iowa.[80] The *Patriotic American* rejoiced that St. Louis had chosen twenty-eight out of forty-five candidates approved by the A.P.A., with only eleven "papists" succeeding at the polls. Bloomington, Indiana, assertedly elected a four-man

school board slate approved by the order, and the "purifying effect" of the A.P.A. was felt in Detroit, Bay City, Saginaw, Grand Rapids, and Jackson, Michigan, and at Cleveland and Minneapolis.[81] The standard for victory, however, was that non-Catholics were chosen, not necessarily that men committed to the A.P.A. were elected. This flexible interpretation, which was almost meaningless, was always to prove useful to the order in expanding its political effectiveness.

The *Catholic Record* of Indianapolis, faced with an alleged A.P.A. success in that city, asked if Catholics were not spending too much time and good ammunition on the A.P.A. and warned that free advertising and publicity gave to it an importance it had not earned. "If you want to notice them, you might give them the benefit of a smile," it advised its readers.[82] For the time being, this sensible advice went unheeded.

Protestant opposition to the A.P.A. was outspoken on occasion. Washington Gladden's attack on the Columbus A.P.A. in the fall of 1892 continued to have consequences there. An assistant pastor in his church was removed by Gladden because the man belonged to the "malicious, devilish, and perfectly asinine" organization. The assistant then publicized his removal, charging that Gladden had violated the "congregational" spirit of his church by assuming that hiring and firing were in his, and not the congregation's, jurisdiction. Gladden came to feel that his attitude toward the A.P.A. accounted for his failure to be offered the presidency of Ohio State University, because anti-Catholics controlled the state legislature.[83] In Omaha, an Episcopal minister, the Reverend John Williams, attacked the A.P.A. in his *Parish Messenger,* demonstrating the falsity of A.P.A. charges, defending the loyalty of Catholics, and pointing to the "Orange" origin of many A.P.A. leaders.[84]

In labor circles also there was recognition of the order as a divisive and disturbing force. A belief that the order prospered in some way as a result of the favor of railroad management cropped up from time to time.[85] The Rock Island lines were supposed to be using the order as a means to divide employees along religious lines. In the beginning of its career, the entry of

the order into Chicago was said to have been managed by a railroad lawyer, while the earliest members were supposed to have been railroad employees.[86] It is true that the Union Pacific railroad was a constant, though not a large, advertiser in the Omaha *American*.[87] The attitude of the order itself was such that it could hardly be called favorable to unity among organized labor. In its press, "American" working men were warned to beware of the Knights of Labor because of Powderly's Catholicism.[88] The papal encyclical of 1891, *Rerum Novarum,* was looked on by A.P.A. leaders as having as its objective the unification of "papist labor," to secure the same advantages for priestly control of labor that the order already believed was enjoyed by the hierarchy in politics.[89] Within the Brotherhood of Locomotive Firemen, A.P.A. members did threaten the cohesiveness of the union sufficiently to draw the condemnation of Eugene Debs.[90] Since the A.P.A. was most successful in urban areas, undoubtedly the charge of its divisive influence on industrial labor contained an element of truth. The danger was not that the A.P.A. might be actually encouraged by management; it was that it might operate to turn one laborer against another to prevent labor unity.

Catholic opposition to the order was localized and sporadic. On the evening of March 27, 1893, in Saginaw, a public meeting was held and addressed by three prominent speakers. The subject was the A.P.A. and the serious effects rising from its local career. Religious hatreds were blamed for the business depression, one speaker stating that the "blossoming for rent" signs in Saginaw were the result of boycotts and counterboycotts, instead of the product of the Panic of 1893. Another speaker described the A.P.A. as the "Associated Political Assassins," while he turned the tables of nativism on them by stating that the order's members were trying to conduct the affairs of the United States with the dust of Canada still clinging to their coattails.[91] The meeting may have caused some comment in Saginaw, but it could hardly convince doubters of anything much except that one group of zealots disliked another.

The idea that there was no middle ground, often expressed

by A.P.A. enthusiasts, was also expressed by the editor of the *Catholic Citizen* of Milwaukee in his editorial, "There is no Neutrality for Good Men." In order to retain claims on the adjective "good," the editor believed, all public figures would have to express themselves either for or against the order. This same editor was shortly to charge that the rural pulpit of America was the source of anti-Catholicism, saying that the ignorance and credulity of rural Protestantism fed upon such misinformation as the forged papal encyclicals.[92] Actually, unless the editor had private information that he was not divulging, the sources and expressions of anti-Catholicism about him showed that an urban population was very susceptible and more willing than its country cousin to take political action. Moreover, members of the Protestant pulpit were willing to speak out strongly, perhaps with even more force, than were Catholics at the moment.

The target of the A.P.A., the Catholic Church in the United States, did not present a unified front at this period in its history. Probably at no other time were American Catholic leaders so divided among themselves as in the decade of the nineties. In January of 1893, the *Nation* hailed this Catholic controversy as evidence of the "rising might of democracy" that was shifting power everywhere from the conservatives to the liberals. False as this joyous statement proved to be, it illustrated the *Nation's* belief that the "liberal" members of the hierarchy were winning the struggle within the church.[93] Controversy within Catholic leadership was an obvious disproof of the anti-Catholic's picture of monolithic "Romanism, but this fact disturbed him not a bit; in fact, he sought to turn it to his advantage.

One instance of this was the A.P.A. reaction to the settlement of the Father McGlynn affair. Absolved from his excommunication, McGlynn was generally regarded as proof of the liberal's victory. By a reasoning process difficult to understand, an article in the *Patriotic American* of January 7, 1893, reported McGlynn's reinstatement as a "jesuitical trick" to strengthen the hierarchy by utilizing McGlynn to weaken his superior bishop and to strengthen the position of Archbishop Ireland and his

adherents within the church.[94] Thus, observing the breach within the hierarchy, and noting the leaders of the contending sides, the A.P.A. saw it as a devious conspiracy to strengthen the church.

Another source of controversy was the desire on the part of some German Catholics to retain their language in America. The first conference of the *Deutsch-Amerikanischer Priester-Verein* had been held in Chicago in 1887, and from it had come plans for organizing a German-American Catholic Congress. In 1890, Peter Cahensly, a priest in Germany who felt that German immigrants in the United States were lost to the church because American bishops could not provide German-speaking priests to serve them, presented a memorial to an assemblage at Lucerne, Switzerland, to suggest a remedy. "Cahenslyism" was thus born in Europe, but its suggestion that greater autonomy be granted to foreign-language groups within the Catholic church in America made its effect felt in the United States. Archbishop Corrigan and Bishop McQuaid, among others of the hierarchy, attended a meeting of the German-American Catholic Congress at Buffalo in 1891. Archbishop Ireland did not attend, although he was responsible for informing newsmen of the character of the meeting. He suggested that a reporter be sent and that his reports be given wide publicity so that the purposes of the meeting should be known. The results were satisfactory to Ireland, although the prelate did not desire that his connection with the publicity should be revealed.[95]

In April of 1892, Senator Cushman K. Davis of Minnesota rebuked the Cahensly movement on the floor of the Senate; he refused to retract when asked to do so by a meeting of German-American Catholics in Dubuque. The Senator was thereupon deluged with congratulatory messages, some of which were from A.P.A. councils. The general tone of these was that Davis' stand had popular support and that, though a "few Limburger priests may pass resolutions," the real Catholic power in Davis' state was Ireland, who was known to oppose the Cahenslyites and would "batter their heads with his crosier if they continued contumacious." Senator Allison of Iowa advised Davis that the

German-Catholics were Democrats anyhow and that the news-papers supporting them were Democratic, too, and so could be ignored.[96]

Still further division came within the Catholic fold over the Faribault school compromise, and Ireland was again the center. The Archbishop's speech to the National Education Association set off a dispute between the two camps. The Reverend Thomas Bouquillon of Catholic University prepared a pamphlet, *Education: To Whom Does It Belong?,* in which he conceded to the state greater authority over education than had any other Catholic, going beyond even Ireland's position, generally re-garded as liberal. Another priest answered immediately with a denial, *The Parent First: An Answer,* saying that parental rights were supreme and that the state had no right to enforce com-pulsory education laws and that it even had no proper right to instruct. So severe did the argument become that Ireland felt obliged to go to Rome to defend himself, inasmuch as he was the central figure involved. The Papal Propaganda in April of 1892 finally announced that arrangements such as those at Faribault could be tolerated. This, it was hoped, would end the argument. It only added fuel. Ireland's supporters regarded it as a victory, while his opponents saw it as a rebuke from the Pope.[97]

The controversies among the American prelates had become so troublesome that a papal representative was appointed to smooth them over. First arriving in 1889 to represent the Pope at the centenary celebration of Catholicism in America and at the inauguration of Catholic University, Archbishop Francis Satolli was designated a second time in 1892 to represent the Pope at the Chicago World's Fair. While in the country during this second visit, he was designated Apostolic Delegate, in Janu-ary of 1893. Satolli had a difficult mission. But as the symbol of the papal authority appearing in person at a time when the church was under attack, his designation and his subsequent residence at Washington were singularly ill-timed.[98]

Announcing that "in Mr. Satolli the Pope is here!" a bishop of the Methodist Church aired his disturbance. A Catholic an-swered that opposition to Satolli was motivated by jealousy be-

cause the Catholic Church was using methods that would insure a new generation of "believing Christians." The *Nation* welcomed the delegate as a benevolent despot who would put down the "nice little intrigues and cabals which have been arraying the Catholic Church against some of the most fundamental principles of our Government." Looking back from the vantage point of some years, Henry Bowers wrote:

> We looked upon Satolli as a representative of the Propaganda at Rome to direct and influence legislation in this country, more especially his settling down in the city of Washington, and several moves which were made, which I cannot just now call to mind, which gave rise to an opinion at least that he was interfering with the public institutions of this country.[99]

In each instance, then, where one Catholic group differed from another, and in each of the problems that Catholicism faced in the nineties, the A.P.A. was prepared to take advantage of the situation.

Nor had the public school debate yet been resolved. A clear proposal for dividing public school funds, so that parochial schools would receive a share, was made. Both Pennsylvania and New Jersey legislatures faced such proposals, though neither legislature enacted them into law. The National Education Association heard former President Harrison advocate the teaching of the "morality of the Ten Commandments" and then passed a resolution stating that the promotion of "Americanism" would be a good thing.[100]

From another direction came even more pertinent information that would stimulate discussion. The census of 1890 had attempted to gather information on the religious affiliation of the population. Figures were obtained from pastors, or the governing bodies, of each church, so that the results were in no true sense a numbering of individuals. But the director of the census had summarized the findings and his figures had permitted him to illustrate Catholic "claims" to growth. He was cautious, however, recognizing that Catholic figures were greater than his count. He reported a figure of 6,367,330, while the *Catholic Directory* reported 7,885,000 and noted that a figure close to

ten million was probably closer to the truth. Even the census figures were bad enough, and the census director added fuel to the flames by stating, with figures, "New England is Roman Catholic." Immigration had brought Catholics to the region, while migration had taken Congregationalists out.[101] The Protestant weekly *Independent* warned of the unreliability of the figures but described Catholic growth as the trend. A Philadelphia lawyer, referring to the effects of immigration, concluded his discussion:

> The modern movement against immigration, if it go on increasing and take definite form, will have many advantages over the Know-Nothingism of 1850. It will avoid the absurdity of being a secret organization and the absurdity of recommending that the foreign-born shall never hold office. It will be entirely free from attacks on the Roman Catholics and all the violence and bitterness which that involved.[102]

Anti-Catholicism could not be divorced from the problem of immigration, however, even in the general discussions of the subject.

In May of 1893, when the annual meeting of the A.P.A. was held at Cleveland, the delegates had only to look around them to find many reasons that, for them, justified their being there; they could also find proof that their organization had made an impression. Delegates from twenty-two states and Canada were in attendance, representing a claimed million people. The claim was an exaggeration, but it had a truth in it. The man elected president of the order at this meeting reported some years later that membership had never exceeded seventy thousand before the 1893 meeting and that it was only sparsely scattered through twenty states at that time.[103] The difference between seventy thousand and one million was great but can be partly explained. The figure of seventy thousand probably revealed the total dues-paying membership of the A.P.A., while the million "represented" at Cleveland were very likely that intangible, "influence," and denoted the total members in the various "American orders" for which the A.P.A. was by this time taking action.

The claim of twenty or twenty-two states was probably less of an exaggeration. Iowa, Nebraska, Illinois, Michigan, Ohio, Wis-

consin, Missouri, and Minnesota were certainly represented; during 1892 "patriotic" weekly newspapers were founded in Colorado, Kansas, Kentucky, and Massachusetts, which suggests that the A.P.A. had already extended itself into those states. Indiana could hardly have been missed. A total of thirteen could thus be accounted for without much trouble. Since it may be conjectured that the 1893 meeting was attended by representatives of other "patriotic orders," and since the A.P.A. had been preceded frequently by other such groups in its organizing, this meeting probably provided a means by which the order was spread still further in the months following, when the delegates returned to their homes.

During 1892, in addition to the weeklies that had already appeared, the *Rocky Mountain American* was begun in Denver, *Liberty* was started at Galesburg, and the *American Blade* began printing at Rock Island, Illinois. In Kansas the *American Eagle* appeared in Kansas City, and *Freedom's Banner* was inaugurated at Louisville, Kentucky. Boston added the *American Citizen* to its list of publications; the *True American* circulated in St. Louis, and the *Wisconsin Patriot* became the A.P.A. spokesman from Milwaukee.[104]

The convention elected a new national president. Although it proved to be a turning point in the order's history, the replacement of Henry Bowers should not be assumed to represent any degree of dissatisfaction with his administration. He continued to attend all national conventions afterward and was always ready to resume the presidency if called upon. He served on committees, was elected president of the Iowa superior council in 1894 and 1895, and as a result of his previous position occupied a place on the supreme council of the order.[105]

The new regime did represent a different spirit operating within the order. More publicity, greater organizational effort, and larger political influence followed. Whether the delegates explicitly intended it or not, the new officers had broader organizational affiliations among the patriotic orders. This meant a growth of unity among the various groups and enhanced the role of the A.P.A. as the political vehicle for the "Americans."

Heading the new set of officers was William James Henry Traynor of Detroit, as supreme president.[106] Luckily for a man who would make much of his patriotism, Traynor was born on the Fourth of July, 1845; unluckily, he was born in Brantford, Ontario. Unlike Bowers, Traynor had a public school education, but the failure of his father's contracting business curtailed the son's opportunities for further schooling, and he went to work on a farm. Late enough to avoid service in the Civil War, but close enough to the age of discretion to prove his choice the wisdom of maturity, Traynor left Ontario and moved to Detroit in 1867. For the next six years he was in the livestock and lumber business. Then he started publishing, with the *Public Ledger,* the Detroit *Graphic,* the *Daily Times,* the Detroit *Courier,* and the *Patriotic American* as the titles of his various publishing ventures. Of these, the *Patriotic American* served the patriotic cause.[107]

Whereas Bowers' pre-A.P.A. lodge experience was limited to the Masons, Traynor was an enthusiastic joiner. Also a Mason, he affiliated with the Independent Order of Good Templars at the age of seventeen; he joined the Maccabees, the National Union, and the Royal Arcanum, among fraternal beneficiary lodges. His patriotic fervor was demonstrated by membership in the Order of the American Union, the Crescents, the American Patriotic League, and the American Protestant Association. His British origin revealed itself in his most comprehensive lodge membership, which was in the Loyal Orange Institution, where he reached high rank, with membership in the American Orange Knights, the Royal Black Knights of the Camp of Israel, and the Illustrious Order of the Knights of Malta. In 1890–91, Traynor was Deputy Grand Master of the Grand Orange Lodge of the United States, and Grand Master of the Michigan Grand Orange Lodges. He also served as vice-president of the triennial council of the world for the Loyal Orange Institution.[108] His entry into the A.P.A. was through his position as publisher of the *Patriotic American.* Traynor had been in attendance at the conference of patriotic societies in Chicago in 1891 and had been elected treasurer of that group then. Moreover, he had been the first

president of the Michigan superior council of the A.P.A. and was responsible for introducing the order to that state.

Without a doubt, Traynor was a promoter, and his election was partially the result of personal ambition, for his attachment to the A.P.A. gave him a status as a loyal citizen that his membership in the Orange lodges with their known British origins and sympathies could never do. His newspaper ventures had provided him with a facility in language, and his lodge work had prepared him for leadership. His personality was obviously suited to the work of salesmanship, and he had no family ties to any particular place. His contribution to the career of the A.P.A. was his attempted diversion of it from its negative anti-Catholicism, which found "victory" in defeating Catholics and their sympathizers for office, into a positive vehicle for electing men to office who would put its program into effect. In this he failed, although the order's name became a byword during his term of office.

Another member of the new administration was Charles Tupper Beatty, the new supreme secretary. A graduate of the University of Michigan in the class of 1872, Beatty taught school for twelve years after his graduation, meanwhile preparing himself for the bar. In 1884, he began to practice law at Saginaw, and held public office as assistant prosecuting attorney and as a member of the local school board. He succeeded Traynor as superior president of the Michigan council in 1892, a position which he continued to fill after his election to the supreme secretaryship. During his incumbency as secretary, Beatty conducted as a sideline business a land-development scheme in Florida, the "American Home Colonization Company," which was intended to provide "Florida homes for Patriotic American citizens." In order to give this venture an authentic tone, his mother lived in the community.[109] These two men, Traynor and Beatty, retained their offices until the annual convention of the order in 1896, so that they were the principal officers during the years of the order's greatest successes.

Thus, by the spring of 1893 the A.P.A. had become established as the most prominent of the "patriotic orders," and its initials were already being used to identify the whole program of anti-

Catholicism and nonsectarianism. Politically, the order was also becoming known as a factor to be considered by office seekers and party managers within the major parties, for the A.P.A. had learned early in its career that third-party movements were not likely to succeed. The order's publicists had learned the value of a plausible lie, and had also learned that figures indicating membership and "influence" had a way of meaning the same thing. Even the daily press had already demonstrated a tendency toward slipshod methods of reporting A.P.A. "successes" that gave greater importance to the order than it had earned. Most importantly, however, the A.P.A. had got hold of an issue on which it could capitalize—that of the termination of contract payments of government funds to church, now mostly Catholic, Indian mission schools. On this political issue, the order was in agreement with a broad public sentiment that had already manifested itself in the enactment of legislation on the state level. With these advantages, the order was to enjoy its period of greatest prestige and growth, from the spring of 1893, at the end of its annual convention for that year, until the elections of 1894.

4 National Success, 1893-94

In the interval between the annual convention of 1893 and preparations for the fall elections of 1894, the A.P.A. experienced its greatest organizational successes. Riding currents of popular opinion and capitalizing on passing events, the new leadership spread the order from coast to coast. Working arrangements with other patriotic societies were stabilized. Fortuitously, these developments occurred between the presidential election of 1892 and the state and congressional elections of 1894, so that only local political contests and issues subjected the order to the stress of controversy, and full attention could be given to promoting its success.

During this important interval the spread of the A.P.A. was marked by the appearance of many additions to the roster of the "patriotic press." In the national capital, the *United American* began publication in 1894; at Lansingburg, New York, the *Republic* appeared, and at Lowell, Massachusetts, the *Herald* opened. In the Rocky Mountain states, the Denver *Rocky Mountain American* maintained the fight alone until the Butte, Montana, *Examiner* appeared in the spring of 1895. On the Pacific Coast, Los Angeles had the *Tocsin* in 1894, and San Franciscans could read the *American Patriot* or the *California Standard*. In Spokane, the *American Pope* had a brief life, and Oregonians read the *Portlander* or found populism mixed with anti-Catholicism in the Eugene *Broad-Axe*. For a short time the *Justice* circulated in Louisville, Kentucky.[1]

As a stimulus to their circulation growth some of these organs conducted salacious campaigns against the Houses of the Good Shepherd. Often, lacking proper facilities for women lawbreakers in city and county jails, the courts sentenced them to terms

that were served in the custody of the Catholic sisters operating these refuges. Other inmates were occasionally children of broken homes in court custody. The A.P.A. press treated both categories as prisoners of Catholic conspirators outside the authority of the law and sought to bring them within the law by seeking legal means to provide for public inspection of the refuges. In the meantime, the houses were charged with being unfit places for the innocent, and lurid stories were repeated of priests' taking advantage of the female inmates to satisfy their allegedly unlimited carnal appetites. An "open the nunneries" campaign was the usual result, and the circulation of the newspaper increased.[2]

The World's Fair of 1893 also provided an opening for the patriots to gain publicity by joining advocates of immigration restriction. Restrictionists favored a temporary closing of the gates to allow Congress time to discuss the question, and they gave as a reason the supposed threat to the fair of cholera brought in by infected immigrants. This was the specific point on which the press recommended action, but Ella Wheeler Wilcox' poem, "To Columbia on Immigration," was approved as a good statement of the order's views on the subject. On this topic, too, the A.P.A. was in agreement with a growing sentiment among many groups to stem the tide of immigrants.[3]

In yet another way, the World's Fair provided an opportunity to attack "Romanism." Mayor Carter Harrison of Chicago was assassinated in the fall of 1893 during ceremonies at the fair opening. The *Patriotic American* pointed out that his assassin was a "Romanist" and gave its readers a quick review of other political murders each of which, the paper stated, had been perpetrated by a Catholic.[4] During the same months a discussion of Lincoln's assassination was taking place. The priest who had attended Mrs. Surratt stated his conclusion in 1891 that very few people any longer believed that she had known of the plot; a member of the commission that had heard the case replied to this statement by insisting that the evidence had shown the conspiracy to be a "Romanist plot." Thereupon, a Minneapolis publisher brought out a book using the commission

member's reply to prove that the Civil War would need to be fought once more, this time between the true patriots and the blind followers of the "Romanist conspiracy." [5]

Next, the forged papal encyclical that had predicted a Catholic uprising on the Feast of Ignatius Loyola, July 31, or on the date of the convening of the Catholic Congress at the World's Fair on September 5, 1893, was proved false when those two dates came and went with no rising and no evidence of an intent to undertake a massacre of Protestants by Catholics. But the circumstances of the forgery and its plausibility had created what appeared to be a genuine fear. For example, the governor of Nebraska received a letter that said:

> The people of this part of the State are greatly alarmed over rumors of an uprising soon to take place by the Roman Catholics, in which all protistants [sic] are to be slain. Many of our people are nearly frantic with fear and are doing all they can to prepare a defense.
>
> I have no knowledge of anything of the kind, but rumor has it that Catholics are constantly receiving consignments of arms and ammunition for the purpose named.

The letter writer asked the governor for advice, and—more practically—for arms to defend his neighborhood. The governor replied that he had no knowledge of such an uprising and did not believe there was any real occasion for fear. In another instance, Senator Davis of Minnesota received with a letter a clipping of the forged encyclical cut from the *Patriotic American*. His correspondent reported that arms were being shipped to priests in Kalamazoo and Battle Creek, Michigan, in boxes labeled "holy wine," and to a priest in Blair, Nebraska, in coffins. This letter clearly stated that unarmed Protestants would be at the mercy of the "insidious foe of our liberties" without arms for defense. The Reverend Washington Gladden reported that whole communities in Ohio were gripped with fear growing out of belief in the truth of the forged encyclical. When the appointed days passed without a massacre, the *Independent* sought to show how baseless the fears had been:

> The men who were unscrupulous enough to concoct that ridiculous Papal encyclical and then persist in standing by it and asserting its

genuineness, are quite capable of backing up the forgery by any amount of additional falsehood. And this they are doing. . . . All these stories are told as evidence that the Roman Catholics are preparing to inaugurate a rebellion and seize the Government. In one breath we are told that the Catholic ecclesiastics are the most astute of men; and then these stories are told as if to prove they are unconscionable fools. The invention of such tales is criminal and dastardly.[6]

Seventeen Protestant ministers and college professors of Columbus, Ohio, published a circular stating that the alleged encyclical was the product of imagination. To answer the supposed A.P.A. allegation that 95 per cent of the public employees in Columbus were Catholics, these men found upon investigation that of 349 teachers, 13 were Catholic; of 112 policemen, 45 were Catholic; and of 20 county officials, 3 were Catholic. One of the signers of the circular, the Reverend Alexander Milne, a Congregationalist, wrote a letter to the *Nation* to give nationwide publicity to the falsehoods and to ask for a Congressional investigation of the A.P.A. For the benefit of his neighbors in Columbus, Milne continued to denounce the order: "In the name of freedom it stabs freedom in the heart; in the name of Christianity it cultivates an un-Christian spirit; in short, it uses the weapons of the devil in the professed cause of Christ." Eloquent and pertinent as the circular or Mr. Milne's words were, the *Independent,* while it congratulated the authors for their stand, commented sagely that the "ignorant people who take the A.P.A. papers will never believe them." [7]

Within five months a news story broke that made the entire encyclical affair ridiculous. At Toledo, Ohio, in February of 1894 a court action was instituted in order to collect payment from an A.P.A. council for sixty Winchester rifles purchased to defend its membership against Catholics. The basis for the suit was a dispute about the number of rifles, between the dealer and the council's purchasing agent. On its investigation, the Toledo *Blade* found that the A.P.A. members believed that publication of the encyclical had prevented the uprising. Further investigation showed that the mayor of Toledo had been so convinced that

a massacre was threatened that he had called out the members of the Sixteenth Regiment of the Ohio National Guard. For his pains, the mayor was now called the "richest joke of the year"; the news story was carried by news services to the rest of the country.[8] The *Blade,* however had pointed out the manner in which an A.P.A. member could explain the absence of an uprising, and the publicity with its emphasis on the ridiculous apparently did not harm the growth of the order.

Coincidental with the events surrounding the forged encyclical, there had been a move on the floor of Congress to institute an investigation of the A.P.A. Congressman Weadock, a Democrat of Michigan, had presented a petition in behalf of former Congressman Youmans, defeated by William Linton in 1892, alleging that Linton's election was invalid. The petition was referred to the Committee on Elections after minor floor debate. Linton stated that he welcomed the investigation, but opposition to Weadock's petition was expressed by Congressman Albert J. Hopkins of Illinois, who argued that three months had elapsed since the session had begun, and that nearly a year had gone by since the disputed election. After so long a delay, he said, there was no justification for an investigation. Weadock replied that Linton's support had come from the "un-American, illegal, and treasonable" A.P.A., but the matter was quietly dropped.[9]

Former Indian Commissioner Thomas J. Morgan lent his name to the order and described his experiences with Catholics to A.P.A. councils; his firsthand story of the "despotism of Rome" was thus brought to the support of A.P.A. growth. As editor of the *Baptist Home Missionary Monthly,* Morgan discussed his Indian policy, argued the necessity of a "Renaissance of Patriotism," and discussed "Rome in Politics." His collected views on the "aggressions of Romanism" were published in 1894 by the American Citizens Library of Boston.[10]

Thus, with its own press creating sensationalism, its platform statement on immigration restriction coinciding with a widespread sentiment, and with the publicity attaching to its forgery, the A.P.A. boom was under way. As its growth through the coun-

try is surveyed, promotional activities on the part of its leadership and the ability to capitalize on local incidents can be seen to account for the spread of the organization.

On the East Coast, the order entered a region well prepared for its program. So many other patriotic societies were already in operation there that the A.P.A. was never clearly differentiated in newspaper accounts for the general public. This fact operated to benefit the A.P.A., since, no matter which specific group was actually intended, the label "A.P.A." came to be generally applied.

The first councils of the A.P.A. in New England were established in Massachusetts. A Boston school election in December of 1892 had been carried by a coalition of Republicans and anti-Catholics. The A.P.A. very shortly became the center about which the existing patriots clustered for political guidance. Here, apparently, a concentration of Orangemen were willing to accept leadership from one of their own—W. J. H. Traynor. By 1895, an estimated two hundred councils had been established in Massachusetts, with 75,000 members. The *New York Times* found that A.P.A. strength was strongest in the cities of Springfield, Boston, Worcester, Fitchburg, Cambridge, Brockton, Somerville, Chelsea, Haverhill, Lowell, Lawrence, and Northampton.[11]

One of the victims of A.P.A. wrath was Superintendent of Schools Albert P. Marble of Worcester. His trouble was the result of well-meaning but damning misstatements on the part of the Catholic press. Marble had been superintendent for twenty-five years, and had been recognized for his educational leadership by being elected president of the National Education Association in 1889. The Boston *Pilot* reported in error that Marble was a Catholic and a graduate of Holy Cross College; too late, the paper discovered and apologized for its error. As a result of the original misstatement, Marble became the target of the "brainless idiots" of the A.P.A.[12] Once again, coincidence played into the hands of the order. J. M. Rice's *The Public School System of the United States,* a general scholarly survey published in 1893, criticized the Marble administration of the Worcester schools as resulting in a "mechanical . . . cut and dried" curriculum. In

the campaign for a school election these two issues were mixed, and the result was the removal of the superintendent.[13] Marble was, thus, the victim of misinformation; but at the same time, he was the means by which the A.P.A. gained luster as the champion of more modern educational methods.

In New York State, the A.P.A. was given credit for the work and accomplishments of the National League for the Protection of American Institutions. Since its origin in 1889 the N.L.P.A.I. had maintained headquarters in New York City, where its strength was largely concentrated. It opposed all efforts to expend governmental funds in support of any sectarian charitable or educational institution and was making a determined stand against a "freedom of worship" bill in the state legislature of 1892. The bill would have permitted inmates in detention institutions to select pastors of their own choice, and was regarded by the league as a step toward public support of denominational chaplains. The proposal was supported by Catholics. In identifying the opponents of the measure, Catholics tended to use the initials A.P.A., and their mistake was compounded by the daily press.[14]

Actually, there was an A.P.A. state council operating within the state in 1894. Its president was A. G. Van Schaick of Lansingburg, the editor and publisher of the *Republic*.[15] It would appear likely that the A.P.A. operated most successfully on its own in upstate New York rather than in the city. At Rochester a school arrangement that predated the Minnesota Faribault plan but operated on the same principle provided a possible rallying point for anti-Catholic activity.

Pennsylvania, too, was vexed with school questions in 1894. Since that state was pre-empted by the Patriotic Order of the Sons of America and the Junior Order of United American Mechanics, growth of the A.P.A. there was somewhat unlikely. These two organizations were active; they took a test case to the state supreme court in 1894 that involved garbed nuns as teachers in the schools. The courts upheld the practice as not violating the law. In the following year, the legislature changed the law. Maryland and New Jersey were concerned with contro-

versies over the use of school funds in support of church schools, and each St. Patrick's Day brought fears of anti-Catholic riots.[16]

Although the A.P.A. was first organized in Washington, D.C., sometime in 1892, a friendly newspaper did not appear there until August of 1894. Then, the *United American,* with Andrew Jackson Boyer as editor, was established to "meet the demand for a journal in the capital to present the policies of the various patriotic orders." Its principles were announced to be those of the A.P.A., but it also endorsed the principles of the Patriotic Order of the Sons of America and the Junior Order of United American Mechanics. By the time the paper was established, seven councils of the A.P.A. were already operating within the District of Columbia, four in the northwest section, two in the northeast, and one in Georgetown. An advisory board to which each council elected delegates was in operation,[17] but the W.A.P.A. was not organized until February of 1895. Chairman of the advisory board, and hence leader for the District, was John G. Burchfield. Of North Irish descent, Burchfield had been born in Tennessee; he served in the Union Army from 1863 to 1865 and had lived in Illinois and Kansas. He had held a door-keeper's job in the Kansas state senate in 1889 and had come to Washington as a member of the Capitol police force under the patronage of Senator Preston Plumb of Kansas in 1890. Federal employees were thought to be likely adherents of the order, which appealed particularly to those in the Bureau of Engraving and Printing, since they felt that by joining they would gain protection against the nuns who stood each payday at the exit of the building to collect alms, supported by the assistant chief of the Bureau and a priest.[18]

On the whole, the success of the A.P.A. on the East Coast was not remarkable; more notable successes were attained in the West. From its Mississippi Valley origins, the order moved westward and became established in Denver as early as May of 1892. Allison Stocker, a charter member of the Denver Patriotic Order of the Sons of America unit, was elected president of the Colorado state council of the A.P.A. in August of 1893. A railroad employee, F. M. Beckwith, was the first state secretary.[19] It was

the Populist daily in Denver, the *Rocky Mountain News,* desiring to relieve Populists of a charge that the order worked with them, that took a leading part in publicizing the order. A priest, Father Malone, had been responsible for making the charge of Populist affiliation, apparently in the interest of the Democrats. Republican Mayor Marion Van Horne was said to have been a member of the A.P.A. when he was elected to office; in office, he had appointed a Catholic as police inspector, whereupon the A.P.A. council published a circular depicting the mayor as a "Jesuit" and a "traitor." The *News* was informed by a former A.P.A. member that the order was really Republican rather than Populist in its affiliation. According to this man, three groups of people joined the order: (1) a few "dead-in-earnest crazy fanatics," (2) some unprincipled office seekers, and (3) a very large number of dupes. In the county election that fall, the Republican candidate for sheriff was identified as an A.P.A. member and was elected. The *News,* meanwhile, had assured its readers, "No Populist can be an A.P.A.," and was commended for its statement by the *Coming Crisis,* the state Populist organ. After the fall election, a "Society of Liberty and Equality," with a membership limited to Protestants, was organized to combat the A.P.A. The Reverend Myron Reed, a popular Congregationalist minister, was one of the board of governors for this new group.[20]

Elsewhere in the Rocky Mountain states, Montana was a scene of activity. The origins here were obscure. Perhaps the impetus came from a visit of President Traynor on his way to the Pacific Coast in 1893. That year would appear to be the one in which the order was established within Montana. In any case, the turbulent city of Butte was the center of the organization when it came. Butte was an Irish-Democratic miners' town and was noted for the vehemence of its political squabbles. The A.P.A. soon made its contribution to the picturesque excesses of Butte.[21]

In preparation for the Fourth of July celebration in 1894, the proprietor of Hauswirth's Columbia Saloon included the letters A.P.A. in bunting as a part of his decoration.[22] Another saloon, the Sazerac, exhibited small national flags arranged so as to form

the same three letters. Butte's Independence Day celebration began early in the morning with the dynamiting of the plate glass windows at the Columbia. After a parade, in which the local Patriotic Order of the Sons of America exhibited a "little red schoolhouse" float as their entry and in which the A.P.A. had no entry at all, a considerable crowd gathered before the windowless saloon, since the bar was more accessible than usual. The mayor arrived and, finding that the initials in the bunting were the source of trouble, asked that they be removed; they were not. He called the fire department to dampen the crowd's enthusiasm with fire hoses. A general free-for-all ensued in which rocks, clubs, fists, revolvers, knives, and fire hose were wielded by the police, some militia, and the high-spirited miners. An Irish-Catholic policeman was killed, a miner was left dying, and two more men were seriously injured before the brawl terminated. All of Butte's saloons were closed for nearly a week while the town sobered.[23]

Butte's daily press deplored the disastrous result of injecting religion into public affairs and labeled the affair the "A.P.A. Riot," and the name stuck. Inaugurated with such fanfare, the career of the A.P.A. in Montana was off to a rousing start. Within six months a claim was made that there were eight thousand members within the state; J. C. Caldwell was state president, and J. J. Anderson of Butte was state secretary.[24]

Further west on the Pacific Coast, the growth of the A.P.A. was a consequence of a visit of the papal delegate, Satolli, who made a western trip in the summer of 1893.[25] In July he visited Spokane, Seattle, and Tacoma, on his way to Portland, Oregon, and San Francisco. His visits were the occasion for an outpouring of Catholics, and, perhaps for the first time, many westerners saw some evidences of Catholic strength in their communities. Satolli's chief greeter in Seattle, for example, claimed that one sixth of that city's population was Catholic. Almost as if to substantiate its critics' charges that his church was "foreign," Satolli answered his welcomers in Italian, which was then translated into English. A prominent Presbyterian clergyman

in Seattle devoted his following Sunday's sermon to a denunciation of Catholicism.[26]

President Traynor of the A.P.A. visited the Pacific Coast in the
fall and winter of 1893–94 on an organizing trip. The A.P.A. had
made its initial appearance on the Coast at Portland in July of
1893, before he arrived, but Traynor organized the first council
in San Francisco in September and then proceeded to Washington State and organized there in December and January.

From an original seven men who introduced the order into
Oregon, membership had increased to 3,100 within the city of
Portland by March of 1894. A goal of at least one council for
each town within the state by June was set with councils already
in existence at Salem, Oregon City, and Oswego in the Willamette
Valley, at The Dalles and Astoria on the Columbia River, and
at Pendleton and Baker City in eastern Oregon. The June goal
was not achieved, as councils at Corvallis and Medford were not
in existence until March of 1895. A state council came into operation early in 1894, with A. W. France of Oregon City as
president and H. G. Mathies of Portland as secretary. The *Portlander,* "official organ" of the Oregon A.P.A., began publication
under the editorship of J. T. Hayne and launched a campaign
against the local House of the Good Shepherd. Charges of criminal libel against the editor resulted, but they were not sustained.
The membership of the order heard lectures given by the Reverend J. B. Daly, an "ex-priest"and then a Methodist, who was
accompanied by his wife as he spoke on the lack of freedom
within Catholicism.[27]

Once again, opponents of the A.P.A. met to organize. In the
news columns of the Portland *Oregonian* it was reported that a
group met at Hibernian Hall, "mostly Roman Catholic," to organize an "American Defensive Association" against the "Orangeism and foreignism" of the A.P.A. The *Oregonian* cautioned its
readers to avoid discussing religion and politics, and said that
the "exposure" of the A.P.A. was a device being used to draw
crowds to hear particular religious dogmas explained. The editorial continued:

The American Protective Association is built on none of these wire-drawn theological abstractions. All of its motives are material; and all its objects are practical. Many elements enter into it, some mean, narrow, and selfish; others sincere, but mistaken. Many persons believe honestly that the growth of the Catholic Church in this country is fraught with danger to our national institutions. If this were true, no oath-bound secret society would be necessary to protect American institutions. Sharp and short measures would be taken to meet any palpable danger, through the usual agencies of public opinion and action. Indeed, such measures have been taken by the localities interested, whenever the school fund has been threatened by Catholic aggression.

This is the only case in which American institutions ever have been threatened by the Catholic Church. This danger is only local and is nowhere considerable. It can be met and defeated, whenever and wherever necessary, by ordinary agencies. The other legitimate objects sought by the American Protective Association—such as restriction of immigration and limitation of suffrage to persons completely naturalized—not only can be brought about without the interposition of any secret order, but are likely to be delayed and defeated by being entangled with the mean and unworthy object of religious proscription. What is apparently the main object of the order—to keep Catholics out of office—is too petty and proscriptive to be endured by the American sense of fair play.[28]

Despite this rather sane analysis, which demonstrated opposition from Oregon's leading daily newspaper, the A.P.A. continued to flourish in Oregon.

When President Traynor went to California in 1893, he arrived opportunely. California had as recently as 1888 and 1892 experienced a nativistic third party in state politics. That this party had originated with the Patriotic Order of the Sons of America was entirely probable. Following the arrival of President Traynor, a rapid succession of events stimulated growth for the A.P.A. Long-time jibes at Catholicism appearing in the columns of the *Argonaut* perhaps accounted for a reservoir of anti-Catholic feeling. San Francisco was also one of those cities which anti-Catholics regarded as under Catholic political rule. A protracted argument was currently under way over whether a statue should be erected to honor Sir Francis Drake in Golden Gate Park. A Catholic priest had written a letter to the local newspapers op-

posing the statue, describing Drake's role in the subjection of Ireland, and making a disparaging comparison between the qualities of Drake and Columbus as "Christian explorers." In February and March of 1894, Meyer's history text, *Outlines of Medieval and Modern History,* in use in the public schools, was attacked because of its treatment of the Reformation. The text was retained for school use, but individual teachers were to be permitted to omit at their discretion the objectionable passages. Next, two of the daily newspapers were drawn into conflict after the *Examiner* had made arrangements for school children to attend a fair as guests of the paper. A priest pointed out that the *Examiner* had deliberately ignored parochial school children, and the *Examiner* thereupon turned on M. H. DeYoung, manager of the fair and also owner of the rival *Chronicle,* for permitting the situation to develop. The newspaper melee was broadened when Father Peter C. Yorke was designated a member of the editorial staff of the *Monitor,* a recently established Catholic diocesan newspaper. Father Yorke was to prove a vituperative writer in his campaign to eliminate the A.P.A. from San Francisco.[29]

The first A.P.A. council in San Francisco, organized on September 12, 1893, was soon joined by additional councils. Within a year, the order claimed (probably extravagantly) there were seventeen thousand members in San Francisco with an additional fifteen hundred clamoring to join each month. At the other extreme, Father Yorke "corrected" the claim by estimating that between four and five thousand members in San Francisco, and a total of eighteen thousand in California, were more likely figures. Regular weekly meetings of the councils were reported in the daily press. The newspapers were said by Yorke to favor the order by thus giving it publicity, insisting that publicity attracted adherents. He maintained a constant and vitriolic attack on the A.P.A. for the next two years, arguing that there was no middle ground—one was either openly opposed to the order or was to be accounted in favor of it. A local Baptist preacher, the Reverend John Quincy Adams Henry, was a prominent enthusiast and lecturer for the order; former priest Slattery ap-

peared as a guest speaker in April of 1894, while the former Indian Commissioner, Morgan, also lectured in San Francisco. On the opposite side, prominent lay Catholics were organized into the "American Liberal League" to combat the A.P.A.[30]

J. B. Daly, the traveling former priest, appeared in San Diego for a lecture, and was accosted by a priest, who, resenting Daly's refusal to argue with what Daly called a "drunken man," thereupon administered a "handsome drubbing" to the lecturer. Five days in jail and a hundred-dollar fine for assault were levied on the priest.[31]

A California state council was set up, with the Reverend Benjamin F. Hudelson as president and M. T. Brewer as secretary. Two other men prominent in the southern California A.P.A. were J. J. Gosper, national chaplain in 1894–95, and Lionel A. Sheldon. Gosper had been secretary for the territory of Arizona at one time and attained newspaper notice in 1894 by charging that five hundred stands of arms were stored in the basement of the Catholic cathedral of Los Angeles. Sheldon, who would shortly become the political adviser for the California A.P.A., was one of the organizers of the "United Sons of America," which stood for patriotism, anti-Catholicism, and free silver. In Los Angeles, Sheldon was an attorney, but he had a political record that included a term from 1869 to 1875 as a carpetbag congressman from Louisiana, friendship with President Garfield, and an appointment as governor of New Mexico Territory from Garfield.[32]

After inaugurating the order in California, President Traynor visited the state of Washington, which was to prove a fertile field. Catholic growth within the state was reflected in the increasing number and enrollment of Catholic schools. Among Catholics in Tacoma there was a controversy between the Irish and the German groups over the use of German in the parochial schools and the practice of the priests' using German in their parish work.[33]

In January and February of 1894, Traynor busied himself organizing new councils. His work resulted in two councils in Tacoma, four in Seattle, and one each in Olympia, Everett, Port

Angeles, Forks, Fremont, Puyallup, and Orting. Six hundred members were said to have joined during a single month in Tacoma. Traynor also presided over the establishment of a state council in February at Seattle. George Washington Van Fossen of Tacoma was chosen state president, while Fred Taylor, also of Tacoma, became secretary. Regular weekly meetings of local councils were held on Sundays, without newspaper publicity; news of them was spread from one interested person to another by what one observer called the "telephone of the air." [34]

George Van Fossen had come to Tacoma in 1888 and had been a frequent candidate for minor public offices on the Democratic ticket. Born in Pennsylvania, he became a lawyer after trying the Methodist ministry. He was said to have been a prosecuting officer during the Molly Maguire trials in the mining regions of his native state. As he moved west, he resided for a time in Kansas City and then in Pueblo, Colorado. Van Fossen was a Mason and was, at the time of his entry into A.P.A. affairs, Washington state organizer for the Orange lodges; these associations probably account for his availability to Traynor.[35] Fred Taylor, the state secretary, was a former Republican city comptroller for Tacoma, had served in the Union army at the age of fourteen, and had come to Tacoma in 1876. He ran a logging camp at first, then established a soda works and started the first steam laundry in Tacoma.[36]

As elsewhere in the nation, Washington's daily newspapers did not sponsor the A.P.A. Editorially, the Tacoma *Daily Ledger* might be said to have treated the order softly, for it blamed the Catholic Church for having created its opposition, and implied that the criticism of the church would cease when it disclaimed a desire for a share of public school funds. The Seattle *Post-Intelligencer* was denounced as a "sheet of the papacy" for its opposition. Until its own weekly was established in January of 1895, the Seattle A.P.A. enjoyed some favor from the *Argus*, a strongly Republican weekly that was friendly only so long as the A.P.A. supported the Republican cause.[37]

Members had opportunities to listen to visiting lecturers like the Reverend John Q. A. Henry of San Francisco, dubbed

"Ananias" by his critics, who spoke in Tacoma on two occasions in 1894, the second time in the First Baptist Church. His lectures were the occasion for denunciations of the order by a Congregationalist, who called it "un-Christian and unconstitutional," and by an Episcopalian, who said that the practices denounced by the A.P.A. were aspects of medieval, rather than nineteenth-century, Catholicism.[38] In March of 1894, former priest George Rudolph of Ohio arrived in Spokane. On two separate evenings he spoke on "Romanism, the Foe of American Liberty," and "Why I Left the Roman Priesthood," charging admission to both meetings. The burden of his message was quoted as follows: "We will take all the religion the pope desires to send us, but we will take no politics from the old Dago over there." Rudolph then proceeded to Seattle and Tacoma. Spokane was also privileged to hear another "ex-priest" and his wife, a "former nun." This couple spoke to segregated audiences, Mrs. Slattery to women only, he to men only, on what they had seen while within the church. Their admission charges were higher than Rudolph's.[39]

The A.P.A. took a fairly active part in local political contests from the beginning. In Tacoma's municipal election of 1894, the order did not succeed in uniting itself behind any one of the candidates for mayor. For councilmen, however, their support was given to Republicans. With their men elected, officers of the order attended council meetings and opposed continuance by the city of a contract with the local Catholic and Episcopal hospitals for the care of indigent cases. The contract was terminated, and charity cases were thereafter sent to the city-county hospital, maintained primarily for contagious diseases, and where the death rate was reportedly three times as great as in the church-supported hospitals. In the words of the local daily newspaper, the result was not a "gratifying spectacle." [40]

The Seattle A.P.A. quite generally supported Republican municipal candidates against the incumbent Democrats, who were said to have hired "hundreds of foreign laborers" to dig city sewers while patriotic Americans applying for work were given the "cold shoulder." By large majorities, the Republicans were

elected to office.[41] Hospitals in Seattle were also a subject for discussion, though not a political issue as in Tacoma. The Catholic hospital was being cut off from public funds for charity cases with the construction of a new county hospital for the indigent sick. Even so, the hospital facilities of Seattle were such that members of the A.P.A. rejoiced in 1895 when a new general hospital was opened and they no longer were in the position of going to the Sisters of Providence for hospital care if the need arose.[42]

Since Washington State permitted women to vote in school elections, the W.A.P.A. took part in school board contests. In the fall of 1894, officials acceptable to the A.P.A. were chosen in both Seattle and Tacoma. Spokane, also, saw the "A.P.A. choices" run well ahead of their opponents, and the newly constituted school board of Spokane foreclosed a mortgage it held on a former public school used by the local Catholic parish.[43]

Thus, the A.P.A. was established in the West, with its success deriving from its ability to capitalize on local incidents and to pursue rather limited objectives. The region in which the A.P.A. found the least success was the South. Tennessee, Kentucky, and Texas were apparently the sites of considerable activity but of minor strength, and Georgia was another center. Some Protestant pastors in Memphis announced themselves as supporters of A.P.A. principles in 1894 and threatened to carry the issue into local elections in order to defeat "Catholic candidates." The new national president of the W.A.P.A., Mrs. Carrie Oostdyk, organized two councils of the women's group in Nashville, and then proceeded to set up a state council of women representing the eleven W.A.P.A. councils in Kentucky. The first and only general council of the A.P.A. in Louisiana was organized, probably at New Orleans, in August of 1894. Former priest Slattery appeared in Georgia in February of 1895 to be greeted at Savannah with threats of violence; he did speak and there were some explosions near the hall.[44]

During 1893 and 1894, while the A.P.A. was being inaugurated in the East, the West, and the South, the order prospered in those Middle Western states where it had begun, on occa-

sion testing its strength in political contests. Both the parent organization and the women's auxiliary were extended into Kansas. Mrs. J. W. Hile, wife of the editor of the Kansas City *American Eagle,* was the moving spirit for the W.A.P.A. Its rolls were open to all "worthy ladies," except Roman Catholics and those with Catholic husbands.[45] In August of 1893, the state council for the A.P.A. petitioned the Secretary of State for a twenty-five-year charter, giving as the purpose of the order the protection of "our country and its free institutions against the secret, intolerant and aggressive efforts that are persistently being set forth by a certain religio-political organization. . . ." The application was signed by F. H. Barker, the secretary of the state council, and four others. Reviewing the petition, the state's Attorney General recommended that it be denied because the A.P.A. established a religious test for public office. The Secretary of State then returned the application to the petitioners with the suggestion that, if they did not agree with the legal opinion, they could take the matter into the courts.[46] Since both the Secretary of State and the Attorney General were Populists, the A.P.A. was thereafter avowedly anti-Populist in Kansas, and its support was sought by a Republican candidate for governor, who also advocated women's suffrage in order to appeal to the W.A.P.A.[47]

Kansas City was also the headquarters of the Missouri state council in 1893, with the Reverend J. A. Dearborn as state president. In January of 1894, J. M. McNamara, "ex-priest of Rome," appeared in Kansas City to lecture. He armed himself with rifle and revolver for his platform appearance, but the only disturbance occurred outside the hall, where some two thousand people gathered and some stones were thrown.[48]

A serene existence characterized the councils of Iowa, the order's birthplace. At the state convention of 1894 in Keokuk, Osceola B. Jackman was the outgoing state president and Ellis Pierce was state secretary. Jackman's home was Boone and Pierce's residence was in Des Moines. "Oce" Jackman had been born in California in 1859; he was a lawyer, insurance man, Republican, and member of the Disciples of Christ Church.[49] In his

speech to the delegates, Jackman recommended that former priests be banned from speaking under the auspices of the order:

The average ex-priest is simply a leech, sucking the life-blood of the councils for his own enrichment. We claim in our principles that we attack no man's religion and make no warfare on the religious tenets of the Roman Catholic church, and yet we hear these ex-priests abuse all the peculiar observances of this church, and vilify and make fun of its observances. We thereby stultify ourselves and bring reproach upon the order and its principles.[50]

The convention proceeded to adopt a resolution suggesting a nationwide ban on former priests as a rule to be adopted at the next national convention. The action may be interpreted in either of two ways, both of them implicit in Jackman's speech. One was that the former priest encouraged the order to violate its stated principles, the other was that he was a "leech," who deprived the sponsoring council of its rightful revenues. Which of these considerations was the more important in the minds of the supporters of the resolution may be left to conjecture. Success in ridding the order of the leeches, however, depended on factors not within the legislative control of the A.P.A. proper, since any other of the patriotic orders could sponsor them, or the former priests could operate entirely on their own. As the A.P.A. was getting credit for every anti-Catholic activity, it would also very likely get the blame. The order was, consequently, saddled with the former priests, willing or not.

The convention next proceeded to choose Henry F. Bowers as state president for 1894.[51] Membership for Iowa in 1894 was placed at forty-three thousand, and there were reports that the Grand Army of the Republic posts of the state were aiding the work of the A.P.A. by providing it with meeting places.[52]

In Minnesota, the expansion of circulation for the weekly *Loyal American* was a measure of A.P.A. growth. Started in December of 1892, the paper at first competed with *The North,* a Scandinavian-American "patriotic weekly," until the two were combined, in January of 1894. Just before the consolidation, the *Loyal American* reported a weekly circulation of 17,750 for

postal purposes, but raised the figure to 50,000 for advertising purposes. Ole Byorum, an undertaker, was the advertising man for the weekly, and one of his consistent advertisers was Sears, Roebuck, and Company, on whose reliability, the paper said, "our readers may depend." [53]

Edwards Doyle, editor of the *Loyal American,* was the organizer for the Twin Cities area, and his first work was in Minneapolis. He advised those interested in the A.P.A. who were outside his reach to write to the state secretary, Thomas Clark of Duluth. By January of 1894, Doyle claimed twelve thousand A.P.A.-minded voters, but the order was not to be found listed among the "Fraternal Assemblies" in the Minneapolis *Tribune,* which showed a unit of the Patriotic Order of the Sons of America, a council of the Junior Order of United American Mechanics, and a Ladies' Orange lodge.[54]

Of the Twin Cities, St. Paul had much the larger Catholic population. "Exposing" the A.P.A. to this group was the objective of the St. Paul *Globe,* which, in November of 1893, published the entire ritual, oaths, and routine for joining the order. In addition, it provided its readers with a list of officers and members. Extra copies of this edition had to be printed to meet the demand, and the exposure resulted in a boycott of the businessmen listed as members as well as of the advertisers in the *Loyal American.*[55]

The investigation conducted by the *Globe* leading to this exposure, which it assured its readers produced authentic information, permitted it to state that the A.P.A. in Minnesota was the stepchild of Orangeism, and that "the English government has devoted some of its secret service fund to the organization of the A.P.A. councils and the dissemination of their peculiar doctrines, with the further intention of introducing its influence into American politics. . . ." Moreover, said the *Globe,* the A.P.A. had a special appeal to Scandinavians.[56] This series of statements was obviously intended to appeal to the anti-English sentiment among Irish-Catholics, and apparently intended also to appeal to the anti-Scandinavian opinion of non-Catholics; it was a demon-

stration of the uses to which nativism could be put in that it turned prejudice upon prejudice.

In January of 1894, shortly after the *Globe's* revelations, the first meeting of the Minnesota state council was held in Minneapolis. Ninety-seven councils within the state were represented there, and a total of fifty-two thousand members was claimed. The report was broken down to show twenty-nine councils in Minneapolis, seven in St. Paul, eight in Duluth, and nine others scattered through the northern part of the state, twenty-six in the southwestern section, and eighteen in the central region.[57]

During the spring campaign of 1894, the A.P.A. joined with other "reform" elements to elect a mayor of Minneapolis. The order's preference was noted on the advisory ballot with a letter "P," and an "R.C." was printed before the name of the man they opposed. When their man gained office, however, the membership was notified that a mistake had been made and that another contest to attain a "clean, moral business administration" would be necessary. In fact, the A.P.A. never did accomplish much in Minnesota, despite its claims and the fact that other patriotic societies were active there.[58]

Nativism, as distinguished from anti-Catholicism, affected A.P.A. propaganda in both Minnesota and Wisconsin. The *Loyal American and the North,* for example, disapproved of the qualification of native birth required for members of the Junior Order of United American Mechanics. At the same time, the weekly was not favorable to unrestricted immigration, holding that the test of Americanism was a desire for citizenship.[59] The reason for these distinctions was the necessity of appealing to the overwhelmingly Protestant Scandinavians in Minnesota and Wisconsin, as well as to the Protestant Germans in Wisconsin. Swedish Baptists of Minnesota, in convention, adopted a formal resolution denouncing "Romanism" as a threat to free institutions;[60] their action demonstrates that the A.P.A. did not inspire Scandinavians with a dislike for Catholicism. Moreover, Swedish Lutherans had never been as concerned about establishing their own parochial schools as were the German Lutherans; as a conse-

quence, Minnesota Swedes tended to oppose the Faribault arrangement as a threat to the public schools, which they supported. They did not find it necessary to make the same kind of alliance with Democrats as had the Wisconsin Germans, Lutherans and Catholics alike, against the Bennett Law.[61] The result was that in Minnesota the struggle for votes between Republicans and Democrats did not play as successfully on religious prejudice and nativism as it did in Wisconsin.

By 1893, the A.P.A. had councils in a dozen or more Wisconsin towns. Milwaukee had a minimum of three to five hundred members, and Janesville, Portage, LaCrosse, Kaukana, Oregon, Stevens Point, and Elroy were centers of activity.[62] Where there was an active Catholic weekly to deflate excess membership claims, the maximum set forth by the supporters of the order could be compared with the minimum granted by its enemies. In December, for example, the supporters claimed thirteen to fifteen thousand members in Milwaukee, while the *Catholic Citizen* conceded three thousand, organized into ten councils. The *Citizen* counted 282 persons in attendance at one of these council meetings, and warned its Catholic readers, "That's enough to control a caucus." Within two weeks, however, the Catholic weekly was forced to report thirteen councils in operation with strength increased to an estimated 4,215 members. By the fall of 1894, it had to admit that Milwaukee had twenty councils, and Oshkosh had four; Racine, LaCrosse, and Eau Claire each had two; and Fond du Lac, Sheboygan, Manitowoc, Marinette, Madison, Kenosha, Ashland, Janesville, Merrill, Wausau, West Superior, Appleton, Waupaca, and several other towns each had one.[63]

The Reverend David B. Cheney of Racine was chosen Wisconsin's state president at the convention held in Milwaukee in March of 1894. Franklin B. Hopkins, an attorney of Milwaukee, became vice-president, and George D. Fry, Jr., of Milwaukee, secretary.[64] Cheney had been born in San Francisco some thirty years before, was a graduate of the University of Chicago and the Divinity School at Morgan Park, and had held pastorates in Stillwater, LaCrosse, West Superior, and Racine. A year later at the

annual convention in Madison he was re-elected to office, and state headquarters were established in Madison. At that convention, E. C. True replaced Fry as secretary; True was also a college graduate and had taught school and been superintendent of schools for Columbia County, Wisconsin.[65]

Some violence occurred within the state. An A.P.A. lecturer was mobbed at Kaukana in January of 1894 and was provided with an escort for his protection on leaving town.[66] Former priest Slattery and his wife appeared in the autumn to lecture at La-Crosse. Mrs. Slattery announced that she represented the Loyal Women of American Liberty, Margaret Shepherd's group, while her husband admitted his A.P.A. membership. The local newspaper advised people to pay no attention to the couple, but they drew a full house.[67] The *Catholic Citizen* advised its readers to boycott A.P.A. businessmen as early as January of 1894, suggesting as a measure of affiliation that its readers be guided by advertisements in the *Citizen*. It also encouraged its readers to "organize watch parties and spot the sneaks." [68]

An approaching breach in the political alliance between Germans and Democrats was forecast when the Milwaukee *Lucifer-Arminia*, a German-language magazine, asked local Germans why they did not oppose the real enemies of freedom—the papal syllabus, Catholic prejudice, and violence such as had occurred at Kaukana.[69] But the alliance proved effective through another mayoralty campaign, with Milwaukee Democrats again utilizing the A.P.A. as a bogeyman to keep Lutherans in their league.[70] In Ashland, however, the alliance was actually broken by a surprisingly large outpouring of voters who chose Republicans. The victor at Ashland as mayor, C. M. McClintock, was to become state vice-president of the A.P.A. at the annual convention in 1895, in what might very well be regarded as recognition of his achievement.[71]

Political and personal ambitions within the order provided another forecast of future discord. Vice-president Hopkins apparently had plans for using the order for his political advancement and was also attempting to organize financial backing to establish another newspaper to compete with the *Wisconsin*

Patriot for readers; his efforts were not to be successful, but the attempt created distrust.[72]

Next door in the state of Illinois, the A.P.A. was arraigned by the Secretary of State for its anti-Catholicism and its detrimental effect on politics. The state president, J. H. Elward, and the state organizer, Leo Richardson, had brought state membership to a total of eighty-five thousand by May—or so they claimed. In June of 1894, state officers incorporated the order under the laws of Illinois; in the proceedings, Clarence P. Johnson of Springfield was listed as the new state president, and Will D. Newton was listed as secretary. Johnson had been secretary of the state Board of Livestock Commissioners from 1885 to 1893, was a newspaperman, and was affiliated with the Grand Lodge of the Knights of Pythias. Secretary Newton was in the real estate business, a member of the Improved Order of Red Men, and also a member of the Knights of Pythias.[73]

Chicago's municipal election for a successor to Mayor Carter Harrison provided the A.P.A. with an opportunity to support a Republican, George Swift. A campaign dodger printed with "George B. Swift, Protestant," and "John B. Hopkins, Romanist," was circulated in an appeal to anti-Catholic sentiment by Republican headquarters, but the results were not as hoped, since Swift was defeated. In Rockford, where the mayor was supposed to favor the A.P.A., the city council successfully opposed him in a patronage struggle over the office of fire marshal.[74]

For the remainder of the Middle West, routine organizational affairs were mixed with foreshadowings of trouble. The Indiana state council, for example, agreed with the Iowa convention in denouncing the use of former priests as lecturers. Indiana members faced the possibility of public exposure and boycotts, however, when they discovered that a council meeting place had been rifled of membership lists. A leader of an Indianapolis council was forced to resign as city street commissioner because his administration was "honeycombed with corruption"; this episode discredited the order.[75]

The Kalamazoo Catholic weekly expressed the hope that A.P.A. membership in Michigan was declining. Within the week,

however, the state council met at Grand Rapids with two to three hundred delegates in attendance and made a denial of disruptive internal dissension. Resolutions were passed asking for taxation of church property and the abolition of the practice of courts sentencing women to serve terms in custody of the Houses of the Good Shepherd. Before long, though, some members of the Detroit school board for whose election the order had been quite willing to accept credit were awaiting trial for bribery, and the order's members were warned that a "tree is judged by its fruit." [76]

Strictly routine matters concerned the Ohio councils. David T. Ramsey of Columbus was president during 1893, with David K. Watson as secretary. In January of 1894, C. O. Wildasin of Springfield became president, and he held the office for the next two years. R. N. Mercer of Cincinnati became the new secretary.[77] State organizer Thomas C. Ryan of Toledo had been secretary of the state Canal Commission in 1889 and was Inspector of Immigration at Toledo in 1893.[78]

The coming man in Ohio Republican political circles, Governor William McKinley, provided the A.P.A. with an opportunity to gain a superficial reputation as a political factor. Coming as it did in an "off year," 1893, the state election attracted national attention. McKinley had been first elected governor in 1891. Up for re-election in 1893, he recognized the fact that A.P.A. support usually went for the Republican candidate unless it was rejected outright.[79] When faced with the issue directly, McKinley temporized, permitting others to make the moves. In the early fall of 1893, he was called upon by an A.P.A. committee, which asked him to discharge two Catholic guards at the state penitentiary. The committee agreed to return a few days later for his reply. In the interim, McKinley asked for advice and got help. His adviser suggested that he tell the committee to "go to h——l." But McKinley, "a devoted Methodist," said he could not use such language but would defend the constitutional guarantee of religious liberty and retain the men until their performance on the job warranted a discharge. Soon Mark Hanna was informed of the interchange; without consulting McKinley, Hanna sent for a Catholic chaplain stationed at Fort Thomas, Kentucky,

who admired the governor. This priest quietly visited a large number of parishes within the state, telling his fellow clergymen what McKinley had said to the committee. Within a few days of the time the chaplain went into action, Catholic bishops in Cincinnati and Cleveland gave interviews commending McKinley for his wise administration of the public institutions of Ohio.[80]

During the campaign, both Lawrence Neal, the Democratic candidate, and McKinley were asked to state whether they were members of the A.P.A. Neal gave an unqualified "no" as his answer, as he could very well afford to do; McKinley refused to comment. The Columbus *Record,* spokesman for the A.P.A., listed the complete state and county tickets for both parties, showing lodge affiliations, church memberships, and previous political experience for each man on the ticket, plus the church and lodge ties of each candidate's wife and parents. It advised that the "safe course is to vote for Protestants only," and it promised to advise particularly in its next issue on the governorship. In the next issue, the paper identified as A.P.A. members the Republican candidates for county auditor and sheriff, but made no mention of its promise to advise on the governorship.[81]

From outside the state, there was also advice of the kind that aided the confusion; the New York *Irish World,* on the one hand, recommended McKinley, "whose name is insolubly wedded to the protective tariff," apparently because a high tariff would be anti-British in its effect. On the other hand, the Minneapolis *Loyal American* commented favorably on McKinley's capacity and qualifications.[82]

The poll provided Republicans with a general victory, and the Columbus *Record* utilized the usual criterion for measuring political success—since there were no Catholics on the Republican ticket, a Republican victory was an A.P.A. success.[83]

Even though his own emphasis during the campaign had been on "Democratic hard times," McKinley's temporizing had paid off, for he unquestionably received A.P.A. support; Democrats charged that he could not have been elected without it and that he had set the fashion for other Republicans.[84] Undoubtedly, McKinley and his close advisers had learned a lesson that could

be used in the future; but the lesson was not as simple as the Democrats alleged, for McKinley had also been able to gain Catholic support. How to juggle both Catholic and anti-Catholic sentiment, and to retain both groups, was the real lesson learned by McKinley's practical advisers.

The Ohio legislature elected along with McKinley offered nothing in the way of accomplishment that could be construed as an anti-Catholic victory. It considered three bills that could be viewed as acceptable to the A.P.A. One called for an amendment to the compulsory education law of 1893, "to compel the elementary education of children." It passed the lower house by a vote of 57 to 0, but died in committee in the upper chamber. A second bill would have required foreign-born persons to be naturalized six months before voting; the bill was amended to shorten the time to sixty days, and was defeated in this form by a vote of 29 to 44. The last of the three, a bill to exempt works of theology from the provisions of the state law on obscenity, died in committee.[85]

Another indication that the Ohio A.P.A. had been pushed to its limit appeared when financial difficulties beset the mouthpiece of the order in March of 1894. The Columbus *Record* had to announce that its editor had skipped town. This weekly had existed before the career of the A.P.A. and had been taken into the van by its now absent editor. The owners thus had dumped in their laps a paper with an anti-Catholic policy, a Catholic boycott of its advertisers, and a debt of some twenty-two thousand dollars. Without its friendly columns, the A.P.A. would lose an important publicity agent. Former state president Ramsey attempted to raise money to make continued publication possible for the owners, but he was unsuccessful. The owners then attempted to soften the anti-Catholic tone of the *Record* and to maintain an increasingly critical attitude toward the A.P.A. in hopes of attracting readers, but they were not successful and the paper did not last out the year of 1894.[86]

Thus, when the national convention of 1894 was held in May at Des Moines, Iowa, it appeared to represent a highly successful organization at the very crest of its career. The welcome in Des

Moines for its delegates, however, was not as warm as the success of their cause must have seemed to warrant. The *Iowa State Register* greeted the convention with a frank statement that it could not endorse the fundamental principles and methods of the order because they applied a religious test for officeholding.[87] Secretary Beatty reassured the members of their success, however, by telling them that over a thousand new councils had been formed since their previous annual convention. He claimed that Michigan had 65,000 members, Ohio had 93,000, Illinois, 60,000, Iowa, 45,000, New York, 50,000, Wisconsin, 15,000, and California, 12,000, in very round numbers. The Iowa and Indiana resolutions favoring prohibition of the former priests and nuns became the will of the national body by formal resolution, while the delegates accepted the statement to them that Coxey's Army was a Vatican-inspired attempt to disrupt American life.

Every resolution brought before the convention on topics such as the money question, labor, suffrage, or temperance was tabled so that the delegates could concentrate the fire of the A.P.A. on what it regarded as the vital issues of the day. Taxation of church property, the public schools, restrictions of immigration to exclude paupers, public inspection of sectarian charitable institutions, and continued opposition to "ecclesiasticism" with its fingers itching for the public purse were to be the goals of the society.[88] Thus, the negative single-minded anti-Catholicism that had been the mainstay of the A.P.A.'s career so far was somewhat muted as the order endorsed formally the more positive and generalized goals of the various patriotic groups. Whether the reputation of the order could be altered so easily was another question.

President Traynor and Secretary Beatty were re-elected. Selections to the other national offices reflected the Midwestern strength of the order, but the appearance as officials of men from both seacoasts showed that these regions were also being recognized.[89] One of the new officers, Francis Campbell, was to be chosen to serve in other national positions in succeeding years; at the time of his choice as trustee in 1894, he was Master of the Grand Orange Lodge of the United States and would be re-elected

to that position shortly. The Reverends Justin B. Fulton of Boston, Oliver E. Murray of Chicago, and George P. Rudolph of Ohio were designated "patriotic lecturers." [90] Since both Fulton and Murray had begun their anti-Catholic careers as leaders of local groups, their choice showed—along with that of the Orangeman Campbell—how the A.P.A. was absorbing other "patriotic" societies. The choice of Rudolph, a former priest turned Protestant, demonstrated how seriously the delegates took the resolution on the use of former priests.

At the same time, the W.A.P.A. was in session, and it also chose its national officers. Mrs. Carrie Oostdyk of Detroit replaced Mrs. Reynolds as president, and Mrs. Belle Kempster of Saginaw continued as secretary.[91]

In its relationship with the other patriotic societies, the A.P.A. had now attained the dominating position. When the conference of American patriotic orders had met in Chicago in October of 1893, the organizations represented there were only ten in number, while two years before there had been fifty-nine.[92] This process of concentration into the A.P.A. continued so that, in December of 1895, only ten delegates participated in the conference of that year and five of the ten were from the A.P.A.[93] Yet the founding of new patriotic societies was still going on. At Boston, Augustus Bedford announced the formation of the "American Flag Protectors" to secure laws preventing the use of the national emblem for advertising purposes, and to prevent flags of other nations from being flown. The president of this new group, moreover, was the same E. H. Dunbar who had been chosen sergeant-at-arms for the A.P.A. only five months before.[94]

The alliance among the patriotic orders was an informal one, recognized in part by the sharing of officials and amounting to a recognition of the A.P.A. as the superior tactician among them. In the minds of many, both within and without the order, these patriotic societies were all part of the same "movement," a fact that had been recognized by the cooperation in the annual conference of patriotic societies. But the A.P.A. had taken over the functions of that conference by 1894–95 and had become the dominating influence of the entire anti-Catholic movement, with

its accompanying nativistic overtones. The idea of unity was well expressed by the chaplain of the order in 1896:

> The American Protective Association is an aggregation and federation of various patriotic orders of the country, under a new name and strengthened by the addition of thousands who do not belong to any organization, whose aim and objects are to save America for Americans, native-born and naturalized, by educational and moral agencies, and who accord the freedom of religious belief to all, and that fly the Stars and Stripes, and to one Government, the Government of the United States.[95]

The A.P.A. created problems of identification for its critics, because it was both an individual organization—with a secret ritual, dues-paying members, and regular meetings—and what appeared to be a "federation" of groups apparently held together by the positive force of patriotism. Actually, the binding cement was the negative factor of anti-Catholicism. Politicians were disturbed by its appearance in their calculations simply because they could not immediately determine its political influence or its numerical size.

In their campaigns of opposition to the A.P.A. and kindred groups, Catholic publicists contributed a share to the false identification of the order. Thus, the "A.P.A. conspirators" were described as a "hybrid conglomeration of British and other foreign subjects, disgruntled party-whips, apostates from all denominations, Ingersollites, Chiniquites, Fultonites, Cookeites, anarchists among the orders of labor . . . ," all of whom were led by John Jay, Edwin Mead, and Justin D. Fulton.[96] In the same Catholic publication that brought this jumble together there appeared a further statement that the National League for the Protection of American Institutions was "too close to the Congregationalists," while it was at the same time backed by its masked auxiliary, the A.P.A.[97] The Catholic George Parsons Lathrop, in the *North American Review,* confused the issue further by placing the Order of American Mechanics, the League for the Protection of American Institutions, and the Evangelical Alliance in the same category as the A.P.A. The Episcopal Bishop of Albany joined Lathrop in his condemnation of the A.P.A., but he tried to sort

out the correct identities by writing that the League was a separate and distinct organization and that he knew it was because he was a member of it.[98] Despite the corrections and criticisms that intervened between the original publication of the article in the *Catholic World* and its later appearance as a pamphlet, the listing of the "A.P.A. conspirators" was unchanged when it appeared in the latter form.[99]

The carelessness with which these identifications were made, and the inclusiveness of them that, in effect, made the A.P.A. the spokesman for Protestantism, secularism, rationalism—in fact, non-Catholicism—irritated the editors of the Protestant weekly *Independent* into making a corrective statement: "We have criticized the falsehoods and forged documents published by the A.P.A. against Catholicism. We have one here on the other side which deserves similar criticism. A pamphlet comes to us entitled 'An Inquiry into the Objects and Purposes of the So-Called "American Protective Association."' [These statements are] entirely false." The particular part of the pamphlet that was false was that which listed the national officers and headquarters of the A.P.A. The facts given in the pamphlet were actually the names of officials and offices of the National League for the Protection of American Institutions.[100] This factual error occurred at a time when the correct information was appearing in the daily newspapers. The A.P.A. could hardly be expected to object to being granted such widespread influence by its enemies. But even more distressing than false identification at a time when clarification would have helped was the appearance of a letter in the *North American Review* from a prominent Catholic layman, in which he said the only controversy between Catholics and their opponents concerned the public school fund, and that this matter was simply one to be determined by a majority of the votes. This, of course, was no less than the language of the A.P.A. in reverse.[101]

In an editorial addressed to the Protestant clergy, the *Catholic Citizen* of Milwaukee asked them to define their positions on the A.P.A., which, the *Citizen* said, was sometimes the "American Protective Association" and sometimes the "American Protestant

Association." [102] Muffing this chance at clarification, the *Citizen* then attempted to formulate "Our Platform," or the Catholic position, on the issues:

1. Separation of church and state.
2. Maintenance of a free, unsectarian public school system.
3. The interpretation against sectarianism to be as was construed by the Supreme Court of Wisconsin in the Edgerton Bible Case.
4. The largest liberty of private enterprise in education conformable with existing laws.
5. No state support of private or parochial schools. No state supervision or control of private or parochial schools.
6. No religious lines in politics.
7. No religious prejudice in business.
8. No secret political societies.
9. No religious test in politics.
10. Prohibition by law of all secret political societies prescribing by oath or otherwise a religious test in politics.
11. Indictment and punishment of the members of such societies for criminal conspiracy.[103]

Under the circumstances as they existed in the years 1893 and 1894, such a program was not the end of controversy, or even its clarification; it was the beginning, simply because there was no general agreement as to the meaning of the words contained in it.

The *Citizen* then published letters from various public officials and prominent men expressing their views on the A.P.A. Governor Peck of Wisconsin felt the order could not succeed; Senator Vilas said that it was not the "peculiar duty" of the *Citizen* to deal with the A.P.A., but that the citizens of Wisconsin would take care of it; Governor Altgeld of Illinois, with characteristic bluntness, stated that Protestants were too intelligent for the order to be broadly diffused among them, but he felt that Catholics were partly responsible for the existence of the order since certain well-known priests flouted American sensitivity on the school question. The mayors of Eau Claire, Fond du Lac, Appleton, Beaver Dam, Hudson, and Prairie du Chien joined in condemning the order.[104] Since nearly all the men quoted were Wisconsin political figures, and since they were Democrats, the comments

could be considered local rather than national, and partisan rather than dispassionate.

A writer in the *Forum* provided, at this point, a brief accurate history of the founding of the A.P.A. and a summary of its platform. He stated that the general non-Catholic population was not out of sympathy with the broad aims of the organization. On the question of the public schools, the author said that Illinois, Wisconsin, and Minnesota had each presented violations of the well-established tradition, and maintained that Catholics were in no better position to argue the issues than were non-Catholics, since the Catholic position on schools was not as clear as it should be. On the matter of prejudice, the writer asked for tolerance:

Consider whether in truth there be not something of fault on the Catholic side of this controversy as they ask others to recognize that their prejudices against Catholicism have tinged their conclusions, as it may be with the writer. If they can control the intolerant within their own communion, they can reckon on support from many without it who on points of doctrine have little in common with them. And in joint action against extremists lies the only possibility of peace.[105]

Divided as it was, the Catholic community seemed unable to find an authoritative spokesman. Dr. Edward McGlynn submerged his recent antagonism with the hierarchy so that he could apply his reputation to the defense of his church. He asked the question, "Does the Pope know it all? Not at all! I had the cheek to try and teach him a thing or two myself." [106] Archbishop Ireland chose to ignore the existence of the A.P.A. and to speak in generalities, saying that the "safety of the Republic lies in the vigilant and active patriotism of the American people. There is danger in the ignorance of the voters." He repeated his support of compulsory school attendance laws.[107] At a time, thus, when anti-Catholics were emphasizing in their propaganda the monolithic quality of the Catholic Church, there was no concerted counterattack from it or its people.

In general, the attitude of the A.P.A. itself toward criticism

was that "any news is good news." On this basis, the patriotic press welcomed any publicity. A congressional investigation such as that proposed by the Michigan congressman and endorsed by the Reverend Mr. Milne was approved because the publicity would serve to make the principles of the order known.[108] Flourishing, and quite willing to be the subject of controversy, the A.P.A. faced its critics; the variety of criticism and the sources from which it came demonstrated that effective opposition at this time came from non-Catholics, rather than from Catholics.

Among non-Catholics, criticism was active and widespread. Ignatius Donnelly met an A.P.A. lecturer, Walter Sims, at Minneapolis in April of 1894 in a public debate. Their exchange was marked by uniform courtesy on both sides and by an absence of disturbances in the audience. The newspaper account reported that Sims had more of "the dry bones of the argument; and Donnelly more of the oratorical flesh and blood of wit and eloquence." Sims presented stock anti-Catholic arguments; Donnelly presented ridicule.[109] Since Donnelly was a "member of no church but a respecter of all," his views could be regarded as more or less impartial on religious questions; he was not, however, to be regarded as a political unknown.

Robert Ingersoll, professed agnostic, whose followers were said by Catholics to be among the "A.P.A. conspirators," doubted papal infallibility but could see no need of secret political societies; he said, "I think it is better to fight in the open field." His belief in religious liberty, free speech, and a free press, and his patriotism made him believe that the Catholic Church would grow weaker as mankind became more enlightened. "The free secular school is the enemy of priestcraft and superstition," he said, in what he considered a favorable comment on the public schools, but he also believed that Catholics in general placed their loyalty to country above their allegiance to their church.[110]

At Plymouth Church in Brooklyn, the Reverend Lyman Abbott, who supported the abolition of sectarian appropriations, read the A.P.A. oath to his congregation and analyzed it. He stated that its indictments were true of some Catholics, but he

maintained that the church should not be held responsible for the acts of its members. Abbott was also a speaker at the golden jubilee services for Father Sylvester Malone, Father McGlynn's friend and supporter. Speaking on "Civil and Religious Liberty," the Rabbi Joseph Silverman roundly condemned the A.P.A. to his Jewish congregation.[111]

The ease with which the apparently definite opinions of any prominent person could be utilized to serve the purposes of one side or the other was demonstrated in the case of Theodore Roosevelt. Roosevelt welcomed the immigrant to become an American, saying there were certain ideas that the immigrant must give up and certain concepts, such as the complete separation of church and state, which he must accept. "Know-Nothingism, in any form, is as utterly un-American as foreignism. It is a base outrage to oppose any man because of his religion or birthplace, and all good citizens will hold any such effort in abhorrence." These remarks, appearing in a popular magazine at the height of the A.P.A. movement, were applauded by Catholics, while the statement, "We have no use for the German or Italian who remains such," in the article was singled out and italicized so as to emphasize the "who remains such" and applauded by the "patriots." [112]

In general, organized labor groups were unequivocal in condemnation. The Typographical Union of Milwaukee resolved that no member of the A.P.A. could be a member of their union, while in the official organ of the Federated Trades Council of Milwaukee was expressed the hope that the union ranks contained no A.P.A. members. The Boston Central Labor Union denounced the order as unworthy of the support of labor. Since it saw a tendency for the A.P.A. to divide labor along religious lines, the Boston union preferred not to associate itself with any group that did have A.P.A. membership. The Missouri State Federation of Labor condemned the order in 1894, and the national convention of the American Federation of Labor in the same year was told that the greatest need of the day was the abolition of the order.[113]

Organized labor's opposition may have stemmed from its belief

that employers cultivated religious strife among their employees as a means of keeping them divided. This charge was made by Eugene Debs during the Pullman strike of 1894, when he stated that the A.P.A. was sponsored by railroad owners and iron manufacturers. An A.P.A. newspaper replied that the charge was "palpably false," and countered it by stating that labor leaders were "Romanists and tools of the Jesuits." Members of the order were assertedly not eligible for membership in the American Railway Union led by Debs, who was described as being so strongly opposed to the order that his "principles become Romanist." According to the *Wisconsin Patriot,* the Pullman strike had been sponsored by priests, working through foremen who, in turn, were the natural enemy of the laborer. President Traynor, who had another version of the relationship, felt compelled to send out an open address to the order in September of 1894 in which he replied to the charge he said the daily newspapers were making that the Pullman strikers were getting A.P.A. support: "While maintaining your own legal rights, perpetuate our time honored name as most loyal of citizens by scrupulously respecting all property and rights of others during present trouble for which Congress is criminally responsible." Moreover, he continued, when labor's demands were "honorable and American," it might expect to receive the support of the A.P.A.[114]

On Labor Day, September 10, 1894, the *United American* of Washington, D.C., reported the capital's labor parade as follows:

The workingmen of Washington celebrated Labor Day for the first time on Monday the third instant. There was an imposing parade in which all the trades of the city were represented, the number of men in line being estimated at 7,000. Among the most conspicuous leaders were [and here followed a list of Irish names]. These names are very suggestive. They sound strangely like the names of city officials of New York, Boston, Chicago, and San Francisco, and indicate that in the trade unions, as in the municipalities of the country, the Protestant elements have been reduced to the ranks by the more aggressive Irish Papists, who never forget Pope Leo's injunction to make themselves felt as active elements in the daily political life of the communities in which they live. . . .

Thus, the charge that the A.P.A. tended to split labor's ranks was borne out by its own press, although the charge that employers encouraged it to do so cannot be substantiated.

The public importance the order had achieved was demonstrated by the number of magazine articles about it appearing during the course of the year 1894. Both Secretary Charles Beatty and President Traynor made their appearances as authors. Beatty wrote an explanatory article for the *Independent* that was not notable. Traynor appeared in the pages of the *North American Review* with an exposition of the "Aims and Methods of the A.P.A.," which amounted to little more than a repetition of the usual propaganda—the temporal rather than the spiritual purposes of the papacy, the "godless" public schools, arms in Catholic churches, and so on. Similar charges appeared in an article in the *American Journal of Politics* that implied that pope-directed priests controlled politics in large cities.[115]

Traynor's article was surveyed and found wanting by the *Independent*, which said that attention to a dictionary along with his study of Catholic literature would straighten out Traynor's misconceptions, because he was applying his own meanings to church documents. George Parsons Lathrop answered Traynor in the *North American Review*, praising the loyalty of Catholic citizens. From the sidelines, the *Outlook* commented that "assault provokes counterassault" and predicted that the A.P.A. would never gain as much influence as had the Know-Nothings.[116]

Washington Gladden's ideas, first expressed in his sermons in Columbus, were gathered together and presented to the nation in an article in the *Century*. He called for the Protestant clergy to speak out against the A.P.A., because it was so ill-timed in that it came at a time when Catholics were being enlightened.[117] Elbert Hubbard analyzed "A New Disease," paranoia, as one of the penalties of civilization and progress. Fear of someone's plotting against us and ours, coupled with suffering and want because of the current economic depression, had resulted in a campaign of falsehood, he wrote. "The A.P.A.," he continued, "seeks to spread hate, it thrives by fear, and its only weapon is

untruth," and he further charged that there was financial and political advantage to be gained by so utilizing fear. He believed that the only conqueror of these fears was the "light of reason" sending forth "gleams of glorious truth through all religions," including the Catholic.[118]

Even before Gladden's article was published, the editor of the *Forum,* who did not believe it had "much importance as a corrective," was looking for someone to write another article that would show that the order "claims to have done more . . . than it can be proved that it has done." Senator William Vilas was asked to supply the need from his own experience, but he did not have the time to compose an article. Frederic R. Coudert, a New York lawyer, apparently did have the time and his "corrective" appeared. In passing, Coudert admitted as true the charge of Irish participation in the Democratic party. The only practical method for the A.P.A. to carry out its program, he said, was in job discrimination against individual Catholics, and political discrimination against Catholics in general.[119] Even though Coudert was correct in his analysis, his article had not fulfilled the need expressed by the editor when he originally wrote to Vilas.

Still another writer found it incredible that a society founded on prejudice should appear in strength during the advanced nineteenth century, but there it was for all to see. Its chief promoters, he said, were Orangemen, its members were foreign-born, and it was working within the Republican party. "The course to pursue, therefore," he concluded, "is to hold the Republican party responsible for its existence, and to punish it accordingly." [120]

A "liberal" Catholic, Bishop John Lancaster Spalding of Peoria, writing in the *North American Review,* felt disposed to find men evil because of their acts, not because of their ideas. He would hold the A.P.A. responsible for what it had done, and he thought that correct information about the church would be the Catholics' best aid in downing their detractors. He admitted that there was jealousy of the rapid growth of Catholicism in America and that within the church itself there were divisions that helped produce external criticism; he suggested that the arrival of the

Apostolic Delegate was a mistake in church affairs and a mistake in timing, but he said that these facts did not justify the kind of attack the A.P.A. was making. He hoped that hatred would pass, but he did not expect Catholics to be patient under attack.[121]

Querulousness and martyrdom, not patience, were the reaction of a writer in the *Catholic World*. The Catholic Church was the "surest bulwark of American principle," he wrote, because it was so opposed to the supremacy of the state:

> The struggle must come sooner or later. The Catholic Church cannot expect to find in America the rest denied her, wholly or in part, in every country under the sun. But many would tell us that our apprehensions are groundless. It is said that the better class of Protestants will frown down the roughs that lurk in such societies as the A.P.A. Maybe! But so far have they done this? If as a body they disapprove of such associations, why will they not denounce them before the world?

To his way of thinking, the Catholic Church had a history of thriving under persecution, and this antagonism to it, like all the previous ones, was the "mark of the church's divinity." [122]

One of the coincidental, but minor, results of the interest in the subject of anti-Catholicism was the attention given by scholars to earlier manifestations of it in American history. John Bach McMaster, the historian, reviewed briefly the history of the Know-Nothing movement, comparing it with the A.P.A.; of the latter, he said, "Never was the name 'American' more misapplied." [123] Another writer, comparing the old Know-Nothingism with the new, found that both were conceived in "jealousy of the church's progress." [124]

As the year 1894 drew to a close, the Protestant *Independent* announced that the "American Protective Association is dead; killed by the patriot hand of reputable Protestantism." Men like Washington Gladden and periodicals like the *Independent* deserved the credit for this accomplishment, the magazine claimed on January 3, 1895. This announcement of death was premature, for the A.P.A. still had life in it. It is true that the "movement" the A.P.A. represented, the federation of "patriotic" or anti-Catholic societies, was too loose to withstand external or internal

pressures. But these pressures had not yet been applied and the façade stood to all appearances before a stable structure.

Against this background of fact, misinformation, misinterpretation, appearance, and the many attempts on all sides to gain religious or political advantage, the materials from which the A.P.A. would attempt to multiply political capital in the congressional and state elections of 1894 were gotten together. Two separate, but similar, legislative instances furnished the materials; one was in New York State and the other was in the United States Congress. In neither case was the A.P.A. responsible for creating the situation, and in neither was it the sole sponsor of the legislation that came to be identified with it.

New York held a constitutional convention from May to September of 1894 to revise its constitution. An amendment similar to that proposed as the Sixteenth Amendment to the federal Constitution forbidding the use of public money for sectarian purposes was introduced. The measure, which was to be accepted in a slightly altered form, was properly identified as a proposal submitted by the National League for the Protection of American Institutions.[125] During the convention, the first mention of the A.P.A. came at a time when a memorial to Congress suggesting complete citizenship before suffrage was being discussed. This memorial had some opposition, not on its merits, but because it was part of the A.P.A. platform; nevertheless, it was approved by a vote of 64 to 48.[126]

Other controversies developed over two proposals: Section XI of Article VII, creating a state Board of Charities with general supervisory authority over all charitable institutions, incorporated and otherwise, private or public;[127] and Section IV of Article IX, forbidding the use of public funds in support, except for inspection purposes, of any school under the control or direction of any religious denomination.[128] Among the many petitions from groups throughout the state in support of the second of these proposals, none was from an A.P.A. council.[129] Even before the convention adjourned, the men who submitted these proposals were being attacked for "injecting sectarianism" into politics.

Elihu Root and Joseph H. Choate were two of the men so attacked. When the convention adjourned with these two sections included as part of the constitution to be submitted to the voters, the *New York Times* stated that the convention had ended its "driveling existence," and sneered at its "beautiful piece of work." [130]

In addition to being supported by the N.L.P.A.I., the two sections were approved and desired, particularly the clause on charities, by leaders in public welfare work. To Catholics, public institutions under the control of the state were just as Protestant in character as were those operated by individual Protestant denominations. The contest was obviously one between two differing conceptions of the role of government in welfare work.[131]

Even before the convention adjourned, the Catholic position was being presented. Because charitable institutions under private management were sometimes controlled by no single denomination, they could claim to be "nonsectarian," while Catholic charities would be the only ones seriously affected, said one writer. In another's presentation, the differing concepts of charity were discussed; to the Catholic, poor relief was a creation of Catholic charity; to put it under the supervision of the state was to degrade the recipients of aid. The proposed amendment was described as the work of "agnostics," while the supposed kinship between anarchism and agnosticism was utilized to attack the amendments as "subversive." [132] These arguments did not make the mistake of giving credit for the constitutional amendments to the A.P.A.; a connection between the proposals and the order had been utilized during the convention itself, however, and it was this kind of argument that was to be used during the political campaign of 1894 when the proposals were submitted to the voters.

The groundwork for the other campaign issue to be utilized by the A.P.A. during the elections of 1894 was laid by Congressman William S. Linton during his first term in Congress.[133] In June of 1894, Linton rose to speak during debate on appropriations for Indian school services. He said:

Mr. Chairman, it is high time to call a halt in the expenditure of the nation's money either directly or indirectly toward support of any sectarian school, or to enrich the coffers of any religious society at the expense of many others, and we should here and now, by striking out portions of the pending bill and placing safeguards around the remainder, discontinue such perilous and unconstitutional appropriations.

He called the attention of Congress to the fact that one church had received over two million dollars, while all others had received less than half that amount from the government. In making his remarks, he did not wish to be thought to intend an "attack" on any particular religious denomination. He argued that Indians should be educated so as to be self-supporting, but he pointed to the fact that "for more than a century the Mission Indians have been under Jesuit control, education, and influence, and today are as incapable of self-support as citizens of our country as babes." He then reviewed the history of the general movement toward cutting off the contract school system, relating that the various Protestant church conventions had voluntarily decided not to continue their contractual obligations for Indian schools. He ended by pleading that the Congress make plans to replace the contract school system with one modeled after the public school system.

The next day, Democratic Congressman Weadock of Michigan replied that Linton's speech was not his own, that it was in fact prepared for him as a part of the "un-American, illegal, traitorous, lamentable operations that we have had from an oath-bound secret political society for some time in this country." Weadock then read from the petition for a congressional investigation that he had offered, and failed to secure, the previous October. This petition contained the oaths of the A.P.A., a letter from an A.P.A. council in Saginaw, an excerpt from Gladden's *Century* article, and various newspaper reports on activities of the order; but it did not have a direct bearing on the legislation at hand. He ended his argument for continuation of the Indian contract schools with a reference to the loyalty of Catholics on the Civil War battlefields.

Five days later, Linton rose to answer Weadock. No one else wrote his speech, he said; he was not a "mouthpiece of the A.P.A." He continued, "I was aware at the time, Mr. Chairman, that sectarian appropriations and privileges were delicate subjects to speak on," and he knew that he would be abused for his position; "But I care nothing for those things." His purpose was to raise the question of whether "certain church influences" were stronger than party, laws, or the Constitution. Weadock then withdrew his charge that Linton was a "mouthpiece," but he insisted that Linton spoke the language of the A.P.A. Linton, asked directly whether he was a member, replied that he did not "propose to be catechized at this time."

The next day, Congressman John Gear of Iowa came to Linton's support by presenting a petition from the National League for the Protection of American Institutions that contained an amendment to the bill under discussion. Its object was to prevent the use of any money appropriated under it for the education of Indians in sectarian schools. This petition contained the names of Hubert Howe Bancroft, Joseph Medill, Josiah Strong, Henry C. Lea, Levi P. Morton, Russell Sage, Frederick Law Olmsted, and Moses Coit Tyler, among many others. After Gear spoke, the debate lapsed into confusion, with some congressmen indicating that they did not understand the differences between the contract school system and the government trade and special schools like Carlisle. In any case, the House now faced a decision on amendments that would cut off all sectarian appropriations for contract schools.

In the debates just preceding the vote, a Democratic party leader announced that any contracts now made were to be regarded as temporary since government policy was to get away from them as quickly as possible and to establish government Indian schools. On June 16, the House voted against the amendments, and then passed the appropriation bill without them by a vote of 158 for, 58 against, and 135 not voting.[134] In the majority for passage were 147 Democrats, 6 Republicans, and 5 Populists. These men were immediately put on the A.P.A. "black-list" of Congressmen to be defeated as the agents of the papacy. In the

minority were 54 Republicans, 2 Democrats, 1 Populist, and 1 Populist-Democrat. These men became the "A.P.A. Roll of Honor." [135]

In the Senate, a resolution to do away with the contract school system as rapidly as possible and to replace it with government schools, a policy already announced for the Democratic administration by a party leader in the House, was presented by Senator Jacob Gallinger, Republican of New Hampshire; the resolution was supported by Senator Platt of New York, another Republican. The proposal was accepted. Meanwhile, petitions from Florida, Tennessee, Illinois, Minnesota, Massachusetts, Michigan, Connecticut, and Kentucky were received protesting against the "union of church and state." These were referred to the Senate Committee on Indian Affairs.[136]

Congress passed on August 15, 1894, a directive to the Secretary of the Interior requesting him to investigate the propriety of discontinuing the contract school system and substituting for it a governmental school system in a fashion that would not be detrimental to Indian pupils while the change was taking place.[137]

These congressional debates had succeeded in making a demagogic connection between the A.P.A. and the proposal to abolish sectarian appropriations to contract schools. The identification was hardly fair to the many other supporters of the proposal. Opposition to continuance of the contract school system was quite clearly accepted by Republicans in both houses of congress as a party issue; but the Democratic congressional leadership was not insistent on the contract system, except that it did not desire to abolish it without adequate preparation for its replacement. Informed individuals and groups concerned with the welfare of the Indians were in favor of withdrawing government aid from the contract schools.[138] Despite the evidence, which would give the credit for specific proposals to the National League for the Protection of American Institutions, and despite the fact that groups concerned with Indian welfare also supported the proposals, the A.P.A. got the blame—or the credit—for the eventual termination.[139] For the time being, the A.P.A. intended to utilize the issue in the coming campaign.

Thus, with an organization that had lodged itself in the Middle West and the West in strength, but which had councils in nearly every state in the Union, the A.P.A. was prepared to take an active part in the elections of 1894. For good or bad, accurately or not, its name was well known and its initials identified almost any activity or proposal that could by any stretch of the imagination be called anti-Catholic.

5 The A.P.A. and the Elections of 1894

In a review of the politics of the years in which the A.P.A. was active, certain generalizations can be made. The victory of either major party was never a foregone conclusion; the margin between victory and defeat was a narrow one, demonstrated by the frequency with which control of Congress had shifted from one party to another since Reconstruction. The decade of the nineties brought with it the disturbing question of depression on the one side and the growing demand for reform that was utilized by the Populists. Minor issues—anti-Catholicism was never a major one—could attain stature and a transitory importance in such a situation. To some extent, anti-Catholicism can be considered an attempt to avoid major problems, in this particular instance the problems arising from industrialization and rapid urbanization. The A.P.A. was a politically minded organization from the beginning and sought the arena of political controversy.

With local variations, the A.P.A. operated within the Republican party. Active members were frequently lifelong Republicans, and the similarities between A.P.A. and Republican party heroes were remarkably close; the Lincoln idolization and the "Catholic conspiracy" legend in connection with his martyrdom, the use of Grant as a major opponent of "Romanism" because of his support of the proposed Sixteenth Amendment, and the emphasis on Harrison's defeat at the hands of his Catholic "enemies" were three instances; but the admitted fact that Irish-Catholics usually voted for Democrats and that this had been true for many years

was the most prominent piece of evidence explaining the A.P.A. affinity for the Republican party. The so-called "Catholic vote," however, had shown signs of changing its allegiance, and as prominent a Catholic leader as Archbishop Ireland of St. Paul was a known Republican. The unofficial cooperation between Republicans and the A.P.A. was as important to Democrats in maintaining themselves in office as it was to Republicans in gaining votes. The test of the importance of the A.P.A. to Republicans was whether it brought them votes that the party had not had; the importance of the order to Democrats was that, by opposing it and by making sure the Republicans carried responsibility for it, Catholics would be kept from slipping into Republican columns.

The role of the Populists was a complicating element. The A.P.A. was strongest numerically in those areas where the Populists were also strong. In general, the order has been shown to be unwelcome within Populist ranks. The appearance of the third party, however, meant that a group of votes such as the ones the A.P.A. claimed to control could be more important to the older parties than it would have been in a two-party contest. A loosening of party ties was also evident in the middle nineties, a fact that contributed to the supposed eminence of the A.P.A.

Methods of nomination, the caucus and the convention, presented an opportunity for a well-knit and disciplined group. The welcome offered to the order within the Republican party by practical politicians would persist only if it could deliver its vote in return for any concessions to it on nominations. Here was the difficulty. Anti-Catholicism, by its nature, was a divisive force, not a cohesive one; it thrived on suspicion. However united anti-Catholics might be on one issue, they differed on many others. "Swinging the A.P.A. vote" was an operation easily accomplished when the person involved was a Catholic or a known anti-Catholic. But the hard game of politics thrives on neutrality and noncommitment. When a candidate or a party sought its vote without a commitment, the A.P.A. ran the risk of a "sellout"; if one of its leaders tried to utilize the group for his own gain or to support someone who was not a member or

who had not committed himself, the order ran the risk of being "sold out," with the attendant loss of confidence among its own members.

Another test of accomplishment would come in the legislative halls. Appointment of Catholics to office, the position of Catholics in public affairs, attention paid to Catholics or to anti-Catholics by the political parties, and—not least of all—the passage of laws by state legislatures and the national Congress provide the material on which any conclusion as to the effectiveness of the A.P.A. must be based. The elections of 1894 put the order to this test. By working with Republicans, anti-Catholics remained loyal to the same party they had supported in 1892, but now they were working with a party on the upgrade; once the heat of the campaign was past, the newly elected officeholders would have a chance to demonstrate whether the A.P.A. was anything more than a device to obtain office.

The appointment of Senator Edward White of Louisiana to the Supreme Court confirmed once again the suspicion among anti-Catholics that the Democratic party was too sympathetic to Catholics. President Cleveland had first nominated Wheeler Peckham, a member of the law committee of the National League for the Protection of American Institutions, for the vacancy. But this recommendation had been blocked by Senator David Hill of New York, a Democrat, and the anti-Catholics lost a man who would have been acceptable to them. White was then nominated. Forgetting Roger Taney's Catholicism, the *Loyal American and the North* termed White the first "Jesuit" to get such an appointment.[1] Senator Vilas was criticized for voting to confirm this appointment by a correspondent who did not like the man from "the state where the alligators make their home, a Southerner, an ex-Rebel, and what is still worse a Catholic, who received his early training by those hated, but eminent Jesuit Fathers."[2] Cleveland eventually did appoint Peckham to the Court, but not until the election was over.

Later in the year, in preparation for the Congressional elections, the A.P.A. made several moves. The "Roll of Honor,"[3] derived from the vote on Indian contract school appropriations,

was refined so that voters could tell which congressmen voted "Yes," which voted "Nay," and which were present but not voting, as well as which were absent.[4] Indicating a desire to tighten up on recommendations, the supreme executive council in September drew up an agreement form that candidates desiring A.P.A. support were supposed to accept and sign. A formal procedure for endorsement by councils was also established. The local units were supposed to make recommendations to their local advisory boards. That group would then investigate the recommended men and report findings to the full council, which would make the endorsement.[5] A practical warning note of caution crept into the advice given by the *Patriotic American* on August 25, when it advised its readers as well as prospective candidates as follows: "The man who pretends to carry the A.P.A. vote in his pocket is a liar; he who tries to sell it is a knave; he who buys it is a fool; for he buys goods that no man can deliver." So prepared, the A.P.A. was ready for the campaign to come.

The character of the campaign was demonstrated early. The former Speaker of the House Thomas B. Reed, Republican, was put on the spot by the *Catholic Record*. He was quoted therein on August 16 as being opposed to any union between the A.P.A. and the Republican party: "I would a thousand times go down to honored defeat with the unsullied flag of the Grand Old Party waving over me than to victory obtained by any such aid. And the man who rests his political hopes on this foreign-born un-American league is foredoomed to disaster, dishonor, and defeat."

Reed denounced the quotation, saying that he had never so criticized the A.P.A. and that the Catholic weekly had been taken in. The paper replied on September 13, "Goodbye, Tom Reed; the A.P.A. can have you." Another Republican made an attempt to rid his party of the A.P.A., which was not committed to any party and which corrupted politics, he asserted. This man, Richard C. Kerens, was a Catholic and a member of the party's national committee from Missouri; he thought the G.O.P. should get rid of the "lot of bushwhackers, politicians, and badgers" who controlled the A.P.A. in order to avoid losing thousands of votes.[6]

To prove that the Republican party had a working agreement with the A.P.A., the *New York Times* began on September 28 the publication of a series of reports from Washington, D.C. Congressman Linton's speech on sectarian appropriations had been printed at the Government Printing Office. Senators Gallinger of New Hampshire, Platt of New York, and Patton and McMillan of Michigan were reported to have ordered additional copies. With Linton's allotment, a total of two and one-half million copies of the speech were said to be ready for distribution through the Republican National Congressional Committee. The executive committee of the Republican National Committee then met and refused to condemn the A.P.A. as it was requested to do by Patrick Egan and Mr. Kerens, both Catholic Republicans. A carefully worded resolution was accepted, however, stating that "the Republican party, as it always has been, is in sympathy with the largest liberty of religious opinion, and is in favor of entire freedom in this respect, standing on the ground of no religious test." [7] Thus the Republicans moved officially into the field where broad generalizations obscure sharp differences.

The *Times* repeated its original charges, giving names of individuals working in the mailing room for the Congressional Committee and saying that Green Clay Smith was the A.P.A. man in charge there. Smith actually was an A.P.A. leader in Washington, D.C.; he had been a Union congressman from Kentucky from 1863 to 1866 and governor of the Territory of Montana from 1866 to 1869, he was an ordained Baptist minister, he had been candidate for president for the National Prohibition Party in 1876, and he was after 1890 minister for the Metropolitan Baptist Church in Washington. The *Times* continued to assert that its story was true and that there was a connection between the Committee and the A.P.A. A few days later, the Albany correspondent of the paper found a subdepot in the New York State House at Albany from which copies of the speech were also being mailed. Despite a formal denial from the Republican party chairman, the *Times* maintained that its facts were true. The Reverend Green Clay Smith admitted that he was in charge of the Washington mailing room, but denied

that there was any official connection between his actions and the Congressional Committee.[8]

Theodore Roosevelt became quite concerned over the charges and made a personal investigation. He wrote to a Catholic friend that there was no truth in the charge of cooperation, and that the only people who had come to the Committee seeking material to show such a connection were "Democratic decoys." He asked his correspondent, Bishop Keane of Catholic University, to go with him to the mailing rooms to see for himself. He further asked Keane to get proof from the Democrats, for that was where Keane had first heard the story, if the charges were not to be considered as purely campaign propaganda.[9] Across the country that fall, the story of Republican-A.P.A. cooperation was to be repeated many times with variations. The only answer that could satisfy those who made the charge was an outright denial and a denunciation of the order, with consequent loss of A.P.A. votes. Countering the charge was the belief that the Democrats were utilizing the A.P.A. as a whip to keep Catholic voters within the fold. Both charges had a measure of truth in them.

The election in New York State presented three different issues on which there was controversy between Democrats and Republicans involving the "Catholic vote" and anti-Catholicism. One was the acceptance or rejection of the new constitution, with its proposals on charities; another had to do with the election of regents for the state university; and the third was the state election with the governor's office as the objective. In the immediate background was a division between two factions within Catholic ranks, and the investigation into vice conditions conducted by the Lexow Committee.

Personalities were added to the campaign when Republicans nominated for one of the vacancies on the Board of Regents Father Sylvester Malone, friend and biographer of Father Edward McGlynn. Father Malone was supported for office by Fathers Lambert and Ducey, both of whom were at odds with their ecclesiastical superiors because they had testified before the Lexow Committee without permission. The Democrats, not to be outdone in the quest for Catholic votes, nominated Bishop

Bernard McQuaid of Rochester, friend of Archbishop Corrigan, who was the superior of Fathers Malone, Lambert, and Ducey. Thus, face to face, exponents of the "liberal" and the "conservative" wings of the Catholic clergy sought public support. Bishop McQuaid desired the defeat of Malone because one's worst enemy was "always one of his household." [10] During the campaign, Archbishop Ireland of St. Paul came to New York and gave his support to the Republican Catholic candidate. Bishop McQuaid felt that if Ireland could not aid his brother prelate, he should have kept quiet; in any case, Ireland had no business interfering in the affairs of a diocese not his own. The Bishop managed to contain himself publicly until the votes were counted and Father Malone was announced victorious. Then he made a public statement in his cathedral stating that Ireland had come to New York supporting Republicans in order to pay a debt to the Republican party for its financial assistance to him. In McQuaid's mind, Ireland was doing the work of the A.P.A. [11]

Bishop McQuaid's public outburst was too shocking for non-Catholic comment to be withheld. The *Outlook* stated that it was impossible to read McQuaid's sermon "and not realize anew the tremendous blunder and wicked injustice of the miscalled American Protective Association, which involves all Roman Catholics in a common condemnation. There are no worthier members to be found for any association for the protection of true Americanism than Father Ducey and Archbishop Ireland." [12]

The A.P.A. could have enjoyed sitting on the sidelines and watching such internecine warfare without commitment, but the necessities of politics did not afford this luxury. The Republicans had refused to denounce the order at their state convention. [13] Their gubernatorial nominee was Levi P. Morton, a member of the League for the Protection of American Institutions but, as he was to prove in 1896, an enemy of the A.P.A. The Democrats nominated David B. Hill and denounced the A.P.A. by implication, although not by name. [14]

State president Van Schaick of the A.P.A. attended the Republican convention and reported that there were one hundred thousand voters sharing his views who watched its deliberations.

He was reported by the *New York Times* as being in consultation with party leaders and working with them, producing a slogan, "Go Papa," signifying the union of the "G.O.P." and the "A.P.A." Van Schaick announced his support of Mr. Morton, saying, "Mr. Hill, having openly denounced the A.P.A., has naturally antagonized our organization. The natural conclusion is that the members of the Association will oppose him at the polls." [15]

Actually, Hill had not denounced the A.P.A. by name. He had merely condemned an "un-American spirit of intolerance" exhibited by a group that he failed to identify, for which sympathy was to be found in Republican ranks.[16] Carl Schurz, for one, regarded this kind of argument as "nonsense." [17] As election day approached, the *Times* reported several instances in which priests advised their congregations from the pulpit to vote straight Democratic because of the A.P.A.[18]

Election day brought victory to the Republicans and also acceptance of the proposed sections of the state constitution. For the first time in the memory of the Republican boss, his party carried both the city and the upstate.[19] As proof that the election illustrated the need for reform, the *United American* interpreted the results to mean voter rejection of Tammany and "Roman Catholic villainy in connection with New York city politics," as shown by the Lexow findings.[20]

In office, the new legislature enacted a law forbidding the display of any flag other than the national colors over public buildings, except when ranking foreign visitors were present.[21] Such a law was intended to prevent the flying of green emblems on St. Patrick's Day, and had been previously endorsed by the New York A.P.A. A similar bill had been vetoed in June of 1894 by Governor Flower.[22]

Looking toward New England, the *New York Times* found that there, too, the Republicans were in the "grasp of the A.P.A." At the Massachusetts Republican convention, Senator Hoar was a proxy delegate because he had been defeated by A.P.A. strength as a regular delegate, it was reported. Senator Lodge was expected to denounce the order in his nominating speech for Governor Greenhalge, but he did not. As chairman of the resolu-

tions and platform committee,[23] Senator Lodge presented a plank on the public schools that was expected to retain A.P.A. support but was not expected to be completely satisfactory to the order.[24] On election day, Greenhalge was chosen governor along with a Republican legislature. The majority in the legislature turned out an experienced clerk and replaced him with an alleged incompetent, one supposedly acceptable to the A.P.A.[25] The *Nation* commented on this minor concession: "When Massachusetts is determined to disgrace herself, she certainly knows how." [26] Both Governor Greenhalge and Senator Hoar were to reveal their antagonism toward the A.P.A. in the following year.

In other New England states, New Hampshire Democrats condemned the order, and their Connecticut brethren did likewise, insisting that the Republicans follow suit or be charged with complicity with the A.P.A. A Republican candidate for Congress and another for governor were said to be "in league" with the order, although only the governorship aspirant took time to deny it.[27]

Across the country, the A.P.A. had become a partisan issue. Governor Matthews, Democratic governor of Indiana, attacked the order in his speech to that state's convention, after which the delegates inserted a condemnation plank into the platform. Former President Benjamin Harrison, visiting in New York City, was asked whether there was any A.P.A. strength in his home state. He replied, "I have not heard of any in our state, except as our Democratic friends talk of it. I do not think there is any." [28]

On occasion, a Catholic priest expressed political advice. In South Dakota, Bishop Marty recommended to his priests that Senator Richard Pettigrew and the two Republican candidates for the House be elected.[29] Neither of South Dakota's congressmen had voted for the sectarian appropriations bill, but one of these men was not a candidate for re-election. All three of the Republicans endorsed by the Bishop were elected. Many states furnished election results that were said to favor the A.P.A. Walter Evans, Republican of Louisville, broke the Democratic hold on Kentucky by being elected as congressman, with A.P.A. support.[30] His victory forecast a real political turnover, which

became pronounced in 1895, when the state chose a Republican governor.

In Ohio, where a prospective Republican presidential candidate was to be groomed for two years hence, Republicans were playing calculated politics to the hilt. Governor McKinley, speaking as a party supporter in Missouri on the safe subject of the tariff, was asked, "What's the matter with the A.P.A.?" He did not appreciate this attempt to make him commit himself; he paused for a moment and then replied, "The question we have to settle now is, what is the matter with the country." His audience cheered.[31] At his party's state convention, boss George B. Cox blandly pointed out that the party did not need to concern itself with Congressman Bellamy Storer, who was not in attendance. Storer, whose wife was a recent Catholic convert, had earned a place on the A.P.A. "Roll of Honor" by voting for the sectarian appropriations bill, but he was opposed by the order as a nominee because of his wife.[32] The Democrats formally condemned the A.P.A., and the *Catholic Columbian* advised its readers that "a vote for the candidate of the People's party means a full vote against the outspoken opponents of proscription and half a vote for the A.P.A. ticket. Make your vote count for all it is worth!"[33] A few days later, Ohio voters rejected this pro-Democratic argument and elected the Republicans.

The career of the A.P.A. in Michigan politics was a confused one, in which the leadership played with the McMillan forces within the Republican party while the membership apparently saw in Hazen Pingree the man they desired in the governor's office. Governor Rich was the McMillan group's candidate for renomination. In December of 1893, Senator McMillan had received a letter from a supporter suggesting that the vice-president of the state A.P.A., John Glassford, be relieved from his regular employment for four weeks to frustrate the tendency of the rank and file in the order to support Pingree. The letter was "confidential."[34] McMillan replied that he was not in favor of manipulating the order in such a fashion but, if it were necessary, he did believe it would be a good thing to "control the organization so as to do what is right and proper." He asked that

an estimate of the costs involved be made and volunteered to pay his share.[35]

As election time approached, J. H. D. Stevens, who was to become state secretary of the Michigan council in 1895, was traveling around the state lining up A.P.A. support behind the candidacy of Rich and, also, seeking some recognition of himself.[36] A little later, Stevens ran into some difficulties with the Republican State Central Committee, which assigned him to work elsewhere.[37] Another A.P.A. leader, canvassing in the Ninth Congressional District, also for the McMillan group, asked the Senator for a thousand dollars to cover expenses.[38] The total effort of the McMillan faction was rewarded when their man received the nomination at the convention.

Congressman Linton was also nominated to succeed himself,[39] and Rousseau O. Crump, mayor of West Bay City, was nominated to run against Congressman Weadock in the Tenth District. The *Patriotic American* on September 1 announced that if Crump were elected, Michigan would have two congressmen pledged to A.P.A. principles. In addition, Roswell P. Bishop, David D. Aitken, and Dr. Henry F. Thomas were identified as other Republican congressional nominees who had A.P.A. blessing, but this last information appeared in a Catholic weekly.[40]

A constitutional amendment providing that foreign-born voters should be either naturalized citizens or have declared their intention of becoming citizens two years and six months prior to November 8, 1894, appeared on the ballot and was adopted by the voters with a margin of three to one.[41] Michigan voters adopted this restrictive law in spite of the fact that at the time three-fourths of the voters in the upper peninsula were foreign-born, and 55 per cent of the potential voters in Wayne County (Detroit) were also foreign-born.[42] The issues of the election, consequently, were quite well defined on the twin subjects of anti-Catholicism and nativism.

When the votes were counted for the various offices, Michigan went Republican with a vengeance. Only one Democrat succeeded in gaining a seat in the state legislature; all the rest went to Republicans; all the congressional seats went to Republicans,

and Governor Rich was re-elected. The A.P.A. laid claim to 60 per cent of the legislature, and all the congressmen-elect were now enclosed within the arms of the order.[43] But this apparent victory was soon to be clouded by charges from within the organization that its leadership had acted corruptly during the campaign.

In Wisconsin, the Democratic state chairman understood that his party enjoyed a tenuous hold, which had been obtained through the windfall of the Bennett Law. He was determined to maintain and increase his party's grasp on the state.[44] Chairman Wall began as early as May of 1893 to prepare for the contest of 1894. His plans were outlined in a letter to Senator Vilas. In this analysis, he credited the Bennett Law with having placed the party in its present position, but the past was past; now the party had to make plans to retain its lead. For continued success he believed that Democrats would need to "over-come prejudice by prejudice," and the A.P.A. would provide the means. To retain the German Protestants and to be assured of the entire Catholic vote, Democrats needed to attack the order. Perhaps, incidentally, he continued, "through it we may be able to keep out of the campaign the annoying 'local option' controversy." His procedure was, first, to blame the A.P.A. for the Bennett Law, then to provide state newspapers with materials on the evils of secret societies. When the ground was laid and the time was ripe, he would open fire all along the line. "It would not be dangerous then, because the Republicans would not know which horn of the dilemma to accept. If they support the A.P.A.'s, they would lose the German voters; if they attack them, they would lose others." Conferences with the Archbishop and other Catholic leaders, diplomacy toward the Lutherans, a "German Bureau" to conduct the campaign among that language group, and finances to the amount of ten thousand dollars a year for the next two years— this was the plan of attack proposed and the price of victory estimated.[45]

That Wall's plan would not go smoothly soon became apparent. First, the German-language newspaper *Germania,* which represented the "liberal" position in Wall's analysis, was getting

ready to expose those who were too friendly to Catholics "whilst declaring their disapproval of A.P.A.ism." [46] Then, Wall's ingenious plan was revealed to the public on January 16, 1894, in an editorial in the Kenosha *Independent*. The plan seemed to be working, however, when a Lutheran minister reported that his people would remain with the Democrats,[47] who were trying to divest themselves of anyone who might be considered an A.P.A. sympathizer.[48]

Meanwhile in the Republican camp Congressman Nils Haugen, the only Republican member of Congress from Wisconsin to survive the Democratic landslide of 1890, was releasing a trial balloon on his chances for the governorship. He was informed that the state president of the A.P.A. was for him [49] but was also told by a Catholic supporter to stay in Congress and not to try for the governorship because Catholics would vote for Peck's re-election "on account of this A.P.A. foolishness." [50] Haugen was advised to be prepared for questions on the A.P.A.,[51] at the same time that he was being informed that the rank and file of the order were supporting him.[52]

Unity among members of the A.P.A. was impossible, however. H. M. Stark, national treasurer in 1894 and a national trustee in 1895, was supporting another candidate, Scofield, in the hopes of getting back his old job as Labor Commissioner.[53] Franklin Hopkins, state vice-president and already suspected of having personal political ambitions at the organization's expense, was supporting William Upham.[54] At the convention, A.P.A. support insofar as it can be determined went to Upham, who got the nomination.[55]

In drafting their platform, Republican leaders had to decide whether they would include the principles of the Bennett Law or not, and just how much emphasis should be placed on it if they did.[56] Their decision was to present as the substance of their campaign the reapportionment of legislative districts for the legislature.[57]

As the campaign grew heated, the A.P.A. became aware that it was being used by the Democrats as a bogeyman.[58] With few exceptions, however, the A.P.A. refrained from endorsing specific

men until the last days of the campaign. In August, Theobald Otjen received the endorsement of the *Wisconsin Patriot* in his race for Congress.[59] At the same time as the Democrats were charging that the A.P.A. found its natural home within Republican ranks, former state Democratic chairman Ellis Usher, now editor of a LaCrosse newspaper, could find only one real A.P.A. man on his county's Republican ticket.[60]

Fissures began to appear in the carefully constructed structure built by Chairman Wall. The *Germania* was more concerned with national than with local issues, and was solidly Republican on them. It stated that when Democrats nominated men like David B. Hill, Tammanyite New Yorker and the *"Mephistopheles der partei,"* it was doomed to fail, and it further warned that German Protestants should not be willing to fall into the arms of Rome in order to defeat the A.P.A., which was ephemeral anyhow.[61] A Catholic priest announced himself publicly for Upham, and Rasmus Anderson, President Cleveland's minister to Denmark in the first administration, came out for a Republican victory because he, too, could not stomach Hill of New York. A former Democratic newspaper announced that the free public school was the bulwark of the Republic, not of the Democrats, and should no longer be a political football.[62]

Wall's projected plans were carried out in some respects. *Der Seebote,* a German-language newspaper and in Wall's mind the spokesman for Catholic Germans, reminded its readers that the Democrats had stood with them in 1890 on the Bennett Law, and that the anti-Catholic A.P.A. was now in union with the Republicans.[63] Usher's LaCrosse *Chronicle* used the symbol of the "little red school house" for the Democrats; but at the same time could not resist taking a swipe at the Irish, saying they were responsible, in their narrowness, for the rise of the A.P.A.[64]

On October 27, only a few days before election day, the *Wisconsin Patriot* published the now familiar advisory ballot with candidates listed on both tickets. An "R" or an "R.S." meant "Romanist" or "Romanist sympathizer," and a "P" indicated a "Protestant." All Republicans were shown with a "P," while all Democrats were either "R" or "R.S." In addition to the

specific mention of congressional candidate Otjen as a choice, Henry R. Cooper was endorsed in his congressional race in recognition for his vote on the sectarian appropriations bill, while Democratic Peter Somers was specifically denounced for his.[65]

When the voters had recorded their choices, the *Wisconsin Patriot* cheered the victory of Otjen and claimed that every county where an A.P.A. council existed had gone Republican.[66] The *Abend Post* was also pleased, calling the results *"Die Nemesis"* and *"Des Volkes Protest,"* [67] while the Beloit *Daily Free Press* wrote that "when principles are at stake, isms invariably take a seat very far back." [68] Democratic Chairman Wall believed that his defeat was a result of "national issues and national issues solely." [69] Actually, the unnatural alliance of German Lutherans and German Catholics in league with the Democratic party had been broken. The alliance had been forged in 1890 in opposition to the Bennett Law, but Wisconsin in 1894 returned to its traditional place within the Republican fold.

In postelection months, the A.P.A. tried to capitalize on its support of the victors. One "patriot" wanted the appointment as state Attorney General and offered the endorsement of state A.P.A. president Cheney as recommendation.[70] State vice-president Hopkins sought a patronage interview with the Republican state leader, former Senator John C. Spooner.[71] On the other hand, it was thought good politics to appoint at least one Irishman to some job in Iowa County so that Irish Republicans would know that the A.P.A. did not dominate Republicans.[72] On the day after election, Governor-elect Upham announced the appointment as his private secretary of a well-known anti-A.P.A. Republican; he thereby disappointed the *Wisconsin Patriot*. After his inauguration, Upham was considered a bad loss by the *Patriot* because of this man's influence over him.[73] Apparently the A.P.A. had secured little in postelection months that was satisfying to it.

In Minnesota, the Republicans renominated Governor Knute Nelson, who was not unsatisfactory to the A.P.A., as was shown by the "P" following his name on their advisory ballot. Along with Nelson, all but two of the Republican candidates for Congress were listed as "P," and even the two exceptions were listed

as "doubtful." [74] One of the "doubtful," Charles Towne of Duluth, was declared to be unacceptable to the order by his home town paper.[75] Of the approved candidates, Joel P. Heatwole was a newspaperman and a former chairman of the state Republican central committee.[76] His newspaper reported the entire campaign without mentioning the A.P.A. but did express editorially, after election day, that the Republicans had stood for "patriotism." His paper also expressed a diluted nativism when it spoke favorably of literacy requirements for voting, whether in northern states as applied to immigrants or in southern states as applied to Negroes.[77] Heatwole was apparently regarded somewhat as was Senator Cushman K. Davis of Minnesota by the A.P.A.—favorably in return for certain very general statements —but there is no indication that either of them stepped out of his way to come to any kind of terms with the order.[78]

When Republicans again carried Minnesota, the *Loyal American and the North* hailed the election results as a victory for "thorough Americans" and cried that "victory perches upon the banners of the American Protective Association." The paper, however, was not so jubilant over the fact that Republican party managers had placed advertisements in Catholic newspapers.[79]

The part played in these various state contests was always determined by local conditions and political alignments usually within the Republican party. Nebraska, for example, was experiencing a struggle for power between railroad and antirailroad factions within the party. Dominating at the convention, the railroad candidates were nominated. Edward Rosewater, who considered himself the leading Republican opposed to railroad domination, thereupon publicly denounced the party's candidate, resigned his position as Republican national committeeman, and supported the Democrat Silas Holcomb for governor on the Democrat-Populist ticket. Holcomb was elected, but all other state offices and the control of the legislature went to the Republicans. Thomas Majors, the Republican gubernatorial candidate, had not denied a connection with the A.P.A., although he admittedly had the support of some Catholics.[80] The A.P.A. did

find some comfort in the defeat of Congressman William Jennings Bryan because of Bryan's support of non-English language teaching in the territorial schools of New Mexico.[81] The defeated Bryan became editor of the Omaha *World-Herald* and thus Rosewater's newspaper competitor and still a factor in Omaha politics.

In the new legislature, Governor Holcomb was shorn of his control over the police and fire commissioners of Omaha. This was accomplished by the enactment of a bill cutting the size of the police and fire board to three members, consisting now of the Governor, the Attorney General, and the Land Commissioner. Both the others, unlike the Governor, were Republican and acceptable to the A.P.A.; with their majority, the Governor would be outvoted. Holcomb tried to veto the bill, but it was enacted over his veto; he then instituted a test case that was eventually appealed and lost in the State Supreme Court. In the meantime, the issue was a struggle over patronage in the Omaha police and fire departments, which would be in the control of the police and fire board under the law, and in the hands of the mayor otherwise. The mayor of Omaha was not acceptable to the A.P.A., and the order thus became involved in a struggle for patronage at the same time it was in the difficult position of opposing "home rule" for the city. Republicans defended themselves by saying that the "gambling fraternity" of Omaha supported the Governor, and they denied that the issue was patronage.[82] Rosewater's *Bee* regarded the affair as "A.P.A.-sectarianism, bigotry, and sub-rosa, subterranean, gum-shoe, peanut politics." [83] The colorful language and the personalities involved made it a good story for local consumption, but it was this Rosewater version that was published elsewhere in the nation, for his paper was the source of wire-service news.[84]

In Colorado, for local reasons, the election was characterized by an attempt to blame the Populists for the A.P.A. Populist Governor Waite ("Bloody Bridles") was up for re-election; his defeat was urged by the Republicans and by an active priest, Father Malone, who had discovered, he said, the A.P.A. within Populist ranks. According to his opponents, Waite's attitude on

the silver question or any other problem was secondary to the fact that he had earned his nickname by using the state militia to protect striking miners during some labor trouble. On this issue, a Catholic paper had reported an A.P.A. gang supporting the mine owners, and reported that the strikers were generally Populist in sympathy.[85] Moreover, during the campaign two former officers of the "Republican League" announced their support for the Populists because, they said, the Republican-A.P.A. alliance was so strong and because Republicans were opposed to free silver.[86] Thus, in Nebraska and Colorado there appeared some evidence of confusion as to the role of the A.P.A. and the Populists; yet the evidence still indicates considerable Republican party regularity.

California did not adhere to the usual pattern, either. There, the A.P.A. endorsed the Democratic candidate for governor as punishment imposed on the Republican nominee, who would not dismiss his Catholic secretary, as the order had asked as the price of their endorsement. Father Yorke, editor of the Catholic *Monitor* and bitter opponent of the A.P.A., unaware of the endorsement also came out for the Democratic candidate.[87] One Democratic editor described the resulting confusion: "Half of our forces have gone over to the Populists and the A.P.A.'s are raising the d——l with all the parties." [88] This crossing of party lines probably meant that the A.P.A. did not operate together, but at least one man satisfactory to them, Samuel G. Hilborn (who would appear as a speaker for the order at the national convention of 1896), retained his seat in Congress.

The state of Washington adhered rigidly to the pattern. Democrats in convention avoided any possible misunderstanding by condemning the A.P.A. by name. Each candidate was sent a copy of the principles of the A.P.A. with a request for comment. Both incumbent congressmen were on the A.P.A. "Roll of Honor," but one of them, John L. Wilson, was interested in elevation to the Senate by the legislature being elected. In Spokane, Wilson's friends worked with the A.P.A.; in Seattle, A.P.A. men worked in preconvention caucuses with the anti-"ring" Republican faction, but in the convention itself they came to terms with

the "regulars" who controlled the "ring" and were rewarded with the nomination for County Superintendent of Schools. In Tacoma, the state secretary of the order, Fred Taylor, secured a nomination for the state legislature and won his seat. Election day brought Republican victories.[89]

Just before election day, Archbishop Ireland of St. Paul had permitted an interview, which was published nationally. In it he denied the general accusation of a Republican-A.P.A. alliance. He stated that the Republican party had not officially shown itself as sustaining "the movement which has been set afoot by anti-Catholic bigots to abridge the civic and religious liberties of Catholics." He knew that the movement existed, but was willing to "remit it confidently to the good sense and spirit of justice of the American people." He disagreed with those who felt that Republican silence amounted to acceptance of A.P.A. principles, and concluded that "a great political party cannot be expected to take notice of every fleeting wind that passes over the fields of American politics, and dignified silence was most in keeping with the dignity of these conditions and was the strongest rebuke to the pigmy form of this vile bigotry." He maintained that political parties were not the keepers of the individual consciences of their adherents, and he ended his remarks by advising Catholics to vote always for principles, which was for him the true Catholic way.[90]

When the Republican victories throughout the nation became known, President Traynor rejoiced in the name of the A.P.A. Twelve congressmen from Michigan were elected, he said, eight of whom were "our men," while the remaining four were "in sympathy." He also claimed that 50 per cent of the Michigan legislature was A.P.A.-minded, and that 50 to 90 per cent of all local officials elected in Michigan were also. He pointed joyously to the defeat of many Democrats who had voted against Linton on the sectarian appropriations bill.[91]

In viewing these election results, certain qualifications should be made; the A.P.A. claims were large, and they were in many cases substantiated by news reports. In fact, the A.P.A. claimants may very well have based their estimates of victory on a reading

of the daily press. But the psychology behind the A.P.A. claim was not that the men elected were members of the order; their postelection joy was that Catholics or "Catholic sympathizers," a rather vague entity, had been defeated. In nearly every instance where claims can be tested, actual members of the order were successful only in minor offices. Undoubtedly, the A.P.A. did support Republicans and did contribute to the victory of 1894. But the effect of its support on the outcome was another matter. In general, anti-Catholic votes had gone Republican in 1892, too, so there was no change of allegiance in 1894. A nonexistent A.P.A. switch to the Republican column in 1894 would hardly have accounted for the Republican victory. The success should be attributed rather to the far-reaching and thoroughgoing political turnover that was in the making for 1896.

As for the charge that the A.P.A. "controlled" the Republican party, it was a campaign tactic used by the Democrats. After the experience of 1892, it would have taken some stupidity for a party wheel horse to overlook the "Catholic vote." Between them and for different reasons, Democratic sympathizers and Catholics asserted that the A.P.A. controlled the Republican party.[92] In making the charge, enthusiasts overlooked the fact that prominent Catholics, such as Archbishop Ireland, Bishop Marty, and Richard Kerens, continued to support Republicanism and were undoubtedly joined by many other Catholics in doing so.[93]

One test of the truth of the claims, however, can be found in the records of those elected once they were in office. In the state legislatures and in Congress the claims could be put to the test, first in choosing United States senators and then in the enactment of legislation. At least one of the A.P.A. newspapers had already endorsed the direct election of senators, reasoning that the "people's choice" would thereby be less likely to owe his election to "Roman power" operating secretly in caucuses, and less likely to submit to "Jesuitical" wiles once elected.[94]

As in the election, the A.P.A. was to be credited with influence on the choices of senators by state legislatures. Stephen

B. Elkins was chosen senator in West Virginia despite alleged opposition because his daughter had married a Catholic.[95] Congressman John Gear, who had supported Linton on the sectarian appropriation debate, was raised to a senatorship from Iowa.[96] In Michigan, Congressman Julius C. Burrows, who had assertedly been initiated into the A.P.A. in a private ceremony at the Capitol and who had also voted with Linton, was designated a senator. Newly elected Congressmen Crump and Thomas, both of whom were claimed by the A.P.A., as well as Congressman Linton, were said to have managed Burrows' campaign on the floor of the state legislature. Crump was a member of the state legislature before he entered on his term as congressman, and Thomas was a former legislator; both were experienced in legislative circles.[97]

In California, George Perkins was elected senator to serve out the term of Leland Stanford. One of his opponents for the position was M. H. DeYoung, owner of the San Francisco *Chronicle*. Apparently the A.P.A. supported Perkins, for one of its councils formally denounced legislators who voted for DeYoung.[98] Oregon's Senator Joseph Dolph was defeated for re-election, with the local Catholic weekly charging that two A.P.A. members of the legislature from Multnomah County (Portland) were responsible.[99]

In both Washington and Montana, A.P.A. councils were disgusted with the votes of their men in senatorial contests to the point of charging bribery. Republican Congressman John L. Wilson of Washington, on the "Roll of Honor," was chosen senator only after twenty-eight ballots. Fred Taylor, the state secretary of the A.P.A. and a member of the lower house of the legislature, did not cast his vote for Wilson until the final ballot, although Wilson allegedly had the support of the A.P.A. councils in his home town of Spokane.[100] During the long struggle between Wilson's supporters and the Levi Ankeny faction, a communication was published expressing the attitude of some A.P.A. members:

Friends, attend your councils. Common report has it that at the next meeting of Council number 2, certain schemers will seek endorsement

of their effort to deliver the American Protective Association vote to Levi Ankeny. It is well known that money has been paid to certain high officers, or officer, for the purpose of consummating this nefarious scheme. Can it be made to work? Let none but true Americans be put on guard. Down the frauds who are using the order for the purpose of selling it to the highest bidder.

(Signed) Thirteen friends.

At the same time, Taylor was asked, "Is it true that the silent yet oft times potent influence, sometimes called the sock, has found lodgement in your breast?" [101] State president Van Fossen, as though he had been the person referred to in the letter, denied the implication.[102] Whether bribery was used cannot be determined, but the charge of bribery undoubtedly did damage to the order. There were indications that the men involved did believe there was an A.P.A. "influence" operating: when John Wilson appeared in the Senate after his election, he was asked, "Is there any A.P.A. sentiment in your state?" "Is there?" he replied, "Why, I didn't dare congratulate Tom Carter when he was elected because it would have defeated me." [103]

Thomas Carter, Catholic and former Commissioner of the General Land Office as well as former Republican National Chairman, was chosen Montana's senator. In spite of his Catholicism, he received the votes of the A.P.A. members in the legislature in an incident receiving nationwide publicity. Carter had prepared his position with one A.P.A. member in the legislature by asking former Republican Chairman James Clarkson of Iowa to intercede for him. Naming a legislator who was an old friend of Clarkson's, Carter designated the man as "a member of the American Protective Association, but still not violently committed to the theories of that organization. This suggestion, however, will probably convey to you some idea of the difficulty to be overcome in this case." [104] During a legislative caucus, several A.P.A. men were said to have voted for Carter, and the state president of the order protested. Then an A.P.A. delegation from Butte descended on Helena to work against Carter's election, but it was shunted into the galleries and not permitted to operate on the floor of the legislature.[105] Carter was

chosen; afterward, Howard Paschal of Butte, the subject of the
letter from Carter to Clarkson, received the following communication from members of the A.P.A. dissatisfied with his
vote for Carter, a letter intended not only for him but for other
A.P.A. men who had also voted for Carter:

> You traitors—Understand we, an oath-bound band of 13, will await
> with pleasure your arrival in Butte either during or after your legisla-
> tive duties have expired. You despised bribe-takers, traitors to your
> constituents and traitors to your religion; you Rome-bought abor-
> tions, dare you call yourselves Americans or confront those to whom
> you owe your offices? Sincerely then we wait your arrival in the
> "greatest mining camp on earth." You will find upon investigation
> there are no traitors in our mystic number.
>
> Signed, James Mellen.[106]

Faced with a threat to one of its members, the lower house of
the legislature appointed an investigating committee to look
into the letter, but nothing came of it.[107] The Butte *Bystander,*
a local labor paper, added some more verbal color to an already
highly colored story by commenting: "The American Protective
Association, conceived by the republican party and born of a
jackass, has fizzled off its little wad of 'sincerity.' Its spectral
form will loom up in the dismal, visionary imaginings at pellucid
intervals, but its extemporaneousness will be enshrouded in the
robes and cross of Rome." The *Bystander* did not believe that
Carter had found it necessary to purchase the votes of A.P.A.
men with anything substantial, as had been implied by less charitable sources; rather, Republican party leaders had been able to
get the "foolish votes for comparatively nothing." It suggested
that the order disband, for its sincerity as an anti-Catholic group
was now doubtful and its affiliation with the Republican party
was indissoluble.[108]

One month after the elections, the lameduck Congress met.
Congressman Linton was greeted as it opened by a shower of
flowers from his A.P.A. supporters, and he was responsible for
the introduction of two bills, one to forbid the misuse of the
national flag for advertising purposes, and the other relative to

immigration and naturalization. Both bills were referred to committees and remained there.[109]

Somewhat querulously, Representative Charles Grosvenor, Republican of Ohio, reported to the House that his failure to vote on the sectarian appropriations bill in the previous session had resulted in an unpleasant campaign for him. Despite his Protestant heritage, which he felt the A.P.A. people could very well have taken into account, he had been called a fit companion for Catholic cardinals, but he wanted his colleagues to know that he had won his seat in 1894 by a greater vote than he had gotten in 1892.[110]

Whether it was a reaction to election results, or the result of thought in repose, this lameduck session acted somewhat differently on contract school matters than had the pre-election session. An amendment was introduced to the appropriation bill, reducing the amount to be spent on Indian schools to 80 per cent of the last appropriation. Thereafter, it was to be the objective to abolish the system within five years by reducing appropriations by 20 per cent each year. The purpose of the concession was to permit the Secretary of the Interior to carry out the substitution of a federal school system within a reasonable time. With only minor quibbling on the mandatory and discretionary features of the amendment, the face-saving gesture and the bill were finally accepted by Congress.[111]

Legislative activity in the states of Michigan, Minnesota, and Washington provided an opportunity to test A.P.A. claims to victories in the elections of 1894. The new legislature of Michigan, which President Traynor had stated was "50 per cent" A.P.A., met in January of 1895. State Senator Julius Jamison of Grand Rapids was identified as the leader of the A.P.A. forces.[112] Traynor himself was in Lansing during a part of the session. Three bills were reported by the daily press as constituting the proposed legislative program of the order: one was an alteration in the 1867 law permitting a Catholic bishop to hold real property as a corporation sole for his diocese; another was a church taxation bill; and a third would have repealed the law

permitting commitment of children to the custody of the House of the Good Shepherd in Detroit.[113]

The first bill, on the bishop's power over diocesan property, was transferred to a committee of which Jamison was chairman and later reported favorably; the committee of the whole in the Senate recommended passage, and on final vote the bill was passed by a vote of twenty-six to one. The lower house, however, refused to concur.[114] Jamison tried again, but his second trial also failed after a favorable report.[115]

Despite a tacit promise during the campaign to introduce such a bill, and despite the fact that the public apparently believed such a bill was in the hopper, judging from the petitions sent to the legislature endorsing it, no bill taxing church property was introduced into either house.[116] The House of the Good Shepherd bill was introduced by State Senator Herbert Smalley of Detroit. It was reported from committee with a "do pass" recommendation and was approved by the Senate to take effect immediately. Again, the lower house refused to concur.[117]

Two other bills, not on the A.P.A. program but acceptable to it, were enacted. One was a compulsory education law.[118] The other required display of the national flag over all school buildings,[119] a law much easier to enact than to enforce. It made no provision for funds to purchase flags, so that the state Superintendent of Schools was moved, upon failures among local school boards to appropriate local funds for purchases, to say that "nothing save stinginess of the smallest type, mulishness of the long-eared variety, or copper-headism of the rankest kind, can long keep the schools from owning and unfurling the flag." [120] The innocuous flag law, or the compulsory school attendance law, could hardly be used to distinguish A.P.A. strength. Moreover, local school boards would undoubtedly have bought flags enthusiastically if A.P.A. strength in their communities had made itself felt. It is difficult to believe under these circumstances that a legislature that was actually composed of members "50 per cent" committed to a specific legislative program could have failed to complete it more decisively.

In the Minnesota legislature, two attempts at compulsory

education and school attendance laws were indefinitely post-poned.[121] An attempt to amend the constitution to forbid the use of public funds in support of institutions not under public control was passed by the lower house, where it was opposed by four men, two of whom were Catholics and Democrats, and one of whom was Republican and of Norwegian birth.[122] In the upper house, the bill was favorably reported from committee and read a second time. By a technical maneuver, it was then referred to another committee, where it died. The man responsible for the technical maneuver was a former Republican Superintendent of County Schools from Lake City, Minnesota.[123]

A bill providing for taxation of church property, amending the state constitution, got to its second reading in the House. Then a committee of the whole recommended an indefinite postponement and was upheld.[124] Another bill, undoubtedly an outgrowth of the Faribault school situation, would forbid the use of any sectarian device or insignia within the public schools, a prohibition obviously directed at nuns' garbs. The bill passed the lower house by a vote of sixty-one to twelve. In the Senate, the bill was outmaneuvered by the man who had also stopped action on the proposed constitutional amendment.[125]

During the session, some remarks were made on the House floor that public officials were not permitted to make inspection visits to the House of the Good Shepherd in St. Paul, where certain convicted persons were being held. A resolution, appointing a committee to conduct an investigation, was enacted and a committee was appointed, but no report was made; [126] the only purpose served by the gesture, apparently, was to prove that the legislature had a right to investigate. In summary, then, if the order had any number of men or any influence in the Minnesota legislature, the number was small and the men were not disciplined, or they were inept parliamentarians.

In the state of Washington, where the state secretary of the A.P.A. was a member of the lower house of the legislature from Tacoma, more success was attained in securing legislation satisfactory to the order. Just before the session took up its business, the state advisory council of the A.P.A. met to map out a legisla-

tive program, and laid claim to control of the lower house either through members committed to the A.P.A. or through sympathizers.[127] Legislator as well as state A.P.A. secretary, Fred Taylor and his affiliation were publicized by the daily press; the handbook of legislative members made mention of his membership in the A.P.A.; and on the first day of the session his desk was decorated with the national flag as well as with an emphatic announcement of his membership.[128]

Taylor introduced four memorials to be sent to the national Congress. Three had to do with naturalization and immigration, calling in turn for a longer term of residence prior to naturalization, for permitting entry into the country only to those who desired citizenship, and for closing off all immigration for a period of ten years so that "starving immigrants" would not compete with native labor. These three memorials were adopted by the legislature and forwarded to Congress,[129] but they represented opinion rather than actual lawmaking. The fourth memorial requested Congress to order the removal from the country of Papal Delegate Satolli, "the said ablegate or delegate of the Pope of Rome." This petition was referred to the Committee on Public Morals for consideration, and was reported from it with a recommendation for passage, but no further action on it was taken.[130]

Perhaps because Taylor's use of the flag at his desk on the first day of the session had made it incongruous, his proposed bill to forbid the use of the flag for advertising purposes failed to secure passage. Another attempt, the creation of a state board of charities to oversee all charitable activities within the state, also failed directly,[131] but its objective was indirectly accomplished otherwise.

Washington's constitution was very definite in its prohibition of expenditures of public money in support of religious purposes,[132] but there was no clause in the constitution concerning tax exemption for real estate used by religious or charitable organizations.[133] Exemption had been a perplexing problem during the six years since the state had achieved statehood.[134] Several attempts were made in 1895 to amend a law of 1893 and thus

permit taxation, but none of these amendments succeeded as introduced.[135] Mr. Taylor, however, was a member of the House Committee on Revenue and Taxation to which all bills of this nature were referred.[136]

A bill, which eventually became law and which contained a legislative victory for the A.P.A., originated in the Senate as a general revenue bill for the support of state government; it went to third reading in that house before it was amended so as to exempt church and charitable properties provided their accounts were open for public inspection. The bill was amended further in the House, referred to the Senate, and then sent to a conference committee to iron out conflicts. It was finally adopted in both houses by large majorities without the recording of individual votes.[137] During the period of its discussion in committee, the daily newspapers reported occasionally on it in general terms, but otherwise no record was made of its compromises.[138] Since it was a general revenue bill without which state government would have no revenue, and since the session was constitutionally limited to a sixty-day period, an individual legislator who voted against it because of one of its minor provisions placed himself in the position of an obstructionist.

The pertinent sections that constituted the A.P.A. victory provided for tax exemption for all property used exclusively for church purposes to the extent of a plot 120 by 200 feet, if the church were supported by donations and did not charge pew rent, and for all charitable institutions, hospitals, homes for fallen women, orphanages, and homes for the aged and infirm, if supported by charity and if profits or income were returned to charitable purposes. The victory for the A.P.A. was contained in the provision that these exemptions were not automatic. To secure the benefits of the law, institutions were required to open their books to the inspection of the state Board of Health and to the county and city officials wherever the institutions were located. Furthermore, the chairman of the Board of County Commissioners and/or the mayor of the city must be included as *ex officio* members of the boards of trustees of such institutions, and the superintendents were required to make annual reports

to the state Board of Health with complete statistics for publication.[139] On the surface, these provisions—if enforced—would appear to contain about all the A.P.A. could hope for in the way of punitive legislation.

But, while the same provisions were enacted into every revenue law passed by the Washington state legislature until 1939, there apparently was no attempt made to enforce them. The Catholic Providence Hospital of Seattle paid its taxes in 1896,[140] which would seem to indicate that it preferred to pay rather than submit to the law. But the legislature of 1899 modified the law, and made its modification retroactive, so that exemption could be granted without inspection if other provisions of the law were met.[141] In the end, then, the law had almost no punitive effect.

This piece of legislation was accomplished, most certainly, with the aid of non-A.P.A. legislators. The same can be said for the memorials introduced by Taylor that were sent to Congress. In total, the record would seem to demonstrate that, whatever victories may be granted to the A.P.A., the legislation itself was not contrary to the growing activity of state government in the supervision of private charities. The explanation for the failure to carry out the punitive features of the tax exemption clauses probably lies in the circumstance that the law was general in its application, and that the local tax assessor would need to levy on Protestant as well as Catholic churches and charities. To enforce the law to the letter would have been political suicide. Perhaps this letter-of-the-law feature, with its political consequences, offers an explanation as to why it was so difficult to write specific antagonisms into general legislation.

Thus, despite all the claims made for it by its own press and friends, as well as the credits that the general newspapers gave it, the A.P.A.'s political successes, when measured by its legislative record, were overrated, even at a time when its friends and its enemies admitted it to have its greatest influence.[142]

After the elections of 1894, and before the legislative record was written, the "patriotic press" discussed the election outcome as it would affect the order's future, in the light of its experiences. Third-party sentiment had existed for some time and now was

discussed again.[143] Pointing to Archbishop Ireland's statements in favor of the Republicans, the *United American* on November 24 warned that the prelate's purpose was to force the A.P.A. out of Republican ranks and into a party of its own. Such a step would be, in the editor's estimation, a mistake. On December 1 the paper reported President Traynor's belief that patriotism was the "alchemy which will hold the A.P.A. together in politics." The winning of office, not legislation, had so far been the mistaken emphasis misdirecting the order, he said; his point was that the A.P.A. should have no allegiance to either party. The *Loyal American and the North,* on December 15, and *Doyle's Paper,* on April 15, 1895, joined the discussion. Both opposed the third-party proposals, and both cited the Prohibition party as an example of placing principle before victories. Both papers described and discussed a tactic called "balance of power," which they believed to be the explanation of A.P.A. influence; that is, the order should swing its weight to the candidate or the party from which it would obtain results. Traynor continued to insist that real independence of the two major parties would operate best for the order, and in this continued to disagree with the *United American.* As the editor carried on the discussion, he found himself disagreeing with Traynor on more and more points; finally, he charged that Traynor was attempting to destroy the *United American.*[144] On the subject of third parties, the Butte *Examiner,* in an article on June 15, 1895, maintained a neutral position, presenting the arguments of both sides but preferring to let its readers make up their own minds.

As a case in point, the anti–third-party editors pointed to Illinois for an example of foolhardiness; there, Walter F. Sims, the A.P.A. lecturer, had inaugurated an Independent American Party to take part in the election of 1894. It was hinted that his expenses were paid by the Democrats in order to take A.P.A. support from the Republicans.[145] Several candidates had been nominated, a platform had been written opposing sectarianism in education and advocating literacy tests for voting, and several planks were included that could have had some appeal to populist-minded voters.[146] When this venture fizzled on election

day, the Milwaukee German paper, *Der Seebote,* reported the dismal showing, and stated that the party's principles were those of the A.P.A., hinting that the parent order would eventually end up the same way: *"Es geht los."* [147]

In the midst of this discussion, which might have been regarded as a healthy sign if the order had really exhibited political independence during the election just past, the A.P.A. showed that it could still take advantage of Catholic announcements. A papal edict condemning secret societies was issued in 1894; specifically, the Knights of Pythias, the Odd Fellows, and the Sons of Temperance were listed on it.[148] Some American Catholic bishops pondered whether this edict should be publicized because of the encouragement it might give to the A.P.A., and their decision was to withhold publication. However, Cardinal Satolli communicated to them the papal wish for immediate publicity in December of 1894.[149] The announcement was regarded as a "tactical blunder" and an infringement of the "personal liberty of choice" for Catholics by non-A.P.A. Protestants. It was said not to distinguish between the immoral and vicious secret societies and those which were not and was also said to apply best in "medieval" Europe rather than in America.[150]

In Tacoma and Seattle, for example, the edict was received with amazement. The *Ledger* of Tacoma on December 28 asserted in an editorial, "It has long been known that the Roman Catholic church was opposed to such secret societies as could not be governed by it," and somewhat indignantly gave unasked-for advice to Catholics: "Americanize thyself before thou venture to control Americans." According to an article in the *Daily Ledger* on December 29, a Tacoma priest refused to accept the edict as genuine until he had a copy with the Pope's signature on it.

In both cities, A.P.A. councils made plans for a general conclave of local patriotic orders and secret societies to protest. In Tacoma, all three of the condemned lodges had representatives at a meeting with A.P.A. state president Van Fossen presiding. The Temperance group found nothing odd in the condemnation, said one speaker; after all, three fourths of the saloon keepers in the country were Catholics, as were most of the "dive keepers

and gamblers," and one does not bite the hand that feeds one. The Pythian representative chided the A.P.A. as the obvious favorite of the Pope since it was not condemned. In Seattle, a similar meeting was well attended. One speaker was John Bushell, a prominent Temperance man, who forthwith became an A.P.A. leader in Seattle and who was soon publishing a weekly newspaper, the *Spirit of Seventy-Six*. The friendly *Argus* commented that the storm over the edict was the result of having a "macaroni-eating Dago" like Satolli to carry out the Pope's every whim in America.[151]

Despite the evidences of strength and growth elsewhere, the backbone of the A.P.A. had apparently been broken in the Midwest, where it had its first success. In February of 1895, Edwards Doyle resigned as editor of the *Loyal American and the North* and moved to Portage, Wisconsin, where he began *Doyle's Paper*,[152] another venture into anti-Catholic journalism that lasted only until May 1, 1895.[153] Replacing Doyle in Minneapolis was James P. Koll, a former proofreader on the Minneapolis *Tribune,* but the first issue of March, 1895, was the last of the *Loyal American and the North.*[154]

Trouble appeared also within the state council of Ohio. Wildasin, the state president, found that his position did not guarantee to him or to other officers the domination of policy that he thought should attach to the positions. In fact, he said, the order's political activity was controlled, not by its membership, but by an "inner circle" of politicians and officeholders in Cincinnati, Columbus, and Toledo, who manipulated the order to suit themselves. The Columbus *Record,* now somewhat a critic of the A.P.A., added its comment from bitter experience, "He ought to visit Columbus." [155]

Sims's third party was the reason for open disagreement within the Illinois state council. President Johnson disapproved of the venture, after it had failed, as a case of attempted personal aggrandizement on the part of Sims. The two men fought bitterly for control of the delegates to the order's state convention in 1895. President Johnson favored the Republican alliance, while Sims advocated more flexibility in political action. Sims carried

his fight to the convention floor, but Johnson utilized his power as presiding officer to adjourn the convention one day ahead of schedule, so the issue was not decided by the delegates. Sims thereupon led his supporters from the hall; his walkout signaled the beginning of a rapid decline of the A.P.A. in Illinois.[156]

When he was making arrangements for the annual Michigan state convention for the spring of 1895, state president Beatty, who was also national secretary, announced that the objective of the A.P.A. was eventually to form a third party. The convention met in Saginaw with three delegates from each council in the state, one hundred in all. The reason for the marked difference in numbers between 1894 and 1895 was explained by Walter Sims, the Illinois troublemaker now visiting Michigan to bring "light" to the membership. He charged that Beatty's claims as to members were, and always had been, vastly inflated; that instead of the one hundred thousand members claimed, something like five thousand was more like the real truth. For his own state of Illinois, he reported that only 120 councils remained of the 300 that had once existed and were still claimed to be operating. The reason for decline, Sims said, was the fact that appeals to prejudice concentrating on Catholicism were accepted mostly by "protestant illiterates" who were not interested in real principles. He offered his own recently organized "Loyal Patriotic League" as a haven for those disgruntled A.P.A. members who agreed with him that the real issue was patriotism. He also implied that he could demonstrate that the Michigan A.P.A. had been sold out by its leadership to the Republican politicians.[157]

Another source of criticism, also from outside the order, was the daily press of Detroit. The *News* published facsimile letters purporting to show a financial tie-up between certain Republican aspirants for office and the political advisers of the A.P.A. The source of the letters was not mentioned, but the likelihood was that Sims provided them. This revelation also came while the state convention was in session. According to the story, Beatty had been promised six thousand dollars by Colonel A. T. Bliss for the support of the order in Bliss's bid for the governorship nomination at the Republican state convention in 1894. Of this,

only one thousand had actually changed hands, the newspaper reported. In managing the financial affairs of the order, Beatty had been equally unscrupulous, it continued. He had maintained his hold on the national secretaryship by personally appointing ten of the twenty-six delegates from Michigan to the last national convention. Moreover, if Beatty's figures showing 125,000 members in Michigan were true, there should be an annual income from dues of $37,500; but the convention had already been told that the treasury was empty. A financial accounting was suggested. When Colonel Bliss made a routine and immediate denial, the *News* said it was not to be considered unusual under the circumstances, and declared the Colonel to be "dead politically." [158]

In reply to the charges of mismanagement and misinformation, which must have disturbed the delegates, Beatty explained to the convention that Sims was out to ruin the A.P.A. and would take any means to do so. Beatty assured the convention that the stories were simply not true; in fact, he said, the real sellout involved A. E. Gammage, former secretary of the state council, who had attempted to sell his influence to Hazen Pingree. When Gammage had gone to collect the three hundred dollars promised in this version, Pingree's manager had righteously kicked him out of the office.[159] Implicating, as it did, another state officer in charges of political manipulation, the explanation could hardly have eased the delegates' minds.

Beatty, however, was re-elected to the office of state president. J. H. D. Stevens, who had supported Governor Rich's successful bid for renomination while in the pay of the McMillan faction, was chosen vice-president. Stevens thus replaced John Glassford, who had been named in the *News* story as Beatty's right-hand man in the sellout to Bliss, but who had actually been a party to the McMillan group's operations in Rich's favor. Gammage, who was apparently the main spokesman for Pingree within the Michigan A.P.A. leadership, was replaced by S. D. Gage of Kalamazoo.[160] On the whole, then, Beatty came out on top, but so did the partisans of the McMillan machine. Beatty's success did not mean that the delegates accepted his story as true. Mean-

while, Protestant and Catholic church leaders in Bay City joined in a "Christian Unity" movement to attack the A.P.A. as "un-American, un-Christian-like, unbrotherly, and opposed to the best interests of the cause of Christ." [161]

Walter Sims carried his exposures still farther. While the annual national convention was meeting in May of 1895 at Milwaukee, Sims conducted a public evening meeting in another hall. With him on the platform sat A. E. Gammage, deposed secretary of the Michigan council. With only a small amount of heckling from the floor, the meeting proceeded, with Sims charging that instead of the two or three million members claimed by the order, only about one hundred thousand members were really in good standing. He repeated his statement that some officials had used the order to obtain money for their personal uses, and dated his own disagreement with the order from the time of the forged papal encyclicals, which he said were known to be forgeries by the men who used them.[162] Sims's purpose was to present as logical and as reasonable a position for himself as was possible, but he was being somewhat less than truthful, since he had been a recognized A.P.A. lecturer after the forged encyclicals had been printed.

There was evidence coming from the national convention that Sims's charges did not disturb the delegates. President Traynor and Secretary Beatty were elected once again to their respective offices. J. H. Jackson of Fort Worth became vice-president; E. H. Dunbar of Boston was chosen secretary of state; Francis Campbell, the Orangeman of Minneapolis, treasurer; the Reverend J. M. Taulbee of Covington, Kentucky, chaplain. The new officials represented the West Coast, the East, and the South, indicating that the relative importance of the Midwest was now declining within the order. Completing the list of officers were J. H. Woodman of San Diego, sergeant-at-arms; W. B. Howard of Omaha, sentinel; with W. J. Palmer of Butte, J. M. Snyder of Washington, D.C., and H. M. Stark of West Superior, Wisconsin, as trustees.

Convention formalities included the presentation to Congressman Linton of a "little red schoolhouse" made of everlasting

flowers, and the gift of a jeweled medal to former president and founder Henry Bowers. In his acknowledgment, Bowers displayed his characteristic oratorical style:

On March 13, 1887, there was born, upon the banks of the Mississippi River, in a western city, the child I love and admire, and cherish with a father's care, and we named it the American Protective Association. It too has had its springtime and summer and the harvest with a bounteous yield, and yet we hear the music of the sickle and the songs of the reapers voicing the sentiments of their patriotic souls, "My country 'tis of thee, sweet land of liberty," and all the world inclines an ear to catch the sweet refrain. We see the frost that is rapidly approaching upon our land, we can feel the effect of the finger of the Tiber's noted pontiff, Rome's plague and Italy's potent curse, while he sits weaving a garland of the advantages gained in this country. We can see the leaves dropping one by one by his cruel and blasting touch, and so we hear the cry and despair and desolation coming up from the people, "Save us, save us from this monster!" [163]

Representation at this convention was at its broadest. Every state in the Union, except Mississippi, was said to be represented,[164] although not every state had a state council at this time; Arkansas, for example, had only one delegate in attendance. Three Negroes were present in an official capacity.[165] Two hundred and seventy delegates in all were present. Canadian guests worked with these delegates to set up plans for an International Protective Association and worked out a declaration of principles for it.[166] Two months later, at Detroit, Canadian representatives met with the supreme council of the A.P.A. to establish the International formally.[167] Its objective was to press the development of the order in the British Isles particularly.[168]

In preparation for the presidential election of 1896, the convention designated five men to meet in December with representatives of other patriotic societies to plan a concerted campaign effort. Members of this group were George Van Fossen of Tacoma, Allison Stocker of Denver, A. V. Winter of Tennessee, State Senator H. A. Gibson of Pennsylvania, and Colonel E. H. Sellers of Detroit. These men were expected to operate somewhat as did the national committees of the two major parties; it was in effect a national advisory board.[169]

In his speech to the delegates, President Traynor reviewed the accomplishments of the preceding year and issued some warning words for the coming year. He reported membership gains on the Atlantic Coast and in the Far West, while he also pointed with pride to a successful invasion of the South. Politically, he referred to the overwhelming victories in 1894, particularly to that in Michigan; but he warned that Michigan's experience should be a lesson to other state groups on what to avoid in political action. Too much blind cooperation with an unscrupulous political machine in Michigan, he said, had led to the denial of satisfactory legislation by A.P.A.-supported men once they were in office. Opposition to individuals and institutions was not enough to assure continued political success, Traynor said, but what the order should do was to demonstrate that its political course was independent of any established party and that its members intended to seek positive legislation rather than merely to defeat unsatisfactory men. He advised local councils to be ever vigilant that troublesome men should not be admitted to membership; pointing to the experience with Sims, he declared that "rule or ruin" men had destroyed other groups and that they would ruin the A.P.A. if the membership were not vigilant. Legislatively, he commended Utah for incorporating a women's suffrage clause in its constitution. He advocated the passage of convent inspection laws, immigration restriction, the abolition of sectarian appropriations, and the restriction of the suffrage to persons who were already full-fledged citizens. He spoke vehemently against the recently established Catholic University in the national capital.[170] Thus, while Traynor did not specifically acknowledge the truth of Sims's charges, he did admit that the order had worked with the political machine of Michigan to its own detriment. On the whole, Traynor showed an awareness of the problems his organization faced and also indicated an awareness of the disintegration already threatening it from within.

Certainly, the A.P.A. was at its peak of membership and influence in the last months of 1894 and the early months of 1895. The news of the legislative shortcomings was unlikely to catch up with the excessive claims that were made as to victories in the

elections of 1894. Actually, of course, the order had merely capitalized on election returns that were not exclusively of its own making. The Republican party had won the elections of 1894, not the A.P.A.

Membership figures and influence for the A.P.A. were always inexact; for example, they were never given except in totals rounded off to five. For another thing, figures were often given as representing "membership," or "voters," or "influence." The last of these three, the most intangible of the lot, was the best figure to use when dealing with political matters, but it was the one most susceptible to testing by party politicians. How either of the last two could be accurately measured was something best left for the person or persons desiring to utilize one or both of them. From certain bits of evidence, it can be concluded that the first figure, "membership," represented the number of persons who had joined the organization in its lifetime, whether each of these people had kept up on his dues or not, and whether the person concerned considered himself any longer a member or not. It can also be concluded that reports from individual states were inaccurate, even of memberships on this very elastic basis.[171]

Any estimate of the membership of the A.P.A. must take into account the fact that the order was at one and the same time a secret society with its own distinct membership list, and a federation for political purposes of self-styled "patriotic societies." The total membership of the federation was probably somewhere near the two and one-half million figure; the actual membership of the A.P.A., that is the distinct lodge, was perhaps one hundred thousand.[172] But it should be remembered that it was the larger figure that was referred to when its contemporaries spoke of the "A.P.A. movement."

The membership table has the virtue of demonstrating relative strength by states for the federation. That the concentration of strength was in the Midwest cannot be doubted. But there was a surprising show of strength on the Pacific Coast, while Massachusetts, New York, and Pennsylvania were strong. Claims of expansion in the South were perhaps encouraging to the membership when they were made. But aside from Louisiana, Arkan-

TABLE 1

MEMBERSHIP OF THE AMERICAN PROTECTIVE ASSOCIATION

State	Membership Total *	State Population †
Maine	6,500	722,000
New Hampshire	3,800	385,000
Vermont	4,750	337,000
Massachusetts	100,000	2,472,749
Rhode Island	2,700	375,000
Connecticut	3,800	790,000
New York	150,000	6,690,842
New Jersey	78,000	1,689,400
Pennsylvania	165,000	5,745,574
Delaware	2,500	179,700
Maryland	18,000	1,122,890
West Virginia	7,500	857,325
Ohio	163,500	3,825,000
Indiana	75,850	2,406,504
Michigan	125,000	2,241,500
Kentucky	85,000	2,000,000
Illinois	125,000	4,500,000
Missouri	138,000	3,000,000
Wisconsin	176,850	2,000,000
Minnesota	12,500	1,500,000
North Dakota	4,325	200,000
South Dakota	3,000	390,000
Montana	18,000	185,000
Idaho	7,500	125,000
Iowa	76,000	2,010,000
Nebraska	84,500	1,250,000
Wyoming	19,000	80,000
Kansas	65,325	1,450,000
Colorado	100,000	425,000
Utah	10,500	252,834
Virginia	5,600	1,750,000
North Carolina	3,500	1,700,000
South Carolina	3,675	1,270,000
Tennessee	85,000	1,800,000
Georgia	6,500	1,956,000
Florida	2,350	425,000

State	Membership Total *	State Population †
Alabama	3,785	1,600,000
Mississippi	2,500	1,352,800
Louisiana	15,800	1,200,000
Arkansas	25,650	1,300,000
Indian Territory	1,535	. . . .
Oklahoma	3,250	250,000
Texas	65,000	2,650,000
New Mexico	2,500	190,000
Alaska	2,545	32,000
Washington	115,000	395,589
Oregon	84,000	350,000
California	175,650	1,350,000
Nevada	8,450	44,000
Arizona	3,850	68,000
District of Columbia	. . . . . .	
United States Total	2,448,540	
Europe Total	7,850	
WORLD TOTAL	2,456,390	

* The order of arrangement of the above follows the chart given in Albert C. Stevens, *The Cyclopedia of Fraternities* (New York: Hamilton Printing and Publishing Company, 1899), p. 114, which states that these figures are "official but do not seem to be sufficiently in accord with the situation to be of great value for comparison." This statement appeared in 1897.

† These figures are the actual figures or the estimates reported by state governors for 1895, and given in the *World Almanac, 1895*, p. 473.

sas, and Texas, the claims must be written off as publicity rather than accurate reporting of the facts. Kentucky, Tennessee, and Missouri provided some strength in the old border states. Of individual states, probably Wisconsin provides the greatest surprise. Compared with Illinois, a state that had much the same background in population and in school controversies, Wisconsin probably gained stronger A.P.A. membership because of the

identification there with the Republican party fortunes and the virulence of the Democratic attack. Again, Wisconsin's total membership is noteworthy when compared with that of Minnesota, another state where large foreign-born Protestant populations lived. Catholic leadership in Wisconsin was German and conservative, and it did not hesitate to collaborate with the Democrats on the Bennett Law issue in 1890 and in subsequent campaigns. On the other side, Minnesota's Catholic leader was Archbishop Ireland of St. Paul, a staunch Republican and a Catholic who believed the best thing to do in opposing anti-Catholicism was to ignore it. Despite a parochial school problem potentially as explosive as that in Wisconsin, Minnesotans failed to accept the A.P.A. anywhere nearly as strongly as did Wisconsinites.

Perhaps the most significant fact that the membership table reveals was that the A.P.A., and consequently anti-Catholicism and Catholicism as issues in political struggles, was strongest in the same states where the Catholic population was the largest.[173] Probably nothing was so important in explaining the growth of the order as the fact that Catholics were taking a more active part in national and local affairs. Immigration was not the only source of irritation stemming from Catholicism's growth; probably more significant than increase in numbers was the increasing activity of Catholic citizens and the recognition by politicians that they were a political force.

In a very real sense, the A.P.A. was an organization in which the mass of individual members remained almost anonymous. In the group, the individual behaved rather typically except for his disposition to accept suspicion as a guide to political behavior.[174] The leadership of the order was not comparable in quality to that in other national organizations.[175] It was inferior and selfish. Except for Bowers, who stayed with the organization until he died, its leaders were willing to use it only as long as it served their purposes.

6 Riding the Crest, 1895

Between the annual convention of the A.P.A. in 1895 and its meeting one year later during the summer of a presidential campaign, the order continued to experience some dissension from within, and consistent criticism and opposition from outside, its ranks. The source of internal dissension and distrust was suspicion of the leadership, fostered by evidence that these leaders had used the organization for their own purposes, and kept alive by repeated references to the incidents by certain members of the "patriotic press." Ironically enough, suspicion of Catholicism was the source of the order's growth in the first place, and now suspicion of its own members was to be a reason for its decline.

Not only was there distrust among the members and followers, however; there was a general loosening of the ties that bound the A.P.A. into a common purpose with other self-styled patriotic groups, ties that had given meaning to the widely held belief that there was great political strength in the letters A.P.A. In legislation, the principal objective of the order had been to prevent appropriations from government funds in support of sectarian institutions. This objective had been for all purposes attained by the end of 1894. For its accomplishment, the A.P.A. hardly deserved the sole credit, inasmuch as there had been support for such legislation even before there had been an A.P.A. But attainment of the goal lessened the force and directness of the A.P.A.'s appeal. The order was not to be successful in attaining its more punitive objectives in legislation, the laws that were intended to have a detrimental effect on Catholics or Catholicism. Taxation of church property, for example, had sounded reasonable when large and rich cathedrals, schools, and the many other institutions supported by Catholics were considered. But a law

providing for their taxation would apply equally to all religious groups, and moderation was certain to temper a legislator's second thought or an administrator's enforcement. Those laws that called for a specified treatment to be accorded the national flag could hardly have been opposed by anyone, even though many individuals might distrust the efficacy of inculcating patriotism by law. Immigration restriction and qualifications on the suffrage were desired by people within all political parties. The only question involved on these two issues was as to what specific provisions should be written into law to attain the ends. Thus, that part of the A.P.A. success which came because of its ability to capitalize on currently popular legislative reforms could slip away as easily as it had come.

Politically, the order had demonstrated its commitment to the Republican party so strongly that its independence of action was gone, and even shrewd Republicans learned that they need pay no more than passing attention to it. There was little likelihood that Democrats would benefit if anti-Catholics should leave the Republican party for a third-party venture. The Populist threat to the major parties also was lessening, and there was no indication that A.P.A. support would be welcome in Populist ranks. There was, additionally, reason to believe that some Catholics were finding a political home within Republican ranks, an event which meant that party leaders would tend to be cautious not to disturb this new allegiance by too close attention to anti-Catholics.

Nevertheless, despite evidence of distrust within and increasing opposition from without, the year was not solely one of decline and loss of influence. The subtle change that had occurred was recognized by shrewd contemporary observers experienced in such matters, and it is obvious in retrospect. Yet the façade of success and importance, built on easily obtained publicity, still stood and continued to be maintained for another year before it crumbled. In those regions where the A.P.A. had first gained a foothold, the decline was most obvious; in the areas where it had most recently made its appearance, it was still showing signs of growth. Thus, the Midwest showed the first evidence of loss of

prestige at a time when the Pacific Coast region was still showing advances and maintaining strength already gained.

In the states of Oregon and Washington, the order continued to organize effectively, holding regular council meetings, hearing occasional visiting lecturers, and using cryptic advertising such as the following, which appeared in Eugene, Oregon:

A.P.A.
The mills of the gods grind slow, but the product is
Murder, whoredom, ceaseless war, and slavery,
Perpetual HELL and torment.
27-33-69-31-97-L-O-T
Meeting in their dungeon January 1st
At the regular specified time.
AMERICAN PROTECTIVE ASSOCIATION
The innocent sleep, while the keen edge of the razor,
In the hands of the supposed priests' angels
Cut their throats from ear to ear.
YOU BETTER LOOK THE MATTER UP
It's in Eugene
1842–1852   1862–1872
The most secret order in the world is the Roman Catholic Church, and next to that is their friend the A.P.A. There are ten million Catholics in the U.S.A., and there are nearly three million of the A.P.A.'s. Watch results. The greatest truth will surely win.
BETTER GET INTERESTED ENOUGH TO LOOK THE
MATTER UP
1892–1902   1912–1922 [1]

The Reverend E. B. Sutton, state organizer for Washington, had the unpleasant experience of being pelted with rotten eggs on two occasions, but his activities were not curtailed thereby. He carried the order into Idaho, where, at Wardner, it soon became involved in a fight with organized labor. In this Idaho mining region, the Knights of Labor unit passed a resolution reporting to friends of labor everywhere that the local A.P.A. council was in favor of reducing miners' wages in the Coeur d'Alene region, a reduction that was eventually successful. On the other hand, mine owners in Montana were reported to be threatening with discharge any man who joined the order.[2]

California members began to support the publication of a

fairly large monthly, the *A.P.A. Magazine,* in June of 1895. It offered its readers special rates on the purchase of Lew Wallace's *Ben Hur,* Chiniquy's *Fifty Years in the Church of Rome,* and Maria Monk's *Awful Disclosures,* and many other titles, while it also advertised as an "anti-Catholic" book Mandell Creighton's five-volume *History of the Papacy during the Period of the Reformation.*[3]

The miscellaneous but minor incidents that had accompanied the career of the order in previous years continued. The *American Pope* of Spokane discontinued publication in June of 1895 after a very short career,[4] and the editor of the *United American* of Washington, D.C., found himself arrested for libel after asserting that a local merchant would hire no one but Catholics. This editor then sought to invoke sympathy for himself as a victim of the "Romish conspiracy."[5] While it continued a campaign to "expose" convent life, the Butte *Examiner* replaced its editor several times. Surprisingly, this paper editorialized in support of academic freedom in the case of Professor Bemis at the University of Chicago,[6] even though there was no question of Catholicism involved. At Seattle, an anonymously published list of local members was broadcast for purposes of inaugurating a boycott of businessmen listed thereon; a counterboycott resulted when A.P.A. members sought to "fight fire with fire." The effect of the contest on the community's business life was then deplored. Seattle's *Spirit of Seventy-Six* conducted a campaign against the local House of the Good Shepherd, while the local councils asked the city to investigate the matter. The City Council asked for legal advice from the city attorney and were told that no legal basis for an investigation existed, so the issue was officially closed.[7]

The discussion of the merits of a third-party venture now bubbled over into a serious criticism of A.P.A. leadership. Unlike the case of Walter Sims of Illinois, who had left the order to criticize it from outside, the controversy now concerned individuals within the order who insisted that their organizational loyalty was greater than that of the leaders they criticized. Mrs. Oostdyk, president of the Women's A.P.A., had appointed a deputy. Not

only was there no constitutional provision for such an officer, there was likewise no authority for the appointment, rather than the election, of any officer. Her action, thus, produced an immediate outcry to restore the ladies to proper constitutional procedures and limit executive highhandedness.[8]

Much more serious than this was the campaign waged against the administration of President Traynor by the editor of the *United American*. This was a continuation of a third-party discussion in which Traynor favored political independence and editor Boyer desired to continue working within the Republican party. But the editor enlarged the area of his disagreement to include certain occurrences at the national convention of 1895. Quoting the Louisville *Justice*, which was also apparently concerned with "America first," the *United American* asked with reference to the internationalization of the A.P.A., "What need Americans care if the people of other countries see fit to kneel at the feet of Rome?" Moreover, the editor maintained, President Traynor's re-election to office was an illegal manipulation of executive power, since only the California, Massachusetts, and District of Columbia delegates at the convention had represented councils whose financial obligations to the order were currently paid. Not Traynor, consequently, but Judge Jackson of Fort Worth should have become supreme president. Specifically, Traynor was charged with jobbery for the benefit of his friends in Michigan, Maryland, and District of Columbia councils. The charge involving Michigan was based on Walter Sims's charges already publicized; in Maryland, Traynor was said to have appointed a state president who was neither a Maryland voter nor employed within the state (he worked in the District of Columbia); within the District, Traynor's personal zeal was said to have amounted to an attempt to get a *United American* subscription list so as to use it to increase the circulation of his own *Patriotic American* of Detroit. Some of these charges were picayunish and personal, but the allegations as to the order's treasury revealed publicly for the first time that the order was nearing bankruptcy because of failure to collect dues. On this point, editor Boyer asked Traynor to account for the money

already expended, and what specifically had happened to the dues from three million members. The *United American* announced its determination to continue fighting Catholicism and corruption: "We'll fight Rome 'till hell freezes over, and then fight it on the ice; but we'll not do so under the leadership of William John Henry Traynor." [9]

Several months later, the Reverend Thomas C. Easton, president of an A.P.A council in Washington, D.C., joined Boyer and wrote an open letter expressing his disagreements with Traynor and citing many of the same charges. Traynor, he wrote, was an "autocrat, a despot and a veritable czar," and he too requested complete reorganization of the order, with an accompanying financial accounting. His letter was reported to the nation by regular news services.[10] Disturbed by the unfavorable publicity incident to these revelations of dissent, the Butte *Examiner* wrote a "Harmony in the Order" editorial asking that dirty laundry be washed in private.[11]

Another series of incidents indicated a different attitude toward the organization by outsiders. Unlike the Butte A.P.A. riot, which had little nationwide publicity and had no effect except to stimulate the order locally, there occurred in Boston on July 4, 1895, a riot that produced disparaging publicity and led to condemnations of the A.P.A. by newspapers and national figures. A general parade to celebrate the Fourth had been held in the morning. Permission for the entry of a "little red schoolhouse" float in this parade had been denied. When the "patriotic orders" asked for a parade permit for an afternoon procession all their own, it too was denied. They then appealed to Governor Greenhalge, who advised them that no permit was necessary so long as the streets were not blocked; at the same time he advised them against holding the parade. The governor, however, promised police protection to the marchers if it were held,[12] and it was. Trouble began when the controversial float appeared escorted by a carriage in which a woman was seated wearing an orange dress. A member of the governor's guard attempted to quell the outbreak, but his yellow-plumed hat only incited more

trouble. In the general melee that followed, one man was killed and many others were injured.[13]

The evidence did not indicate that the A.P.A. was responsible for the riot, although the "patriotic orders" were responsible for the parade that had set it off. Seeing fault on both sides, the *New York Times* deplored the resort to violence and hoped that the "Irishness" of the Irish as well as the "Orangeism" of the anti-Catholics could be submerged in "Americanism," which neither group seemed to be encouraging.[14] The *Outlook* placed the initial responsibility on the Board of Aldermen of Boston for denying the first parade permit and thus producing a riot situation. But it also deplored violence, and stated that though the rioting broke out when the "patriots" were attacked, fanaticism was not characteristic exclusively of the Irish and the Catholics involved.[15]

Among some of the patriots, the emphasis on "Orangeism" was too much; thus, a former president of an A.P.A. council in Chelsea, Massachusetts, announced his withdrawal from the order, saying, "It is come now to such a point that patriotism is put back in second place and the one object seems to be pitching into the Roman Catholic church. . . . This patriotic order should not be something to give alien-born residents of this country an excuse to engage in religious fights." Since Traynor was an Orangeman, and since Orangemen were never satisfied until they were "cracking at some Irish Catholic head," this writer preferred to leave the A.P.A. and to seek a patriotic society that had Americans as its officers.[16]

From outside, the riot produced strong criticism directed at the A.P.A. In the spring of 1895, Republican Senator George Hoar of Massachusetts had spoken at the opening of Clark University's summer session. His remarks had contained a rather general denunciation of religious proscription in politics. For this, he had been taken to task by letter. Hoar's answer to the letter writer was made public after the riot and contained his detestation of the A.P.A. and its methods. Hoar reminded his correspondent that he had always been a zealous supporter of the

public schools and that he fully supported the Massachusetts Republican platform on matters of schools and sectarian appropriations. He preferred, however, to do his fighting in support of his beliefs in the open, he said and hoped that eventually he could attract Catholics to his way of thinking. The A.P.A., on the other hand, was a means that would drive Catholics into supporting the ideas of the most extreme members of their clergy on these issues, and he continued, "I think your method will result in driving and compacting together, in solid mass, persons who will soon number nearly or quite 50 per cent of the voting population of Massachusetts. Nothing strengthens men, nothing makes them so hard to hear reason, nothing so drives them to extremity in opinion or in action as persecution and proscription." He ended his letter with a plea not to force the defense of American principles into the "damp malarial atmosphere of dark places," and to remember that the emblem of the Republic was the "eagle and not the bat." [17]

Senator Hoar received much support for his statement as a clarification of the situation.[18] But the *New York Times* could not resist the opportunity to remind Hoar that it disapproved of his retention of "anti-Southern" prejudices while it approved his views on anti-Catholicism in politics. Public approval of his statement, the *Times* wrote, ought to remind Hoar "how much more efficacious and reputable he is when he is giving his intellect a fair chance than when he is airing his prejudices." [19] The St. Paul *Globe,* moreover, recognized that the effect of Hoar's declaration was to take a potent weapon from the hands of Democratic newspaper editors, and tried immediately to prevent it by saying that the public could not be sidetracked into relieving the Republican party of its responsibility for the A.P.A.[20]

At a time when it was being weakened internally by its own supporters, and while it was undergoing sharp attack, the A.P.A. was the subject of many books and pamphlets. These were not official publications, to be sure, but they were approved by one or another of the order's officers, in most cases. A series of lectures given at Toledo, Ohio, was presented in printed form in 1895 in John L. Brandt's *America or Rome: Christ or the*

Pope?,[21] for which W. J. H. Traynor wrote the introduction. The book contained essays making the familiar distinction between religious and political "Romanism," references to the public schools, idolatry, and the adaptability of the confessional to seduction of innocent girls by lust-maddened priests. Traynor asked the readers of the book to become once again "stewards of the nation" in order to preserve liberty by eternal vigilance against its deadly enemy, the papal hierarchy.

J. W. Hile, publisher of the Kansas City *American Eagle,* wrote another pamphlet, *The A.P.A. Must Go,*[22] in which he asserted that the objective of the order was to purify politics, to elect tolerant men to public office, and to keep religion out of politics. These objectives were explained by his statements that Irish-Catholics controlled most large cities with political machines, priest-ridden public officials were notoriously intolerant, and the union of Catholics and officeholders would only be eliminated if the A.P.A. were victorious. National vice-president J. H. Jackson produced still another pamphlet, *The American Protective Association: What It Is, Its Platform and Roman Intolerance Compared*, in which the thirteen planks of the order's platform were listed, each of them followed by an explanatory note.[23] Another, *The Roman Catholic in American Politics,* by W. H. Thomas, proceeded by question-and-answer to solve the problem of "Why do Roman Catholics vote as a solid body?" without ever showing that they did.[24] It presented as working mottoes for loyal Americans who opposed Catholicism the following: "Romanism Ruins Republics" and "Popery Pollutes Politics." Another attempt to play upon the assassination of Presidents Lincoln and Garfield at the hands of "Romanists" appeared when an address by Edwin A. Sherman, given at Boston in 1889, was published in pamphlet form as *Lincoln's Death Warrant: or, The Peril of Our Country* by the A.P.A. weekly, the *Wisconsin Patriot;* this, too, included the principles of the order.[25]

A more substantial volume, physically, was a collection of essays by various men, *Errors of the Roman Catholic Church.*[26] Published with a publisher's note stating that the work did not

"proceed from any ill-feeling toward those who belong to the Roman Catholic Church," it contained essays by a number of Protestant ministers, mostly Baptists and Southern Methodists, among whom were the Reverend Madison C. Peters, whose position on Catholicism was already fairly well known, and Richard Salter Storrs, pastor of the Church of the Pilgrims in Brooklyn, whose views on the subject were not so well known. Storrs was to secure election as president of the American Historical Association the following year in recognition of his work, *Bernard of Clairvaux*.[27] The first essay in the cooperative work was an account of the A.P.A.'s origins and purposes, ignoring the part played by Henry Bowers in its origin and emphasizing the later career of the order as a "cooperative" association of patriotic societies. Some fifty or so of these patriotic organizations were said to be in existence to oppose the "un-Americanism of the Catholic Church." The A.P.A. served the function of a "coordinate" society that would "push the battle for relief from political Romanism through the ballot." The other patriotic societies were said to be mainly defensive; the A.P.A. was "mainly offensive." The writer admitted some faults: "When it is considered that this wonderful movement of organized patriotism is but a few years old, and has grown with a rapidity the like of which no movement at any time has enjoyed in our country, it will not seem strange if in its work, or methods, there be found signs of minor weaknesses, impracticabilities, and crudeness." But the writer looked to the future with confidence, sure that the order would "belt the globe" and succeed in making "Rome tremble."

Another chapter, on "Political Romanism in Washington," repeated the charge that the national capital was under the domination of Jesuits working through government officials subservient to them, and operating out of the papal delegate's residence, Georgetown University, or the newly established Catholic University of America. Former Indian Commissioner Thomas J. Morgan contributed a section on his Washington experiences, and the Reverend Mr. Peters wrote on "Romanism, Illiteracy, Illegitimacy and Crime," stating that the "most marvelous supporter of Romanism is ignorance," and that Catholic

countries were noted for supremacy in illiteracy, illegitimacy, and crime. The historian Storrs considered "The Appeal of Romanism to Educated Protestants," finding that the church's authoritarianism had a satisfying consistency. But he pointed out that this was only half the story—like the dome of St. Peter's in Rome, which was illuminated, he said, on only that side which faced the city. On its reverse, the dome was "frowning and stern" in its dimness; yet he warned his readers that to understand the appeal of Catholicism, they must pay attention to some other aspect of the church than its dark side.

President Traynor appeared again as author in the pages of the *North American Review* on the subject of "The Menace of Romanism." [28] In his article he tried to demonstrate that Catholics did not disagree on any important subject. Archbishop Ireland, although usually termed a "liberal" Catholic, was as consistently a follower of the Pope as was Bishop McQuaid, wrote Traynor. "There is no such thing as a 'Liberal Catholic'; if they are 'liberal' they are not Catholic," he argued. Pointing to the recent attack on Ireland by McQuaid, or to the instances when Catholic priests advised their parishioners how to vote in New York City, or to the instance when the Bishop of South Dakota counseled his priests to vote Republican, Traynor maintained that Catholic political activity could be clearly seen.

The year 1895 also saw the appearance of pamphlets and books defending Catholics and counterattacking the A.P.A. Alfred Young's *Catholic and Protestant Countries Compared* was written during 1894 but not published until 1895.[29] The book was intended as a statistical reply to the charge that ignorance, crime, and poverty were characteristic of Catholic countries. Comparisons were made in tabular form between Catholic and Protestant countries, with the result that Catholic nations were found to be the most moral and most literate. Ireland was classified among the "Protestant" countries because it was dominated by Protestant England. French Canada, on the other hand, was classified among the "Catholic" nations, as distinct from the remainder of Canada, because its customs were French and Catholic.[30] Otherwise, the book contained a general

attack on those Protestant ministers who supported the A.P.A. and the various patriotic orders with which it was associated. Young concluded his book with a list of recent converts from Protestantism to Catholicism and asked that his readers compare their abilities with those of the anti-Catholic leadership.

From Kansas City came a pamphlet, *Why I Am Not an A.P.A.* by Joe Speyer,[31] editor of the Kansas City *Reform*. It asked all men to declare themselves on this new "political fungus," and pointed to the undisputed fact that "no brave man of national power and authority" was in the ranks of the A.P.A., saying that the order was in fact composed of "hopeless failures" who were seeking to secure opportunities for themselves by sowing the seeds of dissent and discord.[32]

An outspoken Protestant lawyer, Patrick Henry Winston of Spokane, politically independent to the extent that, though he was raised a Democrat and had fought for the South in the Civil War, he had become a Republican in 1883 and was to be elected in 1896 as a Populist-Fusion candidate for Attorney-General of the state of Washington, wrote an attack on the A.P.A. and paid for its publication out of his own pocket.[33] In vigorous and straightforward language, Winston attempted to destroy the charge that Catholics split their allegiance between the nation and the Pope. He classified members of the A.P.A. into five groups: (1) those who had become members in ignorance of the real principles of the order, (2) those who were intrigued by the mysteries and secrecies of the ritual, (3) honest fanatics who really believed what was said about Catholicism, (4) business and professional men who entered because they thought it would be good for their businesses, and (5) small caliber politicians who desired political preferment but could not obtain it on merit. At another period in his career, Winston had noted that unscrupulous individuals could utilize any one of three "merchantable" assets to conceal motives: religion, patriotism, and the public schools.[34]

Controversial, but not partisan in its intention, opinion also appeared on subjects that concerned the two camps. During 1895, a scholarly account of church-state relations appeared that em-

phasized individual choice while it deplored paternalism, whether governmental or otherwise. Its comments, consequently, on such matters as sectarian school appropriations were not favorable to the most extreme Catholic position. In general, however, in tone and point of view the book was an expression of that secularism which had at one time seemed to coincide with A.P.A. goals.[35] Now, though, the book could assist toward a clarification of issues.

Two articles also pointing toward clarification appeared in national magazines having to do with the Irish and the numerical growth of Catholicism. The *Atlantic Monthly* presented an analysis of the Irish in America. Exhibiting some of the characteristics of a "conquered race," Irishmen were described in it as "morbidly sensitive." The writer deplored the religious antagonisms engendered by the A.P.A. but thought the order was less effective than the Know-Nothings had been and would prove to be more transitory in its effects. Politically, the author admitted that there was a well-known alignment of Irish and Democrats and said that the facts of the alignment had never been seriously challenged. But dishonesty in politics was "hardly more of a crime to an Irishman than smuggling is to a woman," he said, and should not lead to any more distress. Somewhat more hopefully, the author felt that the Irish would no longer be quite so able to disturb peaceful relationships between the United States and Britain.[36] Less inflammatory in its statement of the "facts," a more moderate article appeared in *Outlook*. Its author cautioned that the so-called Catholic threat of numerical supremacy was easily overemphasized and misunderstood: "Now, there is no occasion in any section for either Catholic hopes or American Protective Association fears of Catholic political ascendancy," since the number of church communants and the total of voters were figures in which Protestants still outnumbered Catholics.[37]

Thus, throughout the year 1895 the order was getting publicity and was being subjected to criticism in print by its enemies whether they were Catholic or Protestant or neither. Surveying the daily newspapers, *Public Opinion* reported in August of

1895 with regard to the A.P.A. that "press indorsements of that association's tenets and methods are not easily found." [38] The daily press had never endorsed the A.P.A., but it had contributed to the façade of its success by a failure to report political news objectively. For a while to come, the daily press continued to label Republican candidates who were willingly or unwillingly supported by the A.P.A. as the "A.P.A. candidates," an appellation that was hardly just.

Local political contests continued to be those in which avowedly A.P.A. people most frequently achieved success. In school board and municipal affairs, however, these officials were faced with the necessity of providing government, a necessity which produced uncomfortable results in some instances. Despite attempts on the part of President Traynor to alter the political emphasis of the order from negative opposition to particular candidates toward positive legislative goals and a third party, the membership and its political advisers continued usually to support Republicans. Since the elections of 1895 were "off year" contests and consequently were a time for testing, and because Republican victories were the order of the day, the order's facility for capitalizing on victories and being credited with achieving them continued. After elections, and in the legislation achieved by the men elected, the A.P.A. influence was most obvious by its nonappearance.

On the Pacific Coast, where the A.P.A. was still flourishing, its candidates were elected to school boards in Seattle and Tacoma. In November of 1895, Seattle chose three board members acceptable to the order, so that with the one already on the board a majority of members were said to be favorable to the A.P.A. Within a very short time, however, the board was creating a job for a relative of one of them and dismissing all school janitors so as to provide further patronage. There was no agreement among A.P.A. people as to who should get the vacated jobs, and within the year the board members were considered disloyal by the members of the local council. At Tacoma, where an A.P.A. school board was already in office, the voters were called upon to approve a bond issue in order to keep the schools

open. Poor management, which made additional funds necessary, was charged to the incumbent board. In the bond election, the W.A.P.A. worked diligently to secure approval of the bond issue, and it was approved. But that fall, when board members were up for re-election, the A.P.A.-sponsored candidates were defeated by nearly four to one.[39]

At Spokane, an election in the fall of 1895 placed two men favorable to the order on the school board. As the spring term was drawing to a close, teachers were hired for the following year. Each teacher was asked his religious affiliation, and only non-Catholics were rehired. Two Catholic teachers, both in primary grades, were among six teachers dismissed in this fashion. Despite the board's statement that religion was no more involved in the dismissal of the two Catholics than it was in the case of the four others, the local daily newspaper continued to probe the matter. Soon it revealed that a committee of the board had inserted the objectionable question on religion in the application blanks, and in dismissing the two had gone over the head of the superintendent, who had wished to retain them. That fall, the incumbents did not choose to face re-election campaigns on their records.[40]

In Portland, Oregon, a member of the Junior Order of United American Mechanics became a candidate for the school board with the support of the A.P.A. His campaign favored state publication of textbooks and in it he had the support of some school principals and teachers. After a well-publicized campaign, in which the *Oregonian* tried to explain the issues, the so-called "A.P.A. man," who had incidentally denied membership in the order, was defeated.[41]

The Milwaukee Catholic diocesan paper reported that four Irish-Catholic teachers were dismissed in Newport, Kentucky, by an A.P.A. school board.[42] Such incidents led a writer in the *Atlantic Monthly* to warn that the public schools might be "burned up in the fire" kindled by controversies between strongly partisan and religious groups.[43]

Two months later, the *Atlantic* published the results of a questionnaire it had sent to teachers and superintendents all over the

country. The subject of the investigation was "improper influences" in hiring and firing practices and their effect on tenure. Responses indicated that improper pressures from textbook publishers, favoritism by school board members, political "pull," and demagoguery were reported by over 40 per cent of the teachers involved. Where religion entered the picture, teachers reported that membership in the prevailing church in the community was important, but there was no indication in this poll that A.P.A. influences were of anything but minor importance to the educators responding. In fact, one of them had a good word to say for an A.P.A. school board that had retained a Catholic teacher.[44] On the face of this summary, despite some scattering evidence to the contrary, it would appear that the A.P.A. had little effect on the hiring practices of school boards in general; at least the effect of the A.P.A. was not strong enough to surmount influences that teachers found more distasteful.

In municipal affairs, the A.P.A. was on occasion linked to unsavory patronage squabbles, corruption, and bribery, and charged with inability to focus its support at the crucial moments. From Louisville, Kentucky, came news of a conflict between the mayor and the A.P.A.-dominated city council. At issue were patronage in city departments and paving contracts. Before the struggle for power was over, four members of the council were indicted by a grand jury, but the news stories incident to the events indicated that Democrats, Populists, and Republicans were engaged in a three-way struggle for political control, with the A.P.A. the whipping boy of both Democrats and Populists in their attacks on Republicans.[45]

At Omaha, the *Bee* and the *World-Herald,* under the editorship of Rosewater and William Jennings Bryan, respectively, tried to outdo each other in opposing the A.P.A. Each newspaper attempted to demonstrate that the candidates supported by the other were anti-Catholic. Between the two, Omaha's mayoralty election in 1895 was somewhat confused. The *Bee*'s "reform" candidates were defeated, and the *World-Herald*'s Republicans were victorious. Charges of ballot-box stuffing were made, but no investigation of their truth followed. The local A.P.A. councils

were shortly said to be in process of disintegration, perhaps because they couldn't compete with so paradoxical a situation as an erstwhile Republican supporting Populist-Democrats and a former Democratic congressman, now an editor, supporting Republicans.[46]

Seattle A.P.A. councils were apparently strong enough to determine who should be chosen as municipal candidates from among the Republicans, but not strong enough to name one of their own people. Inept handling of delegates in caucuses and in nominating conventions, with the local A.P.A. leader's insisting that his support would be given only to a temperance advocate, resulted in Republican derision directed at the order, terming it a "mass battery" whose function was as "a sort of derrick to lift nincompoops and nonentities into office." An anti-A.P.A. man was chosen as mayor; he resigned his office soon and was replaced by another Republican also unsatisfactory to the order.[47]

The incumbent mayor of Tacoma, elected two years before with A.P.A. support, was opposed openly in his bid for re-election by George Van Fossen, state A.P.A. president. A local newspaper called the meetings of the order "Van Fossen's Sunday School," because they met on Sunday afternoons. For thus poking fun at him, Van Fossen described the daily as "venal, corrupt, and Jesuitical." Despite the derision, Van Fossen's candidate was elected, but by the narrow margin of two votes. The A.P.A. councils, however, then rebuked Van Fossen for his "extravagant" activities during the campaign and implied that he had misused the name of the order.[48]

Spokane's Populist mayor, whose election two years before had been approved by the A.P.A., was not favored by it for re-election in 1895. One charge made during the campaign was that the mayor's street superintendent had hired none but Irish-Catholics. Shortly before election time, the A.P.A. minority on the city council had attempted to promote a "flag resolution" forbidding any flag but the Stars and Stripes to be flown over Spokane buildings. Its inclusiveness probably accounted for its failure to be enacted, for there was support enough for limiting the restriction to public buildings. Despite charges that the in-

cumbent mayor was the candidate of the "vice ring," he was re-elected; the local Republican daily attributed his victory to an "unnatural combination of saloon and church," because the saloon forces had supported him while the church people had worked with the A.P.A. for the Citizen's ticket instead of supporting the regular Republican. Sure of his office for another term, the mayor was shortly again at odds with his city council in a struggle over the police department. "Politics and religious bigotry" were the qualities that the council desired in police administration, according to the mayor's police chief. The council appointed its own police chief while the mayor insisted on retaining his; and the case eventually ended with a court decision upholding the mayor.[49]

Pre-election forecasts in Oregon tended to predict an A.P.A. victory in scattered spring municipal elections. Once the votes were counted, however, the newspaper reports showed that the victors actually represented other issues. In Roseburg, however, the A.P.A. was apparently active enough to split the town into two warring factions, disrupting fraternal lodges, and arraying friends against friends.[50]

In other municipal elections across the country, there was now less willingness among Republicans to accept the support of the order than previously, yet three-way contests often resulted in the A.P.A.'s obtaining some credit for victories. Kansas City news stories reported a former mayor running for election with the support of Populists, Democrats, and anti-A.P.A. Republicans. In the race, the regular Republican came out victor.[51] Republicans and Democrats combined in Youngstown, Ohio, to defeat the regular Republican, who assertedly had the support of the order.[52] In Butte, the anti-A.P.A. Republicans had their own candidate, while the Democrats and Populists combined. The regular Republican won in this three-way contest, with the aid of the A.P.A.[53] The Butte *Examiner,* on May 25, 1896, explained how this could be termed an A.P.A. victory in the following fashion: "The reason why this should be known as an A.P.A. success, is that the other side declared for the opposing ticket, and supported it almost to a man." Thus, once again, the

A.P.A. press defined victory as the defeat of Catholics, "the other side."

In the few gubernatorial elections of 1895, the order played an indefinite role, though its actions were well publicized. Governor Greenhalge of Massachusetts, who had been supported by the order in his previous election and had ruled favorably at the time of the Boston July Fourth parade, was renominated by the Republicans, although he had spoken out in the meantime against the A.P.A. and had taken an active part in the golden jubilee celebration for Archbishop John Williams. His platform, however, was still opposed to the use of public funds for any sectarian purpose and he charged during the campaign that Democrats were responsible for injecting religion into politics. At the last moment, A.P.A. councils announced their support for Greenhalge, who was re-elected but with a Democratic legislature.[54]

In Kentucky there now occurred the first major victory for Republicans in any southern state since Reconstruction days. The race for the governorship was a three-way affair among Democrats, Populists, and Republicans; the Democrats openly denounced the A.P.A., so that its vote went quite solidly to the Republican candidate, William O. Bradley. The victorious Bradley was taken over immediately by members of the A.P.A. press as a promising national figure.[55] Bradley assertedly appeared at some A.P.A. meetings as a guest speaker in acknowledgment of its support,[56] and Sam P. Jones, the evangelist, hailed the Republican victory as an "indication that the American conscience can be reached on the Romish problem," and gave credit for victory to the A.P.A., "the dire need of the age." [57] Kentucky's entry into the Republican camp was of some importance as a reminder of the political turmoil of the times, and the A.P.A. connection with it was another example of the ability of the order to be in the right place at the right time to explain a political overturn in simple terms. Actually, of course, the order was not finding easy victories where there was real work to be done, nor was it finding successes it could claim in the Midwest. As early as mid-1895, the Far West and the South were the areas where its tactics were still successful.

In Ohio, where Senator Foraker and Mark Hanna were struggling for control of the Republican party, the state convention met in May of 1895. A large number of A.P.A. delegates, though clearly not enough to control decisions, was reportedly ready to support Foraker's candidate, Asa Bushnell, for governor. Hanna was asked his impression of A.P.A. strength in the convention and replied, "I don't know anything about it, don't want to say anything about it, and it will be a waste of time to talk about it." [58] Bushnell, himself, denied any knowledge of the order except what he had read in the newspapers, but the A.P.A. state president announced that he believed Bushnell to be in "sympathy" with its principles.[59] Bushnell was nominated and secured election as well, admittedly receiving A.P.A. votes. Commenting on the facts, the *United American* stated that Governor McKinley could not have gotten the support of the order if he had been a candidate, but that Bushnell was acceptable and that his mentor, Foraker, was "the coming man in Ohio. He is as true as steel." [60] Immediately after the election, a report was published that one of the A.P.A. men elected to the new legislature would sell his support for the U.S. senator to be chosen at a price of $1,500. There were no takers.[61]

The new legislature did, however, provide an example of how the A.P.A. received credit in the newspapers even though the facts did not warrant it. Philip M. Ashford, a lawyer from Salineville, introduced into the lower house a bill providing specifically for public inspection of all private and public hospitals, reformatories, houses of detention, convents, seminaries, schools, or other institutions within the state. Such a bill was obviously acceptable to the A.P.A., but in the legislative process a very general substitution was made, which altered the original bill so as to provide inspection only of institutions exercising a "reformatory or correctional influence over individuals." In this modified form, the Ashford Bill was passed by both houses.[62] In reporting passage, however, the *Ohio State Journal* inexplicably described the bill as it had been originally without its changes.[63] Thus through newspaper imprecision the A.P.A. received credit for accomplishing a major legislative victory, when

actually the bill as enacted was a technical defeat in that the really punitive teeth of the law had been extracted.

The same legislature enacted two flag laws, one providing that the national emblem be flown over all public buildings, the other forbidding foreign flags over public structures.[64] Neither of these laws, though they were certainly approved by "patriots," could serve as an effective demonstration of A.P.A. strength.

Illinois also enacted a flag law, which was not approved by Governor Altgeld, but which became law without his signature. Incipient opposition to it by German Lutherans and Catholics was halted by the Catholic chancellor of the Diocese of Chicago, who called it "needless and grandmotherly legislation," described it as a good thing for the "bunting trust," but who cautioned his people not to oppose it.[65] Derisively, a Catholic weekly asked why the legislators did not also require loyal citizens to spend a specified amount for fireworks to celebrate the Fourth of July and cartooned an animate flag saying, "Save me from my A.P.A. friends!"[66] The author of the bill was aggrieved when the state attorney general ruled that the law could not legally be applied to parochial or private schools.[67]

The *True American* of St. Louis found that A.P.A. sympathizers in the Missouri state legislature could not surmount their basic political allegiances in order to unite forces against the advances of "Rome" and for the safety of the Republic. Tariff and financial questions seemed to be the more important issues which kept the "patriots" in the legislature from agreeing.[68]

In preparation for the convening of the Congress elected in the fall of 1894, as well as to get ready for the coming presidential election of 1896, the national advisory board of the A.P.A. met in St. Louis in October of 1895. Nearly a year had elapsed since the election, and a lameduck session had met in the meantime. The effect of the A.P.A. victories of 1894 had subsided, and the growing difficulties faced by the order made a survey of the situation necessary. The board that met in St. Louis consisted of two members from each state, one of whom was the state president; the other was designated by the state council. Where no state council existed, the delegate was appointed by the na-

tional president. Fifteen states and the District of Columbia sent representatives: Massachusetts, New York, Kentucky, Maryland, Ohio, Michigan, Illinois, Iowa, South Carolina, Louisiana, Missouri, Arkansas, Nebraska, Washington, and California. A permanent national advisory board was formed, with Judge J. H. D. Stevens of Michigan as its chairman, George W. Van Fossen of Washington as vice-chairman, and the Reverend James Dunn of Boston as secretary. Henry F. Bowers warned the delegates that the avenue for Catholic control of the country lay in the electoral college and the Catholic justices of the Supreme Court. A resolution was accepted stating that there was no official press for the order, that the "patriotic press" had its hearty cooperation, but that no individual was authorized to speak for the body.[69] Another resolution set forth the current legislative goals of the order:

Resolving—That the Executive Board advises the members of the order to vote for nominees on the tickets of the party they affiliate with, and to vote for the election of candidates who are in thorough accord with, and will, if elected, support the reduction of immigration, extension of time for naturalization, and educational qualification for the suffrage; maintenance of general non-sectarian free public systems; no public funds nor public property for sectarian purposes; taxation of all property not owned and controlled by the public; opening to public official inspection of all private schools, convents, monasteries, hospitals, and all institutions of an educational or reformatory character; no support for any public position to any person who recognizes primal allegiance in civil affairs to any foreign or ecclesiastical power; public lands for actual settlement by American citizens only, and that the order demands the thorough enforcement of all existing laws by legally constituted authorities.[70]

Additional stocktaking and words of advice formed the substance of a letter from President Traynor to the membership in December as the Congress convened. First, he stated that a sufficient number of the "exponents of our principles" had been elected to the Fifty-fourth Congress to insure the passage of measures "most dear to us and to maintain the balance of power." If there was failure under these circumstances, it would be because of "their treachery or our negligence." He listed as desirable

goals the bill to establish a national university, measures to restrict immigration and to regulate naturalization, a law to prevent the use of the national flag for advertising purposes, a law to
open all monastic institutions to public inspection, a restriction
on diplomatic recognition of representatives from any ecclesiastical body, prohibition of sectarian appropriations either for Indian
education or in support of charities in the District of Columbia,
and opposition to the appointment of men to government positions who owed "primal allegiance" to a foreign power.

As presidential possibilities, Traynor practically eliminated
any Democrat, because he regarded the unsuitable Cleveland as
a sure nominee and did not expect that "priest-ridden" party to
produce any other candidate. Among Republicans, he approved Congressman Linton and Governor Bradley of Kentucky.
He said the order would be willing to accept Senator John Gear
of Iowa, because of his support for Linton during the Fifty-third
Congress, or former President Benjamin Harrison, because of
his loyalty to former Indian Commissioner Morgan. But before
the Republican party could expect the continued support of the
order, he warned that it must rid itself of men such as Senator
Thomas Carter of Montana.

Lest the order regard the papacy as the only enemy, Traynor
looked into the future to predict a potent combination of
"plutocracy and priestcraft," which would arise from a unity of
interest within the existing financial monopoly. He advised his followers to beware of professional politicians and political trick-
sters, to be careful of the lecturers they heard in their councils,
and to work for women's suffrage because "patriotism and
reform" would surely follow when women voted.

On international affairs, Traynor cautioned calm in the excitement arising from the Venezuela incident, since disruption
of friendly relations with England would be a "mutual calamity
and an international sin." [71] Thus, Traynor provided the order
with rather sound advice and a program of legislation and exhibited an awareness of new issues that might be exploited if
properly joined with anti-Catholicism, issues such as the financial
monopoly or emphasis on women's suffrage. That part of the

program listing legislative goals to be achieved could be tested in the Congress then convening.

Sentiment for a national university had risen in the Fifty-third Congress with the argument that "we need today an education in Americanism" and that a university in the national capital would complete the structure of the public educational system. Anti-Catholics saw in it an answer to Catholic University of America, recently established in Washington, D.C., but there was widespread support for a national university on the graduate level from professional educators.[72] Two bills providing for such a university were introduced into the Fifty-third Congress, but both of them died with the end of the session.[73] In the Fifty-fourth Congress, the measures were reintroduced, with Congressman Eugene Hainer of Nebraska, Senator Gallinger of New Hampshire, Senator Thurston of Nebraska, Senator Kyle of South Dakota, or Senator Hawley of Connecticut either introducing them or speaking favorably on the floor. A committee on the university was appointed, but more pressing business intervened whenever Congress was about to discuss the specific proposals.[74]

An immigration restriction bill was introduced into the House that would have excluded male migrants between the ages of sixteen and sixty who could not both read and write English or some other language. The House passed the measure by a vote of 195 to 26, but the Senate did not vote on the measure during the session. Debate, however, did take place, occurring coincidentally with the 1896 national convention of the A.P.A. in Washington, D.C. At that time, Senator Gibson of Maryland, a Democrat, stated that restriction sentiment was strongest in those regions where the A.P.A. and the Boston Anti-Immigration League were strongest, and stated furthermore that the A.P.A. was

. . . a secret, oath-bound, red-lettered, left-handed, dark lantern association . . . the child of envy, hatred and malice—the offspring of a pestilential brood of mischief-makers, who lurk about the doors of legislative halls, and hang on the flanks of political parties, seeking to lure lawmakers from the wide paths and open day of rectitude into the devious ways and darkness of evil doing—breathing threatenings and vengeance where they cannot cajole and deceive.

In reply, Senator Knute Nelson of Minnesota, Republican, denied that the bill had been inspired by the A.P.A. or that it was necessarily antagonistic to Catholics. No action, other than talk, took place on the measure until after the presidential election of 1896, and then the bill was finally passed only to be vetoed as "illiberal, narrow, and un-American" by President Cleveland two days before he left office.[75]

Not until the second session of the Fifty-fourth Congress, which convened after he had been defeated for re-election, did Congressman Linton introduce a bill to "prevent desecration of the national flag." At that time, the bill was referred to a committee and nothing more was heard of it.[76]

Senator Gallinger was responsible for introducing again the proposed sixteenth amendment to the Constitution outlawing use of public money for any sectarian purpose, but the measure secured only its first and second reading before it was placed on the table.[77]

Of all the pieces of legislation for which the A.P.A. received credit from its contemporaries, that concerning appropriations for Indian contract schools secured the most attention. Actually, the issue in the Fifty-fourth Congress was not so much whether, but when, the appropriations could be cut off without doing harm to the continuing education of Indian children. After the Fifty-third Congress had decided to make regular reductions in amounts appropriated, so that the contract schools would be eliminated in five years to be replaced by a government school system, the only action left for the A.P.A was to demand immediate and complete denial of further funds. This was their position during the Fifty-fourth Congress. The argument used on the floor of the House was that if eventual termination were correct in principle, any postponement amounted to a compromise. From the standpoint of administration, the Indian Commissioner let it be known that he wanted time to effect the orderly shift from contract to government schools, of which there were not yet enough in existence to accommodate the Indian children. Congressman Linton suggested that voluntary public subscriptions would provide the money to keep the schools operating in the

meantime. Linton sponsored an amendment to forbid the use of any money appropriated by the Fifty-fourth Congress in support of sectarian institutions, which if accepted would cut off the contract schools immediately. There then followed debate on the merits of immediate termination, with little reference to the principle involved. On the final vote, Linton's amendment was accepted and the amended appropriation bill then passed the House.[78]

The victory was welcomed by the "patriotic press," and those congressmen who had supported Linton on the floor were commended. Henry Cooper of Wisconsin, Eugene Hainer of Nebraska, and David Watson of Ohio were singled out to receive special praise.[79] Linton was also subjected to condemnation, which took the form of a challenge to a duel from a man who suggested Bladensburg as a proper site for a meeting of honor. Linton quite properly ignored the communication.[80]

The moderating influence of the Senate was soon felt. Senator Lodge of Massachusetts announced that he was weary of the statement that Indians would go uneducated if Linton's amendment were accepted by the Senate. He maintained that the effect of the bill would not be to cast Indian children out "onto the prairies" without schooling. Senator Hoar asked for time enough to make the change from contract to government schools, which he favored but which he thought required patience. Indian Commissioner Browning informed the Senate that he would like to have two or three years to make the change, while Senator Cockrell, Democrat of Missouri, thought that 1898 would be a judicious terminal date. This suggestion was made formal and accepted by the Senate.[81]

Thenceforward, the issue was threshed out in conference committees, with each of the houses conceding somewhat. The resulting proposal permitted the Indian Commissioner to negotiate contracts for 1897 to the amount of 50 per cent of the expenditures made in 1895. The bill became law in June of 1896. During the course of debate on it, in this final form, Congressman Cooper of Wisconsin argued that the issue was one of conscience and principle and thus not subject to compromise.

Congress had a right and an obligation, he said, to deny funds for the teaching of "Catholicism to a Comanche or Methodism to a Modoc." [82] In its essentials, then, the measure was an expression of the firm belief that public funds should not be expended in a fashion so as to benefit any religious group; wide public support for this kind of legislation and enactment of it into state laws and constitutions existed before the A.P.A. had come into existence. [83]

Another instance involving expenditure of government funds in support of sectarian institutions concerned charitable activities within the District of Columbia. Since reforms in government for the District had been initiated in 1875, the action of Congress in 1896 was supplementary to a series of preceding actions. Child-care cases were placed under the jurisdiction of the District Commissioners in 1875; the position of Superintendent of Charities was created in 1891, and in 1892 a Board of Children's Guardians was established to place wards of the courts in homes and to pay for their care. [84] As its contribution to the charitable institutions within the District, Congress had for many years appropriated money in lump sums to Catholic, Protestant, or nondenominational groups as partial support for their charitable operations. In the Fifty-fourth Congress, these appropriations, by now fairly routine matters, came up for discussion when the District of Columbia appropriation bill was considered. Congressman Eugene Hainer of Nebraska announced that he intended to object to each of these specific allocations on principle, maintaining that the proper procedure was to appropriate the money to the Board of Children's Guardians to distribute as it saw fit for child care, rather than to give money directly to each of the institutions as a direct grant in a lump sum. [85]

In the debates engendered by his determination, Hainer found it necessary to explain his actions. Although he had been born a Catholic, he no longer considered himself one and he was not opposed to proper child care for charity wards. But he did feel that government control should be exercised over the expenditure of government money. He denied specifically that he was, or had been, a member of the A.P.A. or any of its kindred organiza-

tions.[86] The views which he expressed on the floor during these debates indicated that he was a convinced secularist at least, and perhaps an agnostic.

Hainer proceeded to carry out his announced intention. Objecting to each of the specific allocations of funds as it came up, he was supported by his colleagues with votes varying from two to one to four to one. The charitable operations struck from the bill as recipients of government gifts were Catholic, Episcopalian, and Lutheran in their management. Soon he had made his point abundantly clear. He then made a general motion amending the appropriations bill to shift the power of distribution of the funds to the Board of Children's Guardians. His amendment was accepted. Thereupon, Congressman Linton moved onto the field of victory and sought to add a further clause forbidding the use of any money appropriated under the bill for the support of "sectarian institutions." The Linton amendment was accepted, but with it the bill was defeated in a close vote; there was agreement, however, to reconsider. A Democrat took this opportunity to chide the Republican majority for its inability to accomplish even routine public business.[87]

Reworked by a committee, the bill was again submitted. In revised form it placed all funds in the custody of the District Commissioners, and included an amendment forbidding the use of any money for support of institutions under "sectarian or ecclesiastical control." Debate flared up again, with the amendment receiving the brunt of the attack; its wording was called identical with A.P.A. terminology. The vote accepting the amendment, however, was 134 to 21, and the bill with its amendment was passed by the House without a record vote and forwarded to the Senate.[88]

Senate committee action recommended rejection of the House amendment and the restoration of appropriations to the individual charities. Senator Platt of New York asked why the committee had reopened the "vexing" question when public opinion seemed to regard the House solution as proper. Despite his question, the Senate passed its version of the appropriation bill. After many

conference committees, considerable bickering on the floor, and some compromising, a bill forbidding either money or property to be appropriated for the use of church or religious institutions or societies was agreed to; but the restriction was not to be placed in force until after 1897. Democratic Senator Vest of Missouri objected that such a decision would amount to a "contract" and would forbid future Congresses to take action on the subject. Republican Senator Sherman of Ohio replied that one Congress could not bind another and said that the Senate was using the device "merely as a way of getting out of a dilemma." Vest countered that such action was unworthy of the Senate and that the concession would permit the conclusion that senators had yielded "to this religious clamor that has been raised," while "we wink at each other and say we don't mean it." When the Senate voted on the bill as proposed by the committee and accepted it, individual votes were not recorded.[89]

In the second session of the same Congress, meeting after the election of 1896, Congressman Hainer brought up the issue again in connection with another District appropriation bill. Hainer said he was out to eliminate the "custom of ladies (of both sexes, dilettante very largely) gossiping over their little cups of tea and organizing societies to dispense so-called charity at the expense of the government." What he desired by his action was to bring about a thoroughgoing reform of charity administration in the District. In the meantime, the Senate had come to almost the same decision on a wider scale. An investigating committee was appointed under the chairmanship of Senator McMillan of Michigan to look into all matters concerning the government and administration of the District.[90]

The last item on Traynor's list of legislative goals for the A.P.A. was the prevention of appointments for Catholics, and in this the order was unsuccessful. One individual concerned was Colonel Coppinger, a Catholic of Irish birth and a son-in-law of James G. Blaine, who had been nominated to become a brigadier general. Coppinger's appointment was confirmed in the Senate by a vote of forty-four to seventeen. Opposing it were

such Republican Senators as Burrows of Michigan, Gear of Iowa, Perkins of California, Teller of Colorado, Pettigrew of South Dakota, Squire and Wilson of Washington.[91]

Additional evidence of A.P.A. legislative activity and of interest in government policy may be found. The most publicized concerned a statue of Father Marquette proposed as Wisconsin's contribution to the Hall of Fame at the national Capitol. Preliminary steps had already been undertaken by prominent Catholics of Milwaukee, one of whom was the editor of the Milwaukee *Catholic Citizen*.[92] Congress authorized the acceptance in 1893, but the statue was not completed and ready for installation until February of 1896.[93] Congressman Linton, ever ready to protect America from Rome, introduced a resolution into the House protesting the inclusion of a "Jesuit" among the nation's heroes, and a deluge of "patriotic" petitions arrived to support him. The presentation and acceptance of the statue, however, went forward without incident,[94] except for the case of a New Yorker who was apprehended by Capitol police for threatening to disfigure the statue after its unveiling.[95] The governor of Wisconsin continued to receive protesting petitions long after the statue was in place.[96]

As though a statue were not enough to rub salt into the wounds of the A.P.A., a commemorative postage stamp bearing a picture of Father Marquette was authorized in 1898. This, too, the A.P.A. protested. A comment on the protests, containing more than an element of glee at the insult to the order, was received by an A.P.A. official in the national capital. It read:

Dear Major and comrade:
The last time I had the pleasure of a talk with you was in Statuary Hall in the National Capitol. You pointed to the Marquette Statue and said, "Pat, that must go." I have been looking for the removal of the statue almost every day since but so far there has been no sign of its going.
Now my dear Major, I want to invite your attention to a newer and more extensive outrage perpetrated on the American people than the erection of the Marquette statue at the National Capitol. I enclose for you a United States postage stamp which has a facsimile of the

Rev. Father Marquette attired in his priestly robes with a Catholic cross and beads in full view.

Just think of the members of the great American Protective Association being compelled to lick the back-side of Father Marquette every time they mail a piece of literature to enlighten the American people concerning the disloyalty of their Catholic fellow citizens.

Yours dolefully. . . .[97]

The proposed "God in the Constitution" amendment to the Constitution also caused some fear in A.P.A. ranks. Its purpose was to secure recognition of the Deity as the source of all law, so that the United States could properly be called a "Christian" nation. The *A.P.A. Magazine* saw in it an attempt by the papacy to unite church and state and termed it a "diabolical" piece of legislation.[98] Traynor was quoted in another place as saying that the proposal was a "remarkable and dangerous" one that could have emanated from the Pope.[99] Actually, the measure had been sponsored by the National Reform Association, an evangelical Protestant group.[100]

In the matter of the Cuban struggle for independence from "Catholic Spain," the A.P.A. state council of Nebraska memorialized Congress to grant belligerent status to the insurgents, while Congressman Linton actually proposed a resolution to that effect. It was referred to the Committee on Foreign Affairs and was not heard of again.[101]

Thus, the A.P.A. wrote its legislative record and made its impression on government. Neither "treachery" of congressmen nor "negligence" of membership explained the order's lack of success. These were the two dangers that, President Traynor had warned, would prevent the A.P.A. from writing its principles into law with the friendly Congress he claimed after the elections of 1894. Only in the matter of prohibitions of sectarian appropriations could there have been cause for rejoicing. Despite the statements of partisans on the floor of Congress that these were "A.P.A. measures," it would be improper to label them as such; it would be equally improper to regard their passage as evidence of A.P.A. strength, although the role of Congressman Linton in

their enactment should not be overlooked. Labeling them as A.P.A. legislation, however, gave continued prestige to the order when it was already definitely on its downward path. Consequently, the order found itself able to go into the presidential year of 1896 with its reputation still somewhat intact, although the fissures that would eventually destroy it from within were already in evidence.

7 Decline and Dissolution

The decline in the fortunes of the A.P.A., which had been notice-able through 1895, became pronounced and unmistakable from the convention of 1896 onward. Within a few months after that convention in the spring, the stresses of the presidential election of 1896 tore the order apart and the decline then proceeded into the long slow process of dissolution.

As the summer of 1896 approached, the inability of the order to focus its membership or to lead its adherents into battle dur-ing the presidential election illustrated its decline. To continue the cooperation among the various patriotic orders under A.P.A. leadership—the "movement"—a meeting of representatives from each cooperating order was called for Washington in December of 1895. Whereas in previous meetings delegates had attended these conferences from many different organizations, the 1895 conference of the National Council of Patriotic Organizations was attended only by representatives from the A.P.A., the parent and the Junior Order of United American Mechanics, and the Loyal Orange lodges. This remnant, however, appointed a joint committee to attend the nominating conventions of all major parties; its purpose was to obtain recognition for the principles of the "patriotic orders" in party platforms. Members of this committee were E. H. Sellers of Michigan, George Van Fossen of Washington State, Francis Campbell of Minnesota, A. V. Winters of Tennessee, and Stephen Collins of Pennsylvania.[1] These men held membership in two or more of the participating organizations: Van Fossen and Campbell were Orangemen as well as A.P.A. officials, and Collins was a strong Junior Order leader; but the fact that they represented so few of the orders

showed how seriously the effectiveness of joint action among the patriots had declined.

Even before this conference was held, the *United American* was sponsoring the "American Liberty League" to emphasize new and more current reform measures such as a national initiative and referendum and the placing of all governmental power in the House of Representatives so that the "judicial plutocracy" of the Supreme Court and the "monarchical Senate" could no longer dominate the government under the guidance of the "papacy and the money power." The Court's decision declaring an income tax unconstitutional was the special instance cited to demonstrate this joint control of government.[2] The conference, thus, failed to unite the patriots and amounted to the first public fissure in the façade of the A.P.A. movement. Apparently, the success of the legislation it had chosen to assist to fulfillment had left the movement without pressing issues it could agree on.

In March of 1896, the executive committee of the A.P.A. itself met in Washington to consider the various candidates for president.[3] Disregarding the leading contenders, this committee considered as most acceptable to the order such men as Congressman Linton, Governor Bradley of Kentucky, Robert Todd Lincoln, and former President Harrison. Of these, Linton was recommended, and the order was advised to begin organizing "Linton for President" clubs.[4]

In making this announcement to the membership, moreover, the committee chairman, J. H. D. Stevens of Michigan, reported that Governor McKinley had forfeited the favor of the A.P.A. by refusing to meet with its representatives either in person or by letter.[5] Consequently, a decision was reached to oppose his nomination on the grounds that he had appointed Catholics to state positions in Ohio and that he was a member of the Young Men's Institute (the Y.M.I.), a Catholic men's organization. To answer this allegation, a denial of McKinley's membership in the A.P.A., the Ancient Order of Hibernians, or the Y.M.I., plus a statement as to his church affiliation and his lodge affiliations, was put out by his supporters as a part of his preconvention publicity.[6] Mark Hanna replied to the charge that McKinley had

refused to meet with representatives of the A.P.A. by saying that no one had ever approached him or sent him a letter concerning the matter, and that he would know if McKinley had been approached personally because he, Hanna, was managing McKinley's campaign.[7]

The editor of the Portland, Oregon, *Portlander,* a man who was also state A.P.A. secretary for Oregon, maintained that McKinley was a member of the Y.M.I., despite the denial, and was therefore not entitled to A.P.A. support. However, a Portland officer of the Junior Order of United American Mechanics took it on himself to write to Ohio. From the head of his organization in that state he received word that McKinley was worthy of the support of the Junior Order. In commenting on these interchanges, the Portland *Oregonian* noted that "in newspaper reports, the term A.P.A. usually means any or all of the different well-known organizations which are opposed to the Catholic Church," thus admitting a newspaper practice which was now beginning to lose its validity.[8]

As time for the order's annual convention neared, more of the story behind the executive committee's announcement became clear. It now appeared that only seven members of the entire committee, which had comprised thirty members in October of 1895, had actually participated in the Washington meeting.[9] Thus, the announced opposition to McKinley did not represent the thinking of the executive committee, probably did not represent the order's majority wish, and only served to drive one more wedge into the widening breach dividing the "patriots."

Except in Michigan, the annual state conventions of the order in the various states showed that the Republican party was still the chosen political home of the order. The Michigan meeting decided that unless the major parties accepted A.P.A. principles in their platforms the order should set about forming an independent party. In Wisconsin, the incumbent state president was overthrown because of his friendship with the Republican governor, but the new man had Republican ambitions of his own. Texas held its first state meeting,[10] and the California A.P.A. acknowledged Lionel Sheldon, who would be one of California's

delegates to the Republican convention, as its political adviser.[11] From Illinois, where internal stresses had shown up a year before, came word that state president Johnson was condemned by the assembled delegates because he opposed McKinley and in doing so had "assailed with baseless accusations the good name and untarnished character of the foremost statesman of the day." Furthermore, the resolution denounced any attempt to bring McKinley into disrepute with the order. State president C. E. Sapp of Kentucky, a visiting speaker, was said to be responsible for these actions.[12]

Indications that McKinley would be an issue at the A.P.A. convention were borne out when it met in May of 1896. Head-quarters were at the National Hotel in Washington, and dele-gates apparently were able to secure special railroad rates in order to attend.[13] Two hundred delegates heard Secretary Beatty announce that 963 new councils had been established during the preceding year. During the six-day session, the order dis-patched a committee to Ohio to call on McKinley. It was re-ported that McKinley had talked to the group and expressed his sympathy with the principles of the A.P.A. Many delegates wore McKinley badges on the floor of the convention, and some of the state officers in attendance were committed to him. Some of the Ohio delegates explained that McKinley was not opposed by his own state's council. The convention's decision was to over-ride the recommendation of the executive committee and to include McKinley on the list of "acceptable" candidates along with others whom Republicans were considering: Allison, Reed, Quay, Cullom, Harrison, and Morton, in addition to the A.P.A. favorites Bradley and Linton.[14]

A minority of the total delegates would not consent to the decision to include McKinley among the acceptable, and this group held a "rump" convention to condemn the action of the majority. Delegates from twenty states attended the rump session, which adopted the following self-explanatory resolution:

Whereas, The supreme council of the American Protective Asso-ciation of the United States at its session Saturday evening, by a unanimous vote, adopted the report of the national advisory board,

which report endorsed the action of the executive committee of said board, and in plain language said that the executive committee was justified in publishing the political affiliation of McKinley with the Roman political hierarchy, which affiliation is proved by the affidavits of reputable members of the order and which affidavits have never been controverted except by the unsworn statement of Major McKinley himself, and

Whereas, Major McKinley did, on May 14, 1896, to a committee of the national advisory board, in the city of Canton, O., state that he heartily approved the principles of the American Protective Association and on the following day gave an interview to the press denying that he had met such a committee, which was composed of honorable and truthful men, and

Whereas, The members of the supreme council, during its session have been hounded and badgered by a large McKinley lobby, composed of members and non-members to discredit the advisory board and to turn the supreme council into a McKinley ratification meeting, and having signally failed to clear McKinley in consequence of his papal political record, to-day, after two-thirds of the delegates had started for home, attempted to take revenge by abolishing the national advisory board and accomplishing the same by a vote of 30 to 29,

Resolved, That we, the delegates in condemnation meeting assembled, denounce the unwarranted interference of the paid McKinley lobby with the affairs of the order and denounce the cowardly denial by McKinley of his endorsement of the principles of the order given by him to our committee, and

Resolved, That because of his record as reported by the national advisory board, we herewith pledge ourselves to use our influence and efforts to accomplish his defeat.[15]

The obvious division among the delegates, representing as it did a similar division among the membership on the issue of McKinley, was criticized by the Philadelphia *American,* a Junior Order paper. This paper placed the ultimate responsibility on McKinley, who, it said, should have followed his accustomed practice and said nothing when approached for a statement.[16] But no amount of reasoning could shift attention away from the fact that the A.P.A. was split, and that the real responsibility rested within the order.

Almost incidental to the charges of political misuse of the A.P.A. and to the name-calling over McKinley, the order had

come to a decision to replace President Traynor. So bitter was the opposition to him that some delegates refused to remain at the convention after its first day. In his speech to the order, Traynor had warned it concerning conflicts in authority among the various committees and boards. He recommended a change in the constitution so as to eliminate confusion. The delegates replied by abolishing the advisory board, the very group that had created the fuss over McKinley by opposing him.[17] Traynor's role in all of this was not clear, but he was likely to have been among those opposed to McKinley, so that he was with the minority in the convention.

While it was the signal for organizational disruption, the convention was also the opportunity for the order to display its greatest evidence of attraction to public officials. Five congressmen spoke at various sessions; four of them were identified while one remained anonymous: Linton and Crump of Michigan, Hilborn of California, and Howard of Alabama, all Republicans except the last, who was a Populist. Of them, only Crump was to retain his seat beyond 1898.[18]

Before reaching its decision on McKinley and creating the subsequent division among the delegates, the convention had already made up its mind on a new national president. Several men were available to succeed Traynor—Henry Bowers was willing to become the symbol of organizational unity, Judge Stevens of the advisory board undoubtedly split the Traynor forces, Vice-President Jackson of Fort Worth represented personal ambition, and the Reverend James Dunn of Boston stood for continued cooperation among the various patriotic orders. A newcomer, John Warnock Echols, was also available. Because he was a lifelong Democrat and therefore uncommitted on the McKinley matter, Echols was the convention's choice. He served also as a symbol of the new importance to the A.P.A. of the South, because his home state was Georgia, where he had been first state president of the superior council. Secretary Beatty lost his position when William J. Palmer, a former trustee from Butte, became his successor. Francis Campbell, the Orangeman, remained as treasurer, but the rest of the new officers were hold-

ing national offices for the first time, and they represented the entire country pretty well.[19]

The new president, Echols, was a lawyer from Atlanta. Aside from his lack of previous attachment to any faction within the order, he represented a region in which the A.P.A. hoped to make an impression. He had been born in 1849 and was reported to have read law in the office of Robert Toombs in preparation for his legal career; this report would indicate that Echols' formative years were spent in Reconstruction Georgia under the influence of one of the Confederacy's great men. In 1890, he was chairman of the executive committee of the Scotch-Irish Society of America, and his legal career had brought him to the position of counsel to the Fidelity Banking and Trust Company of Atlanta in 1893. Mr. Echols apparently had an amateur's interest in history, which, with his Scotch-Irish affiliation, suggests the source of his anti-Catholicism; he apparently applied his prejudice to historical fact in order to obtain his interpretation of past events.[20]

This was the leadership that led the A.P.A. into the campaign of 1896 and to its rather sudden disappearance from public view. Their responsibility, however, was limited. The facts were apparent to almost anyone who cared to survey its career during the previous year that the order was not as successful as it was reputed to be, that it could be opposed without reprisal, that its members were so loosely united, both within the secret society and with other patriotic societies, that but a slight disagreement could flare into suspicion and dissension, and, worst of all because it was so apparent to politicians, that the order could not deliver its vote to any candidate.

Almost as though he were writing the swan song of the order, former President Traynor published an article in June of 1896. The thought and writing were actually a warning and prediction rather than a report of events, for Traynor had written and submitted the article before the May convention met and thus before its outcome was known. In the article, Traynor reviewed the difficult ten-year history of the order, recalling the early years and the period of ascendancy and apparent political success, and then he issued some warnings for the future. He showed how

candidates elected to office with the assistance of the order had repudiated it once in office; he stated that most of these men were first of all "party men," and only secondarily loyal to the A.P.A. "Half-a-loaf" compromises in legislation were "pernicious and enervating," while the strong spirit of "partyism" within the order did not permit the freedom of political movement necessary for the accomplishment of goals. He maintained that once the votes of the order were within the control of any one person, party, or interest, the dissolution of the order would commence. If an independent party were necessary to preserve the order without compromises, he was in favor of such a gesture on the part of the order even should it lead to organizational suicide. He placed responsibility for the incipient troubles of the order in politics on the system of advisory boards, whose function was to "advise," not to decide, on the political course to be taken by the association. In taking the power of decision, he said, the boards had usurped to a minority of the members and to a group of politically minded leaders the power that should legitimately rest with members.[21] Traynor's summary, apt as it was and so clearly demonstrated as true by the events of May, reviewed what had been occurring within the order for some time. His view on advisory boards was gained from experiences in state and local councils, rather than from the operations of the national board, for it had been functioning only during the time Traynor's article was in process of writing or in the press. Not to be overlooked, then, in the sensational fiasco at Washington in the spring of 1896 were the facts of the order's structure and its method of procedure in politics on the local level, where it had repeatedly behaved in a fashion similar to that which was so harmful when performed on a national stage.

In preparing for the national party conventions, members of both major political parties in their state conventions followed the pattern of 1894 with regard to the A.P.A. Democrats wrote resolutions seeking to demonstrate again that there was an identity between Republicans and anti-Catholicism. Michigan Democrats, in particular, took it on themselves to retire Congressman "Linton the little" to private life. On the other side, Repub-

licans tried to play it safe, retaining the A.P.A. vote for whatever it was worth while not offending those who opposed the order if it could be avoided. California Republicans endorsed a resolution stating, "We heartily recognize the right to establish schools through private enterprise, but we demand that none but non-sectarian public schools shall receive public aid," [22] thus demonstrating a technique by which A.P.A. support could be held in line without conceding much to it.

Hopeful candidates and their managers also sought to gather in support. In seeking delegates pledged to McKinley for the Republican national convention, Mark Hanna was ready to contradict the A.P.A. charges against his man, but was also quite concerned that nothing should be done to lose A.P.A. support if it could be had.[23] Washington State A.P.A. leadership was supporting the ambitious Senator John Wilson's control of the Republican party because of his past legislative record on the order's legislative program in Congress. His brother, Henry Lane Wilson, later the diplomatic representative of the United States in Mexico,[24] was the local manager while the senator was in the capital.[25] At the Republican state convention, the A.P.A. delegates were corralled by the Wilson managers with a platform statement to this effect: ". . . we oppose any union of church and state and we recognize loyalty, intelligence and honesty as the main requirements of good citizenship, and we denounce any attempt to create a religious disqualification for office as un-American, unjust and unconstitutional." [26]

Since active A.P.A. people regarded Catholics as the offenders in injecting religion into politics, the last clause of the plank, which had a double meaning, was a proper statement of their views. Just before the election of 1896, however, the Washington state president of the A.P.A. died; he was replaced by John Bushell of Seattle. Bushell had demonstrated that his political judgment was likely to warp whenever temperance was an issue, and his actions in 1896 illustrated that the silver issue was also more important to him than political commitments made before he assumed office. Consequently, many Washington State A.P.A. people followed him in voting for candidates on a fusion ticket of

Populists and silver Democrats.[27] Thus, while Republican leaders demonstrated that they were aware of the order, they were also forced to acknowledge that the order's continued support could not be taken for granted. But they also learned that the A.P.A. could be ignored without any particular harm.

This practice of awareness with no concessions was demonstrated as well at the Republican national convention in St. Louis in June. There the invocation was offered by a rabbi; reportedly, this was the result of a compromise made in the belief that either a Protestant or a Catholic would have offended someone or some important group.[28] McKinley's managers worked out their plans in detail so that there would be no unpleasant alliterative reference made by any of his supporters to anything like "Silver, Sacerdotalism and Sedition" to disturb the even tenor of his progress toward nomination and election.[29]

From the Catholic side before the convention met, Cardinal Gibbons made a public statement asking that both major parties "express themselves, without any equivocation, on the principles of religious freedom which underlie our Constitution." He acknowledged that Catholics were to be found in both parties, and that he would regret the "entire identification of any religious body with any political party." However, when their political rights were attacked, the Cardinal fully expected the members of any religious group under attack to "espouse the cause of the party which has the courage openly to avow the principles of civil and religious liberty." He concluded with the statement, "Patience is a virtue. But it is not the only virtue. When pushed too far it may degenerate into pusillanimity." [30] Despite this clear statement of an obvious fact, only one of the presidential possibilities at St. Louis was willing to be unequivocal on the issue of religious discrimination. This man was Governor Levi Morton of New York, who had been elected to his position in 1894 ostensibly with A.P.A. support. The *Nation* commented on this turn of events, "What a curious light it throws on the McKinleyized political situation that no other candidate finds himself able to say it"—to say, that is, that he was opposed to religious discrimination.[31]

If the candidates were unwilling to declare themselves, so was the platform committee; but here circumstances entered to prevent the "patriots" from getting even a token recognition. The Reverend James King, secretary of the National League for the Protection of American Institutions, had prepared a statement to be submitted to the platform committee stating the position of his organization on the use of tax funds for support of non-public institutions. In preparing his statement, King said he did not consult any member of the A.P.A., and in fact he believed that his statement was no less than the Republican party position adopted in 1876. Yet his statement was labeled an "A.P.A. proposal," quite improperly, King believed in retrospect, when he found time to assess the reasons for its failure to be accepted.[32]

Meanwhile, the committee of "patriots," dominated by A.P.A. men, delegated by the National Council of Patriotic Organizations to attend both conventions was at St. Louis trying to see Mark Hanna for a platform statement but was unsuccessful in its objective, as Hanna "flitted from hotel to hotel." [33]

While the convention was in session and before the platform committee had completed its work, Senator Thomas Carter of Montana, whose position among the higher party officials was always disturbing to the A.P.A.,[34] received a telegram from Archbishop Ireland stating that

[any clause inserted into the proposed platform] opposing the use of public money for sectarian purposes and union of church and state is unnecessary and uncalled for. It is urged by the A.P.A. Its adoption will be taken as a concession to them, will awaken religious animosities in the country, and will do much harm. The Republican party should not lower itself to recognize directly or indirectly the A.P.A.[35]

The plank was not inserted, and the failure of the platform committee to accept it was regarded as an "act of treachery" by its supporters. The Democratic party likewise rejected a platform statement of the same nature.[36] This was the first time since 1876 that the Republican party had not included some statement in its platform on the issue of the public schools, and this served as an indication of the extent of the "patriots' " defeat.[37] And so, with neither party making a statement on the subject dearest to

the heart of the A.P.A., and with McKinley nominated by the Republicans and Bryan by the Democrats, the order faced the election of 1896.

With no acceptable platform statement, the A.P.A. and its press were put in the position of having to make a decision between the nominees. The problem on this score had been forecast at the convention in May when McKinley's name had disrupted the meeting. President Echols at first announced that his participation in the campaign would be to seek the defeat of Congressmen Joseph Cannon of Illinois, Joseph Wheeler of Alabama, and James D. Richardson of Tennessee. Wheeler and Richardson were Democrats, while Cannon had been helpful in securing termination of contract school appropriations during the congressional struggle. Why Cannon should have been singled out for defeat was explained only when he was combined with the other two as "dangerous men in the papal combine," and singled out as a specially vicious "tool of the papacy." [38]

Inevitably, however, the order divided on the presidential candidates. The Boston *Standard* described McKinley as a "public man of absolutely unstained integrity and commanding ability," [39] while the *A.P.A. Magazine* announced its support of him "fully and unequivocally." [40] On the other hand, the Butte *Examiner,* apparently conceding to the silver affections of its constituents, published on July 23 a picture of "BRYAN, Our Next President" reminding its readers that his name was "Bryan, not O'Brien."

Aware that many A.P.A. men opposed McKinley, Republican leaders probed the possibility of saddling the Democrats with the burden of the A.P.A. Mark Hanna, for example, desired to win "to the support of the Republican ticket many thousands of Roman Catholics," and considered this to be of "prime importance" in a McKinley victory. Hanna also secured the services of Father Stephan of the Catholic Indian Bureau, who had worked so diligently against Harrison in 1892, and Stephan retraced his footsteps of 1892, this time supporting the Republicans. [41] Senator John Gear of Iowa, only recently regarded with approval by the A.P.A., now expressed his opinion that a Bryan connection with the A.P.A. could be shown, writing to another Republican, "I

have written to find out about Bryan. I do not know whether he is an A.P.A. or not, but he is such an infernal fool, that I would not be surprised to find it so." [42] Theodore Roosevelt also looked for evidence to support his private assumption that the A.P.A. would be "eager to support Bryan." [43] Actually, Bryan had never had A.P.A. support in Nebraska during his congressional races; in fact, he had been condemned by it for his votes in Congress. The only suspicion that might have been aroused could have come from the circumstances of his participation as editor of the *World-Herald* during the municipal election of 1895 in Omaha.[44]

Beginning in August, the division within the A.P.A. became wider than before, and there appeared charges of a conspiracy among the leaders to sell the support of the order to the highest bidder. President Echols, Chaplain Gottwald, and C. W. Macune, who was a leader of the National Farmers' Alliance from Georgia and suffered unjustly the reputation of "selling out" that group to the Democrats in 1892,[45] were the alleged leaders of the move.[46] Since the charge was made by the *Wisconsin Patriot,* a staunch Republican supporter, the likelihood was that the "sell-out," if there were any truth to the charge, would have meant A.P.A. support for Democrats. The Populist *Bystander* of Butte was just as able to discern that Republican A.P.A. men had sold out their support to the "sound money" crowd and were merely "doing the bidding of the men who furnish the money to promote the organization." [47]

As election day came closer, others of the "patriotic press" came out with their decisions. A "Patriotic Press Bureau" appeared, with headquarters in the nation's capital, to publicize Bryan's congressional voting record in support of the "papal program." [48] Attempting to put the record straight, another paper pointed out that Bryan was never a member of the A.P.A. and that he had received considerable Catholic support in his congressional races.[49] The Omaha *American* first made it known that Bryan and "Romanism" were, and always had been, hand-in-glove, and shortly it confirmed this analysis by announcing its support for McKinley and Hobart.[50] President Echols, erstwhile Democrat and only recently charged with willingness to sell out

the order to the Democrats, now announced his opposition to Bryan, although he did not specify a positive preference, and said that he believed three fourths of the A.P.A. members would vote against Bryan.[51] Former President Traynor, an enthusiast for a third party when the major parties should turn "patriotism" away from their doors, now came out for "Bryan and reformed democracy." [52] Under the circumstances, any political manager who was willing to purchase the support of the entire order at any price would have been paying for goods that could not be delivered.

Capping the charges and countercharges of sellouts, the *United American* asserted that it stood for Bryan because the "pope and the money power" were joined together in a conspiracy against American liberty and for McKinley. But believing that the order was still being prostituted to the partisan purposes of its supreme officers, the paper pleaded with its readers that "no American becomes a slave by becoming a member of a patriotic order. Vote as you please!" [53]

Meanwhile, some Catholics took part in the campaign. Archbishop Ireland denounced the Democratic platform as a resuscitation of the old secession doctrines in its condemnation of interference in the affairs of the states by federal officials. Destruction of the social order and property rights were said by the prelate to follow from the lawlessness and anarchy accompanying arraignment of class against class as the Democrats had done.[54] For his pains, Ireland was opposed by other priests who felt that injection of a Catholic statement only stimulated the dying A.P.A. One of them said: "The best proof of the happy condition of affairs is that one section of the A.P.A. is flooding the country with circulars to prove that McKinley is a Papist in disguise, and another section of the A.P.A. is flooding the country with Linton's speeches to prove that Bryan keeps a cageful of tame Jesuits in the cellar of his Nebraska home." He believed that Ireland's announcement was characteristically fearless, but was also characteristically ill-timed.[55]

Amid the cries and charges, one member of the A.P.A. took

the trouble to reason his way to a political decision and to write it down. Everywhere he found that havoc was being created in the ranks by "selfish and designing politicians." This was always the history of patriotic movements: "As the churches are full of hypocrites who steal the livery of heaven to serve the devil in, so our orders are infested with men who seek to serve their selfish political ends under the garb of pretended patriotism." Every patriot should, in his mind, consider himself free to make his own choice, since the supreme council and officers had not gone on record officially in favor of any candidate. Caution was needed with regard to any Republicans, he said, since Catholics supported McKinley: "Remember that Republican politicians work on the same principles as do the storekeepers: Protestants will trade with us anyway; but we have to cater to the Roman Catholics." For himself, he would vote for Bryan, since the hierarchy "worships at the shrine of gold" and because money was on the side of McKinley. If other patriots could not follow him in this reasoning, he hoped that they would vote Prohibition.[56]

Under the circumstances, the A.P.A. vote—if there was any such thing left—dissipated among the various candidates. The charges of a sellout were undoubtedly part of campaign enthusiasm on the part of editors among the patriotic press. No official public commitment of the order to either side was made. Faced with a number of candidates other than Bryan or McKinley, a conscientious member of the order could have avoided a choice on the two controversial candidates. There was evidence that most of them did not do so, that they remained with the Republican party. On the other hand, the appearance of silver as an issue and the emphasis on the "money question" took many members, most notably in the Rocky Mountain states, into the Bryan camp.[57] As has already been indicated, Washington State members were split; undoubtedly many in other western states followed to support Bryan and silver. The Democrats in Texas, however, tried to prove an alliance between the Populists and the A.P.A., although the allegation was difficult to establish convincingly.[58] From this situation, the slight influence of the order

in the South may be projected as anti-Bourbon and possibly pro-Populist, although the evidence was too scant for clear conclusions.[59]

Congressman Linton of Michigan was defeated in a close race for re-election. The campaign against him was a concentrated one, since he was the most clearly identified congressional supporter of the A.P.A. His victorious opponent was supported by a fusionist group calling itself the "Democratic People's Union Silver party." But the Republicans carried the governorship, electing Hazen Pingree to that office.[60] On the whole, Republican victories across the country were not hailed in 1896 as "A.P.A. victories" as they had been in 1894 or 1895; the newspapers apparently recognized the rapid decline in the effectiveness of the order either as a factor in votes or as a convenient label.

There were many other indications of the decline. One was the failure of the Boston *Daily Standard,* the only patriotic newspaper that attained the status of a daily. Another was the cessation of the *Patriotic American,* Traynor's own weekly, in October of 1896. The *Wisconsin Patriot* had been in financial difficulties with irregular appearances during the early months of 1896, but it made a recovery in October in time to continue its usual support for the Republican ticket. The size of the Butte *Examiner* was cut in half on August 13, 1896, and it managed to stay in business to support Bryan. The Washington, D.C., *United American* was revived from its circulation doldrums in October to support Bryan, but its last issue appeared shortly after the election on November 28, 1896. The renegade patriot, Walter Sims, also had trouble with his *Northwest American* of Sioux City; even before the election was completed, he had re-established himself in Chicago as editor of a stockyards paper called the *Hog-Raiser.* Reporting the demise of the A.P.A. newspaper in Seattle, its erstwhile Republican friend commented that *"The Spirit of Seventy-Six* failed to survive the spirit of '96." [61] This epitaph summarized succinctly an event, but by no means did it explain what there was in the "spirit of '96" that was so inimical to the further life of the order.

The election of 1896 marked the end of the coalition of patriotic societies under the leadership of the A.P.A. The termination of this federation, which had always been somewhat providential, had been forecast as early as 1894 and had drawn closer throughout 1895 and 1896. Since the federation was a political one, only the test of an election could demonstrate how completely it had disintegrated. In McKinley and his managers, the A.P.A. met superior tacticians; but the real fault lay with the ridiculous spectacle of internal squabbling and name calling that had come to a head at the time of the May convention in Washington and continued through the campaign of 1896. For many years to come the order continued to function in a limited way, never regaining the prestige or the power that it had reputedly enjoyed during the years of its heyday. Anti-Catholicism, however, continued to exist.[62]

Unable to comprehend that the effective political career of the A.P.A. was a thing of the past, the remnants of the federation continued to seek recognition in several instances. The patriotic press offered gratuitous advice to president-elect McKinley in order to guide him in selecting his official family. Benjamin Harrison was recommended for Secretary of State, Thomas J. Morgan for the Treasury, Robert Todd Lincoln for War, William S. Linton for Interior, Henry Bowers for Postmaster General, Richard W. Thompson once again for Navy, and John L. Webster of Nebraska for Attorney General.[63] McKinley was aware of the necessity for considering religious affiliations in making political appointments;[64] one of his most criticized choices was Terence Powderly as Commissioner of Immigration, a choice which both Catholics and anti-Catholics disliked.[65]

But McKinley paid little attention to A.P.A. recommendations. As though it were deliberate, he failed to keep an alleged pre-election promise to the California A.P.A. adviser, Lionel Sheldon. A longtime Republican and one of California's delegates to the Republican convention of 1896, Sheldon had believed that his services would be rewarded; in the postelection turmoil he was overlooked.[66] Yet A.P.A. men were not entirely

forgotten for their services to the party. Former Congressman Linton was appointed postmaster of Saginaw, a position he held through successive reappointments until 1914.[67] Kentucky's A.P.A. leader, C. E. Sapp, was recommended as Collector of Internal Revenue for the Louisville district by the state's newly elected senator, William J. Deboe, who had assertedly been initiated into the order by Sapp in a private ceremony sometime previous to the appointment.[68]

The political ineffectiveness of the A.P.A. was further demonstrated in 1897 and 1898 by the fact that candidates paid little or no attention to it. Wisconsin A.P.A. men supporting Robert La-Follette in his opposition to the Republican machine in that state were charged with inconsistency by the *Wisconsin Patriot* because LaFollette had never rejected Catholic assistance in his campaigns against the "ring." [69] Yet LaFollette's star was rising. Furthermore, a Fusion candidate for governor of Oregon found that his past membership in the A.P.A. neither helped nor hindered his career.[70]

Ineffective for its own purposes, the A.P.A. could still be used by its enemies. Three incidents in San Francisco demonstrated this. Just before the election of 1896, the vitriolic priest-editor of the San Francisco *Monitor* had exposed what he believed to be an agreement between the A.P.A. leaders and John D. Spreckels, owner of the San Francisco *Call*, by the terms of which Spreckels was to be chosen in the state legislature as United States senator.[71] According to the charge, state A.P.A. president B. F. Hudelson and other leaders were receiving $2,500 per month until election day, with a promise of $30,000 in addition to be paid when Spreckels became senator. Spreckels called the entire story a piece of blackmail, but the source for Father Yorke's story was one of the collaborators who had been, he said, cut out by Hudelson, who wanted the entire booty for himself. In a rather puzzling turn of events, Hudelson was indicted for criminal libel, denied the charge, but was faced by his erstwhile collaborator, who testified against him.[72] The objective in this series of events was obviously not truth but votes.

During the latter part of 1896, Father Yorke also engaged in

a controversy with the Reverend Charles W. Wendte, a Unitarian minister of Oakland, who was admittedly not a member of the A.P.A. Wendte objected to the virulence of Yorke's language in the *Monitor,* and sought to bring Yorke into a discussion of the primacy of the Pope as a subject more worthy of time and attention. In answer to the charge of intemperate language, York stated that Wendte's "plumage might not now be so unruffled" if he had fought the misrepresentations, forgeries, and lies of the A.P.A. as had Yorke. When faced with such enemies, Yorke believed that "it is possible that he [Wendte] could have maintained that calm and dignified tone with which a professor on an iceberg might address a young woman's seminary. It is possible, if Dr. Wendte has the temper of an angel. I haven't." In the course of his presentation, Yorke alleged in his unangelic temper that the Oakland Public Library was anti-Catholic because it did not subscribe to the *Monitor,* and that the Sutro Library of San Francisco was managed by anti-Catholics because he could not get from it the necessary materials to support his controversy with Wendte.[73] The Unitarian minister was joined by a prominent Unitarian, John P. Irish, who defended his pastor by stating that Yorke was unable to distinguish between legitimate criticism and anti-Catholicism and that in his crusades Yorke used a "waterfront vocabulary."[74]

Yorke carried his technique of classification into the state and municipal elections of 1898. According to him, the two Democratic candidates, former Congressman James Maguire, now a candidate for governor, and James Phelan, now running for mayor of San Francisco, were both receiving A.P.A. support without repudiating it. The issue, as Yorke saw it, involved a sailors' home operated by a nonsectarian committee that Yorke said discriminated against Catholic seamen. To Yorke, thus, the campaign was entirely one of "religious freedom," although the two men he opposed were both Irish and Catholic, and although the Republican candidates were called "corporation" men. If his antagonists cared to argue about railroad corporation control, Yorke was ready to reply that the A.P.A. was friendly with the "sugar trust," a reference to the Spreckels affair. When the Re-

publicans won control of the state, Yorke received appointment as one of the regents for the University of California. His campaign was regarded as the source of the extra votes which brought victory to the Republicans, and his appointment was viewed as an acknowledgment and payment for services rendered to the Republican party. Yorke's health, however, had been so badly shattered by his strenuous activities that he left to spend a year in Europe after the campaign.[75] What Yorke had done was to continue the type of editorial campaign against the A.P.A. that had characterized its peak career into a time when the order was practically defunct. His inability to see shades of difference in opinions had been a handy device during the period of A.P.A. ascendancy; when the order was finished, the device amounted to political demagoguery.

The A.P.A., meanwhile, continued to hold its annual conventions, but they illustrated that what had once been a "movement" was now reduced to a small and ineffective secret society. Its remnant membership expressed dissatisfaction with the emphasis on personalities that had so characterized the order in its political career. In at least four states, Oregon, Wisconsin, Kansas, and Kentucky, state conventions were held in 1897, and the membership found it expedient to emphasize nativism by denying that it was an offshoot of the Orange lodges.[76]

The annual national convention was held in Washington in May of 1897. To those attending, officers reported an "encouraging increase" of members, but no specific instances of growth were provided except in the case of Oregon, where sixty-seven councils were said to have been organized during the preceding year. President Echols and Secretary Palmer were re-elected, but, because the membership was "so large as to be unwieldy," it was thought proper to reduce the number of officers so that money paid out in salaries could be saved. This was an apparent attempt to save face by making a brave outward appearance, but its unreality was shown toward the end of the year when the Washington, D.C., headquarters were closed for lack of funds, an event that was described to the faithful as "only an incident—not an end." [77]

Looking forward to another presidential campaign in 1900, one member of the patriotic press envisaged a "true-blue" ticket composed of former Congressman Linton for president with Thomas E. Watson of Georgia as his running mate.[78] The Omaha *American* polled its readers on their choices and found that Linton was their preferred candidate, too. William Jennings Bryan ran second in this poll, while President McKinley placed fifth. For vice-president, the self-designated patriots preferred Henry Cabot Lodge, Tom Watson, Garret Hobart in that order and followed by Henry Bowers in sixth place.[79] These men were offered as possibilities to the Republican and the Democratic parties should either of them be willing to accept the guidance of the patriots. For the remnant of the order, then, the major political parties continued to be the preferred vehicle for attaining political victory.

But for former President Traynor and his friend, E. H. Sellers of Detroit, the "corrupt alliance of the old political parties with corporate power" was now complete. The two issued a call for a new "American Party" to be formed in St. Louis on August 25, 1897. Every year, it was stated in the call, immigration reinforced the alliance because the immigrant vote was purchasable. The new party's objective was to be constitutional reform so that state legislatures, which were the "special prey of trusts," would lose their legislative powers to the national Congress. This was the device and means by which corporate power's reign would be ended.[80] The call did not lead to a new party, but it did demonstrate that anti-Catholicism had lost its force for two of the men who had once led the A.P.A.

Accompanying the dissolution of the A.P.A. after 1896 was a decline in the number of members among the self-styled "patriotic press." The *Wisconsin Patriot* continued to appear with intermittent lapses in publication until April of 1898, always as a staunch supporter of the regular Republicans against the inroads of the LaFollette group. The Omaha *American* managed to hang on until 1899. The *A.P.A. Magazine,* which had been inaugurated in San Francisco in 1895, began to experience financial problems in November of 1896. At that time, it accused news

dealers of being under Catholic influence since they assertedly ordered more copies than could be sold. "Romanists" were also blamed for the magazine's failure to secure advertising. Continuing to struggle along, however, the magazine offered special low rates for club subscriptions, rates so low that it described itself as "practically the cheapest magazine in the world." The December, 1896, and the January, 1897, issues were skipped. The last issue appeared in June of 1897. In January of 1898, a new monthly magazine, the *American Advocate* of Mechanicsville, Iowa, began a brief career as a spokesman for any organization that took as its slogan "No pope for America." The *Advocate* revived the charge that the daily press was in "abject slavery to political ecclesiasticism" and provided the dying A.P.A. with its last favorable organ.[81]

As the press accompanied the A.P.A. down the road to dissolution, the careers of some of its editors seemed to follow a parallel course. In April of 1897 the editor of the *A.P.A. Magazine*, W. E. Price, was sent to San Quentin state prison for selling salacious literature. His offense had consisted of publishing materials "exposing" certain aspects of the Catholic confessional. He was willing to become a "martyr" to the cause if his case would only raise public indignation.

Price's prison experience furnished evidence for his supporters to argue that "Rome" neither forgave nor forgot the crusaders against it. At San Quentin, Price was made gatekeeper of the prison jute mill, to count the other convicts as they went in or out. Apparently resenting this favoritism toward a new prisoner, the older convicts attacked him. The incident "proved" to his friends that the "long arm of the Jesuits" could reach through prison walls so that imprisoned "papist thugs" could do the church's bidding. His friends asked that Price be transferred to the county jail where he would be safe from such persecution. Released finally, Price was lost until the final note of martyrdom was reached. Pursued and hounded constantly by his "Romish persecutors," the "martyr" Price died in a flophouse in New York City so that the "inquisition had another victim to its credit." [82]

Another leader, A. D. Hubbard, the former state president and board member for the Kansas A.P.A., also became a victim of "persecution." Hubbard had been appointed a receiver for a bankrupt printing plant in 1895. In 1897, he was convicted of embezzlement and sentenced to three years in the state penitentiary. Despite his cries of "persecution," he served a portion of his term but did secure release after four months on the order of the state supreme court.[83]

Before it disappeared, the patriotic press continued to utilize current topics to illustrate the influence of Catholicism and, at the same time, revived many of the old propaganda stories. These devices, which had accompanied the rise of the A.P.A., likewise accompanied its decline, thus tending to disprove their effectiveness as an explanation for the appearance of anti-Catholic movements. Protection of the American working man from competition with foreign-born labor was said to be of more importance than the protective tariff. Taxation of church property continued to receive national advocacy. Assassination as a means of getting rid of its enemies continued to be regarded as one of Catholicism's methods. In this connection, McKinley's failure to accede to the A.P.A. led the *A.P.A. Magazine* to ask an unwittingly prophetic question, "Did Rome's assassination of Abraham Lincoln make William McKinley afraid?"[84]

Another revival of sensationalism appeared in St. Paul. A Miss Seline Clewett instituted suit against the House of the Good Shepherd there, charging unjust imprisonment on the grounds of a Minnesota Supreme Court ruling that municipal courts should no longer sentence women to serve sentences in the custody of the Sisters. Miss Clewett's suit was sensationalized, with the St. Paul *Breeze* alleging that the church provided training for lives in "sporting houses" to girls in its custody. The argument also included the charge that keepers of disorderly houses, who were "universally Catholic," made the contributions that supported the preparatory work of the Houses of the Good Shepherd. Miss Clewett finally lost her case. Trying to make capital of it, the notorious Mrs. Margaret Lisle Shepherd appeared as a speaker in St. Paul to describe once again her experiences,

imagined or real.[85] There was no indication of a revival of interest in organized anti-Catholicism.

The publicized distress of Cuba provided anti-Catholics with another opportunity. The Cuban insurgents were praised because Catholic Spain was the oppressor. Protests were made against Spanish policies with the slogan that the "Spaniards are mad and the Americans are glad of it." [86] When the battleship *Maine* was sunk, the Omaha *American* asked the question, "Was it treachery or an accident?" Answering its own query, the weekly announced that "opinion generally prevails among patriots that Spain's treacherous Roman sons did the deed." The paper also advised its readers to enlist in the volunteers and to "prefer death to Roman Catholic success." [87] To emphasize their point that Catholics sympathized with the Spanish, anti-Catholics disapproved of the designation by the Pope of Archbishop Ireland as an emissary to prevent conflict between the United States and Spain.[88] A cartoon on this subject appeared in the Omaha *American* showing a reluctant McKinley held by Mark Hanna, who was covered by dollar signs, and Ireland, saying, "This is my favorite son," as he pointed to Spain. Hanna was, in turn, in the hands of a Semitic-looking person who was pictured as saying, "Mein Gott! Mark, don't shpeak of war or der shtocks vill drop!" [89] Thus, an attack on the money power, anti-Catholicism, and anti-Semitism were joined. Yet there was no revival of organized anti-Catholicism in strength.

In 1899 appeared the Reverend James M. King's *Facing the Twentieth Century,* which attempted to show the beginning of the new century as a decisive point in world history in much the same fashion as had Josiah Strong's *Our Country* in 1885. The book did not catch on.

Henry F. Bowers, founder of the A.P.A. and its president again after 1898, also saw the year 1900 as a year of destiny. The tone of his remarks showed that he intended to create a revival of the fears of a conspiracy such as had been generated by the forgeries of 1893:

There are great and constantly accumulating reasons for believing that the year 1900 is to mark the most important epoch in all the

history of our country, if not, indeed, of the whole world. That year is to witness what is destined to be the final desperate contest of the papal hierarchy for political supremacy; the supremacy that they claim to make as dogmatic with Protestants as with papists, and which shall, therefore, bring to the papacy the full reward for its long years of treasonable efforts.

Bowers was referring to a "conspiracy" he said had been hatched in Europe some seventy years before, which had as its goal the capture of America for Catholicism. He regarded the presidential election of 1900 as the final contest to achieve this "grand design." For obvious reasons, however, his plans to defeat the conspiracy could not be made public, and he asked his prospective supporters to send him money to make up the funds necessary to combat the Jesuits, who were working "night and day." Secrecy was an essential for success. Bowers ended his appeal, "Let us prove to Rome we can focus our energies and successfully scrape the papal barnacle off the ship of state." [90]

Kansas City was the site of the annual convention of the A.P.A. in 1899, and Augusta, Georgia, was honored as host in 1900. At this first meeting of the new century, Bowers was elected to a five-year term as president. Thereafter, the order planned to hold full conventions only at five-year intervals; the executive council would handle business during the intervening period. In general, the thirteen-point statement of principles adopted in 1894 was adhered to, but the emphasis in 1900 seemed to focus on the securing of legislation to tax all church property.[91] Thus, with the order back in the hands of its founder and admitting that it could no longer afford an annual convention, the extent of its decline was confirmed.

In 1908, Bowers was the subject of an interview published in an Iowa newspaper. In it, he claimed to have played a decisive role in the re-election of President McKinley in 1900. Before election time, Bowers was quoted as having expressed friendship and support for Bryan. But just before election day Bowers was offended when Bryan, instead of writing himself, allegedly permitted his son to reply to a letter from Bowers. Insulted, Bowers said he had then sent out three hundred thousand letters to A.P.A.

members advising them to vote for McKinley. In December, after his victory, McKinley was said to have sent for Bowers and acknowledged that the swing of A.P.A. votes to his banners had determined the outcome. Bowers then told the interviewer that there were two and one-half million members on the membership rolls.[92] Exaggeration was always a technique of the A.P.A. during its height, and Bowers was always able to convince himself that his wishes were truth. When Bowers' version of the election victory of 1900 appeared, however, President McKinley was dead; his version of the story could not be obtained, therefore, even if he had bothered to give one. On the other hand, Bryan's son was an essential element by which the story could be tested. Since William Jennings Bryan, Junior, was only eleven years old in 1900, it would hardly seem likely that he took care of any part of his father's correspondence.

Two days after the original interview, another Iowa newspaper repeated the story without questioning its accuracy. Moreover, this second newspaper commented on the career of the A.P.A., referring to it as exclusively anti-Catholic in its program and saying:

It appealed to the unjust prejudice of protestantism, it fanned it into flame, and there resulted acts of intolerance, bigotry, and un-Americanism that were strangely out of harmony with the American tenets of religious freedom and tolerance.

Of course there were members of the organization who did not countenance this extremism, nor the violence and rioting that followed in many cities. They held to what they claimed to be the original tenet of the society—the separation of the church and school. It is claimed that such men as these today make up the society and that the extremists are no longer its dictators. They point to the original platform as a vindication of their society and in the face of the claim that the A.P.A. is dying out, declare that there will always be room for an organization on the fundamental principles declared by Colonel Bowers twenty-one years ago.

A fairly complete list of officers for the order as of 1908 was given as a part of the story.[93]

Despite Bowers' claim to a membership of two and one-half million, the A.P.A. existed without an organ of publicity and

lacked any of the public notice that it had attracted during the years from 1893 to 1896. The newspaper report quoted above had a bemused quality that perhaps intentionally depicted the reporter's attitude toward the elderly Bowers. Long since, the A.P.A. had become again what it had been in the beginning—the personal property of its founder and president, an organization existing only on paper, supporting the ego of its founder. Its only claim to recognition in 1908 rested on the reflected glory of a past reputation. From the coldly practical excesses of its effulgent years, when that reputation had been exaggerated by both its friends and its enemies, during the long slow decline into memory, the excesses became those of dream and unreality.

Henry Bowers died of a heart attack quite suddenly and unexpectedly in Clinton on November 9, 1911. His obituary referred to his life and to his organization in terms of kindly sentiment and finality.[94] His passing marked the end of the A.P.A., for its heart was gone.

During a campaign for the mayoralty of New York City in November of 1913, a George P. Newman disclaimed responsibility for a circular appearing under the name of the A.P.A. In his denial, Newman revealed that he had been notified sometime before of his election to the presidency of the association. His consent had not been obtained before the event, however; he did not desire the office, and he had never been installed, he continued. Apparently, Mr. Newman was a newcomer to the ranks of the "patriots," for the context of his remarks showed that he believed the American Protective Association had only recently been established.[95] With this news story, the career of the A.P.A. terminated. The circumstances at the end were noteworthy: the scene was political, and there was a note of false identification and misinformation. These—political setting, false identification, and misinformation—fittingly enough were the hallmarks of the entire career of the American Protective Association.

8 Epilogue

Although the A.P.A. was dying, anti-Catholicism continued to be a feature of political campaigns. Presidential elections after 1896 were consistently troubled by concern over the "Catholic" vote and the "anti-Catholic" vote—one seemed to generate the other in politics. In 1900, McKinley's re-election was opposed, though the Democratic candidate who would supposedly benefit by this opposition had not at the moment been selected, in a pamphlet that pointed out that liberty was not safe in the custody of the McKinley administration. Its anti-Catholic tone was shown by its references to the defection of McKinley from a status of "pure Protestant." A "glittering array of power held out to him by the cunning hand of Rome [had] throttled and paralyzed the intentions that perhaps were good" and had made him order protection for Catholics and their properties during the recent war with Spain, or so it was charged. This pamphlet stated that the general voter was not wise enough to understand issues such as free silver, the tariff, or free trade, but that the average man could understand and make his wishes known when less profound issues, such as those already mentioned, were laid before him.[1] The pamphlet was not identified as the work of the A.P.A. remnants, nor did it agree with Henry Bowers' support of McKinley.

Four years later, Theodore Roosevelt was faced with Catholic displeasure over his administration's treatment of lands formerly belonging to Spanish friars in the recently annexed Philippine Islands.[2] The same problems of the Spanish friars' lands haunted William Howard Taft during his campaign in 1908. Taft had been a member of the commission sent to the Philippines to investigate the land question. During his campaign,

Taft was accused from one side of being a slave of the Pope and from another of being anti-Protestant because of his Unitarianism.[3] Theodore Roosevelt, always ready to tilt with windmills, described this injection of religion into politics as the work of the A.P.A.,[4] as though religion in politics were the identifying mark of the order.

Woodrow Wilson, as well, was subjected to charges of anti-Catholicism in 1912 to the extent that his party thought a pamphlet to counteract the rumor was a necessity. But from the other side, Wilson was described as an honorary member of the Knights of Columbus.[5] Wilson's choice of Joseph Tumulty as his secretary also produced a rash of charges that there would develop a funnel from the Vatican to the Presidency through Tumulty. The A.P.A. itself was credited with protesting the appointment of a Democratic national committeeman from Iowa to a district court position during the Wilson administration,[6] and in New York State, State Senator Franklin D. Roosevelt received anti-Catholic pamphlets that used the name of the A.P.A.[7]

Accompanying the continued use of anti-Catholicism in election contests was a desire on the part of its former friends to dissociate themselves from the A.P.A. In 1898, the *American Mechanics' Advocate,* speaking for the Order of United American Mechanics, denied that it was "just the same as the A.P.A." and scoffed at the verbal patriotism of A.P.A. men who would not back up their sentiments by joining volunteer regiments against Spain in defense of Cuba.[8] It was true that the senior Order of American Mechanics had never been as closely associated with the A.P.A. as had the Junior Order. But in 1911 the United States Senate held hearings on a proposed immigration restriction bill and the Junior Order witness also denied that it was the "old decadent A.P.A." operating under a new name. The charge that it was had been made by a Catholic weekly, exhibiting once again that eagerness of some Catholics to identify opposition to immigration with anti-Catholicism and to classify all anti-Catholic sentiment under one general heading. The Junior Order man stated that his society was not anti-Catholic because

of its stand on immigration restriction and was in fact no more anti-Catholic than the Knights of Pythias, the Elks, or the American Federation of Labor, each of which favored imposition of tighter restrictions on immigrants. His order's motto was "Virtue, liberty, and patriotism," he said in its defense.[9]

Organized anti-Catholicism in strength reappeared during the second decade of the twentieth century in the form of the Ku Klux Klan. One anti-Catholic publicist, whose career extended from the days of the A.P.A. through those of the Klan, looked back to his A.P.A. experience in order to advise the Klan. He blamed the failure of the A.P.A. on unscrupulous politicians and on the implacable enmity of the Catholic hierarchy. The fight to keep America free was a continuous one, he said, and he hinted darkly that only unceasing vigilance would prevent a Jesuit victory. Martyrdom was, to him, the mark of the true patriot. As true descendants of the A.P.A. he listed the Guardians of Liberty and the Ku Klux Klan as the groups that would man the defenses.[10] His interpretation of the reasons for the failure of the A.P.A. was of some interest. But he did not mention whether the "unscrupulous politicians" who had brought failure were inside or outside the A.P.A. If he meant that they were within, it should be recalled that the A.P.A. leadership that led the order to its downfall was the same that had led it to its success.

The leader of the A.P.A. at its height, William James Henry Traynor, reappeared in the ranks of anti-Catholics during the Klan era with a booklet containing a "concise digest of Roman Catholic principles" and his commentary on them, gathered from "standard works, text books, and canon law." In question-and-answer form, Traynor's pamphlet was merely a reworking of the standard charges of Catholic claims of superiority to laws of the national state.[11] Traynor demonstrated by his reappearance not only the persistence of anti-Catholic sentiment but also the unchanging content of anti-Catholic arguments.

Still a durable symbol of anti-Catholicism, the "A.P.A." in 1923 was reported to be in existence and willing to throw its support to Henry Ford in a race for president, in order to secure a general house cleaning in the national capital.[12] Its initials were

utilized to designate a new organization titled the "American Political Alliance" in 1926. This new order faced the old enemy, Catholicism, and the term "political Romanism" was once more used to distinguish the religious from the political designs of the hierarchy. Prohibition of intoxicating liquors again appeared as one of the objectives in a first step against the "Jesuits." The founder of this society stated that the initials "only happened" to be the same as those of the extinct A.P.A., which had made the mistake of opposing the "official Roman Catholic system and discriminated against Roman Catholics as such" and thus had failed.[13]

During the flare-up of anti-Catholicism incident to the presidential campaign of 1928, the A.P.A. was once again listed among those honored and "strongly anti-Romanist forces" that had contributed to arousing the rank and file of "American Nationalists." [14] But when a new organization calling itself the "Protestants and Other Americans United" made its appearance after World War II, its organizer preferred that it not be confused with such preceding organizations as the "fanatical A.P.A. or the vicious Ku Klux Klan." [15]

Thus, the friends and enemies of the A.P.A., in its own time and in later years, and those who regarded it as a success or as a failure or sought to find guidance in its career demonstrated that the meaning of the A.P.A. varied according to time and circumstance.

A divergence of interpretation can also be found in the conclusions of thoughtful and scholarly men who viewed the A.P.A. and its career. First appearing in 1897, the *Encyclopedia of Social Reform* listed and discussed the order among the "reform" movements of its time.[16] Apparently convinced that there was some sort of "Catholic threat" to the public school system and to American democracy, the *Encyclopedia* was unconvinced that the methods of the A.P.A. were the best to combat the threat. Organizing against Catholics, in the opinion of the editors, only made the church stronger and tended to drive Catholic children into parochial schools.

Placing the order among reform movements had some merit.

The most obvious qualification was the opposition to corrupt municipal politics. But, too, the emphasis on women's suffrage, the tendency to support prohibition, the view expressed by some members of the patriotic press that more direct participation of the voter in governmental affairs was necessary, and the support of measures to reform Indian administration and the growing public welfare movement, demonstrate that the A.P.A. could very well be considered a reforming group. This judgment, however, takes no cognizance of the motives it had for supporting such reforms.

On the other hand, the fears expressed by the *Encyclopedia* that the methods of the A.P.A. might strengthen Catholicism should also be considered. Cardinal Gibbons, for example, held that the "periodical whirlwinds" of opposition to the church were not an unmixed evil; they were, he said, "winnowing winds" that separated the wheat from the chaff.[17] A conclusion concerning the effect of the A.P.A. on Catholic growth and strength in the United States was thus not one to be sought only in terms of numbers. Catholic growth continued and the political influence of Catholics was certainly no less after the demise of the A.P.A. than it was before. In fact, the importance of Archbishop Ireland within the Republican party was enhanced by his role in the election of 1896.[18]

In spite of the appearance of reform tendencies in the A.P.A., however, it—or anti-Catholicism in general—could not be regarded as a test to determine "liberalism" or "conservatism" of participants in it or in the campaign against it. Washington Gladden was a case in point. Without laboring Gladden's convictions with regard to the "social gospel," and without ignoring his commitment to the tax-supported public school system, both of which may be construed as "liberal" attitudes, he was pronouncedly anti-A.P.A. In general, the liberal Protestant ministry and press, as evidenced by the weekly *Independent,* was opposed to the A.P.A. But opposition to the order did not mean even faintly that the Catholic attitude on the public schools was accepted or that the position of some Catholics on sectarian appropriations was conceded. In general, too, it must be pointed

out that the Protestant ministers who supported the A.P.A. were usually religious fundamentalists.

Among political figures, aside from the possibility of Hazen Pingree of Michigan, no person who would eventually be associated as a leader with the reforms of the Progressive Movement could be identified with the A.P.A. in his earlier career. Robert LaFollette of Wisconsin was aware of the order's existence and of the role it played supporting the Republican party in his state. But the newspaper spokesman of the A.P.A. in Wisconsin favored that wing of the Republican party which LaFollette fought. Among Populists, John P. Altgeld of Illinois was the Democratic governor when the order was at its peak; yet he was clearly not the choice of the A.P.A. as a gubernatorial candidate. In no instance has it been shown that the A.P.A. was clearly to be affiliated with the Populists to the exclusion of the Republican affiliation, but there must be some reservations on the score as to whether the Populists maintained independence at all times; this is particularly true when it is recalled that the names of Thomas Watson and C. W. Macune of Georgia tantalizingly suggest Populist behavior in the South and that both were men approved by some A.P.A. people in 1896.

Some years after the *Encyclopedia*'s summary of the A.P.A. career, and at a time when the Ku Klux Klan was stimulating anti-Catholicism, a commission of the Catholic Knights of Columbus published a report of an investigation into the origins and manifestations of religious prejudice. The purpose of the analysis, printed in 1915, was to rid the country of prejudice by exposing it. With nice discrimination, the commission reported that an occasional Protestant minister departed from his proper duties to malign and vilify Catholics, but that such instances were not representative of the great body of non-Catholics. It admitted that some Catholics contributed to the aggravations which created anti-Catholic campaigns. After close investigation, the commission reported that the name of William Jennings Bryan as an anti-Catholic apparently derived from the activity of a man with the same name from Chicago who permitted his name to be used so as to convey the impression that the more famous man was

responsible. This method of deception was found typical of anti-Catholic activity, along with the practice of issuing dodgers and pamphlets purporting to come from some Catholic authority. As a conclusion to its investigation, the commission reported that general attacks on Catholicism came from three sources: (1) those who fail to appreciate the constitutional provisions regarding freedom of religious worship, and who fail to understand religious professions not their own; (2) those whose purpose it was to destroy not only the Catholic religion, but all religion and all duly constituted government; and (3) those, the worst class of all, who were actuated solely by "sordid, mercenary considerations, despite their expressed motives." [19]

As generalizations, the conclusions of the commission as to the sources of anti-Catholicism were perhaps acceptable to Catholics. The first generalization, of course, depended for its truth or falsity on differing interpretations as to what the provisions of the Constitution on religious freedom meant. The second amounted to condemnation of anti-Catholics by associating them with anarchists and atheists. The third generalization, and the only one which really dealt with the question at hand, suggested that profiteering on prejudice was a motive for anti-Catholic leadership. No evidence warranted the application of the third generalization to the A.P.A. As far as can be learned, the lack of funds that caused so much controversy at the convention of 1896 was due more to the failure of the order to collect dues than it was to misuse of funds. Salaries paid to A.P.A. officials were not large enough to make the jobs unduly attractive. Lecturers perhaps made a living out of their purveying of malice and salaciousness, but probably little more than that. The financial problems and failures of the "patriotic press" suggest that none of the editors experienced unusual profits from their newspaper ventures. Sensational charges of "selling out" the political influence of the order to the highest bidder were made, and they probably accounted for a part of the distrust that led to dissolution, but there was no positive indication that the men concerned received more than their actual expenses. These reservations on the applicability of the commission's third generalization to the

A.P.A., however, do not eliminate the possibility that there was a chance for reward that drew mercenary men into the A.P.A. movement but that did not materialize as they hoped. Neither do they overlook the possibility that anti-Catholic leaders may have been satisfied with a meager income derived from playing on prejudices at a time when the nation was in the throes of a depression and jobs were few.

The commission's report did coincide with the appearance of the Ku Klux Klan, although that organization did not grow rapidly until after 1920.[20] But in finding the Ku Klux Klan a lineal descendant of the A.P.A. its interpreters were likely to read back and give to the A.P.A. the same antagonisms as the Klan. Thus, the A.P.A. was described as anti-Semitic and as opposed to all foreign-born people. The first of these charges was simply not true; only one rather farfetched example of anti-Semitism has been found in the career of the A.P.A. The second charge needs refinement to show that the A.P.A. admitted foreign-born members to its rolls, that it was frequently called a foreign importation by its nativistic Catholic enemies, that it had a foreign-born president, and that it flourished on, rather than engendered, sentiment for immigration restriction.[21]

Generalizations as to the concrete results of the A.P.A. in its short career must be qualified. It provided little that was new or different in anti-Catholic propaganda or literature, and its use of standard propaganda was as much characteristic of its period of decline as it was of its period of growth. Unlike pre-Civil War anti-Catholicism, the A.P.A. did not lead its members into third-party ventures, choosing instead to utilize existing Republican party machinery; the reason, however, for this dissimilarity probably lies in the different political circumstances of the two eras.

If the name "A.P.A. movement" is applied to the entire campaign for immigration restriction, elimination of appropriations for sectarian institutions, and the extension of state control over charitable activities, then the "A.P.A. movement" was an overwhelming success. These were reform measures and were adopted on both state and federal levels. The groundwork for

defining the A.P.A. in these terms was laid by the self-hypnosis and fevered enthusiasm of the patriotic press, by the editors and writers in many Catholic diocesan newspapers and magazines who apparently preferred to classify all non-Catholics with anti-Catholicism, and by the daily press, which permitted itself to accept easy labels to identify quickly, but carelessly. What reputation the order attained by these methods was to a considerable extent the product of unrestrained and uncritical references in the nation's press, for its own partisan, religious, or personal reasons. This broader reputation of the "movement" had the concrete result of preventing the Republican party from including in its platform for 1896 a statement on the public schools for the first time since 1876, although it must be admitted that the statement was little more than a platitude at any time.

If the test is more severe, however, the results of the "movement" appear to be less significant. Legislation that was punitive, the preventing of any number of Catholics from obtaining employment either on the public payroll or in private business concerns, any act that in fact discriminated against Catholics—if these become the standards by which results are to be tested, the A.P.A. was far from an unqualified success. In creating personal animosities and in stimulating antagonisms among neighbors, and among members of the same unions, the order did immeasurable damage to the social structure; but it should be recalled in all fairness that anti-Catholic feeling existed before the A.P.A. enjoyed its brief career and afterward as well.

Essential to an estimate of the effectiveness of the A.P.A., then, is the distinction between the order as a secret society with a limited membership as it began its career and ended it, and on the other hand as the "A.P.A. movement," which was a cooperative and voluntary arrangement among the various self-styled "patriotic orders" for transient political purposes. By their apparently common consent, the limited, secret-society A.P.A. came to be the symbol and leader. The frequency with which the initials identified the "movement" could very well have been due to the fact that they suited the demands of typesetters and headline writers so well. But candor makes it essential to say that the

"movement" had a political usefulness to both major parties in the turbulent years of the 1890's.

The student who seeks to summarize the career of the A.P.A. must be sure that he distinguishes between the lodge or secret society, on the one side, and the "movement" on the other, and that he describes it in one set of terms and evaluates it in the same context. It would be rather unfair to say that the "A.P.A. movement" was of no importance in United States history, but the American Protective Association as a secret lodge scarcely rippled the surface of its times and differs little from hundreds of other such groups that have been organized in the country, pursued a brief career of distrust and suspicion, and died for no apparent reason other than that the times were not ripe for them to flourish.

Appendixes

Appendix I

National Officers of the American Protective Association

Year	President	Vice-President	Secretary of State	Secretary	Treasurer
1887–1892	Henry F. Bowers Clinton, Iowa				
1893	W.J.H. Traynor Detroit	David T. Ramsey Columbus		Charles T. Beatty Detroit	
1894	W.J.H. Traynor Detroit	Adam Fawcett Columbus	Osceola B. Jackman Boone, Iowa	Charles T. Beatty Detroit	H. M. Stark Milwaukee
1895	W.J.H. Traynor Detroit	J. H. Jackson Fort Worth	E. H. Dunbar Boston	Charles T. Beatty Detroit	Francis Campbell Minneapolis
1896	John W. Echols Atlanta	Henry S. Williams Boston	H. H. Swayne California	William J. Palmer Butte	Francis Campbell Minneapolis
1897	John W. Echols Atlanta	E. J. Stickle Canton, Ohio	Harry C. Sawyer Pennsylvania	William J. Palmer Butte	C. J. Stockman Maryland
1898–1911	Henry F. Bowers Clinton, Iowa				
1908	Henry F. Bowers Clinton, Iowa	R. J. Edenfield Augusta, Georgia	A. Campbell St. Louis	M. H. Bacon Kenosha, Wisconsin	G. W. Stubblefield Bloomington, Ill.

Year	Chaplain	Sergeant at Arms	Guard	Trustees	Sentinel	International President
1894	J. J. Gosper Los Angeles	E. H. Dunbar Boston	(unknown)	Francis Campbell Minneapolis N. C. McDonald Cheyenne W. H. Nichols Braddock, Penn.		
1895	J. M. Taulbee Covington, Ky.	J. H. Woodman San Diego	John King Missouri	W. J. Palmer Butte J. M. Snyder Washington, D.C. H. M. Stark West Superior, Wis.		
1896	W. H. Gottwald Washington, D.C.	J. W. Ellis S. McAlester, I.T.	W. B. Howard Omaha	Allison Stocker Denver George Hester Cleveland W. J. White Richmond, Virginia	T. S. Benson Ohio	
1897	W. H. Gottwald Washington, D.C.	C. E. Taylor Bath, Maine	E. T. Davis Springfield, Mass.	T. B. Haughwat T. N. Losie J. N. Nickson	R. M. Chambers Maryland	
1908		Emil Stamm St. Louis	J. B. Borke Chevy Chase, Md.		J. W. Reid Hartford, Conn.	George Evan Vancouver, B.C.

Appendix II

The "Patriotic Press"

The basic list of titles below was obtained from the inside cover of the *A.P.A. Magazine,* published in San Francisco, showing members of the "patriotic press." To this basic list titles were added that were found from time to time in other periodicals used in preparation of this study. Each item was checked against the *American Newspaper Directory,* ed. George P. Rowell (New York, 1894–96).

Where it was possible, claims made for members of the so-called "patriotic press" by other members of it were tested against the columns of the periodical, when files exist. Some claims were discarded as a result of this search, and the titles do not appear. For most of the titles below, however, no files are apparently in existence.

ARKANSAS
Brinkley
Mirror

CALIFORNIA
Colusa
Guard

Los Angeles
Tocsin

Oakland
Sentinel of Christian Liberty
American Sentinel

Oroville
American Guardian

San Diego
American and Seaport News

CALIFORNIA (cont.)
San Francisco
A.P.A. Magazine
American
American Patriot
California Standard
Light

COLORADO
Denver
Rocky Mountain American
Mercury
Pueblo
Individual

CONNECTICUT
Bridgeport
Independent-Leader

DISTRICT OF COLUMBIA
Washington
Commonwealth
United American

GEORGIA
Atlanta
Southern Eagle

ILLINOIS
Aurora
Blade

Chicago
American
Native Opinion
Patriot
Sentinel
True Protestant

Fairbury
Fair-Dealer

Galesburg
Liberty

Jacksonville
Our True Friend

Rock Island
American Blade
W.A.P.A.

INDIANA
Fort Wayne
American Eagle

IOWA
Des Moines
American Idea

Mechanicsville
American Advocate

Sioux City
Northwest American

KANSAS
Kansas City
American Eagle

KANSAS (cont.)
Topeka
Western Patriot

KENTUCKY
Louisville
Freedom's Banner
Justice

LOUISIANA
New Orleans
Visiting Friend

MARYLAND
Baltimore
Public Spirit

MASSACHUSETTS
Boston
American Citizen
British-American Citizen
American Protestant
Daily Standard
Women's Voice and Public School Champion

Everett
Orange Blossoms

Lowell
Herald

Worcester
Light

MICHIGAN
Detroit
Patriotic American

MINNESOTA
Duluth
Liberty

Minneapolis
Loyal American and the North

St. Paul
Breeze

MISSOURI
  Kansas City
  American

  St. Joseph
  American

  St. Louis
  American Monitor
  True American

  Springfield
  Protestant American

MONTANA
  Butte
  Examiner

NEBRASKA
  Kearny
  Central Star of Empire

  Omaha
  American
  Nation

NEW HAMPSHIRE
  New Hampshire Protestant

NEW JERSEY
  Camden
  American Patriot

  Philipsburgh
  Patriot

  Washington
  American Advocate

NEW YORK
  Albany
  Red Schoolhouse

  Brooklyn
  Primitive Catholic

  Buffalo
  Empire State American

  Lansingburg
  Republic

OHIO
  Cincinnati
  American Constitution
  American Protestant

  Cleveland
  Allied American

  Columbus
  People's Voice
  Record

  Minerva
  American Watchman

  Toledo
  American

ONTARIO (Canada)
  London
  Patriotic Canadian

OREGON
  Baker City
  American

  Eugene
  Broad-Axe

  Portland
  Portlander

PENNSYLVANIA
  Altoona
  Independent Loyal American

  Erie
  Advertiser

  Lebanon
  Progressive American

  Philadelphia
  American Mechanic's Advocate
  Protestant Standard

  Pittsburgh
  American
  True Flag

TENNESSEE
Memphis
American

Nashville
Patriotic Herald

TEXAS
Cleburne
Banner of Liberty

WASHINGTON
Seattle
Spirit of Seventy-Six

WASHINGTON (cont.)
Spokane
American Pope

Tacoma
True American Citizen

WISCONSIN
Kenosha
Independent

Milwaukee
Wisconsin Patriot

Portage
Doyle's Paper

Appendix III

American Protective Association
Congressional "Roll of Honor" *

Name	Party	State	Election of 1894
Silas Adams	Republican	Kentucky	Defeated
James F. Aldrich	Republican	Illinois	Re-elected
Henry M. Baker	Republican	New Hampshire	Re-elected
Henry H. Bingham	Republican	Pennsylvania	Re-elected
Henry W. Blair	Republican	New Hampshire	Not a candidate
William H. Bower	Democrat	North Carolina	Defeated
William W. Bowers	Republican	California	Re-elected
Julius C. Burrows	Republican	Michigan	Became U.S. Senator
Joseph G. Cannon	Republican	Illinois	Re-elected
Henry A. Cooper	Republican	Wisconsin	Re-elected
Robert G. Cousins	Republican	Iowa	Re-elected
Charles Curtis	Republican	Kansas	Re-elected
Jonathan G. Dolliver	Republican	Iowa	Re-elected
William R. Ellis	Republican	Oregon	Re-elected
Benjamin F. Funk	Republican	Illinois	Not renominated
John J. Gardner	Republican	New Jersey	Re-elected
John H. Gear	Republican	Iowa	Became U.S. Senator
Alva L. Hager	Republican	Iowa	Re-elected
Nils P. Haugen	Republican	Wisconsin	Not a candidate
Thomas J. Henderson	Republican	Illinois	Not renominated
William P. Hepburn	Republican	Iowa	Re-elected
Albert C. Hopkins	Republican	Pennsylvania	Not a candidate
Thomas J. Hudson	Populist	Kansas	Not a candidate
George W. Hulick	Republican	Ohio	Re-elected
John A. T. Hull	Republican	Iowa	Re-elected
Henry U. Johnson	Republican	Indiana	Re-elected
Martin N. Johnson	Republican	North Dakota	Re-elected
Andrew R. Kiefer	Republican	Minnesota	Re-elected

* The list of these men is to be found in the Washington, D.C., *News* for August 22, 1894. The remainder of the information was taken from the *Biographical Directory of the American Congress, 1774–1949.*

Name	Party	State	Election of 1894
John F. Lacey	Republican	Iowa	Re-elected
William S. Linton	Republican	Michigan	Re-elected
Eugene Loud	Republican	California	Re-elected
Henry C. Louderslagen	Republican	New Jersey	Re-elected
Thaddeus M. Mahon	Republican	Pennsylvania	Re-elected
Benjamin F. Marsh	Republican	Illinois	Re-elected
Francis Marvin	Republican	New York	Not renominated
Stephen A. Northway	Republican	Ohio	Re-elected
Thomas H. Paynter	Democrat	Kentucky	Elected as a state judge
Lafayette Pence	Pop.-Demo.	Colorado	Defeated
George D. Perkins	Republican	Iowa	Re-elected
Philip S. Post	Republican	Illinois	Died Jan., 1895
George W. Ray	Republican	New York	Re-elected
John B. Robinson	Republican	Pennsylvania	Re-elected
Thomas Settle	Republican	North Carolina	Re-elected
George B. Shaw	Republican	Wisconsin	Died Aug., 1894
George W. Smith	Republican	Illinois	Re-elected
Samuel W. Stephenson	Republican	Michigan	Re-elected
Charles Warren Stone	Republican	Pennsylvania	Re-elected
William A. Stone	Republican	Pennsylvania	Re-elected
Bellamy Storer	Republican	Ohio	Not a candidate
Luther M. Strong	Republican	Ohio	Re-elected
Willis Sweet	Republican	Idaho	Not a candidate
James A. Tawney	Republican	Minnesota	Re-elected
Henry F. Thomas	Republican	Michigan	Re-elected
Thomas Updegraff	Republican	Iowa	Re-elected
Henry C. Van Voorhis	Republican	Ohio	Re-elected
Daniel W. Waugh	Republican	Indiana	Not a candidate
John L. Wilson	Republican	Washington	Became U.S. Senator

Notes

Chapter 1

1. Ray Allen Billington, *The Protestant Crusade* (New York: The Macmillan Company, 1938), is the standard account of the origins of nativism in the United States. Billington's choice of title indicates that he regards Protestantism as the key to anti-Catholic nativism. This is perhaps true for the earlier period; I do not find, however, that it is true to the same degree in the postwar period. See his chap. i, "The Roots of Anti-Catholic Prejudice," for his discussion.

2. George M. Stephenson, *The Puritan Heritage* (New York: The Macmillan Company, 1952), p. 8.

3. Richard Hofstadter, *Social Darwinism in American Thought, 1860–1915* (Philadelphia: University of Pennsylvania Press, 1945), p. 16.

4. The use of the term "sect" here is made with the full knowledge that to Catholics it is a term applicable only to Protestant groups. Stephenson, in *Puritan Heritage,* p. 214, makes this point parenthetically.

5. Robert H. Lord *et al., History of the Archdiocese of Boston in Its Various Stages of Development, 1604 to 1943* (New York: Sheed & Ward, 1944), III, 63–65.

6. *The Bible in the Public Schools: Arguments in the Case of John D. Minor, et al., versus the Board of Education of the City of Cincinnati, et al., Superior Court of Cincinnati* (Cincinnati, Ohio: Robert Clarke Co., 1870), pp. 19–20. Exhibit I is a cartoon showing Purcell making his objection in 1842.

7. *The Bible in the Public Schools,* p. 310.

8. Harold M. Helfman, "The Cincinnati 'Bible War,' 1869–1870," *Ohio State Archeological and Historical Quarterly,* LX, 369–86. Helfman says that 1870 marked the high point of support for Bible reading and that after that date the secularization trend speeded up.

9. Bernard Mandel, "Religion and the Public Schools of Ohio," *Ohio State Archeological and Historical Quarterly,* LVIII, 185–206.

10. "Anti-Catholic Movements in the United States," *Catholic World,* XXII, 810–22.

11. The list is to be found in Florence E. Gibson, *The Attitudes of the New York Irish toward State and National Affairs, 1848–1892* (New York: Columbia University Press, 1951), pp. 283–85. Leon B. Richardson, in *William E. Chandler: Republican* (New York: Dodd, Mead & Co., 1940), p. 149, discusses the 1872 campaign; Chandler was Grant's manager.

12. Gibson, *Attitudes of the New York Irish,* chaps. ix–x; see also Albert Bigelow Paine, *Th. Nast, His Period and His Pictures* (New York: The Macmillan Company, 1904), pp. 139, 190, for cartoons.

13. William B. Hesseltine, *Ulysses S. Grant: Politician* (New York: Dodd, Mead & Co., 1935), pp. 304–5, for Grant's religious beliefs; pp. 390–91, for views on Grant's reason for making the Des Moines speech.

14. "The President's Speech at Des Moines," *Catholic World,* XXII, 433–43. Grant's speech was made on September 29, 1875, and was reported in newspapers. There is apparently no complete text of it in existence. From the reports of it, however, the speech appears to agree in many respects with the message sent to Congress on December 7, 1875, cited in note 15, below.

15. *Congressional Record,* 44th Cong., 1st Sess., pp. 175 ff. Also to be found in James D. Richardson, *A Compilation of the Messages and Papers of the Presidents, 1789–1897* (Washington, D.C.: Government Printing Office, 1896–1900), X, 4288 ff.

16. *Congressional Record,* 44th Cong., 1st Sess. (Dec. 14, 1875), House Resolution No. 1. See also Sister Marie Carolyn Klinkhamer, "The Blaine Amendment of 1875: Private Motives for Political Action," *Catholic Historical Review,* XLII, 15–49.

17. Charles Richard Williams, *The Life of Rutherford Birchard Hayes* (Boston: Houghton Mifflin Company, 1914), I, 387–89, 397–401; for Hayes's correspondence on this episode, see Charles Richard Williams (ed.), *Diary and Letters of Rutherford Birchard Hayes* (Columbus: Ohio State Archeological and Historical Society, 1926). See also Harry Barnard, *Rutherford B. Hayes and His America* (Indianapolis, Ind.: The Bobbs-Merrill Company, Inc., 1954), pp. 272–74, 310–12.

18. Williams, *Life of Hayes,* I, 410; Clifford H. Moore, "Ohio in National Politics, 1865–1896," *Ohio State Archeological and Historical Quarterly,* XXXVII (April–July, 1928), 220–427.

19. Williams, *Life of Hayes,* I, 476–78. See George D. Ellis (comp.), *Platforms of the Two Great Political Parties, 1856–1928* (Washington, D.C.: Government Printing Office, 1928), p. 45, for the platform of the Republicans in 1876 favoring the proposed Sixteenth Amendment and the public schools.

20. Irving Brant, in *James Madison, Father of the Constitution*

(Indianapolis, Ind.: The Bobbs-Merrill Company, Inc., 1950), pp. 268–73, has no doubt that Madison intended "absolute separation of church and state and total exclusion of government aid to religion" as the meaning of the First Amendment.

21. Allen Sinclair Will, *Life of Cardinal Gibbons, Archbishop of Baltimore* (New York: E. P. Dutton & Co., Inc., 1922), I, 160.

22. *Congressional Record*, 44th Cong., 1st Sess., pp. 5189, 5205, 5214, 5245–46, 5580–95. See also William A. Russ, Jr., "Anti-Catholic Agitation during Reconstruction," *Records of the American Catholic Historical Society*, XLV, 312–21.

23. Charles Roll, *Colonel Dick Thompson: The Persistent Whig* (Indianapolis: Indiana Historical Bureau, 1948), pp. 197–99. See also H. J. Eckenrode, *Rutherford B. Hayes: Statesman of Reunion* (New York: Dodd, Mead & Co., 1930), p. 242.

24. Richardson, *Messages and Papers*, XI, 4771, 4840, for President Arthur's words on education; Harrison's, XII, 5489; Burke A. Hinsdale, *The Works of James Abram Garfield* (Boston: J. R. Osgood & Co., 1882–83), II, 782–87, for acceptance of nomination; II, 783, for a precise statement on separation of church and state and the uses of public funds. See Ellis, *Platforms of the Two Great Political Parties,* pp. 51 (1880), 75 (1888), and 89 (1892) for Republican party platforms.

25. Eva Ingersoll Wakefield (ed.), *The Letters of Robert Ingersoll* (New York: Philosophical Library, 1951), pp. 88–89.

26. Frank Swancara, *The Separation of Religion and Government* (New York: Truth Seeker Co., 1950), pp. 148–51, a publication of the National Liberal League. See Joseph L. Blau (ed.), *Cornerstones of Religious Freedom in America* (Boston: Beacon Press, 1949), pp. 202–7, for a short account of the two organizations. Papers "to further the cause of absolute separation" were published by the National Religious Liberty Association; see William Addison Blakely (comp.), *American State Papers Bearing on Sunday Legislation* (New York: National Religious Liberty Association, 1891).

27. Wakefield, *Letters of Ingersoll*, pp. 163–64, 637. Ingersoll was not a nativist; see pp. 650–51, for his statement, "We have room here —plenty of room—for five hundred millions of people."

28. Anson Phelps Stokes, *Church and State in the United States* (New York: Harper & Brothers, 1950), II, 260.

29. Wakefield, *Letters of Ingersoll*, pp. 696–97.

30. Richard J. Gabel, *Public Funds for Church and Private Schools* (Washington, D.C.: Catholic University Press, 1937), pp. 548–49. Gabel does not list the state of Washington (1889), which, along with the other "omnibus states" admitted in the same year, was required by Congress to write such a clause into its constitution. See

also Conrad Henry Moehlman (comp.), *The American Constitutions and Religion* (Berne, Ind.: n.p., 1938), pp. 112 ff.

31. Samuel Windsor Brown, *The Secularization of American Education* (New York: Columbia University Press, 1912), pp. 69, 120–34; Howard K. Beale, *A History of the Freedom of Teaching in American Schools* (New York: Charles Scribner's Sons, 1941), pp. 213, 218. See also Kurt Leidecker, *Yankee Teacher: The Life of William Torrey Harris* (New York: Philosophical Library, 1945), pp. 290–92, for a description of Harris' early career and difficulties on this point.

32. Brown, *Secularization of American Education,* p. 1.

33. Quoted in Gabel, *Public Funds for Church and Private Schools,* p. 487.

34. Joseph Jackson Smith, *The Impending Conflict between Romanism and Protestantism in the United States* (New York: E. Goodenough, 1871).

35. Rev. Walter Elliott, "Honest Protestants and the Public Schools," *Catholic World,* XXXIX, 420–26.

36. James Anthony Froude, "Romanism and the Irish Race in the United States," *North American Review,* CXXIX, 519–36.

37. Peter Guilday, *A History of the Councils of Baltimore, 1791–1884* (New York: The Macmillan Company, 1932), pp. 222–23. See Theodore Roemer, *The Catholic Church in the United States* (St. Louis, Mo.: B. Herder Book Co., 1950), pp. 282–83, for growth in the West.

38. Guilday, *Councils of Baltimore,* pp. 233–34, 240–41. See also Apollinaris W. Baumgartner, *Catholic Journalism: A Study of Its Development in the United States, 1789–1920* (New York: Columbia University Press, 1931), and Frank Luther Mott, *A History of American Magazines, 1741–1885* (New York: D. Appleton & Co., 1930–38), III, 67–69, 329–30.

39. Guilday, *Councils of Baltimore,* pp. 238, 248–49.

40. Peter Guilday, *The National Pastorals of the American Hierarchy (1792–1919)* (Washington, D.C.: National Catholic Welfare Council, 1923), pp. 234 ff., 250.

41. Oscar Handlin, *The Uprooted* (Boston: Little, Brown & Co., 1951), pp. 132–38.

42. Sister Mary Evangela Henthorne, *The Career of the Right Reverend John Lancaster Spalding, Bishop of Peoria, as President of the Irish Catholic Colonization Association of the United States, 1879–1892* (Urbana: University of Illinois Press, 1932); Howard Eston Egan, "Irish Immigration to Minnesota, 1865–1890," *Mid-America,* XII, 133–66, 223–41; and James H. Moynihan, *The Life of Archbishop Ireland* (New York: Harper & Brothers, 1953), p. 22.

43. Samuel W. Barnum, in *Romanism As It Is* (Hartford: Connecticut Publishing Company, 1879), p. 764, is aware of the unreliability of his statistics.

44. Kirk H. Porter, *A History of Suffrage in the United States* (Chicago: University of Chicago Press, 1918), pp. 119–31; John Palmer Gavitt, *Americans by Choice* (New York: Harper & Brothers, 1922), p. 5; Frederick W. Van Dyne, *Citizenship of the United States* (Rochester, N.Y.: Lawyer's Cooperative Publishing Company, 1904).

45. Leon E. Aylesworth, "The Passing of the Alien Suffrage," *American Political Science Review*, XXV, 114–16.

46. Dudley O. McGovney, *The American Suffrage Medley: The Need for a National Uniform Suffrage* (Chicago: University of Chicago Press, 1949), pp. 49–60.

47. Luella Gettys, *The Law of Citizenship in the United States* (Chicago: University of Chicago Press, 1934), pp. 32–33.

48. George M. Stephenson, *A History of American Immigration, 1820–1924* (Boston: Ginn & Company, 1926), is basic, but Roy L. Garis, in *Immigration Restriction: A Study of the Opposition to and Regulation of Immigration into the United States* (New York: The Macmillan Company, 1927), provides the evidence from which the above conclusion is made.

49. Raymond Corrigan, in *The Church and the Nineteenth Century* (Milwaukee: Bruce Publishing Company, 1938), presents this conflict.

50. Roemer, *Catholic Church in the United States*, pp. 264 ff.

51. Dieter Cunz, in *The Maryland Germans, A History* (Princeton, N.J.: Princeton University Press, 1948), pp. 320–21, 335–36, 350–61, shows how Germans in Baltimore acted on school questions and what part they took in politics.

52. See Billington, *Protestant Crusade*, chap. xiv, "The Literature of Anti-Catholicism," to see how timeless anti-Catholic literature was and how little attention was paid in it to the passing scene.

53. Charles Howard Hopkins, *The Rise of the Social Gospel in American Protestantism, 1865–1915* (New Haven, Conn.: Yale University Press, 1940), and Henry F. May, *Protestant Churches and Industrial America* (New York: Harper & Brothers, 1949), are two studies of this movement in Protestantism.

54. (New York: Baker and Co., 1885). I have used the 1891 edition, which reports the sale of 167,000 copies between 1885 and 1891. Strong added materials on the public schools question in the 1891 edition.

55. James M. King, *Facing the Twentieth Century* (New York: American Union League Society, 1899), pp. 409–11. King had been

one of the Protestant ministers escorting Blaine when the incident occurred. Later, he was to become secretary of the National League for the Protection of American Institutions, for which see below.

56. John Gilmary Shea, "No Actual Need of a Catholic Party in the United States," *American Catholic Quarterly Review*, XII, 705–13.

57. Dexter A. Hawkins, *Archbishop Purcell Outdone! The Roman Catholic Church in New York City and Public Land and Public Money* (New York: Phillips & Hunt, 1880). Gibson, *Attitudes of the New York Irish*, pp. 16–17, shows figures telling how many Irish were on the charity rolls of New York City from 1848 to 1891.

58. Allan Nevins, *Grover Cleveland: A Study in Courage* (New York: Dodd, Mead & Co., 1932), p. 170; Gibson, *Attitudes of the New York Irish*, p. 384. See Rev. George Deshon, "An Impudent Fabrication Exposed," *Catholic World*, XXXIX, 114–19, for a reply to Hawkins, and Rev. George M. Searle, "Religious Liberty as Understood by the Evangelical Alliance," *Catholic World*, XXXIX, 400–6, for comment on the bills before the New York legislature.

59. David Saville Muzzey, *James G. Blaine, A Political Idol of Other Days* (New York: Dodd, Mead & Co., 1934), p. 309; Albert T. Volwiler (ed.), *The Correspondence between Benjamin Harrison and James G. Blaine* (Philadelphia: American Philosophical Society, 1940), p. 9. Harrison C. Thomas, in *The Return of the Democratic Party to Power in 1884* (New York: Columbia University Press, 1919), believes that the Burchard incident can easily be overdrawn because of its dramatic qualities.

60. Gibson, *Attitudes of the New York Irish*, p. 392.

61. Allan Nevins, *Abram Hewitt: With Some Account of Peter Cooper* (New York: Harper & Brothers, 1935), pp. 510–14; Abram Hewitt to Daniel Connolly, Sept. 25, 1888, in *Selected Writings of Abram Hewitt*, ed. Allan Nevins (New York: Columbia University Press, 1937). See also Gibson, *Attitudes of the New York Irish*, p. 408.

62. John Higham, "The American Party: 1886–1891," *Pacific Historical Review*, XIX, 37–46; Priscilla Knuth, Nativism in California, 1886–1897 (Master's thesis, University of California, 1947), gives a discussion of the American Party in California. Edward John Byrne, in "The Religious Issue in National Politics," *Catholic Historical Review*, VIII, 329–64, improperly identifies the American Party as the American Protective Association; Henry Minor, in *The Story of the Democratic Party* (New York: The Macmillan Company, 1928), p. 358, correctly calls it a forerunner of the A.P.A.

63. Nevins, *Cleveland*, pp. 428–30; Muzzey, *Blaine*, p. 386.

64. See his *Rome in America* (Boston: The Pauline Propaganda, 1887), Introduction, for biographical information on Fulton. Of North of Ireland stock, Fulton was born in 1828, graduated from the University of Rochester in 1851, wrote books on subjects other than the menace of Catholicism, and died in 1901. His *Washington in the Lap of Rome* was published in Boston by W. Kellaway, 1888.

65. Fulton, *Washington in the Lap of Rome,* p. 11.

66. This charge of a wire from Cardinal Gibbons to Cleveland was repeated during the campaign of 1892 so often that Cleveland felt compelled to deny it publicly; see John Tracy Ellis, *The Life of James Cardinal Gibbons* (Milwaukee, Wis.: Bruce Publishing Co., 1952), II, 507, and Will, *Life of Gibbons,* I, 411, 417, for instances of communication between Cleveland and Gibbons.

67. Fulton, *Washington in the Lap of Rome,* Preface.

68. Lord, *History of the Archdiocese of Boston,* III, 85–87.

69. *Ibid.,* III, 100–133. *Why Priests Should Wed* was reprinted in 1912. Lord says the British-American Association had 40,000 members by 1887 in Boston. Alvin Packer Stauffer, in Anti-Catholicism in American Politics, 1865–1900 (Ph.D. dissertation, Harvard University, 1933), p. 256, says that it had fifty-five branches by October, 1888, with an average membership of 300, extending from Maine to Chicago. Caution advises that Stauffer's total of 16,500, approximately, be accepted, but Lord's statement on the "bitter, arrogant, and truculent" spirit exhibited by these people indicates that perhaps they *seemed* like 40,000

70. Margaret Lisle Shepherd, *My Life in the Convent* (Toledo, Ohio: Book and Bible House, 1949). Mrs. Shepherd's book first appeared in 1892 and was republished twice as recently as 1938 and 1949. Her recollections of the Boston incidents are contained in the Appendix of the 1949 edition. M. J. Brady, *A Fraud Unmasked: The Career of Mrs. Margaret L. Shepherd* (Woodstock, Ont.: n.p., 1893), gives one revelation of her career; see also Lord, *History of the Archdiocese of Boston,* III, 107–9.

71. Lord, *History of the Archdiocese of Boston,* III, 114, 126, 133.

72. *Ibid.,* III, 75–85.

73. *Ibid.,* III, 118–26.

74. Boston Committee of One Hundred, "An Open Letter to the Friends of Free Schools and American Liberties," and "The Pope's Last Veto in American Politics." These two pamphlets were published in 1888 and 1890, respectively, and are a part of a series published by the Committee of One Hundred. See also Lois B. Merk, "Boston's Historic Public School Crisis," *New England Quarterly,* XXXI, 172–99.

75. G. W. Anderson, "Politics and the Public Schools," *Atlantic Monthly*, LXXXVII, 433–47, gives a dispassionate account of the long struggle.

76. Daniel Dorchester, *Romanism versus the Public School System* (New York: Phillips & Hunt, 1888).

77. Mason Wade, *Francis Parkman: Heroic Historian* (New York: The Viking Press, Inc., 1942), p. 436.

78. *Who's Who in America, 1908–1909.*

79. Edwin D. Mead, *The Roman Catholic Church and the Public Schools* (Boston: George H. Ellis, 1890).

80. Philip Schaff, "Church and State in the United States; or, The American Idea of Religious Liberty, and Its Practical Effects," *Papers of the American Historical Association*, II, 391–543.

81. *Congressional Record*, 45th Cong., 1st Sess., p. 4615; 2nd Sess., pp. 421, 433–34, and for petitions in favor of the amendment, pp. 371, 2033; John Whitney Evans, "Catholics and the Blair Education Bill," *Catholic Historical Review*, XLVI, 273–98.

82. National Education Association, *Journal of Proceedings and Addresses*, for 1887, see pp. 45–47, 192–95, 615; for 1888, pp. 156–58; for 1889, pp. 37, 111–79. See also the symposium in *Forum* during the year 1888 on "What Shall the Public Schools Teach?" Contributors included Lester Ward, S. Edward Warren, Austin Flint, and others. A pamphlet published for the Session of the Westminster Presbyterian Church, undated, by David James Burrell, *The Roman Catholic Church vs. The American Public School* (Minneapolis, Minn.: Session of the Westminster Presbyterian Church, n.d.), probably relates to this controversy.

83. Gibson, *Attitudes of the New York Irish*, chap. xii; Sylvester Malone, who wrote *Dr. Edward McGlynn* (New York: Dr. McGlynn Monument Association, 1918), was another priest equally disliked by the Archbishop. Malone will reappear in this study as a candidate for office in 1894.

84. Anna George DeMille, *Henry George: Citizen of the World* (Chapel Hill: University of North Carolina Press, 1950), pp. 144–45, 156–57. See *The Letters of Theodore Roosevelt*, ed. Elting E. Morrison (Cambridge, Mass.: Harvard University Press, 1951), I, 122–23, for a letter from Roosevelt to Henry Cabot Lodge, Feb. 15, 1887: "I have regarded with dispassionate enjoyment the Corrigan-McGlynn-George-Davitt-Papal controversy. May each vanquish all the others! It is one of those few contests in which any result is for the good."

85. See Edward McGlynn, *Father Lambert, a Priest Who Went to Rome, and What He Got There* (New York: Anti-Poverty Society, 1888), for McGlynn's version of what happened to recalcitrant priests.

86. Malone, *McGlynn,* p. 87; Frederick J. Zwierlein (ed.), *Letters of Archbishop Corrigan to Bishop McQuaid and Allied Documents* (Rochester, N.Y.: The Art Print Shop, 1946), pp. 124–25; pp. 90–126 are concerned with the McGlynn affair.

87. DeMille, *George,* p. 220; see also Charles Albro Barker, *Henry George* (New York: Oxford University Press, Inc., 1955), pp. 486–93.

88. Henry J. Browne, *The Catholic Church and the Knights of Labor* (Washington: Catholic University Press, 1949), pp. 262 fn., 285.

89. Terence V. Powderly, *The Path I Trod* (New York: Columbia University Press, 1940), chap. xxvii in particular.

90. Browne, *Catholic Church and the Knights of Labor,* pp. 22–23, 48, 78–79, 155. The cartoon from *Puck* is reproduced opposite p. 275.

91. Gibson, *Attitudes of the New York Irish,* pp. 446–47.

92. *The Papal Controversy Involving the Claim of the Roman Catholic Church to be the Church of God between the "American Baptist" and the "Church Progress"* (St. Louis, Mo.: National Baptist Publishing Company, 1892).

93. Isaac J. Lansing, *Romanism and the Republic* (Boston: Arnold Publishing Company, 1890). The 1890 printing was reported to have been preceded by 9,000 copies.

94. *Dictionary of Canadian Biography,* ed. W. Stewart Wallace (2nd ed.; Toronto, 1945), lists Charles Paschal Telesphore Chiniquy as born in 1809, educated at Quebec Seminary, ordained in 1833; he deserted the church in 1858 to become a Presbyterian minister, married in 1864, and died in Montreal in 1899. His books were translated into many languages, the two autobiographical volumes being the *Fifty Years in the Church of Rome* for his Catholic years, and the *Forty Years in the Church of God* for his Protestant years. Some of his other books are simply excerpts from these two; for example, *The Assassination of Lincoln* is taken from the *Fifty Years.* The account of the alleged visit with Lincoln may be found on pp. 714–15 of the 40th edition of *Fifty Years,* published by Adam Craig in Chicago, 1891.

95. John Ireland, *The Church and Modern Society: Lectures and Addresses* (St. Paul: Pioneer Press Manufacturing Company, 1905), I, 73, 81, 97.

Chapter 2

1. Arthur Meier Schlesinger, *The Rise of the City* (New York: The Macmillan Company, 1933), pp. 288–90.
2. Charles W. Ferguson, *Fifty Million Brothers* (New York: Farrar & Rinehart, Inc., 1937), p. 301.
3. Maurice F. Egan and John B. Kennedy, *The Knights of Columbus in War and Peace* (New Haven, Conn.: Knights of Columbus, 1920), II, 42–45, 156
4. James M. King, *Facing the Twentieth Century* (New York: American Union League Society, 1899), p. 559, lists these and many others as "Patriotic orders," a term which had a special meaning to him. On the G.A.R., see Mary R. Deering, *Veterans in Politics: The Story of the G.A.R.* (Baton Rouge: Louisiana State University Press, 1952); see also Wallace E. Davies, *Patriotism on Parade* (Cambridge, Mass.: Harvard University Press, 1955).
5. King, *Facing the Twentieth Century,* pp. 563–65.
6. Ray Allen Billington, *The Protestant Crusade* (New York: The Macmillan Company, 1938), pp. 183–84.
7. Florence E. Gibson, *The Attitudes of the New York Irish toward State and National Affairs, 1848–1892* (New York: Columbia University Press, 1951), pp. 245–50; see also Dennis Tilden Lynch, *The Wild Seventies* (New York: D. Appleton-Century Co., 1941).
8. Albert C. Stevens (comp. and ed.), *The Cyclopedia of Fraternities* (New York: Hamilton Printing and Publishing Company, 1899), pp. xviii–xix.
9. There are organizational charts reproduced in Stevens, *Cyclopedia of Fraternities,* but the complexity of relationships is beyond verbal description.
10. Ferguson, *Fifty Million Brothers,* pp. 174, 320–25; see also the undated pamphlet put out by the Order of the American Union (organized 1875), *The Future Conflict: An Address to the American People* (n.p., n.d.), published sometime after 1878 according to internal evidence.
11. *Age* (Clinton), Feb. 11, 1887, had a three-column promotional spread on the town's future. Statistics on Iowa and Clinton County were taken from the U.S. Bureau of the Census, *Tenth Census of the United States: 1880,* I, 432, and the *Eleventh Census: 1890,* I, pt. 2, 600, 628. *Age* on Jan. 28, 1887, reports Catholic growth.

12. Charles F. Griffith, "The Erection of the Diocese of Davenport," *Mid-America*, XIV, 335–43.

13. See footnote in Josiah Strong, *Our Country: Its Possible Future and Its Present Crisis* (New York: Baker and Taylor, 1891), p. 108, referring to the Dubuque development.

14. Election results for 1886 and 1887 are to be found in *Age* (Clinton), Feb. 18, 1886, for Walliker's election, and March 11, 1887, for his defeat. There is a noticeable difference in results from the Fourth Ward. The Knights of Labor decision not to support Walliker is reported in the *News* (Clinton), March 3 and 5, 1887. Knights of Labor materials and manuscripts at the Catholic University Library, including the Terence Powderly Papers, do not indicate that the Clinton affair became a subject of official correspondence.

On the lumber company as an issue, see *News* (Clinton), March 6, 11, 23, 1887. For the school election, *Age* (Clinton), March 4, 18, and *News*, March 15, 1887.

Arnold Walliker was interviewed before his death, and the material gained thereby appeared in Ruth Knox Stough, The American Protective Association (Master's thesis, University of Nebraska, 1931). Another thesis, that of Sister Mary Callista Hynes, The History of the American Protective Association in Minnesota (Catholic University of America, 1939?), agrees that Walliker blamed Catholic influence; her source, however, was another old-time Clinton resident who was not a member of the A.P.A.

15. Bowers was chairman of a Walliker meeting during the campaign; he also notarized Walliker's final report to the City Council, *News* (Clinton), March 6 and 23, 1887.

16. The number of founders is usually given as seven, and I have seen no good reason for changing it. However, there are three different lists of names of the men in attendance at the founding, the most reliable of them listing eight names. The list in the Stough thesis, for which Arnold Walliker is the source, gives eight names. Another is to be found in the Hynes thesis; it agrees with Stough on four names; the source in this instance was Edmund Burke, an old Clinton resident, and was obtained by letter. The third list is to be found in Fritiof Ander, "The Swedish-American Press and the A.P.A.," *Church History*, VI, 165–79, with duplication of some names on both lists; Ander's source is not cited, although he apparently made a visit to Clinton. I interviewed Mrs. C. C. Bowers, daughter-in-law of Henry F. Bowers, at the family home in Clinton during the summer of 1952, and at that time she could add nothing to clarify the differences. The three lists are given below for comparative purposes. The Stough list is probably the most reliable of the three:

Hynes List	Stough List	Ander List
H. F. Bowers	H. F. Bowers	H. F. Bowers
Jacob H. Walliker	Jacob H. Walliker	Jacob H. Walliker
Arnold Walliker	Arnold Walliker	Ernest Walliker
Simon Woldenburg	Simon Woldenburg	Charles Huzzey
Socrates Bates	William Andrews	William Andrews
L. W. Miller	Philip Mudgett	Philip Mugett
Dr. H. S. Rathbun	Louis Emmons	Charles Flanigan
	—— Wilson	

17. The quotation, a letter from Bowers, is in Stevens, *Cyclopedia of Fraternities,* pp. 293–98. The same statement is to be found in the *American Advocate,* II, 373, where it is treated as an original interview with Bowers. Other versions, less complete but substantially the same, are to be found in the *Wisconsin Patriot,* May 14, 1895, the *Loyal American and the North,* March 10, 1894, and in Richard Wheatly, "The American Protective Association," *Harper's Weekly,* Oct. 27, 1894.

18. Photographs of Bowers are to be found in *Harper's Weekly,* Oct. 27, 1894, and in *Wisconsin Patriot,* May 14, 1895.

19. Lawrence F. Schmeckebier, in *History of the Know-Nothing Party in Maryland* (Baltimore, Md.: Johns Hopkins University Press, 1899), gives no instance of the sort that Bowers described.

20. Biographical information on Bowers is to be found in *Who's Who in America* for the years 1899–1900 through 1911; Benjamin F. Gue, *Biographies and Portraits of the Progressive Men of Iowa* (Des Moines, Iowa: Conway and Shant, 1899), I, 201–2; *American* (Omaha), April 6, 1894; *Loyal American and the North,* March 10, 1894; *American Advocate,* II, 373. See also John Higham, "The Mind of a Nativist: Henry F. Bowers and the A.P.A.," *American Quarterly,* IV, 16–24, for a psychological interpretation. A frustrated and unsuccessful youth resulting in paranoia and delusions of persecution is the explanation that Higham presents for Bowers' anti-Catholicism.

21. Obituary, *Herald* (Clinton), Nov. 9, 1911. After Bowers' death, his widow disposed of his museum collections and whatever "papers" there were for $25.00, without consulting his surviving children by his first wife. The children were outraged—not at the disposal but at the price. This family information and that in the text above was supplied by Mrs. C. C. Bowers, daughter-in-law. Some of Bowers' paintings were in her home.

22. *American Advocate,* II, 373.

23. *Who's Who in America* lists Bowers as a "widower" until the 1903–5 edition. The obituary cited above reported that he married

a Miss Eliza Wilson, daughter of an Iowa pioneer, but gives no date for the marriage.

24. Hynes, History of the A.P.A. in Minnesota, pp. 2–4, 132.

25. Gue, *Biographies and Portraits,* I, 201–2.

26. "The American Protective Association," in *Encyclopedia of Social Reform,* ed. William D. P. Bliss (New York: Funk & Wagnalls Co., Inc., 1897), pp. 48–52; Charles T. Beatty, "The American Protective Association," *Independent,* XLVI, 69.

27. The description of the structure of the A.P.A. that follows depends on inferences and direct statements drawn from scattered citations. They have been gathered together here so as to permit a "constitutional" description. No copy of the order's constitution has been reported under review by any previous investigator, and I have not seen one. The card catalogues at the Michigan Historical Collections in Ann Arbor and at the Nebraska Historical Society in the library of the University of Nebraska both list a constitution among their holdings; but neither library was able to produce a copy when asked for it. Stough's thesis, already cited, was completed at the University of Nebraska in 1931; that she does not cite the constitution seems to indicate that it was missing at that time. A librarian at the Montana Historical Society recalled that many years ago a book had been given to the Society's library with a copy of the A.P.A.'s constitution in it as a bookmark; a search of their pamphlet files did not reveal the item, however.

28. Annual conventions were held as follows: Belle Plaine, Iowa, in 1889; Chicago, 1890; St. Louis, 1892; Cleveland, 1893; Des Moines, 1894; Milwaukee, 1895; Washington, 1896 and 1897; Augusta, 1900. The 1891 meeting was probably held at Detroit. For reports of conventions, see *A.P.A. Magazine,* July, 1895, p. 167; *American* (Omaha), May 5, July 7, 1893, May 11, 1894; *Loyal American and the North,* May 12, 1895; *Wisconsin Patriot,* May 11, 1895, May 15, 1897; *Breeze,* May 20, 1897; *Examiner* (Butte), April 30, 1896; *American Advocate,* June, 1900, pp. 199 ff. In the daily press, see *News* (Milwaukee), May 7–11, 1895; *Sentinel* (Milwaukee), May 6–11, 1895; *Post* (Washington, D.C.), May 12–18, 1896. *Public Opinion* gathered news reports; for example, see May 16, 1895, p. 553, for reports on the 1895 convention.

29. *Loyal American and the North,* May 12, 1894; *Catholic Citizen,* May 12, 1894; *Wisconsin Patriot,* Dec. 4, 1897.

30. State conventions are reported in *American* (Omaha), June 8, 1894; March 27, 1896; *Loyal American and the North,* Jan. 27, March 17, 1894; *Patriotic American,* March 3, 1894; *Record* (Columbus), Jan. 18, 1894; *Doyle's Paper,* March 15, 1895; *Wisconsin Patriot,* Feb. 23, 1895, Feb. 22, 1896, Feb. 20, 1897; *True Amer-*

ican, Feb. 15, 1896; *Tribune* (Minneapolis), Jan. 26, 1894; *News* (Detroit), Feb. 27, March 21, 1895; *Call* (San Francisco), March 8, 1896; *Oregonian,* Jan. 21, 1897. The distinction between "Supreme" and "Superior" is made most clearly in *Breeze,* May 20, 1897.

31. *Record* (Columbus), Jan. 4, 1893, and *American Eagle,* Aug. 19, 1893, contain sample petitions for inaugurating a new council with twenty-five charter members.

32. *A.P.A. Magazine,* June, 1895, p. 88, President Traynor's statement.

33. *World Almanac,* 1895, p. 115, gives the complete platform. J. H. Jackson, *The American Protective Association: What It Is, Its Platform and Roman Intolerance Compared* (n.p., n.d.), a pamphlet by the supreme vice-president elected in 1895, gives the platform with explanations of each plank.

34. H. R. Howe, *The Patriotic American Songster* (Rockford, Ill.: The Author, 1895), p. 7.

35. Negro delegates attended the national convention of 1895 from Missouri, Illinois, and Washington; see *Wisconsin Patriot,* May 11, 1895; the separate councils for Negroes are mentioned in the *A.P.A. Magazine,* July, 1895, p. 136.

36. The conclusion on anti-Semitism is the result of my search of the "patriotic press"; the only example found will be cited in the appropriate place.

37. First mention of the W.A.P.A., with Mrs. Reynolds as president, is in *Patriot* (Chicago), Sept., 1891, p. 231. The W.A.P.A. is discussed rather frequently in the patriotic press, so I feel confident of the name; however, Stevens in his *Cyclopedia of Fraternities* discussion of the A.P.A., refers to the women's organization as the "Women's Historical Society" and implies that its first function was to encourage American history in the schools. See Oliver E. Murray, *The Black Pope* (2nd ed.; Chicago: The Patriot Company, 1892), table of contents, for Mrs. Reynolds' connection with the Orange Institution.

38. An exchange of letters on this disagreement is published in the *American* (Omaha), July 7, 14, 1894.

39. The Junior A.P.A. and the International Protective Association are mentioned in the accounts of the 1895 convention as well as in Stevens, *Cyclopedia of Fraternities.* The Mexican club is mentioned in *The Lake Breeze,* Sept. 12, 1895; the Manchester group, in the *Wisconsin Patriot,* March 23, 1895. See J. S. Willison, *Sir Wilfrid Laurier and the Liberal Party* (Toronto: G. N. Morang, 1903), II, 207–8, footnote, for mention of the Canadian Protestant Protective Association and the Manitoba school question.

40. Two newspaper "revelations" formed the basis for this survey;

see *Ohio State Journal* (Columbus), Nov. 7, 1892, and *Globe* (St. Paul), Nov. 6, 1893. The *Congressional Record,* 53rd Cong., 2nd Sess. (June 8, 1894), pp. 5997–6005, contains much the same material, introduced there as part of a contested election case.

41. Alvin Packer Stauffer, in Anti-Catholicism in American Politics, 1865–1900 (Ph.D. dissertation, Harvard University, 1933), says the part of this oath on collaboration with Catholics during strikes was inserted in 1893, so that the A.P.A. served as an anti-union organization. The exposés of 1892, however, contained the clause, so Stauffer's dates are wrong, although his interpretation of the organization may be correct.

42. See the *Oregonian,* May 16, 1896, for a news service report.

43. The matter of insignia is in the *Ohio State Journal* exposé. The meaning of "F.P. and P." is revealed in Murray, *The Black Pope,* p. 203. Montana's addition is found in the *Examiner* (Butte), June 8, 1895. An example of the symbols and "Friend" used in correspondence with a nonmember is to be seen in W. J. Willis to C. K. Davis, Oct. 16, 1892, in the Cushman Kellogg Davis Papers at the Minnesota Historical Society in St. Paul.

The phrase "little red schoolhouse," meaning the free public school, may well be a product of this period; Mitford M. Mathews, in *A Dictionary of Americanisms on Historical Principles* (Chicago: University of Chicago Press, 1951), II, 1372, gives 1862 as the date of the first use of "red skool house" in literature. His next citation is for 1901, to *World's Work,* where the phrase has gained the meaning above. The patriotic orders used the phrase constantly during the decade of the nineties and thus may be responsible for giving currency to it.

44. *News* (Milwaukee), May 8, 1895.

45. *Wisconsin Patriot,* Jan. 19, 1895; *Doyle's Paper,* March 15, 1895.

46. *A.P.A. Magazine,* I, 87.

47. Howe, *Patriotic Songster,* p. 24.

48. *Record* (Columbus), Aug. 31, 1893.

49. *Oregonian,* Aug. 15, 1895.

50. *United American,* April 3, 1895.

51. *Patriotic American,* Aug. 6, 1892; *United American,* Sept. 28, 1895; *American* (Omaha), Nov. 1, 1895; *True American,* Feb. 15, 1896.

52. Stough, American Protective Association, p. 3; H. F. Bowers to H. J. Desmond, March 1, 1899, in Humphrey J. Desmond, *The A.P.A. Movement* (Washington, D.C.: New Century Press, 1912), pp. 13–14, 64–66; Stauffer, Anti-Catholicism in American Politics, p. 192; *American* (Omaha), April 14, 1893.

53. Stough, American Protective Association, p. 86.

54. It is strange that such a condition existed. The strangeness lies, not in the lack of publicity between 1887 and 1892, but in the fact that the friendly press after 1893 did not mention other members of the Pantheon of the order.

55. Allen W. Burns, The A.P.A. and the Anti-Catholic Crusade: 1885–1898 (Master's thesis, Columbia University, 1947), p. 21. Burns has made good use of the papers of these conferences, which are on file at the New York Public Library as Conference of American and Protestant Organizations, 1889, Papers.

56. José McCready, Platform of the Papal Party (Cambridge: The Author, 1890).

57. John Jay wrote Rome, The Bible and The Republic, published in 1879; he was president of the American Historical Association in 1890.

58. King, Facing the Twentieth Century, is in the nature of a final report of the N.L.P.A.I., although King was much narrower in his personal views than the men whose names gave prestige to the league; following p. 519 is a review of the history of the league. Encyclopedia of Social Reform, p. 917, also discusses the league; John Moffett Mecklin, in The Ku Klux Klan (New York: Harcourt Brace & Co., 1924), refers to the league as an "upper class A.P.A.," which is a rather good description.

59. This is the interpretation placed on "Amorean" in the St. Paul Globe exposé.

Chapter 3

1. W. J. H. Traynor, "Policy and Power of the A.P.A.," North American Review, CLXII, 658–66. Traynor was president of the A.P.A. after 1893; this article suggested the periodization utilized for chapter divisions in this study.

2. Patriotic American, Oct. 25, 1890, Aug. 6, 1892; W. J. H. Traynor to Henry Baldwin, March 3, 1891, Baldwin MSS, New York Public Library; Alvin Packer Stauffer, Anti-Catholicism in American Politics, 1865–1900 (Ph.D. dissertation, Harvard University, 1933), p. 198.

3. U.S. Congress, House of Representatives, Report of the Select Committee, 50th Cong., 2nd Sess., Rep. 3792 (also called the "Ford Committee Report").

4. On Pingree, see the sketch by Raymond C. Miller in the Dictionary of American Biography; for background, see Arthur Chester

Millspaugh, *Party Organization and Machinery in Michigan Since 1890* (Baltimore, Md.: The Johns Hopkins Press, 1917).

5. W. R. Bates to James McMillan, April 7, 1892, James McMillan Papers, Burton Historical Collections, Detroit Public Library. Biographical information on Linton may be found in *Who Was Who in America;* the *Biographical Directory of the American Congress; American* (Omaha), April 10, 1896; and James Cooke Mills, *History of Saginaw County, Michigan* (Saginaw, Mich.: Seemann and Peters, 1918), II, 35–39.

6. W. R. Bates to McMillan, April 6, 1892, McMillan Papers. Bates was a former secretary to McMillan and was, in 1892, the secretary of the Republican state central committee.

7. E. R. Phinney to Harrison Geer, May 7, 1892, Harrison Geer Papers, Michigan Historical Collections, Ann Arbor. Phinney was postmaster at Saginaw, while Geer was federal collector of customs for Michigan; they were both McMillan men.

8. *Michigan Catholic,* July 28, 1892; several letters on the election are in the McMillan Papers: Junius E. Beal to McMillan, Nov. 15, 1892, and Charles P. Collins to McMillan, Nov. 5, 1892, are two examples.

9. G. W. Hill to Harrison Geer, Dec. 14, 1892, Geer Papers; *Times and Expositor* (Adrian, Mich.), Jan. 13, 1893. At this time, presidential electors in Michigan were chosen by congressional districts. Also see the letter, H. S. Brown to Geer, Dec. 14, 1892, Geer Papers, which says in part: "Mr. Linton owes his great success mainly to the careful fostering of an underground sentiment, which was judiciously handled by his Congressional Committee, and the strength from that element, helped our whole ticket, and particularly Mr. Rich throughout our District, as in our canvass we ranked Rich along with Linton in making our plea on the lines referred to, and which you will understand without my being more explicit."

10. *American* (Omaha), Oct. 14, 1892.

11. Victor Rosewater, The Life and Times of Edward Rosewater, unpublished biography, written by a son, Nebraska Historical Society, undated, p. 195.

12. *American* (Omaha), Nov. 5, 1891.

13. *Ibid.,* April 8, 1892; *Patriotic American,* Jan. 7, 1893. The Miller case was never solved, apparently, although investigations were prolonged. The judge who conducted the investigation was opposed by the A.P.A., and the order apparently had a difficult time finding explanations for the fact that much of the evidence supplied in the hearings came from prostitutes and gamblers, who altered their stories each time they told them.

14. *Bee* (Omaha), Nov. 6, 1892; Stauffer, in Anti-Catholicism in

American Politics, p. 322, says that David H. Mercer was elected to Congress from the Nebraska Fourth District largely through A.P.A. efforts. I have found no corroboration for the story and have consequently not used it.

15. Bryan's candidacy was discussed in T. S. Allen to W. J. Bryan, Jan. 22 and 30, 1893, William Jennings Bryan Papers, Library of Congress. On the other hand, there is no mention of the A.P.A. in Charles G. Dawes, *A Journal of the McKinley Years* (Chicago: Lakeside Press, 1950), although the entry for March 10, 1893 (p. 19), mentions a school board election in Lincoln, an opportunity not likely to be ignored by an active A.P.A. council. The entries in the *Journal* for 1894 were not made by the day, but are general reminiscences.

16. George W. Covell, Chairman, to Lorenzo Crounse, Jan. 2, 1893; Covell to Crounse, Jan. 12, 1893; Frank R. Knapp to Crounse, March 7, 1893; Platte Valley Council No. 45, A.P.A., to Crounse, March 8, 1893; C. B. Campbell to Crounse, March 10, 1893, Nebraska Governors, Executive MSS, Boxes 33 and 35, Nebraska State Historical Society; *American* (Omaha), May 26, 1893.

17. William B. Shaw, "Compulsory Education in the United States," *Educational Review*, IV, 129–41; United States Bureau of Education, *Compulsory School Attendance*, Bulletin 1914, No. 2 (Washington, D.C., 1914), p. 10.

18. Minnesota, Iowa, Michigan, and Illinois also went Democratic, so something more than the Wisconsin school law was operating; current opinion, however, held the Bennett Law responsible; see John Bascom, "The Bennett Law," *Educational Review*, I, 48–52, or J. J. Mapel, "The Repeal of the Compulsory Education Laws in Wisconsin and Illinois," *Educational Review*, I, 52–57; Mapel was from the State Normal School in Milwaukee. Nils P. Haugen, the surviving Republican congressman, wrote his views in his memoirs, "Pioneer and Political Reminiscences," *Wisconsin Magazine of History*, XI, XII, XIII; Robert M. LaFollette, also a defeated congressman, wrote his opinion in his *Autobiography* (6th ed.; Madison, Wis.: The Robert M. LaFollette Co., 1913), p. 134.

19. Theodore Roemer, *The Catholic Church in the United States* (St. Louis, Mo.: B. Herder Book Co., 1950), p. 300.

20. Louise Phelps Kellogg, "The Bennett Law in Wisconsin," *Wisconsin Magazine of History*, II, 3–25; and, by a participant, William F. Whyte, "The Bennett Law Campaign," *Wisconsin Magazine of History*, X, 363–90.

21. See Vilas' article, "The Bennett Law in Wisconsin," *Forum*, XII, 196–207.

22. Mr. Wall's dilemma is stated in his letter to Senator Vilas,

Aug. 25, 1891, William F. Vilas Papers, Wisconsin Historical Society, Madison, in which he identifies the German language newspaper *Germania* as representative of the liberal position, with *Der Seebote* representing the Catholic "narrow policy."

23. E. C. Wall to Vilas, March 18, 29, 1892, and telegram April 6, 1892, Vilas Papers; on the Irish in Wisconsin, see Sister M. Justille McDonald, *History of the Irish in Wisconsin in the Nineteenth Century* (Washington, D.C.: Catholic University Press, 1954).

24. Wall to Vilas, May 11, 13, 1892, Vilas Papers.

25. Editorial, *Educational Review,* IV, 95.

26. B. N. Robinson to J. C. Spooner, Oct. 23, 1892, John Coit Spooner Papers, Manuscript Division, Library of Congress. This letter is labeled by the recipient, "Anti-Catholic letter."

27. Harry Barnard, *Eagle Forgotten: The Life of John Peter Altgeld* (New York: Duell, Sloan & Pearce, Inc., 1938), p. 160.

28. Theodore Roosevelt to Henry Cabot Lodge, Sept. 25, Oct. 11, 1892, *The Letters of Theodore Roosevelt,* ed. Elting E. Morrison (Cambridge, Mass.: Harvard University Press, 1951), I, 290–93; William Henry Smith to William Walter Phelps, Oct. 7, 1892, Letterbooks, v. 32, William Henry Smith Collection, Ohio State Archeological and Historical Society, Columbus.

29. Patrick Francis Quigley, *Compulsory Education* (New York: Robert Drummond, 1894). For news reports, see *Plain Dealer* (Cleveland), May 29, 1892, and *Blade* (Toledo), Oct. 1, 1892.

30. *Catholic Columbian,* Nov. 12, 1892.

31. Sister Mary Eunice Murphy, The History of the American Protective Association in Ohio (Master's thesis, Catholic University, 1939), pp. 13–15; Ross Seymour Johnson, The A.P.A. in Ohio (Master's thesis, Ohio State University, 1948).

32. *Plain Dealer* (Cleveland), March 12, 28–29, April 5, 1892.

33. *Catholic Columbian,* April 9, 23, July 2, 30, Aug. 6, 1892; *Ohio State Journal* (Columbus), July 1, 1892; *Record* (Columbus), March 23, July 7, 1892. The *Record* was not originally an anti-Catholic weekly; for example, see its editorial on June 12, 1891; however, on May 18, 1893, it boasted of its certification as a "true blue" A.P.A. newspaper, although it had been publicizing the order before that date.

34. Telegram, A. Fawcett, Chairman, and B. B. Holland, Secretary, to C. K. Davis, Sept. 22, 1892, Cushman Kellogg Davis Papers, Minnesota Historical Society, St. Paul.

35. *Ohio State Journal,* Oct. 3, 1892; *Catholic Columbian,* Oct. 8, 1892. The collection of sermons by Gladden now on deposit at the Ohio State Archeological and Historical Society does not include this sermon.

36. *Record* (Columbus), Oct. 13, 1892.

37. *Ibid.,* Nov. 10, 1892; *Ohio State Journal,* Nov. 9, 1892.

38. Dated Nov. 7, 1892.

39. Helen Clapesattle, *The Doctors Mayo* (New York: Garden City Publishing Company, 1943), pp. 253–54, 264–65. On the Faribault plan, this study follows William Watts Folwell, *A History of Minnesota* (St. Paul: Minnesota Historical Society, 1930), IV, 174–83.

40. Ireland's speech to the National Education Association at St. Paul in 1890, see *N.E.A. Journal,* 1890, pp. 179–85; see also James H. Moynihan, *The Life of Archbishop Ireland* (New York: Harper & Brothers, 1953).

41. H. F. Bowers to H. J. Desmond, March 1, 1899, in Humphrey J. Desmond, *The A.P.A. Movement* (Washington, D.C.: New Century Press, 1912) pp. 13–14.

42. Sister Mary Callista Hynes, The History of the American Protective Association in Minnesota (Master's thesis, Catholic University, 1939?), pp. 34–35. The "Austrians" were probably the South Slavic group then entering the iron ore district; *Tribune* (Minneapolis), Jan. 26, 1894.

43. *Patriotic American,* Aug. 6, 1892; *Loyal American,* July 29, 1892; see the following letters to Nelson in the Knute Nelson Papers, Minnesota Historical Society, St. Paul: Charles Kittelson, July 9, 1892; Allen J. Greer, July 16, 1892; N. Grevstad, July 18, 1892; and William Bickel, Aug. 18, 1892. The Grevstad letter estimated anti-Catholic strength in Minneapolis at two thousand. See also Winifred G. Helmes, *John A. Johnson: The People's Governor* (Minneapolis: University of Minnesota Press, 1949), p. 72, for the Democratic governor candidate who opposed the A.P.A.

44. A Spokane *Review* (later the *Spokesman-Review*) editorial, March 2, 1892, said "The republican party could hardly afford to go before the country with a candidate having upon his hands a quarrel with the Catholic church."

45. Donald Marquand Dozer, "Benjamin Harrison and the Presidential Campaign of 1892," *American Historical Review,* LIV, 49–77. See also the statement, "The Minneapolis Convention of June 7th to 10th, 1892," in the Louis T. Michener Papers, Manuscript Division, Library of Congress. There is a report in the *Catholic Record* (Indianapolis), Nov. 30, 1893, that W. J. H. Traynor had sent a telegram to the Republican convention opposing Blaine; Traynor was not president of the order in June of 1892, convention time. The Thomas Carter Papers in the Manuscript Division, Library of Congress, do not contain material on his conduct of the office of chairman. There are nine letters in the Don M. Dickinson Papers,

Burton Historical Collections, Detroit Public Library, written by someone who signed himself "C.D.," as chief deputy of some "secret
religio-political order." The writer claimed to have operated through
John C. New against the "Quay, McKinley, Blaine Papal programme"
at the Republican convention, and was now offering his services
through Dickinson in aid of Cleveland at the Democratic convention.
Dickinson's response is not indicated. If authentic, these letters illustrate the cross-purposes at which anti-Catholics sometimes worked,
and also suggest that some anti-Catholics were willing to put their
"influence" on the auction block.

46. Thomas J. Morgan, *Ethics of Americanism* (Boston: American
Citizen Company, 1894). In this pamphlet, Morgan reports that
former President Hayes at Lake Mohonk in Oct. of 1893 predicted
that an "unprecedented tide" of Americanism would sweep the country if Harrison were defeated. Since Hayes died on Jan. 17, 1893,
the date given by Morgan was wrong.

47. Loring Benson Priest, *Uncle Sam's Stepchildren* (New Brunswick, N.J.: Rutgers University Press, 1942), chap. iii. Priest says that
an "anti-Catholic bias" was present in the administration of Indian
policy, no matter who was president. See also Martha L. Edwards,
"A Problem of Church and State in the 1870's," *Mississippi Valley
Historical Review,* XI, 37–53.

48. Lake Mohonk Conference of the Friends of the Indian, *Proceedings,* 1894, pp. 126–30; see also Lyman Abbott, *Reminiscences*
(Boston: Houghton Mifflin Company, 1914), pp. 42–49.

49. See Kurt Leidecker, *Yankee Teacher: The Life of William
Torrey Harris* (New York: Philosophical Library, 1945), pp. 458–
61, for information on the appointment.

50. *N.E.A. Journal,* 1887, pp. 192–96; for 1888, pp. 156–58,
188. To see how Morgan's ideas were accepted by other professional
educators, see the files of the *N.E.A. Journal* and the *Educational
Review.* To see that his policies on Indian education were widely
approved, see the following: Frank Blackmar, "Indian Education,"
Annals of the American Academy of Political and Social Science, II,
813–37; the annual reports for 1887 through 1900 of the Board of
Indian Commissioners, an advisory group; the Lake Mohonk Conference of the Friends of the Indian, *Proceedings,* for 1890–1900;
the Indian Rights Association, *Annual Reports,* and miscellaneous
pamphlets; Women's National Indian Association, *Annual Reports,*
1893–1902; "The Government and Sectarian Schools," *Nation,* LVI,
22–23. Morgan's own reports are to be found in the annual reports
of the Commissioner of Indian Affairs to the Secretary of the Interior,
1889–92, and these may be compared with the reports of his predecessor and his successor to see the continuity of administrative policy.

After the turmoil died down, Morgan produced *The Negro in America: and The Ideal American Republic* (Philadelphia: American Baptist Publishing Society, 1898), which gives another aspect of his ideas.

51. Thomas J. Morgan, *Studies in Pedagogy* (Boston: Silver, Burdett & Co., 1888), p. 94, a textbook for prospective teachers.

52. Conrad Henry Moehlman is the author of the sketch in the *Dictionary of American Biography*.

53. Father Stephan Scrapbooks, I, 58–59, 61, in the possession of the Bureau of Catholic Indian Missions in Washington, D.C.; Harry J. Sievers, "The Catholic Indian School Issue and the Presidential Election of 1892" *Catholic Historical Review*, XXXVIII, 129–55. For Morgan's military career, see Dudley Taylor Cornish, *The Sable Arm: Negro Troops in the Union Army, 1861–1865* (New York: Longmans, Green & Co., Inc., 1956), pp. 226–43, 283–84, 289. There is no mention of the court-martial in Cornish. For the court-martial, see the *Official Records of the War of the Rebellion*, XXXIX, Part I, 714–16. Morgan's subsequent promotion in March of 1865 suggests that he was not disqualified because of the court-martial. A letter from Elvero Persons, Morgan's adjutant at the time of the incident, to Senator Allison, Dec. 27, 1889, is to be found in the William Boyd Allison Papers, Iowa State Department of History and Archives, Des Moines. Persons said the court-martial was the result of personal animosity toward Morgan and deplored the use of the incident to prevent Morgan's confirmation as Indian Commissioner.

54. U.S. Office of Indian Affairs, *Report of the Commissioner of Indian Affairs*, 1894, compiled by Morgan's successor, shows that Catholic allotments *increased* during Morgan's tenure of office; Protestant mission schools were almost nonexistent by that time. Catholic contracts in 1889 were $247,957, and in 1892 were $394,756, an all-time high.

55. Father Stephan Scrapbooks, I, 77–79.

56. John Tracy Ellis, in *The Life of James Cardinal Gibbons* (Milwaukee, Wis.: Bruce Publishing Co., 1952), II, 390–92, says that the Catholic press was "intemperate" in attacking Morgan and that Gibbons regretted it. See also Charles S. Lusk, "A Retrospect of Fifty Years," *Indian Sentinel*, IV, 3–6, by the man who was the secretary for the Catholic Indian Bureau at the time; Lusk thinks that Stephan's zeal might better have been tempered with discretion. On Lusk, see William Hughes, "Charles Lusk's Life and Death," *Indian Sentinel*, VIII, 172–73.

57. Morgan's letter to Gibbons, July 16, 1891, is published as an appendix to the sixtieth *Annual Report* of the Commissioner of Indian Affairs.

58. *Patriotic American,* Aug. 1, 1891; see the *Review* (Spokane), July 31, 1891, for a wire service story on the misappropriation charge.

59. For example, see *Catholic Columbian,* Oct. 15, 29, Nov. 5, 1892; *Catholic Record,* Nov. 3, 1892. Father Sievers, in "The Catholic Indian School Issue," gives more examples of Catholic press opinion and places the responsibility for the attacks on Michael Walsh, editor of the *Catholic Herald* and of the *Sunday Democrat,* both of New York City. See the 1894 article by L. W. Reilly, "The Weak Points of the Catholic Press," *American Ecclesiastical Review,* X, 117–25, which says that Catholic newspapers generally supported Democratic party candidates and that their editors were usually unable to separate fact from fiction in political discussions.

60. *Independent,* Sept. 1, 22, 1892.

61. Arthur Wallace Dunn, *From Harrison to Harding* (New York: G. P. Putnam's Sons, 1922), I, 82–85; George Harmon Knoles, *The Presidential Campaign and Election of 1892* (Stanford, Calif.: Stanford University Press, 1942), pp. 217–18.

62. Knoles, *Presidential Campaign,* pp. 231–32; Dunn, *From Harrison to Harding,* I, 97–98; *Catholic Columbian,* Nov. 12, 1892; *Catholic Record,* Nov. 17, 1892; "A Triumph of Right," *Ave Maria,* XXXV, 578; Arthur R. Kimball, "The Religious Issue in Politics," *North American Review,* CLV, 633–63.

63. Knoles, *Presidential Campaign,* p. 229; Walter Ellsworth Nydegger, "The Election of 1892 in Iowa," *Iowa Journal of History and Politics,* XXV, 359–449.

64. There was a persistent story that James S. Clarkson, Republican national committeeman from Iowa and former national chairman, had given money to the A.P.A. for its support in the election of 1892. The Clarkson family newspaper, the Des Moines *Iowa State Register,* did *not* write favorably of the A.P.A., and there is nothing in the James S. Clarkson Papers, Manuscript Division, Library of Congress, to support the story. On the Clarksons, see George Mills, "The Fighting Clarksons," *Palimpsest,* XXX, 283–89.

65. Morgan became editor of the *Baptist Home Missionary Monthly,* and its April, 1893, issue published his picture in welcome.

66. To illustrate this point, one may cite the Enabling Act providing for the admission of the "Omnibus States" in 1889, which required that the state constitutions of Utah, Montana, South and North Dakota, and Washington include prohibitions on expenditure of public money for any sectarian purpose.

67. One faces here the same necessity as is confronted for the earlier anti-Catholic and nativistic movements. To call all pre-Civil

War movements "Know-Nothing" is to do the same violence to historical fact as to label all anti-Catholic, nativist (and secularist) movements of the 1880's and 1890's as the "A.P.A. movement."

68. Stauffer, Anti-Catholicism in American Politics, p. 224.

69. Oliver E. Murray, *The Black Pope* (2nd ed.; Chicago: The Patriot Company, 1892), p. 63; *Patriot* (Chicago), March, 1891, pp. 20–21, 38–40. On Carter Harrison, see Claudius O. Johnson, *Carter Henry Harrison I: Political Leader* (Chicago: University of Chicago Press, 1928).

70. *Patriot* (Chicago), March, 1891 pp. 21, 43.

71. *Ibid.,* p. 19; Allen W. Burns, The A.P.A. and the Anti-Catholic Crusade: 1885–1898 (Master's thesis, Columbia University, 1947), p. 21, lists the organizations participating in 1891. Of the officers chosen at this meeting, W. J. H. Traynor, treasurer, would become president of the A.P.A., and Mrs. Blanche Reynolds, wife of the secretary, would become president of the W.A.P.A.

72. *Patriotic American,* Jan. 7, April 15, 1893.

73. Smith to the Rev. Addison P. Foster, Feb. 19, 1892, Letterbook 1890–92, William Henry Smith Collection, Ohio State Archeological and Historical Society, Columbus.

74. *Patriotic American,* Oct. 22, 1890; the forgery referred to Pope Leo XIII as "of blessed memory" although he lived until 1903.

75. *Catholic Columbian,* Nov. 12, 1892, reproduced the document and called it a forgery; *Patriotic American,* Jan. 7, 1893, continued to use it.

76. *Patriotic American,* Aug. 1, 1891.

77. *Catholic Record,* April 6, 1893, for Slattery; *Patriotic American,* Jan. 7, 1893, for Rudolph; Paul Walton Black, "Lynchings in Iowa," *Iowa Journal of History and Politics,* X, 151–254.

78. This man's reminiscences, which are a jumble of excerpts from his various publishing ventures over a period of forty years, are the only example of personal memoirs found for an A.P.A. member; see William Lloyd Clark, *The Story of My Struggle with the Scarlet Beast* (Milan, Ill.: Rail Splitter Press, 1932), pp. 30–31.

79. *Catholic Record,* March 9, 1893, said that the A.P.A. supported Harrison; Johnson, in *Carter Henry Harrison,* pp. 156, 194, 201–3, 222, shows Irish-Catholic support for him, and shows furthermore that the Rev. Isaac J. Lansing, whose book *Romanism and the Republic* has been previously cited, campaigned against Harrison.

80. *Record* (Columbus), March 23, April 6, 1893.

81. *Patriotic American,* April 15, 1893.

82. *Catholic Record,* April 27, June 1, 1893.

83. *Ibid.,* March 8, 1893; *Record* (Columbus), Feb. 9, 16, 23, 1893. How Gladden justified his own action in discharging a man for

A.P.A. membership at a time when he was critical of the A.P.A. for opposing employment of Catholics is not known. Gladden, in *Recollections* (Boston: Houghton Mifflin Company, 1909), pp. 414–15, states that anti-Catholics in the legislature prevented his appointment as university president, and gives former President Hayes in the spring of 1893 as the source; Hayes died in January of 1893, so the date is obviously wrong. Williams, *Diary and Letters of Hayes,* V, 81, 94, shows Gladden under consideration for the appointment in May and July of 1892.

84. *Michigan Catholic,* March 30, 1893.

85. The charge appears in the *Catholic Citizen,* July 1, 1893, with Bishop Spalding of Peoria as the source. Spalding repeated the charge in his article, "Catholicism and Apaism," *North American Review,* CLIX, 278–87.

86. Stauffer, Anti-Catholicism in American Politics, pp. 185–91; the attorney was Harry C. Gano.

87. *American* (Omaha), see any issue.

88. *Patriotic American,* Aug. 1, 1891.

89. W. J. H. Traynor, "The Menace of Romanism," *North American Review,* CLXI, 129–40.

90. Ray Ginger, *The Bending Cross* (New Brunswick, N.J.: Rutgers University Press, 1949), pp. 68–69.

91. *Proscription vs. Americanism,* Addresses of the Hon. Dan P. Foote, Hon. Timothy E. Tarsney, and Jas. H. Davitt (n.p., n.d.). Tarsney was the Democratic congressman defeated by Linton in 1892.

92. *Catholic Citizen,* Dec. 9, 1892, June 3, 1893.

93. "The Catholic Controversy," *Nation,* LVI, 44–45; "The Schism in the Church of Rome," *Illustrated American,* Feb. 4, 1893. Peter E. Hogan, *The Catholic University of America, 1896–1903* (Washington, D.C.: Catholic University Press, 1949), p. viii, defines "conservative" and "liberal" as the terms applied to the conservative Archbishop Corrigan and Bishop McQuaid, on the one side, and to the liberal Archbishop Ireland and Bishop John Keane, rector of Catholic University, on the other. See also Roemer, *Catholic Church in the United States,* chap. xviii, for another discussion.

94. *Independent,* Dec. 29, 1892, Jan. 5, 1893; *Patriotic American,* Jan. 7, 1893.

95. See the two articles by John J. Meng, "Cahenslyism: The First Stage, 1883–1891," *Catholic Historical Review,* XXXI, 389–413, and "Cahenslyism: The Second Chapter, 1891–1910," *Catholic Historical Review,* XXXII, 302–40. John Ireland to B. S. Cowan, Sept. 1, 1891, John Ireland to William H. Smith, Sept. 25, 1891, July 17, 1892, and William H. Smith to Ireland, July 23, 1892, in the William Henry Smith Collection.

96. C. K.. Davis Papers, beginning in August of 1892 and continuing through October; identifiable as A.P.A. in origin are A. Fawcett, Sept. 22, 1892, G. M. Higbee, Oct. 2, 1892, W. J. Willis, Oct. 16, 1892; see "E.S.G." [E. S. Goodrich] to Davis, Sept. 23, 1893. See also Moynihan, *Life of Ireland,* p. 70, where Ireland is given credit for inspiring Davis' action.

97. *Educational Review* carried a series of articles in 1892 on the Catholic controversy in education. The whole general subject of the preceding paragraphs is discussed under the general heading of "Americanism"; see the article by James M. Gillis, "Americanism: Fifty Years After," *Catholic World,* CLXIX, 246–53, for a summary.

98. Archbishop Francis Satolli, *Loyalty to Church and State* (Baltimore, Md.: John Murphy, 1895), pp. 11–12; Ellis, in *Life of Cardinal Gibbons,* I, 625, says that Satolli's appointment played directly into the hands of the A.P.A.

99. *Forum,* XV, for the following: John H. Vincent, "The Pope in Washington," 261–67; Leonard Woolsey Brown, "An American Viceroy from the Vatican," 268–74; Dr. James F. Loughlin, "Rome a True Ally of the Republic," 272–82; *Nation,* LVI, Jan. 12, Feb. 9, 1893; Bowers to Desmond, March 1, 1899, in Desmond, *A.P.A. Movement,* p. 15.

100. Morgan M. Sheedy, "The School Question in the Pennsylvania Legislature," *Catholic World,* LIII, 485–96; A. B. Poland, "The New Jersey Parochial Free School Bill," *Educational Review,* V, 491–94; Rt. Rev. Monsignor Bernard O'Reilly, "How to Solve the School Question," *North American Review,* CLV, 569–74; James M. King, "The American Common Schools," *North American Review,* CLVI, 254–56; *Independent,* Jan. 14, 1892; *N.E.A. Journal,* 1892, pp. 23, 41; and the three articles by John L. Spalding, George M. Grant, and Lewis G. Janes, on "Religious Instruction in State Schools," *Educational Review,* Vols. II–IV (1891–92).

101. Henry K. Carroll, "What the Census of the Churches Shows," *Forum,* XIII, 529–38; Carroll was also religious editor of the *Independent.* A Catholic study, Gerald Shaughnessy, *Has the Immigrant Kept the Faith?* (New York: The Macmillan Company, 1925), reports that there has never been an accurate census of the Catholic population of the United States; his estimate for 1890 was 8,909,000; see pp. 33, 166. The *Catholic Directory* figure in its 1890 edition is on p. 200.

102. Sydney G. Fisher, "Alien Degradation of American Character," *Forum,* XIV, 608–15.

103. *American* (Omaha), May 5, 1893; W. J. H. Traynor, "Policy and Power of the A.P.A.," *North American Review,* CLXII, 658–66.

104. An extensive file of the *Wisconsin Patriot* was used in this

study, and the scant files of the *American Eagle* and the *True American* were also used. Apparently there are no files in existence for the others.

105. *American* (Omaha), April 6, 1894, March 21, 1895.

106. Basic biographical information is to be found in *Who's Who in America,* for 1899–1900 through 1903–5; *Wisconsin Patriot,* May 4, 1895; Albert C. Stevens (comp. and ed.), *The Cyclopedia of Fraternities* (New York: Hamilton Printing and Publishing Company, 1899), pp. 293–98.

107. No files, except for the *Patriotic American,* exist.

108. *Patriotic American,* Oct. 25, 1890.

109. Biographical information is in a letter to the author from Margaret Smith, Reference Librarian, University of Michigan Library, April 1, 1952, derived from university alumnus records. Beatty died in Pittsburgh in 1910. The Florida venture is described in *United American,* Aug. 17, 1895, and in *Wisconsin Patriot,* July 4, 1896. The townsite was named Linton, and it was seventeen miles south of West Palm Beach, Dade County, Florida; Congressman Linton aided Beatty in securing the land for development.

Chapter 4

1. See Appendix II.

2. *Record* (Columbus), Aug. 24, 1893; *Loyal American,* Nov. 18, 1893; *Patriotic American,* March 3, 1894; see *Catholic Columbian,* Aug. 26, 1893, for a denunciation of this "war on women."

3. *American* (Omaha), March 9, 1894; W. E. Chandler, "Shall Immigration Be Suspended?" *North American Review,* CLVI, 1–8; Chandler was chairman of the Senate Committee on Immigration; see John Higham, "Origins of Immigration Restriction, 1882–1897: A Social Analysis," *Mississippi Valley Historical Review,* XXXIX, 77–88.

4. *Patriotic American,* Jan. 6, 1894; *American* (Omaha), Aug. 17, 1894.

5. Rev. J. A. Walter, "The Surratt Case: A True Statement of the Facts Concerning This Notable Cause," read before the U.S. Catholic Historical Society, May 25, 1891, and reprinted as a pamphlet; T. M. Harris, *The Assassination of Lincoln: A History of the Great Conspiracy* (Boston: American Citizen Company, 1892); Burton Huntington, *The Coming American Civil War* (Minneapolis, Minn.: E. J. Doyle?, 1893); Edwin A. Sherman, *Lincoln's Death Warrant: Or, The Peril of Our Country* (Milwaukee: The Wisconsin

Patriot, 1889). See the article by John Bigelow, "The Southern Confederacy and the Pope," *North American Review,* CLVII, 462–75, which appears to be an attempt to set the record straight.

6. J. A. Fleming to Gov. Crounse, Aug. 7, 1893, Nebraska Governors, Executive MSS, Box 36; Gov. Crounse's intended reply is penciled on the incoming letter; Edward Savage to Davis, May 28, 1893, Cushman Kellogg Davis Papers, Minnesota Historical Society, St. Paul; Washington Gladden, *Recollections* (Boston: Houghton Mifflin Company, 1909), pp. 359–65; *Independent,* Sept. 28, 1893.

7. *Ohio State Journal,* Oct. 9, 1893; *Catholic Record,* Oct. 19, 1893; *Nation,* Nov. 9, 1893; *Catholic Columbian,* Dec. 9, 1893; *Independent,* Nov. 2, 1893.

8. *Blade* (Toledo), Feb. 22, 24, 28, 1894; *Public Opinion,* March 29, 1894; *Catholic Columbian,* March 3, 1894. The mayor may have been unfairly treated in this episode; the Guard was in the Armory from Sept. 5, 1893, until the Labor Day parade, and may not have been called out for special duty.

9. *Congressional Record,* 53rd Cong., 1st Sess. (Oct. 27 and 30, 1893), 2893–94, 2960–61.

10. *Record* (Columbus), Jan. 11, 1894, describes Morgan's visit to Jacksonville, Ill.; *Baptist Home Missionary Monthly,* Oct., 1893, Dec., 1893, and June, 1894; see his *Ethics of Americanism,* unpaged pamphlet, for Morgan's venture with the American Citizens Library.

11. Robert H. Lord *et al., History of the Archdiocese of Boston in Its Various Stages of Development, 1604 to 1943* (New York: Sheed & Ward, 1944), III, 139–43; *New York Times,* Oct. 1, 1894.

12. *Pilot* (Boston), Jan. 20, 1894.

13. See *Educational Review,* VI, 516–17, and VII, 104, for discussions of the incidents. Rice's book was reviewed in the December, 1893, issue, pp. 498–503. An article by Marble appears in the September, 1894, issue (VII, 154–68), but it refers only incidentally to the case above.

14. See Frederick Zwierlein, "The Catholic Contribution to Liberty in the United States," in United States Catholic Historical Society, *Historical Records and Studies,* XV, 112–36; see also the *New York Times,* Oct. 22, 1894, where an A. N. Martin of the American Patriotic League objected to his organization's identification as "A.P.A."

15. *New York Times,* Oct. 22, 1894; there is no file of the *Republic* in existence.

16. Carl Zollman, *American Civil Church Law* (New York: Columbia University Press, 1917), pp. 35–36; *Nation,* LVII, 441.

17. *United American,* Aug. 11, 27, 1894.

18. *Ibid.,* Feb. 27, March 13, 1895.

19. *American* (Omaha), June 8, 1894.

20. *Rocky Mountain News,* Oct. 1, 3, 4, 6, Nov. 8, 9, 26, 1893, Jan. 25, 1894; *Republican* (Denver), Nov. 7, 1893. Reed prepared a history of Denver, which is on file at the Denver Public Library; based on newspaper stories, it serves as an index to Denver newspapers.

21. C. B. Glasscock, *War of the Copper Kings* (New York: Grosset & Dunlop, Inc., 1935), pp. 113–14.

22. Nearly a year later an advertisement appeared in the *Examiner* (Butte), on May 18, 1895, inviting members of the A.P.A. to make the Columbia Saloon their Butte headquarters.

23. *Inter Mountain* (Butte), July 5, 1894; *Bystander* (Butte), July 7, 1894.

24. *Examiner* (Butte), Nov. 2, 1895. One of the owners of the Sazerac Saloon was named Anderson, but whether this was the same man who was the local A.P.A. secretary is not known.

25. See *Harper's Weekly,* Jan. 20, 1894, for discussion of the delegate's visit; see also Thomas Bouquillon, "The Apostolic Delegation," *American Catholic Quarterly Review,* XX, 112–30.

26. *Review* (Spokane), July 1, 4, 1893; *Ledger* (Tacoma), July 2, 3, 5, 1893. Satolli's interpreter was Dr. Thomas O'Gorman, historian.

27. *Oregonian,* March 2, 1894, Feb. 5, March 16, 18, 1895; *Patriotic American,* March 3, 1894; *Ledger* (Tacoma), Dec. 4, 1894, March 14, 1895. Daly said that he had been converted to Methodism at Boston in 1888; he also claimed to have been ordained a priest by "Bishop Wheeler" of West Virginia, according to the news report; a Bishop Whelan was in charge of the Wheeling Diocese from 1850 to 1874.

28. *Oregonian,* Feb. 26, 27, 1894.

29. Priscilla Knuth, Nativism in California, 1886–1897 (Master's thesis, University of California, 1947), pp. 78, 117–18. Two articles on the career of the A.P.A. in San Francisco, both based on the Yorke Scrapbooks at the University of San Francisco, appeared almost simultaneously in 1951: Joseph F. Brusher, "Peter C. Yorke and the A.P.A. in San Francisco," *Catholic Historical Review,* XXXVII, 129–50; and David Joseph Herlihy, "Battle Against Bigotry: Father Peter C. Yorke and the American Protective Association in San Francisco, 1893–1897," *Records of the American Catholic Historical Society of Philadelphia,* LXII, 95–120. On Yorke, see Bernard Cornelius Cronin, *Father Yorke and the Labor Movement in San Francisco, 1900–1910* (Washington, D.C.: Catholic University Press, 1943), pp. 25–26.

30. *New York Times,* Oct. 9, 1894.

31. Reported in *Ledger* (Tacoma), Nov. 25, 1894.

32. *New York Times,* Oct. 1, 1894, reports Gosper as "ex-governor" of Arizona Territory; Earl S. Pomeroy, in *The Territories and the United States, 1861–1890* (Philadelphia: University of Pennsylvania Press, 1947), p. 132, shows him as territorial secretary. *Patriotic American,* Aug. 25, 1894; biographical information on Sheldon is to be found in the *Biographical Directory of the American Congress,* and the Garfield friendship may be followed in Theodore Clarke Smith, *The Life and Letters of James Abram Garfield* (New Haven: Yale University Press, 1925), pp. 173, 179, 204, 447, 616, 947, 1153, 1171.

33. Sister Mary Agnes Balfe, The Catholic High School in the State of Washington (Master's thesis, Gonzaga University, 1935); *Review* (Spokane), July 6, 1893; *Ledger* (Tacoma), Sept. 8, 1893.

34. *Ledger* (Tacoma), Jan. 27, 28, Feb. 17, 1894.

35. Neither Anthony Bimba, *The Molly Maguires* (New York: International Publishers, 1932), nor J. Walter Coleman, *The Molly Maguire Riots* (Richmond, Va.: Garrett & Massie, Inc., 1936), mentions Van Fossen; letter to the editor, *Ledger* (Tacoma), Jan. 31, 1894; Van Fossen's obituary gives biographical information, see *Ledger,* Oct. 7, 1896.

36. *Ledger* (Tacoma), Aug. 20, 1894; W. P. Bonney, *History of Pierce County, Washington* (Chicago: Pioneer Historical Publishing Company, 1927), III, 334; *Legislative Souvenir Manual for 1895–1896* (Seattle, Wash.: Steel and Searl, 1895), p. 116.

37. Editorials in *Ledger* (Tacoma), March 20, Sept. 6, 24, Oct. 14, 21, 1894; *Post-Intelligencer* (Seattle), April 1, 28, 1895, identified hereafter as *P.-I.; Argus* (Seattle), Oct. 1, 1894, June 23, 1895; *Patriotic American,* March 3, 1894.

38. *Ledger* (Tacoma), March 12, 19, 26, Oct. 8, 18, 19, 22, 1894.

39. *Review* (Spokane), March 23–25, May 19, 1894; *Ledger* (Tacoma), March 28, 29, 1894; see *Argus* (Seattle), March 31, 1894, for a photograph of Rudolph.

40. *Ledger* (Tacoma), March 2, 21, 28, 29, Nov. 18, 22, Dec. 16, 17, 1894; *Review* (Spokane), April 4, 1894.

41. *Argus* (Seattle), March 10, 1894; *Ledger* (Tacoma), March 4, 6, 7, 1894.

42. Washington, King County, County Commissioners' Record, II, 323, reveals the original agreement between the county commissioners and the Catholic hospital. In VIII, 209, some bids for the new county hospital are recorded. Erected in 1892, the new county hospital was four miles from downtown Seattle. See the *P.-I.* (Seattle), Jan. 3, 1897, for an account of the county hospital. Seattle's Providence Hospital (Catholic) was quite generally referred to as the

"poor house" because of its care of indigent before the county hospital was built; see Robert Snodgrass, "A History of St. James Cathedral Parish," in *Silver Jubilee, St. James Cathedral Parish* (Seattle: 1929?), p. 90. For jubilation at the opening of the "protestant refuge," Seattle General Hospital, see *Argus* (Seattle), March 10, 1894, and July 6, 1896.

43. *Ledger* (Tacoma), Oct. 23, Nov. 4, 1894; *P.-I.* (Seattle), Nov. 4, 1894; *Spokesman-Review,* Oct. 13, 18, 30, 31, Nov. 1, 2, 4, Dec. 21, 1894, Jan. 12, 1895.

44. *United American,* Aug. 27, Sept. 17, 1894; *Loyal American and the North,* Aug. 25, 1894; *Spokesman-Review,* March 8, 1894, Feb. 27, 1895.

45. *American Eagle,* Aug. 19, 1893.

46. Charter application, Edwin Locke and others, Aug. 13, 1893; John T. Little, Attorney General, to R. S. Osborne, Secretary of State, Sept. 20, 1893; R. S. Osborne to F. H. Barker, Sept. 20, 1893, Executive MSS, Kansas State Historical Society. F. H. Barker had been city clerk and member of the Board of Education in Atchison, and he was a member of the Disciples of Christ Church; see *Western Patriot,* Sept. 1896, p. 95.

47. *Loyal American and the North,* June 30, 1894; *Catholic Citizen,* Sept. 16, 1893; *Catholic Columbian,* Sept. 23, 1893.

48. *American Eagle,* Aug. 19, 1893; *American* (Omaha), May 4, 1894; news report in *Review* (Spokane), Jan. 18, 1894.

49. *American* (Omaha), April 20, 1894.

50. *Loyal American and the North,* March 17, 1894.

51. *Record* (Columbus), March 22, 1894.

52. *Catholic Review,* Feb. 10, 1895; *American* (Omaha), May 4, 1894.

53. *Loyal American,* July 29, Dec. 2, 30, 1893.

54. *Ibid.,* July 29, 1893, Jan. 20, 1894; *Tribune* (Minneapolis), Jan. 21, 28, 1894.

55. *Globe* (St. Paul), Nov. 6, 1893; *Loyal American,* Dec. 30, 1893.

56. *Globe* (St. Paul), Nov. 6, 1893. Publication of members' names permits investigation of the persons who joined A.P.A. councils. The St. Paul president was a book agent and real estate man; the secretary was a printer; and the chaplain was a dentist; another official was chief clerk in one of the railroad yards, and the sergeant at arms was a former fire chief. Of twelve others identified in the St. Paul *Directory* for 1895, three owned their own businesses: one owned a metal-working plant, another was a clothing manufacturer, and the third was a manufacturing jeweler. A tailor, a bookstore operator, and a blacksmith for a railroad company complete the list

of those to be identified from the *Directory*. Nearly a year later, *Town Talk,* a Minneapolis weekly, on Sept. 1, 1894, also published an exposure, listing several members of the Minneapolis Fire Department; if surnames are proof, the charge that Scandinavians formed the nucleus of the A.P.A. in the Twin Cities does not hold up.

57. *Tribune* (Minneapolis), Jan. 26, 1894; *Loyal American and the North,* Jan. 27, 1894.

58. *Loyal American and the North,* April 28, July 21, 1894. *Tribune* (Minneapolis), Feb. 22, 23, 1894, reports the state convention of the Patriotic Order of the Sons of America, which denied any connection with the A.P.A.

59. *Loyal American and the North,* Feb. 17, April 21, 1894.

60. *Patriotic American,* Aug. 25, 1895.

61. Fritiof Ander, "The Swedish-American Press and the A.P.A.," *Church History,* VI, 165–79.

62. *American* (Omaha), April 14, 1893, quoting a *Catholic Citizen* statement. The *Catholic Citizen,* Oct. 28, 1893, gave a figure for membership in Milwaukee that was much lower than A.P.A. claims. Only infrequently was a Catholic weekly willing to make its own investigation to provide a corrective for the expansive A.P.A. claims.

63. *Catholic Citizen,* Dec. 16, 1893, Jan. 6, Sept. 22, 1894.

64. *Patriotic American,* March 3, 1894. Other officers chosen were Hugh Rogers of Tomahawk, secretary of state, the Rev. J. H. McManus of Washburn, chaplain, William H. Coles of Whitewater, treasurer, L. L. Thayer of Ontario, sergeant at arms, R. L. Rudolph of Milwaukee, guard, and E. H. Whittier of Kaukana, sentinel.

65. *Wisconsin Patriot,* Feb. 23, March 23, May 4, 1895.

66. The Herbert B. Tanner Papers at the State Historical Society in Madison do not contain information on this point; Tanner was mayor of Kaukana, 1888–96.

67. *Chronicle* (LaCrosse), Oct. 28, 30, 1894; this paper was edited by Ellis B. Usher, prominent Democrat, whose papers are in the State Historical Society at Madison. They do not reveal specific information on A.P.A. activities but do supplement the Vilas collection on Democratic party affairs.

68. *Catholic Citizen,* Jan. 20, 1894.

69. *Lucifer-Arminia* (Milwaukee), March 1894, p. 83.

70. L. W. Nieman to Vilas, March 6, 1894, William F. Vilas Papers, Wisconsin Historical Society, Madison. See also Bayrd Still, *Milwaukee: The History of a City* (Madison: State Historical Society of Wisconsin, 1948), pp. 301–2, for mayoral election of 1894.

71. John H. Knight to Vilas, Vilas Papers, April 4, 1894; see *Wisconsin Patriot,* April 6, 1896, for McClintock.

72. *Wisconsin Patriot,* Nov. 24, 1894.

73. *Record* (Columbus), Feb. 15, 1894; *American* (Omaha), May 4, Sept. 14, 1894; *Loyal American and the North,* June 30, 1894.

74. *Catholic Citizen,* Jan. 6, 1894; *Nation,* Jan. 4, 1894; *Loyal American and the North,* May 12, 1894.

75. *Loyal American and the North,* Feb. 24, April 28, 1894; *Catholic Record,* Jan. 31, 1895.

76. *Augustinian* (Kalamazoo), Feb. 24, 1894; *Patriotic American,* March 3, Aug. 25, 1894.

77. *Record* (Columbus), Jan. 18, 1894; I have not been able to identify the David K. Watson, who was secretary of the A.P.A., with David Kemper Watson, lawyer, Ohio Attorney General from 1887–89, and Republican congressman elected in 1895 for one term.

78. Letter, J. B. Foraker to John Sherman, Nov. 9, 1889, in *Correspondence of J. B. Foraker* (n.p., n.d.), I, 80.

79. Eugene H. Roseboom and Francis P. Weisenburger, *A History of Ohio* (New York: Prentice-Hall, Inc., 1934), p. 364, asserts that A. P. A. support contributed to McKinley's victory in 1893.

80. Told by Kohlsaat, the person involved, in H. H. Kohlsaat, *From McKinley to Harding* (New York: Charles Scribner's Sons, 1923), pp. 18–20.

81. *Catholic Citizen,* Sept. 30, 1893; *Record* (Columbus), Oct. 19, 26, Nov. 2, 1893.

82. *Irish World,* Nov. 4, 1893, clipping in Father Stephan's Scrapbook, Vol. II; *Loyal American,* Nov. 4, 1893.

83. *Record* (Columbus), Nov. 9, 1893; this same reasoning was applied to the results of the spring municipal elections in the *United American,* April 3, 1895.

84. *Nation,* Nov. 23, 1893, p. 389, for an immediate comment; Sept. 27, 1894, p. 226, for a delayed reaction.

85. Ohio General Assembly, *Journal of the House of Representatives of the State of Ohio for 1894,* pp. 45, 95, 103, 207, 214–15, 559, 678, 1006; *Journal of the Senate of the State of Ohio for 1894,* pp. 871, 878.

86. *Record* (Columbus), March 15, 22, 1894.

87. *Iowa State Register,* May 4, 1894.

88. *Loyal American and the North,* May 12, 1894; *American* (Omaha), May 11, 1894; *Catholic Citizen,* May 12, 1894.

89. See complete list of officers in Appendix I.

90. *Loyal American and the North,* June 16, 1894; *American* (Omaha), July 7, 1893; Richard Wheatley, "The American Protective Association," *Harper's Weekly,* Oct. 27, 1894, which published photographs of the officers.

91. *Patriotic American,* March 3, Aug. 18, 1894.

92. *Catholic Citizen,* Oct. 28, 1893.

93. Allen W. Burns, The A.P.A. and the Anti-Catholic Crusade: 1885–1898 (Master's thesis, Columbia University, 1947), p. 50.

94. *United American,* Sept. 17, 1894.

95. Chaplain W. H. Gottwald in the *A.P.A. Magazine,* Sept. 1896, p. 1377; see also Albert C. Stevens (comp. and ed.), *The Cyclopedia of Fraternities* (New York: Hamilton Printing and Publishing Company, 1899), p. 294, for same view.

96. Thomas J. Jenkins, "The A.P.A. Conspirators," *Catholic World,* LVII, 685–92.

97. Rev. Alfred Young, "The Coming Contest—with a Retrospect," and "The Coming Contest—Have Catholics a Political Enemy?" *Catholic World,* LVIII, 457–72 and 694–708.

98. "Hostility to Roman Catholics," *North American Review,* CLVIII, 563–82.

99. An American, *A.P.A.: An Inquiry into the Objects and Purposes of the So-Called "American Protective Association"* (n.p., n.d.).

100. *Independent,* XLVI, 301; at this time, A.P.A. national headquarters were in Chicago.

101. Letter to the editor from Maurice Francis Egan, *North American Review,* CLVIII, 745–47.

102. *Catholic Citizen,* Oct. 7, 1893.

103. *Ibid.,* Dec. 9, 1893.

104. *Ibid.,* Jan. 6, 13, 20, 1894. Senator Vilas was criticized for his statement; see the following letters in the Vilas Papers: R. V. Hooper, Jan. 11, "Anonymous," Jan. 11, J. Sprague Wilkins, Feb. 14, J. H. Berkstrasser, Feb. 28, 1894.

105. E. M. Winston, "The Threatening Conflict with Romanism," *Forum,* XVII, 425–33.

106. *New York Times,* Oct. 8, 1894.

107. John Ireland, *The Church and Modern Society: Lectures and Addresses* (St. Paul: Pioneer Press Manufacturing Company, 1905), I, 176, for address delivered to the New York Commandery of the Loyal Legion, April 4, 1894.

108. *American* (Omaha), Sept. 1, 1893; *Loyal American,* Nov. 4, 1893.

109. *Tribune* (Minneapolis), April 12, 1894; *Loyal American and the North,* April 7, 1894. The Ignatius Donnelly Papers in the Minnesota Historical Society collections do not contain any more pertinent materials than can be found in the newspaper reports.

110. *United American,* Sept. 17, 1894.

111. *New York Times,* Oct. 15, Nov. 5, 1894.

112. Theodore Roosevelt, "What Americanism Means," *Forum,* XVII, 196–206; Roosevelt's private opinions were much clearer, see *The Letters of Theodore Roosevelt,* ed. Elting E. Morrison (Cambridge, Mass.: Harvard University Press, 1951), using index entry "A.P.A." for examples. The *Catholic Columbian* applauded a Roosevelt speech in which ideas similar to those in the *Forum* article were expressed, Nov. 25, 1893; see James M. King, *Facing the Twentieth Century* (New York: American Union League Society, 1899), p. 482, for the italicized phrase.

113. *Catholic Citizen,* Dec. 16, 1893; K. Gerald Marsden, "Patriotic Societies and American Labor: The American Protective Association in Wisconsin," *Wisconsin Magazine of History,* XLI, 287–94; for wire service reports, see *Spokesman-Review* for Sept. 17, Oct. 4, Dec. 16, 1894.

114. *Wisconsin Patriot,* Aug. 11, 18, 1894; *Loyal American and the North,* July 7, 21, 1894; *Patriotic American,* Sept. 1, 1894. See United States Strike Commission, *Report on the Chicago Strike of June–July, 1894* (Washington: Government Printing Office, 1895), pp. 44–45, for the testimony of George W. Howard, a Protestant, who said that corporations placed men in labor groups in order to foment religious divisions between Catholic and Protestant working men. Senator C. K. Davis refused to support a resolution in the Senate favoring the strikers; there are many letters in his papers from A.P.A. people congratulating him on his "patriotism."

115. *Independent,* XLVI, 69; *North American Review,* CLIX, 67–76; Rev. E. D. McCreary, "The Roman Catholic Church as a Factor in Politics," *American Journal of Politics,* IV, 119–31; this magazine had been previously called "un-American"; see "An Un-American Journal," *Ave Maria,* XXXVII, 20–21. See also Madison C. Peters, "The American Protective Association," *Converted Catholic,* XI, 153–55, for a friendly account of the A.P.A.

116. *Independent,* XLVI, 924–25; *Outlook,* L, 493; George Parsons Lathrop, "Catholic Loyalty: A Reply to the President of the A.P.A. and to Bishop Doane," *North American Review,* CLIX, 218–24.

117. Washington Gladden, "The Anti-Catholic Crusade," *Century,* XLVII, 789–95; later, Gladden sent a letter to the editor; see "Secret Societies in Politics," *Century,* XLVIII, 954–55. His article was commended in *Outlook,* L, 439.

118. Elbert Hubbard, "A New Disease," *Arena,* June, 1894, pp. 76–83.

119. Walter H. Page to Vilas, Feb. 24, March 24, 1894, Vilas Papers; Frederic R. Coudert, "The American Protective Association," *Forum,* XVII, 513–23.

120. Charles Robinson, "The Threatened Revival of Know Nothingism," *American Journal of Politics,* V, 504–25.

121. J. L. Spalding, "Catholicism and Apaism," *North American Review,* CLIX, 278–87; on Spalding, see Sister Agnes Claire, *The Social Thought of John Lancaster Spalding* (Washington: Catholic University Press, 1944).

122. Lucian Johnston, "Americanism and Ultramontanism," *Catholic World,* LIX, 731–43.

123. John Bach McMaster, "The Riotous Career of the Know Nothings," *Forum,* XVII, 524–36. For another historian and how he fared, see Edward Scully Bradley, *Henry Charles Lea: A Biography* (Philadelphia: University of Pennsylvania Press, 1931). Lea's *History of the Inquisition* came out in a second edition in 1895, and his *History of Auricular Confession* appeared in 1896. Both books were severely criticized by Catholics and hailed with delight by "professional Protestant polemicists," according to Bradley, pp. 266 and 301.

124. Thomas J. Jenkins, "Know Nothingism in Kentucky and Its Destroyer," *Catholic World,* LVII, 511–22.

125. *Harper's Weekly,* April 28, 1894, p. 387.

126. *Revised Record of the Constitutional Convention of the State of New York, May 8, 1894 to September 29, 1894* (Albany, 1900), I, 618–47.

127. *Ibid.,* II, 948–57.

128. *Ibid.,* V, 693–707.

129. *Ibid.,* I, 23, 25, 34, 133, 192, 282, 314–15, 326–28, 347, 349, 351, 392–93, 441, 452–54, 469, 499, 512, 526, 537, 652–53, 712, 805, 874, 931, 935.

130. *New York Times,* Sept. 2, 5, 30, 1894.

131. David M. Schneider, *The History of Public Welfare in New York State, 1609–1940* (Chicago: University of Chicago Press, 1941), pp. 125–28. These clauses remained in the constitution until 1916 and 1934, respectively; see New York State Constitutional Convention Committee, *Amendments Proposed to the New York Constitution, 1894–1937* (New York: 1938), pp. 774, 790–94. See John O'Grady, *Catholic Charities in the United States: A History and Problems* (Washington, D.C.: National Conference of Catholic Charities, 1930), p. 147.

For Elihu Root's part in the convention, see his *Addresses on Government and Citizenship* (Cambridge, Mass.: Harvard University Press, 1916), pp. 137–40; for Choate's convention work, see Edward Sandford Martin, *The Life of Joseph Hodges Choate* (New York: Charles Scribner's Sons, 1927), I, 458–60, 464–67, as well

as Theron G. Strong, *Joseph H. Choate* (New York: Dodd, Mead & Co., 1917), pp. 85–86.

132. "The Attack on Catholic Charities in New York," *Catholic World,* LIX, 702–9; Rev. M. O'Riordan, "The Church vs. The State in the Concerns of the Poor," *Catholic World,* LX, 145–57; Rev. Thomas McMillan, "The Proposed Agnostic Amendment to Our State Constitution," *Catholic World,* LX, 267–75. The controversy continued after the election; see Richard H. Clarke, "Catholic Protectories and Reformatories," *American Catholic Quarterly Review,* XX, 607–40.

133. Linton was a member of the House Committee on Ventilation and Acoustics, *Congressional Record,* 53rd Cong., 1st Sess., p. 555.

134. *Congressional Record,* 53rd Cong., 2nd Sess. (June 7–16, 1894), pp. 5928–32, 5997–6005, 6238–39, 6309–15, 6423–24, 6434–35.

135. *News* (Washington, D.C.), Aug. 22, 1894.

136. *Congressional Record,* 53rd Cong., 2nd Sess., pp. 7706, 7816, 7877.

137. U.S. Congress, *Twenty-eight Statutes at Large,* 53rd Cong., 2nd Sess., p. 311.

138. U.S. Office of Indian Affairs, *26th Annual Report of the Board of Indian Commissioners,* 1894, pp. 9–10. In 1895, Cleveland's appointee reported that he intended to transfer Indian children to public schools, pp. 5–6, *27th Annual Report.* His report for 1896, *28th Annual Report,* would indicate that his long-term policies were identical on this score with those of Commissioner Morgan. See the editorials in the *Indian's Friend* supporting the termination of sectarian appropriations; this magazine was published by the Women's National Indian Association. Cardinal Gibbons' views may be found in his *Retrospect of Fifty Years* (Baltimore, Md.: John Murphy Company, 1916), in the essay "The Claims of the Catholic Church in the Making of the Republic."

139. Secretary King of the National League for the Protection of American Institutions made his claim at the Lake Mohonk Conference in 1894; see *Proceedings,* 1894, pp. 126–30. On the other hand, Allen Sinclair Will, in *Life of Cardinal Gibbons, Archbishop of Baltimore* (New York: E. P. Dutton & Co., Inc., 1922), I, 492–94, and Francis E. Leupp, in *The Indian and His Problem* (New York: Charles Scribner's Sons, 1910), pp. 29–30, give the credit to the A.P.A. Leupp was Theodore Roosevelt's Indian Commissioner.

Chapter 5

1. *Loyal American and the North,* March 3, 1894.
2. Theo Kersten to Vilas, Feb. 21, 1894, William F. Vilas Papers, Wisconsin Historical Society, Madison.
3. See Appendix III.
4. *United American,* Sept. 3, 1894.
5. *Wisconsin Patriot,* Oct. 6, 1894.
6. Reported in *Spokesman-Review,* Sept. 28, 1894.
7. *New York Times,* Sept. 28, Oct. 5, 1894.
8. *Biographical Directory of the American Congress; New York Times,* Oct. 6, 13, 18, 19, 1894.
9. *The Letters of Theodore Roosevelt,* ed. Elting E. Morrison (Cambridge, Mass.: Harvard University Press, 1951), I, 404–5, Roosevelt to John Joseph Keane, Oct. 15, 1894. Roosevelt had heard of Keane's concern from Mrs. Bellamy Storer, whose husband was a Republican congressman from Ohio.
10. Frederick J. Zwierlein (ed.), *Letters of Archbishop Corrigan to Bishop McQuaid and Allied Documents* (Rochester: The Art Print Shop, 1946), p. 166; see pp. 171–73 for another example of confusion of the A.P.A. with the N.L.P.A.I.
11. Frederick J. Zwierlein, *The Life and Letters of Bishop McQuaid* (Rochester: The Art Print Shop, 1927), III, 206–15, 220, 244–45. The debt referred to was apparently a consolidation of Ireland's diocesan debt. McQuaid believed that Ireland's financial difficulties were caused by unwise speculation in railroad stocks; he did not believe that the money was a loan, saying that some of the men who contributed to the fund did so in the belief that it was a gift. See also Zwierlein, *Letters of Corrigan to McQuaid,* pp. 179–80, 182, 184–85, 187; and Father George Zurcher, "Foreign Ideas in the Catholic Church in America," *Roycroft Quarterly,* Nov. 1896; Zurcher says that Father Malone represents "Irish Nativism and A.P.A.ism" within the Catholic Church, and that the A.P.A. "in any shape is at home in the G.O.P."
12. *Outlook,* Dec. 1, 1894, p. 896. See James M. King, *Facing the Twentieth Century* (New York: American Union League Society, 1899), pp. 276–79; and the *Independent,* Dec. 6, 1894, p. 1577, for comments.
13. Zwierlein, *Letters of Corrigan to McQuaid,* pp. 174–77.
14. *New York Times,* Sept. 27, 1894.
15. *Ibid.,* Sept. 19–20, Oct. 22, 24, Nov. 1, 1894.

16. *Ibid.,* Oct. 12, 1894.

17. Frederic Bancroft (ed.), *Speeches, Correspondence, and Political Papers of Carl Schurz* (New York: G. P. Putnam's Sons, 1913), V, 242.

18. *New York Times,* Nov. 5, 1894, reports sermons to this effect at St. Patrick's, Elizabeth, New Jersey, and the Church of the Sacred Heart of Jesus, New York City; the Nov. 6, 1894, issue reports the Church of the Paulist Fathers on 9th Avenue and the Church of St. Francis Xavier on West 16th Street, as well as the East Third Street Roman Catholic Church.

19. Thomas C. Platt, *Autobiography* (New York: B. W. Dodge & Co., 1910), pp. 297–98. Harold F. Gosnell, in *Boss Platt and His New York Machine* (Chicago: University of Chicago Press, 1924), p. 39, reports that Republican victories in New York in 1894 were not so much the result of Republican effectiveness as they were of Democratic disorganization.

20. *United American,* Dec. 29, 1894.

21. *Nation,* Feb. 28, 1895.

22. *Pilot* (Boston), March 24, 1894; *Illustrated American,* June 9, 16, 1894.

23. *New York Times,* Oct. 1, 7, 1894.

24. *Letters of Theodore Roosevelt,* I, 401–2, Roosevelt to Henry Cabot Lodge, Oct. 11, 1894.

25. Solomon B. Griffin, *People and Politics* (Boston: Little, Brown & Co., 1923), pp. 370–74. Griffin was a newspaperman working on the Springfield *Republican.*

26. *Nation,* Jan. 9, 1895, p. 23.

27. *New York Times,* Sept. 7, Oct. 16, 19, 1894.

28. *Ibid.,* Aug. 16, Oct. 25, 1894.

29. Reported in *Ledger* (Tacoma), Oct. 31, 1894.

30. *New York Times,* Nov. 2, 1894; on Tennessee, see J. Eugene Lewis, "The Tennessee Gubernatorial Campaign and Election of 1894," *Tennessee Historical Quarterly,* XIII, 99–126, 224–43, 301–28.

31. *Tribune* (Chicago), Oct. 3, 1894.

32. Everett Walters, *Joseph Benson Foraker, An Uncompromising Republican* (Columbus: Ohio History Press, 1948), p. 120.

33. *Catholic Columbian,* Nov. 3, 1894.

34. E. W. Meddaugh to McMillan, Dec. 11, 1893, James McMillan Papers, Burton Historical Collections, Detroit Public Library.

35. McMillan to Meddaugh, Dec. 13, 1893, McMillan Papers.

36. W. R. Bates to McMillan, July 2, 1894, McMillan Papers.

37. J. H. D. Stevens to Charles Wright, Oct. 6, 1894, McMillan Papers.

38. F. C. Chamberlain to McMillan, Oct. 17, 1894, McMillan Papers.

39. W. R. Bates to McMillan, Oct. 30, 1893, for a summary of Linton's chances as they appeared in 1893.

40. *Catholic Citizen,* Sept. 1, 1894.

41. *Official Directory and Legislative Manual, 1895–1896* (2nd ed.; Lansing, Mich., 1895), p. 454.

42. Arthur Chester Millspaugh, *Party Organization and Machinery in Michigan Since 1890* (Baltimore, Md.: The Johns Hopkins Press, 1917), p. 10.

43. *Wisconsin Patriot,* Nov. 10, 1894. Millspaugh, in *Party Organization and Machinery in Michigan,* p. 39, says primary corruption was at its height in 1894.

44. Horace S. Merrill, in *Bourbon Democracy of the Middle West, 1865–1896* (Baton Rouge: Louisiana State University Press, 1953), pp. 225–27, introduces Mr. Wall, saying there was "nothing amateurish or sentimental in the political approach of Chairman Wall."

45. E. C. Wall to Vilas, May 12, 1893, Vilas Papers. Several other letters along the same line are in the Vilas Papers: E. C. Wall to Vilas, Sept. 13, 1893, and its enclosure, E. B. Usher to Wall, Sept. 11, 1893; E. C. Wall to Vilas, Jan. 31, 1894; and E. C. Wall to Vilas, June 30, 1894.

46. J. Schlerf to Vilas, Aug. 8, 1893, Feb. 10, 1894, Vilas Papers.

47. Christian Popp to Vilas, April 23, 1894, Vilas Papers.

48. Herman Stromp to Vilas, May 4, 1894; Frank P. Coburn to Vilas, June 23, 1894, Vilas Papers.

49. G. L. Rice to Haugen, May 16, 1894, Nils Haugen Papers, Wisconsin Historical Society, Madison.

50. Arthur Gough to Haugen, May 25, 1894, Haugen Papers.

51. "Bob" LaFollette to Haugen, June 7, 1894, Haugen Papers.

52. L. N. Clausen to Haugen, June 16, 1894, Haugen Papers.

53. Frank A. Flowers to Haugen, June 25, 1894; Haugen to Nicholas Grevstad, June 30, 1894; "Bob" LaFollette to Haugen, July 16, 1894, Haugen Papers.

54. H. J. Finstad to Haugen, July 6, 1894, Haugen Papers.

55. C. W. Mott to Spooner, July 27, 1894, John Coit Spooner Papers, Manuscript Division, Library of Congress; *Pilot* (Boston), Aug. 4, 1894; *Catholic Citizen,* Aug. 4, 1894.

56. George Koeppen to Haugen, June 23, 1894, Haugen Papers. Koeppen was editor of *Germania.* See also Henry C. Thom, Republican State Chairman, to Spooner, July 17, 1894, Spooner Papers.

57. H. C. Thom to Spooner, Aug. 22, 1894, Spooner Papers.

58. *Loyal American and the North,* Aug. 11, 1894.

59. *Wisconsin Patriot,* Aug. 18, 1894.

60. *Chronicle* (LaCrosse), Sept. 7, 16, 1894; when the votes were counted, the A.P.A. man ran about two hundred votes ahead of the Republican candidate for governor; see the *Chronicle,* Nov. 7, 1894.

61. *Germania,* Oct. 9, Nov. 2, 1894.

62. *Daily Free Press* (Beloit), Oct. 10, 1894; *Abend Post,* Oct. 10, 1894.

63. *Der Seebote,* Oct. 19, 1894.

64. *Chronicle* (LaCrosse), Oct. 25, 26, 1894. See also W. White to Usher, Oct. 29, 1894, Ellis T. Usher Papers, Wisconsin Historical Society, Madison, asking advice on how to treat A.P.A. lecturers in the paper's news columns.

65. *Wisconsin Patriot,* Oct. 27, Nov. 3, 1894.

66. *Ibid.,* Nov. 10, 1894.

67. *Abend Post,* Nov. 7, 1894.

68. *Daily Free Press* (Beloit), Nov. 7, 1894.

69. E. C. Wall to Vilas, Nov. 9, 1894; Rev. E. O. Giesel to Vilas, Feb. 28, 1895, Vilas Papers.

70. Ira Harris to Spooner, Nov. 3, 13, 1894, Spooner Papers. Harris was City Clerk of West Superior. Protesting the appointment is Julius Oleson to Spooner, Jan. 1, 1895, Spooner Papers.

71. F. B. Hopkins to Spooner, Nov. 10, 1894, Spooner Papers.

72. Saul Reese to Spooner, Nov. 30, 1894, Spooner Papers.

73. *Wisconsin Patriot,* Nov. 10, 1894, Feb. 9, 1895.

74. *Loyal American and the North,* Oct. 27, 1894.

75. *Press* (Duluth), Aug. 18, 1894.

76. *Pioneer Press* (St. Paul), July 29, 1892.

77. *News* (Northfield), Sept. 29, Nov. 17, 1894; there is no mention of the A.P.A. in this newspaper during the election and for two months afterward.

78. A. C. Hawley to Davis, April 1, 9, 1895, Cushman Kellogg Davis Papers, Minnesota Historical Society, St. Paul.

79. *Loyal American and the North,* Nov. 10, 1894.

80. *Bee* (Omaha), Nov. 4, 1894.

81. F. I. Ellick to Bryan, Oct. 13, 1894, William Jennings Bryan Papers, Library of Congress. The Rosewater version of this campaign is to be found in Victor Rosewater, The Life and Times of Edward Rosewater, unpublished biography, written by a son, Nebraska Historical Society, undated, pp. 184–88, as well as in the news and editorial columns of the *Bee.* See the article by a personal friend of Holcomb, N. C. Abbott, "Silas A. Holcomb," *Nebraska History,* XXVI, 187–200.

82. *Evening Call* (Lincoln), April 2, 4, 1895.

83. *Bee* (Omaha), April 4, 1895.

84. Rosewater, Life and Times of Edward Rosewater, pp. 194–95.

Gov. Holcomb's veto message is in Nebraska Governors, Executive MSS, Box 40, dated April 1, 1895. The recommendation from the A.P.A. for the appointment of Attorney General Churchill to the Police and Fire Board is cited in footnote 16, chap. 3. For examples of national news coverage on this story, see *Public Opinion,* Aug. 15, 1895, pp. 202–3.

85. *Republican* (Denver), Nov. 3, 1894; *Catholic Citizen,* Aug. 11, 1894.

86. See *Public Opinion,* Oct. 18, 1894, p. 693.

87. Bernard Cornelius Cronin, *Father Yorke and the Labor Movement in San Francisco, 1900–1910* (Washington, D.C.: Catholic University Press, 1943), pp. 30–31.

88. Quoted in Harold F. Taggart, "Thomas Vincent Cator, Populist Leader of California," *California Historical Society Quarterly,* XXVII, 311–18; XXVIII, 47–55.

89. *Ledger* (Tacoma), Aug. 18, Sept. 1–3, 5–6, 27, 1894; *Spokesman-Review,* Oct. 10, 1894.

90. *Irish World* (New York), Nov. 10, 1894, in Father Stephan Scrapbook, Vol. II.

91. *American* (Omaha), Nov. 23, 1894.

92. L. W. Reilly, "The Weak Points of the Catholic Press," *American Ecclesiastical Review,* X, 117–25; written before the election, this article said in part, "The Church is not Democratic with a big 'D', but a majority of the Catholic papers are."

93. Of the fifty-eight congressmen on the "Roll of Honor," three had been defeated for nomination, three were defeated for re-election, seven were not candidates, two died, and three were elected to the Senate. None of the Democrats or Populists on the list was re-elected, one of them had not attempted re-election, and one ran for another position. Evidently, A.P.A. support, if it helped anyone, aided only Republicans.

94. *Wisconsin Patriot,* Jan. 19, 1895.

95. *United American,* Dec. 29, 1894.

96. Dan Elbert Clark, *History of Senatorial Elections in Iowa* (Iowa City: University of Iowa Press, 1912), pp. 222–23.

97. *News* (Detroit), Jan. 23, 1895. Senator Burrows' connection with the A.P.A. is questionable; he was a shrewd politician and may have come to some sort of terms with the order. However, he was awarded an honorary Doctorate of Laws by Notre Dame University in 1912, so that his reputation as an anti-Catholic did not last; see William Dana Orcutt, *Burrows of Michigan and the Republican Party* (New York: Longmans, Green & Co., Inc., 1917), II, 334.

98. Reported in *Oregonian,* Jan. 28, 1895.

99. *Spokesman-Review,* Feb. 27, March 1, 1895, quoting the *Catholic Sentinel.* Theodore T. Geer, in *Fifty Years in Oregon* (New York: Neale Publishing Company, 1912), p. 387, says that Dolph was defeated in 1895 because he was for the gold standard.

100. *Spokesman-Review,* Jan. 6, 10, 12, 1895.

101. *Ledger* (Tacoma), Jan. 18, 1895.

102. *Ibid.,* Jan. 20, 1895. See the *Senate Journal of the Legislature of the State of Washington* (Olympia, Wash., 1895), for the various votes on the senatorship.

103. Arthur Wallace Dunn, *From Harrison to Harding* (New York: G. P. Putnam's Sons, 1922), I, 154.

104. T. H. Carter to Clarkson, Nov. 23, 1894, James Clarkson Papers, Box 2, Folder "j," Manuscript Division, Library of Congress.

105. *Standard* (Anaconda), Jan. 13–16, 1895.

106. *House Journal of the Legislative Assembly of the State of Montana* (Helena, Mont., 1895), pp. 100–1. See the news reports in the *Oregonian,* Jan. 18, and the *Spokesman-Review,* Jan. 15–16, 1895, and the letter from "A Staunch Protestant," in the *Nation,* Jan. 31, 1895, p. 90.

107. Montana *House Journal,* 1895, p. 85.

108. *Bystander* (Butte), Jan. 19, 1895.

109. *Loyal American and the North,* Dec. 15, 1894; *Congressional Record,* 53rd Cong., 3rd Sess., pp. 192, 1763.

110. *Congressional Record,* 53rd Cong., 3rd Sess., pp. 1115–17.

111. *Ibid.,* pp. 993–96, 1110 ff. For text of the amendment, see *U.S. Congress, Twenty-eight Statutes at Large,* 53rd Cong., 3rd Sess. (1895), p. 904.

112. *Loyal American and the North,* Jan. 5, 1895.

113. *News* (Detroit), Jan. 10, 1895.

114. *Journal of the Senate of the State of Michigan, 1895* (Lansing, Mich., 1895), pp. 339, 444, 762, 764–65, 933, 1734.

115. *Ibid.,* pp. 328, 483.

116. *Patriotic American,* Sept. 1, 1894. See Madison C. Peters, "Why Church Property Should Be Taxed," and John N. Farley, "Why Church Property Should Not Be Taxed," *Forum,* XVII, 372–79, 434–42; Michigan *Senate Journal,* 1895, pp. 253, 317, 338, 378, 418, 476, 482, 521, 585, 602, 624, 654, 699, 736, 850.

117. Michigan *Senate Journal,* 1895, pp. 53, 320, 428, 460, 1734; *Journal of the House of Representatives of the State of Michigan* (Lansing, Mich., 1895), pp. 776, 920, 1082, 1099.

118. Michigan *House Journal,* 1895, pp. 175, 423, 1296, 1568, 1604, 1655. A bill to abolish "sectarianism" from the public schools was also introduced, Senate Bill 340. This was not an A.P.A. bill,

however, since the "sectarianism" it sought to abolish was that of the M.D.'s, in favor of the location of a homeopathic college of medicine at the state university.

119. Michigan *Senate Journal,* 1895, pp. 288, 524–25, 612, 846, 857, 886.

120. Michigan Superintendent of Public Instruction, *60th Annual Report* (Lansing, Mich., 1897), p. 5.

121. Minnesota Legislature, *Journal of the House, 29th Session* (St. Paul, Minn., 1895), pp. 178, 358, 487–88.

122. *Ibid.,* pp. 243, 363, 376, 580, 641. Biographical data are to be found in *Portrait Gallery of the Twenty-ninth Legislature of the State of Minnesota* (Minneapolis, Minn., 1895).

123. Minnesota Legislature, *Journal of the Senate, 29th Session* (St. Paul, Minn., 1895), pp. 577–79, 736, 746, 763–64.

124. Minnesota *House Journal,* 1895, pp. 373, 612, 618, 781–82.

125. *Ibid.,* pp. 527, 627, 633, 781, 813; Minnesota *Senate Journal,* 1895, pp. 702, 716, 752–53.

126. Minnesota *House Journal,* 1895, p. 547.

127. *Ledger* (Tacoma), Jan. 13, 1895; *Spokesman-Review,* Jan. 13, 1895.

128. *Ledger* (Tacoma), Jan. 10, 1895; *P.-I.* (Seattle), Jan. 10, 1895; *Legislative Souvenir Manual for 1895–1896* (Seattle, Wash., Steel and Searl, 1895), p. 116.

129. *House Journal of the Legislature of the State of Washington* (Olympia, Wash., 1895), pp. 39–40, 42, 79, 155, 207, 349, 393, 497; Washington *Senate Journal,* 1895, pp. 134, 147, 185, 230, 239, 259, 302, 358, 407.

130. Washington *House Journal,* 1895, pp. 295, 697.

131. *Ibid.,* pp. 71, 202, 349, 364–66, 452–53, 468.

132. Art. I, sec. 11.

133. Art. VII, sec. 2.

134. Fred Leghorn, Spokane County Assessor, had levied taxes on Catholic church property because, he said, pew rents were admission charges; see *Review* (Spokane), March 18, 1892, Aug. 1, 15, 1893. Discussion of the subject in the state legislature before 1895 is to be found in *Session Laws of the State of Washington, 1889–1890,* chap. xviii, sec. 5; *Session Laws, 1891–1892,* chap. cxl, sec. 5; *Session Laws, 1893–1894,* chap. cxxlv, sec. 5; while rebates were authorized in King County (Seattle) to certain local churches, see Washington, King County, *County Commissioners' Record,* VII, 416, 451, VIII, 8, 65.

135. House Bills 188, 194, 327, Senate Bill 163.

136. Washington *House Journal,* 1895, pp. 129, 138, 164, 234, 491.

137. Washington *Senate Journal,* 1895, pp. 3–14, 355, 504, 524, 675, 677, 721, 756–57.

138. *Ledger* (Tacoma), Jan. 29 to Feb. 8, 1895; *Argus* (Seattle), April 14, 21, 1895.

139. *Session Laws, 1895,* chap. clxxvi, sec. 2.

140. Washington, King County, County Treasurer's Office, Real Property Assessment Roll, 1896, V, 880. The hospital and its tract were assessed at $44,000 and paid a tax of $1,181.40 in two install-ments.

141. *Session Laws, 1899,* chap. xxxvi; for the 1939 law, see *Session Laws, 1939,* chap. ccvi, sec. 8. A man who served as a county assessor in the state from 1935–43, thus holding office when the clause was removed, assured the author that to his knowledge the law had never been enforced.

142. The record of the Ohio legislature of 1896 will be reviewed in its chronological place in the next chapter.

143. *American Eagle,* Aug. 19, 1894.

144. *United American,* Dec. 1, 1894, March 6, 13, 1895.

145. *Tribune* (Chicago), Oct. 5, 1894. *Inter Ocean* (Chicago), Oct. 28, 1894, stated that Harry C. Gano, who had been the first state president of the Illinois A.P.A. and was now the secretary of this third party, had been paid $750 by Democratic Mayor Hopkins of Chicago.

146. *Wisconsin Patriot,* Sept. 22, 1894.

147. *Der Seebote,* Nov. 9, 1894.

148. Fergus McDonald, *The Catholic Church and the Secret Societies in the United States* (New York: United States Catholic Historical Society, 1946), is the standard work on this subject.

149. John Tracy Ellis, *The Life of James Cardinal Gibbons* (Milwaukee, Wis.: Bruce Publishing Co., 1952), I, 467.

150. *Independent,* Dec. 27, 1894.

151. *Ledger* (Tacoma), Jan. 1, 7, 1895; *Argus* (Seattle), Jan. 5, 19, Feb. 2, 1895; *Spokesman-Review,* Jan. 21, 1895.

152. *Loyal American and the North,* Feb. 1, 1895.

153. *Doyle's Paper,* March 15–May 1, 1895.

154. *Loyal American and the North,* Feb. 15, March 1, 1895. Written in pencil on the last issue in the file at the Minnesota Historical Society is this notation: "Petered out, apparently. Stopped coming anyway."

155. *Record* (Columbus), March 15, 1895.

156. *American* (Omaha), Feb. 1, 1895.

157. *News* (Detroit), Feb. 27, March 5, 12, 1895.

158. *Ibid.,* March 13–14, 1895. Colonel Bliss's career was not ended; he became governor in 1900, and was re-elected in 1902.

159. *American* (Omaha), April 5, 1895.

160. *Doyle's Paper,* March 15, 1895; this friendly weekly reported two hundred delegates, where the reporter from the *News* saw one hundred.

161. *News* (Detroit), Jan. 28, 1895.

162. *Sentinel* (Milwaukee), May 9, 10, 1895.

163. *News* (Milwaukee), May 10–11, 1895.

164. *A.P.A. Magazine,* June, 1895, p. 82.

165. *Wisconsin Patriot,* May 11, 1895.

166. *Journal* (Milwaukee), May 10, 1895.

167. *New York Times,* July 2, 1895.

168. *Sentinel* (Milwaukee), May 12, 1895.

169. *Wisconsin Patriot,* May 18, 1895.

170. Traynor's speech is reported in *Public Opinion,* May 16, 1895, and in the Milwaukee daily papers. Its full text is to be found in the *A.P.A. Magazine,* July, 1895, pp. 160–80.

171. For example, Michigan membership in the 1897 table is the same as that given by state president Beatty for the year 1895. Further support for my conclusion will appear during 1895, when the *United American* began a criticism of the order's national officers for mismanagement of its financial affairs. The discrepancy between actual and reported membership suggested by comparisons such as the one above probably means that dues income was considerably less than membership reports indicated that it should be.

To assess the accuracy of the various state figures, notice that Colorado, Oregon, and Washington are credited with membership totals approximately one fourth of the state population. There would appear to be considerable inflation in these membership totals when compared to population totals that include all ages, where A.P.A. membership at its broadest could include only adult males and the wives of some of them.

172. This figure was arrived at by using Walter Sims's ratio of one dues-paying member to twenty-five reported members.

173. This conclusion derives from a comparison of membership given here with Plate I in Vol. IX of the 1890 Census Reports, which shows church membership by denominations.

174. This conclusion of typicality comes from two very limited analyses: one was my breakdown of occupations given in the exposé of Minnesota membership mentioned previously. The other, with many reservations, since the names do not mean membership in the A.P.A. but represent simply people who were willing to sign petitions sponsored by the order, comes from a series of petitions arising from the Father Marquette statue controversy (discussed in Chapter 6).

These petitions are to be found in the Wisconsin Governors, Executive Papers, Archives, Wisconsin Historical Society, Madison, and were addressed to Governor Upham. Petitions from Seattle, Tacoma, Snohomish, and Port Angeles, Washington, were checked against the respective city directories, and identification was made in perhaps half the cases (illegible signatures or no directory entry account for the other half). Occupations of those found were as follows: of 116 identified, 4 were farmers, 22 were unskilled workers, 21 were skilled workers, 9 were white-collar employees, 25 were in business for themselves or managed businesses, 25 were holders of elective public positions or their employees, and 10 were professional people. Carpenters, plasterers, boatbuilders, a millwright, a janitor or two, a porter, and railroad laborers, undertakers, insurance men, roominghouse proprietors or operators, real-estate men, grocerymen and butchers, a dentist, several lawyers, a physician, a public school teacher, a minister, and an actor, city and county officials and their deputies and clerks—these are full examples. Two conclusions from this very limited sample strike me: the occupations represented were heavily urban, and the proportion of politically oriented individuals was high.

See also John J. Louis, "Shelby County: A Sociological Study," *Iowa Journal of History and Politics,* II, 82–101, 218–55, for a survey of an Iowa community shortly after A.P.A. days that refers to its effect.

175. This is Desmond's conclusion in his *A.P.A. Movement.* Desmond, the editor of the Milwaukee *Catholic Citizen,* was in Washington, D.C., at the time of the A.P.A. convention of 1896 and stayed at a hotel where delegates were housed. Desmond's book, as well as his newspaper, tended to discount A.P.A. strength in Wisconsin, where he knew and understood politics and opinion, and at the same time to refer to Ohio, Indiana, southern Illinois, Iowa, and Nebraska as the "A.P.A. belt." Since his own Wisconsin would appear from the membership table to have been the state where membership was largest of all states regardless of size, one might conclude that Desmond was able in his own mind to distinguish between secularism, the A.P.A. actual membership, and Republican or Democratic campaign tactics in familiar territory, but could not do so clearly elsewhere. Consequently, he used the more inclusive term "A.P.A. movement" elsewhere in the Middle West, but for Wisconsin his firsthand knowledge encouraged him to use the number of actual dues-paying members, or something close to that total, as a guide to A.P.A. strength there.

Chapter 6

1. *Oregonian,* Oct. 10, 1895, Jan. 13, Feb. 2, 20, 1896.

2. *Argus* (Seattle), June 29, 1895, July 6, 1896; *Examiner* (Butte), Nov. 9, Dec. 15, 1895; *Spokesman-Review,* June 9, Sept. 23, 1895, April 29, 1899.

3. *A.P.A. Magazine,* June, Sept., 1895, March, 1896.

4. *Spokesman-Review,* June 21, 1895.

5. *United American,* Aug. 31, 1895.

6. *Examiner* (Butte), Sept. 7, 21, Oct. 12, 1895, Feb. 20, June 26, 1896.

7. *Argus* (Seattle), April 3, 10, 21, 1895; *P.-I.* (Seattle), Aug. 12, 1895; Seattle City Clerk's Office, *House of Delegates of the City of Seattle,* VI, 299 (Aug. 19, 1895), and 307 (Aug. 26, 1895).

8. *Examiner* (Butte), Nov. 9, 1895.

9. *United American,* June 1, 15, 1895.

10. *News* (Detroit), Nov. 9, 1895; *American* (Omaha), Nov. 22, 1895.

11. *Examiner* (Butte), April 23, 1896.

12. Robert H. Lord *et al., History of the Archdiocese of Boston in Its Various Stages of Development, 1604 to 1943* (New York: Sheed & Ward, 1944), III, 145–56.

13. *New York Times,* July 5, 1895; *Public Opinion,* July 11, 1895, for an evaluation of newspaper reports; no single paper gave a true picture of the affair, it reported. See also *The Letters of Theodore Roosevelt,* ed. Elting E. Morrison (Cambridge, Mass.: Harvard University Press, 1951), I, 466–67, for Roosevelt to Henry Cabot Lodge, July 14, 1895, describing how Roosevelt took measures to prevent a similar incident in New York City.

14. *New York Times,* July 6, 1895.

15. Editorial, *Outlook,* July 13, 1895, p. 45.

16. *New York Times,* Aug. 18, 1895.

17. George F. Hoar, *Autobiography of Seventy Years* (New York: Charles Scribner's Sons, 1903), II, 278–93 (chap. xxix, "The A.P.A. Controversy"). Senator Hoar perhaps had been interested in this subject for some time; see his letter to John C. Spooner, Dec. 3, 1894 (John Coit Spooner Papers, Library of Congress), asking for information from Spooner on the "Catholic issue" in a Spooner election campaign.

18. *Nation,* Aug. 22, 1895; *Independent,* Aug. 22, 1895; *New England Magazine,* XIII, 254–55.

19. *New York Times,* Aug. 18, 1895.

20. *Public Opinion,* Aug. 22, 1895, p. 22.

21. (Toledo: Loyal Publishing Company, 1895).

22. (Kansas City: The Author, 1895).

23. (n.p., n.d.). My dating was arrived at from the fact that Jackson is listed as vice-president of the A.P.A. in the pamphlet, and was such in 1895.

24. (Boston: Albion Printing Co., 1895).

25. (Milwaukee: *Wisconsin Patriot, n.d.*).

26. (St. Louis: J. H. Chambers & Co., 1895). The full title includes: ". . . and Its Insidious Influence in the United States and Other Countries by the Most Profound Thinkers of the Present Day, and the History and Progress of the American Protective Association Including the Sufferings and Death of the Protestant Martyrs, under Popish Persecutions."

27. Herman Ausubel, *Historians and Their Craft* (New York: Columbia University Press, 1950), pp. 197, 264–66.

28. CLXI, 129–40.

29. (New York: The Catholic Book Exchange, 1895). The ninth edition, 1898, was utilized in this study. See a friendly review of the book in *American Catholic Quarterly Review,* XX, 421–24, and another calling it "special pleading" in *Independent,* March 7, 1895.

30. Alfred Young, *Catholic and Protestant Countries Compared in Civilization, Popular Happiness, General Intelligence, and Morality* (9th ed.; New York: Catholic Book Exchange, 1895), pp. 230, 248–49, 435. See J. Thomas Scharf, "The Catholic Church the Parent of Republics," *Catholic World,* LXI, 290–304, for another definition of a "Catholic country"; Scharf says there are no "Protestant countries" because a mixture of Catholics and Protestants makes a country non-Protestant.

31. (Kansas City: *Kansas City Reform,* 1895).

32. A pamphlet by R. M. Ryan, *The New KnowNothingism* (New York: The Author, n.d.), may be dated 1895 from internal evidence.

33. Patrick Henry Winston, *American Catholics and the A.P.A.* (Chicago: Charles H. Kerr Co., 1895). Mr. Winston edited a weekly in Spokane, *Winston's Weekly,* after the turn of the century; a file of this newspaper in the University of Washington Law Library contains a scrapbook of clippings relative to Winston's career. I also interviewed Mrs. Virginia Jackson of Seattle, Mr. Winston's daughter, who told me that there had been some difficulties in the sale of the book, which she did not recall clearly; the *Spokesman-Review,* Nov. 4, 1895, reports that the American News Company was not cooperative in distributing the book, but this report did not seem to be the one Mrs. Jackson referred to.

34. Obituary notice in the scrapbook clippings in *Winston's Weekly.*

35. Isaac Cornelison, *The Relation of Religion to Civil Government in the United States* (New York: G. P. Putnam's Sons, 1895).

36. Henry Childs Merwin, "The Irish in American Life," *Atlantic Monthly,* LXXVII, 289–301.

37. *Outlook,* Aug. 10, 1895, p. 209.

38. *Public Opinion,* Aug. 15, 1895, p. 201.

39. *Argus* (Seattle), Oct. 5, 26, Nov. 2, 9, 1895, Jan. 4, Feb. 1, Nov. 14, 1896; *Ledger* (Tacoma), Jan. 20, 24–26, Feb. 9, 11, 15, Nov. 7–8, 10, 1896.

40. *Spokesman-Review,* Oct. 30, Nov. 2–3, 1895, May 26–31, June 1–5, Nov. 5–6, 1896.

41. *Oregonian,* Feb. 15, March 5, 7–10, 1896.

42. *Catholic Citizen,* July 11, 1896.

43. Horace E. Scudder, "The Schoolhouse as a Center," *Atlantic Monthly,* LXXVII, 103–9.

44. G. Stanley Hall, "Case of the Public Schools," and L. H. Jones, "The Politicians and the Public Schools," *Atlantic Monthly,* LXXVII, 402–13, 810–22.

45. *New York Times,* June 17, 1896; *Ledger* (Tacoma), Oct. 31, 1896; Ben J. Webb, *Sham Patriotism in 1896: Know Nothingism As It Was and A.P.A.ism As It Is* (Louisville, Ky.: Charles A. Rogers, 1896).

46. Told from Rosewater's viewpoint in Victor Rosewater, The Life and Times of Edward Rosewater, unpublished biography, written by a son, Nebraska Historical Society, undated, pp. 195–202. See Edgar Howard to Bryan, Nov. 13, 1895, and H. M. Hinkle to Bryan, Nov. 18, 1895, in William Jennings Bryan Papers, Library of Congress, for suggestions that Bryan resign from the *World-Herald* position for the sake of his political future. Bryan's connection with this episode is discussed in an unidentified clipping in the Terence Powderly Scrapbooks, Campaign Book No. 1, Catholic University of America Library, Washington, D.C., pp. 15–16, where Bryan's actions are called "unstable." The clipping was intended to indicate Bryan's stability potential as president. See also *Bee* (Omaha), Oct. 31, Nov. 2–8, 1895, and the *World-Herald* (Omaha), Nov. 4, 1895.

Further description of A.P.A. influences in Omaha as seen through the eyes of the Catholic leader at the local university may be found in M. P. Dowling, *Creighton University: Reminiscences of the First Twenty-five Years* (Omaha: Burkley Printing Company, 1903), pp. 131–37.

47. *Argus* (Seattle), Jan. 11, Feb. 8, 15, 22, April 11, June 20, 1896. See also Clarence B. Bagley, *History of Seattle* (Chicago: S. J.

Clark Publishing Company, 1916), II, 552, and Thomas Wickham Prosch, A Chronological History of Seattle from 1850 to 1897, unpublished manuscript in the University of Washington Library, 1901, p. 457.

48. *Ledger* (Tacoma), Jan. 28, March 8–19, April 4–8, 1896; *Herald* (Tacoma), Feb. 15, 29, March 7, 28, April 4, 11, 18, 25, 1896.

49. *Spokesman-Review,* Feb. 6, 27–28, March 6, April 12–14, 18, 27, May 5, 7–9, Sept. 4, 16–19, 24, Oct. 12–13, 30–31, 1895, March 6, 1896; N. W. Durham, *History of the City of Spokane and Spokane County* (Chicago: S. J. Clark Publishing Company, 1912), I, 475.

50. *Oregonian,* March 1, 10, 1896.

51. News report in *Spokesman-Review,* April 8, 1896.

52. *Plain Dealer* (Cleveland), April 7, 1896.

53. *Examiner* (Butte), April 2, 9, 1896.

54. *Public Opinion,* Oct. 10, 1895, p. 454, for the platform; *New York Times,* Nov. 6, 1895; *Outlook,* Nov. 9, 1895, p. 743, editorial.

55. *Bee* (Omaha), Nov. 5, 1895; *Catholic Advocate,* Nov. 7, 1895; *United Americ n,* Nov. 9, 1895.

56. *Americ n* (Omaha), April 3, 1896.

57. *Wiscon in Patriot,* Dec. 7, 1895. There is nothing in Jones's biography to support this assertion; see Laura M. Jones, *The Life and Sayings of Sam P. Jones* (2nd ed.; Atlanta: Franklin-Turner Co., 1907).

58. *Plain L eader* (Cleveland), May 27, 1895.

59. *Ohio State Journal,* May 27, 1895.

60. *United American,* Nov. 9, 1895; see Herbert Croly, *Marcus Alonzo Hanna: His Life and Work* (New York: The Macmillan Company, 1912), p. 176.

61. *Catholic Citizen,* Nov. 2, 1895.

62. Ohio General Assembly, *Journal of the House of Representatives of the State of Ohio for 1896,* pp. 108, 114, 483, 615, 769; *Journal of the Senate of the State of Ohio for 1896,* pp. 556, 567, 609, 665, 69 .

63. *Ohio State Journal,* April 15, 1896.

64. Ohio *House Journal,* 1896, pp. 67, 70, 222, 248–49, 488, 506 (for one), and 303, 326, 478, 523, 563 (for the other of these laws); Ohio *Senate Journal,* 1896, pp. 237, 425, 465–69 (for one), and 47, 55, 232, 259, 476, 500, 506 (for the other).

65. *Tribune* (Chicago), Aug. 16–17, 1895.

66. *Catholic Review,* Aug. 31, 1895.

67. *Inter Ocean* (Chicago), Aug. 17, 1895; *Journal* (Milwaukee), Aug. 31, 18 5.

68. *True American,* Feb. 15, 1896.

69. *United American,* Oct. 19, 1895.

70. *Public Opinion,* Oct. 24, 1895, p. 522.

71. William J. H. Traynor, *Letter of the Supreme President Traynor to the Order* (Detroit: The Author, 1895).

72. Simon Newcomb, "Why We Need a National University," *North American Review,* CLX, 210–16; Edgar Bruce Wesley, *Proposed: The University of the United States* (Minneapolis: University of Minnesota Press, 1936); and U.S. Senate, *University of the United States,* 57th Cong., 1st Sess., Senate Rep. 945 (Washington, D.C.: Government Printing Office, 1902).

73. *Congressional Record,* 53rd Cong., 1st Sess., p. 1277; 3rd Sess., pp. 76, 271, 283, 344, 585, 2744.

74. *Ibid.,* 54th Cong., 1st Sess., pp. 50, 239, 252, 334, 650, 958, 2636.

75. *Ibid.,* pp. 3531, 5218–21, 5417, 5470, 5478, 5485; 2nd Sess., pp. 233–34, 247, 1937–38, 2667, etc. These page citations are illustrative but are not the complete record of the bill in Congress.

76. *Ibid.,* 2nd Sess., p. 846.

77. *Ibid.,* 1st Sess., p. 3164.

78. *Ibid.,* pp. 1982–85, 1987–94, 2079–89, 2124.

79. *A.P.A. Magazine,* April, 1896, pp. 1127–28.

80. *Breeze,* March 19, 1896.

81. *Congressional Record,* 54th Cong., 1st Sess., pp. 3812–22, 4208–14, 4255–59.

82. *Ibid.,* pp. 4386, 5076–78, 5093, 5174, etc. For the text of the law, see U.S. Congress, *Twenty-nine Statutes at Large,* 54th Cong., 1st Sess., p. 345.

83. In the second session of the Fifty-fourth Congress, after the election in November of 1896, permission was granted to the Commissioner to make contracts where government schools were not yet ready for use; see *Congressional Record,* 54th Cong., 2nd Sess., pp. 1139–45, 1255–68, 1314, 1761, etc. See also U.S. Congress, *Thirty Statutes at Large,* 55th Cong., 1st Sess., p. 79, for the law. The annual reports of the Commissioner of Indian Affairs for 1896, pp. 14–17, for 1898, pp. 15–16, and for 1900, pp. 23–28, show how this policy was carried out. Even after this, however, Catholic mission schools, supported by private donation and by tribal funds administered by the government, continued in operation.

84. Louis G. Weitzman, *One Hundred Years of Catholic Charities in the District of Columbia* (Washington, D.C.: Catholic University Press, 1931), pp. 7–9; Walter Fairleigh Dodd, *The Government of the District of Columbia* (Washington, D.C.: John Byrne & Co., 1909), pp. 153–66; the *Annual Report* for 1915 of the District of

Columbia Board of Children's Guardians gives a short historical summary of the board's activities.

85. *Congressional Record,* 54th Cong., 1st Sess., pp. 1126, 1170–88, 1221–25, 1240 ff.

86. *Ibid.,* pp. 1244, 1295 ff.

87. *Ibid.,* pp. 1339–40.

88. *Ibid.,* pp. 3780–90.

89. *Ibid.,* pp. 3812, 4962, 5177, 5296, 5348, 5365, 5393, 5401–7, 5415, 5478, 5487, 5510, 5926, 6087, 6122, 6239, 6243, 6270, 6300, 6354, 6367, 6383.

90. *Ibid.,* 2nd Sess., pp. 1255, 1447–62, 1532–52, 1619–28, 1642, 1918, 2525–35, 2648, 2696, 2739, 2941–42, 2979. See U.S. Congress, *Twenty-nine Statutes at Large,* 54th Cong., 1st Sess., p. 411, and 2nd Sess., p. 683, for text of the laws.

91. *Wisconsin Patriot,* Feb. 8, 1896.

92. H. J. Desmond to Vilas, Feb. 7, 18, 1893; W. J. Onahan to Vilas, Feb. 13, 1893; William Fox to Vilas, Feb. 13, 1893; William F. Vilas Papers, Wisconsin Historical Society, Madison. The writer of the first letter cited is the same H. J. Desmond who wrote *The A.P.A. Movement.* See K. Gerald Marsden, "Father Marquette and the A.P.A.: An Incident in American Nativism," *Catholic Historical Review,* XLVI, 273–98.

93. U.S. Congress, *Twenty-eight Statutes at Large,* 53rd Cong., 1st Sess., p. 12; W. H. Upham, Gov. of Wisconsin, to Vilas, Feb. 14, 1896; Vilas to Upham, Feb. 20, 1896; Upham to Vilas, Feb. 26, 1896, Vilas Papers.

94. *Congressional Record,* 54th Cong., 1st Sess., pp. 2314, 2911, 3161, 3313, 3465, 3648, 3739, 3890, 3977, 4146, 4189, 4294, 4346, 4398, 4451, 4546–52, 4570, 4589, 4909, 4917, 4918, 4959, 5091, 5152, 5273, 5320, 5439, 5600.

95. *Post* (Washington), March 1, 1896.

96. These petitions have already been mentioned in Chapter 5. They are contained as an enclosure in Knowles to Gov. Upham, March 30, 1896, Wisconsin Governors, Executive Papers, Archives, Wisconsin Historical Society, Madison.

97. Patrick O'Farrell to Major Jerome Bourke, June 21, 1898, Mary T. O'Farrell Manuscripts, Catholic University of America Library, Washington, D.C.

98. *A.P.A. Magazine,* April, 1896, p. 1089.

99. *Examiner* (Butte), May 14, 1896.

100. *Public Opinion,* April 12, 1894, pp. 46–47; see the *Congressional Record,* 53rd Cong., 2nd Sess., pp. 3762–63, for petitions opposing the amendment.

101. *Congressional Record,* 54th Cong., 1st Sess., pp. 446, 1020.

Chapter 7

1. *United American,* Dec. 12, 1895.
2. *Ibid.,* Sept. 7, 1895.
3. *Post* (Washington), March 26, 1896.
4. *American* (Omaha), April 3, 1896; *Examiner* (Butte), Nov. 16, 1895; *New York Times,* Nov. 8, 1895.
5. *American* (Omaha), April 10, 1896.
6. *Public Opinion,* April 16, 1896, p. 489, and April 23, 1896, p. 522. See also Patrick Egan, *Recollections of a Happy Life* (New York: George H. Doran Company, 1924), p. 198, for a Catholic Republican's denial that McKinley was anti-Catholic. See also Margaret Leech, *In the Days of McKinley* (New York: Harper & Brothers, 1959), pp. 76–78, on McKinley and the A.P.A.
7. *Plain Dealer* (Cleveland), April 15, 1896.
8. *Oregonian,* April 17, 23, 1896.
9. *Star* (Washington), May 5, 1896.
10. *American* (Omaha), Feb. 21, March 27, 1896; *Wisconsin Patriot,* Feb. 22, April 18, 1896.
11. *Call* (San Francisco), March 8, 1896.
12. *American* (Omaha), May 15, 1896.
13. *Examiner* (Butte), April 30, 1896.
14. *Post* (Washington), May 17, 1896. Reports on the convention are in the *Post,* May 12–18, 1896.
15. *American* (Omaha), May 22, 1896.
16. *American* (Philadelphia), May 23, 1896.
17. *Post* (Washington), May 12, 1896.
18. *Ibid.,* May 16, 1896; the congressmen were William S. Linton, Samuel Hilborn, Rousseau Crump, and Milford W. Howard. The fifth one was probably Josiah D. Hicks of Pennsylvania.
19. *Ibid.;* see Appendix I for list of officers.
20. Biographical information was obtained from *Western Patriot,* Sept. 1896, p. 95; a letter to the author from Ella May Thornton, State Librarian of Georgia, Sept. 11, 1952; Library of Congress card number 18-18086, which lists Echols' *The Man Behind the Gun: An Address Delivered before the Historical Society of Fairfax County, Virginia, on Washington's Birthday, 1917* (Washington, D.C.: Judd and Detweiler, Inc., 1917).
21. W. J. H. Traynor, "Policy and Power of the A.P.A.," *North American Review,* CLX, 658–66.
22. Wire service reports in *Ledger* (Tacoma), April 22, 23, 30, May 6, 7, 1896, and from *Spokesman-Review,* for same dates.

23. See the letter from Mark Hanna to W. R. Holloway, April 25, 1896, in A. Dale Beeler (ed.), "Letters to Colonel William R. Holloway, 1893–1897," *Indiana Magazine of History,* XXXVI, 371–96. Holloway was an Indiana Republican supporting McKinley.

24. See Henry Lane Wilson, *Diplomatic Episodes in Mexico, Belgium, and Chile* (New York: Doubleday, Page & Co., 1927), pp. 217–18, for Wilson's later views on the relationship of church and state, specifically in Mexico.

25. N. W. Durham, *History of the City of Spokane and Spokane County* (Chicago: S. J. Clark Publishing Company, 1912), I, 478–79; *Spokesman-Review,* April 9, 22–30, May 2–10, 1896.

26. *Spokesman-Review,* May 14–15, 1896; *Ledger* (Tacoma), May 14–16, 1896.

27. *Ledger* (Tacoma), Sept. 22, 1896. The defection of the Seattle A.P.A. from Republican ranks may be followed in the unfriendly columns of the *Argus* (Seattle), Aug. 1, 22, Sept. 12, 19, 26, 1896. The *Argus* had always been a Republican cheerleader and favored the A.P.A. only as long as the order supported Republicans; when John Bushell demonstrated his preference for silver and temperance over party regularity, the *Argus* attacked him. In Washington, the Gold Democrats utilized the regular Democratic machinery and its ballot position, while the Bryan Democrats appeared on the ballot under the Fusion Party label.

28. *New York Times,* June 17, 1896.

29. Herbert Croly, *Marcus Alonzo Hanna: His Life and Work* (New York: The Macmillan Company, 1912), p. 215.

30. *Public Opinion,* June 11, 1896; John Tracy Ellis, *The Life of James Cardinal Gibbons* (Milwaukee: Bruce Publishing Co., 1952), II, 37, footnote.

31. *Nation,* June 18, 1896.

32. James M. King, *Facing the Twentieth Century* (New York: American Union League Society, 1899), pp. 263–68. King's account gives the text of his proposed platform statement; he was disturbed that his efforts should now be condemned by association with the A.P.A.

33. Thomas Beer, *Hanna* (New York: Alfred A. Knopf, Inc., 1929), pp. 142–43. Beer says that St. Louis at convention time was full of "religious busybodies"; his version of the Ireland telegram is that Hanna sent a messenger to St. Paul to a lawyer who got in touch with the Archbishop, who in turn sent the message.

34. *A.P.A. Magazine,* Nov., 1896, p. 1615, lists Carter as an example of Catholic influences operating within both major parties.

35. The text is in King, *Facing the Twentieth Century,* pp. 263–68; see also James H. Moynihan, *The Life of Archbishop Ireland* (New

York: Harper & Brothers, 1953), pp. 263–64, where the communication is discussed without reference to its background.

36. *American Advocate,* Oct., 1899.

37. George D. Ellis (comp.), *Platforms of the Two Great Political Parties, 1856–1928* (Washington, D.C.: Government Printing Office, 1928), pp. 41, 45, 49, 51, 75, 84–85, 89.

38. *Wisconsin Patriot,* June 27, 1896; Congressman Richardson, a Mason, was the compiler of the *Messages of the Presidents.*

39. *Public Opinion,* June 25, 1896.

40. *A.P.A. Magazine,* Aug., 1896, p. 1313.

41. Hanna to Louis T. Michener, July 20, 1896, Louis T. Michener Papers, Library of Congress. See also Arthur Wallace Dunn, *From Harrison to Harding* (New York: G. P. Putnam's Sons, 1922), I, 197, for the story of how Hanna secured the services of Father Stephan.

42. John H. Gear to Michener, July 20, 1896, Michener Papers.

43. *The Letters of Theodore Roosevelt,* ed. Elting E. Morrison (Cambridge, Mass.: Harvard University Press, 1951), I, 547–48, Roosevelt to Henry Cabot Lodge, July 14, 1896.

44. One would be hard put to it to find much substantiation in Bryan's career to support the Republican statements of an A.P.A. connection. Paxton Hibben, in *The Peerless Leader* (New York: Farrar & Rinehart, Inc., 1929), p. 74, relates that as a college debater Bryan maintained that Catholicism was more dangerous to the United States than communism; on p. 126, Bryan rejected anti-Catholic support in his first race for Congress. In the Bryan Papers is a letter on the letter-head of the "Patriots of America" that mentions secret meetings and which lists "trusts and organizations of selfish," without naming Catholics, as the enemy; see W. H. Harvey to Bryan, Jan. 4, 1896, William Jennings Bryan Papers, Library of Congress.

45. Solon J. Buck, *The Agrarian Crusade* (New Haven, Conn.: Yale University Press, 1921), p. 115; C. Vann Woodward, *Origins of the New South, 1877–1913* (Baton Rouge: Louisiana State University Press, 1951), p. 236. Both accounts show that Macune's role in Georgia politics was not quite as lurid as the above statement of "sellout"; Macune was a conservative who was not willing to desert the Democratic party for a third-party venture.

46. *Wisconsin Patriot,* Aug. 1, 1896.

47. *Bystander* (Butte), Oct. 22, 1896.

48. *Breeze* (St. Paul), Aug. 6, 1896.

49. *Wisconsin Patriot,* Aug. 22, 1896.

50. *American* (Omaha), Oct. 23, 30, 1896.

51. *Star* (Washington), Oct. 1, 10, 1896.

52. *Examiner* (Butte), Oct. 24, 1896.

53. *United American,* Oct. 31, 1896.

54. Moynihan, *Life of Ireland,* p. 261; *Public Opinion,* Oct. 22, 1896.

55. *Examiner* (San Francisco), Oct. 13, 17, 1896.

56. This advice is given in an oversized and lengthy document included, without date, in the Bryan Papers. It is titled, "The Presidential Situation: The A.P.A. Attitude Thereto," and accompanies a letter from J. W. Reynolds to the Rev. C. C. Cline of Clintonville, Kentucky.

57. *Examiner* (Butte), July 16, 1896, said the Montana A.P.A. had been for "silver all the time." Probably the same could be said for Colorado, but the lack of files for any member of the "patriotic press" in that state makes this conjecture.

58. See Roscoe C. Martin, *The People's Party in Texas: A Study of Third Party Politics* (Austin: University of Texas Press, 1933), pp. 87, 107, 232–33.

59. See Jasper Berry Shannon, *Presidential Politics in Kentucky, 1824–1948* (Lexington: University of Kentucky Press, 1951), p. 70, for a breakdown on presidential voting for 1896 in Jefferson County (Louisville), where the A.P.A. was strongest; Shannon does not mention the A.P.A. in his analysis. James A. Barnes, in "Myths of the Bryan Campaign," *Mississippi Valley Historical Review,* XXXIV, 367–404, emphasizes the same factor as Shannon, urbanization. Rowland T. Berthoff, "Southern Attitudes toward Immigration," *Journal of Southern History,* XVII, 328–60, states that few southerners were in the A.P.A., a statement that appears to be true when the entire South is included in the generalization. A.P.A. strength, what there was of it, seems to have been an urban affair in the South, with most evidence coming from the border states.

60. *Official Directory and Legislative Manual, 1897–1898* (Lansing, Mich., 1897), pp. 473–78, for election returns. Linton was defeated by a vote of 20,992 to 20,158. There is an unsupported assertion in Arthur Chester Millspaugh, *Party Organization and Machinery in Michigan Since 1890* (Baltimore, Md.: The Johns Hopkins Press, 1917), p. 142, that a person who helped manage the Republican campaign said that the Republican National Committee repaired every Roman Catholic Church in Monroe County in 1896. If this statement should be true, it is the most practical evidence that Republicans were more interested in gaining Catholic support in 1896 than they were in retaining A.P.A. allegiance.

61. *Wisconsin Patriot,* Oct. 10, 17, 1896; *Catholic Citizen,* Oct. 3, 1896; *Examiner* (Butte), Aug. 13, 1896; *United American,* Nov. 28, 1896; *Argus* (Seattle), Nov. 14, 1896.

62. See the comment, "Is Anti-Catholic Prejudice Dying Out?" *Ave Maria*, XLIII, 470–72, where the answer given is "No."

63. *American* (Omaha), Nov. 13, 1896.

64. On the projected appointment of the Catholic Joseph McKenna of California to be Secretary of Interior, see H. H. Kohlsaat, *From McKinley to Harding* (New York: Charles Scribner's Sons, 1923), pp. 59–60; Fremont Older, *My Own Story* (San Francisco: Call Publishing Company, 1919), pp. 16–20; Col. T. Bentley Mott, *Myron T. Herrick: Friend of France* (New York: Doubleday, Doran & Co., 1929), pp. 58–59; Edith Dobie, *The Political Career of Stephen Mallory White* (Palo Alto, Calif.: Stanford University Press, 1927), pp. 225–26; and Richard J. Purcell, "Justice Joseph McKenna," *Records of the American Catholic Historical Society,* LVI, 177–223. For Bellamy Storer's difficulties in obtaining an appointment to office, see Everett Walters, *Joseph Benson Foraker, An Uncompromising Republican* (Columbus: Ohio History Press, 1948), p. 145, and the entries in the *Letters of Theodore Roosevelt* under Storer's name.

65. Clippings from *Truth* (Scranton), July 19, 1897, and *Journal* (Dayton), Sept. 15, 1897, in the Terence V. Powderly Scrapbooks, Catholic University of America Library, Washington, D.C. See also Terence V. Powderly, *The Path I Trod* (New York: Columbia University Press, 1940), pp. 298 ff. and 369.

66. Letter from C. I. Shumway to the editor, dated April, 1900, in *American Advocate,* June, 1900.

67. *Biographical Directory of the American Congress.*

68. *Wisconsin Patriot,* May 29, 1897.

69. *Ibid.,* March 5, 1898.

70. *Oregonian,* May 9, 1898.

71. *Examiner* (San Francisco), Oct. 6, 1896. See John P. Young, *Journalism in California* (San Francisco: Chronicle Publishing Company, 1915), for California newspaper owners.

72. *Oregonian,* Jan. 22, 1897.

73. Rev. Charles Wendte and Rev. Peter C. Yorke, *The Yorke-Wendte Controversy: Letters on the Papal Primacy and the Relations of Church and State* (San Francisco: Monitor Publishing Company, 1896). For Wendte's viewpoints in general, see his autobiography, *The Wider Fellowship: Memories, Friendships, and Endeavors for Religious Unity, 1844–1927* (Boston: Beacon Press, 1927). After leaving Oakland Wendte became Foreign Secretary of the American Unitarian Association, and became also the first General Secretary of the National Federation of Religious Liberals, which included those religious groupings not included within the Federal Council of Churches of Christ in America.

74. *Examiner* (San Francisco), Jan. 2, 1897; the Yorke Scrapbooks contain clippings on this interchange from Dec. 31, 1896, until late in Jan., 1897.

75. Bernard Cornelius Cronin, *Father Yorke and the Labor Movement in San Francisco, 1900–1910* (Washington, D.C.: Catholic University Press, 1943), pp. 32–35. Yorke's attacks on Maguire and Phelan were published as Republican campaign pamphlets and are in the Yorke Scrapbooks. According to Harold F. Taggart, in "The Election of 1898 in California," *Pacific Historical Review,* XIX, 357–68, the Republican State Committee paid for their publication. Taggart also says, in his article, "Thomas Vincent Cator: Populist Leader of California," *California Historical Society Quarterly,* XXVII, 311–18, and XXVIII, 47–55, that Yorke's appointment as regent was a return for his services to the Republican cause. There is a reply to this assertion in the *Quarterly* for June, 1949, in a letter from the Hon. Joseph Scott objecting to Taggart's comment, and saying that Yorke was qualified for the appointment—which was hardly Taggart's point.

76. *Breeze,* Nov. 12, 1896; *Wisconsin Patriot,* Feb. 20, 1897; *A.P.A. Magazine,* Nov., 1896, p. 1578; *Oregonian,* Jan. 21, 1897.

77. *Oregonian,* May 12, 1897; *Breeze,* May 20, 1897; *Wisconsin Patriot,* May 15, 22, Dec. 4, 1897.

78. *United American,* Nov. 28, 1896. C. Vann Woodward, in *Tom Watson: Agrarian Rebel* (New York: The Macmillan Company, 1938), has little to say about anti-Catholicism in this early phase of Watson's career.

79. *American* (Omaha), Feb. 18, 1898.

80. Form letter, E. H. Sellers and W. J. H. Traynor, "To All Loyal American Citizens," July 7, 1897, Henry Baldwin MSS, New York Public Library.

81. *Wisconsin Patriot,* April 23, 1898; *A.P.A. Magazine,* Nov., 1896 (note "To Our Readers" at end of issue), Feb., 1897, pp. 1730–32; *American Advocate,* July, 1899, p. 346.

82. *A.P.A. Magazine,* April, 1897, p. 1930, June, 1897, pp. 34–37; William Lloyd Clark, *The Story of My Struggle with the Scarlet Beast* (Milan, Ill.: Rail Splitter Press, 1932), p. 159.

83. *Wisconsin Patriot,* Aug. 7, Dec. 18, 1897.

84. *True American,* Feb. 15, 1896; *A.P.A. Magazine,* April, 1897, pp. 1887–88, 1907; Speed Mosby, "Taxation of Church Property," and Madison C. Peters, "Taxation of Church Property," *North American Review,* CLXIII, 254–56 and 633–34.

85. *Breeze,* Feb. 11, May 6, 1897, April 14, May 5, 1898; *Wisconsin Patriot,* Nov. 20, 1897.

86. *True American,* Feb. 15, March 7, 1896.

87. *American* (Omaha), Feb. 1, 1898; see also King, *Facing the Twentieth Century,* pp. 155, 461–62.

88. Dunn, *From Harrison to Harding,* I, 235; John T. Farrell, "Archbishop Ireland and Manifest Destiny," *Catholic Historical Review,* XXXII, 269–301; Richard J. Purcell, "Archbishop Ireland: An Appreciation," *Records of the American Catholic Historical Society,* LX, 95–105.

89. *American* (Omaha), April 15, 22, 1898.

90. *American Advocate,* Nov., 1899, p. 489; Bowers' reference was apparently to the Leopold Association, which had been the object of Samuel F. B. Morse's attacks; see Ray Allen Billington, *The Protestant Crusade* (New York: The Macmillan Company, 1938), pp. 121 ff.

91. *American Advocate,* June, 1900, pp. 198–200.

92. *Journal* (Sioux City), March 6, 1908.

93. *Register and Leader* (Des Moines), March 8, 1908.

94. *Herald* (Clinton), Nov. 9, 1911.

95. *New York Times,* Nov. 24, 26, 1913.

Chapter 8

1. Robert S. McCallen, *Strangled Liberty, or, Rome and Ruin* (St. Louis, Mo.: Columbia Book Concern, 1900).

2. H. H. Kohlsaat, *From McKinley to Harding* (New York: Charles Scribner's Sons, 1923), pp. 110–18.

3. Henry F. Pringle, *The Life and Times of William Howard Taft* (New York: Farrar & Rinehart, Inc., 1939), I, 220–31, 243–44, 374; II, 834, 888.

4. *The Letters of Theodore Roosevelt,* ed. Elting E. Morrison (Cambridge, Mass.: Harvard University Press, 1951), VI, 1318, Roosevelt to Kermit Roosevelt, Oct. 24, 1908.

5. Arthur S. Link, *Wilson: The Road to the White House* (Princeton, N.J.: Princeton University Press, 1947), pp. 499–500.

6. John N. Blum, *Joe Tumulty and the Wilson Era* (Boston: Houghton Mifflin Company, 1951), pp. 51, 89. Tom Watson was the one who made the charge.

7. Frank Freidel, *Franklin D. Roosevelt: The Apprenticeship* (Boston: Little, Brown & Co., 1952), p. 106. An attempt was made to investigate the editorial career of Warren Harding during the A.P.A. days. The opportunity looked too good to miss because of Harding's strong Republicanism, his conviviality, and his inability to say "No." But files of the crucial years, according to the records

of the Ohio State Archeological and Historical Society, are non-existent.

8. *American Mechanics' Advocate,* Feb., June, 1898.

9. U.S. Immigration Commission, *Statements and Recommendations Submitted by Societies and Organizations Interested in the Subject of Immigration,* 61st Cong., 3rd Sess., Senate Doc. No. 764, Vol. XLI (Washington, D.C., 1911), pp. 15–29.

10. William Lloyd Clark, *The Story of My Struggle with the Scarlet Beast* (Milan, Ill.: Rail Splitter Press, 1932), pp. 159, 164.

11. W. J. H. Traynor, *The Devil's Catechism* (New York: Peter Eckler Publishing Company, 1920). After his A.P.A. presidency, Traynor became a real estate man in Chattanooga, and in 1903–5 he was located in Pasadena, California. From then until 1920 there is no information on his whereabouts.

12. Howard Carl Lundvall, in The American Protective Association: A Study of an Anti-Catholic Organization (Master's thesis, University of Iowa, 1950), pp. 90–91, reports that the *Fellowship Forum* of June 23, 1923, reports a Col. Arthur Petersen of Bakersfield, California, as the "Grand Master" of the A.P.A. The title of the office eliminates the possibility that this organization was the old American Protective Association. Lundvall also reports, pp. 109–10 in a footnote, that he had an interview with a person who had participated in an attempt in 1923 to renew the A.P.A. in Illinois.

13. William H. Anderson, *American Protestant Alliance: A Comprehensive Introductory Working Outline* (New York: The Author, 1926).

14. Paul M. Winter, *What Price Tolerance* (Hewlett, N.Y.: All-American Book, Lecture and Research Bureau, 1928), pp. 53–54. See Edmund A. Moore, *A Catholic Runs for President* (New York: Ronald Press, 1956), for the most recent study of anti-Catholicism in the election of 1928.

15. Joseph Martin Dawson, *Separate Church and State Now* (New York: Richard R. Smith, 1948), p. 86.

16. *Encyclopedia of Social Reform,* ed. William D. P. Bliss (New York: Funk & Wagnalls Co., Inc., 1897), pp. 48–52; a new edition, 1908, also includes the article on the A.P.A. Note that Eric Goldman, in his *Rendezvous with Destiny* (New York: Alfred Knopf, 1953), p. 454, says that Paul Blanshard's *American Freedom and Catholic Power* (Boston: Beacon Press, 1949), is the "first important liberal criticism of the way the Catholic hierarchy was functioning in the United States." Mr. Goldman apparently believes that, if Blanshard's is to be called "liberal," earlier anti-Catholicism was "illiberal."

17. John Tracy Ellis, *The Life of James Cardinal Gibbons* (Milwaukee: Bruce Publishing Co., 1952), II, 598–99.

18. James H. Moynihan, *The Life of Archbishop Ireland* (New York: Harper & Brothers, 1953), pp. 258–59, for examples.

19. Knights of Columbus, Supreme Council, Commission on Religious Prejudices, *Report* (Louisville, Ky., 1915).

20. John Moffatt Mecklin, *The Ku Klux Klan: A Study of the American Mind* (New York: Harcourt, Brace & Co., 1924), is a popular rather than a scholarly treatment, and it makes attempts to analyze the "mass mind" that weaken its conclusions.

21. See for example André Siegfried, in *America Comes of Age* (New York: Harcourt, Brace & Co., 1927), pp. 130–31, who is correct in placing the A.P.A. among extreme nationalistic groups.

Bibliography

Apparently no organizational "records" of the American Protective Association have survived to the present. The principal source for information used in the preceding study was the files of remnants of the "patriotic press" friendly to the organization. There were enough of these periodicals in various libraries to provide adequate geographical coverage as well as to support a narrative. The list supplied below includes the name of the library where a file exists. These periodicals were supplemented by Catholic diocesan newspapers, by the daily press, and by weekly, monthly, and quarterly magazines, to lend perspective. Specific references to articles used from these periodicals are indicated in the footnotes; the list that follows contains only the titles of the periodicals used and a location for some of them.

There are many references in passing to the general subject of anti-Catholicism in the late nineteenth century as well as to the specific topic of the A.P.A. to be found in various biographies, memoirs, special studies, monographs, as well as in the published papers of significant figures in public life of that era. None of them, however, has provided enough of the material on which this study is based to warrant repeating their titles in a bibliographical listing. The only information on number of members, other than that scattered through the press reports, can be found in Albert C. Stevens, compiler and editor, *The Cyclopedia of Fraternities* (New York: Hamilton Printing and Publishing Company, 1899). The small book by Humphrey J. Desmond, *The A.P.A.: A Sketch* (Washington, D.C.: New Century Press, 1912), written by the editor of a Catholic diocesan paper shortly after the height of the A.P.A. career (though not published for several years), is still useful for its generalizations

and its information; it does, however, tend to emphasize the midwestern locale, and it does not provide sufficient detail. For background on nativism in the late nineteenth and early twentieth centuries, John Higham's *Strangers in the Land: Patterns of American Nativism* (New Brunswick, N.J.: Rutgers University Press, 1955), provides the best information.

The legislative record of the A.P.A. may be traced in the *Congressional Record* for the sessions of the 1890's; the laws enacted will be found in the United States *Statutes at Large* for the same years. Specific depth and background on the legislative issues that the A.P.A. involved itself in may be obtained from the annual reports of the Board of Indian Commissioners, Interior Department, for the years 1887 to 1900, supported by the annual reports for 1890–94 of the Indian Rights Association (Philadelphia), the annual reports of the Women's National Indian Association for 1883–1901 (Philadelphia), and the *Proceedings,* 1890–1900, of the Lake Mohonk Conference of the Friends of the Indian (Philadelphia), on the issue of Indian schools. For public school matters, the debates in the *Proceedings* of the National Education Association for 1887–96 (Washington, D.C.), are informative. There is a historical summary of charities in the District of Columbia in the Board of Children's Guardians *Annual Report,* 1915–16 (Washington, D.C.: Government Printing Office, 1917). State legislative journals for both houses of the state legislatures of Michigan, Minnesota, Montana, and Washington for the 1895 sessions, and for Ohio in the sessions of 1894 and 1896 were checked to follow news stories appearing in the "patriotic press"; the alterations of the state constitution of New York were found in the *Revised Record of the Constitutional Convention of the State of New York, May 8, 1894, to September 29, 1894* (Albany, N.Y.: The Argus Company, 1900), as well as to the New York State Constitutional Convention Committee, 1938, *Amendments Proposed to the New York Constitution, 1895–1937* (New York, 1938).

The bibliography which follows, then, lists in order those unpublished materials—theses, dissertations, manuscripts, interviews, miscellaneous scrapbooks, and the papers of public figures

whose careers touched that of the A.P.A. at some point. There is an alphabetical arrangement by title of all contemporary periodicals utilized; the student interested in specific citations from these will find them in the footnotes. Because a great deal of interesting materials were found of the sort I am calling "The Contemporary Controversy"—those ephemeral publications of anti-Catholicism and anti-anti-Catholicism!—a list of pamphlet and hard cover publications is also included; it does not claim to be complete but represents merely those which this author found in his searches and used.

A full listing of all other published materials, either in magazines or book-length, which were useful would be too lengthy and indiscriminate; may I refer the interested scholar to the footnotes.

Unpublished Materials

MANUSCRIPTS AND COLLECTED PAPERS

Allison, William Boyd. Papers in the Iowa State Department of History and Archives, Des Moines.

Baldwin, Henry. MSS in the New York Public Library, Manuscript Division.

Balfe, Sister Mary Agnes. The Catholic High School in the State of Washington. Master's thesis, Gonzaga University, 1933.

Bryan, William Jennings. Papers in the Library of Congress, Manuscript Division.

Burns, Allen W. The A.P.A. and the Anti-Catholic Crusade: 1885–1898. Master's thesis, Columbia University, 1947.

Carter, Thomas H. Papers in the Library of Congress, Manuscript Division.

Clarkson, James Sullivan. Papers in the Library of Congress, Manuscript Division.

Davis, Cushman Kellogg. Papers in the Minnesota Historical Society, St. Paul.

Dickinson, Don M. MSS in the Detroit Public Library, Burton Historical Collections.

Donnelly, Ignatius. Papers in the Minnesota Historical Society, St. Paul.

Geer, Harrison. Papers in the Michigan Historical Collections, Ann Arbor.

Gladden, Washington. Collection in the Ohio State Archeological and Historical Society, Columbus.

Hantke, Richard Watson. The Life of Elisha William Keyes. Ph.D. dissertation, University of Wisconsin, 1942.

Haugen, Nils P. Papers in the Wisconsin Historical Society, Madison.

Holmes, Byron Marshall. The American Protective Association Movement. Master's thesis, University of California, 1939.

Hynes, Sister Mary Callista. The History of the American Protective Association in Minnesota. Master's thesis, Catholic University of America [1939?].

Johnson, Ross Seymour. The A.P.A. in Ohio. Master's thesis, Ohio State University, 1948.

Knuth, Priscilla Frances. Nativism in California, 1886–1897. Master's thesis, University of California, 1947.

Lundvall, Howard Carl. The American Protective Association: A Study of an Anti-Catholic Organization. Master's thesis, State University of Iowa, 1950.

McMillan, James. Papers in the Detroit Public Library, Burton Historical Collections.

Michener, Louis T. Papers in the Library of Congress, Manuscript Division.

Morton, J. Sterling. Papers in the University of Nebraska Library.

Murphy, Sister Mary Eunice. The History of the American Protective Association in Ohio. Master's thesis, Catholic University of America, 1939.

Nebraska Governors, Executive MSS, in Nebraska State Historical Society, Lincoln.

Nelson, Knute. Papers in the Minnesota Historical Society, St. Paul.

O'Farrell, Mary T. MSS in the Catholic University of America Library, Washington, D.C.

Prosch, Thomas Wickham. A Chronological History of Seattle from 1850 to 1897. Typewritten, University of Washington Library, 1900–1901.

Rosewater, Victor. The Life and Times of Edward Rosewater. Manuscript biography, typewritten, no date, Nebraska State Historical Society, Lincoln.

Smith, William Henry. Collection in the Ohio State Archeological and Historical Society, Columbus.

Spooner, John Coit. Papers in the Library of Congress, Manuscript Division.

Stauffer, Alvin Packer. Anti-Catholicism in American Politics, 1865–1900. Ph.D. dissertation, Harvard University, 1933.

Stough, Ruth Knox. The American Protective Association. Master's thesis, University of Nebraska, 1931.

Tanner, Herbert B. Papers in the Wisconsin Historical Society, Madison.
Usher, Ellis T. Papers in the Wisconsin Historical Society, Madison.
Vilas, William F. Papers in the Wisconsin Historical Society, Madison.
Watterson, Henry. Papers in the Library of Congress, Manuscript Division.
Wisconsin Governors, Executive Papers, in the Archives, Wisconsin Historical Society, Madison.

SCRAPBOOKS

Allen, William V. Scrapbook. Nebraska Historical Society, Lincoln.
Miscellaneous Scrapbooks. Oregon Historical Society, Portland.
Powderly, Terence V. Scrapbooks. Catholic University of America Library, Washington, D.C.
Stephan, Father Joseph. Scrapbooks. Bureau of Catholic Indian Missions, 2021 H Street N.W., Washington, D.C.
Winston, Patrick Henry. Scrapbook. University of Washington Law Library, Seattle. (Contained in the file of *Winston's Weekly*.)
Yorke, Father Peter. Scrapbooks. University of San Francisco Library.

INTERVIEWS

Mrs. C. C. Bowers, 618 6th Avenue South, Clinton, Iowa.
Robert Bushell, 705 North 50th Street, Seattle, Washington.
Mrs. Virginia Jackson, 6306 21st Avenue N.E., Seattle, Washington.

GOVERNMENT RECORDS

Seattle City Clerk's Office. House of Delegates of the City of Seattle. Records, 1894–96.
Washington State, King County, County Commissioner's Office. County Commissioners' Record, 1892–96.
Washington State, King County, County Treasurer's Office. Real Property Assessment Roll, 1896–1900.

Published Materials

PERIODICALS

Abend Post (Milwaukee), 1893–96.
Age (Clinton, Iowa), 1886–87.
American (Omaha), 1891–99. Nebraska Historical Society.
American (Philadelphia), 1895–96.
American Advocate (Mechanicsville, Iowa), 1898–1900. University of Washington Library.

American Catholic Quarterly Review (Philadelphia).
American Eagle (Kansas City, Kansas), 1893. Kansas Historical Society.
American Ecclesiastical Review (Philadelphia).
American Journal of Politics (New York).
American Mechanics' Advocate (Philadelphia), 1898–1905.
A.P.A. Magazine (San Francisco), 1895–97. Stanford University Library.
Arena (Boston).
Argus (Seattle), 1893–97.
Atlantic Monthly (Boston).
Augustinian (Kalamazoo), 1894–96.
Ave Maria (South Bend), 1892–98.
Baptist Home Missionary Monthly (New York), 1893–95.
Bee (Omaha), 1892–98.
Blade (Toledo), 1892–93.
Breeze (St. Paul and White Bear Lake, Minnesota), 1896–98, also published as *The Lake Breeze*. Minnesota Historical Society.
Bystander (Butte), 1894–96.
Call (San Francisco), 1896.
Catholic Advocate (Louisville), 1895–96.
Catholic Citizen (Milwaukee), 1892–97.
Catholic Columbian (Columbus), 1892–96.
Catholic Record (Indianapolis), 1892–96.
Catholic Review (New York), 1892–96.
Catholic World (New York).
Century (New York).
Chronicle (LaCrosse), 1894–95.
Converted Catholic (New York), 1893–96.
Daily Free Press (Beloit), 1894.
Doyle's Paper (Portage), 1895. Wisconsin Historical Society.
Educational Review (New York).
Evening Call (Lincoln, Nebraska), 1894–95.
Examiner (Butte), 1895–96. Historical Society of Montana.
Examiner (San Francisco), 1896–97.
Forum (New York).
Germania (Milwaukee), 1893–96.
Globe (St. Paul), 1893.
Harper's New Monthly Magazine (New York).
Harper's Weekly (New York).
Herald (Clinton, Iowa), 1911.
Herald (Tacoma), 1896.
Illustrated American (New York), 1893–97.
Independent (Kenosha), 1894.

Independent (New York), 1892–97.
Indian Sentinel (Washington, D.C.)
Indian's Friend (Philadelphia), 1888–1900.
Inter Mountain (Butte), 1894–95.
Inter Ocean (Chicago), 1896.
Iowa State Register (Des Moines), 1894.
Journal (Milwaukee), 1895.
Journal (Sioux City), 1908.
Ledger (Tacoma), 1891–98.
Lend a Hand (Boston).
Loyal American (Minneapolis), 1893–96, retitled *Loyal American and the North,* January 27, 1894. Minnesota Historical Society.
Lucifer-Arminia (Milwaukee), 1894–96.
Michigan Catholic (Detroit), 1892–94.
Miner (Butte), 1894–95.
Monitor (San Francisco), 1894–97.
Nation (New York).
N.E.A. Journal (Washington, D.C.).
News (Clinton, Iowa), 1887.
News (Detroit), 1895.
News (Milwaukee), 1894–95.
News (Northfield, Minn.), 1894.
News (Washington, D.C.), 1894–95.
News Tribune (Duluth), 1893–94.
New York Times, 1893–97, 1913.
North American Review (Boston).
Ohio State Journal (Columbus), 1892–96
Oregonian (Portland), 1891–99.
Outlook (New York).
Patriot (Chicago), 1891. Chicago Historical Society.
Patriotic American (Detroit), 1890–96. University of Michigan Library.
Pilot (Boston), 1894.
Pioneer Press (St. Paul), 1892–94.
Plain Dealer (Cleveland), 1892–95.
Post (Washington, D.C.), 1896.
Post-Intelligencer (Seattle), 1894–97.
Press (Duluth), 1892–94.
Public Opinion (New York), 1892–98.
Record (Columbus), 1890–94. Ohio State Archeological and Historical Society.
Register and Leader (Des Moines), 1908.
Republican (Denver), 1893–95.
Review. See *Spokesman-Review.*

Rocky Mountain News (Denver), 1893–95.
Roycroft Quarterly (East Aurora, N.Y.).
Der Seebote (Milwaukee), 1893–96.
Sentinel (Milwaukee), 1893–96.
Spokesman-Review (Spokane), 1890–1900, formerly the *Review*.
Standard (Anaconda), 1895–96.
Star (Washington, D.C.), 1896.
Times and Expositor (Adrian, Mich.), 1892–94.
Town Talk (Minneapolis), 1894–95.
Tribune (Chicago), 1894.
Tribune (Minneapolis), 1894–95.
True American (St. Louis), 1896. Missouri Historical Society.
United American (Washington, D.C.), 1894–96. Library of Congress.
Western Patriot (Topeka), 1896–97. Kansas Historical Society.
Winston's Weekly (Spokane), 1903–4.
Wisconsin Patriot (Milwaukee), 1894–98. Wisconsin Historical Society.
World-Herald (Omaha), 1895.

BOOKS AND PAMPHLETS

"An American." *A.P.A.: An Inquiry into the Objects and Purposes of the So-Called "American Protective Association."* n.p., n.d.
Anderson, William H. *American Protestant Alliance: A Comprehensive Introductory Working Outline of Its Philosophy, Principles, Purposes, Policy, and Program.* New York: The Author, 1926.
Balmes, Jaime Luciano. *European Civilization: Protestantism and Catholicity Compared in Their Effects on the Civilization of Europe.* Baltimore, Md.: John Murphy, 1850.
Barnum, Samuel W. *Romanism As It Is: An Exposition of the Roman Catholic System, for the Use of the American People.* Hartford: Connecticut Publishing Company, 1879.
The Bible in the Public Schools: Arguments in the Case of John D. Minor, et al., versus The Board of Education of the City of Cincinnati, et al., Superior Court of Cincinnati. Cincinnati, Ohio: Robert Clarke Co., 1870.
Blakely, William Addison (comp.). *American State Papers Bearing on Sunday Legislation.* New York: National Religious Liberty Association, 1891.
Boston Committee of One Hundred. *An Open Letter to the Friends of Free Schools and American Liberties.* Boston: Committee of One Hundred, 1888.
Brady, M. J. *A Fraud Unmasked. The Career of Mrs. Margaret L. Shepherd. "Ex-Romanist," "Ex-Nun," "Ex-Penitent," and Biga-*

mist. *Her Own Confessions Attested by Most Reliable Witnesses.*
Woodstock, Ont.: n.p., 1893.

Brandt, John L. *America or Rome: Christ or the Pope.* Toledo, Ohio:
Loyal Publishing Company, 1895.

Burrell, David James. *The Roman Catholic Church vs. the American
Public School.* Minneapolis, Minn.: Session of the Westminster
Presbyterian Church, n.d.

Chiniquy, Charles Paschal Telesphore. *Fifty Years in the Church of
Rome.* 40th ed. Chicago: Adam Craig, 1891.

Clark, William Lloyd. *The Story of My Struggle with the Scarlet
Beast.* Milan, Ill.: Rail Splitter Press, 1932.

Cornelison, Isaac A. *The Relation of Religion to Civil Government
in the United States of America: A State without a Church, but
Not without a Religion.* New York: G. P. Putnam's Sons, 1895.

Dorchester, Daniel. *The Problem of Religious Progress.* New York:
Phillips and Hunt, 1881.

————. *Romanism Versus the Public School System.* New York:
Phillips and Hunt, 1881.

Dunn, James B. *The Pope's Last Veto in American Politics.* Boston:
Committee of One Hundred, 1890.

Echols, John Warnock. *The Man Behind the Gun: An Address.*
Washington, D.C.: Judd and Detweiler, 1917.

*Errors of the Roman Catholic Church, and Its Insidious Influence in
the United States and Other Countries by the Most Profound
Thinkers of the Present Day, and the History and Progress of the
American Protective Association: Including the Sufferings and
Death of the Protestant Martyrs, under Popish Persecutions.* St.
Louis, Mo.: J. H. Chambers and Company, 1895.

Fulton, Justin D. *Rome in America.* Boston: The Pauline Propaganda, 1887.

————. *Washington in the Lap of Rome.* Boston: W. Kellaway,
1888.

Harris, T. M. *Assassination of Lincoln: A History of the Great Conspiracy.* Boston: American Citizen Company, 1892.

Hawkins, Dexter A. *Archbishop Purcell Outdone! The Roman Catholic Church in New York City and Public Lands and Public Money.*
New York: Phillips and Hunt, 1880.

Hile, J. W. *The A.P.A. Must Go.* Kansas City, Kans.: The Author,
1895.

Howe, H. R. *The Patriotic Campaign Songster.* Rockford, Ill.: The
Author, 1895.

Huntington, Burton Ames. *The Coming American Civil War. Washington's Words of Warning. Lincoln's Apprehension and the Prophecy of General Grant.* Minneapolis: n.p., 1893.

Jackson, J. H. *The American Protective Association: What It Is. Its Platform. And Roman Intolerance Compared.* n.p., n.d.

Jones, Alonzo T. *The Two Republics: Or, Rome and the United States of America.* Battle Creek, Mich.: Review and Herald Publishing Company, 1891.

King, James M. *Facing the Twentieth Century, Our Country: Its Power and Peril.* New York: American Union League Society, 1899.

Lansing, Isaac J. *Romanism and the Republic: A Discussion of the Purposes, Assumptions, Principles and Methods of the Roman Catholic Hierarchy.* Boston: Arnold Publishing Company, 1890.

Lewis, Abram Herbert. *Sunday Legislation: Its History to the Present Time and Its Results.* New ed. New York: Appleton, 1902.

McCallen, Robert S. *Strangled Liberty, or Rome and Ruin. A Bombshell to the McKinley Administration. A Revelation to the Protestant World.* St. Louis, Mo.: Columbia Book Concern, 1900.

McCready, José. *Platform of the Papal Party.* Cambridge, Mass.: The Author, 1890.

McGlynn, Edward. *Father Lambert, a Priest Who Went to Rome, and What He Got There.* (Anti-Poverty Addresses, No. 42.) New York: Anti-Poverty Society, 1888.

Mead, Edwin D. *The Roman Catholic Church and the Public Schools.* Boston: George H. Ellis, 1890.

Miss Columbia's Public Schools: Or, Will It Blow Over? by A. Cosmopolitan. New York: n.p., 1871.

Morgan, Thomas J. *Ethics of Americanism.* Boston: American Citizen Library, 1894.

————. *The Negro in America: and the Ideal American Republic.* Philadelphia: American Baptist Publication Society, 1898.

————. *The Present Phase of the Indian Question.* Boston: Indian Citizenship Committee, 1891.

————. *Studies in Pedagogy.* Boston: Silver, Burdett, 1892.

Murray, Oliver E. *The Black Pope: Or, The Jesuit's Conspiracy against American Institutions.* 2nd ed. Chicago: The Patriot Company, 1892.

Order of the American Union. *The Future Conflict: An Address by the Order of the American Union to the American People.* n.p., n.d.

Owen, Olin Marvin. *Rum, Rags and Religion: In Darkest America and the Way Out.* Binghamton, N.Y.: The Author, 1891.

The Papal Controversy Involving the Claim of the Roman Catholic Church to be the Church of God between the "American Baptist" and "Church Progress." St. Louis, Mo.: National Baptist Publishing Company, 1892.

Proscription vs. Americanism. Addresses of Hon. Dan P. Foote, Hon. T. E. Tarsney, and Jas. H. Davitt. n.p., n.d.

Quigley, Patrick Francis. *Compulsory Education: The State of Ohio vs. The Rev. Francis Patrick Quigley, D.D.* New York: Robert Drummond, 1894.

Ryan, R. M. *The New KnowNothingism. A Reply to the Charges of Incivism and Want of American Patriotism Made by the A.P.A.* New York: The Author, n.d.

Satolli, Archbishop Francis. *Loyalty to Church and State.* Baltimore, Md.: John Murphy, 1895.

Shepherd, Margaret Lisle. *My Life in the Convent.* Toledo, Ohio: Book and Bible House, 1949.

Sherman, Edwin A. *Lincoln's Death Warrant: Or, The Peril of Our Country.* Milwaukee: Wisconsin Patriot, 1889.

Smith, Joseph Jackson. *The Impending Conflict between Romanism and Protestantism in the United States.* New York: E. Goodenough, 1871.

Speyer, Joe. *Why I Am Not an A.P.A.* Kansas City, Mo.: The Author, 1895.

Strong, Josiah. *Our Country: Its Possible Future and Its Present Crisis.* Rev. ed. New York: Baker and Taylor, 1891.

Thomas, W. H. *The Roman Catholic in American Politics, by an American Journalist.* Boston: Albion Printing Company, 1895.

Thompson, Richard Wigginton. *The Footprints of the Jesuits.* New York: Eaton and Mains, 1894.

Tighe, John J. *Essays, Lectures, Addresses, Sermons, and Miscellaneous and Descriptive Pieces. Including a Discussion of Education.* Arlington, N.J.: Sacred Heart Protectory Print, 1893.

Traynor, W. J. H. *The Devil's Catechism: Being a List of Questions Compiled from Standard Roman Catholic Authorities.* New York: Peter Eckler Publishing Company, 1920.

———. *Letter of the Supreme President to the Order.* Detroit, Mich.: Patriotic American, 1895.

A Voice from the Roman Catholic Laity. The Parochial School Question. An Open Letter to Bishop Keene . . . by An Irish Catholic Layman. Boston: Arnold Publishing Company, 1890.

Walter, J. A. *The Surratt Case: A True Statement of Facts Concerning This Notable Case.* Read before the United States Catholic Historical Society, May 25, 1891. N.p., n.d.

Webb, Ben J. *Sham Patriotism in 1896: Knownothingism As It Was and A.P.A.-ism As It Is.* Louisville, Ky.: Charles A. Rogers, 1896.

Wendte, Charles W., and Peter C. Yorke. *The Yorke-Wendte Controversy. Letters on the Papal Primacy and the Relations of Church and State.* San Francisco: Monitor Publishing Company, 1896.

Weninger, Franz Xaver. *Reply to the Hon. R. W. Thompson, Secretary of the Navy, Addressed to the American People.* New York: P. O'Shea, 1877.

Winston, Patrick Henry. *American Catholics and the A.P.A.: A Complete History of American Catholics in Their Relations to the Government of the United States; and a Review of the Meaning, Methods, and Men of the American Protective Association.* Chicago: Charles H. Kerr and Company, 1895.

Winter, Paul M. *What Price Tolerance.* Hewlett, N.Y.: All-American Book, Lecture and Research Bureau, 1928.

Yorke, Peter C. *The Ghosts of Bigotry: Six Lectures.* 2nd ed. San Francisco: Text-book Publishing Company, 1913.

Young, Alfred. *Catholic and Protestant Countries Compared in Civilization, Popular Happiness, General Intelligence, and Morality.* 9th ed. New York: Catholic Book Exchange, 1895.

Index

Abbott, Lyman, 128-29
Aitken, David D., 150
Allen, William V., 63
Allison, William Boyd, 87
Altgeld, John Peter: governor of Illinois, 67; criticizes A.P.A., 126; mentioned, 245
Amendments to the Constitution: proposed 16th in 1875, 8; comments on, 9; Senator Frelinghuysen on, 9; referred to, 20; proposed 16th in 1895, 205; "God in the Constitution," 211
American Citizens Library, 99
American Defensive Association, 105
American Flag Protectors, 123
American Historical Association, 28, 190
"Americanism," 14
American Liberal League, 108
American Liberty League, 214
American Minute Men, 54
American Party: 1888, 21; 1897, 233
American Political Alliance, 243
American Protective Association: idea of Catholic conspiracy, 16; founding, 35; advisory boards, 44, 201-2; constitutional aspects, 41, 44, 49, 273n27; motto, 50; insurance feature, 53-54; criticism of, 127-28; leadership quality, 180; Catholic attack on, 191-92; "martyrs," 234-35; as reform movement, 243-44; effect, 244; founding members, 271-72n16. See also Women's American Protective Association
— Conventions, national: 1889, 55; 1893, 90; 1894, 122; 1895, 174-76; 1896, 216-19; 1897, 232; 1899-1900, 237; summarized 273n28
— Conventions, state: 113, 119, 172-74, 232
— Dissension: in Clinton, 1889, 55; in

Ohio, 171; in Illinois, 171-72; in Michigan, 172; over third party, 169, 171-72; mentioned, 181, 185-86
— Growth, 54-55; on East Coast, 1893-94, 100; in Rocky Mountain area, 102-4; on Pacific Coast, 104-10; in South, 111, 317n59; in Middle West, 112; in West, 1895, 183
— Membership, 90, 122, 172, 177-80, 291n56, 306n171, 306-7n174
— Officers, national: 42, 122-23, 218, 238
— Officers, state: California, 108; Colorado, 102; Illinois, 79, 118; Iowa, 112-13; Kansas, 112; Michigan, 173-74; Minnesota, 73, 114; Missouri, 112; Montana, 104; Nebraska, 64; New York, 101; Ohio, 68, 119; Oregon, 105; Washington State, 109; Washington, D. C., 102; Wisconsin, 116-17
— Platform and goals, 175, 189, 202-4, 211-12
— Propaganda devices. See "Expriests" and "ex-nuns"; Patriotic press; Propaganda devices
American Protestant Association: organized 1843, 34; confused with A.P.A., 125-26
American Railway Union, 130
Amoreans, 57, 70-71
Ancient Order of Hibernians, 30, 214
Anderson, Rasmus, 153
Ankeny, Levi, 160-61
Anti-A.P.A. literature, 191-92
Anti-Catholic literature, 188-91
Anti-Catholic organizations, 34-35
Anticlericalism, 17
Anti-Semitism, 47, 129, 236
A.P.A. riot, Butte, 1894, 103-4
Apostolic delegate, 132. See also Sa-

335